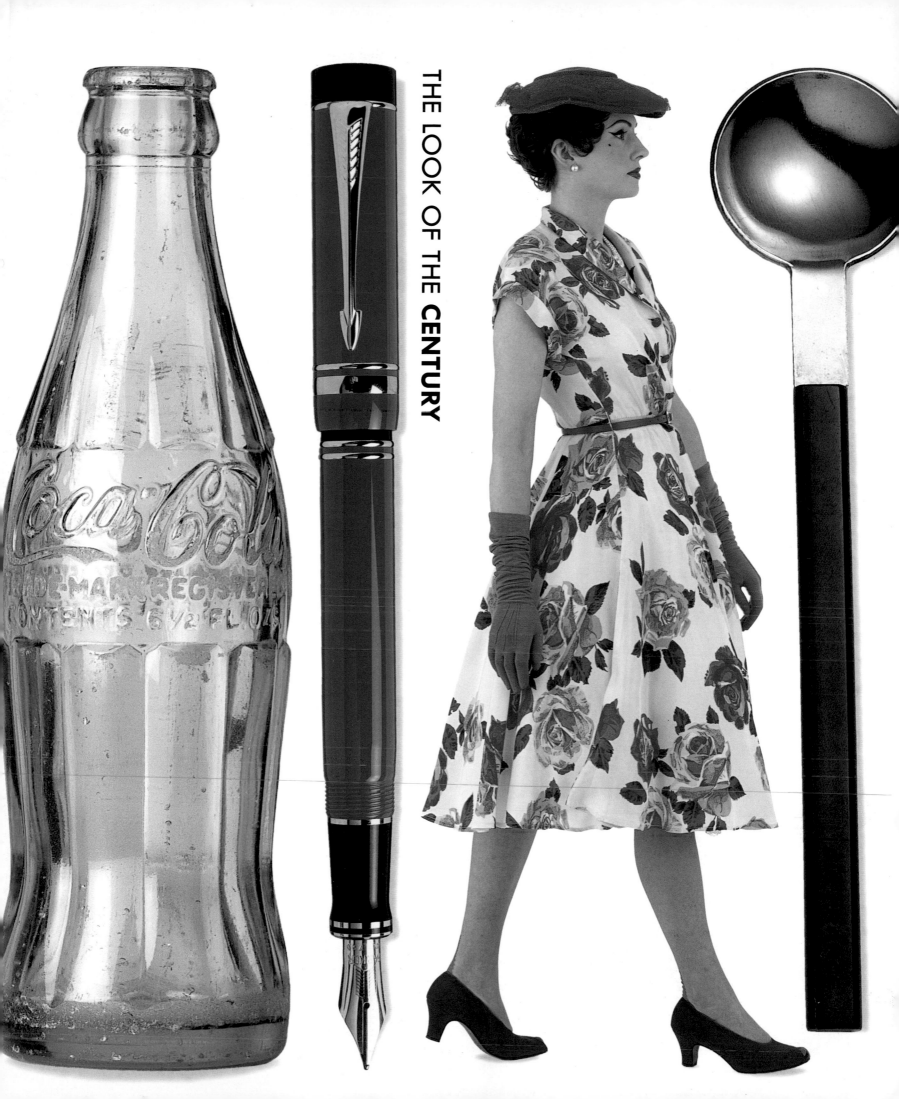

THE LOOK OF THE **CENTURY**

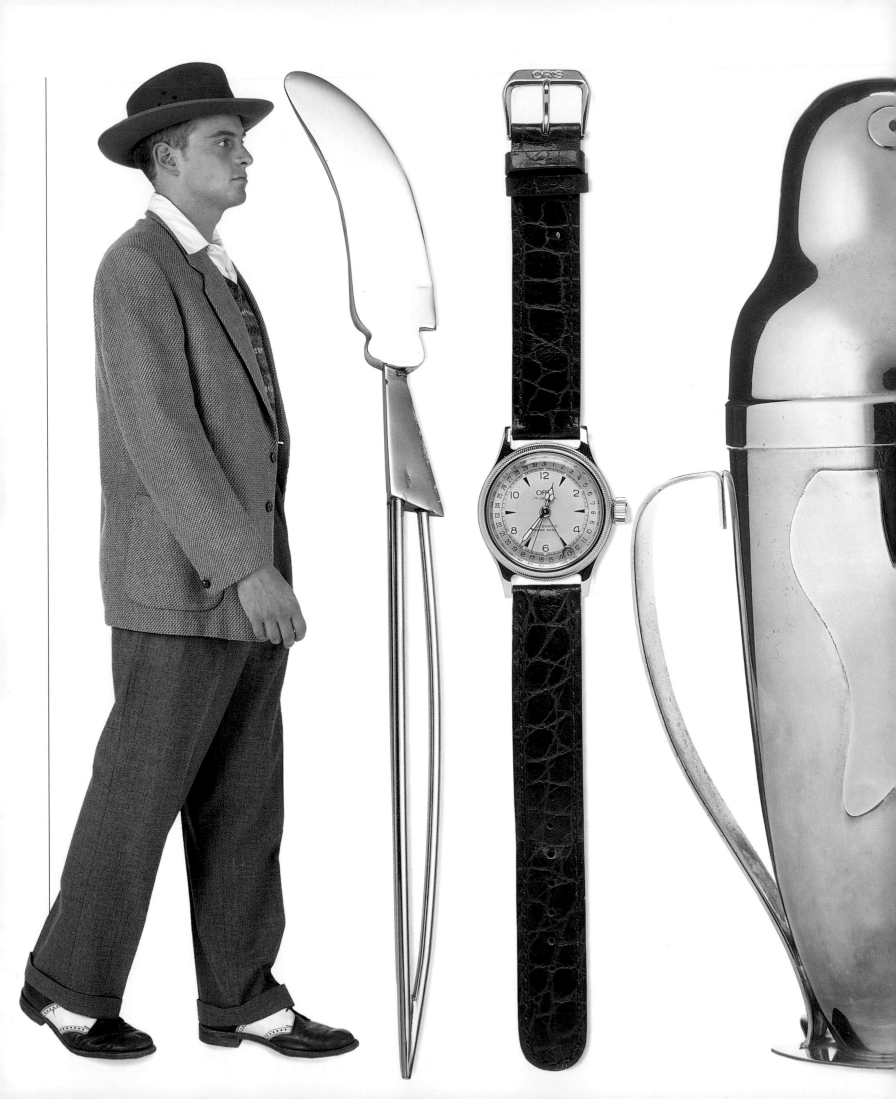

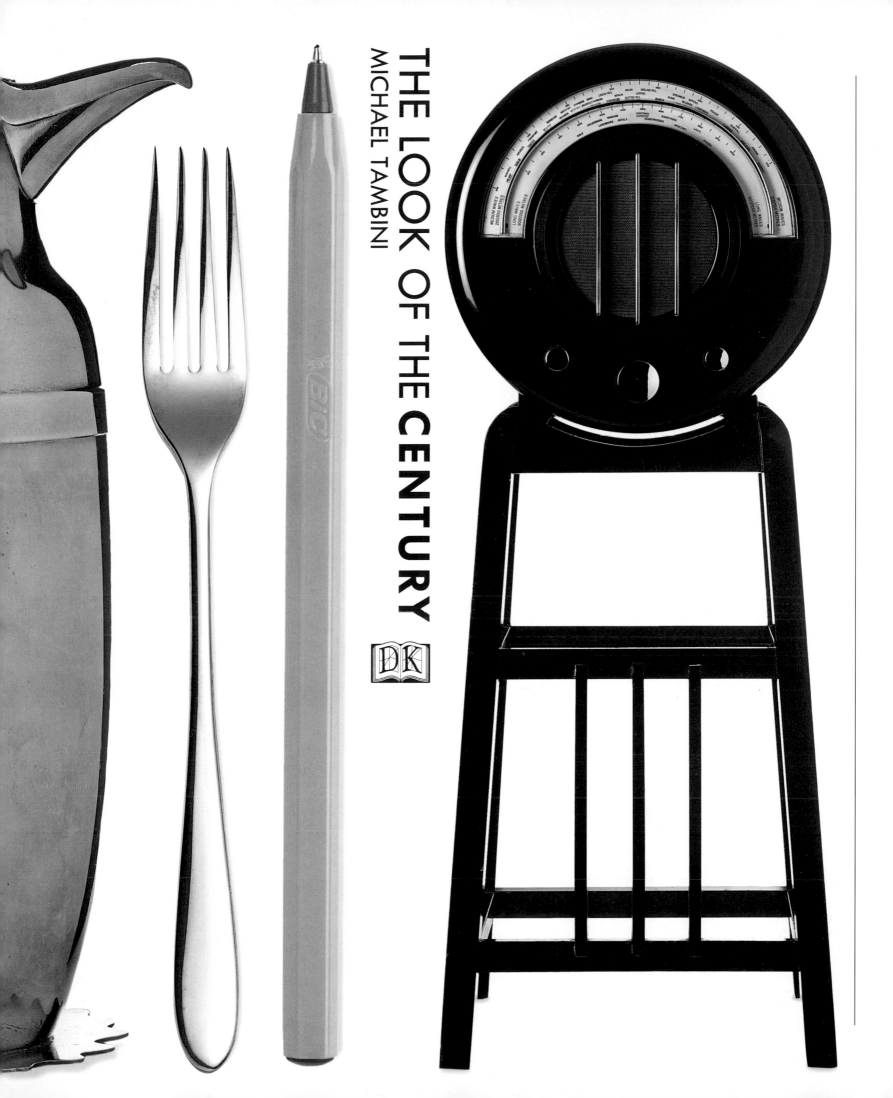

MICHAEL TAMBINI

THE LOOK OF THE CENTURY

DK

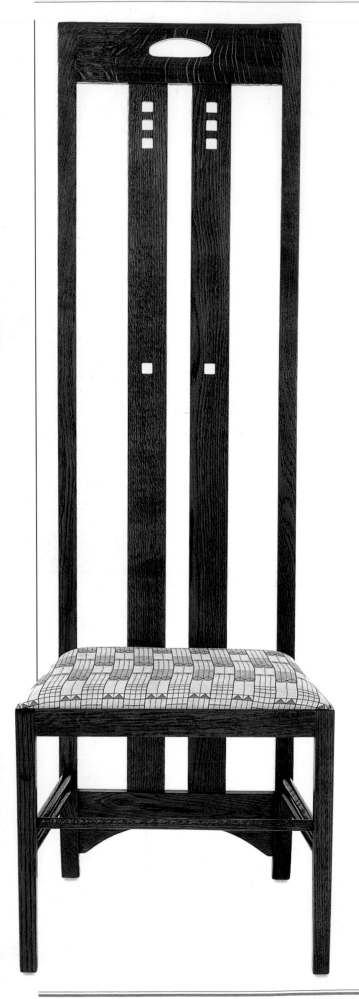

A DK PUBLISHING BOOK

*To Jules and Joseph for their help and patience,
and Mum and Dad for their support.*

Senior Editors Janice Lacock, Louise Candlish
Senior Art Editor Tracy Hambleton-Miles
Project Editor Jo Evans
Art Editor Dawn Terrey
Editors Jane Sarluis, David T. Walton, Caroline Hunt
US Editor Laaren Brown
Designer Carla De Abreu
Design Assistant Stephen Croucher
Senior Managing Editor Sean Moore
Art Director Peter Luff
Production Manager Meryl Silbert
Picture Researcher Jo Walton
DTP Designer Zirrinia Austin
Photography Dave King, Steve Gorton, Andy Crawford
Consultants Robert Opie,
Professor Jonathan M. Woodham

National Design Museum Review Panel
Susan Yelavich, Assistant Director for Public Programs
Gillian Moss, Curatorial Chair, and Assistant Curator, Textiles
Department
Deborah Sampson Shinn, Assistant Curator, Department
of Applied Arts and Industrial Design
Joanne Warner, Assistant Curator,
Wallcoverings Department
Caroline Mortimer, Special Assistant to the Director

First American Edition, 1996
2 4 6 8 10 9 7 5 3 1
Published in the United States by DK Publishing, Inc.
95 Madison Avenue, New York, New York 10016
Visit us on the World Wide Web at http://www.dk.com

Copyright © 1996 Dorling Kindersley Ltd., London
Text copyright © 1996 Michael Tambini

Library of Congress Cataloging-in-Publication Data
Tambini, Michael.
  The look of the century / [Michael Tambini]. -- 1st American ed.
    p. cm
  Includes bibliographical references and index.
  ISBN 0-7894-0950-X
    1. Design. Industrial--History--20th century.   I. Title.
TS171.T35 1996
    745.2′ 09′ 04--dc20   96-11806
                                                        CIP

Reproduced by Colourscan, Singapore
Printed and bound in Italy by A. Mondadori, Verona

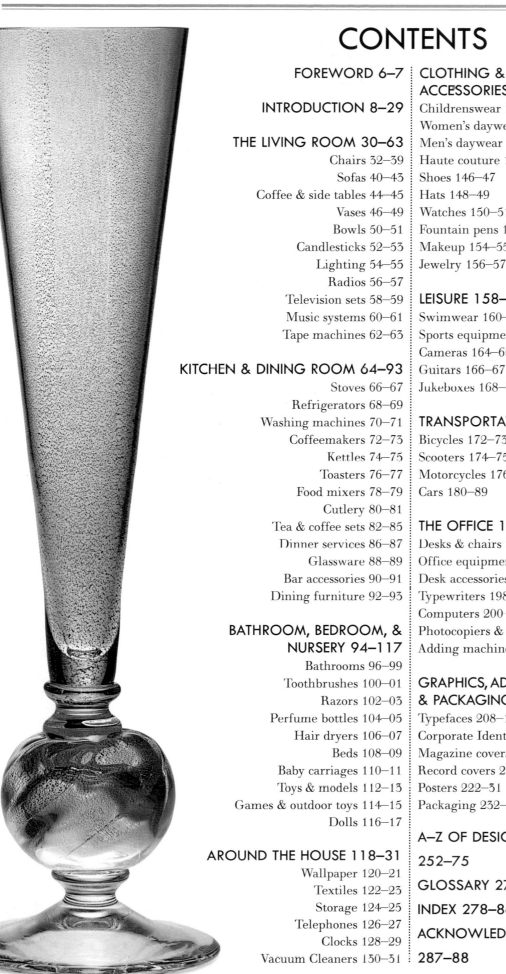

CONTENTS

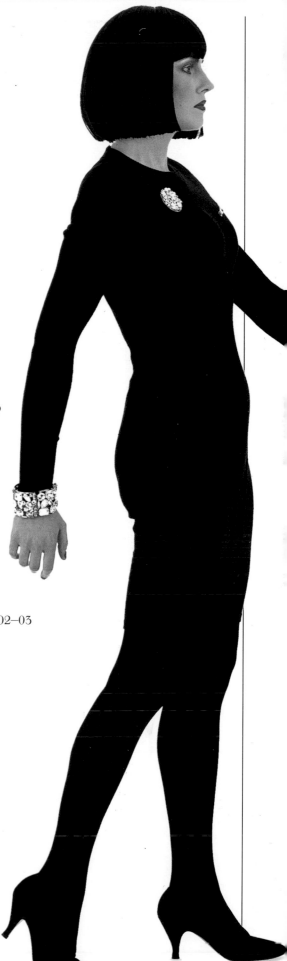

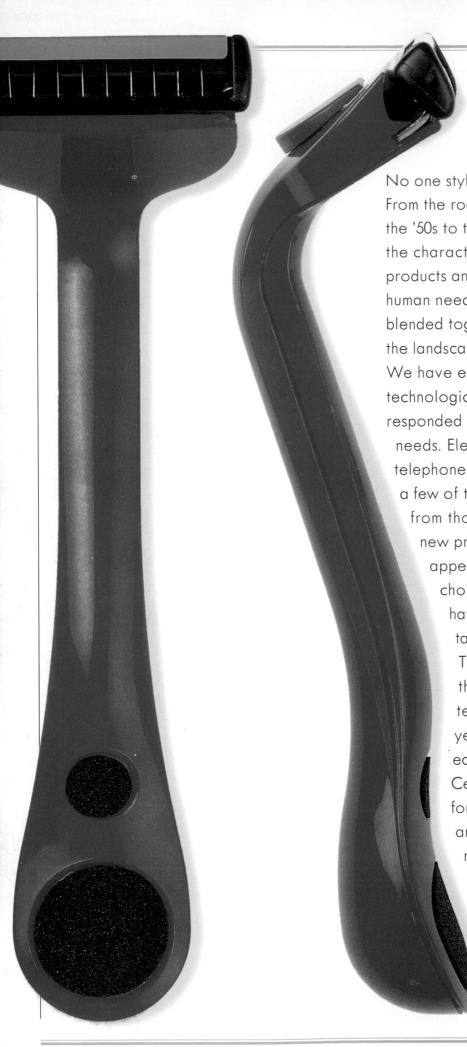

FOREWORD

No one style defines the 20th century, but its look is unmistakable. From the roaring '20s to the streamlined '30s, the amoebic forms of the '50s to the mod look of the '60s and today's high-tech virtuosity, the character of each decade is embodied in the design of its products and places. No longer simply the fulfillment of our basic human needs, like eating and sleeping, form and function have blended together to offer us almost unlimited choice in shaping the landscape of our daily lives.

We have experienced unparalleled social, economic, and technological development during this century. Designers have responded by creating new genres of objects to suit our modern needs. Electronic calculators, personal coffeemakers, cellular telephones, plastic wristwatches, and disposable shavers are but a few of the objects now in our daily use that distinguish our lives from those of our great-grandparents. Besides the array of new products available to us, we find that increasingly their appearances are styled to suit our tastes. We have more choices about the way things look than ever before. We have become a society that expects design to reflect our tastes, our cultures, and our values as consumers and citizens. The look of the 20th century is inextricably linked to the astounding number of innovations and advances in technology we have experienced in the past hundred years. New materials like plastics, originally developed early in the century, found new uses as time progressed. Ceramics, glass, wood, and metal — traditional materials for the objects of our daily lives — were joined by plastic and other synthetic substances that offered strength, malleability, and new potential for design innovation. Recycled materials are used to create furniture, tableware, books, and even buildings. We look to design to reduce strains on our natural resources and promote environmental sustainability.

The innovation that has characterized the 20th century is evident in our homes, our offices, on the roadways, in our towns and cities, and in the newly emerging network of cyberspace. During this century, we have explored the macrocosm of our universe and created whole new worlds through the microcosm of electronic technology. New environments, like the virtual office, are constructed and navigated on the screens of our computers.

In the 20th century, the word "design" has taken on a complex set of meanings, but at its heart the act of design is the process of wedding our ideas about living with the world we live in. Today, design involves both functional and aesthetic problem-solving that is appreciative of cultural and national differences. At the same time, design is an increasingly global affair, participating in the cross-pollination of images and ideas from continent to continent. Clearly, the look of the century is in all of our hands.

Dianne Pilgrim
Director, Cooper-Hewitt,
National Design Museum

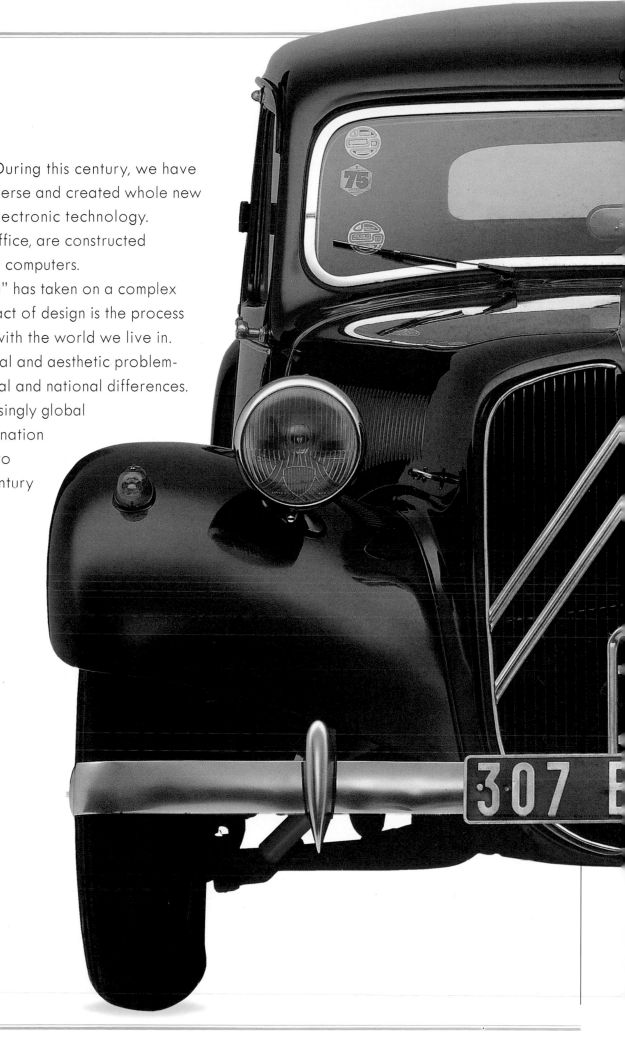

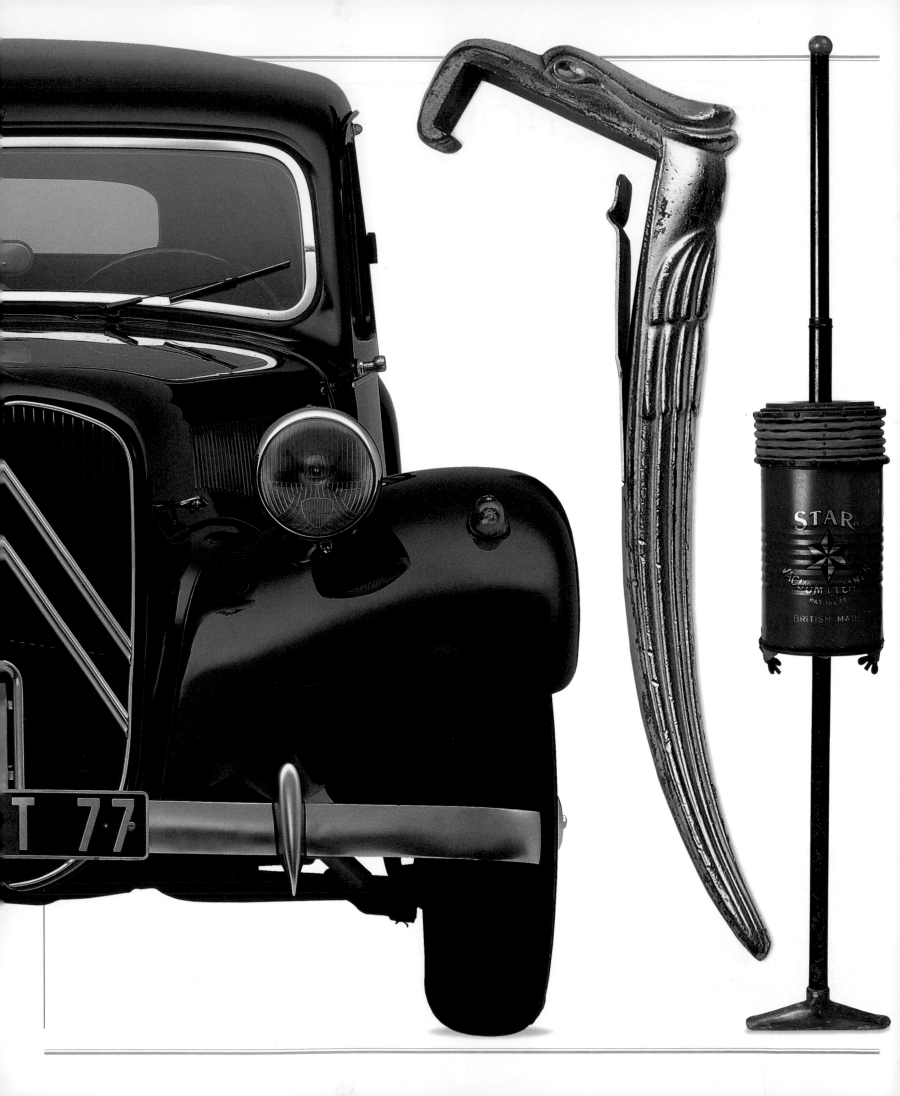

INTRODUCTION

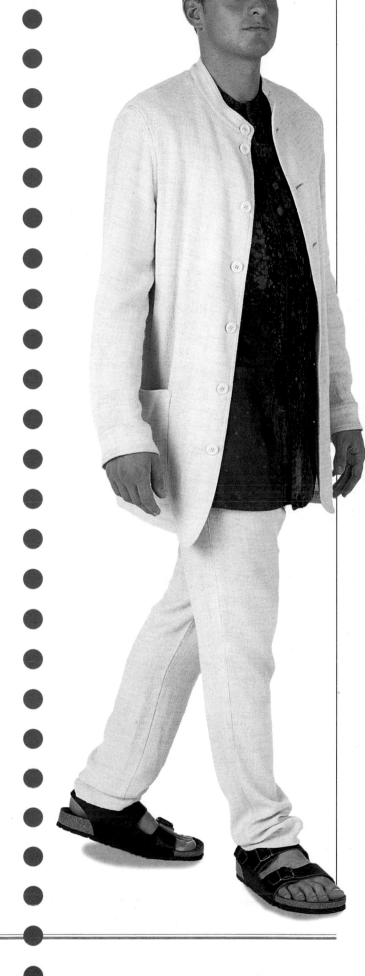

Our world is changing at a dizzying speed, and technology is racing ahead so quickly that many of us are overwhelmed by the multitude of new designs and inventions that are available: videophones, cable television, solar-powered cars, virtual reality, the information super-highway... Yet so many of the things we take for granted, or even feel are becoming outmoded, were the stuff of dreams just one hundred years ago. You have only to look at the two New York street scenes below to see the astonishing progression in clothing, transportation, and architecture. In fact, change has been this century's only constant. In addition to the technical advances that science has contributed to the product designs of the 20th century, designers and craftspeople have also been influenced by a bewildering succession of movements, from Art Nouveau to postmodernism, Bauhaus to Psychedelia. Some, such as De Stijl, were relatively short-lived and affected only a limited number of countries, while others, such as Art Deco, lasted longer and had international exponents.

The following pages, which are divided by decade, give a concise introduction to the most important of these movements and their key designers, as well as some of the most interesting developments and innovations from each era.

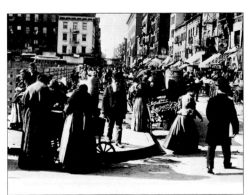

New York, 1900

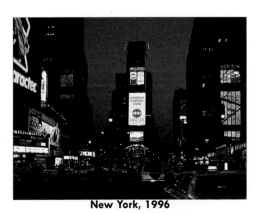

New York, 1996

1900–09

At the dawn of the 20th century, a frenetic series of momentous advances in technology was making a major impact on society. The internal combustion engine, the electric motor, and the rudiments of telecommunication allowed manufacturers to aspire to hitherto unimaginable heights of efficiency. Previously handmade goods could now be made more quickly and cheaply by machine, undermining the role of craftsmanship.

The machine was also revolutionizing the domestic world and, with the advent of the radio, telephone, and television, it was to redefine "communication" completely at home and at work. The assembly line drastically accelerated the production of vehicles, making the motor car affordable to a much wider

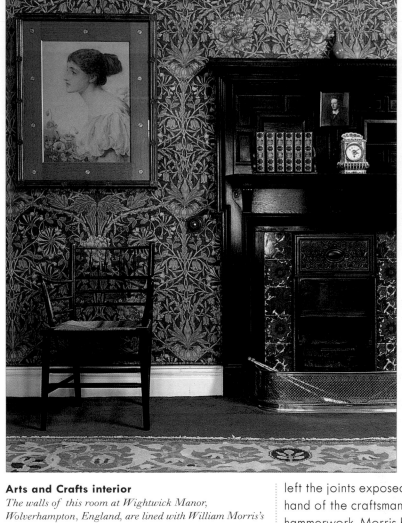

Arts and Crafts interior
The walls of this room at Wightwick Manor, Wolverhampton, England, are lined with William Morris's Honeysuckle printed linen; other items are by his followers.

market. In 1903, the Wright brothers realized the centuries-old dream of flight by traveling 131 feet (40 meters) through the air in their gasoline-powered biplane. Just six years later, Louis Blériot flew his little monoplane 26 miles (42 kilometers) across the English Channel from France to England. Within 30 years, flight would be available to anyone with money, as regular passenger flights crossed the world.

ARTS AND CRAFTS MOVEMENT

Although a product of the Victorian age, the Arts and Craft movement left a legacy that extended deep into the 20th century. The primary concern of its central figures was that "machine-age" manufacturers were driven by quantity rather

Gustav Stickley chair
This beautifully crafted wooden and leather chair was made in 1904–05. Typical of Stickley's work, it was produced using mechanical processes.

than quality. The movement's most influential designer and theorist was William Morris (1834–96). His company, Morris and Co., produced a wide range of items, including furniture, stained glass, wallpaper, fabrics, and ceramics. For Morris, art and craft had equal status, and his designs utilized the skills of craftsmen and artists in collaboration.

Arts and Crafts work is characterized by medieval and gothic references; Morris wanted the craftsman's hand visible in the work, differentiating it from the machine-made. The robust, simply constructed furniture left the joints exposed, and in metalwork the hand of the craftsman is visible in the textural hammerwork. Morris believed that good design was uplifting and would contribute to a happier society — a belief shared by the modernists in the 1920s. Although the Arts and Crafts movement began in Britain, there were European and American counterparts. Workshops, or guilds, following Morris's precepts sprang up in many countries. While American designers, such as Gustav Stickley, followed the British model closely, many Europeans moved away from the fundamental tenets of the Arts and Crafts movement and more readily embraced Art Nouveau and modernism.

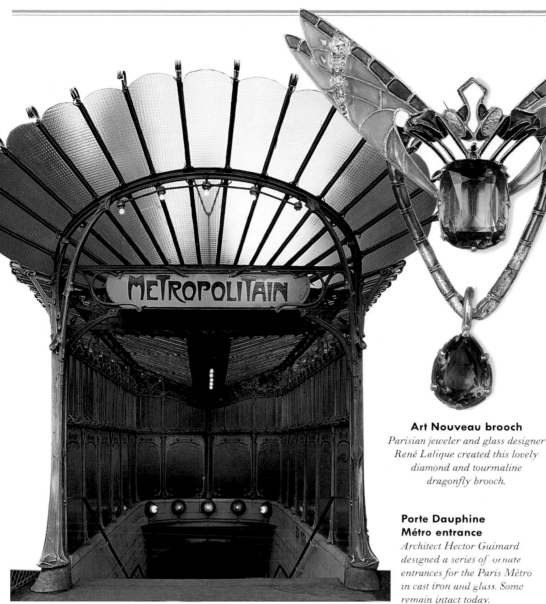

the form and the surface decoration of the object. Its organic fluidity was inspired by nature, particularly plant life. There are also references to past traditions, such as Celtic art and Rococo, to be found in the style. Art Nouveau could be interpreted either naturalistically or abstractly, and its principles could be applied to the design of anything from architecture to jewelry. The most important work took place in France, Belgium, Austria (see p.12), and Scotland.

THE GLASGOW SCHOOL

In Scotland, the Glasgow School, a small but widely recognized group of designers led by the architect and designer Charles Rennie Mackintosh, was producing work that combined the functionalism of Arts and Crafts with the decorative exuberance of Art Nouveau. Its work fused a geometric format with a flowing linear pattern based on organic form.

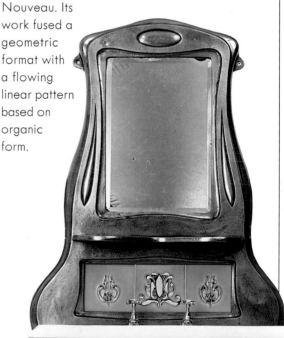

Art Nouveau brooch
Parisian jeweler and glass designer René Lalique created this lovely diamond and tourmaline dragonfly brooch.

Porte Dauphine Métro entrance
Architect Hector Guimard designed a series of ornate entrances for the Paris Métro in cast iron and glass. Some remain intact today.

ART NOUVEAU

By 1900, the dominant movement of the decade, Art Nouveau, was already established, born of the Arts and Crafts movement and the 19th-century Aesthetic movement. Its exponents were much more willing to embrace the use of new materials and mass production than their Arts and Crafts counterparts. While they also drew on the past, they shared an enthusiasm for the future that set them apart from the preceding movement. The name is derived from art dealer Samuel Bing's shop, *L'Art Nouveau*, which opened in Paris in 1895. Leading designers from around Europe were invited to display their work there, including the Belgian Henry van de

Velde (furniture), the American Louis Comfort Tiffany (glass), and Frenchmen Emile Gallé (glass) and René Lalique. The latter was one of the key exponents of Art Nouveau. His exquisite jewelry, often based on plant or insect motifs, used glass, semiprecious stones, and gold.

Although Art Nouveau developed in idiosyncratic ways in many countries (it was closely related to Jungendstil in Germany, Secession in Austria, and Stile Liberty in Italy), the fluid, organic style is easily recognizable. The dominating characteristic is the whiplash curve that influences both

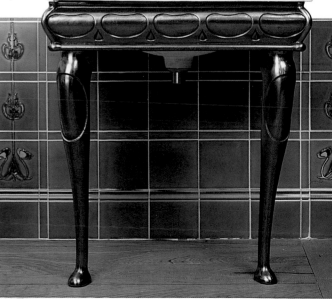

Cast iron wash basin
This highly ornate British wash basin, dating from 1903 to 1911, demonstrates the curving, organic lines of Art Nouveau. Its tiles are typical of the time.

Blériot's Type XI airplane
The plane that Louis Blériot flew over the English Channel in 1909 was constructed from linen stretched over a wooden frame, supported by wire braces.

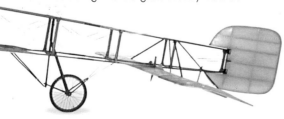

1910–19

Josef Hoffman was one of the leading figures in the group of Viennese artists and architects known as the Vienna Secession. Although most of the art of the Secession was fundamentally Art Nouveau in style, its design is remembered for a more geometric approach to decoration. The Secession published its own journal, *Ver Sacrum*, and held regular exhibitions showing work from many international artists.

WIENER WERKSTÄTTE

In 1903, Hoffmann formed the Wiener Werkstätte with Koloman Moser. This association of workshops owes much to the Arts and Crafts guilds. The Wiener Werkstätte was responsible for producing fine pieces of jewelry, metalwork, textiles, furniture, and architecture. Its designers occupied ground between the decorative Art Nouveau and the austere modernism that was starting to influence the appearance of objects.

THE MACHINE AESTHETIC

As the century progressed, designers became less concerned with the crafts aesthetic and favored instead the aesthetic of the machine. In 1917, a group of Dutch painters, architects, designers, and philosophers formed a collective called De Stijl ("The Style"). Moving away from natural form in architecture and design, the De Stijl group attempted to find a visual language to express a new machine aesthetic by using a limited

Excelsior Auto-cycle, 1911
By 1914, all the major components of the modern motorcycle were already in place; the designs that followed represented a process of refinement.

color palette and geometric shapes and lines only. Of all the work, perhaps Gerrit Rietveld's Red-and-blue chair of 1918 (see p.33) comes closest to achieving this goal. Constructed from standardized lengths of machine-finished wood, it is devoid of all unnecessary ornamentation. De Stijl's influence extended throughout Europe, particularly to the Constructivists in Russia (see p.15) and the Bauhaus in Germany (see right). In Italy, the futurists, who included poet Filippo Marinetti (1876–1944) and artist Giacomo Balla (1871–1958), also glorified the machine.

MASS PRODUCTION

The industralist Henry Ford had founded the Ford Motor Company in 1903, and over the next few years he developed a system of mass production that was to have a permanent effect on the design process: the standardization of parts for easy assembly and, in 1913, the moving assembly line. When these principles were applied to the

Coca-Cola bottle
Based on the shape of the cola nut, the Coca-Cola bottle was redesigned in 1915 (see p.213) and has remained virtually unchanged since.

Model T Ford (see p.180), it was so successful that by the 1920s every second car on the world's roads was a Model T. Mass production made goods affordable to a much wider market, but also left factory workers with a feeling of alienation. Their role in manufacturing was reduced to an anonymous, repetitive task. Some now supported William Morris's argument that the only escape was a return to craftsmanship. But the momentum of mass production was not to be resisted and, in fact, increased as the century progressed. However, the quality of life of the average worker began to be improved by the introduction of a plethora of time- and labor-saving devices, such as washing machines, hair dryers, and irons.

ELECTRICITY

The majority of these newfangled devices did not really save time, but they did save labor, making housework less tiring. Many of the products were electrically

Electricity in the home
As this advertisement shows, by 1917 a variety of electrical appliances was available for the home. With the decrease in the number of domestic servants, housework could be made easier with these devices, which spread across the US and Europe as electricity became more widely available.

designs from 1909 (see p.74), which allowed for 80 variations from just three basic models. Behrens also ensured that there was continuity in all other elements of the company's output, from architecture to advertising. AEG had taken on a corporate identity – a feature to be copied by other companies in the future. Behrens employed some of the most avant-garde designers, including Walter Gropius, Mies van der Rohe, and Le Corbusier. Their work has had an enormous impact on product design and has greatly influenced the debate about art and technology.

THE BAUHAUS

In 1919, an art school was formed in Germany known as the Bauhaus. Under the directorship of Walter Gropius, it became one of the most influential art schools of this century, active until 1933. Its simple aim was to train artists to work for industry, and although its achievements can easily be exaggerated, it has left a lasting impression on 20th-century design. Using modern industrial materials, stripped down to their basic elements and without added decoration, Bauhaus designers attempted to make products that avoided historic reference. Their aspirations were not always achieved. Marcel Breuer's famous Wassily chair (see p.33) has many of the characteristics associated with the Bauhaus

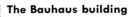

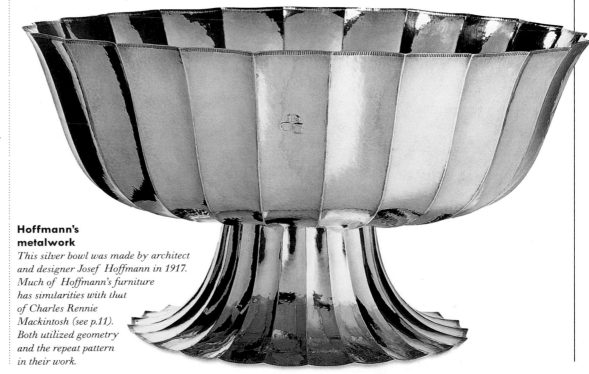

The Bauhaus building
Walter Gropius designed the new school building at Dessau in 1925. It has become a symbol of modernism, with its emphasis on steel, glass, and concrete, and has had a great impact on the development of 20th-century architecture.

style – it is made from tubular steel and with a stripped-down geometric form. Yet its construction still owes more to the craftsman than the machine. The Bauhaus's greatest success was its teaching methods, which have been copied the world over. Gropius attracted highly respected painters, including Wassily Kandinsky (1866–1944), Josef Albers, and Paul Klee (1879–1940), to teach the foundation course. Celebrated architects such as Marcel Breuer and Mies van der Rohe also taught there.

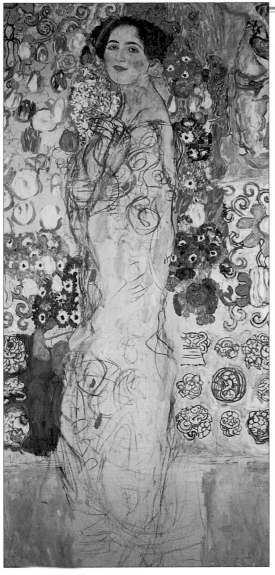

Austrian painting
Gustav Klimt provided a bridge between Art Nouveau and fine art. His richly decorative paintings, with large blocks of flat pattern and heavy use of gilt, were firmly based in the traditions of the Vienna Secession. Entitled Portrait of a Lady, *this painting from 1917–18 is unfinished.*

operated. A relatively new commodity at the beginning of the century, electricity was as yet unavailable to most homes. However, the promise of a clean, odorless energy source, bright lighting at the flick of a switch, and the attraction of new inventions like the electrically powered vacuum cleaner made electricity such a worthwhile investment that it was quickly accepted throughout the Western world.

THE BIRTH OF CORPORATE IDENTITY

In Germany at this time, Peter Behrens was established as artistic director of the electrical manufacturer AEG (Allgemeine Elektricitäts-Gesellschaft). The company recognized the need to unify its design, and Behrens's standardization and interchangeability of components were crucial to AEG's success. The clearest example of this is Behrens's kettle

Hoffmann's metalwork
This silver bowl was made by architect and designer Josef Hoffmann in 1917. Much of Hoffmann's furniture has similarities with that of Charles Rennie Mackintosh (see p.11). Both utilized geometry and the repeat pattern in their work.

1920–29

At the influential 1925 *Exposition Internationale des Arts Décoratifs et Industriels Modernes* held in Paris, the Swiss architect Le Corbusier designed one of the pavilions, naming it *L'Espirit Nouveau*. This was a model of Modernism: its plain white walls, concrete frame, and large expanses of glass were all unified by an uncompromising geometry. The inside was equipped with commercially available, unpretentious furniture, including the bentwood Thonet armchair (see p.32). However, the Exposition is remembered less for the functionalism of Le Corbusier's contribution and more for the look that the rest of the exhibits in the other pavilions encapsulated. For it was from this exhibition that the term "Art Deco" was derived.

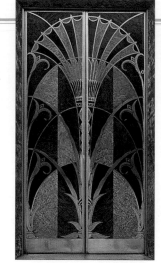

Elevator door
The decorative paneling of these elevator doors from the Chrysler Building is characteristically Art Deco, with its use of overlapping curves and contrast provided by different wood grains.

Torch dancer
This exuberant bronze and ivory figure on an onyx plinth was cast from a model by Ferdinand Preiss. It is typical of Art Deco figurines, which frequently featured acrobatics and dancing.

ART DECO

This decorative style was inspired by non-Western art, particularly that of Africa and Egypt, made popular by the discovery in 1922 of Tutankhamun's tomb by Howard Carter. Diaghilev's Ballets Russes (which first danced in Paris in 1909) and the Cubist paintings of Pablo Picasso (1881–1973) and Georges Braque (1882–1963) captured the imagination of designers. However, Art Deco was not a design movement, but rather a shared approach to styling. The interplay of geometric forms; abstract patterns of zigzags, chevrons, and sunbursts, rendered in brilliant colors; and the use of bronze, ivory, and ebony were all common features. Criticized by some for its opulence, it was seen to distract from the purist theories expounded by the modernists. Furniture designers such as Jacques-Emile Ruhlmann (who designed the interior of one of the pavilions at the 1925 exhibition) used exotic veneers and ivory inlays in a rich decorative design. He was inspired by 18th-century design, but updated the look by using geometry and modern materials.

Art Deco did not remain the preserve of the wealthy. Indeed, new low-cost materials such as Bakelite were flexible and popular. In Britain, Wells Coates used Bakelite to great effect in his radio designs. In architecture, colored glass and chromium created the Art Deco look at relatively low cost and was used successfully in public buildings such as the Odeon cinemas. The cinema itself played an important role in popularizing the Art Deco style, through the exterior architecture and the plush interiors of the picture palaces.

In New York, the greatest monument to Art Deco architecture was William van Alen's Chrysler Building. This skyscraper expresses the glamour of Art Deco both in its interior and exterior decoration and forms. The semicircular pinnacles were faced in Nircosta metal to create gleaming white surfaces reminiscent of platinum (the metal most often chosen for contemporary jewelry).

Many famous designers who had made their names with products featuring the Art Nouveau style now adapted their designs to the new look. For example, René Lalique switched from his trademark organic-looking jewelry to Art Deco glassware, including car mascots, perfume bottles, and statuettes.

1920S FASHION

In the 1920s, the Charleston became the first of many dance crazes to sweep America. To perform such energetic dancing,

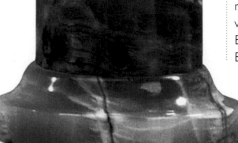

Art Deco architecture
In 1930, New York witnessed the completion of two contrasting Art Deco skyscrapers, the Chrysler Building and the Empire State Building. Public reaction to the more ornate Chrysler was mixed, but no one could deny that the building provided a startling change to the previous skyline.

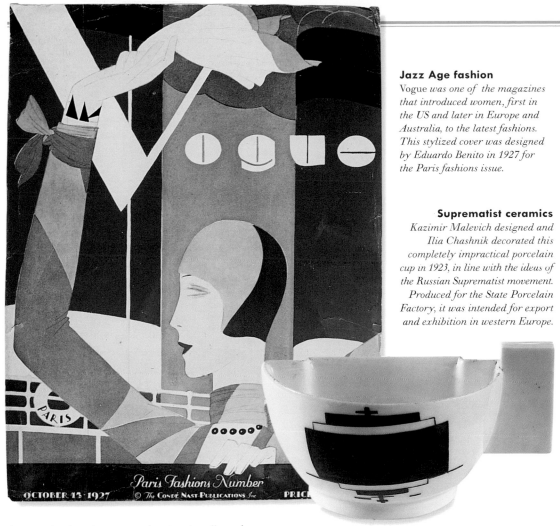

Jazz Age fashion

Vogue was one of the magazines that introduced women, first in the US and later in Europe and Australia, to the latest fashions. This stylized cover was designed by Eduardo Benito in 1927 for the Paris fashions issue.

Suprematist ceramics

Kazimir Malevich designed and Ilia Chashnik decorated this completely impractical porcelain cup in 1923, in line with the ideas of the Russian Suprematist movement. Produced for the State Porcelain Factory, it was intended for export and exhibition in western Europe.

SUPREMATISTS, CONSTRUCTIVISTS, AND VKHUTEMAS

In Russia, a desire similar to that of the Dutch De Stijl designers (see p.12) inspired a number of artists, among them the painter Kazimir Malevich, to attempt to find a universal relationship between geometric forms and pure color. Their work, termed Suprematism, was more concerned with aesthetics and geometry than with functionality. It was superseded by less abstract Constructivist design. The Constructivists, who included the graphic designers El Lissitzky and Aleksandr Rodchenko, eschewed fine art and were committed to the notion of putting art to the service of the emerging socialist state. In 1920, Constructivist ideas strongly influenced the VKhUTEMAS, a newly opened avant-garde design school in Moscow. (Its name is an abbreviation of Higher State Artistic and Technical Workshops.) Like the Bauhaus (see p.13), the school's purpose was to train artists for industry. It shared many of the characteristics of the German school; indeed, Wassily Kandinsky and El Lissitzky were active in both organizations. One of the teachers at VKhUTEMAS, Aleksandr Rodchenko, designed furniture for the Workers' Club at the 1925 Paris Expo. Textiles produced by his wife Varvara Steparnova (1894–1958) and Lyubov Popova (1889–1924) were also put into production. Though the school created many furniture prototypes, none of them became an industrial reality.

dresses had to be worn shorter to allow for greater freedom of movement. Young women, known as "flappers," began to cut their hair into short bobs, and often wore cloche hats or berets. Designer Coco Chanel created a look to go along with women's newfound sense of confidence. Adapting men's clothes, she promoted a flat-chested, boyish silhouette, frequently worn with flamboyant costume jewelry, but above all designed for comfort and style, and to radiate youth.

THE JAZZ AGE

Popular entertainment also influenced public taste. Jazz, which evolved in New Orleans at about the turn of the century, was now mainstream popular music. With the development of swing in Chicago, there were large ensembles playing with written orchestration. Benny Goodman, Count

Basie, Artie Shaw, and Glenn Miller were all major musicians. The interior of Radio City Music Hall in New York, which opened in 1932, was designed in an Art Deco style by Donald Deskey using a jazz motif. Similar patterns were used in textiles, wallpaper, and ceramics.

Photographic advances

Photography was popularized by the Brownie and the Vest Pocket Autographic Kodak cameras, and, by the 1920s, was an increasingly common hobby. The Leica A went into production in 1924 and was the first widely used 35mm camera, producing good-quality black-and-white shots.

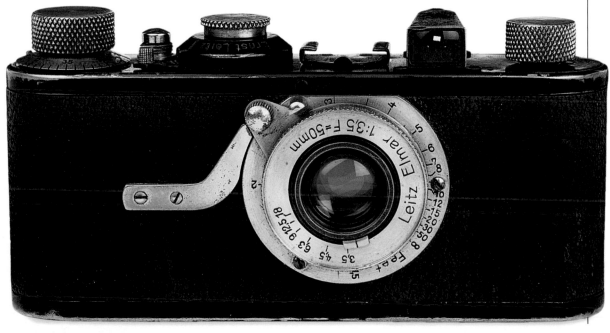

1930–39

Since the beginning of the century, designers had been experimenting with hydro- and aerodynamics. Based on studies of the shape and movement of fish and birds, it was discovered that boats and aircraft could be made more efficient by smoothing and curving the bows or fusilage. In 1933, the Douglas DC1 appeared as a commercial passenger aircraft. Strikingly different from its cumbersome predecessors, it had a streamlined monocoque structure, integrated wings, and a stressed aluminum skin that was strong enough not to need bracing wires. Along with the Boeing 247, it marked the beginning of modern passenger flight. In 1934, Chrysler launched its new streamlined car, the Airflow. Designed by Carl Breer, it was the result of thorough research into aerodynamics. Its curved body, with sloping windshield and extended tail, was so different from previous cars that the public did not take to it and production ended after just three years. However, the car was an engineering success and contributed much to the appliance of aerodynamics to car design, paving the way for car designers such as Ferdinand Porsche to create their aerodynamic sports cars.

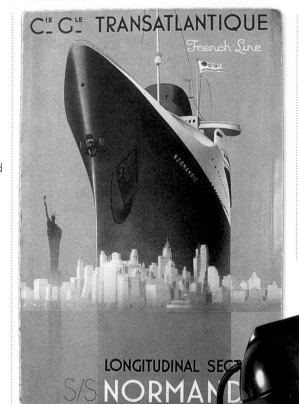

1930s shipping poster
With transatlantic travel becoming popular, product designers such as Loewy and Teague were influenced by the streamlining of ocean liners, as shown on this poster.

of industrial machinery – no attempt had been made to make it pleasing to look at or easy to use. Loewy, using a full-size clay model to achieve the desired effect, enclosed all the working parts within a smooth, unifying body. The duplicator was a great commercial success and, in the US, designers began applying streamlining to a whole range of domestic appliances. Although the restyled products suggested improved efficiency, sometimes all that had changed was the housing.

AMERICAN STREAMLINING
Streamlining suggested speed, efficiency, and, most of all, modernity. Like Art Deco, it had a commercial imperative, for it became obvious that the consumer was attracted, if not to cars, then to other streamlined products. The first sure evidence of this came in 1929 when Raymond Loewy redesigned the Gestetner duplicator (see p.202). Until then, it had been a typical example

Ergonomic design
Henry Dreyfuss designed for human form and in 1937 collaborated with engineers to develop this telephone, making it supremely practical as well as stylish.

City of Salina train
This, the first American streamlined train, was designed in 1935. The torpedo-shaped front and rear ends and the enclosed chassis reduced wind resistance.

London Underground maps

The original maps showing the routes on the London Underground followed a traditional geographical approach (left). Then, in 1933, Henry Beck persuaded the newly formed London Transport to adopt a diagrammatic map (below). The vertical, horizontal, and 45-degree angles reveal Beck's training as an electrical draftsman. Besides being easy to read, the main advantage is that the map permits the crowded central area to be enlarged in relation to the outlying areas. The hugely successful map has been imitated around the world.

US INDUSTRIAL DESIGN

Raymond Loewy was one of the most successful designers ever to work in the US. Essentially a stylist, he was responsible for redesigning the look of numerous products, including the Coldspot Super Six refrigerator (increasing sales by 400 percent), the Lucky Strike cigarette packet, the Silversides Greyhound bus, and the Shell Oil company logo (see p.68, 240, and 212). When it came to streamlining, American designers led the way: in addition to Loewy, Norman Bel Geddes, Walter Dorwin Teague, and Henry Dreyfuss all made contributions that influenced design throughout the world. Eventually, Dreyfuss developed a design theory concerned less with styling and more with the relationship between the machine and the operator. He believed that for a machine to be efficient it had to be adapted to people. He developed this theory into a study of ergonomics (how humans relate to objects) and anthropometrics (the study of body size and strength). Dreyfuss's reputation was established with the Bell 300 telephone. He designed it "from the inside out," carrying out detailed tests to ensure it would be easy to operate. It remained the standard American telephone for over 40 years.

SWEDISH MODERN

Although Art Deco and American streamlining dominated the 1930s, a very separate style was evolving in Scandinavia that was to be of increasing international importance during the 1940s and '50s. The term "Swedish Modern" was coined following the New York World's Fair in 1939. Key designs during the 1930s were the ceramics of Wilhelm Kåge, the glassware of Kaj Franck, and the furniture of Alvar Aalto. The look was characterized by a soft, organic, natural feel influenced by traditional Scandinavian design and a human scale.

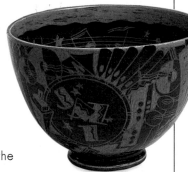

Jazz motif
Victor Schreckengost's 1931 punch bowl is an example of the continuing popularity of jazz.

BAKELITE AND NEW MATERIALS

In the 1930s, Alvar Aalto and Marcel Breuer both experimented with new forms of machine-processed wood such as plywood. Interest in other new materials was strong and centered on Bakelite. Invented and patented in 1907 by the Belgian-born inventor Leo Baekeland, this was one of the first plastics to be used extensively. Its malleable properties were the perfect expression of the smooth, sleek contours of a streamlined product. Initially, it was used as a substitute for wood or ivory and was carved into shape from blocks. As designers began to exploit its own unique properties, it was molded into myriad shapes and used for electrical products. Bakelite, the most successful of the early plastics, gave freedom to designers to style and restyle artifacts.

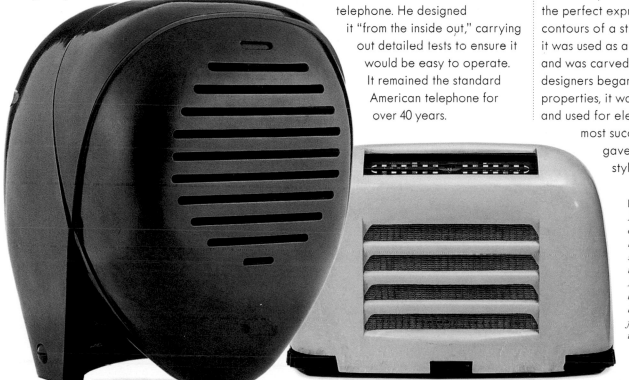

Bakelite products
Bakelite was used for a wide range of goods. The Radio Nurse (shown left) was designed by the Japanese sculptor Isamu Noguchi in 1937 after the sensational Lindbergh kidnapping. It consists of a microphone in the baby's room and a receiver shaped like a stylized nurse's head. The four-valve plug-in radio from 1950 was nicknamed the "Toaster."

1940–49

World War II had a major impact on product design and manufacturing. Countries involved in the hostilities were quick to restrict the use of raw materials, and factories themselves were frequently turned over to military production. In 1941, Britain introduced a "Utility Scheme" in an attempt to ration the use of scarce resources. The Design Panel, which had Gordon Russell as its chairman, was charged with approving designs for production. The panel followed principles derived from the Arts and Crafts movement, but was also influenced by the European Modernists. The furniture was required to be strong and attractive but not wasteful in the use of materials. Some materials, such as silver and aluminum, were completely restricted or not available, and even dyes for textiles had to be approved through the Utility program.

AUSTERITY DESIGNS

Of course, it was not only in Britain that government placed controls on manufacturing. In most of Europe, Japan, and the US government restrictions prevented the unnecessary use of scarce materials. In Germany, under the *Schönheit der Arbeit* ("Beauty in Work") program, designers adopted an Arts and Crafts style, similar to that of Britain, with a particular emphasis on vernacular or rustic designs. In the US and Japan, industries were cut back and price controls were put in place. Designers were put to work on a range of government commissions and often given an unexpected opportunity to try out new materials. This experimentation paid dividends after the war as designers applied the new materials to the products they created for the domestic market. The results of these austerity measures were severely pared-down consumer products made from the most basic materials. Although they were low cost and by and large well made, they tended to be drab and lacked any sense of flair or luxury. In many countries, the regulations lasted long after the end of the war and consumers soon became impatient with the continuing restrictions.

NEW LOOK FASHION

It was, therefore, hugely refreshing when Christian Dior showed off his first Paris collection in 1947. Women, desperate to escape from the sensible clothes of the war

Dior's New Look
After years of rationing and constraint, Christian Dior's New Look made a powerful impact. His clothes made women feel feminine again.

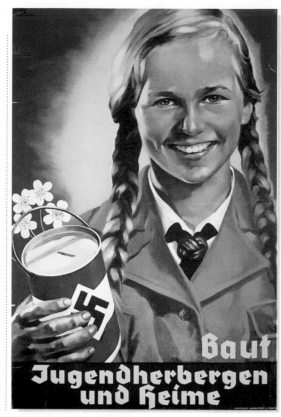

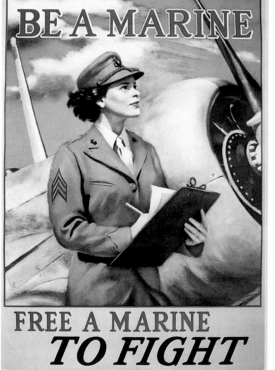

War posters
During wartime, the governments of all the participating countries were quick to commission graphic designers to produce information and propaganda posters. Many encouraged women to work in factories, on farms, or to join the forces.

years, embraced the New Look — powerfully feminine, with softly rounded bodices, tight waists, long, very full skirts, and high-heeled shoes. With rationing still in place in many parts of Europe, the yards of fabric required to construct the huge skirts were mostly unobtainable. Not all women loved it, and some, who saw the look as extravagant and indulgent, picketed the House of Dior, further adding to Dior's reputation. Nevertheless, the more elegant look quickly gained popularity, and manufacturers tried to produce something akin to Dior's vision but using less fabric. For men too, shapeless wartime suits were replaced with a narrower silhouette.

ITALIAN DESIGN

In Italy in 1946, former helicopter designer Corradino d'Ascanio designed the Vespa scooter for Piaggio (see p.175). This exciting, streamlined, modern vehicle became a symbol of postwar *ricostruzione* and attracted worldwide sales. After the war, Italy consolidated its design practice, eventually becoming a world leader. Companies such as Fiat, Olivetti, and Cassina employed avant-garde designers to make products that would hold their own in the world of international commerce.

NEW MATERIALS

Plastics became increasingly important materials after World War II, and their use has significantly changed the way things look. Before then, they had been regarded as substitutes only, but after the war, many designers deliberately chose to exploit the properties of particular plastics for individual projects. The following are just a few examples. Acrylic, such as Plexiglas, had been discovered in the 1930s and was put to use in furniture design and as a lightweight replacement for glass. See-through films, such as PVC, were used to produce waterproof raincoats and umbrellas. Nylon was utilized by the American forces for parachutes. In 1942, Earl Tupper introduced a set of lightweight polyethylene containers with airtight lids. Known as Tupperwear, it was available in a range of pastel colors and was both flexible and hardwearing. One of the most exciting developments was in the use of plastics for modern chairs. The pioneers of this work were the American architect Charles Eames, together with his wife Ray, and Eero Saarinen. During the war, Eames had worked with glass-reinforced polyester to make radar domes for aircraft. By applying the knowledge he had acquired from this work to chair design, he produced a one-piece molded seat shell supported on wire legs, known as the DAR chair, in 1948. Unlike the Womb chair produced earlier by Saarinen (see p.35), Eames's chair was left uncovered so the glass-reinforced plastic construction was exposed. Many of Eames's seating designs were put into production by Herman Miller.

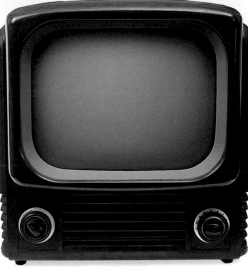

Early television set
This television set by Bush has a Bakelite case molded into a shape reminiscent of the Art Deco radios produced a decade earlier.

RADIO AND TELEVISION

Radio stations had started broadcasting in the early 1920s, and domestic radio became more popular during the following decade. However, it was only with the outbreak of World War II that the various warring governments realized radio's potential for disseminating information and propaganda both to their own civilians and to the enemy. After the war, television began to make an impact on domestic life. A television transmitter had been demonstrated by John Logie Baird in 1926, but it was not until the late 1930s that cathode ray tubes were capable of receiving high-definition broadcasts. As with radios and record players, early televisions were housed in traditional cabinets, giving them the appearance of items of furniture, with no indication as to the true purpose. As the technology improved, designers began experimenting with new materials and finding solutions more fitting to the function. Bakelite could be molded, initially to fit the shape of the screen and subsequently to find expressive forms.

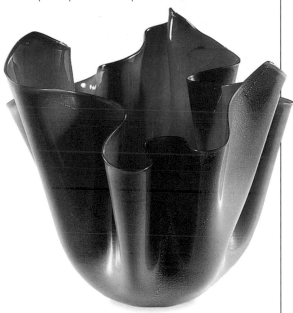

Unconventional vase
Italian designer Paolo Venini combined his bold sense of color and texture with traditional glass-making techniques to produce the Handkerchief vase. First made in 1946, the design became extremely popular.

Eames's DAR chair
This fiberglass chair with wire legs was manufactured by Herman Miller from 1950 on. It was based on an earlier model entered by Eames for a competition held by the Museum of Modern Art, New York.

1950–59

The inferno that was World War II had given way to the chill of the Cold War, played out by the capitalist US and the communist Soviet Union. Competition between the two political systems came to be symbolized by the space program: the frantic race between the superpowers to become leaders in space exploration. The Soviets took the initiative: in 1957, they launched Sputnik 1, the first satellite to orbit the earth, and, in 1961, the Soviet cosmonaut Yuri Gagarin became the first man in space. Just eight years later, American Neil Armstrong took his "giant leap for mankind" by walking on the Moon. Science, space travel, and science fiction became an all-consuming obsession. Scientific motifs came to be associated with modernity and appeared everywhere.

CONSUMERISM

In the 1950s, car design in the US took on a new, extravagant look. Inspired by aircraft and rockets, Harley Earl of General Motors began to change the shape of cars in a way that expressed the postwar confidence of American society. His cars were wide, low, and very long. They had lavish interiors, imaginative tail fins, masses of chromium, wraparound windshields, and striking colors. During this time, the controversial strategy of planned obsolescence emerged in the US. By introducing small stylistic changes, companies could launch new

Music machines
The growing popularity of rock 'n' roll created a huge demand for jukeboxes. In cafes and coffee shops, they could be heard playing the latest hits. Big, brash with flashing lights, jukeboxes borrowed shamelessly from automobile styling.

versions of their products each year, thereby appealing to those conscious of social status by making last year's model stylistically obsolete. Of greater concern was the decision to build in physical obsolescence, so that through a lack of actual durability the product only had a limited lifespan. The debatable defense of this huge waste of resources was increased employment.

INTERNATIONAL STYLE

In contrast to the cynicism of planned obsolescence, some companies, most notably Braun in Germany and Saab in Scandinavia, began to design and market goods on the basis of their durability. In 1955, the Swiss industrial designer, sculptor, and painter Max Bill (1908–) cofounded the *Hochschule für Gestaltung* in Ulm in Germany. Bill had studied at the Bauhaus, and his goal was to continue that school's rationalist approach to design. This revival of the modernist style took the search for a machine

Youth culture
The 1950s marked the emergence of a vibrant new teen culture with its own dress, behavior, music, and language. Singers like Elvis Presley and movie stars like James Dean became role models for this affluent consumer group.

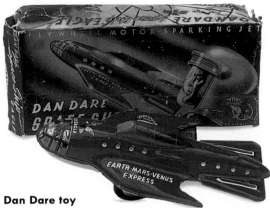

Dan Dare toy
Many manufacturers saw enormous opportunities for product development in the space obsession, and geared product design to this market. A whole line of toys, for example, featured Dan Dare, the hero of the British comic the Eagle (founded in 1950).

aesthetic further than before; it required design to be forward-looking, reflecting modern life, and embracing technology. This functionalist approach, which is often referred to as the International Style, was most clearly represented in product design by the Ulm school. Financed by commissions, the school had close links with industry. Among its first and most important commissions was a series of radios and phonographs for Braun by Hans Gugelot and Otl Aicher. This helped formalize Braun's reductionist design philosophy, and the continued collaboration between Gugelot and Dieter Rams of Braun brought about the development of the "black box syndrome" in modern design. Anything unnecessary to the

function of the product was stripped away. Clean lines, durability, balance, and unification were key requirements. All Braun products are clearly related, often finished in glossy white or black, with the company logo visibly marked on the casing.

TRANSISTORS

One of the most significant developments in the look of electronic equipment was the invention of the transistor in 1947 by Bell Laboratories. Made from silicon and only requiring a low electric current to function, these small components were used for items such as radios, televisions, and record players, in which they replaced the cumbersome vacuum tube. The Tokyo Telecommunications Engineering Corporation (later known as Sony) produced the first mass-produced transistorized pocket radio in 1955, and in 1959 developed the first all-transistorized television with a 8in (20cm) screen. The diminutive size of the transistor gave designers the freedom to miniaturize all other electronic appliances.

An insect on metal legs
Arne Jacobsen's 1951 Ant chair is one of many 1950s furniture designs that incorporated steel rods or steel wire. Harry Bertoia's Diamond chair and Ernest Race's Antelope (see p.36) are others. Jacobsen's chair is still much copied today.

IMPORTANT COUNTRIES

The 1950s mark a high point in 20th-century Italian design. Designers such as Gio Ponti, Marco Zanuso, Marcello Nizzoli, the Castiglioni brothers, "Pinin" Farina, and Ettore Sottsass achieved great success for themselves and Italian companies such as Olivetti, Artemide, and Brionvega. Elsewhere, Denmark became a major player on the international design stage, noted for its mass-produced furniture, luxury silverware, and innovative textiles and wallpapers. Denmark's Scandinavian neighbors Finland and Sweden were also enjoying much design success.

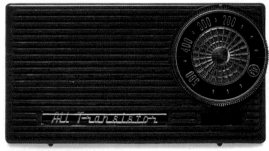

Transistor radio
By replacing radio valves with transistors, which were smaller, more robust, and used less power, radios shrank in size. Their low cost and portability made them popular with teenagers, and bright colors were often adopted to add to their appeal. This particular model was made in the US.

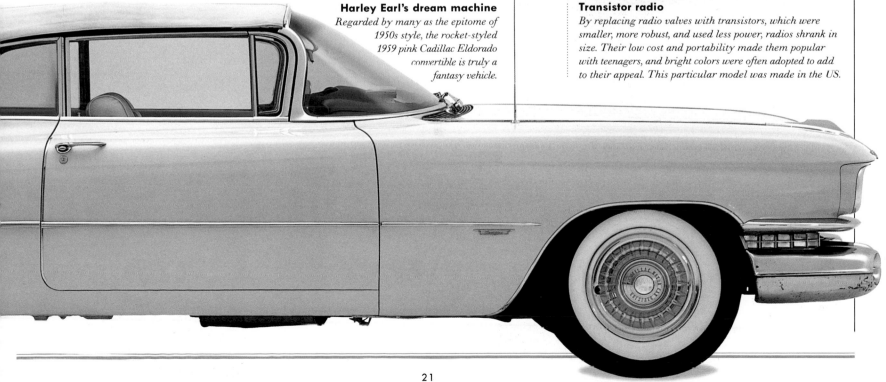

Harley Earl's dream machine
Regarded by many as the epitome of 1950s style, the rocket-styled 1959 pink Cadillac Eldorado convertible is truly a fantasy vehicle.

1960–69

During the 1960s, the postwar baby boomers were growing up, and *en masse* they created a powerful new army of consumers. They were coming of age in a period of unparalelled, unrestrained optimism and self-belief: the war, and the postwar austerity, was over; humans were in space and would soon walk on the Moon; the first heart transplant had taken place; and 60 years after the first flight across the English Channel, the Concorde would be flying faster than the speed of sound across the Atlantic Ocean. "We live," one commentator said, "in a throwaway society. Obsolescence is created by the rapid advances in technology; built-in obsolescence is no longer relevant, so why is the functionalism

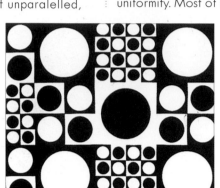

Black-and-white textile
Danish furniture and textile designer Verner Panton designed this Op Art fabric in 1961.

of the International Style relevant?" So began the rejection of Modernism, which was no longer able to meet the demands of this eager new force of consumers, who wanted change and variety in the place of permanence and uniformity. Most of all, they wanted a look they could call their own, that divorced them from their parents, and that reinforced the gap that had grown between the pre- and postwar generations.

MASS CONSUMERISM

During this period, the power of advertising, particularly on television, led to the birth of mass consumerism. Manufacturers quickly recognized the buying power of the teenage population and began to create products aimed specifically at the youth market. A combination of new materials, new shapes, new technology, and new colors vied for the attention of these affluent young people. This manifested itself in all areas of design: in the automobile industry, the Mini (see p.185) was born; in fashion, the miniskirt appeared (see p.139); and in graphics, Wes Wilson produced his barely legible posters (see p.229). There were myriad radical furniture designs: Danish designer Verner Panton produced his bright red molded-plastic stacking chair (see p.37), and Gunner Aagaard Anderson (b.1919) of Denmark created his polyurethane Armchair, an extraordinary item that looks like — and, in fact, is — a huge solidified blob of poured liquid plastic.

PSYCHEDELIA

Youth movements abounded. Each had its own music, its own dress code, and its own visual language. One, Psychedelia, was a short-lived but incandescent revivalist movement that had a far-reaching influence. The Psychedelic

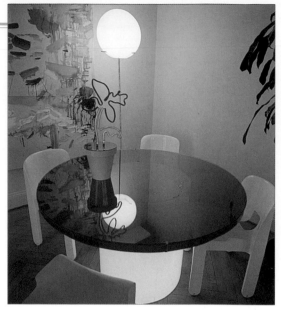

Interior design
This 1960s domestic dining area shows the contemporary fascination with plastics, transparent materials, bright colors, and soft shapes.

Space-age clothes
In 1969, models displayed the latest Martian wigs by French coiffeur Jean-Louis St Roch. "Space-age" clothes were made popular by Pierre Cardin and André Courrèges.

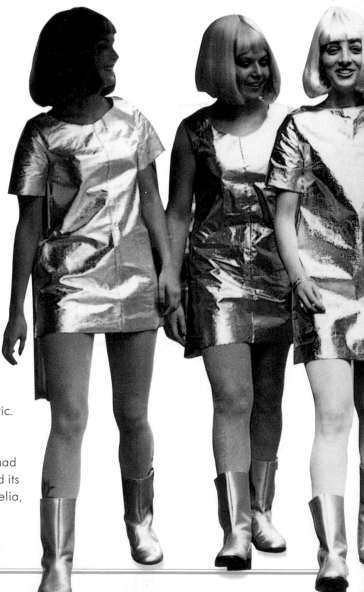

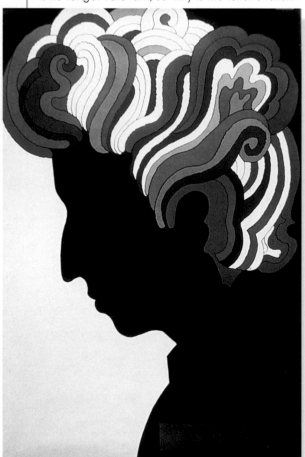

Psychedelic poster for the *Dylan* album
Bob Dylan has himself become an icon of the 1960s. Illustrated here by Milton Glaser in 1966, Dylan's hair is rendered as a pattern of colorful psychedelic swirls.

designers of the day rejected Modernism out of hand. Where the Modernists looked only to the future for inspiration, Psychedelia looked anywhere and everywhere, often through the blur of hallucinogenic drugs. Its artists sought inspiration back at the beginning of the century, incorporating aspects of Art Nouveau and the Vienna Secession into their work; they looked to the East, and as far into the past as ancient Egypt for references; and they looked at their own world, creating a visual drug-inspired language that was aimed at a select audience.

1960s FASHION
In the world of fashion, one of the names that stands out above the others is Mary Quant. Rejecting *haute couture*, she aimed her designs at the young, and produced inexpensive and fun clothes. She remains best-remembered as the designer responsible for introducing the miniskirt and hot pants to Britain.

The space age continued to influence fashion, and designers created outfits in futuristic materials, typified by Courrèges's "silver-foil" suits.

POP ART
Fashion and art have had a huge influence on product design, and no art movement has had a greater impact on commercial design than Pop Art. Pop artists such as Andy Warhol, Jasper Johns (b.1930), Roy Lichtenstein (b.1923), and Robert Indiana were turning the art world on its head by drawing the everyday into their studios and recycling it as ironic, irreverent art. Andy Warhol openly celebrated American consumerism in his repeat-image paintings of iconic images of popular culture, be it Campbell's soup cans or Elvis Presley. Ironically, manufacturers themselves began to use Pop Art in product design, marketing, and advertising — so much so that it soon became a part of everyday life, with, for example, Robert Indiana's "LOVE" image appearing on 40 million postage stamps. Other fine art movements, notably Op Art, were also commandeered by product and textile designers.

THE ITALIAN INFLUENCE
In Europe, the Italian designers had taken the lead role on the international stage, and many acknowledged the influence of the Pop artists in their work. Joe Colombo, Ettore Sottsass, and Marco Zanuso, freed from the constraints of Modernism, absorbed the playfulness of the age and began to toy with the new themes. Their work, dubbed "Radical" or "Anti-Design," drew on popular taste. Joe Colombo experimented with plastic for his furniture designs, as did Sottsass in such classics as the vividly styled orange red and yellow

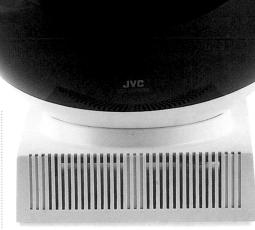

Spherical television
JVC's Videosphere from 1970 has a plastic case and looks like a spaceman's helmet, reflecting public interest in space travel while also challenging traditional shapes.

Valentine typewriter (see p.199). The Italian designers more or less rescued plastic from its reputation as cheap and therefore undesirable, an image that had grown from its use in disposable designs such as the Bic Biro (see p.197). Few could fail to see the beauty and sophistication of Marco Zanuso and Richard Sapper's plastic Grillo telephone, regardless of its material (see p.127). Other Italian designers were making a contribution with innovative furniture designs. Two of the most famous are the Sacco chair by Gatti, Paolini, and Teodoro, a stuctureless, polystyrene-filled bag that is now regarded as the first beanbag chair (see p.38); and the Blow Armchair by de Pas, d'Urbino, and Lomazzi, an inflatable plastic chair that relied on air for its shape and comfort. These radical Italian designers in turn influenced the post-modernist designers of the following decades.

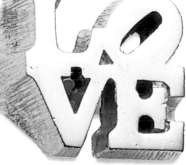

Pop Art jewelry
Pop artist Robert Indiana's LOVE ring was made in gilded metal in about 1966.

1970–79

Italy continued as a center for design excellence into the 1970s and as a leader in Radical design. Many of its chief designers are linked to the most important movement of the decade — postmodernism.

POSTMODERNISM

The term can be applied to many aspects of our lives, cultural and social, but has particular

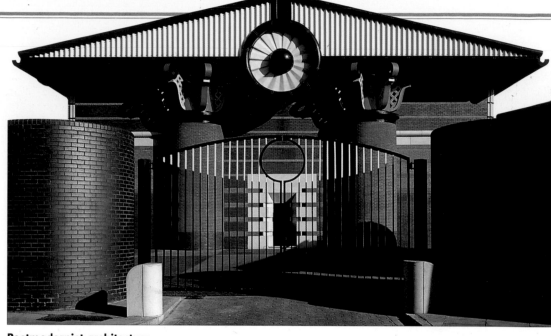

Postmodernist architecture
Architect John Outram's water pumping station at Blackwall, Isle of Dogs, London, is a classic example of postmodernist architecture. Many structures described by this term feature elements borrowed from the architecture of older periods, such as classical columns and pediments.

relevance in the world of art, architecture, and design. It is essentially a rejection of everything entailed in modernism, which detracters argue is elitist, unintelligible, unattractive, and unappealing. The postmodernist's aim was to popularize the highbrow, and to make the intellectual accessible. Exponents borrowed freely from history, reworking the color, texture, or material, often as a witty parody of the original source. While many of the most important protagonists of postmodernism are Italian, it is a truly international movement. Its leaders include Ettore Sottsass, whose work is typified by the Carlton sideboard (see p.124); the American architect Robert Venturi, who designed the classic postmodernist building

Chestnut Hill House in Pennsylvania; and Michele de Lucchi, who created the prototypes shown here. The postmodernists rejected the Modernist's Utopian goals and their search for a universal aesthetic, and instead looked to create a visual language that was made up of signs, visual metaphors, references to the past, and to the work of other designers. As a result, the postmodernists have been accused of continuing the elitism they despise by assuming an understanding of the references made in their work, and for the prevalence of in-jokes. Another criticism that has been leveled at postmodernism is that it has been manipulated by the forces of commerce, and has produced little more than an incoherent mishmash of styles. By the 1970s, manufacturing allowed for limited production,

Fan prototype
Although de Lucchi's colorful prototypes (see also right) never went into production, they encouraged more decorative, fun product design.

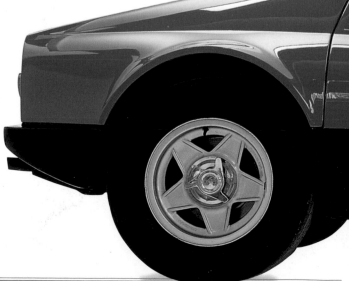

Furniture in Irregular Forms
This wooden chest of drawers is one of the best-known pieces by Shiro Kuramata and was created for Fujiko in 1970 at a time when Japanese design was being recognized as an innovative force on the international stage. It is shaped like an elongated "S."

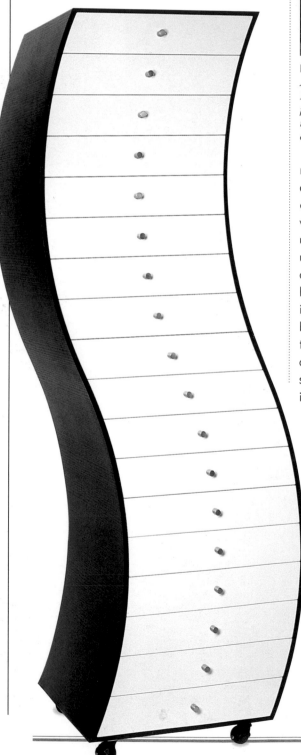

and for all types of products to be tailored to accommodate the demands of a small market. This caused a shift in emphasis away from mass production and toward meeting the needs of the individual.

SPORTS CARS

Another important area of Italian design influence in the 1970s is the sports car. The decade saw the birth of the supercar, with Italian manufacturers Lamborghini, Ferrari, and Lancia competing with the likes of Porsche,

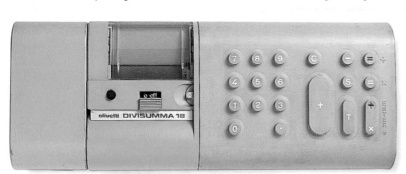

Olivetti Divisumma 18
A leading exponent of Italian design, Mario Bellini has produced many stylish products for Olivetti. This brightly coloured calculator is typical of his work, featuring as it does an expressive surface created by the rubber "skin."

Triumph, and Jaguar to produce the sleekest, lowest, fastest, most powerful car in the world. Cars such as the Lamborghini Countach were capable of 0–60mph (0–96km/h) in 5.1 seconds, and had a top speed of 187mph (301km/h). However, the spiraling gasoline prices that resulted from the oil crisis of 1973 made gas-guzzling cars less popular,

and so manufacturers began to look at more fuel-economic alternatives.

Japan began to emerge as a major player in automobile design in the 1970s and more so in the field of motorcycle design, an area now dominated by the Japanese through the efforts of Yamaha, Honda, Suzuki, and Kawasaki. The Japanese also led the world in the development of new technology, and by the 1970s many of its manufacturing companies, such as Nikon, Olympus, Sony, and Sharp, were growing in commercial stature. Their goods typically featured a "high-tech" look. In graphic design, fashion, and furniture production, too, young Japanese designers were increasingly being recognized as playing an important international role. They were among the first to recognize and exploit the value of computer technology in the design process.

THE MICROCHIP

The theory behind the microchip, one of the most important inventions of the century, was originally devised by an American, Jack Kirby of Texas Instruments. Its development meant that electronic components could be reduced unimaginably in size. By 1970, for example, thousands of components could be printed

Ferrari 365 GT4 Berlinetta Boxer
In production from 1973 to 1976, only 387 Boxers were built. At the time of launching, it was hyped as one of the fastest GT cars ever built. In fact, it was slower than the Ferrari model it replaced, achieving 170mph (274km/h). During the boom of the mid-1980s, when classic cars were highly sought after, the Boxer was selling for double its original price.

on top of a single silicon chip measuring only ¼in (5mm) square. Without this invention, a personal computer would take up the space of a living room and a pocket calculator would be the size of a small car. Microchip technology is now commonplace in the household and workplace: in telephones, washing machines, video recorders, and cars. In industry, its use has seen the monotonous tasks of the production-line worker slowly being taken over by robots.

A classic example of the application of

Toaster prototype
Michele de Lucchi created a series of ten appliance prototypes for Girmi. Made of colored wood, they included a vacuum cleaner, coffee grinder, teapot, and hair dryer, as well as this toaster. They were first shown at the 1979 Milan Triennale.

microchip technology is the Sony Walkman personal stereo (see p.62), which was introduced in 1979. It was originally thought that because it could not record, the product might not be successful, yet it was an instant success, and spawned numerous imitators.

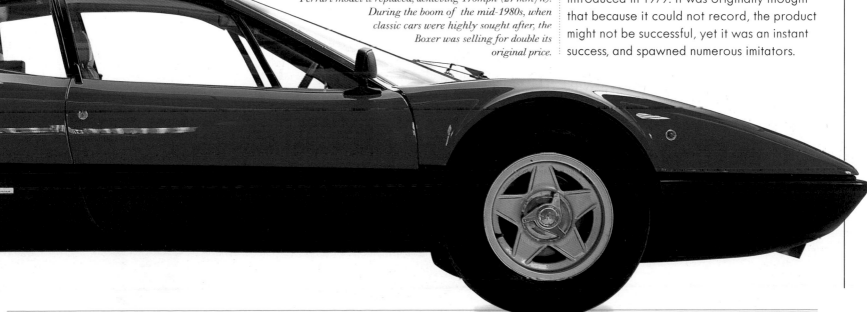

1980–89

Technological advances produced many changes in the penultimate decade of the 20th century. The computer age had definitely arrived and designers were increasingly utilizing sophisticated programs to carry out many aspects of product design that had traditionally been drawn or made by hand. For graphic designers, too, the new technology created myriad new possibilities for manipulating typesetting and image reproduction.

COMPUTER TECHNOLOGY

Home computing began slowly to take off in the 1980s, accelerating astonishingly into the 1990s. The first personal computer (PC) had been developed by IBM in the late-1970s, and was introduced as the IBM PC in 1981. However, the real breakthrough came with the introduction of the Apple Macintosh in 1984 (see p.200). It improved the user-friendliness of the home computer, and introduced the now ubiquitous mouse.

The compact disc (CD), which first appeared in 1982, has revolutionized the music industry. CDs record information digitally as a series of numbers. This stored information is read and translated by a laser beam, which allows the music to be reproduced clearly. CDs have now all but replaced the vinyl record in most homes.

Sound is not the only type of information that can be recorded on CDs; they are also able to store text and pictures, and even video sequences. This ability is utilized in the CD-ROM player. Invented in 1985 by the Dutch electronics manufacturing giant Philips, this innovation was marketed jointly with Sony. Basically a CD adapted for use with a computer, a CD-ROM can store 1,000 times as much information as a floppy disc.

Cellnet mobile telephone
Portable telephones have evolved from large and cumbersome units into sleek, pocket-sized instruments. It has been predicted that their rapidly increasing popularity will one day see the disappearance of fixed-point telephones.

The initials ROM stand for "Read-Only Memory," indicating that the information can only be read, not added to or changed. The CD-ROM did not conquer the domestic market until the 1990s.

THE GLOBAL VILLAGE
The term "global village" began to be used as new technology made possible instant communication with virtually any part of the world. Fax machines became a familiar part of the office, and modems and electronic mail (e-mail) enabled people to communicate cheaply and instantly via computer. Satellites were developed in the US in the 1960s by NASA, the National Aeronautics and Space Administration, and by the 1980s thousands of satellites orbiting the earth were being used for telecommunications and broadcasting. Another invention, the cellular, or portable, telephone, first developed in 1979 by the Swedish company Ericsson, became commonplace during the 1980s.

Marketing phenomenon
In less than ten years the compact disc has established itself as the preeminent method of sound recording for the home entertainment market, despite being more expensive than the vinyl recordings that it has superseded.

Modern vase
Philippe Starck's work often gives an appearance of instability that is confounded by its actual sturdiness. This three-legged vase seems precariously balanced on the tapered, slanting feet. However, the sheer weight of the glass makes the structure rigid and stable.

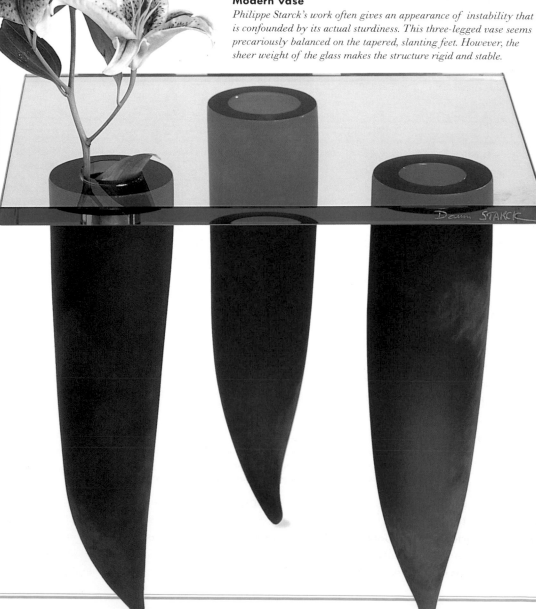

PUNK AND BRITISH DESIGN

In the late 1970s, Britain saw the appearance of a new, aggressive street style — Punk — that was, in tamer forms, to have an influence on graphics, fashion, and culture in the 1980s. In fashion, Vivienne Westwood's 1981 Pirate collection (see p.145) translated the Punk look into successful high-street fashion and marked the revival of British fashion as an international force. Punk also had a great influence on new-wave graphics, exemplified in Britain by Jamie Reid's controversial record covers for the Sex Pistols, and in Terry Jones's *i-D* magazine. Something of the shock appeal of Punk is also evident in the furniture of Ron Arad (see p.254), and the industrial designs of Daniel Weil (see p.57).

MEMPHIS

Undoubtedly the most important design group of the decade was Memphis. It was started in Milan by Ettore Sottsass after he left the radical Studio Alchimia in 1980. He surrounded himself with a group of international architects and furniture, fabric, and ceramics designers, including Andrea Branzi, Martine Bedin, George Sowden (b.1942), Peter Shire, Michael Graves, Javier Mariscal (b.1950), Michele de Lucchi, and Matteo Thun. They first showed their work at the 1981 Milan Furniture Fair, where it was an immediate success, although some critics attacked it for being tasteless. A postmodernist group, Memphis borrowed from an eclectic variety of sources, including anything from classical architecture to 1950s' kitsch. It made startling and innovative use of bold, often outrageous, coloring, and put more emphasis on the look and meaning of the object than on its practical usage. What started out as a polemical venture proved to be an enormous commercial success. However, the ideas of the Memphis group, which typified the more excessive aspects of postmodernism, were quickly exhausted.

UNIVERSAL DESIGN

In total contrast, the industrial design consultancy Ergonomi Design Gruppen was founded in Sweden in 1979 by Maria Benktzon (b.1946) and Sven-Eric Juhlin (b.1940) to specialize in the ergonomic design of everyday tools. A key interest was design for people with limited physical abilities, and one of the group's best-known designs is a range of cutlery called Eat/Drink, which clearly embodies the design philosophy that "the need and desires of the user shall form the basis of the project."

Despite being the focus of increasing concern through the 1980s and '90s, universal design, or design for disability, as it is also known, is still a largely neglected area. Attention is likely to increase as the population balance shifts with more people living into old age. Computer technology is also increasing access and creating opportunities for all people. For example, despite having been disabled at the age of 20 by a crippling disease that left him unable to walk, speak, or write, the eminent British physicist Stephen Hawking has been enabled to work by communicating through a voice synthesizer and computer.

SOCIAL CONSCIENCE

"Design for need" started as an international conference that took place in London in 1976. It pointed to the growing feeling that design should be addressing issues relating to the

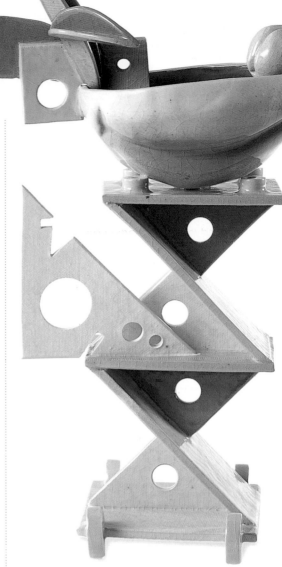

Postmodernist ceramics
Peter Shire, who was a member of Ettore Sottsass's Memphis group, is noted for his eccentric ceramic designs. The California Peach Cup, made in 1980, is typical of his work and a good example of postmodernist design.

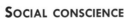

Eat/Drink cutlery
This functional yet attractive cutlery set was designed in 1980 for people with limited strength. The design of the knife is such that pressure is applied with the arm rather than just the wrist.

environment, ecological concerns, and special problems occurring in underdeveloped countries. The problem was that design had for too long been concentrating on production and consumerism. A series of ecological threats in the 1980s provoked designers into focusing more clearly on "green" issues. One result was a move toward designing products that could be recycled. This began to trickle down to affect all areas of design. For example, the French designer Philippe Starck, who became one of the most celebrated designers of the 1980s, created his Louis 20 stacking chairs (see p.193) with the legs screwed rather than glued to the body, so that the parts could be separated and recycled. Designers began to realize that they had an important role to play in finding solutions to large-scale world problems.

THE 1990s

On a visit to Africa in the early 1990s, Trevor Baylis, a British inventor, became aware of the importance of radio for communicating information to remote communities that lacked an electric power supply. Although many village communities had radios, they were more or less useless, since the batteries were prohibitively expensive. This meant valuable information, particularly relating to health, did not always reach those who needed it most. Baylis's response was to invent a wind-up radio that could generate enough power to be self-sufficient. In collaboration with a manufacturer, he produced a model that is now being successfully used across Africa. The wind-up radio highlights two of the most important design imperatives for the 1990s: ecology and communication.

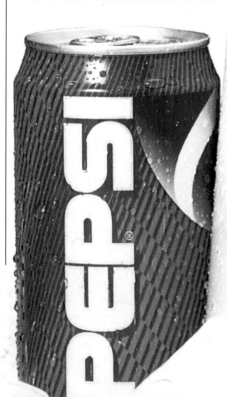

BayGen Freeplay radio
Trevor Baylis's wind-up radio was launched in 1995. It shows how knowledge that has been available for generations can be used as effectively as new technology.

ECOLOGICAL CONCERNS

Some designers in the 1990s have been concerned with undoing the damage that humans have inflicted on the planet with the mass industrialization of the

19th and 20th centuries, or at least with trying to stem future damage.

In 1985, scientists discovered that there was a dangerously large hole in the ozone layer. They contended that if the hole was permitted to grow, the temperature of the planet would increase with catastrophic effects. Governments responded with atypical speed, collaborating with the Montreal Protocol — signed in 1987 and reinforced in 1990 — and imposing controls on items such as aerosols and refrigerators that contained potentially harmful chlorofluorocarbons (better known as CFCs). It became clear in the 1970s and '80s that the world's resources are being exhausted at a rate that cannot be sustained. Fossil fuels will not last forever, so designers are beginning to explore solutions that may slow down and even stop the depletion of raw materials. For example, alternative sources of energy are being devised: solar cars have been developed in California and elsewhere, and the electric car, once an inventor's dream, is now a reality. In response to the rapid depletion of the forests caused by the ever-increasing demand for paper and wood, alternative forms of

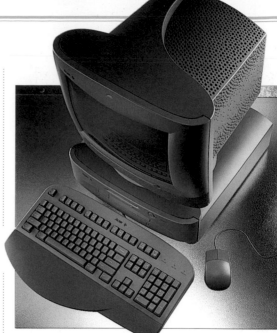

Ergonomic design
As more people work at home, computer companies are improving the external appearance of their products in response to customer demand for better-looking machines.

communication and information storage are being developed in addition to using more recycled paper. However, the idea of a paperless office, relying solely on electronic storage, is still a long way from being realized.

RECYCLED GOODS

Built-in obsolescence is beginning to be replaced by a more responsible approach to product durability. As well as incorporating more recycled materials into their products, designers are creating more energy-efficient products that can be recycled or repaired. A well-designed car is one that uses little fuel, produces few emissions, lasts a long time, can easily be

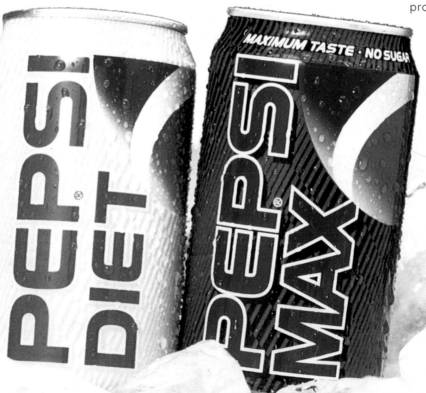

New-look packaging
At the close of the century, as products become more sophisticated and refined, their appearance remains the essence of their success or failure. Pepsi Cola illustrated the continued importance of packaging in 1996, when it spent $40 million on changing the color of its most famous product.

repaired, and at the end of its life can be broken down with the component materials either being recycled or disposed of safely. In the rapidly advancing computer industry, the trend is now to create machines that can be upgraded to keep up with new developments, rather than having to replace the whole machine.

ADVANCES IN MASS COMMUNICATION

The 1990s have also seen the most astonishing advances in communication. The Internet and the information superhighway promise to have as much impact on our lives as the invention of

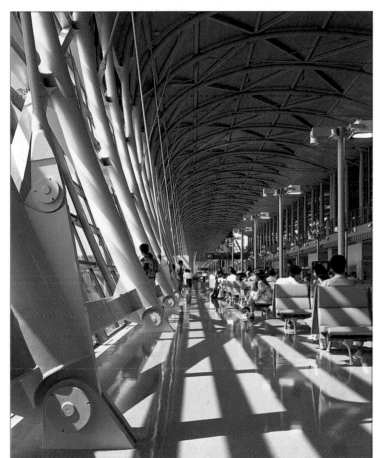

Modern architecture
Kansai International Airport, situated on the Bay of Osaka, Japan, was designed by Renzo Piano. It has been built on a manmade island and has its own train running the length of its mile-long (1.6km) terminal.

the telephone, the television, or the automobile. All you need is a computer to have instant access to information databases around the world. For example, from your own living room in Paris or Sydney or Munich, you could access the Smithsonian Institution in Washington, DC, or have a guided virtual tour of the Natural History Museum in London. At this relatively early stage in its development, it is impossible to guess just how great its impact will be on the

21st century, just as no one could have guessed in 1900 how great the impact of Alexander Graham Bell's telephone would be on our personal and working lives.

THE FUTURE

In the final decade of the century, scientific and technological developments are not slowing down; they are increasing with mind-boggling rapidity. The changes that will take place in the next century will be even more marked than those that took place in the last. Although it is impossible to predict exactly what the future will bring, there are some indicators. For example, machines a mere half a millimeter wide are being created, designed to be injected into the veins to clear blood clots. The Hubble telescope is sending back photographs that are rewriting our understanding of the universe (scientists now estimate that there are at least 50 billion galaxies in the universe, not at least ten billion as was previously thought) and may reawaken interest in space exploration. In the transportation industry, there is talk of a revolutionary new generation of superjets, superseding the Concorde and flying *outside* the earth's atmosphere. They will make transglobal flights possible in a fraction of the time they currently take. With the end of the cold war, the scaling down of the arms race, and the unification of Europe, there is an opportunity for greater international cooperation, and for the world to become a safer place. And with the continuing brilliance and increasing moral responsibility of scientists and designers, we enter the next century with every reason to be optimistic.

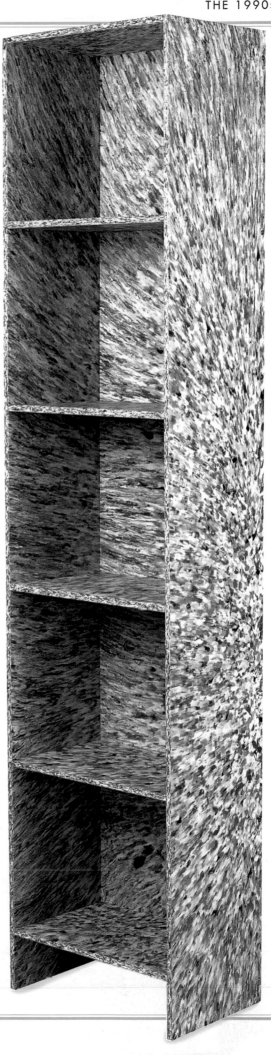

Recycled storage unit
Jane Atfield's shelving unit, made from plastic recovered from used dishwashing-liquid bottles, is an example of the growing trend among designers to produce furniture and other products from recycled materials.

THE LIVING ROOM

CHAIRS

ALL THE MAJOR THEMES OF 20th-century furniture design can be traced through the look, construction, and materials of the chair. Whether it is made by modern or traditional means, the chair has been used by designers to make statements about their personal design philosophy. Gerrit Rietveld's chair from the late 1910s says more about spatial harmony than it does about sitting in comfort (see opposite). Charles Eames, on the other hand, used advanced technology and applied ergonomic theory to make chairs that were better able to support the human body (see p.37). By the 1960s, furniture designers were exploring a less deterministic approach: the Sacco chair, for example, allows each sitter to shape the chair to fit his or her body (see p.38).

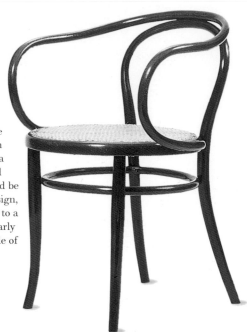

Thonet chair 1902–03

Michael Thonet was an extremely successful mass producer of chairs. His manufacturing process, developed in the 19th century, used steam to bend solid wood into a number of prefabricated components, which could be assembled later. The design, which reduces the chair to a simple structure, is an early and still popular example of machine aesthetics.

Specifications
Country: Austria
Material: Bentwood

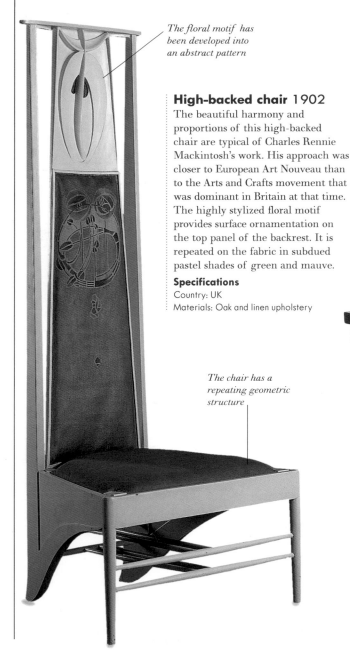

The floral motif has been developed into an abstract pattern

High-backed chair 1902

The beautiful harmony and proportions of this high-backed chair are typical of Charles Rennie Mackintosh's work. His approach was closer to European Art Nouveau than to the Arts and Crafts movement that was dominant in Britain at that time. The highly stylized floral motif provides surface ornamentation on the top panel of the backrest. It is repeated on the fabric in subdued pastel shades of green and mauve.

Specifications
Country: UK
Materials: Oak and linen upholstery

The chair has a repeating geometric structure

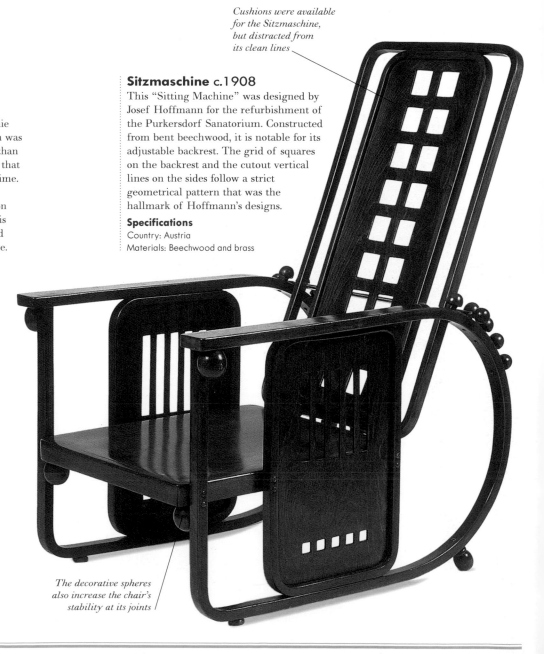

Cushions were available for the Sitzmaschine, but distracted from its clean lines

Sitzmaschine c.1908

This "Sitting Machine" was designed by Josef Hoffmann for the refurbishment of the Purkersdorf Sanatorium. Constructed from bent beechwood, it is notable for its adjustable backrest. The grid of squares on the backrest and the cutout vertical lines on the sides follow a strict geometrical pattern that was the hallmark of Hoffmann's designs.

Specifications
Country: Austria
Materials: Beechwood and brass

The decorative spheres also increase the chair's stability at its joints

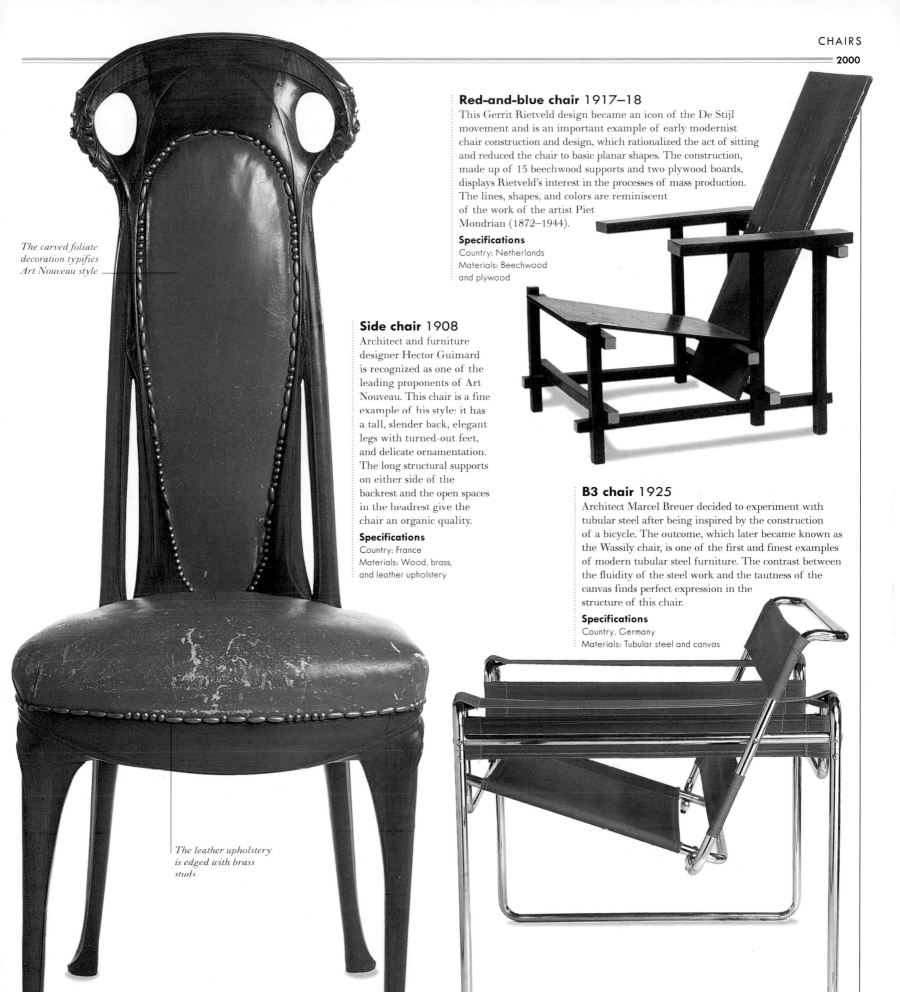

The carved foliate decoration typifies Art Nouveau style

Red-and-blue chair 1917–18

This Gerrit Rietveld design became an icon of the De Stijl movement and is an important example of early modernist chair construction and design, which rationalized the act of sitting and reduced the chair to basic planar shapes. The construction, made up of 15 beechwood supports and two plywood boards, displays Rietveld's interest in the processes of mass production. The lines, shapes, and colors are reminiscent of the work of the artist Piet Mondrian (1872–1944).

Specifications
Country: Netherlands
Materials: Beechwood and plywood

Side chair 1908

Architect and furniture designer Hector Guimard is recognized as one of the leading proponents of Art Nouveau. This chair is a fine example of his style: it has a tall, slender back, elegant legs with turned-out feet, and delicate ornamentation. The long structural supports on either side of the backrest and the open spaces in the headrest give the chair an organic quality.

Specifications
Country: France
Materials: Wood, brass, and leather upholstery

B3 chair 1925

Architect Marcel Breuer decided to experiment with tubular steel after being inspired by the construction of a bicycle. The outcome, which later became known as the Wassily chair, is one of the first and finest examples of modern tubular steel furniture. The contrast between the fluidity of the steel work and the tautness of the canvas finds perfect expression in the structure of this chair.

Specifications
Country: Germany
Materials: Tubular steel and canvas

The leather upholstery is edged with brass studs

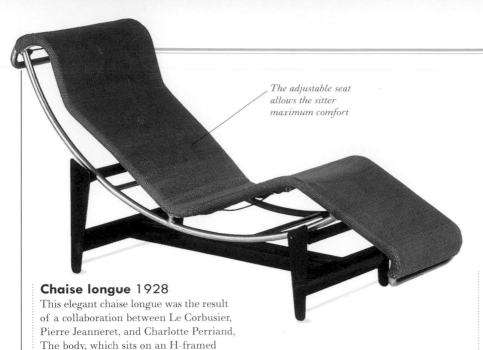

The adjustable seat allows the sitter maximum comfort

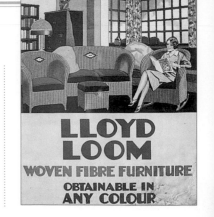

Lloyd Loom
This poster advertises the classic Lloyd Loom furniture suite of sofa, two chairs, and foot stool, displayed against an elegant, colorful Art Deco interior backdrop. The text emphasizes one of the chief advantages of the company's woven fiber – it was versatile enough to be dyed any of the variety of colors.

Chaise longue 1928
This elegant chaise longue was the result of a collaboration between Le Corbusier, Pierre Jeanneret, and Charlotte Perriand, The body, which sits on an H-framed base, is made from tubular steel. An early example of ergonomic design, the chair combines graceful lines with the innovative use of industrial materials.

Specifications
Country: France
Materials: Tubular steel and leather

Gent's chair 1931
The cane furniture produced by Lloyd Loom was particularly popular in the 1920s and '30s. The company was founded in 1919 by an American, Marshall B. Lloyd, who invented a method of weaving a canelike material from twisted paper and wire. This chair is part of a suite that includes Gent's and Lady's chairs and a sofa.

Specifications
Country: US
Materials: Woven fiber and wood

The buttoned-leather cushions are traditionally manufactured

Barcelona chair 1929
Mies van der Rohe's chair was designed for the king and queen of Spain for the opening ceremony of the 1929 International Exhibition in Barcelona. Its modern appearance retains the sense of luxury and ceremony associated with traditional thrones. The frame is made from two flat, chrome-plated steel bars, which cross over to provide back and leg supports.

Specifications
Country: Germany
Materials: Steel and leather

Pressed layers of wood are molded to shape to create the pliancy required for the scrolls

Paimio chair 1932
This armchair was designed by Alvar Aalto for the Tuberculosis Sanatorium at Paimio, Finland. Aalto spent a number of years developing the techniques that would allow his uncompromisingly modern designs to be realized. With the Paimio, he shows that molded plywood has all the properties suited to modern furniture design.

Specifications
Country: Finland
Materials: Laminated birch and birch plywood

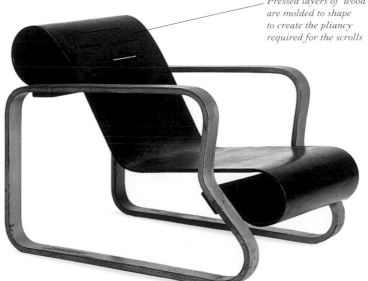

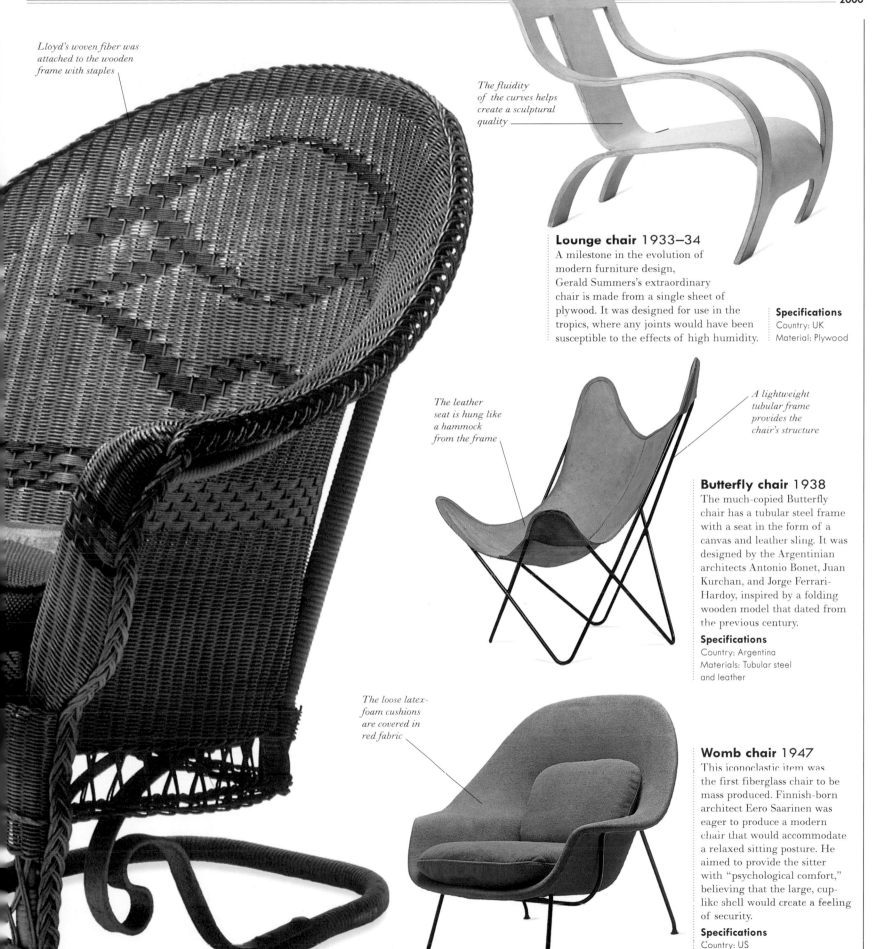

Lloyd's woven fiber was attached to the wooden frame with staples

The fluidity of the curves helps create a sculptural quality

Lounge chair 1933–34

A milestone in the evolution of modern furniture design, Gerald Summers's extraordinary chair is made from a single sheet of plywood. It was designed for use in the tropics, where any joints would have been susceptible to the effects of high humidity.

Specifications
Country: UK
Material: Plywood

The leather seat is hung like a hammock from the frame

A lightweight tubular frame provides the chair's structure

Butterfly chair 1938

The much-copied Butterfly chair has a tubular steel frame with a seat in the form of a canvas and leather sling. It was designed by the Argentinian architects Antonio Bonet, Juan Kurchan, and Jorge Ferrari-Hardoy, inspired by a folding wooden model that dated from the previous century.

Specifications
Country: Argentina
Materials: Tubular steel and leather

The loose latex-foam cushions are covered in red fabric

Womb chair 1947

This iconoclastic item was the first fiberglass chair to be mass produced. Finnish-born architect Eero Saarinen was eager to produce a modern chair that would accommodate a relaxed sitting posture. He aimed to provide the sitter with "psychological comfort," believing that the large, cup-like shell would create a feeling of security.

Specifications
Country: US
Materials: Tubular steel, fiberglass, fabric, and latex foam

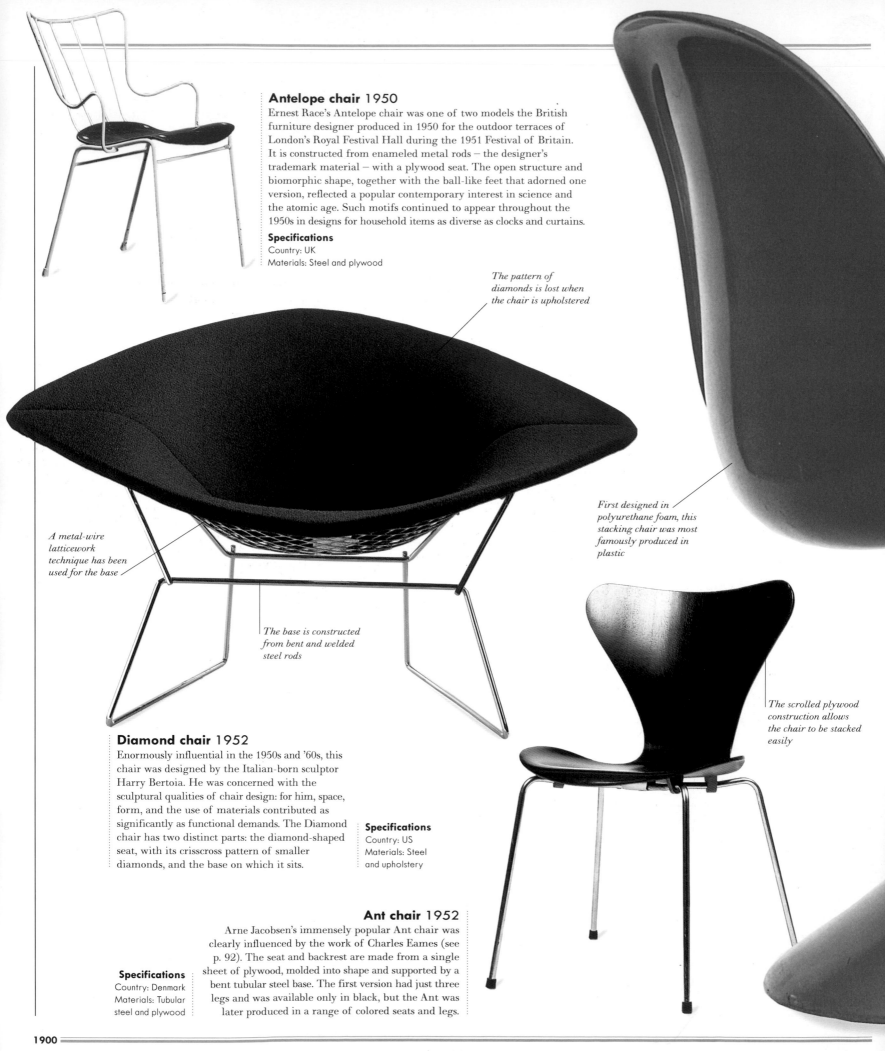

Antelope chair 1950

Ernest Race's Antelope chair was one of two models the British furniture designer produced in 1950 for the outdoor terraces of London's Royal Festival Hall during the 1951 Festival of Britain. It is constructed from enameled metal rods – the designer's trademark material – with a plywood seat. The open structure and biomorphic shape, together with the ball-like feet that adorned one version, reflected a popular contemporary interest in science and the atomic age. Such motifs continued to appear throughout the 1950s in designs for household items as diverse as clocks and curtains.

Specifications
Country: UK
Materials: Steel and plywood

The pattern of diamonds is lost when the chair is upholstered

A metal-wire latticework technique has been used for the base

First designed in polyurethane foam, this stacking chair was most famously produced in plastic

The base is constructed from bent and welded steel rods

The scrolled plywood construction allows the chair to be stacked easily

Diamond chair 1952

Enormously influential in the 1950s and '60s, this chair was designed by the Italian-born sculptor Harry Bertoia. He was concerned with the sculptural qualities of chair design: for him, space, form, and the use of materials contributed as significantly as functional demands. The Diamond chair has two distinct parts: the diamond-shaped seat, with its crisscross pattern of smaller diamonds, and the base on which it sits.

Specifications
Country: US
Materials: Steel and upholstery

Ant chair 1952

Arne Jacobsen's immensely popular Ant chair was clearly influenced by the work of Charles Eames (see p. 92). The seat and backrest are made from a single sheet of plywood, molded into shape and supported by a bent tubular steel base. The first version had just three legs and was available only in black, but the Ant was later produced in a range of colored seats and legs.

Specifications
Country: Denmark
Materials: Tubular steel and plywood

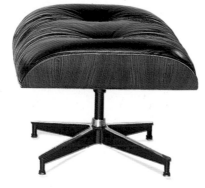

The chair swivels on its stand, allowing considerable flexibility and comfort

Lounge chair and foot stool 1956

This complicated piece of furniture involves three plywood shells padded with upholstery and joined by aluminum supports. Unquestionably placed at the luxury end of the market, the chair was originally designed by Charles Eames as a birthday gift for film director Billy Wilder.

Specifications
Country: US
Materials: Plywood, aluminum, rubber, and leather upholstery

"READY-MADE" STOOLS

Achille and Pier Giacomo Castiglioni's Mezzadro stool is clearly influenced by the "ready-made" sculpture of Marcel Duchamp. The stool consists of a brightly colored, enameled metal tractor seat attached by a wing-nut to a cantilevered bent steel support with a wooden footrest. The original stools, at first considered too radical to be put into production, did not have holes in the seat and had a dark metal base. This revised version did not appear until the 1970s. The name derives from the Italian mezzadro, meaning "tenant farmer."

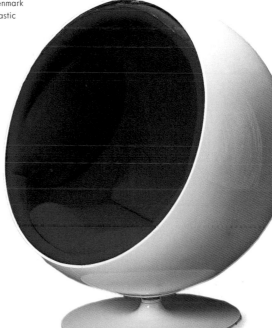

Mezzadro stool, 1957

Stacking chair 1960–67

The Danish designer Verner Panton is credited with having created the world's first single-piece plastic chair. This unusual, cantilevered chair, produced in a range of vivid colors, has become an icon of the 1960s. The original versions were produced in 1960, but it was seven years before technical problems were resolved and the chair was put into production. Strong, comfortable, and with a glossy, brightly colored finish, the piece is a tribute to the unique properties of plastic.

Specifications
Country: Denmark
Material: Plastic

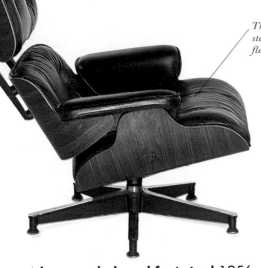

Ball chair 1963–65

Finnish designer Eero Aarnio used state-of-the-art manufacturing processes to produce his space-age Ball, or Globe, chair. It is made from a fiberglass ball, cut in section, and swivels on an aluminum base. It was often equipped with speakers or telephone.

Specifications
Country: Finland
Materials: Fiberglass, aluminum, and upholstery

The ball tied to the foot of Donna was intended to symbolize female imprisonment

Made by Zanotta, the beanbag was available in leather or vinyl

Vivid red nylon is stretched across the contours of the voluptuous structure

Sacco 1968–69

In 1968, Piero Gatti, Cesare Paolini, and Franco Teodoro produced a chair without a fixed form — the first successful beanbag chair. It does not have a frame; instead, a soft skin is filled with tiny polystyrene balls. The idea is that the user should be able to shape the chair to suit his or her body and needs. This reflects a sympathy with the radical anti-design movements prevalent in Italy during the late 1960s.

Specifications
Country: Italy
Materials: Leather or vinyl and polystyrene

Up 5 Donna 1969

One of six designs in his Up series, Gaetano Pesce's Donna chair is made from polyurethane foam and stretch fabric. It was most remarkable for its packaging: compressed to a tenth of its normal volume for packing and shipping, the chair would spring into shape when the purchaser opened the PVC wrapper. Clearly shaped like a voluptuous woman, Donna has no internal structure and relies instead on the high density of the foam.

Specifications
Country: Italy
Materials: Polyurethane foam and stretch nylon

Little Beaver armchair 1987

Frank Gehry is an American architect and designer whose work includes the Vitra Design Museum in Germany, where some of his own chairs are displayed. This armchair and footrest were designed to form part of a series of low-cost pieces of furniture made from corrugated cardboard. Strength has been achieved by using the edges of the cardboard for the chair's surface.

Specifications
Country: US
Material: Laminated cardboard

Proust's armchair 1978

Alessandro Mendini was a leading activist for the radical design group Alchimia when he designed this chair. The group rejected modernist design theory in favor of ornament and craftsmanship. For Proust's armchair (Mendini's aim was to create a chair that Proust might have sat in), the designer took a traditional 19th-century chair and hand-painted it all over in the Impressionist style.

The ornate carved frame is covered in an Impressionist brushstroke pattern

Specifications
Country: Italy
Materials: Hand-painted wood and hand-painted upholstery

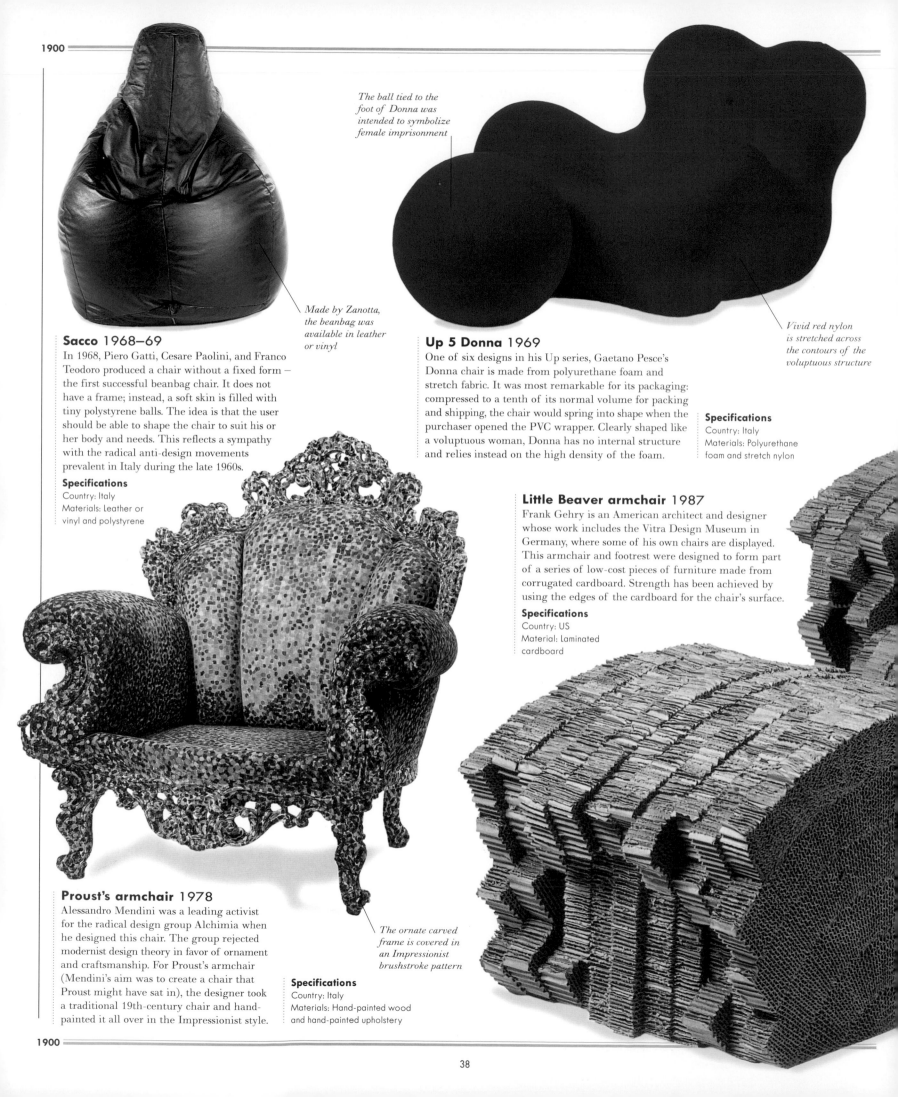

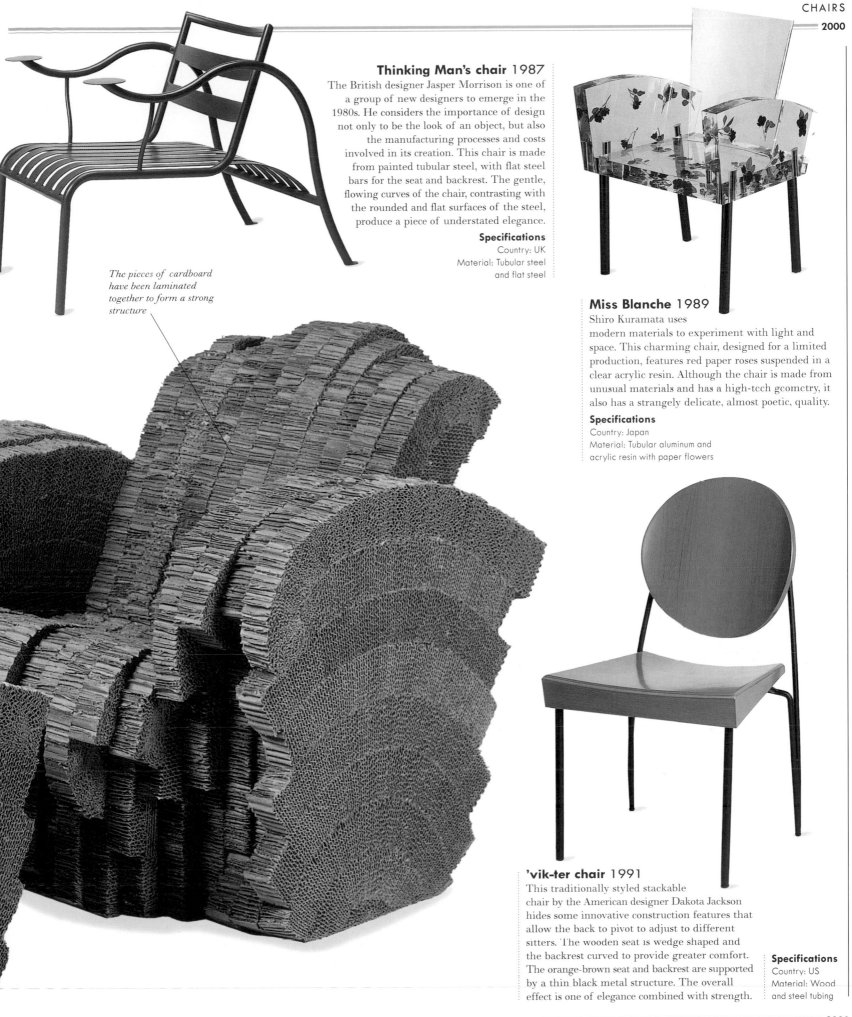

Thinking Man's chair 1987

The British designer Jasper Morrison is one of a group of new designers to emerge in the 1980s. He considers the importance of design not only to be the look of an object, but also the manufacturing processes and costs involved in its creation. This chair is made from painted tubular steel, with flat steel bars for the seat and backrest. The gentle, flowing curves of the chair, contrasting with the rounded and flat surfaces of the steel, produce a piece of understated elegance.

Specifications
Country: UK
Material: Tubular steel
and flat steel

The pieces of cardboard have been laminated together to form a strong structure

Miss Blanche 1989

Shiro Kuramata uses modern materials to experiment with light and space. This charming chair, designed for a limited production, features red paper roses suspended in a clear acrylic resin. Although the chair is made from unusual materials and has a high-tech geometry, it also has a strangely delicate, almost poetic, quality.

Specifications
Country: Japan
Material: Tubular aluminum and acrylic resin with paper flowers

'vik-ter chair 1991

This traditionally styled stackable chair by the American designer Dakota Jackson hides some innovative construction features that allow the back to pivot to adjust to different sitters. The wooden seat is wedge shaped and the backrest curved to provide greater comfort. The orange-brown seat and backrest are supported by a thin black metal structure. The overall effect is one of elegance combined with strength.

Specifications
Country: US
Material: Wood and steel tubing

Canapé LC2 (Petit Confort) c.1928

This sumptuous leather and tubular steel settee is the two-seater version of the famed Grand Confort armchair by Le Corbusier, Pierre Jeanneret, and Charlotte Perriand. A modernist interpretation of the 19th-century overstuffed armchair, Grand Confort Petit Modèle was also available in various other forms. These included single-seater "female chair," which allowed the sitter's legs to be crossed with ease. "Great Comfort" refers to the luxurious leather cushions.

Specifications
Country: France
Materials: Leather, foam, and chromium-plated steel

The steel framework seems slight in contrast with the vast cushions

D70 1953

Italian architect Osvaldo Borsani founded the Tecno SpA Design company to build his sophisticated furniture designs. The D70 divan bed was one of a pair, the other being the lounge chair, P40, reputedly capable of 486 seating positions. The D70 made no such extravagant claims, but its multi-holed side plates meant that the interchangeable back and seat could each be set in several different positions. The sofa can be opened out and used as a bed or closed up for storage.

Specifications
Country: Italy
Materials: Steel frame and foam cushions

The gentle curves of the upholstery prevent the divan from looking too mechanical

The 18-holed side plate allows the user to adjust the back and seat

SOFAS

IN ANY LIVING ROOM, the sofa is the dominant piece of furniture, one that creates competition between aesthetics and comfort. It is frequently used by designers as a vehicle for making a design statement – a conduit through which they can express their individual philosophies. Canapé LC2 (Petit Confort) by Le Corbusier, Jeanneret, and Perriand is a superb example of a sofa that successfully balances all of these concerns: it is elegant and inviting in appearance, it is supremely comfortable to sit on, and it is as uncompromisingly modernist as its creator intended it to be.

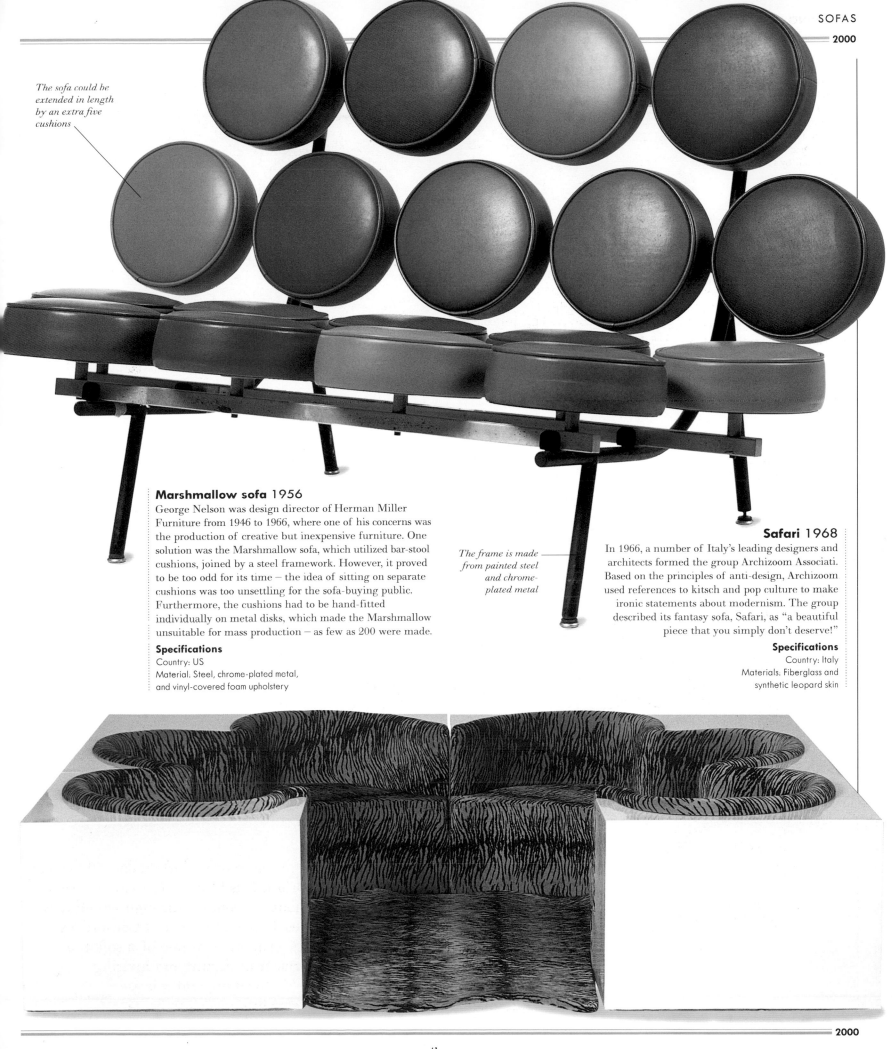

The sofa could be extended in length by an extra five cushions

Marshmallow sofa 1956

George Nelson was design director of Herman Miller Furniture from 1946 to 1966, where one of his concerns was the production of creative but inexpensive furniture. One solution was the Marshmallow sofa, which utilized bar-stool cushions, joined by a steel framework. However, it proved to be too odd for its time – the idea of sitting on separate cushions was too unsettling for the sofa-buying public. Furthermore, the cushions had to be hand-fitted individually on metal disks, which made the Marshmallow unsuitable for mass production – as few as 200 were made.

Specifications
Country: US
Material. Steel, chrome-plated metal, and vinyl-covered foam upholstery

The frame is made from painted steel and chrome-plated metal

Safari 1968

In 1966, a number of Italy's leading designers and architects formed the group Archizoom Associati. Based on the principles of anti-design, Archizoom used references to kitsch and pop culture to make ironic statements about modernism. The group described its fantasy sofa, Safari, as "a beautiful piece that you simply don't deserve!"

Specifications
Country: Italy
Materials. Fiberglass and synthetic leopard skin

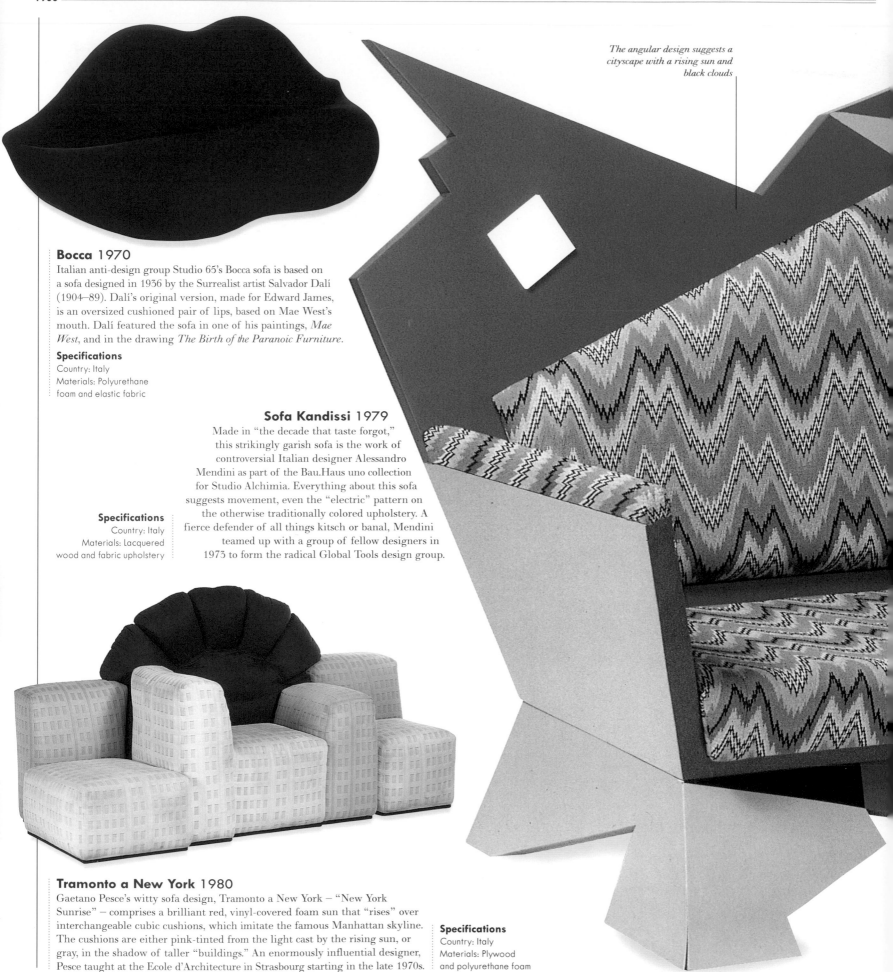

The angular design suggests a cityscape with a rising sun and black clouds

Bocca 1970

Italian anti-design group Studio 65's Bocca sofa is based on a sofa designed in 1936 by the Surrealist artist Salvador Dalí (1904–89). Dalí's original version, made for Edward James, is an oversized cushioned pair of lips, based on Mae West's mouth. Dalí featured the sofa in one of his paintings, *Mae West*, and in the drawing *The Birth of the Paranoic Furniture*.

Specifications
Country: Italy
Materials: Polyurethane foam and elastic fabric

Sofa Kandissi 1979

Made in "the decade that taste forgot," this strikingly garish sofa is the work of controversial Italian designer Alessandro Mendini as part of the Bau.Haus uno collection for Studio Alchimia. Everything about this sofa suggests movement, even the "electric" pattern on the otherwise traditionally colored upholstery. A fierce defender of all things kitsch or banal, Mendini teamed up with a group of fellow designers in 1973 to form the radical Global Tools design group.

Specifications
Country: Italy
Materials: Lacquered wood and fabric upholstery

Tramonto a New York 1980

Gaetano Pesce's witty sofa design, Tramonto a New York – "New York Sunrise" – comprises a brilliant red, vinyl-covered foam sun that "rises" over interchangeable cubic cushions, which imitate the famous Manhattan skyline. The cushions are either pink-tinted from the light cast by the rising sun, or gray, in the shadow of taller "buildings." An enormously influential designer, Pesce taught at the Ecole d'Architecture in Strasbourg starting in the late 1970s.

Specifications
Country: Italy
Materials: Plywood and polyurethane foam

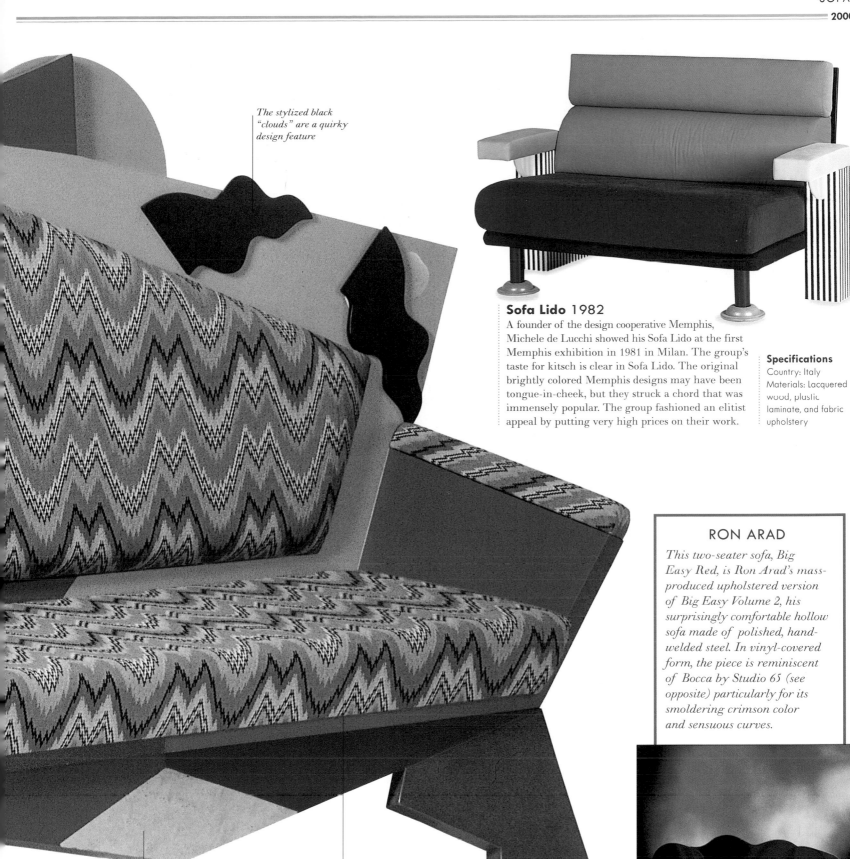

The stylized black "clouds" are a quirky design feature

Sofa Lido 1982

A founder of the design cooperative Memphis, Michele de Lucchi showed his Sofa Lido at the first Memphis exhibition in 1981 in Milan. The group's taste for kitsch is clear in Sofa Lido. The original brightly colored Memphis designs may have been tongue-in-cheek, but they struck a chord that was immensely popular. The group fashioned an elitist appeal by putting very high prices on their work.

Specifications
Country: Italy
Materials: Lacquered wood, plastic laminate, and fabric upholstery

RON ARAD

This two-seater sofa, Big Easy Red, is Ron Arad's mass-produced upholstered version of Big Easy Volume 2, his surprisingly comfortable hollow sofa made of polished, hand-welded steel. In vinyl-covered form, the piece is reminiscent of Bocca by Studio 65 (see opposite) particularly for its smoldering crimson color and sensuous curves.

Big Easy Red, 1989

Unlike the flamboyant backrest, the base of the sofa is a symmetrical structure

Solid blocks of vivid color contrast with the subdued shades and zany patterning of the upholstery

COFFEE & SIDE TABLES

IN THE EARLY PART of the century, the search for pure form found expression in Jacques-Emile Ruhlmann's hand-crafted furniture, made on commission using expensive materials. Eileen Gray, also active in France at that time, was allied with the Parisian avant-garde, who were experimenting with new materials and solutions. Donald Deskey's furniture echoes the American aesthetic that was emerging in 1929 and was to peak in the streamlined 1930s. Isamu Noguchi's and Carlo Mollino's strong biomorphic designs of the late 1940s were influenced by the work of Charles Eames. In the 1970s, there was a renaissance of traditional forms, and it was against this backdrop that the radical, anti-establishment Memphis group came together.

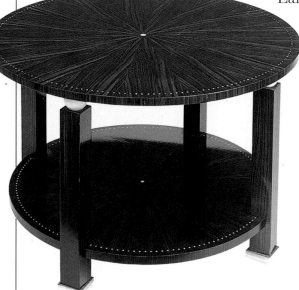

Guéridon en palissandre c.1922

Jacques-Emile Ruhlmann was one of the foremost French furniture makers of this century. Specializing in highly crafted luxury furniture, his classic pieces simplified traditional forms and lent a timelessness to modern design. Ruhlmann was famous for his use of veneers and inlays, and those skills are visible in this beautifully constructed table. Its simplicity is belied by closer inspection of the two table-top surfaces, which reveal a complicated grain effect.

Specifications
Country: France
Height: 19¾in (50cm)
Materials: Rosewood and ivory

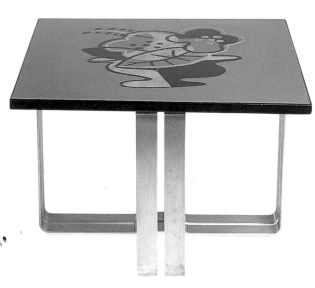

De Lucchi's enthusiastic use of decorated plastic laminate is typical of Memphis designers

The legs and neck of the table are made from blue enamelled tubular metal

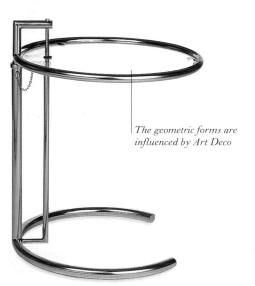

The geometric forms are influenced by Art Deco

E-1027 adjustable table 1927

Designed by Eileen Gray as part of a commission for a villa in Roquebrune, France, this table demonstrates a progressive attitude to the forms and materials of the Machine Age.

Specifications
Country: France
Adjustable tabletop height: 30–35in (53–89cm)
Materials: Tubular steel and glass

Occasional table c.1929

Produced by Deskey-Vollmer, a partnership formed in 1927 between Donald Deskey and Phillip Vollmer, this table is a good example of Deskey's design. His interest in innovative materials and techniques is exemplified by the aluminum strapwork base, and the abstract still life of the enameled top is evidence of his training in fine art.

Specifications
Country: US
Height: 24in (61cm)
Materials: Aluminum, enameled metal, and wood

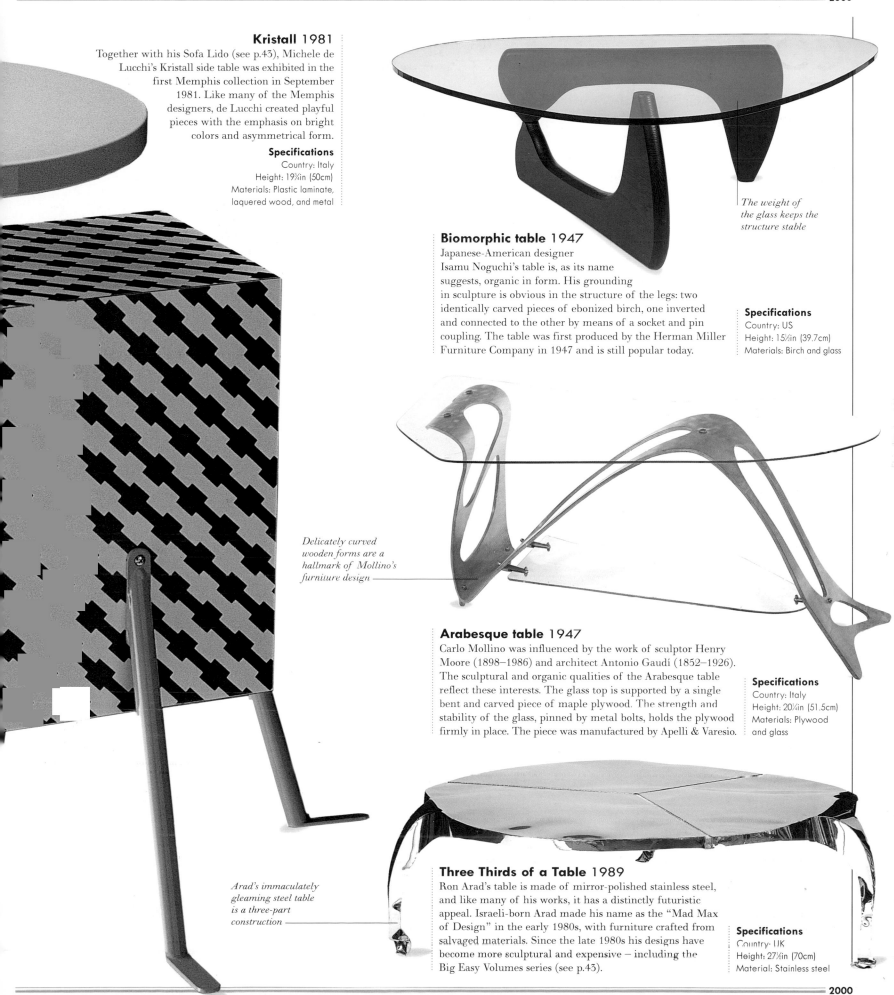

Kristall 1981

Together with his Sofa Lido (see p.43), Michele de Lucchi's Kristall side table was exhibited in the first Memphis collection in September 1981. Like many of the Memphis designers, de Lucchi created playful pieces with the emphasis on bright colors and asymmetrical form.

Specifications
Country: Italy
Height: 19¾in (50cm)
Materials: Plastic laminate, laquered wood, and metal

The weight of the glass keeps the structure stable

Biomorphic table 1947

Japanese-American designer Isamu Noguchi's table is, as its name suggests, organic in form. His grounding in sculpture is obvious in the structure of the legs: two identically carved pieces of ebonized birch, one inverted and connected to the other by means of a socket and pin coupling. The table was first produced by the Herman Miller Furniture Company in 1947 and is still popular today.

Specifications
Country: US
Height: 15⅝in (39.7cm)
Materials: Birch and glass

Delicately curved wooden forms are a hallmark of Mollino's furniture design

Arabesque table 1947

Carlo Mollino was influenced by the work of sculptor Henry Moore (1898–1986) and architect Antonio Gaudí (1852–1926). The sculptural and organic qualities of the Arabesque table reflect these interests. The glass top is supported by a single bent and carved piece of maple plywood. The strength and stability of the glass, pinned by metal bolts, holds the plywood firmly in place. The piece was manufactured by Apelli & Varesio.

Specifications
Country: Italy
Height: 20¼in (51.5cm)
Materials: Plywood and glass

Arad's immaculately gleaming steel table is a three-part construction

Three Thirds of a Table 1989

Ron Arad's table is made of mirror-polished stainless steel, and like many of his works, it has a distinctly futuristic appeal. Israeli-born Arad made his name as the "Mad Max of Design" in the early 1980s, with furniture crafted from salvaged materials. Since the late 1980s his designs have become more sculptural and expensive – including the Big Easy Volumes series (see p.43).

Specifications
Country: UK
Height: 27½in (70cm)
Material: Stainless steel

VASES

DISPLAYING FRESH FLOWERS in the home brings natural beauty to an otherwise man-made environment. Whether plainly understated or flamboyantly decorative, the vessels that hold flowers are, above all else, designed to enhance the splendor of their contents. During the 20th century, vases have provided inspiration for an extraordinary diversity of designs, from the sculptural, organic forms crafted by Art Nouveau designer Hector Guimard to the simplest, most functional pieces typified by Enzo Mari's double vase (see p.45). While a variety of materials from solid silver to lightest plastic have been used, the vase truly remains the showcase of the glassblower's skill.

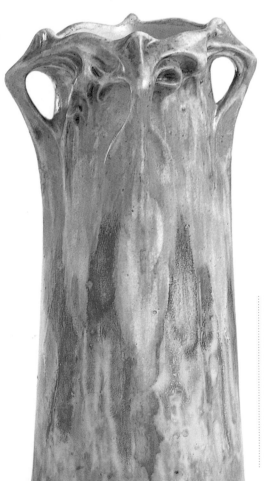

Peacock vase c.1900

Louis Comfort Tiffany was the outstanding producer of Art Nouveau glassware. He developed a method of manipulating color into his blown-glass vases to produce an iridescent effect. These glassworks were known by the trademark Favrile (French for "handmade") and were enormously popular in the US and Europe.

Specifications
Country: US
Material: Favrile glass
Height: 13¼in (33.7cm)

The brilliant iridescent colors and shimmering satin finish are associated with Favrile glassware

Ceramic vase 1908

When the French porcelain manufacturer Sèvres undertook to modernize its output, it employed a number of progressive artists. Among them was Hector Guimard, a renowned Art Nouveau designer best known for his entrances to the Paris Métro. This was one of a number of vases Guimard produced for the company.

Specifications
Country: France
Material: Porcelain
Height: 10½in (26.5cm)

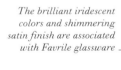

Organic forms are characteristic of Guimard's work

Rookwood vase 1909

Founded in Cincinnati in 1880, Rookwood became one of the most successful art potteries in the US. This hand-painted vase, with its muted tones and yellow and brown coloring, is a typical Rookwood piece. The influence of the company's Japanese painter, Kataro Shirayamadani, is clear in the imagery.

Specifications
Country: US
Material: Glazed
stoneware
Height: 12¾in (32.5cm)

Dark tones characterize the Rookwood style

Rose flute 1926

This extremely refined, blown-glass rose flute was produced by the Austrian company Lobmeyr. Its lines are restrained and unadorned, the long, delicate bowl of the vase tapering almost to a point. The design emphasizes the transparent and fragile nature of glass.

Specifications
Country: Austria
Material: Blown glass
Height: 5in (12.7cm)

Three layers of glass have been used to produce the subtly changing colors

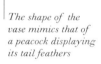

The shape of the vase mimics that of a peacock displaying its tail feathers

Silver vase c1920

Dagobert Pêche designed this wide-bowled solid silver vase for the Wiener Werkstätte. It stands on a fluted base and has a naturalistic floral motif in relief on the surface. Pêche's work came to represent an alternative to the strictly geometric designs originally produced by Josef Hoffmann and Koloman Moser for the Wiener Werkstätte.

Specifications
Country: Austria
Material: Silver
Height: 9½in (23.9cm)

The arabesque pattern of leaves and berries is typical of Pêche's decorative work

Ruba Rombic 1928

Reuben Haley's Art Deco vase, produced by the Consolidated Lamp and Glass Company, has a complex multiplane shape, clearly influenced by Cubism. It is made of green glass that has been blow-molded into shape. The name Ruba Rombic is derived from *Rubyiay* (meaning "poem") and *Rhomboid* (meaning "irregular shape").

Specifications
Country: US
Material: Molded, cased glass
Height: 15in (38cm)

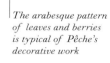

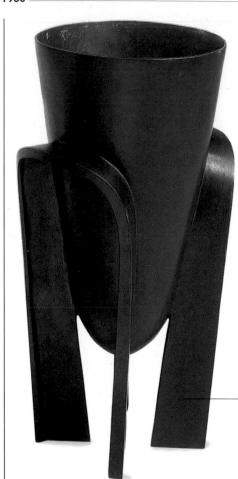

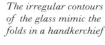

Bronze vase 1930

The work of the German designer Margot Kempe, this heavy bronze vase is cone-shaped, with a rounded base. The vessel is supported by two inverted "u"-shaped legs. An important teacher of ceramics after World War II Kempe arrived in the US via Equador in 1947. She taught at the renowned pottery studio Greenwich House, New York, until 1978.

Specifications
Country: Germany
Material: Bronze
Height: 18½in (47cm)

Orrefors vase 1940

In the 1930s, the Swedish company Orrefors Glasbruk employed three artists, Simon Gate, Edward Hald, and Vicke Lindstrand, to work on its ornamental glass production. Among their designs was this green vase. Made of thick glass, it has a simple, geometric shape that tapers off toward the base. On one of the four sides, there is a flowing figure of a cross-legged woman, who seems to be floating in water.

Specifications
Country: Sweden
Material: Glass with acid-etched decoration
Height: 6½in (16.2cm)

The irregular contours of the glass mimic the folds in a handkerchief

The heavy, dark material and unfussy design make this an austere piece

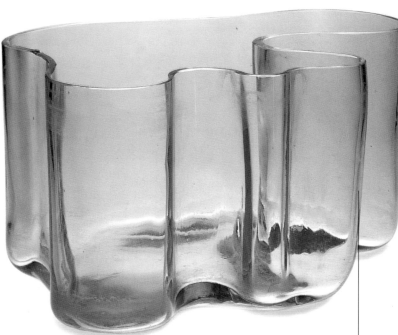

Aalto's vase was also produced in brown, green, and azure blue

Savoy 1936

Designed for the Helsinki Savoy Hotel and made by Karhula Glassworks, this vase is by Alvar Aalto, one of the pioneers of a biomorphic style of furniture. The organic shape is inspired by natural forms and by the work of artists such as Joan Miró (1893–1983). The glass was blow-molded into shape, and the walls vary in thickness.

Specifications
Country: Finland
Material: Blown, molded glass
Height: Not known

Handkerchief vase 1946

In 1921, Paolo Venini became a partner in a Murano glassmaking company, now known as Venini & Co. Originally it concentrated on traditional Venetian forms, but eventually, under Venini's direction, the company adopted more progressive styles. One of the designers, Fulvio Bianconi, worked with Venini to produce this Handkerchief vase. It is made from a square of glass, which is shaped into an irregular form in a manner that inspired its name.

Specifications
Country: Italy
Material: Blown glass
Height: 8¼in (21cm)

Pago Pago 1969

Enzo Mari's Pago Pago vase is cleverly designed to hold both small and large bouquets. It is made from deeply tinted plastic and has a small cone-shaped inner vessel (shown here). By inverting the vase, the outer chamber becomes available for smaller displays. The cutaway clearly reveals the interlocking structure.

Specifications

Country: Italy
Material: Plastic
Height: 11¾in (30cm)

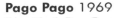

The "rubies" are crafted in smooth, jewel-shaped forms

Made from ABS plastic, the vase is colored a deep glossy purple

Ruby vase 1989

Czech designer Bořek Šípek used both blown and applied glass in the construction of his Ruby vase. It shows an interesting use of textures, colors, and shapes. The clear glass vessel takes on a form reminiscent of an elegant evening dress that is adorned with a belt of red spikes at the waist and a band of red rubies at the neck.

Specifications

Country: Czech Republic
Material: Blown and applied glass
Height: 23½in (60cm)

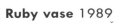

The replaceable glass flower tube is made from a commercial test tube

Flexi vase 1992–93

This vase by Miguel Calvo is notable both for its innovative use of materials and its unusual shape. It is constructed from a bent wire frame onto which translucent yellow vinyl is sewn. This, in turn, has a sewn-on pocket, containing a glass tube for the flowers. The result is a soft, flexible structure that reflects many of the qualities of the flowers it holds.

Specifications

Country: US
Materials: Vinyl, metal, glass, and thread
Height: 14½in (37cm)

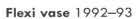

BOWLS

A WIDE RANGE OF MATERIALS and a variety of styles have contributed to the wealth of extraordinary and beautiful bowls produced over the past century. Bowls may serve a functional purpose as containers, but they are often intended to be purely decorative. An expression of the designer's artistic philosophy is often discernible in the form and decoration of the product. Josef Hoffmann, for example, used hammered silver to express the hand of the craftsman, while keeping the bowl free of unnecessary ornamentation. In contrast, Lella and Massimo Vignelli used inexpensive synthetic materials to produce household goods that challenged the principles of functionalist design and celebrated the fresh ideas of an emerging pop culture.

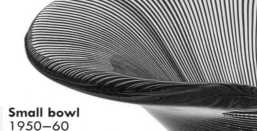

Small bowl
1950–60
Flavio Poli was awarded many prizes for his glassworks, including the Compasso d'Oro in 1954. This heavy, hand-blown glass bowl demonstrates Poli's bold use of sharply contrasting colors.

Specifications
Country: Italy
Material: Glass
Widest point: 7½in (19cm)

*The glass is shaped
to resemble a shell*

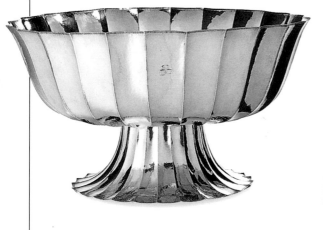

Dragonfly c.1900
One of a limited production run, this delicate centerpiece is by the Royal Copenhagen Porcelain Factory. Perched on the edges of the rim are two dragonflies, whose outstretched wings form the elegant handles.

Specifications
Country: Denmark
Material: Porcelain
Widest point: 12in (31cm)

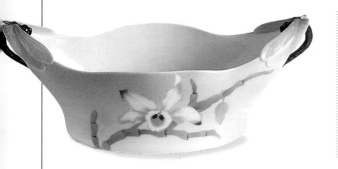

Oval fruit bowl 1917
The architect and craftsman Josef Hoffmann designed this fluted silver bowl for the Wiener Werkstätte. The hammered finish enhances the silver by providing a softly textured surface. The sympathetic use of materials, classical proportions, and lack of ornamentation are typical of the work produced by the Wiener Werkstätte.

Specifications
Country: Austria
Material: Silver
Widest point: 15½in (39cm)

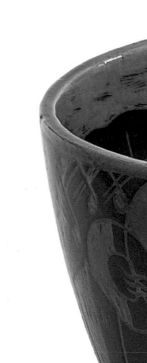

*The sketches depict
a lively jazz theme*

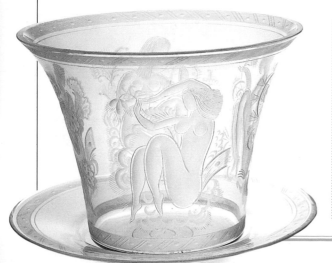

Bowl and stand 1926
Edward Hald designed this attractive glass bowl for the Orrefors Glasbruk, where he was artistic director from 1924 to 1933. It is engraved with the flat, stylized outlines of four seated women and is typical of Hald's work at this time. He had spent four years in Paris studying under Henri Matisse (1869–1954), whose paintings of nudes clearly influenced this piece.

Specifications
Country: Sweden
Material: Glass
Diameter of bowl at rim: 7in (17.8cm)

Jazz 1930–31
In 1930, the American Jazz Age was in full swing. Viktor Schreckengost's punch bowl is decorated with stylized images of New York life. The sgraffito designs were made by scratching through a thin layer of black clay over white ground before applying the glaze. The interior is decorated with musical notations.

Specifications
Country: US
Material: Glazed ceramic
Diameter: 16½in (42.2cm)

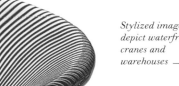

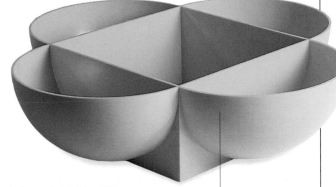

Earthenware bowl 1947

Stylized images depict waterfront cranes and warehouses

The painted black lines and geometric shapes on this bowl are suggestive of an industrial skyline. Detroit-born artist John Foster was probably inspired by the city's major industrial and commercial status. He produced this piece at a time when the automobile industry was recovering from its wartime concentration on the production of armaments.

Specifications
Country: US
Material: Stoneware
Diameter: 9in (23.2cm)

Fruit bowl 1960–70

Produced by Heller Designs, New York, this compartmentalized fruit bowl was created by Italian design team Lella and Massimo Vignelli. The use of plastic, which could easily be formed in bright and unconventional colors, is typical of Italian design of the 1960s.

Plastic allows a greater freedom of color and form

Specifications
Country: Italy
Material: Plastic
Diameter: 16in (41cm)

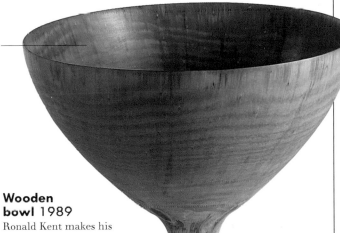

The striated woodgrain is enhanced with turning

Wooden bowl 1989

Ronald Kent makes his exquisite bowls from Norfolk Island pine. Each bowl is a work of art, individually produced on a lathe and turned until it is extremely thin and translucent. Kent then works on the surface with sealant and fine sandpaper to enhance the natural grain and color of the wood.

Specifications
Country: US
Material: Pine wood
Diameter: 14½in (37cm)

Nevada 1987–88

American-born designer Hilton McConnico created this bowl for the established French glassware manufacturer Daum. In an amusing reference to nature, the stem, made from green *pâte-de-verre*, is shaped in the form of a cactus plant. The bowl itself is made from clear thin glass, which is actually pierced by the cactus stem.

Specifications
Country: France
Material: Glass
Diameter: 11¾in (30cm)

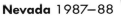

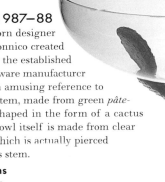

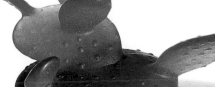

CANDLESTICKS

ALTHOUGH THE FIRST COMMERCIALLY VIABLE ELECTRIC LIGHTBULB, or incandescent bulb, was invented by Thomas Edison in 1879, electric lighting in the home was a luxury beyond the reach of all but the most wealthy for many decades. Instead, kerosene or gas lamps were used along with candlelight. With the eventual widespread introduction of affordable electric lighting, candlesticks were relegated to creating occasional atmospheric lighting for the dining table or used for religious and ceremonial purposes. During the last two decades of the 20th century, candlesticks have once again become fashionable decorative objects in the home. This has encouraged designers to invent new forms and to experiment with different materials to produce objects in a variety of contemporary and classical styles.

Chamberstick 1905

This brass chamberstick was made by the German designer Paul Haustein, who was best known for his enamelwork of the 1920s. Intended for use in the bedroom, it is typical of the handicraft work influenced by the European Arts and Crafts movement.

Specifications
Country: Germany
Height: 4in (9.6cm)
Material: Brass

The finely curved brass was shaped using a spinning technique

Candelabra c.1902

Josef Maria Olbrich was a leading member of the Wiener Werkstätte. This two-armed pewter piece is typical of his use of curved organic shapes. Like much of his decorative work, it illustrates the transition between the naturalistic forms of Art Nouveau and the more abstract geometry of Art Deco.

Specifications
Country: Austria
Height: 14in (36cm)
Material: Pewter

The restrained, slender stick has fluid lines

The tiered, geometric pattern is repeated on each component of the candelabra

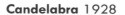

Candelabra 1928

This candelabra was produced by silver manufacturers Reed and Barton, which had started to produce pewterware in 1903. One of a pair, the candelabra's lines are uncompromisingly geometrical and the overall design is functional and devoid of excessive ornamentation.

Specifications
Country: US
Height : 8in (21cm)
Material: Pewter

The symmetrical branches and central post are topped with identical angular candle holders

Rectangular-shaped base is typical of Art Deco styling

Bubble candlesticks 1930s

During the 1930s the Chase Brass and Copper Company was the most successful American producer of chrome and nickel domestic utensils and accessories. These Art Deco candlesticks consist of a polished sphere sitting on a deep blue square of glass mounted on a chromium base.

Specifications
Country: US
Height: 2¾in (7cm)
Material: Chrome-plated metal and glass

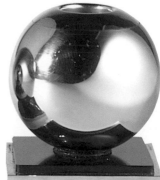

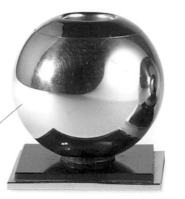

The polished surface is highly reflective

Candlestick 1959

This amusing candlestick was designed for Boda by Erik Höglund. It is made in thick, clear blown glass with a heavy base. Applied to either side of the body are two short arms with four-fingered hands, which are raised in jubilant fashion.

Specifications
Country: Sweden
Height: 4¾in (12cm)
Material: Glass

MODERN CANDLESTICKS

The final decade of the century has seen a revival of interest in candlesticks, and shops selling a dazzling array of candles and receptacles in which to put them. These include original and traditional candlesticks, sconces, lanterns, floorstanding candelabras, garden lamps and pot chandeliers, and bowls for floating candles. Some of the most popular designs are reinterpretations of Gothic wrought iron and pewter pieces, while ethnic influences can be seen in many of the wooden, ceramic, and papier-mâché candlesticks. From the austere to the whimsical, each style attests to the enduring charm of the flickering flame.

The polished finish has a pinkish tinge

Crane 1988

Matthew Hilton's sensuously curved candlestick is made from polished cast aluminum, although it was also available in bronze. It stands on a flared base, from which it develops into an elongated S-shape. The zoomorphic form, in this case derived from the neck of a crane, is carefully controlled and balanced.

Specifications
Country: UK
Height: 16½in (42 cm)
Material: Cast aluminum

Light passing throught the translucent finish illuminates the internal structure

Mirrored wall sconce

Cat's eye 1991

This award-winning candle-holder was designed by Laura Handler for Design Ideas. It is made up of ten separate units, each made from frosted glass. Blue versions were also available. The overall size and look of the finished item is dependent upon the number of units used and how they are interconnected. Here the units have been formed into a slightly curved triangular shape.

Specifications
Country: US
Height: 2in (4.8cm) each unit
Material: Cast glass

The elegant shape is inspired by the graceful arch of the bird's neck

Candlestick with Napoleonic wreath

Selection of glass candlesticks

Tree-shaped candelabrum

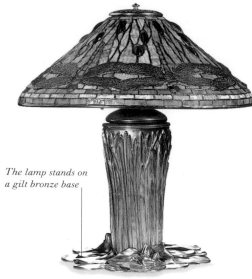

The lamp stands on a gilt bronze base

Dragonfly c.1900–10

Typical of the Art Nouveau work produced by the Tiffany Studios, Clara Driscoll's design employs a theme from nature. A series of dragonflies is positioned around the edge of the shade, and the stem is also inspired by an organic form – waterlilies.

Specifications
Country: US
Material: Glass, gilt bronze, and lead
Height: 26½in (67.5cm)

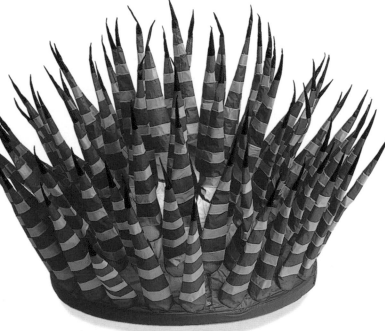

Urchin IL36 1991

GoldmanArts describes its products as "hysterical architecture." This is one of several inflatable lamps designed by Jonathan Goldman. The gently swaying, colorful, and playful nylon structures are intended to resemble a sea urchin as it moves in the ocean's current. The lamp's soft shades have no structural support – a small fan both inflates the shade and cools the bulb.

Specifications
Country: US
Material: Ripstop nylon fabric and metal
Diameter: 25in (64cm)

P H Artichoke 1958

Poul Henningsen's lamp is designed to prevent glare while maximizing reflected light. Overlapping "leaves" achieve this by spreading the light over a large area. Manufactured by Louis Poulsen & Co., it was originally designed to hang in public spaces.

Specifications
Country: Denmark
Material: Copper, steel, and enameled metal
Height: 27in (69cm)

LIGHTING

EARLY SHADES WERE DESIGNED simply to hide the mechanics of the lightbulb. However, Louis Comfort Tiffany's stained-glass lampshades cast a soft, colorful light in the room and were beautiful objects in their own right. The move toward a machine aesthetic, through Art Deco and later modernism, produced lighting designed with geometric forms. The functional design of George Carwardine's 1933 Anglepoise lamp allowed the user to aim the light directly onto the work area. New materials such as plastic became popular for lighting in the 1950s, and, since then, the use of low-voltage technology has allowed greater flexibility.

Copper "leaves" wash the room in a warm light

Eclisse 1966

Winner of the Premio Compasso d'Oro prize at the 1967 Milan Triennale, Vico Magistretti's table lamp, manufactured by Artemide, has an adjustable light. Its title, Italian for "eclipse," refers to the way the light is eclipsed as it revolves.

Specifications
Country: Italy
Material: Enameled metal
Height: 7½in (19cm)

The freestanding lamp may be wall-mounted by hinges on its base

Anglepoise 1933

George Carwardine, the designer of the century's most successful desk lamp, was an automobile engineer by profession. Utilizing his engineering skills, he created a design that lets hinges mimic the joints in a human arm. The Anglepoise is flexible, balanced, and holds any position. This example dates from about 1960; the design has since been modified slightly.

Specifications
Country: England
Material: Steel, enamel, and plastic
Height: 35½in (90cm) extended

The adjustable and movable arm allows the lamp to fold flat

A low voltage is conducted through the arms

Carwardine's hinged system has been widely copied, particularly for office use

Tizio 1972

Low-voltage lamps started to become popular in the 1970s. Richard Sapper's high-tech table lamp is a classic example. A transformer housed in the base greatly reduces the voltage, which is then conducted through the metal arms to power the lamp, eliminating the need for internal wiring. The result is a slender, elegant structure: finely balanced and, with its heavy transformer, perfectly stable.

Specifications
Country: Italy
Material: ABS plastic and aluminum
Height: 46½in (118cm) extended

Jazz c.1990

Ferdinand Porsche is from a family of renowned designers, best known for its contributions to the automobile industry. Made by PAF, his low-voltage halogen table lamp has sensors that electronically regulate the light. The switch is luminous.

Specifications
Country: Italy
Material: Plastic
Height: 25in (63.5cm) extended

RADIOS

THE EARLIEST RADIOS were known as crystal sets. Their workings were left exposed and the listener was required to wear headphones. It was not until the late 1920s that radios were designed to incorporate all the components within a single housing. Initially, these resembled items of furniture, but with the introduction of plastics, radios began to acquire a visual language of their own. In 1955, Sony launched its first transistor radio, and with it began the journey toward miniaturization. Today, it is possible to make radios smaller than a piece of candy.

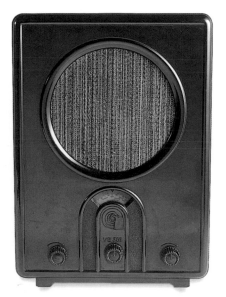

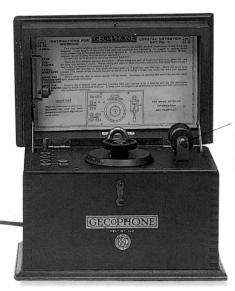

Winding the handle brings a tiny wire into contact with a crystal to detect the radio waves

Gecophone c.1925

Using a horn to amplify sound was a huge advance on the early crystal sets, which required the listener to wear headphones. Apart from the horn, the parts were housed in a plain wooden box, which was better suited to the domestic environment.

Specifications
Country: UK
Height: 6¼in (16cm)
Material: Wood and metal

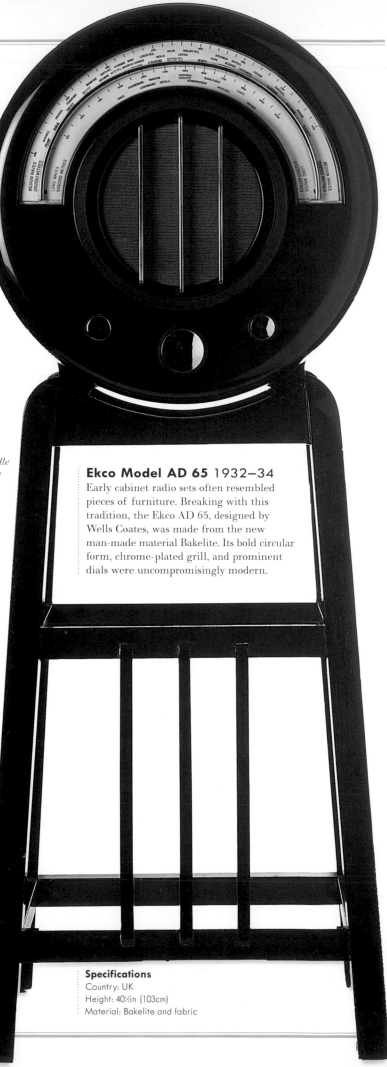

Ekco Model AD 65 1932–34

Early cabinet radio sets often resembled pieces of furniture. Breaking with this tradition, the Ekco AD 65, designed by Wells Coates, was made from the new man-made material Bakelite. Its bold circular form, chrome-plated grill, and prominent dials were uncompromisingly modern.

Volksempfänger VE 301 1928–33

As with the VW Beetle (see p.182), the design for this radio was endorsed by Adolf Hitler. The model number refers to the date Hitler became chancellor – January 30, 1933. The Volksempfänger, meaning "people's radio" bears a symbol of the Third Reich under the dial. For propaganda reasons it was not possible to receive transmissions from abroad on this set.

Specifications
Country: Germany
Height: 15¼in (39cm)
Material: Bakelite and fabric

Specifications
Country: UK
Height: 40¼in (103cm)
Material: Bakelite and fabric

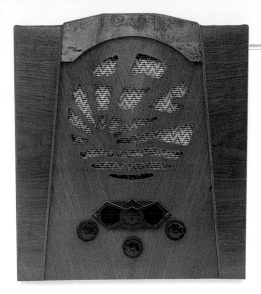

Pye radio early 1930s

The loudspeaker grille gave designers the opportunity to develop a visual identity for the company. Pye used a stylized sunburst, a popular Art Deco motif. The trademark also served as decoration, which increased the consumer appeal.

Specifications
Country: UK
Height: 16in (41cm)
Materials: Wood and Bakelite

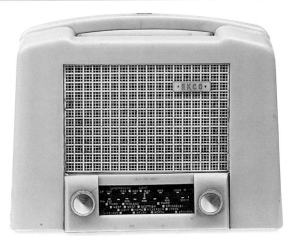

Ekco Type U122 1950s

Plastics radically changed the appearance of radios, which became available in a range of colors and shapes. This process was aided by the miniaturization of the receiver through advances in valve technology.

Specifications
Country: UK
Height: 8¾in (22cm)
Material: Bakelite

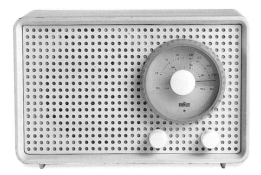

Braun SK 25 1955

In 1954, Fritz Eichler was hired by Artur Braun to modify the company's product line by adopting a more functionalist approach. The basic plastic shell and simple controls of the SK 25 typify the rationality that has come to be associated with Braun products.

Specifications
Country: Germany
Height: 6in (15.5cm)
Material: Plastic and metal

Brionvega Ls 502 1964

In the 1960s, Richard Sapper and Marco Zanuso were commissioned by Brionvega to design a series of radios and televisions. The Ls 502 folding radio, an early example of the application of transistor technology, was a battery powered portable designed to go anywhere. For easy transportation the radio folded up to make a small box.

Specifications
Country: Italy
Height: 5in (12.5cm)
Material: Plastic and metal

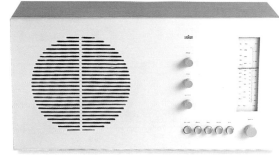

Super RT 20 1961

The range of stereophonic equipment that Dieter Rams designed for Braun in the 1950s and '60s was all executed in the same austere, functionalist style. The Super RT 20 had many of the same characteristics as his earlier Phonosuper record player (see p.61).

Specifications
Country: Germany
Height: 10in (25.5cm)
Material: Plastic, metal, and wood

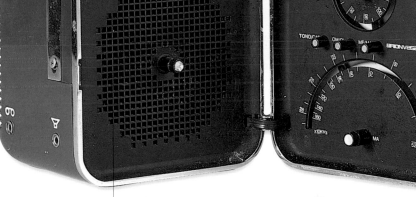

One side of the radio housed the speaker, the other the receiver

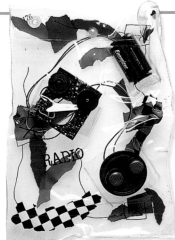

Radio in the Bag, 1981

RADICAL DESIGN

Daniel Weil's bag radio, part of his degree show at the Royal College of Art, London, challenges traditional notions of how a radio should look. Instead of hiding the components within a solid shell, Weil chose to display them in a transparent PVC bag. The exposed workings, combined with the splashes of color, provide an unusual decorative quality.

Hitachi KH-434E 1970s

This portable radio is typical of the wide range of electronic consumables produced in Japan. With its competitive prices, Japan now dominates the radio market. This model can be powered either by battery or electricity.

Specifications
Country: Japan
Height: 4¼in (11cm)
Material: Plastic

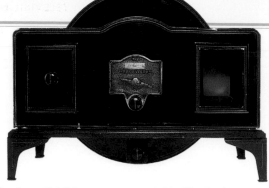

Televisor 1926

The world's first demonstration of television, or "visual wireless," was given by Scottish inventor John Logie Baird in 1926. However, his mechanically operated Televisor, with its small screen positioned on the right, could not broadcast sound and pictures together.

Specifications
Country: UK
Materials: Metal and Bakelite
Height: 22in (56cm)

The hit show I Love Lucy *appeared on television from 1951*

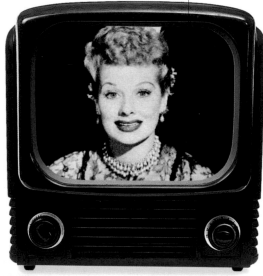

Bush TV12 1949

In the 1930s, mechanical television sets were replaced by electronic models that used cathode ray tubes to project electrons onto the screen. Early sets cost as much as a car, but, by 1949, less expensive models, such as this Bakelite television by Bush, were widely available.

Specifications
Country: UK
Material: Bakelite
Height: 16½in (42cm)

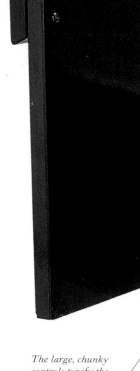

The large, chunky controls typify the uncomplicated styling of the set

TELEVISION SETS

IN A BROCHURE aimed at its retailers, manufacturer E.K. Cole Ltd. predicted that 1939 would go down in history as "Television Year." In fact, it was the radio that dominated homes, as people avidly followed the year's historic international events. Since then, however, the television set has made a greater impact on our domestic lives than almost any other item of electrical equipment. In early form, its sheer size made it the predominant item in any room, but the miniaturization of electronic components in the 1950s facilitated its transformation from large, bulky wooden box to the slim, slickly styled consumer product we know today.

Mullard 1950s

By the 1950s, the television set was part of the furniture – in some cases, literally so. With its two wooden doors, this Mullard set has the appearance of a cabinet, to be opened when its services are required and disguised when not. Its impressive size indicates the dominant presence that television had established in the home as the century entered its second half.

Specifications
Country: UK
Material: Wood
Height: 35⅛in (89.3cm)

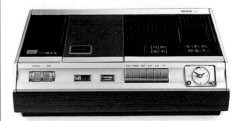

Sony TV8-301 1959

Original in its design, as well as technically innovative, the TV8-301 was the world's first all-transistor television and established Sony as world leader in electronics. Sony was able to utilize the miniaturized parts it had developed for its pocket transistor radios to develop this remarkable-looking portable set.

Specifications
Country: Japan
Material: Metal
Dimensions: Not known

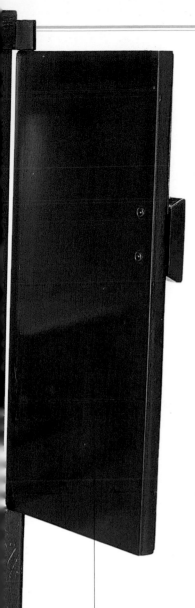

The screen can be both protected and disguised behind cabinet doors

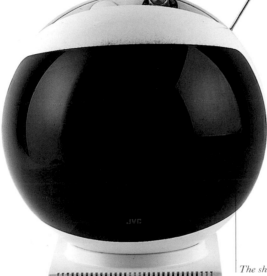

The shape and coloring are reminiscent of an astronaut's helmet

JVC Videosphere 1970

In an effort to distance plastic from its disposable associations, designers used it for expensive consumer items like television sets. A radical rethink of the traditional television shape, the Videosphere looks like a spaceman's helmet, reflecting public interest in space travel. In 1969, 600 million people had tuned in to watch man walk on the Moon.

Specifications
Country: Japan
Material: Plastic housing
Height: 11in (28cm)

Sony wide-screen 1995

Billions of dollars are now spent by electronics companies in an effort to produce the highest-quality television set with the most desirable appearance and price. There has been a vast range of technological innovations in the 1980s and '90s, including the development of flat-screen and wide-screen televisions, exemplified by this sleek, angular Sony wide-screen model.

Specifications
Country: Japan
Material: Plastic
Dimensions: 21¾in (55.2cm)

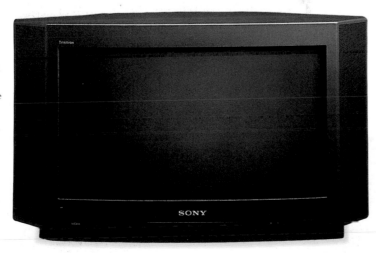

VIDEO CASSETTE RECORDERS

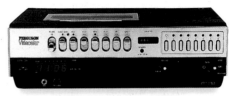

Philips N-1500, 1971

Although a monochrome video recorder was developed in 1956 and a color recorder in 1959, the Philips N-1500, with its mechanical clock, was the first commercially successful video recorder.

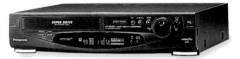

Ferguson Videostar, 1980

After the 1970s "video war" between Sony and Matsushita (the latter's VHS format won the day), video recorders, like the Videostar, became more sophisticated. However, they remained bulky appliances.

Panasonic NV-HD650, 1990

Highly styled, slimline video machines like this Panasonic Ni-cam have dominated the 1990s. Features include remote control, multiprogram operations, long play facilities, and bar-code programming.

CAMCORDERS

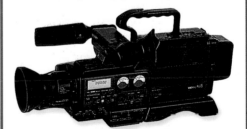

Sony camcorder, 1980

Before the development of the camcorder — a video camera and recorder combined in a portable unit — the recording of moving images involved a 16mm movie-camera or, later, the smaller, more versatile 8mm camera. Although early camcorders were large and unwieldly, they did enable the user to play back recordings immediately through the viewfinder and to edit recordings simply and instantly.

MUSIC SYSTEMS

MECHANICAL, WIND-UP DISK PLAYERS were introduced in 1886 by Emile Berliner, who coined the term "gramophone." Their sound quality was better than the cylinder versions they replaced, and the disks could be mass produced. The huge amplifying horns meant that these first machines were uncased, but designers soon reduced the size of the motor and developed the internal horn, so the whole unit could be housed in a single cabinet. In 1956, Braun transformed the look of the radio-record player with the Phonosuper SK4; with its clear plastic lid and detached speakers, it became the industry standard. Bang & Olufsen's 1972 Beogram 4000 was one of the most sophisticated turntables ever produced – yet it was superseded in the 1980s by the compact disk player. Today, digital technology threatens the record with obsolescence.

The Graphophone is driven by a spring motor

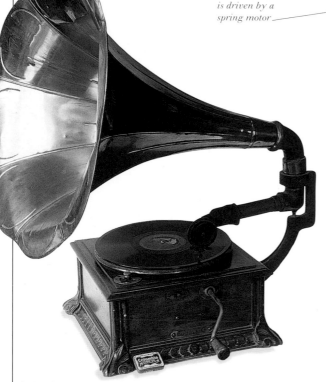

Pathé gramophone c.1908

This gramophone was designed as a piece of furniture – something that would be given a prominent place in the home. A wind-up motor is housed beneath the turntable in a wooden box, which has a carved decorative edging. The influence of Art Nouveau can be seen both in the carving and the attractive flower-shaped horn. This style of horn was known as "Morning Glory," after the flower.

Specifications
Country: France
Height: 26½in (67cm)

Selecta portable 1920s

Portable gramophones changed little in style from the 1920s to the 1950s. This example, housed in its own carrying case, is wound by a spring and has an internal horn. Records can be stored in a pocket under the lid.

Specifications
Country: UK
Height: 5½in (14.3cm)

Bermuda Dansette
1950s

By the 1950s, popular music had become a major industry. With the advent of rock 'n' roll, teenage culture was taking off and new commercial opportunities were beginning to emerge. The Dansette, with its colorful, modern styling, was aimed at this youthful market.

Specifications
Country: UK
Height: 23½in (60cm)

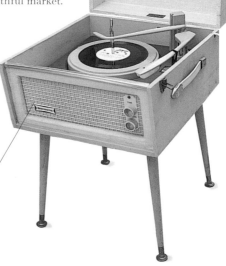

The integrated speaker is hidden behind the open-weave fabric

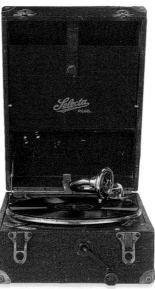

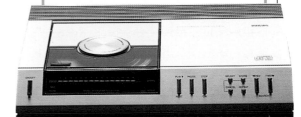

Philips compact disc player, 1983

In a joint venture in 1979, Philips and Sony developed the compact disc. The first commercial compact disc player was launched in Japan in October 1982, and in Europe in March 1983. Sound is recorded onto an aluminum plate in the shape of millions of tiny micro-cells, known as "pits." It is then reproduced by a laser beam scanning across the surface of the disc as it spins, and sending a signal back to the player for decoding. This Philips CD 200 was one of the earliest models available, designed to be compatible with more traditional hi-fi systems.

The horn amplifies sound picked up by the stylus

Graphophone c.1900

The cylinder phonograph was developed by Thomas Edison in 1878. Initially it was sold for dictation, but companies soon turned to the more profitable line of music. The Graphophone worked by picking up vibrations from a cylinder through a stylus, which was connected to an amplifying horn. With this system it was possible to make home recordings, but the sound quality was poor.

Specifications
Country: US/UK
Length of stand: 11½in (29cm)

Decoration is limited to a gold border around the edge of the stand

The use of slick, metallic silver-gray represents a departure from the black styling of the 1980s

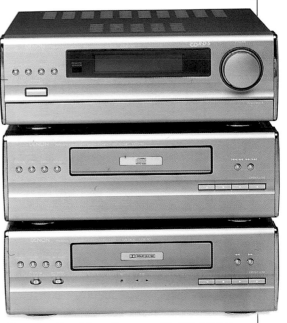

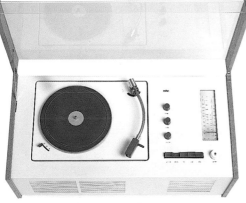

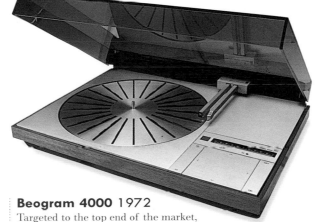

Braun Phonosuper SK55 1956

Also known as "Snow White's Coffin," the SK55 was exhibited at the XI Triennale in Milan in 1957, when Braun was awarded the grand prize. Designed by Dieter Rams and Hans Gugelot, it is a fabulous piece of minimalist design. The clear Plexiglas lid was an innovative concept that radically influenced the hi-fi industry.

Specifications
Country: Germany
Height: 9½in (24cm)

Beogram 4000 1972

Targeted to the top end of the market, Jakob Jensen's Beogram 4000 turntable was designed using the most sophisticated electronics and precision engineering. It was the first record player to have an electronically operated tangential arm, which gives superior sound quality. Widely acclaimed as a state-of-the-art product, it is now featured in prominent museum collections.

Specifications
Country: Denmark
Height: 4in (10cm)

Denon Stacking System D-90 1995

The compact disc has become so popular that in the 1990s most music systems do not include a record player. Integrated stacking systems, like this D90 by the British company Denon, are the most common. This system includes receiver, compact disc player, and cassette tape deck, each styled in the smart silver gray that characterizes Denon products.

Specifications
Country: UK
Height: 11¾in (30cm)

TAPE MACHINES

LATE-19TH-CENTURY EXPERIMENTS with tape recording included Danish engineer Valdemar Poulsen's Telegraphone, the first magnetic sound recorder. However, it was not until the 1930s and the invention of plastic magnetic tape that tape-playing machinery became a practical proposition. The appearance of the machine itself has changed and adapted as technology has advanced. Early reel-to-reel tape machines looked plain, utilitarian, and prohibitively bulky. However, since the launch of Philips's Compact Cassette in 1963, machines have became more portable, more streamlined, and more inventive in design.

Reel-to-reel tape machine 1950

Traditional reel-to-reel, or open-reel, tape machines like this 1950 model had their origins in a system called the Magnetophon, produced by AEG Telefunken in 1935. The design determined that of tape recorders into the 1960s and '70s, with the basic flat, top-loading system challenged only by the introduction of the front-loading rack systems.

Specifications
Country: Not known
Material: Not known
Width: 14¼in (36.2cm)

Philips Model 150 Carry-Corder 1964

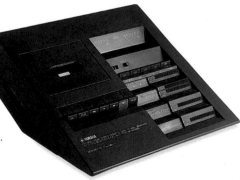

In 1963, Philips introduced the world's first compact tape cassette. This blank cassette measured just 4in (10cm) and could play back both stereo and mono recordings. It was launched with the first cassette recorder, also the first true portable battery-operated recorder, complete with remote microphone.

Specifications
Country: Netherlands
Material: Polystyrene housing
Width: 4½in (11.5cm)

Yamaha TC800D 1975

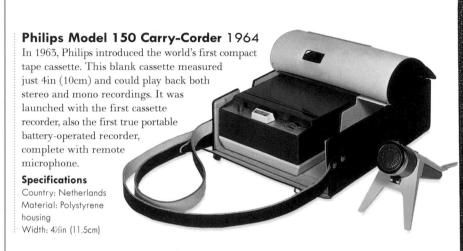

In the mid 1970s, Yamaha commissioned Mario Bellini to design a new cassette recorder. The result was this innovative wedge-shaped "Natural Sound Stereo Cassette Deck." The recorder has a pitch control that can vary the tape speed and a Dolby noise reduction system.

Specifications
Country: Japan
Material: ABS plastic housing
Width: 12in (30.5cm)

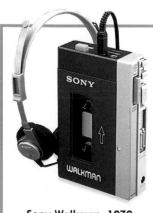

PERSONAL STEREOS

The world's first personal stereo, the Walkman, was launched by Sony in 1979, pioneering a major new product in the audio industry. The Walkman uses advanced microelectronics to produce high-quality, unwavering sound from the smallest possible unit. This original model has anodized-aluminum housing. Personal stereos have become even more portable, incorporating lightweight plastic housing and smaller headphones.

Sony Walkman, 1979

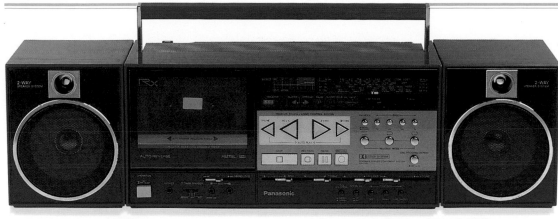

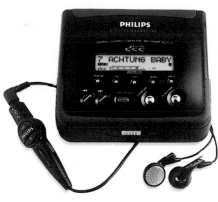

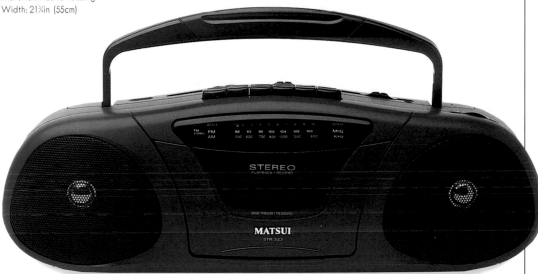

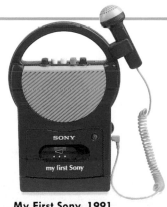

Panasonic boom box 1980s

The generic names "boom box" and "ghetto blaster" derived from the young urban population that was attracted to these large, portable music systems. Produced in hard-edged black or, like this Panasonic model, brightly colored, the rectangular boxes often have detachable speakers. Despite being battery-operated, they produce a powerful sound.

Specifications
Country: Japan
Material: Plastic housing
Width: 21¾in (55cm)

Philips DCC170 1995

In 1992, Philips introduced the Digital Compact Cassette system, an innovation in digital sound recording. The technological sophistication is reflected in the hardworking design of the housing, with its numerous function buttons.

Specifications
Country: Netherlands
Material: Plastic housing
Width: 4¼in (11cm)

Matsui STR323 1996

The 1990s have witnessed the return of softer styling in tape machinery, with rounded forms and pastel colors recalling 1940s streamlining and the car designs of Harley Earl. As the Matsui STR323 demonstrates, the high-tech features that were prominent on models like the Yamaha TC800D have been hidden in favor of retro styling.

Specifications
Country: Japan
Material: Plastic housing
Width: 16¾in (42.5cm)

CHILDREN'S TAPE MACHINES

Low-cost electronics made it possible for companies to develop and manufacture inexpensive tape machines specifically for children. My First Sony is a typical example of the kind of tape machines that attract young users. It is chunky, vividly colored, and has inviting hands-on features – children can use the microphone to record their own sounds or to sing along to music played on a cassette. The styling of this machine has a cheerful, unisex appeal; often, however, machines directed at the young female market are designed in much softer pastel shades.

My First Sony, 1991

THE KITCHEN & DINING ROOM

STOVES

EARLY GAS STOVES resembled the heavy cast-iron ranges of the 19th century. Later, they were raised on slender legs – a feature that emphasized the lighter mechanics of gas appliances. Designs for electric stoves, introduced in the 1920s, tended to emulate their gas counterparts, and by the end of the 1930s, a standard type had been established that was to endure in popularity for decades. This compact, flat-topped stove formed a continuous surface with the kitchen worktop. Today, technical advances make it possible to combine electric oven and gas burners or vice versa, an innovation that coincides with a flexible new kitchen aesthetic catering to the individual's taste.

COMPACT KITCHEN

Designed for the Italian manufacturer Boffi by Joe Colombo, this self-contained mobile mini kitchen consists of two electric burners, refrigerator, cabinet, and drawer space – all housed within an area of approximately 35 cubic feet (one cubic meter).

Mini kitchen, 1963

The simmering and boiling plates have elegant, chromed insulating lids

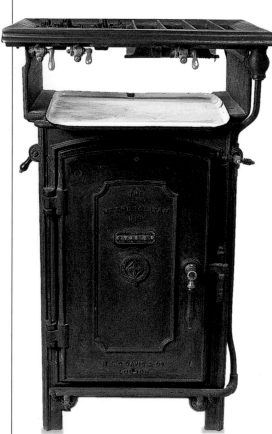

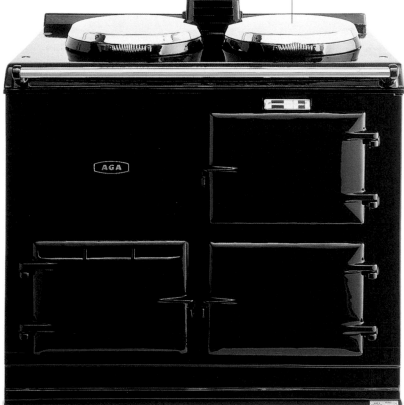

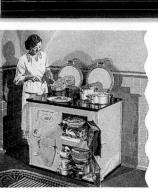

The Metropolitan c.1910
By the 1900s, many urban households had access to a gas supply. This gas stove, constructed from cast iron, is typical of early kitchen appliances. It has a crude, industrial appearance and was difficult to operate. Later, cast-iron enamel replaced the rust prone finish.

Specifications
Country: UK
Height: 33in (84cm)

Aga 1929
Gustaf Dalen, a Swedish Nobel Prize winner, invented the Aga stove in 1922. It was licensed for production in the UK in 1929 and, after several redesigns, it is now available in a range of colors, in addition to the traditional cream enamel finish. The Aga burns fuel constantly, retaining heat for cooking – in its several ovens and on the hotplates – in its cast-iron shell.

Specifications
Country: UK
Height: 33½in (85cm)

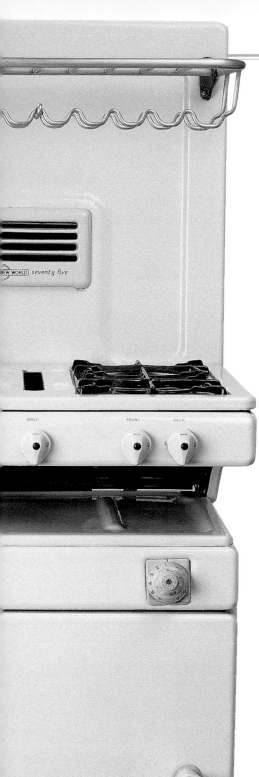

New World stove 1950s

Designed for the modern home, this cream-enameled stove is representative of the standard type established in the late 1930s – a flat-topped box that fitted into the continuous horizontal work surface of the kitchen. It has four burners, a grill, a plate rack, and a thermostatically controlled oven.

Specifications
Country: UK
Height: 56in (142cm)

Saucepans can be stored on hooks at the top of the tree

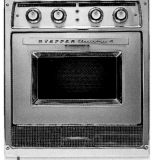

FAST FOOD

The idea of microwave cooking was developed by Percy LeBaron Spencer, an engineer at a radar equipment company in the US. The microwave oven was patented in 1946, but the first models were bulky, expensive, and restricted to industrial use. In the 1960s, domestic models became available.

Microwave oven, 1955

The ceramic burner can be detached from the main stove unit

The kitchen sink occupies the minimum of space

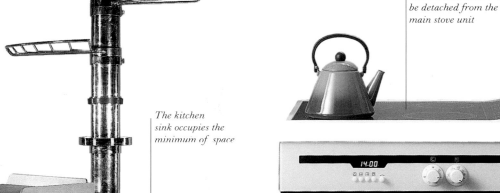

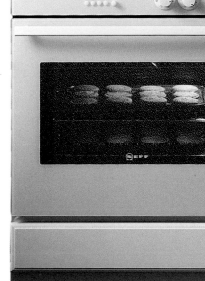

Kitchen Tree 1984

Designed by Stefan Wewerka for Tecta, the Kitchen Tree is the ultimate in space economy, comprising a sink, three electric burners, a work surface, a storage basket, and a hanging area – all extending from a central column. Wewerka's asymmetrical design breaks with convention, challenging the ubiquitous "installed" kitchen.

Specifications
Country: Germany
Height: 77in (196cm)

Neff B1441 oven plus burners 1996

The integral oven and burner unit is no longer the standard in stove design. The two parts can be bought separately and the kitchen layout manipulated to suit the consumer's requirements. Top-of-the-range built-in ovens offer a range of user-friendly features, including a heat-reflective glass oven door, slender bar handle, push-in control knobs, and illuminated dials.

Specifications
Country: Germany
Height: 23in (58.9cm)

STREAMLINING

This refrigerator was designed by Raymond Loewy for Sears Roebuck. Its streamlined, pressed-steel styling resembles the bodywork of an automobile. With its rounded corners and gleaming white finish, it created a brand new "hygienic" look that was widely copied by other manufacturers.

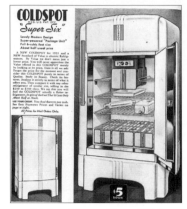

Coldspot Super Six, c.1934

REFRIGERATORS

AT THE TURN OF THE CENTURY, "refrigerators," for those lucky enough to have one, were simply wooden cabinets housing ice boxes. The first domestic refrigerators appeared in 1913. These were cumbersome and had relatively small storage spaces. Some had the cooling mechanism mounted outside the appliance, above the food compartment, earning them the nickname "the beehive." For a long time Europeans considered refrigerators to be an unnecessary luxury. In the US, refrigerators were far more popular with consumers (sixty percent of the population owned one by 1941) and, as a result, many design features originated there. Since the 1950s, refrigerators and freezers have been available in a much wider range of styles, colors, and configurations.

Small-capacity refrigerator 1930s

Made by the British Thomson-Houston Company, this refrigerator is typical of early models. Although it is large and heavy, the cold storage area is small, with the motor occupying considerable space. The two dials at the top of the unit operate the off/on mechanism and the temperature control.

Specifications
Country: UK
Height: 52in (132cm)

The heavy motor takes up the bottom half of the housing

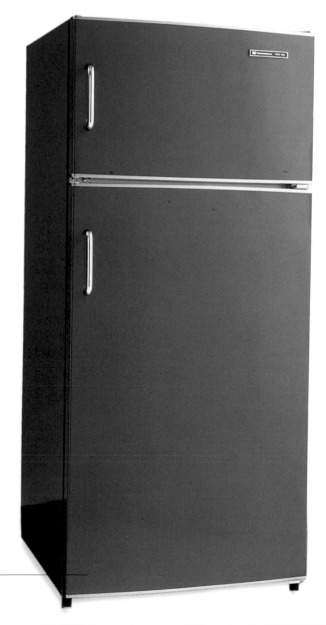

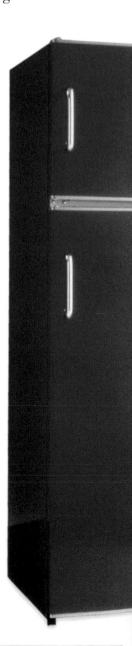

Prestcold refrigerator late 1950s

This Prestcold refrigerator is clearly influenced by Raymond Loewy's Coldspot Super Six. Its shape demonstrates many of the characteristics of the automobile industry's products. The gently curving lines, the handle, and the "radiator cap" logo in the right corner are all reminiscent of car styling.

Specifications
Country: UK
Height: 47in (119cm)

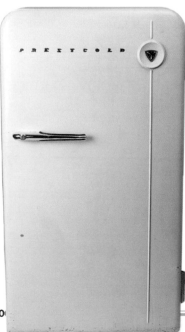

Bold primary colors identify these as products of the 1990s

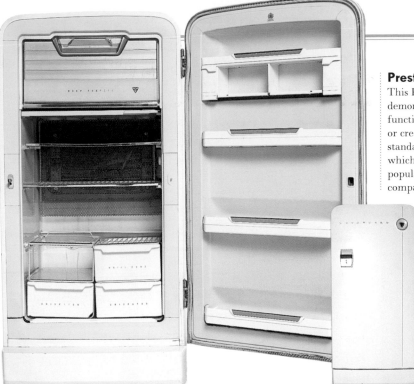

Prestcold refrigerator 1950s

This Prestcold refrigerator demonstrates a move away from the functional, sanitary-looking white or cream finish that had become standard. The inside is light blue, which, along with pink, was very popular. The spacious interior is compartmentalized to separate different food types. A small freezer section is for frozen foods, which had started to become readily available after World War II. The exterior's rounded corners, refined graphics, and square handle give it a modern look.

Specifications
Country: UK
Height: Not known

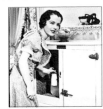
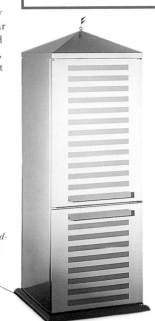

The unusual styling includes a red base plinth and a pyramid-like "roof" complete with flag

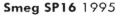

Smeg SP16 1995

During the 1980s the vogue was for refrigerators to be invisible, hidden behind decor panels in kitchens. The Italian manufacturer Smeg is one of a number of companies that is challenging this in the 1990s: its large-capacity fridges and freezers are produced in bold primary colors. The overall shape maintains a simple geometry with clean lines.

Specifications
Country: Italy
Height: 64¼in (164cm)

Zanussi Wizard refrigerators 1987

Roberto Pezetta's postmodernist refrigerators were designed for Zanussi and were not a commercial success. Pezetta used architectural references to produce an appliance that proudly asserts its own identity.

Specifications
Country: Italy
Height: 64¼in (163.5cm)

Amana SRD526SW 1995

The US market has always favored larger-capacity refrigerators than have been standard in Europe. However, large appliances, like this side-by-side Amana unit which measures 35¾in in width (91cm), are gaining popularity with Europeans. The model includes an external coldwater and ice dispenser.

Specifications
Country: US
Height: 68½in (174cm)

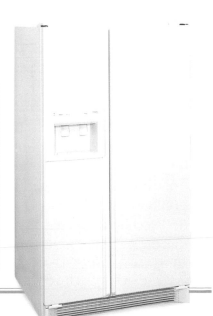

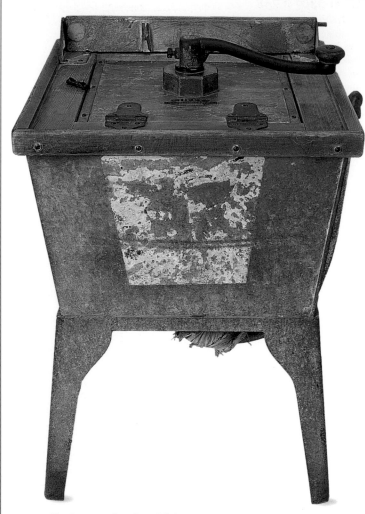

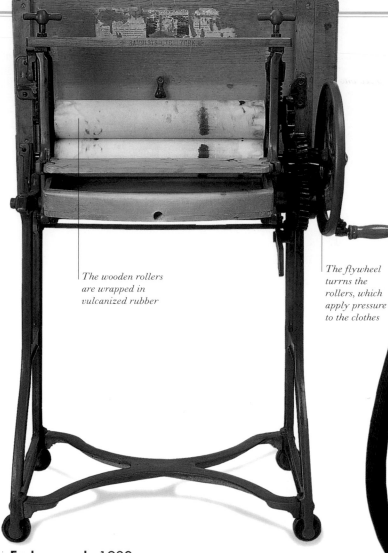

The wooden rollers are wrapped in vulcanized rubber

The flywheel turrns the rollers, which apply pressure to the clothes

Early washtub 1920s
Before electricity became widely available, washtubs were handoperated. There were numerous ways of agitating the wash, including pounding, squeezing, and rocking, which were all very labor intensive. This machine is driven by a handle linked to a central paddle that churns the laundry.

Early mangle 1920s
From the beginning of the century, most households were equipped with a mangle. This was used to squeeze water out of wet laundry and to smooth linen. There were many different styles of mangle, both freestanding and tablemounted. This one is attached to a hinged roller frame, which folds downward to convert into a table.

WASHING MACHINES

WASHING MACHINES HAVE BEEN AVAILABLE in one form or another for more than 200 years. Before the widespread use of electricity, they were aimed at the industrial market, and those who could afford to send their clothes to public laundries. Early tubs had to be filled manually with preheated water, then turned by hand. The soaking-wet clothes then had to be passed through a mangle, or wringer, before being hung on the line to dry. Washers with motorized agitators introduced in the 1930s, and soon followed by automatic front-loading machines, significantly lightened the workload of homemakers. (Still, wringer washers were manufactured until the 1980s.) The latest washing machines keep the impact on the environment to an absolute minimum, attesting to the eco-conscious attitudes of the 1990s consumer.

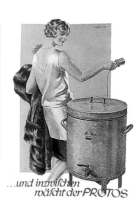

Protos washtub c.1930
Throughout the century, advertisements for domestic appliances have tended to exaggerate their labor-saving properties. This advertisement for the Protos electric washtub implies that the machine will relieve the drudgery of washday, giving the housewife the freedom to pursue other interests.

...und inzwischen wäscht der PROTOS

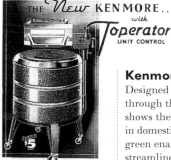

Kenmore Toperator 1933
Designed by Henry Dreyfuss and sold through the Sears catalog, the Toperator shows the growing importance of styling in domestic appliances. Finished in mottled green enamel with chrome trim, the sleek, streamlined body conceals the mechanics.

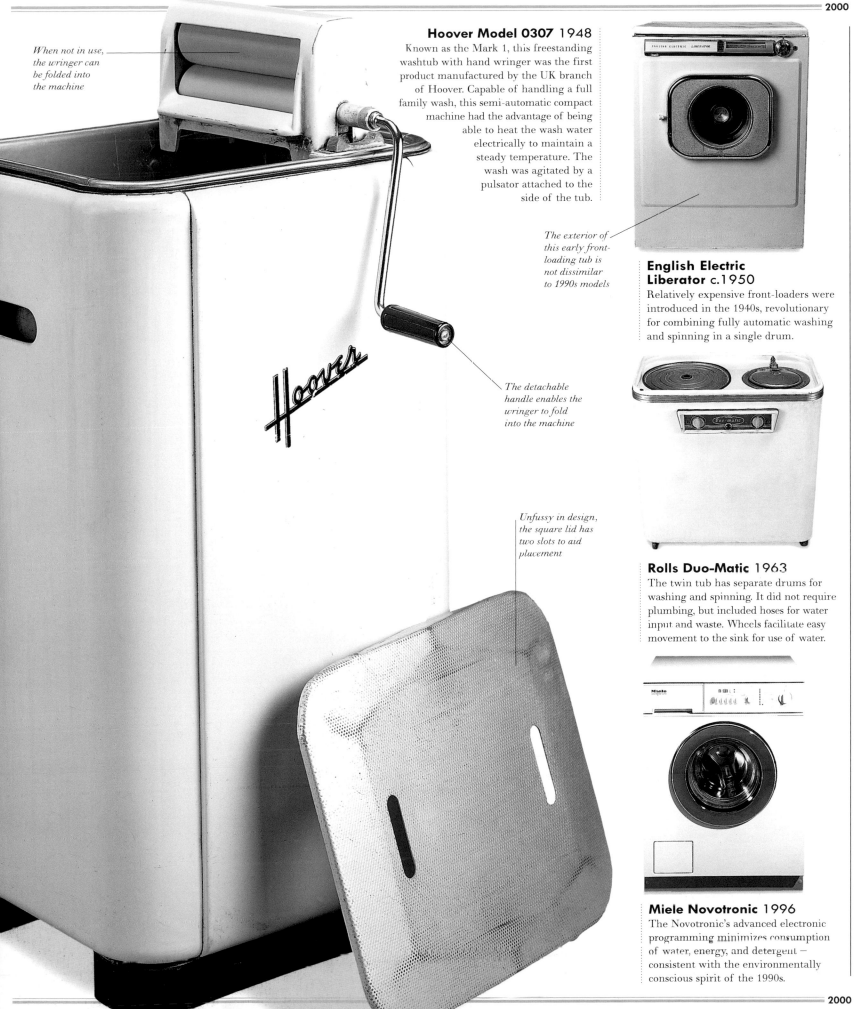

When not in use, the wringer can be folded into the machine

Hoover Model 0307 1948

Known as the Mark 1, this freestanding washtub with hand wringer was the first product manufactured by the UK branch of Hoover. Capable of handling a full family wash, this semi-automatic compact machine had the advantage of being able to heat the wash water electrically to maintain a steady temperature. The wash was agitated by a pulsator attached to the side of the tub.

The exterior of this early front-loading tub is not dissimilar to 1990s models

The detachable handle enables the wringer to fold into the machine

Unfussy in design, the square lid has two slots to aid placement

English Electric Liberator c.1950

Relatively expensive front-loaders were introduced in the 1940s, revolutionary for combining fully automatic washing and spinning in a single drum.

Rolls Duo-Matic 1963

The twin tub has separate drums for washing and spinning. It did not require plumbing, but included hoses for water input and waste. Wheels facilitate easy movement to the sink for use of water.

Miele Novotronic 1996

The Novotronic's advanced electronic programming minimizes consumption of water, energy, and detergent — consistent with the environmentally conscious spirit of the 1990s.

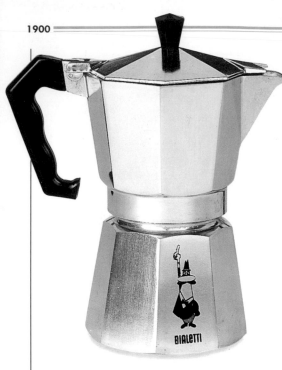

Moka Express 1933

The enduringly popular Moka Express coffeemaker was first designed and manufactured in the 1930s by Alfonso Bialetti. This octagonal-shaped percolator is cast in aluminum and has a plastic handle. It continues to be manufactured today by Alberto Bialetti, grandson of Alfonso.

Specifications
Country: Italy
Materials: Aluminum and Bakelite
Height: 8in (20.2cm)

COFFEEMAKERS

MOST COFFEE CONNOISSEURS have their own preferred – and usually very precise – techniques for making their favorite beverage. This is reflected in the rich assortment of coffee machines available, which includes percolators, drip pots, vacuum pots, cafetieres, and capuccino makers. The Bialetti percolator is favored by families in Italy and makes excellent, strong espresso. Espresso has only been internationally popular since World War II, when Gaggia introduced its domestic espresso machine.

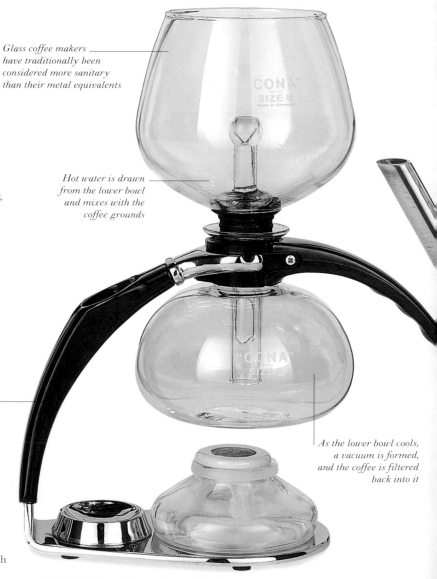

Glass coffee makers have traditionally been considered more sanitary than their metal equivalents

Hot water is drawn from the lower bowl and mixes with the coffee grounds

Wear-Ever coffee pot 1934

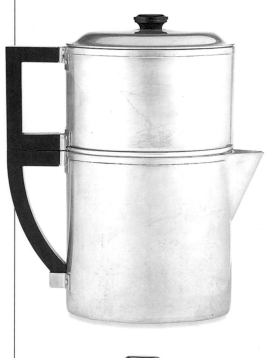

Lurelle Guild was employed by a number of companies in the 1930s to design aluminum kitchen utensils. The form of this well-proportioned, unfussy, cylindrical coffee pot clearly expresses function. Designed by Guild to be manufactured easily, the pot is made from aluminum, with the handles molded in Bakelite.

Specifications
Country: US
Materials: Aluminum and Bakelite
Height: 11in (28cm)

The plastic arm holds the coffee maker above the flame

As the lower bowl cools, a vacuum is formed, and the coffee is filtered back into it

Finel coffee pot 1957

The work of Finnish interior and industrial designer Antti Nurmesniemi, and a product of Wärtsilä, the Finel pot has a cylindrical metal body, which narrows toward the top. It is finished in bright red enamel, with a black plastic handle.

Specifications
Country: Finland
Materials: Enameled metal and plastic
Height: 7⅜in (18.8cm)

"CONA" coffeemaker 1957

Glass coffeemakers have traditionally been considered more sanitary than their metal equivalents. This attractive hourglass-shaped coffeemaker is suspended from a plastic arm, which is mounted on a polished metal base.

Specifications
Country: UK
Materials: Glass and plastic
Height: 11⅝in (29.6cm)

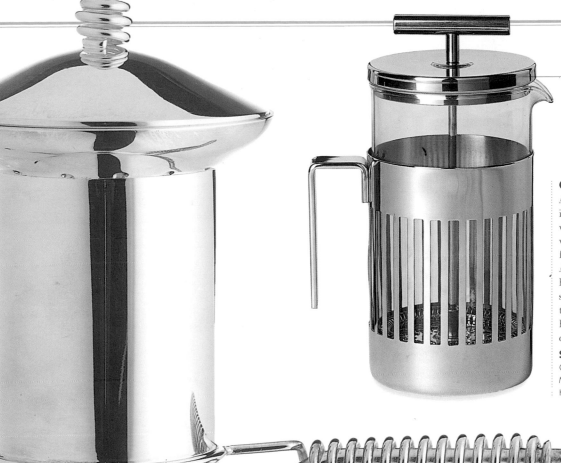

The shape of the lid suggests the top of an architectural column

Cafetiere 1986

Aldo Rossi began working with Alessi in the early 1980s. His method of working is to present the technicians with outline sketches, rather than finished plans. From these, some of Alessi's most successful coffeemakers have been created. This cafetiere shows Rossi's passion for architecture – the elegant lines of the machine have clearly been inspired by classical columns.

Specifications
Country: Italy
Materials: Stainless steel and glass
Height: 8⅔in (22cm)

The innovative radiating spiral design prevents the handles from overheating

The body of the pot is tall and slender, with unfussy, elegant lines

GAGGIA

Although the first espresso machine was patented in 1902 by Italian Luigi Bezzera, the process of forcing hot water through a filter of ground coffee beans was popularized internationally by Milan-based Achille Gaggia in the late 1940s. His purpose-built domestic espresso machine, with its piston and lever system, was introduced in 1948, and became an essential ingredient in the 1950s cult of the coffee-bar.

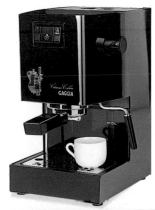

Gaggia "Classic coffee"

Filumena 2 1985

Filippo Alison's design for the tall, elegant Filumena 2, manufactured by Sabattini, was motivated by the Neapolitan tradition of coffee making, which involves using the grounds twice. Coffee is made by first filtering the water through previously used grounds, before passing it through fresh grounds to produce a strong and aromatic drink.

Specifications
Country: Italy
Material: Silver-plated brass alloy
Height: 10⅝in (27cm)

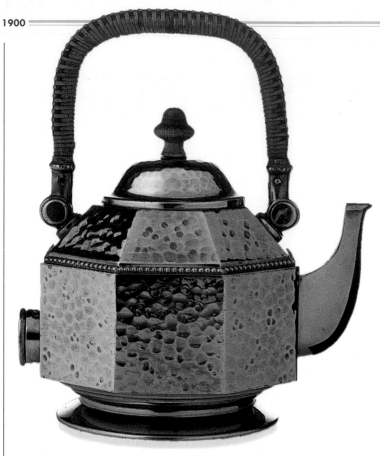

Behrens water kettle 1901

One of the most successful and influential projects by the pioneering German designer Peter Behrens was the line of kettles he introduced in 1901. There were three basic body shapes: octagon, cylinder, and half-oval; three different colors: brass, copper, and nickel; three types of finish: hammered, dragged, and plain; two lid designs, two handle shapes, and two plinth styles. They were all interchangeable, so that 81 different kettle combinations were possible, though only 30 were marketed.

Specifications
Country: Germany
Materials: Plated hammered copper and wicker

KETTLES

EARLY ELECTRIC KETTLES were hazardous appliances: the metal heating element was not waterproof and had to be installed beneath the base of the kettle. Immersible elements first appeared in 1921, 30 years after the first kettle was produced by Carpenter Electric Co. in the United States. However, the electric version never truly replaced the traditional stove-top kettle, which enjoyed a new lease on life in the 1980s, when Alessi produced its Kettle with a Bird-Shaped Whistle. The company has since sold more than 100,000 of these a year.

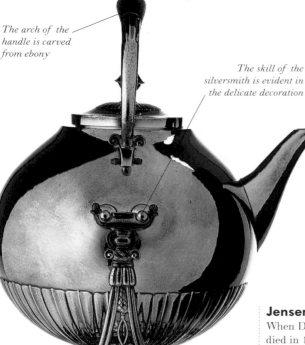

The arch of the handle is carved from ebony

The skill of the silversmith is evident in the delicate decoration

Jensen hot-water kettle 1920s

When Danish silversmith Georg Jensen died in 1935, the *New York Daily Herald* called him "the greatest craftsman in silver of the last three hundred years." This hot-water pot from the 1920s is a fine example of his craft. Although the solid silver pot could be lifted from the base to be filled, to pour water it had to be pivoted forward on the two side arms. The stand included an integral oil lamp that heated the water.

Specifications
Country: Denmark
Materials: Silver and ebony

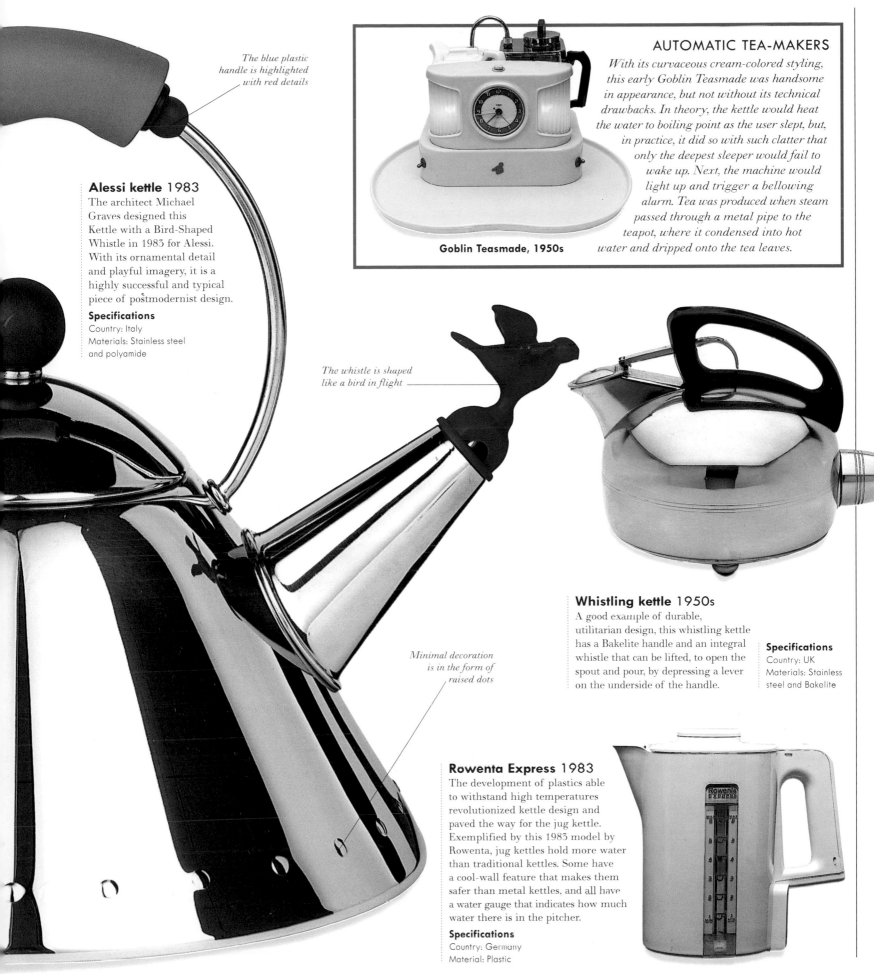

The blue plastic handle is highlighted with red details

Alessi kettle 1983

The architect Michael Graves designed this Kettle with a Bird-Shaped Whistle in 1983 for Alessi. With its ornamental detail and playful imagery, it is a highly successful and typical piece of postmodernist design.

Specifications
Country: Italy
Materials: Stainless steel and polyamide

AUTOMATIC TEA-MAKERS

With its curvaceous cream-colored styling, this early Goblin Teasmade was handsome in appearance, but not without its technical drawbacks. In theory, the kettle would heat the water to boiling point as the user slept, but, in practice, it did so with such clatter that only the deepest sleeper would fail to wake up. Next, the machine would light up and trigger a bellowing alarm. Tea was produced when steam passed through a metal pipe to the teapot, where it condensed into hot water and dripped onto the tea leaves.

Goblin Teasmade, 1950s

The whistle is shaped like a bird in flight

Minimal decoration is in the form of raised dots

Whistling kettle 1950s

A good example of durable, utilitarian design, this whistling kettle has a Bakelite handle and an integral whistle that can be lifted, to open the spout and pour, by depressing a lever on the underside of the handle.

Specifications
Country: UK
Materials: Stainless steel and Bakelite

Rowenta Express 1983

The development of plastics able to withstand high temperatures revolutionized kettle design and paved the way for the jug kettle. Exemplified by this 1983 model by Rowenta, jug kettles hold more water than traditional kettles. Some have a cool-wall feature that makes them safer than metal kettles, and all have a water gauge that indicates how much water there is in the pitcher.

Specifications
Country: Germany
Material: Plastic

TOASTERS

THE AUTOMATIC POP-UP TOASTER was the invention of American mechanic Charles Strite in 1927. His pioneering appliance had a spring device that was operated by thermocontact, which ejected the toast at a set time. Earlier electric toasters did exist, but these were not thermostatically controlled and had to be watched to prevent burning. Today, burned toast is a thing of the past, with electronic timing control enabling toasters to be set to suit any taste.

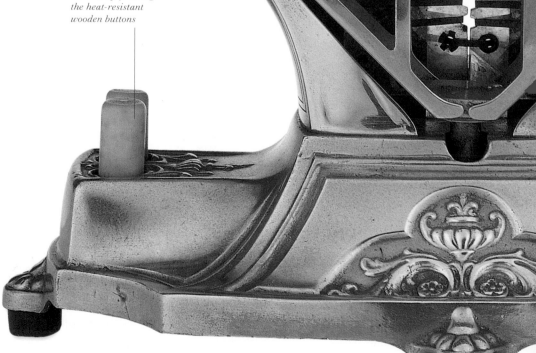

Universal 1920
Designed as a centerpiece for the dining-room table, the Universal toaster was more advanced than earlier machines. Although it could only toast one side of the bread at a time, it turned the bread to toast the second side. The bread was held against a heated metal element by the decorative front plate.

Specifications
Country: US
Materials: Metal and wood

The grilling plates were lowered by pressing the heat-resistant wooden buttons

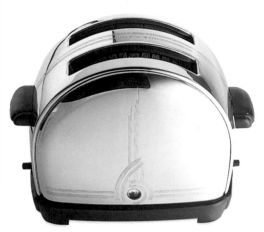

Sunbeam Model T-9 1937
The Sunbeam silent automatic toaster, created by George Scharfenberg, was patented as an "ornamental" toaster, revealing its dual purpose as a practical household appliance and status symbol. Pop-up toasters were available in the US long before they appeared in Europe.

Specifications
Country: US
Materials: Chrome and Bakelite

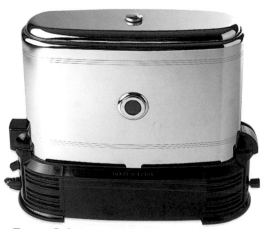

Toast-O-Lator mid 1930s
An innovative solution to toasting both sides of the bread at once was the Toast-O-Lator — the bread was grilled as it traveled from one side of the machine to the other on a small conveyor belt. Another quirky feature was the peephole that allowed the process to be monitored.

Specifications
Country: US
Materials: Chrome and Bakelite

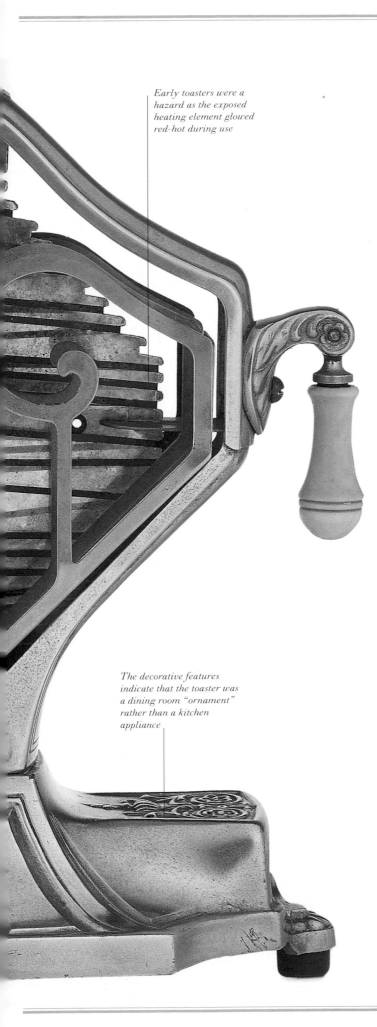

Early toasters were a hazard as the exposed heating element glowed red-hot during use

The decorative features indicate that the toaster was a dining room "ornament" rather than a kitchen appliance

Pye Toaster 1950

Created by Hawkins, this toaster has a Bakelite base and handle designed to protect the user from the heat. The aerodynamic design recalls the Art Deco passion for streamlining. Drop-side toasters of this type were superseded in the 1950s by an American invention, the pop-up toaster.

Specifications
Country: UK
Materials: Chrome and Bakelite

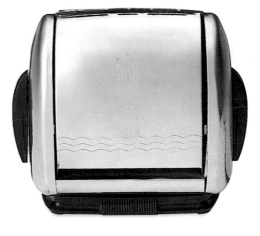

Dualit 1950s

This classic stainless steel toaster is still available today in two-, four-, and six-slice versions. It was originally intended for use in the catering trade, but is now a sought-after domestic design icon. It has not changed since its inception in the 1950s, a tribute to its timeless design.

Specifications
Country: UK
Material: Stainless steel

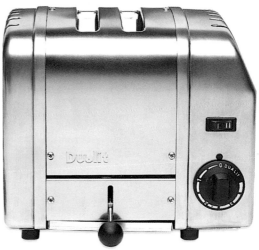

Breville Sandwich Toaster 1980–90

Kitchen gadgets such as sandwich toasters and waffle irons became popular in the 1970s. The Breville toasts, cuts, and seals the sandwich. The plain white exterior reflects the idea that modern kitchen appliances should be both stylish and functional.

Specifications
Country: UK
Material: Plastic

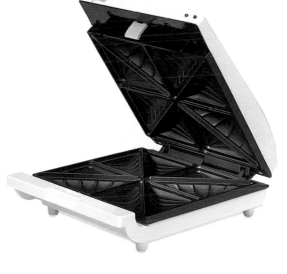

Kenwood Coolwall 1990

So-named because even during use the sides do not get hot, the Coolwall toaster offers a range of novel features, including electronic timing control. Housed in a sleek white shell, the Coolwall is the epitome of rationalized styling for domestic appliances, an approach pioneered by Braun in the 1950s.

Specifications
Country: UK
Material: Plastic

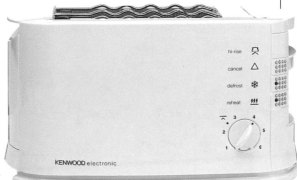

FOOD MIXERS

EARLY FOOD MIXERS tended to be scaled-down versions of industrial appliances from the commercial kitchen. They were reliable, but difficult to operate since they were not designed for domestic use. This industrial form continued until the 1950s, when the mixers began to show stylistic references to motor cars, regarded then as symbols of modernity. At the end of the century, small, versatile, robust, easy-to-use machines, with a vast array of functions, are the norm and are better suited to the modern kitchen.

The unadorned, industrial styling of this early mixer gives it the look of a machine tool

Domestic mixer 1918

Typical of early domestic mixers, this model has a simple, functional design, free from any ornamentation. The frame is hinged to allow the mixer to be turned horizontally. It is a smaller, less complex version of an industrial machine, designed purely to mix.

Specifications
Country: France
Material: Metal

Kenwood Chef 1948

The first Kenwood Chef model retains the industrial features associated with early food mixers. Its metal casing has a rounded form, giving the appliance a solid, heavy appearance, which was criticized for identifying work with housework.

Specifications
Country: UK
Materials: Metal, Bakelite, and porcelain

Sunbeam Mixmaster c.1955

This ingenious design has a detachable mixer unit, which combines the convenience of a handheld mixer with the versatility of a food processor. It has a space-age appearance and uses motifs from the car industry. A wide range of attachments was available.

Specifications
Country: US
Materials: Chrome-plated metal, plastic, and glass

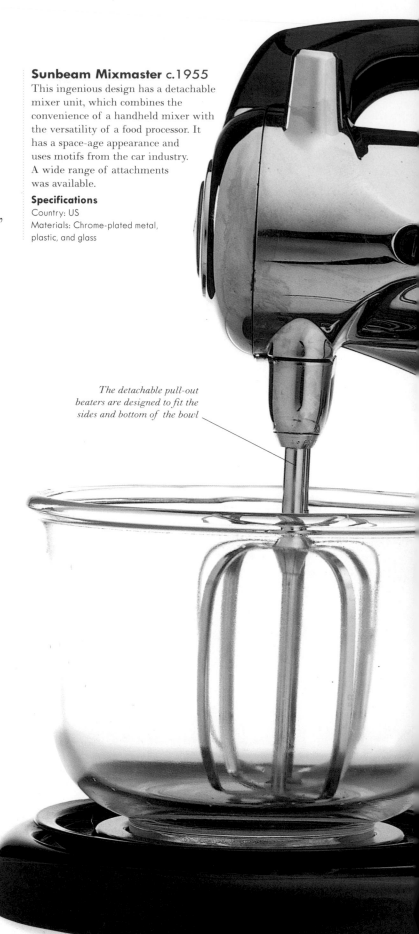

The detachable pull-out beaters are designed to fit the sides and bottom of the bowl

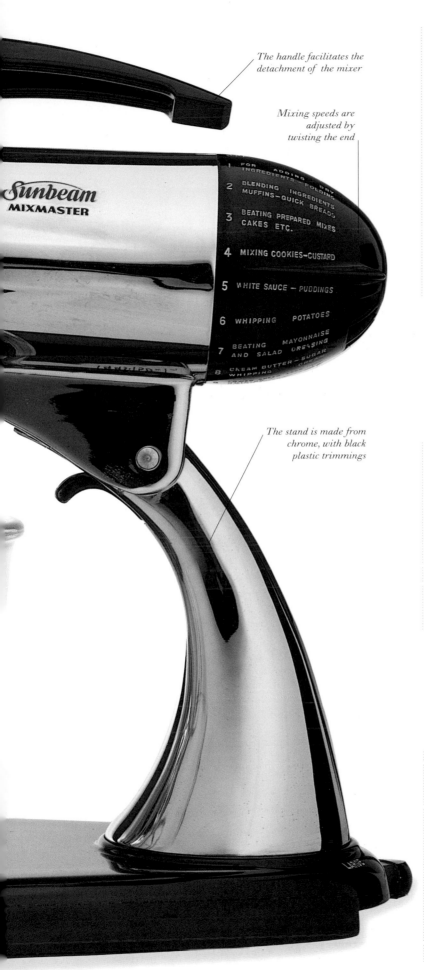

The handle facilitates the detachment of the mixer

Mixing speeds are adjusted by twisting the end

The stand is made from chrome, with black plastic trimmings

Kenwood Chef 1960

Kenneth Grange's redesign of the Kenwood Chef (see left) represents a trend in the late 1950s away from industrial styling and toward a more user-friendly domestic aesthetic. As kitchen appliances became more commonplace, designers began to create a new look for the domestic machine. Grange believed that the design of a product should be incorporated in its manufacture, with the designer as innovator as well as stylist. The lines are sharper than the 1948 model, with a single plastic molding to house the machinery.

Specifications
Country: UK
Material: Plastic

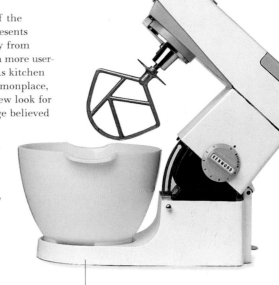

The redesigned Kenwood Chef has harder edges and sharper lines than the original

Magimix c.1978

The compact Magimix marked a radical departure in food mixer design. Designed to carry out a wide range of functions without making the user change attachments, it replaces previous mixers with just one bowl and four blades. It takes up little space in the kitchen since the bowl is housed above the stand. The hard-wearing bowl and attachment are made of toughened, dishwasher-proof plastic, Lexan, making it easy to clean.

Specifications
Country: France
Materials: Plastic and shatterproof Lexan

Soft colors and elegant lines typify Braun's skillful styling of domestic appliances

Braun Multipractic 1983

In the 1950s, the bowl and stand arrangement of Braun's electric kitchen machine was similar to that of the Kenwood Chef. In 1983, Braun introduced a new look with the Multipractic. Its design is closer to the Magimix than previous mixers. The sleek machine has a covered bowl that slots into grooves in the stand.

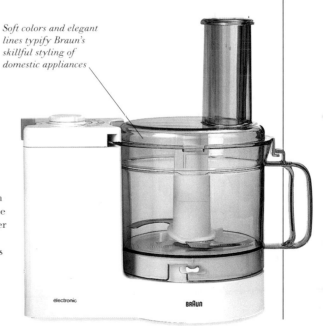

Specifications
Country: Germany
Material: Plastic

CUTLERY

BESIDES ITS OBVIOUS UTILITARIAN purpose, cutlery – or flatware, as it is sometimes known – also plays an aesthetic role in 20th-century living. The look of a dining room or restaurant table can be greatly enhanced by the cutlery settings. The production of metal utensils has a long tradition, particularly in England, and this is reflected in David Mellor's Pride service from the late 1950s. Since World War II, there has been an increase in the use of plastics in cutlery, particularly in the design of disposable items. The postmodern designers of the 1980s and '90s have reintroduced ornament into cutlery: Matteo Thun's decorative Hommage à Madonna elevates knives, forks, and spoons from mere utensils to objects of contemplation.

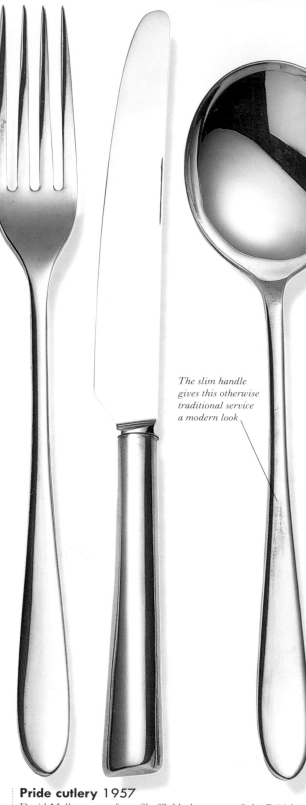

The slim handle gives this otherwise traditional service a modern look

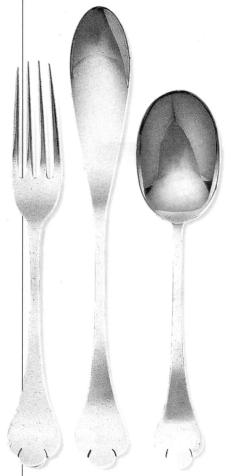

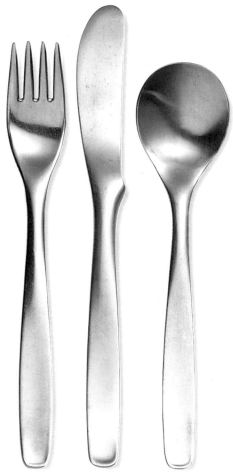

Silver cutlery c.1908
Charles Rennie Mackintosh designed this cutlery for Miss Cranston's Ingram Street Tearooms in Glasgow. The service is simply decorated with a flared floral motif at the end of each piece; otherwise, a clean, gently elongated line is maintained.

Specifications
Country: UK
Material: Silverplate
Length of knife: 8¼in (21cm)

American Modern 1950
This service was designed by Russel Wright to complement his enormously successful American Modern dinnerware (see p.86). The cutlery, characterized by disproportionately long handles, is stamped from single sheets of stainless steel and is completely free of ornamentation.

Specifications
Country: US
Material: Stainless steel
Length of knife: 8¾in (22cm)

Pride cutlery 1957
David Mellor comes from Sheffield, the center of the British steel industry and a city renowned for its flatware. This was his first attempt at cutlery design for the manufacturers Walker and Hall. Although the style is restrained, the light, slender pieces are without decoration. The service was also produced with contrasting celluloid handles. Pride's success was confirmed in 1957, when it received one of the first British Design Council awards.

Specifications
Country: UK
Material: Silverplate
Length of knife: 8½in (21.5cm)

DISPOSIBLE PLASTIC CUTLERY

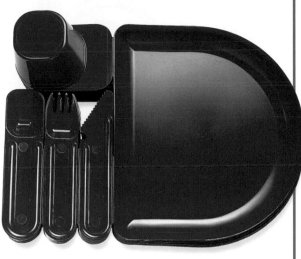

Made from polystyrene, this ingenious disposable picnic set was created by the French designer Jean-Pierre Vitrac in 1979. Plastic has been used as an alternative to wood, metal, and glass since the 19th century, but it has only been with the development of new plastics, such as PVC (polyvinyl chloride), polystyrene, and Lucite that we have seen its full potential. Manufactured by Diam, this bright red, lightweight set is easy to stack and store. The knife, fork, spoon, cup, and plate are joined together – so nothing can be lost in transit – and are then separated by the user.

Plack picnic set, 1979

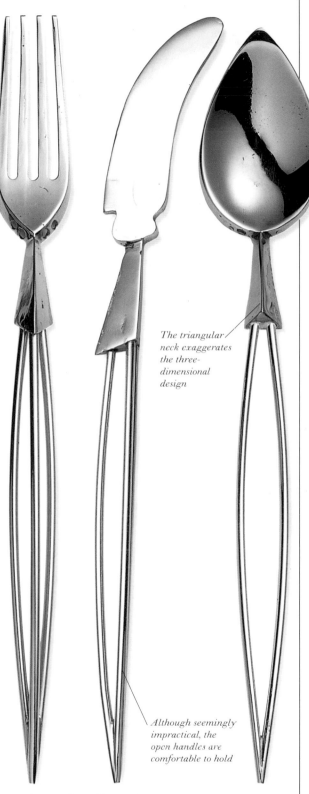

The triangular neck exaggerates the three-dimensional design

Although seemingly impractical, the open handles are comfortable to hold

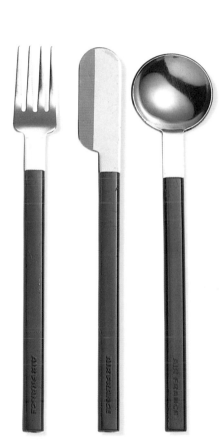

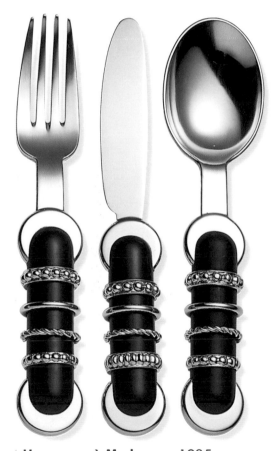

CEI airline cutlery c.1978
In 1952, Raymond Loewy founded the influential Compagnie d'Esthetique Industrielle (CEI) in his native Paris. The company designed this flatware for Air France in the late 1970s. The simple, matching geometry creates an elegant, yet functional, service.

Specifications
Country: France
Materials: Metal and plastic
Length of knife: 6¼in (16cm)

Hommage à Madonna c.1985
Since the 1980s, postmodern designers have been responsible for putting symbolism and metaphor back into design. In his Hommage à Madonna service, made by WMF, Austrian ceramist and designer Matteo Thun applies luxurious decoration to an everyday object, making reference to the famous singer's flamboyant style.

Specifications
Country: Germany
Materials: Gilded brass and PVC plastic
Length of knife: 7in (18cm)

Open-handle cutlery 1991
This is a delightful cutlery service from the Czech designer Bořek Šípek. The heads of each piece are made from stainless steel, while the handles are crafted from gold-plated wire. Instead of the usual solid form conventionally favored for flatware, Šípek has chosen to leave the handles open, each gently bowing in the middle and finishing in a point.

Specifications
Country: Czech Republic
Materials: Stainless steel and gold plate
Length of knife: 8in (20.5cm)

TEA & COFFEE SETS

THROUGHOUT THE WORLD, tea drinking is more than just light refreshment, but an opportunity for ceremony and ritual. Perhaps it is for this reason that so much attention has been paid to the production of tea and coffee services, with contributions made by some of the world's best-known designers. A great diversity of materials has been used, from traditional earthenware to silver, iron, copper, and glass; one of the most celebrated sets, Jan Eisenloeffel's fine Arts and Crafts service, is made from brass. Some designers have applied their artistic concepts to product design, although, as Kazimir Malevich's half cup demonstrates, these are not always practical. In terms of public popularity, it is often the traditional designs, such as Royal Doulton's best-selling Old Country Roses (see p.84), that prove to be the most enduring.

Silver tea service 1928

Jean Puiforcat's tea services from the 1920s and '30s are characterized by their simple geometry. He was interested in a mathematical principle known as the Golden Section, which provided a system of proportion for his work.

Specifications
Country: France
Material: Silver and walnut
Height of teapot: 4½in (11.4cm)

The handle of the teapot is coated in rattan

Brass tea service 1900–03

The Dutch designer Jan Eisenloeffel trained as a goldsmith and silversmith and later went on to study under Fabergé (1846–1920) in St. Petersburg. His work expresses control and harmony: this brass tea service is beautifully made in the Arts and Crafts tradition, with decoration kept to a minimum. A similar set was exhibited to wide acclaim at the first International Arts and Crafts Exhibition, held in Turin in 1902.

The details of the craftsmanship are left exposed to view

Specifications
Country: Holland
Material: Brass, rattan, and ebony
Height of teapot: 8¾in (22.5cm)

Each item is constructed of broad, plain surfaces

Strong, geometric silhouettes typify Eisenloeffel's work

RUSSIAN AVANT-GARDE WORK

Kazimir Malevich was an important avant-garde artist working in Russia during the revolution. His key concept, known as suprematism, attempted to reduce images to universal geometric forms and pure color. This porcelain cup, although serviceable, is more a statement of those beliefs than a practical proposition. The enameled decoration was done by one of Malevich's own students, Ilia Chashnik.

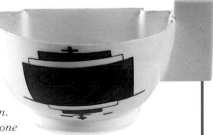

Half cup, 1923

Bizarre coffee set 1929

The British ceramic designer Clarice Cliff is well known for her brightly colored, jazzy designs. She came to fame in the 1920s and '30s, when she was art director for the Wilkinson's Burslem pottery in Staffordshire. Her geometric patterns are firmly associated with the Art Deco style.

Specifications
Country: UK
Material: Ceramic
Dimensions: Not known

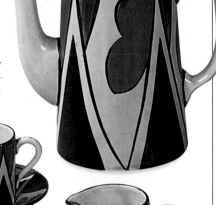

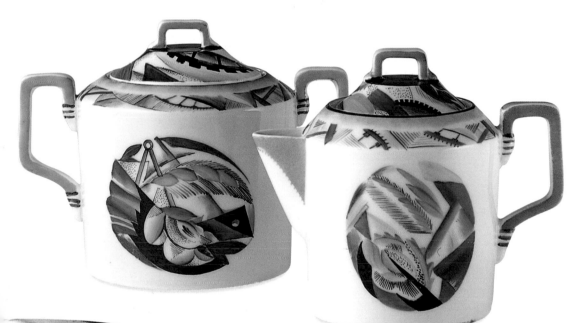

Russian sugar bowl and cream pitcher 1920–25

These two items by Zinaida Kobylestskaya have all the hallmarks of Russian avant-garde design of the early 1920s. The fragmented, semi-abstract images of agricultural and industrial scenes, together with the hammer and sickle, had a powerful symbolic resonance for the post-revolutionary citizens of Soviet Russia. Fragments of cogs, which were used as the State Porcelain Factory trademark, can be seen on both lids.

Specifications
Country: USSR
Material: Porcelain with enameled decoration
Height of sugar bowl: 4¼in (10.6cm)

The sharp lime green shade is typical of Art Deco coloring

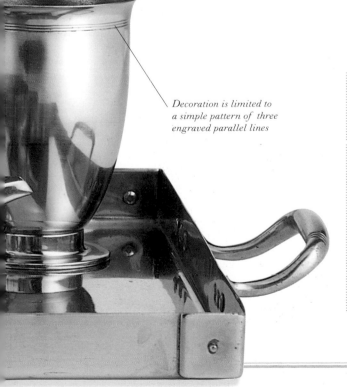

Decoration is limited to a simple pattern of three engraved parallel lines

Japanese teapot and sugar bowl c.1930s

Nowhere is the serving of tea more ritualized than in Japan, where it has been raised to an art form of great ceremony. This teapot and sugar bowl were produced for export to the west. The decoration and geometric styling show the influence of Art Deco.

Specifications
Country: Japan
Material: Ceramic
Height of teapot: 6¼in (16.1cm)

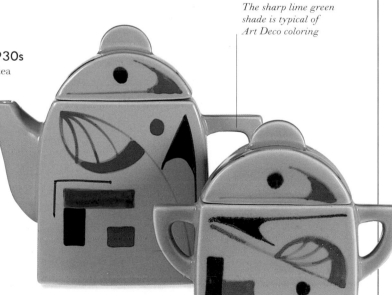

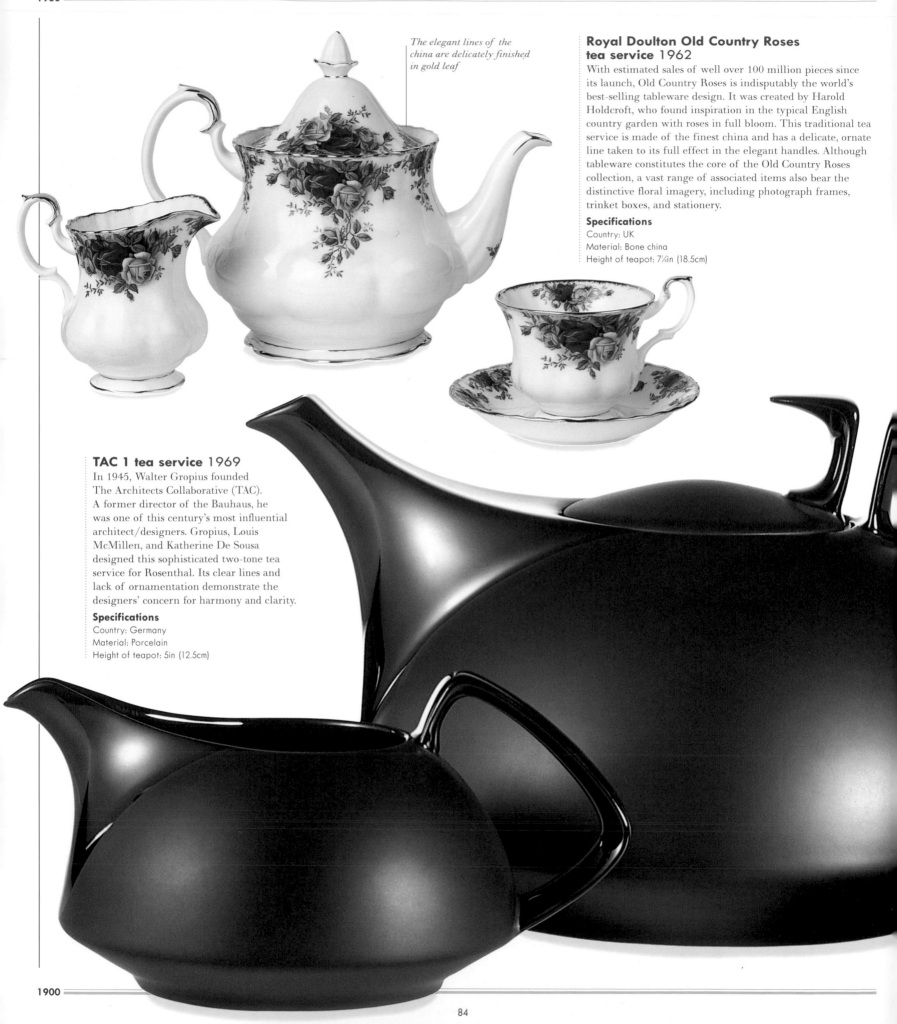

The elegant lines of the china are delicately finished in gold leaf

Royal Doulton Old Country Roses tea service 1962

With estimated sales of well over 100 million pieces since its launch, Old Country Roses is indisputably the world's best-selling tableware design. It was created by Harold Holdcroft, who found inspiration in the typical English country garden with roses in full bloom. This traditional tea service is made of the finest china and has a delicate, ornate line taken to its full effect in the elegant handles. Although tableware constitutes the core of the Old Country Roses collection, a vast range of associated items also bear the distinctive floral imagery, including photograph frames, trinket boxes, and stationery.

Specifications
Country: UK
Material: Bone china
Height of teapot: 7¼in (18.5cm)

TAC 1 tea service 1969

In 1945, Walter Gropius founded The Architects Collaborative (TAC). A former director of the Bauhaus, he was one of this century's most influential architect/designers. Gropius, Louis McMillen, and Katherine De Sousa designed this sophisticated two-tone tea service for Rosenthal. Its clear lines and lack of ornamentation demonstrate the designers' concern for harmony and clarity.

Specifications
Country: Germany
Material: Porcelain
Height of teapot: 5in (12.5cm)

Drop tea service 1971

This inventive, streamlined tea service by Luigi Colani is produced here in white porcelain, but was also available in black or gold. The service was commissioned by Rosenthal for its Studio Line. The flowing forms have an organic quality, particularly evident in the teapot and creamer, which together seem to relate like a parent and child.

Specifications
Country: Germany
Material: Porcelain
Height of teapot: 4¼in (10.5cm)

The teapot handle is positioned near the center to make pouring easy

Alessi tea set 1983

In the 1980s, Alessi commissioned a series of tea services that elevated functional objects to high art. Oscar Tusquets's set cleverly combines the flowing forms of the handles with angular, cutaway spouts.

Specifications
Country: Italy
Material: Silver
Height of teapot: 7½in (19cm)

The choice of black glaze – more often associated with coffee drinking – is an unusual one

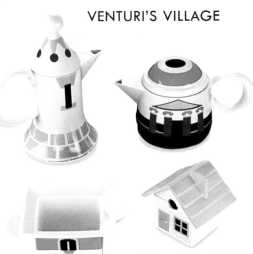

VENTURI'S VILLAGE

Village tea set, 1986

American architect and designer Robert Venturi is a leading proponent of postmodernism. His theories are played out in this 1986 tea service for Swid Powell. References can be seen to classical and vernacular architecture, combined with colors and shapes that might be derived from theme parks and carnivals.

DINNER SERVICES

THE 20TH CENTURY HAS SEEN the introduction of a profusion of interesting dinner service designs alongside traditional, high-quality porcelain sets. During the 1920s, many designers, including Clarice Cliff in the UK (see p.83), chose earthenware in preference to porcelain. At the end of the 1930s, Russel Wright's name became famous for his American Modern service, which was revolutionary for its "mix and match" colored glazes and organic shapes. Eva Zeisel was the other leading contemporary ceramic designer at work in the US, and she too embraced new, more organic shapes. Other designers have retained a formal geometry, and, in the hands of postmodern designers like Aldo Rossi, dinnerware has taken on humorous architectural motifs.

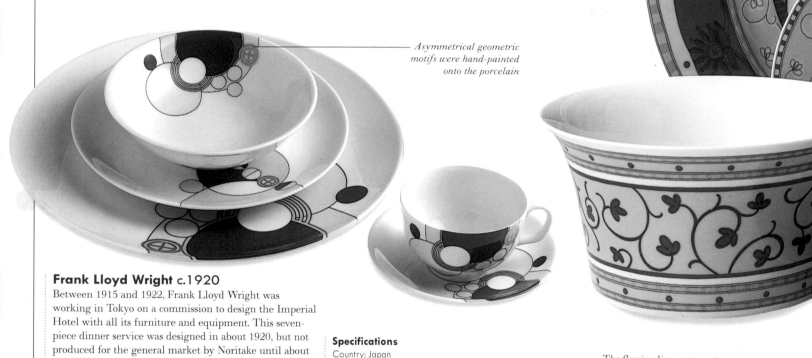

Asymmetrical geometric motifs were hand-painted onto the porcelain

Frank Lloyd Wright c.1920

Between 1915 and 1922, Frank Lloyd Wright was working in Tokyo on a commission to design the Imperial Hotel with all its furniture and equipment. This seven-piece dinner service was designed in about 1920, but not produced for the general market by Noritake until about 1962. It is made from hand-painted white porcelain, with a pattern of red, green, and yellow circles.

Specifications
Country: Japan
Material: Porcelain
Diameter of side plate: 6½in (17cm)

The flowing lines represent a departure from the functionalist aesthetic

Each piece came in a choice of six colors; Seafoam Blue was one

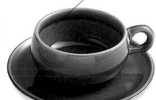

American Modern 1937

Although Russel Wright's unusually shaped dinner service was thought to be daring when it was first introduced in 1939 by Steubenville Pottery, it sold a phenomenal 80 million pieces over 20 years. The soft curves and the use of muted colors that could be mixed and matched created an informal quality.

Specifications
Country: US
Material: Glazed earthenware
Diameter of plate: 10in (25.2cm)

Museum 1942–45

This dinner service was the first modern porcelain service to be produced in the US. It was designed by Hungarian ceramist Eva Zeisel following a recommendation from the Museum of Modern Art, and was produced by the Shenango Company for Castleton China, Inc.

Specifications
Country: US
Material: Porcelain
Diameter of saucer: 6½in (17cm)

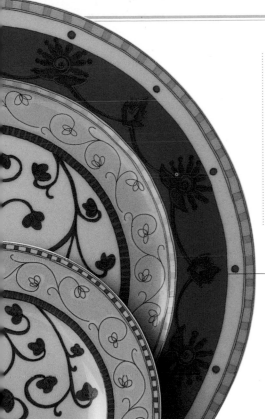

Idillio Bokara 1985

British designer Tricia Guild (1947–) is well known for her radiant color compositions. She was commissioned by Rosenthal to provide the decoration on the elegant Idillio service, designed by Paul Wunderlich. In Bokara she has produced a dazzling pattern of colors in bold reds and yellows.

Specifications
Country: Germany
Material: Porcelain
Diameter of plate: 10¾in (27cm)

Rich primary colors dominate this striking modern service

Decoration is provided by a pattern of circles and squares

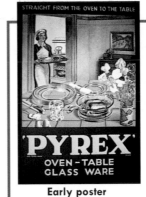

PYREX

Invented by scientists working for Corning Glass Company, these heat-resistant, low-expansion oven dishes were first available for baking and roasting in 1915. Early Pyrex examples used thick glass and had no handles. However, they were easy to clean and were suitable as oven-to-table ware.

Early poster

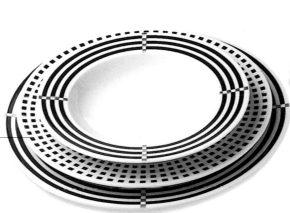

Il Faro Finestra 1994

Architect and designer Aldo Rossi produced this dinner service for Rosenthal. In it he incorporates architectural shapes to humorous effect, making coffee pots as lighthouses, sugar bowls as beach huts, and salt cellars as obelisks. The decoration on this Finestra variation was created by the Indonesian artist Yang (1953–).

Specifications
Country: Germany
Material: Porcelain and glass
Diameter of plate: 12in (31cm)

The domed cover of the vegetable dish is echoed in the salt and pepper shakers

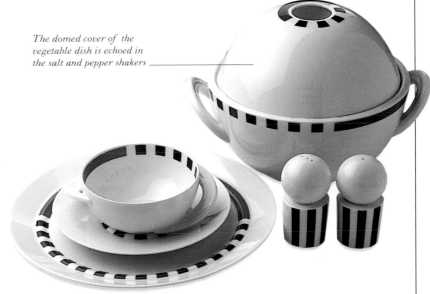

The lively illustrations feature a variety of household items

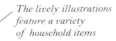

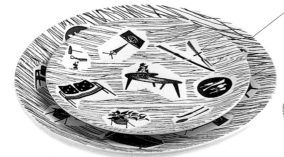

Homemaker 1955

Designed by Enid Seeney for the Ridgeway Potteries, this informal and self-conscious dinner service was clearly aimed at young consumers. The shape of the service remains traditional compared, for example, with Russel Wright's American Modern, but its quirky drawings of modern furniture are typical of the 1950s.

Specifications
Country: UK
Material: Glazed ceramic
Diameter of plate: 10in (25.5cm)

Cupola Strada 1990

The white Cupola dinner service was designed by Mario Bellini and introduced in 1988 as part of the German company Rosenthal's Studio Line. This particular version, featuring black and gray decoration by Yang, appeared in 1990. By adopting a geometric approach, Bellini has produced a well-balanced and extremely attractive service.

Specifications
Country: Germany
Material: Porcelain
Diameter of plate: 10¼in (26cm)

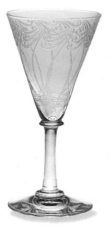

Wine glass c.1900

This elegant wine glass may have been made by the Belgian firm Val Saint Lambert. Around its surface, an interwoven pattern of tendrils forms an almost abstract pattern. The floral decoration is typical of Art Nouveau style.

Specifications
Country: Belgium or France
Height: 5¾in (14.6cm)

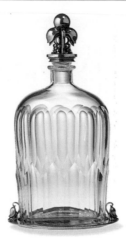

Decanter c.1920

Designed by Harald Nielsen and manufactured by Georg Jensen Sølvsmedie, this decanter has a silver stopper and stand. The intricate detail of the silver vines, fruit, and pods contrasts well with the heavy glass.

Specifications
Country: Denmark
Height: 11in (28cm)

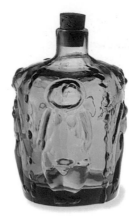

Decanter and glass 1953–59

This highly textured olive green set was produced by the Swedish company Boda. The designer, Erik Höglund, adopted a mold-blown technique to create a relief pattern featuring human figures on the surface of the glass.

Specifications
Country: Sweden
Height: Decanter 5¾in (14.4cm); glass 3⅓in (8.5cm)

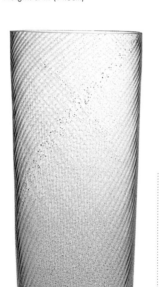

Calici Natale goblet 1990

For centuries, the tiny Venetian island of Murano has been famous for its glassmaking. This elegant goblet was produced there by the Carlo Moretti Studio. Its long, deep bowl has a finely textured surface and rests on a blue base.

Specifications
Country: Italy
Height: 9½in (24cm)

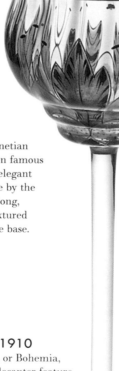

Wine glass and decanter c.1910

Produced in Austria, or Bohemia, this wine glass and decanter feature a beautifully colored leaf motif in yellows, browns, and pinks, with gilded outlines. The classic geometric proportions of the long stem on the glass are echoed in the neck of the decanter.

Specifications
Country: Austria
Height: Decanter 12¾in (32.5cm); glass 7in (17.6cm)

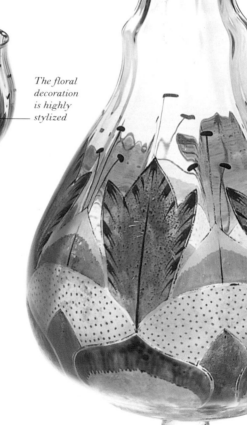

The floral decoration is highly stylized

The gilding on the foot of the decanter echoes that on lip

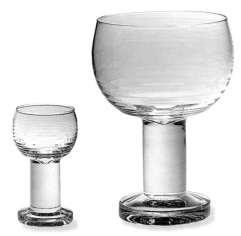

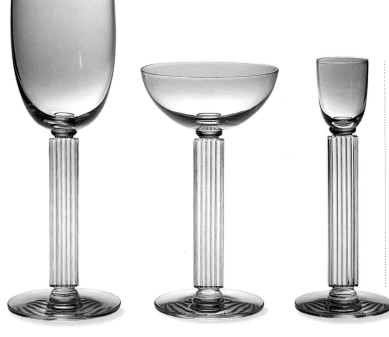

Embassy glasses 1939
These glasses — for water, champagne, and cordials — were designed by Edwin Fuerst and Walter Dorwin Teague for the 1939 New York World's Fair, and made by Libbey Glass Co.. The stem resembles a classical column, remaining the same height for each of the glasses.

Specifications
Country: US
Height: Water glass 8¾in (22cm); champagne glass 6½in (16.6cm); cordial glass 6¾in (17.2cm)

Maaru glasses 1980
Tapio Wirkkala's glassware is renowned for its organic form and fine surface decoration. This set, with short, thick stems, is made at Iittala glassworks.

Specifications
Country: Finland
Height: Large glass 6in (15cm); small glass 8.7cm (3½in)

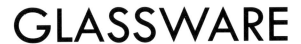

GLASSWARE

THE VENETIAN ISLAND OF MURANO, Orrefors in Sweden, Iittala in Finland, and Corning in the US are four examples of centers of excellence in a long history of glassware design and production. The variety of techniques and finishes developed over the centuries has allowed designers to experiment freely with style and decoration. Glass design in the 20th century began with the outstanding work of the Art Nouveau designers — most innovatively in the form of Louis Comfort Tiffany's high-quality Favrile glassware (see pp.50–51). Since then, other designers have perfected the arts of pressing, layering, engraving, and staining.

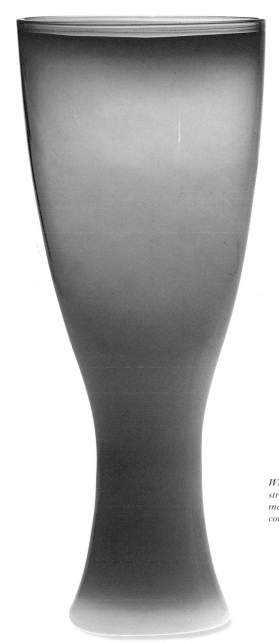

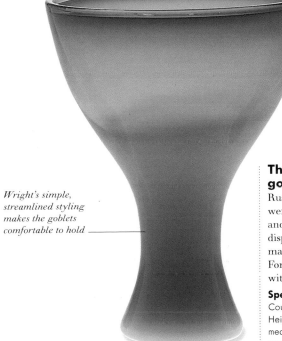

Wright's simple, streamlined styling makes the goblets comfortable to hold

Theme Formal goblets 1950s
Russel Wright's products were typically informal and inexpensive, yet always displayed an innovative use of material and form. His Theme Formal goblets are colored with bands of blue and orange.

Specifications
Country: US
Height: Large goblet 8½in (22cm); medium goblet 4in (10.5cm); small goblet 3¼in (8.5cm)

BAR ACCESSORIES

IT IS NOT UNCOMMON for predominant design movements to influence the look of the most humble of items, and bar accessories are no exception. Craftsmen inspired by Art Nouveau expressed themselves through elaborate floral patterns and curvilinear forms, while Art Deco afforded a sleek, luxurious quality to items that might previously have been given only perfunctory treatment. In the Soviet Union, constructivism (and, later, social realism) was intended to reflect the endeavors of the masses to build a new society. For the modernists, it was new materials that generated particular enthusiasm.

Pitcher 1928–29

This pitcher, which is illustrated with agricultural scenes, was designed at the VKhUTEMAS workshops in Moscow. After the 1917 revolution, designers often adopted themes considered to be important to the survival of the newly formed Soviet Union.

Specifications
Country: Soviet Union
Material: Ceramic
Height: 6¾in (17cm)

The polished, streamlined body is adorned with penguin features

Pitcher 1895–1909

Designed in the Cologne Studio of Engelberg Kayser, this pitcher is influenced by French Art Nouveau. The handle divides and extends to either side of the pitcher, where it develops into a flowerhead.

Specifications
Country: Germany
Material: Pewter
Height: 8in (20.5cm)

Cocktail shaker c.1930

Bar ware was at the peak of its popularity during the 1930s. Manufactured by Napier, this amusing penguin cocktail shaker exhibits all the hallmarks of Art Deco styling.

Specifications
Country: US
Material: Silver
Height: 12¼in (31cm)

Vacuum pitcher 1930

Designed by Nowland and Schladermundt for the manufacturing company American Thermos, this vacuum pitcher was sold in the 1930s. Its black spherical stopper echoes the rounded form of the body.

Specifications
Country: US
Materials: Chrome and plastic
Height: Not known

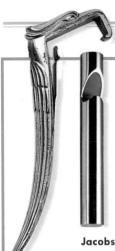

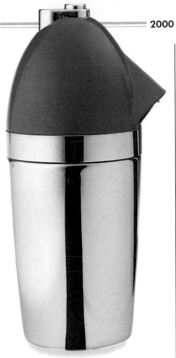

BOTTLE OPENERS

Of all drinks accessories, the corkscrew and bottle opener are among those most subject to reinterpretation. This ensemble of bottle openers shows the designer's inventiveness in remodeling the most prosaic of objects. The Chase Brass & Copper Co.'s elegant Squeezit model is made from chromium-plated brass, while Arne Jacobson's sleek cylindrical opener is crafted from stainless steel. Arne Petersen's refined egg-shaped opener combines brass with stainless steel, and Daniel Ebihara's triangular Open Two is simply formed from a square of folded metal.

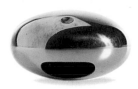

Petersen's opener, 1975

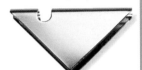

Jacobsen's opener, 1960s

Squeezit, 1930s

Ebihara's Open Two, 1990

Soda siphon c.1930s
The gently curved body of this popular soda siphon demonstrates the industrial designer Norman Bel Geddes's application of streamlining to household objects.

Specifications
Country: US
Materials: Chrome and enamel
Height: 10¼in (26cm)

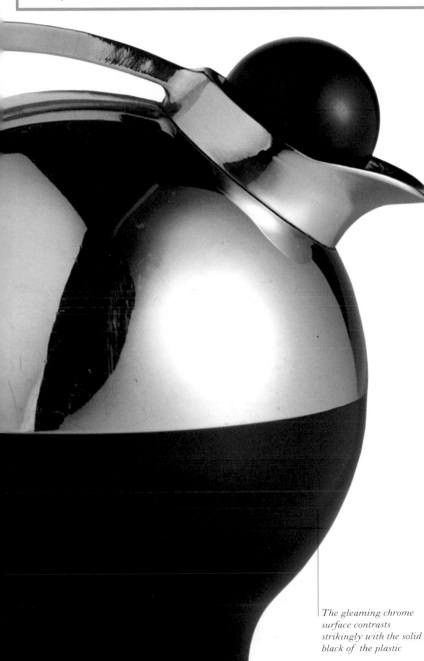

The gleaming chrome surface contrasts strikingly with the solid black of the plastic

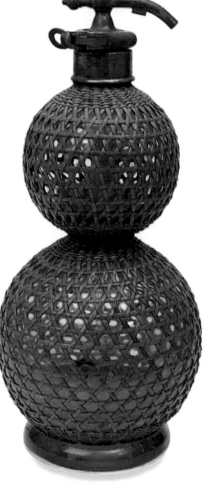

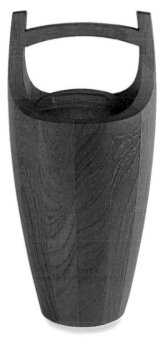

Soda siphon c.1910
A wicker casing creates a decorative geometric pattern on this hourglass-shaped, clear glass siphon. The use of wicker is reminiscent of Chianti wine bottles.

Specifications
Country: France
Materials: Glass, wicker, and metal
Height: 19¾in (50cm)

Ice bucket 1960
Danish modernists such as Jens Quistgaard eschewed the quest for new materials and used traditional ones, in this case teak, to produce beautifully sculpted forms.

Specifications
Country: Denmark
Material: Teak
Height: 15½in (39.5cm)

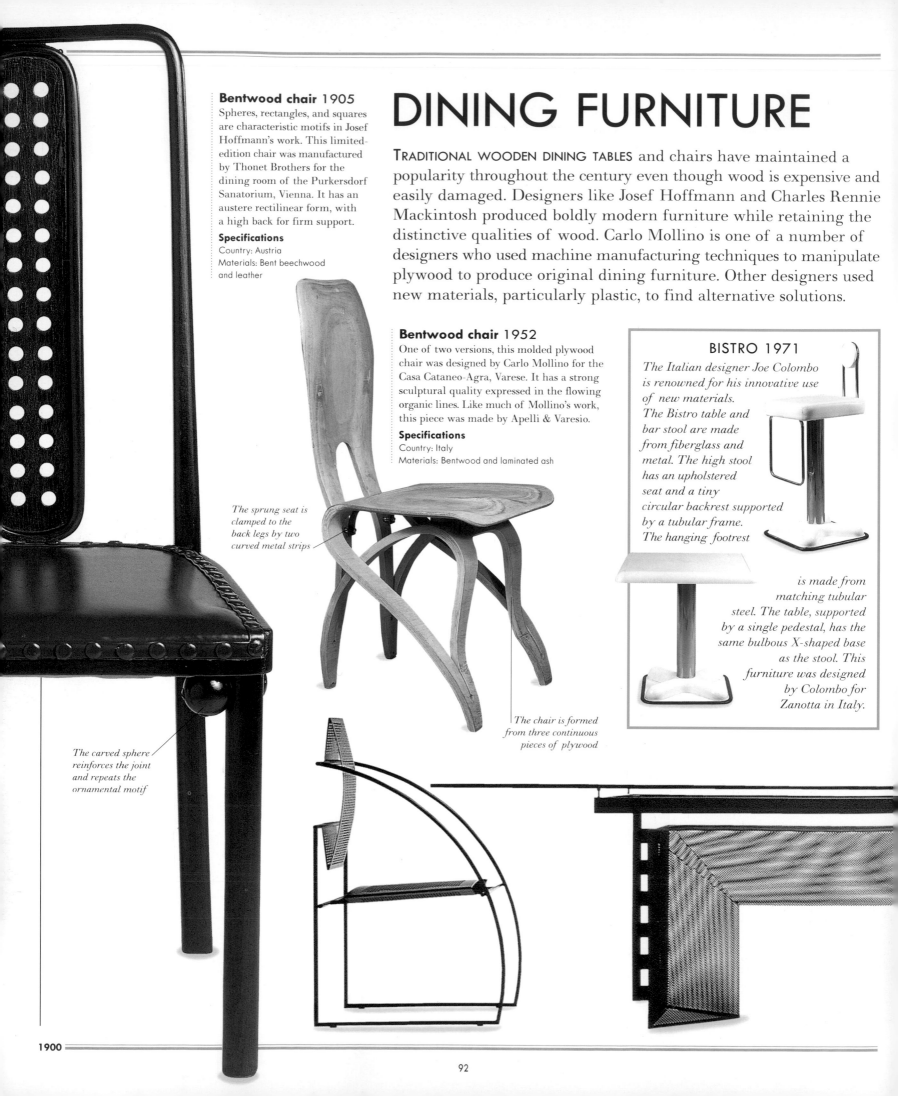

Bentwood chair 1905

Spheres, rectangles, and squares are characteristic motifs in Josef Hoffmann's work. This limited-edition chair was manufactured by Thonet Brothers for the dining room of the Purkersdorf Sanatorium, Vienna. It has an austere rectilinear form, with a high back for firm support.

Specifications

Country: Austria
Materials: Bent beechwood and leather

DINING FURNITURE

TRADITIONAL WOODEN DINING TABLES and chairs have maintained a popularity throughout the century even though wood is expensive and easily damaged. Designers like Josef Hoffmann and Charles Rennie Mackintosh produced boldly modern furniture while retaining the distinctive qualities of wood. Carlo Mollino is one of a number of designers who used machine manufacturing techniques to manipulate plywood to produce original dining furniture. Other designers used new materials, particularly plastic, to find alternative solutions.

Bentwood chair 1952

One of two versions, this molded plywood chair was designed by Carlo Mollino for the Casa Cataneo-Agra, Varese. It has a strong sculptural quality expressed in the flowing organic lines. Like much of Mollino's work, this piece was made by Apelli & Varesio.

Specifications

Country: Italy
Materials: Bentwood and laminated ash

BISTRO 1971

The Italian designer Joe Colombo is renowned for his innovative use of new materials. The Bistro table and bar stool are made from fiberglass and metal. The high stool has an upholstered seat and a tiny circular backrest supported by a tubular frame. The hanging footrest is made from matching tubular steel. The table, supported by a single pedestal, has the same bulbous X-shaped base as the stool. This furniture was designed by Colombo for Zanotta in Italy.

The sprung seat is clamped to the back legs by two curved metal strips

The carved sphere reinforces the joint and repeats the ornamental motif

The chair is formed from three continuous pieces of plywood

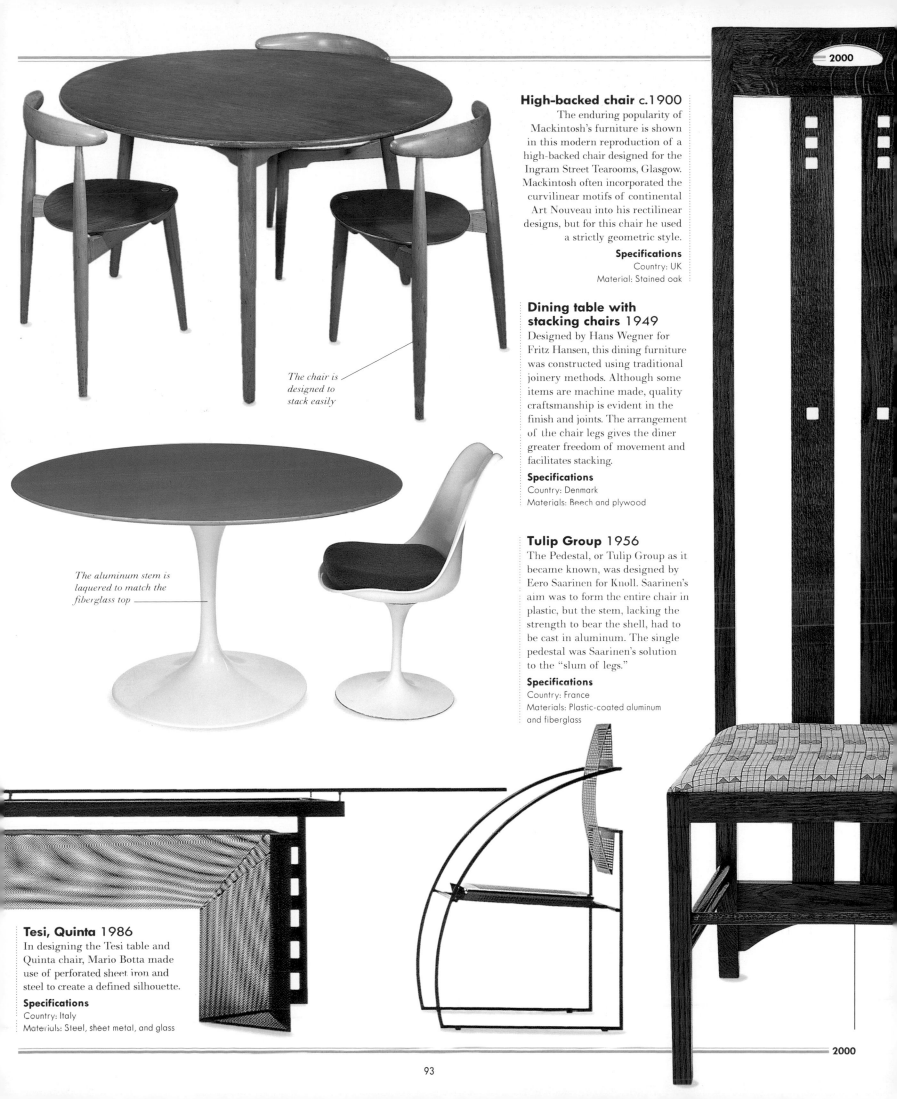

High-backed chair c.1900

The enduring popularity of Mackintosh's furniture is shown in this modern reproduction of a high-backed chair designed for the Ingram Street Tearooms, Glasgow. Mackintosh often incorporated the curvilinear motifs of continental Art Nouveau into his rectilinear designs, but for this chair he used a strictly geometric style.

Specifications
Country: UK
Material: Stained oak

Dining table with stacking chairs 1949

Designed by Hans Wegner for Fritz Hansen, this dining furniture was constructed using traditional joinery methods. Although some items are machine made, quality craftsmanship is evident in the finish and joints. The arrangement of the chair legs gives the diner greater freedom of movement and facilitates stacking.

Specifications
Country: Denmark
Materials: Beech and plywood

Tulip Group 1956

The Pedestal, or Tulip Group as it became known, was designed by Eero Saarinen for Knoll. Saarinen's aim was to form the entire chair in plastic, but the stem, lacking the strength to bear the shell, had to be cast in aluminum. The single pedestal was Saarinen's solution to the "slum of legs."

Specifications
Country: France
Materials: Plastic-coated aluminum and fiberglass

The chair is designed to stack easily

The aluminum stem is laquered to match the fiberglass top

Tesi, Quinta 1986

In designing the Tesi table and Quinta chair, Mario Botta made use of perforated sheet iron and steel to create a defined silhouette.

Specifications
Country: Italy
Materials: Steel, sheet metal, and glass

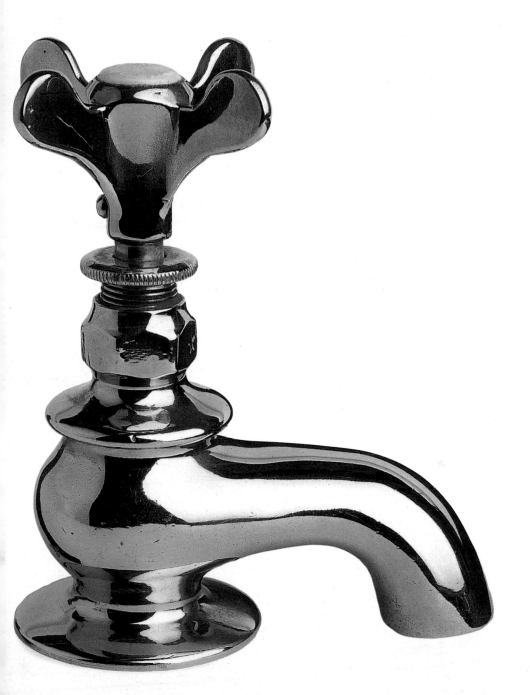

BATHROOM, BEDROOM, & NURSERY

BATHROOMS

THE EARLIEST BATHROOMS were a luxury afforded only by the wealthy, but improved plumbing and increased concern for hygiene led to their inclusion in most homes by the 1920s. Wood and marble gave way to shiny, white nonporous materials, such as ceramic tile and enameled cast iron. By the 1930s, suite ensembles appeared in various colors, enthusiastically adopted in plastic form in the 1950s. Later, shower units were installed and matching accessories became available.

LOW-LEVEL FLUSH TOILETS

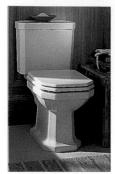

1930s toilet

The cistern of this 1930s Art Deco toilet is low level and completely enclosed, a combination that is still preferred by most bathroom designers today. The toilet bowl is made from white porcelain and has a wooden seat.

EARLY 20TH-CENTURY FAUCETS

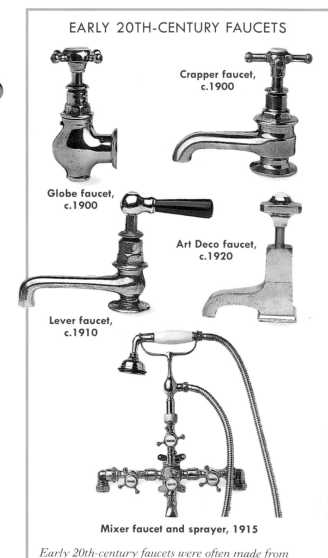

Crapper faucet, c.1900

Globe faucet, c.1900

Art Deco faucet, c.1920

Lever faucet, c.1910

Mixer faucet and sprayer, 1915

Early 20th-century faucets were often made from brass or nickel. Spouts varied in shape and size: the Globe faucet has a short, downward-pointing spout better suited for baths, while the Crapper faucet has a long-reach spout. Four-finial heads were most common, until the lever type was introduced for easier use. Mixer faucets facilitated both the control of the water temperature and the use of a showerhead.

Flush toilet 1902

This high-level flush toilet was manufactured by the Scottish company Shanks, and the water closet by Oneas. The decorative hand-painted floral transfer print is a British government pattern, used for public toilets only. The cast-iron cistern rests on two sunflower brackets.

Specifications
Country: UK
Height with cistern: 89½in (228cm)
Materials: Porcelain, cast iron, nickel, and mahogany

The toilet seat is carved from mahogany

Needle shower c.1910

This luxurious early shower earns its name from the six perforated horizontal bars from which water is forcefully sprayed. Designed predominantly for male use, this large, cagelike shower was referred to as the "morning bracer."

Specifications
Country: UK
Height: 87½in (222cm)
Material: Brass

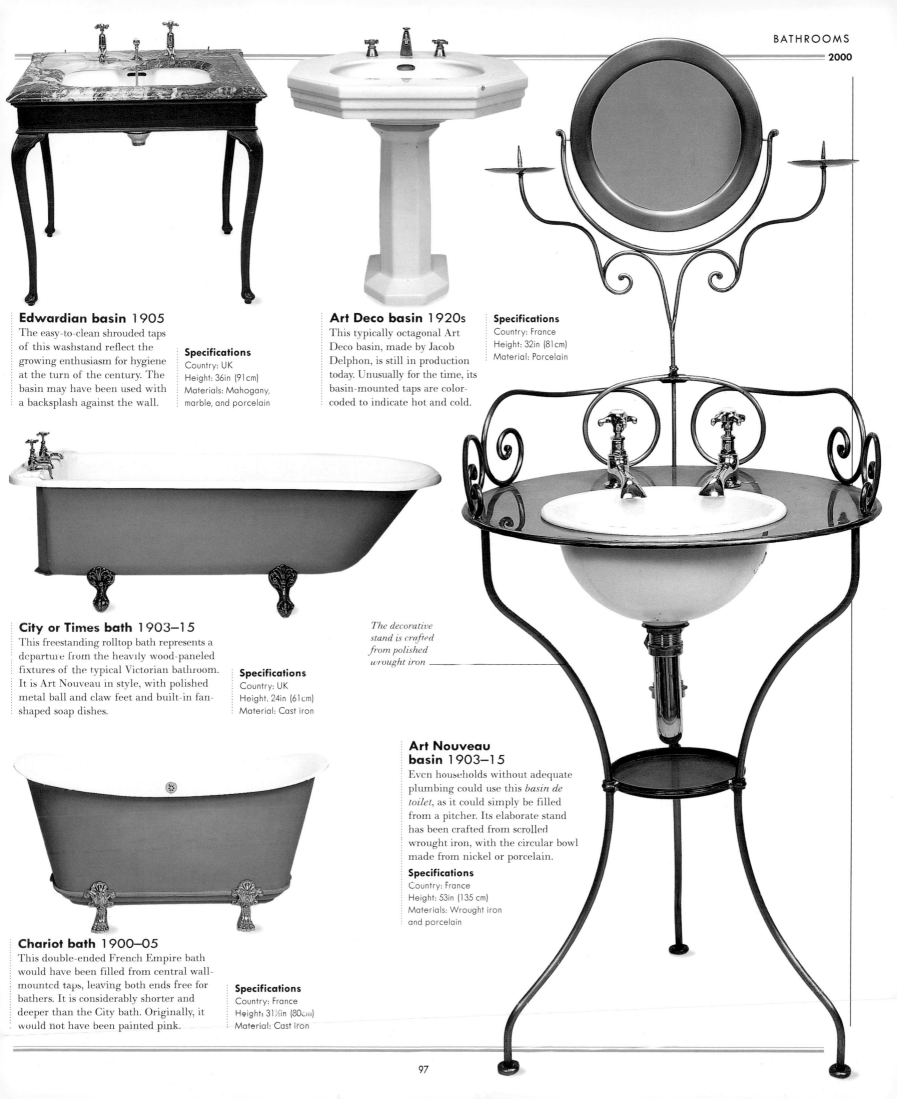

Edwardian basin 1905

The easy-to-clean shrouded taps of this washstand reflect the growing enthusiasm for hygiene at the turn of the century. The basin may have been used with a backsplash against the wall.

Specifications
Country: UK
Height: 36in (91cm)
Materials: Mahogany, marble, and porcelain

Art Deco basin 1920s

This typically octagonal Art Deco basin, made by Jacob Delphon, is still in production today. Unusually for the time, its basin-mounted taps are color-coded to indicate hot and cold.

Specifications
Country: France
Height: 32in (81cm)
Material: Porcelain

City or Times bath 1903–15

This freestanding rolltop bath represents a departure from the heavily wood-paneled fixtures of the typical Victorian bathroom. It is Art Nouveau in style, with polished metal ball and claw feet and built-in fan-shaped soap dishes.

Specifications
Country: UK
Height: 24in (61cm)
Material: Cast iron

The decorative stand is crafted from polished wrought iron

Art Nouveau basin 1903–15

Even households without adequate plumbing could use this *basin de toilet*, as it could simply be filled from a pitcher. Its elaborate stand has been crafted from scrolled wrought iron, with the circular bowl made from nickel or porcelain.

Specifications
Country: France
Height: 53in (135 cm)
Materials: Wrought iron and porcelain

Chariot bath 1900–05

This double-ended French Empire bath would have been filled from central wall-mounted taps, leaving both ends free for bathers. It is considerably shorter and deeper than the City bath. Originally, it would not have been painted pink.

Specifications
Country: France
Height: 31½in (80cm)
Material: Cast iron

Pampas basin 1970s

The 1970s witnessed a proliferation of colored bathroom fixtures. This pedestal basin by Armitage Shanks is equipped with gold-plated taps with plastic dome heads.

Specifications
Country: UK
Height: 30¾in (78cm)
Material: Porcelain

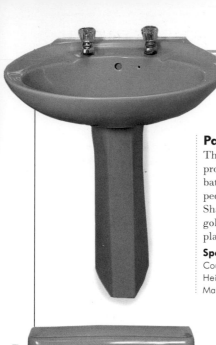

Matching plastic toilet seats and lids were common in the 1970s

Pampas toilet 1970s

Low-tank toilets were a standard feature in most modern bathrooms by the 1950s. The untidy flushing mechanism is completely enclosed, and the chain no longer necessary.

Specifications
Country: UK
Height: 30¼in (78cm)
Materials: Porcelain and plastic

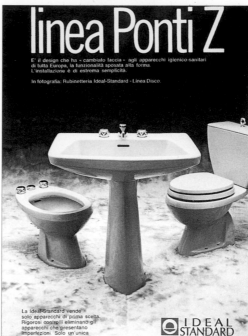

Poster advertising Ponti designs, 1953

Gio Ponti was one of Italy's foremost modern designers, influenced both by classicism and the products of the Wiener Werkstätte. In 1953, he designed this bathroom ensemble for Ideal-Standard, each item carefully shaped and refined to express its function. The sink is particularly successful: the stand tapers toward the curve of the basin to give it perfect support and balance, and the sink itself has a flat surround on which toiletries can be placed.

Shower 1980s

In the 1980s, British manufacturer Aqualisa produced a range of "power showers," which were designed to massage and invigorate the body. The shower includes two body jets, with adjustable water force.

Specifications
Country: UK
Height: 17¼in (44cm)
Materials: ABS plastic and chrome-plated brass

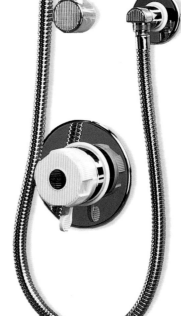

Belvedere toilet 1996

This elegant toilet conceals the tank and bowl in one body, retaining the low-tank principle. Its smooth, streamlined shape gives the unit a sculptural, futuristic quality, which blends discreetly into the bathroom. It is finished in a hardwearing white glaze, which is easy to clean.

Specifications
Country: Italy
Height: 30¾in (78cm)
Material: Vitreous china

The gleaming white finish enhances the sculptural quality of the bathtub

Belvedere bath 1996

This elegant freestanding bath allows the bather total comfort; even the concealed water outlet is within easy reach. The suite is designed by design group Sottini for Ideal-Standard.

Specifications
Country: Italy
Height: 26¾in (68cm)
Material: "Ideal Form" (reinforced acrylic)

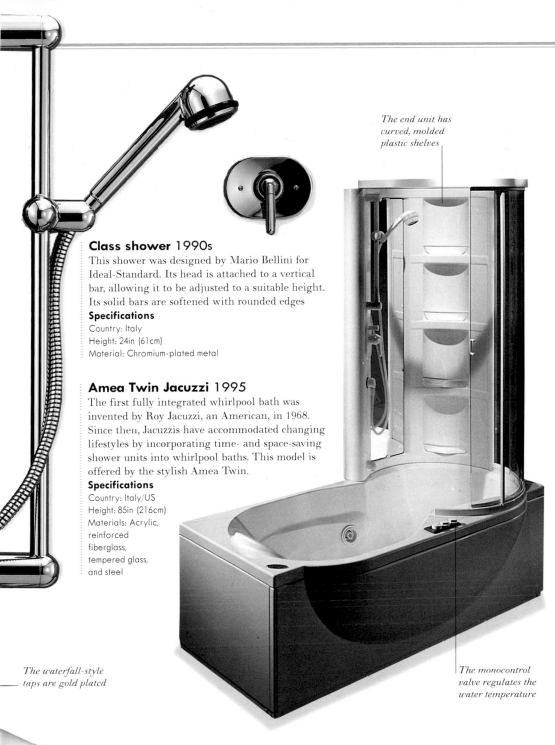

LATE 20TH-CENTURY FAUCETS

Designed by Mario Bellini as part of the Class line for Ideal-Standard, the single-lever mixer shown here has appeared in museum exhibitions. It utilizes ceramic disk technology to allow full pressure water with minimum lever movement. Similarly efficient, the Dallas basin mixer can be fully activated in just a quarter-turn. Chrome- and gold-plated faucets remain favorites in the 1990s, although ceramic and plastic, as used for this dome faucet, have become popular alternatives.

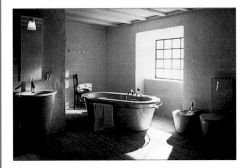

Single lever mixer, 1990s

Dome faucet, 1990s

Dallas basin mixer, 1990s

The end unit has curved, molded plastic shelves

Class shower 1990s

This shower was designed by Mario Bellini for Ideal-Standard. Its head is attached to a vertical bar, allowing it to be adjusted to a suitable height. Its solid bars are softened with rounded edges

Specifications
Country: Italy
Height: 24in (61cm)
Material: Chromium-plated metal

Amea Twin Jacuzzi 1995

The first fully integrated whirlpool bath was invented by Roy Jacuzzi, an American, in 1968. Since then, Jacuzzis have accommodated changing lifestyles by incorporating time- and space-saving shower units into whirlpool baths. This model is offered by the stylish Amea Twin.

Specifications
Country: Italy/US
Height: 85in (216cm)
Materials: Acrylic, reinforced fiberglass, tempered glass, and steel

The waterfall-style taps are gold plated

The monocontrol valve regulates the water temperature

PHILIPPE STARCK

This bathroom suite was inspired by the most basic functional objects — buckets, tubs, and hand pumps. The basin has a pearwood surround, and the bath a built-in towel rail.

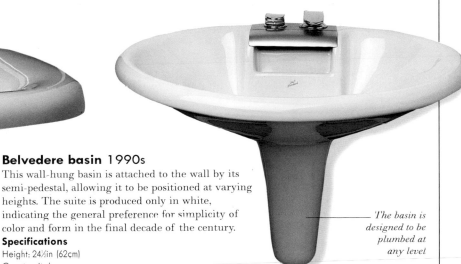

Starck bathroom, 1990s

Belvedere basin 1990s

This wall-hung basin is attached to the wall by its semi-pedestal, allowing it to be positioned at varying heights. The suite is produced only in white, indicating the general preference for simplicity of color and form in the final decade of the century.

Specifications
Height: 24½in (62cm)
Country: Italy
Materials: Vitreous china, chromium, and gold

The base is positioned off center

The basin is designed to be plumbed at any level

TOOTHBRUSHES

FOR THE MODERN CONSUMER, selecting a toothbrush is no easy matter. There is a bewildering range to choose from: "designer" brushes, such as Philippe Starck's Fluocaril; brushes with flexible heads; brushes with multi-angled or multicolored bristles; electric brushes; brushes in any color combination. Before 1953, it was simpler, for that was the year in which plastic-handled, nylon-bristled toothbrushes were first mass-produced. In 1900, the choice was even easier: comparatively expensive, ivory-handled brushes could be afforded only by the well-to-do.

Radius 1984

Designed in the US by Kevin Foley and James O'Halloran, the plastic Radius brush is a successful attempt to rethink established toothbrush design. In three sections, with its large head echoed in the middle thumb plate and wide, rounded handle, the Radius is ergonomically designed to allow the user to apply firm pressure to the teeth while brushing. The size of the head allows pressure to be distributed over a larger area than is conventionally possible.

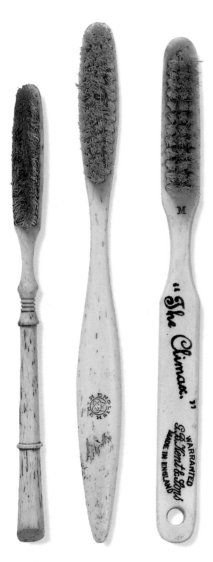

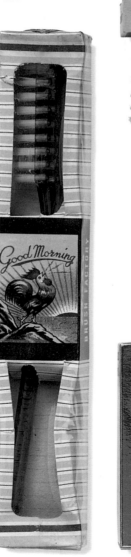

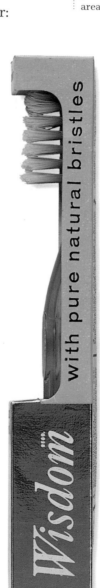

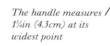

The wide expanse of nylon bristles brushes top and bottom teeth at once

The large central thumb plate repeats the shape of the brush head

The broad contours of the handle allow the fingers a strong grip

The handle measures 1¾in (4.3cm) at its widest point

Early toothbrushes c.1900s

Although toothbrushes had been used for several centuries, by the the beginning of the 20th century they remained expensive items made of bone and bristle, expected to last for a long time. The shape of the handle was much the same as the standard one used today, but the bristle heads were about twice as long as modern versions.

Plastic toothbrushes 1930s–40s

The first plastic toothbrushes were made in the 1930s, but on a small scale. These brushes retained the long heads of their forerunners. Nylon bristles began to replace natural bristles in the late 1940s, but it was not until the plastic handle and nylon bristles were united in 1953 that the toothbrush as we know it was born. Natural bristles continued to be used, marketed as "pure," and therefore healthy, but nylon was cheaper, longer-lasting, and available in various thicknesses – and so prevailed.

TRAVEL TOOTHBRUSHES

The handle of this early plastic travel toothbrush formed a zigzag shape when it was opened, making it difficult to use on any but the inside front teeth. Today, travel toothbrushes tend to come in separate sections, with the thick hollow handle often doubling as the casing for head and neck.

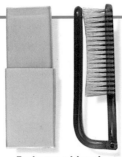

Early travel brush

Fluocaril 1989

Available in a range of subtle, translucent colors, the plastic handle of Philippe Starck's gorgeous Fluocaril toothbrush is sculpted in his trademark flame motif. Bearing Starck's signature on its neck, the item has become known as the ultimate "designer" toothbrush. Starck's intention seems to have been to create something beautiful out of an existing functional design; even so, the handle is remarkably comfortable and well balanced.

The flame motif is shown to best effect when the brush is stored in its base

The designer's signature appears on the neck of the toothbrush

The beautifully proportioned brush measures 7½in (19.3cm) in length

Although a popular design feature, flexible heads have little functional value

Modern toothbrushes 1980s–90s

While plastic has enabled designers to mold handles into any shape, there is little difference between the basic design of these brushes and that of 1950s plastic models. Designers now compete over the details: the most eye-catching colors, the most comfortable grip, the optimum angle and reach, and the best bristle combination.

Electric toothbrush 1990

The most radical innovation in 20th-century toothbrush design is the electric model, first seen in the early 1940s and widely used in the 1950s and '60s. Pressure can be applied in effective degrees to all teeth, without the necessity to "brush" manually.

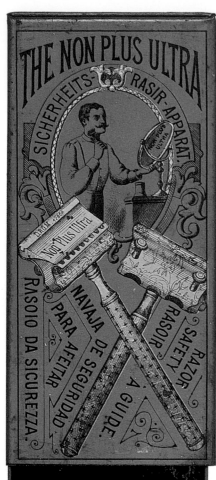

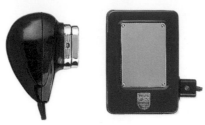

PHILIPS ELECTRIC RAZORS

Philips Philishave, c.1950

Philips razors differ from the standard system of most electric razors, which have a rotating foil head. The battery-operated Philishave has two or three bladed disks, which spin, catch, and cut the beard.

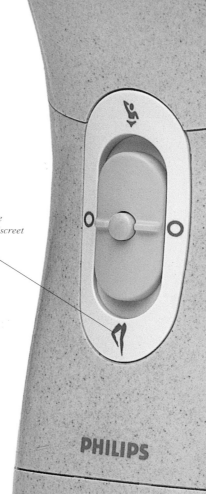

The functions are indicated with discreet pictograms

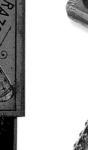

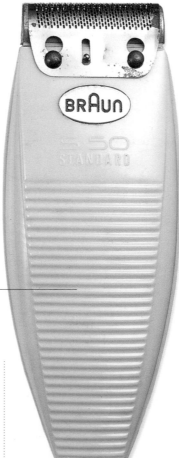

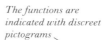

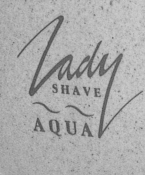

Non Plus Ultra 1910

The safety razor was a remarkable invention: it had a disposable double-edged blade that did not need stropping, and, since only a small sliver of the blade was exposed, serious cuts were impossible. The first safety razor was patented in 1895 by King Camp Gillette, who set up the Gillette Safety Razor Company in 1900. By 1910, Gillette had many rivals, including the ornate Non Plus Ultra.

Specifications
Country: Not known
Material: Metal
Length: 4in (10cm)

The lined grooves on the Bakelite casing give an improved grip

Braun S50 c.1950

Max Braun first developed the S50 electric razor in 1938, but World War II delayed production until 1951. The streamlined body, which tapers elegantly to the electric cord, suggests efficiency and fits comfortably in the hand. The cream coloring is highly unusual; men's razors are produced almost exclusively in black, gray, or silver.

Specifications
Country: Germany
Materials: Bakelite and metal
Length: 4½in (11.3cm)

RAZORS

ALTHOUGH BY MODERN STANDARDS, the "safety razors" available at the beginning of the century did not live up to their name, they were, in fact, a considerable improvement over the "cut-throat" razors that they replaced. Since then, however, the development of wet shave blades has steadily improved, with manufacturers competing to produce a closer, safer, more comfortable shave. New features have been launched regularly over the past three decades: the first twin-bladed razor in 1971; swivel heads and disposables in 1975; lubricating strips in 1986; and protective bars in 1992. Radical progress has also been made with the electric razor. Experiments with mechanized shaving began in early years of the century, but it was Colonel Jacob Schick who, in 1928, patented the first electric razor to be widely accepted. Today, there is a plethora of sleekly styled and multifunctional models for men and women.

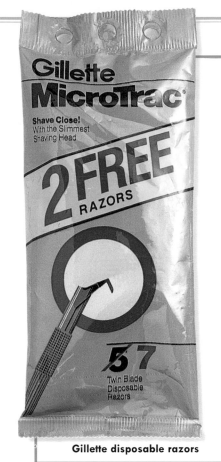

Gillette disposable razors

DISPOSABLE RAZORS

Plastic, which first appeared in the US in the 1930s, made it possible to mass produce a huge array of items and began a craze for cheap, disposable artifacts. In 1953, Baron Bich introduced the first disposable ballpoint pen, the Bic (see p.197). Its phenomenal success encouraged Bich to experiment with razors. He cut the existing blade in half and used the amount saved in manufacturing to produce a cheap plastic handle. The first disposables appeared in 1975, and all the major manufacturers, including Gillette, quickly introduced their own versions.

Philips Ladyshave Aqua 1990s

The key difference between this electric razor and a men's model is the styling. Very few women's razors are made in black, whereas the vast majority of men's are black or a similarly somber "masculine" color. Women's razors are invariably colored pastel or white – here a marbled green has been used. The curvaceous, sleek shape is also intended to be womanly.

Specifications
Country: Netherlands
Materials: Plastic
Length: 5¾in (14.7cm)

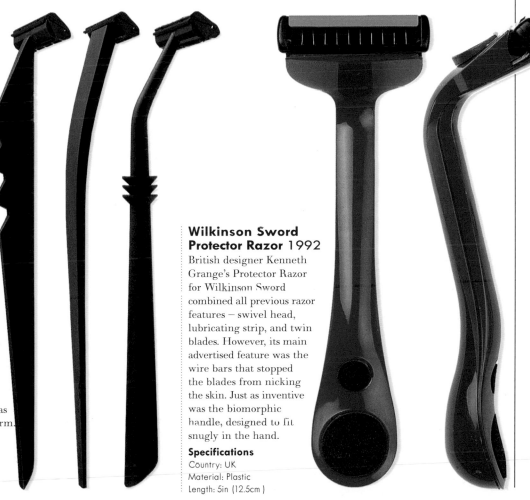

Creazioni Cavari c.1987

The sleek, modern Creazioni Cavari line of "designer" razors was created by Ernesto Spiccolato and Dante Donegani of the Memphis Group. All three razors – from left to right, Sauro, Spazio, and Samurai – are made in matte black. The solid brass handles of the Sauro and Samurai have a pleasing weightiness, while the Spazio, made from coated aluminum, is as light in weight as it is slim in form.

Specifications
Country: Italy
Material: Anodized metal
Length: Sauro 2¾in (7cm); Spazio 3¼in (8cm); Samurai 2¼in (5.5cm)

Wilkinson Sword Protector Razor 1992

British designer Kenneth Grange's Protector Razor for Wilkinson Sword combined all previous razor features – swivel head, lubricating strip, and twin blades. However, its main advertised feature was the wire bars that stopped the blades from nicking the skin. Just as inventive was the biomorphic handle, designed to fit snugly in the hand.

Specifications
Country: UK
Material: Plastic
Length: 5in (12.5cm)

PERFUME BOTTLES

NOWHERE IS PACKAGING more important than in the perfume industry. When Baron Bich, encouraged by the successes of his disposable pens, razors, and lighters, developed a cheaply packaged scent, it failed miserably. The public wanted glamour, sophistication, and expense — a combination never better evoked than when Marilyn Monroe, asked what she wore in bed, replied, "Chanel N° 5," and sent sales of the perfume rocketing. Despite the ultimately decisive power held by the advertisers, a great deal of energy is expended both in the concoction of the scent itself and in the design of the bottle. This can range from the nostalgic, floral excesses of Zenobia to the spare, unfussy angularity of classic Chanel.

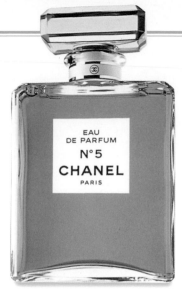

Chanel N° 5 1921
The Chanel N° 5 bottle has changed 15 times since it was introduced by Coco Chanel in 1921, but remains the essence of simplicity. It is square, with a plain wedge stopper and a minimal white label. There are nine stages involved in sealing the fragrance in its bottle, including the placement of the wax-drawn "CC" at the neck.

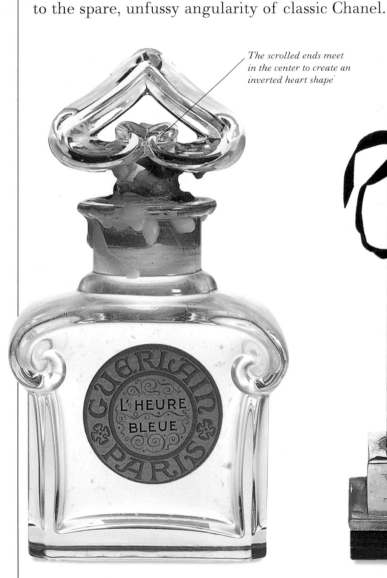

The scrolled ends meet in the center to create an inverted heart shape

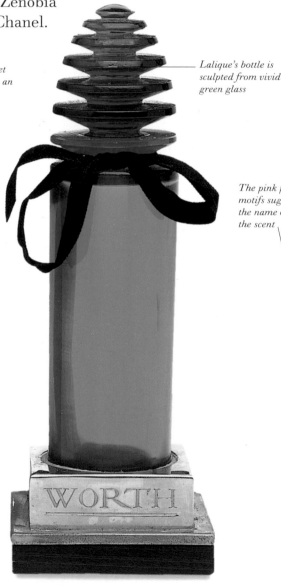

Lalique's bottle is sculpted from vivid green glass

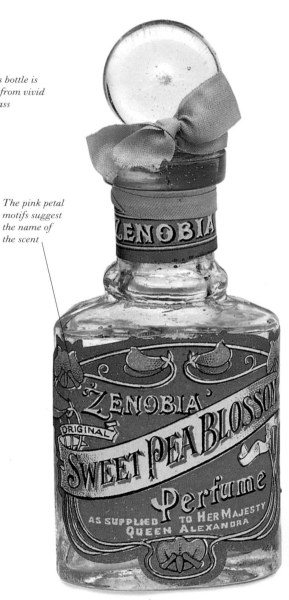

The pink petal motifs suggest the name of the scent

L'heure bleue 1912
In 1912, Pierre Guerlain created L'heure bleue, a blend of roses, irises, vanilla, and musk that was typical of the romantic perfumes produced by this famous parfumier. The Baccarat glass bottle reflects this romanticism. With its heart-shaped stopper, Art Nouveau swirls at the shoulders of the bottle, and delicately drawn label, the design suggests sensuality.

Worth 1920
René Lalique designed this classic, statuesque perfume bottle for Worth. Lalique was a multitalented designer, sculptor, and painter, but it is for his work in glass that he is best known. He was a prolific designer of jewelry, perfume bottles, vases, bowls, lighting, and tableware.

Zenobia pre-1925
The design of this bottle is resonant of nostalgia for the 19th century. Every element is intended to suggest a sweet, natural, floral fragrance, from the syrupy name, Sweet Pea Blossom, to the combination of pastel colors used on the label and the pink bow tied around the neck of the bottle.

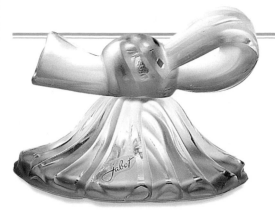

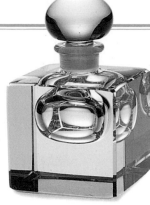

Jabot 1939
Created by Peter Fink, director of design for couturier Lucien Lelong in Paris, this bottle for the fragrance Jabot is a wonderful flight of fancy. The stopper is finished in the shape of a knotted bow, and the base of the bottle resembles the skirts of a petticoat fanned out across the floor.

Lauren 1981
Reminiscent of Chanel N° 5 in its spareness, this bottle by Ben Kotyuk for Ralph Lauren suggests the preciousness of the scent by the very thickness of the glass that protects it.

SCHIAPARELLI 1946
Elsa Schiaparelli rivaled Coco Chanel as the most famous couturier in Paris. Like Chanel, she launched her own perfumes — Shocking, in 1938, and Le Roy Soleil in 1945. The bottle for Le Roy Soleil was designed by Salvador Dalí, with whom Schiaparelli collaborated on many occasions. This poster, which advertises the fragrance, was the work of Marcel Vertes.

Poster for Le Roy Soleil

The bottle is stored in a container that looks like a soup can

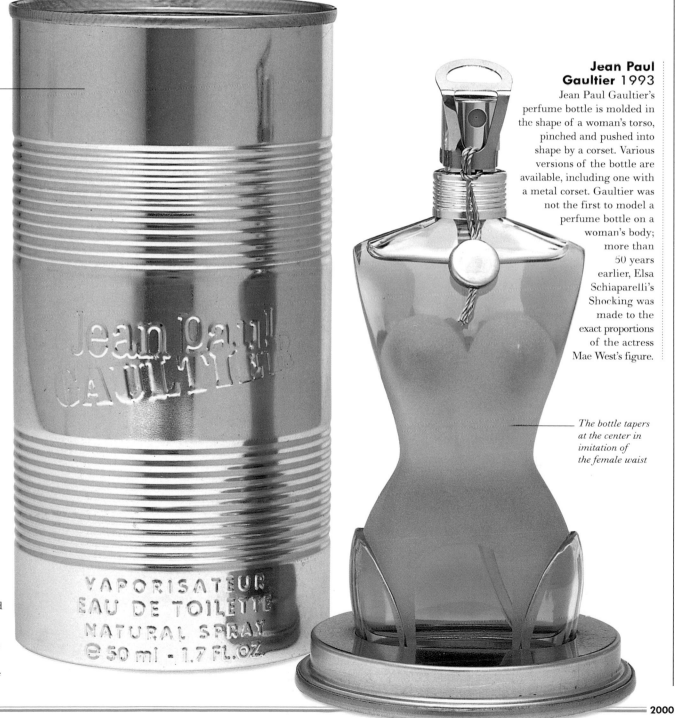

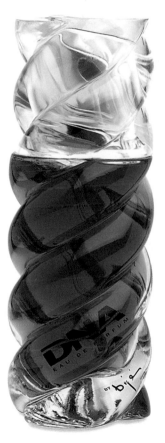

Jean Paul Gaultier 1993
Jean Paul Gaultier's perfume bottle is molded in the shape of a woman's torso, pinched and pushed into shape by a corset. Various versions of the bottle are available, including one with a metal corset. Gaultier was not the first to model a perfume bottle on a woman's body; more than 50 years earlier, Elsa Schiaparelli's Shocking was made to the exact proportions of the actress Mae West's figure.

The bottle tapers at the center in imitation of the female waist

DNA 1993
Just as 1950s design was influenced by public interest in space travel and science fiction, so the name and bottle design of this perfume reflects the 1990s interest in genetics. The bottle is shaped like the double helix form of DNA.

HAIR DRYERS

THE EARLY PART OF THE CENTURY witnessed the introduction of three revolutionary elements in hairstyling: synthetic hair coloring, developed in 1909 by chemist Eugene Schueller, who later founded the L'Oreal company; "the perm," a method of giving hair a lasting curl; and the electric hair dryer. The latter was first designed and manufactured in Racine, Wisconsin, in 1920, and became one of the most desirable electrical gadgets of the following decades. Early models, including the first handheld dryers of 1925, were made of aluminum, stainless steel, or chromium. Modern versions, with their proliferation of attachments and sophisticated controls, are invariably produced in plastic.

HMV HD1 1946
The bulbous curves of the head and base and the lack of a projecting nozzle show the influence of streamlining in the design, popular from the 1930s. Unlike the more versatile handheld models, this dryer has its own stand, which enables the user to devote both hands to styling.

Specification
Country: UK
Height: 9½in (24cm)
Material: Plastic

The dryer is secured on an adjustable stand

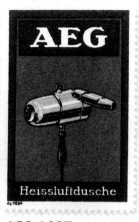

AEG 1927
The iconoclastic chrome plated dryer pictured on this AEG stamp exemplifies Peter Behrens's philosophy that good products should be practical but elegant. As head of design, he had complete control of the company's corporate identity.

Supreme 1938
Bakelite offered the manufacturers of electrical goods some excellent advantages. It was relatively cheap to produce, could easily be molded into shape, and acted as an efficient heat insulator. The Supreme hair dryer, produced by L.G. Hawkins & Co. Ltd., is a fine example of Bakelite design. The pistol-shaped casing is held together by screws, allowing access for maintenance, and the handle can be unscrewed for storage.

Specifications
Country: UK
Height: 8¾in (22cm)
Material: Bakelite

Bakelite was often produced in this wood effect

The dryer is constructed of two identical pieces screwed together

Edir 1936–38
This compact, bright red hair dryer was redesigned in 1936 by Herbert Marloth for Siemens-Schuckertwerke AG. The casing is made from tough, glossy plastic melamine. It has a simple cylindrical shape, with an expanded area to house the electric motor. The case is held together by six screws, which can be removed for maintenance.

Specifications
Country: Germany
Height: Not known
Material: Melamine

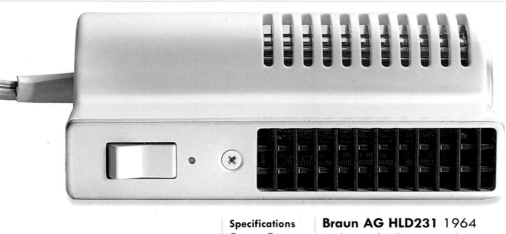

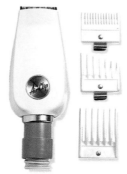

For many years, hairstyling for men relied either on the skilled scissor control of the barber or on the use of manually operated clippers. When electric clippers were first introduced, they ensured a close, precise haircut. This "Air Clip," designed by Henry Dreyfuss Associates, also has a vacuum hose that draws the cut hair away.

Air Clip, 1970

The diffuser has a high-tech, professional appearance

Specifications
Country: Germany
Height: 3½in (9cm)
Materials: Plastic and metal

Braun AG HLD231 1964
As the travel industry started to grow in the 1960s, so manufacturers responded with a range of portable appliances. Reinhold Weiss's portable hair dryer has the minimalist styling associated with Braun's personal care products. The case is made from light gray plastic, with a white switch, and the only color is a single dot of orange to indicate the "on" position.

Sassoon's name is prominently featured on the dryer in his trademark gold lettering

Vidal Sassoon VS-500UK 1995
Vidal Sassoon is one of the world's best-known hairdressers. He made his name during the 1950s and '60s with his radically geometric hairstyles, and has since expanded into product development. This powerful turbo hair dryer has a 6in-long (15cm) spiked attachment called a diffuser, or "volumizer," which diffuses air in the hair to give the style maximum body. The black and gold styling successfully suggests value and luxury.

Specifications
Country: UK
Height: 7½in (19.2cm)
Material: Plastic

The basic nozzle can be swiftly detached and replaced

The handle widens at its base to offer the user a comfortable grip

BEDS

DESIGNERS HAVE RARELY GIVEN the same degree of attention to the design of beds as they have to other items of furniture, yet the bed usually sets the style and tone for the whole room. This is especially true of the elaborate Art Nouveau and Art Deco pieces, represented here by beds designed by Frenchmen Louis Majorelle and Louis Sognot. These imposing forms must have dominated the rooms in which they were placed. The latter's pale green Art Deco bed recalls the first-class cabins of the great ocean liners. A more modest and functional approach to bedroom furniture is evident in the designs of Kho Liang Ie and Carlo Mollino. More recently, Toni Cordero's striking Sospir recalls the long tradition of four-poster beds.

The gilt bronze (ormolu) mounts are inspired by floral images

Majorelle's design uses the grain of the wood to emphasize the curves

Nenuphar bed 1905-09

Louis Majorelle was a key exponent of the School of Nancy Art Nouveau style. Unlike their Parisian counterparts, who tended toward abstraction, these designers favored a literal interpretation of nature. Majorelle's double bed, produced in his factory, displays the flowing lines and elegant carving that earned him such critical acclaim.

Specifications
Country: France
Dimensions: Not known
Materials: Mahogany and gilt bronze

Double bed 1930

Louis Sognot designed the bedroom furniture for the Maharajah of Indore's palace, which was built and decorated by German architect Eckart Muthesius. The materials, symmetry, proportion, and restricted ornamentation of the bed are typical of Art Deco styling.

Specifications
Country: France
Dimensions: h 43½in (110cm), w 128in (325cm), l 86in (218cm)
Materials: Chromium and glass

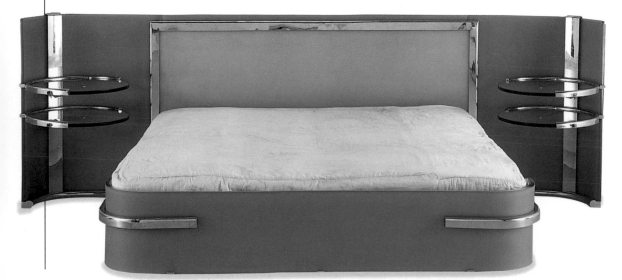

CHARLES RENNIE MACKINTOSH

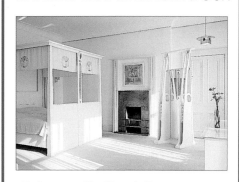

Bedroom at Mackintosh House, c.1906

Charles Rennie Mackintosh designed the entire interiors schemes for a small number of homes. This bedroom in one of his own Glasgow houses features his characteristic painted white furniture with Celtic-inspired motifs.

UTILITY FURNITURE

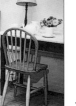

In Britain, World War II brought about harsh restrictions in the use of raw materials. In response, the Board of Trade established a Design Panel, under the chairmanship of Gordon Russell. Its solution to the problem was Utility furniture. Although it aspired to be inexpensive yet well designed and of high quality, in reality the furniture was often drab – largely because of the lack of materials. The design of the furniture owed much to the Arts and Crafts movement.

Utility crib, 1942

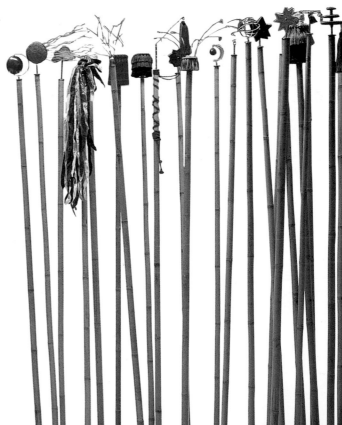

Single bed unit 1970

In this unit, designed by Dutchman Kho Liang Ie, the bed is enclosed by an L-shaped surround of painted cabinets and shelves. The unit is topped with a marble ledge and has a built-in light.

Specifications
Country: Holland
Dimensions: w 65in (165cm), l 78in (198cm)
Materials: Marble, wood, stainless steel, and Lucite

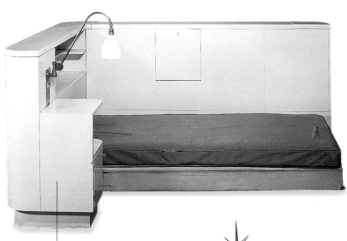

Integrated cabinets and shelves provide useful storage space

Bunk bed c.1954

Carlo Mollino's simple wooden bunk bed has no decoration aside from the brass fittings, but two coat hangers have been added and there is a small laminated table attached to the lower bunk.

Specifications
Country: Italy
Dimensions: h 84in (213cm), w 34in (85.5cm), l 77in (195cm)
Materials: Oak, brass, and laminated plastic

The spearlike rods topped with mythical symbols guard the bed

Sospir 1992

Toni Cordero designed the Sospir double bed for the Italian furniture company Sawaya & Moroni. It has a metal and wooden structure with twin headrests, but its most dramatic features are the four corner lances. Made from bamboo, these come with a variety of decorative finials.

Specifications
Country: Italy
Dimensions: h 83in (210cm), w 68½in (174cm), l 92½in (235cm)
Materials: Metal, wood, and bamboo

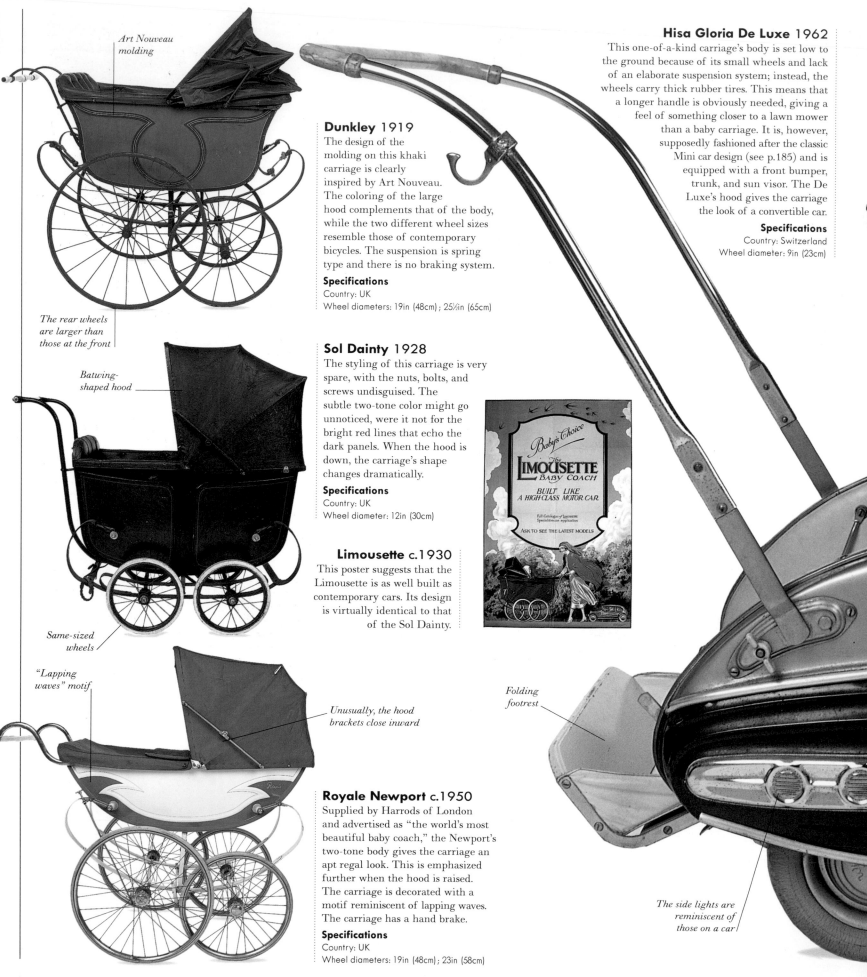

Art Nouveau molding

The rear wheels are larger than those at the front

Batwing-shaped hood

Same-sized wheels

"Lapping waves" motif

Dunkley 1919

The design of the molding on this khaki carriage is clearly inspired by Art Nouveau. The coloring of the large hood complements that of the body, while the two different wheel sizes resemble those of contemporary bicycles. The suspension is spring type and there is no braking system.

Specifications
Country: UK
Wheel diameters: 19in (48cm); 25½in (65cm)

Sol Dainty 1928

The styling of this carriage is very spare, with the nuts, bolts, and screws undisguised. The subtle two-tone color might go unnoticed, were it not for the bright red lines that echo the dark panels. When the hood is down, the carriage's shape changes dramatically.

Specifications
Country: UK
Wheel diameter: 12in (30cm)

Limousette c.1930

This poster suggests that the Limousette is as well built as contemporary cars. Its design is virtually identical to that of the Sol Dainty.

Unusually, the hood brackets close inward

Royale Newport c.1950

Supplied by Harrods of London and advertised as "the world's most beautiful baby coach," the Newport's two-tone body gives the carriage an apt regal look. This is emphasized further when the hood is raised. The carriage is decorated with a motif reminiscent of lapping waves. The carriage has a hand brake.

Specifications
Country: UK
Wheel diameters: 19in (48cm); 23in (58cm)

Hisa Gloria De Luxe 1962

This one-of-a-kind carriage's body is set low to the ground because of its small wheels and lack of an elaborate suspension system; instead, the wheels carry thick rubber tires. This means that a longer handle is obviously needed, giving a feel of something closer to a lawn mower than a baby carriage. It is, however, supposedly fashioned after the classic Mini car design (see p.185) and is equipped with a front bumper, trunk, and sun visor. The De Luxe's hood gives the carriage the look of a convertible car.

Specifications
Country: Switzerland
Wheel diameter: 9in (23cm)

Folding footrest

The side lights are reminiscent of those on a car

Baby's Choice
The **LIMOUSETTE** *BABY COACH*
BUILT LIKE A HIGH-CLASS MOTOR CAR
Full Catalogue of Limousette Specialities on application
ASK TO SEE THE LATEST MODELS

BABY CARRIAGES

THE STORY OF BABY CARRIAGE DESIGN in the 20th century is one of remarkably little change during the first sixty years, followed by a radical redesign to adapt to women's changing lifestyles. During the first period, babies and toddlers were usually transported by perambulator. These were bulky, heavy items. Smaller-wheeled strollers were used for older children. Everything changed with the invention of the Maclaren stroller, patented in 1965. This lightweight, collapsible stroller allowed parents to transport children much more easily and could even fit into a car trunk or be carried onto a plane.

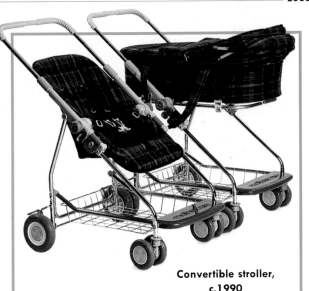

Convertible stroller, c.1990

CONVERTIBLE STROLLERS

Although heavier and less compact when folded than an E-type buggy (see below), the convertible stroller offers a convenient means of responding to the changing needs of a growing child. Newborn babies can travel in safety in the bassinet attachment, and this can be replaced with the chair seat for a baby that can support its head.

The hinges are modeled on the tailfins of 1950s American cars

STROLLER INNOVATIONS

Owen Finlay Maclaren, a retired aeronautical engineer, sold his first lightweight, small wheeled, aluminum stroller in 1967. His revolutionary design incorporated two X-shaped hinges, which, when folded, made the stroller flatter and narrower. The stroller could be folded with just one hand and one foot, and was a huge commercial success. Later versions (this example is from 1994) have various refinements, including improved brakes, reclining seats, and swiveling wheels.

Thick rubber tires have been used instead of a suspension system

Maclaren E-type stroller, 1967

TOYS & MODELS

ALTHOUGH BY THEIR very nature toys and models belong in the nursery, many have also become collector's items for adults. Construction toys were popularized early in the century by Frank Hornby, whose Meccano kits were later joined by the enduringly successful Lego (from the Danish *leg godt*, meaning "play well"). Other celebrated playthings of the century include toy robots, figures based on film and television characters, and, of course, the teddy bear.

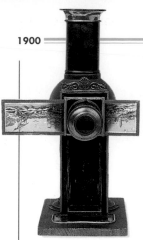

Magic lantern c.1900
Projection devices have been available since the 17th century. This lantern was made by Ernst Plank at the turn of the century. Although intended for children, its oil-powered lamp made no concessions to safety.

Specifications
Country: Germany
Height: 6½in (17cm)
Material: Tin

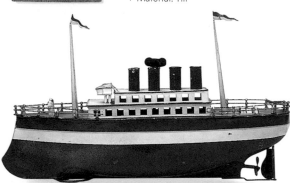

Wind-up ship 1904
Produced by Bing, this delightful ship is propelled by winding it up through one of the funnels. It has an adjustable rudder and a support bracket that allows it to be displayed.

Specifications
Country: Germany
Height: 8½in (21.5cm)
Material: Tin

Steiff teddy bear c.1905
The teddy bear gained its name following US President Theodore (Teddy) Roosevelt's refusal to shoot a bear cub on a 1902 hunting expedition, prompting a New York toy store to display a stuffed bear labeled "Teddy's Bear." The cinnamon-colored bear shown here was made by the Felt Toy Company, which in 1906 became the famous Steiff.

Specifications
Country: Germany
Height: 28in (70cm)
Materials: Mohair plush and excelsior stuffing

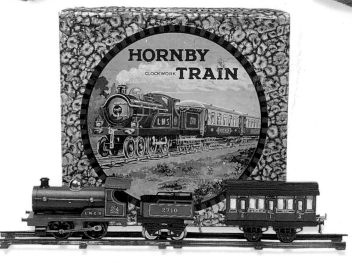

Noah's Ark c.1900
Noah's Ark, complete with wooden animals, was considered a respectable toy for children to play with on Sundays, because of its biblical connections. The ark continues to inspire toy designers today.

Specifications
Country: Germany
Height: 21¼in (54cm)
Material: Wood

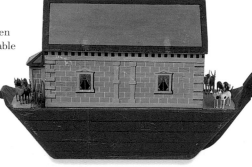

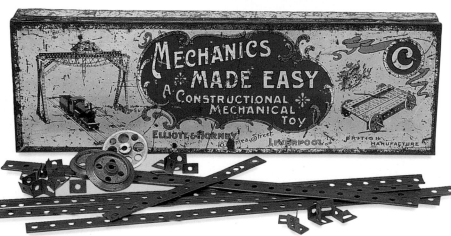

Meccano 1910
Frank Hornby's Meccano is one of the century's great success stories. An infinite variety of vehicles and objects could be built using fully interchangeable components. In 1926, colored parts became available, and, later, electric motors were introduced.

Specifications
Country: UK
Height: Not applicable
Material: Nickel-plated metal

Hornby train set 1920s
By the 1920s, mechanical trains had been in existence for over 30 years, but increased in popularity when Meccano models were widely promoted in toy shops and in *Meccano Magazine*. This model is made from pressed tin and runs on specially made tracks.

Specifications
Country: UK
Height: 3½in (9cm)
Material: Tin

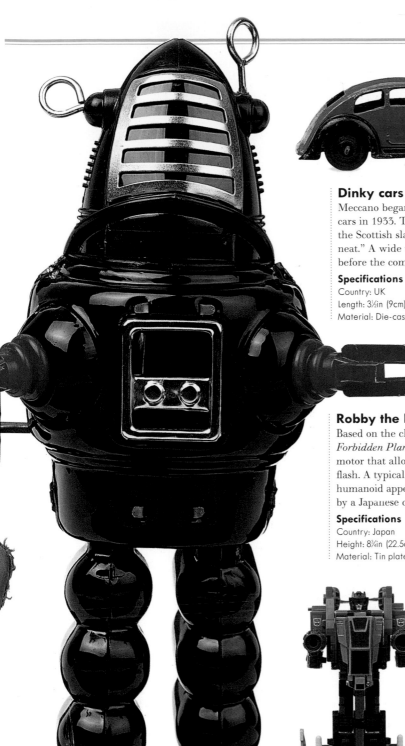

Dinky cars 1930s

Meccano began to produce small, die-cast model cars in 1933. They were christened Dinky after the Scottish slang word meaning "small and neat." A wide variety of vehicles was produced before the company closed in 1980.

Specifications
Country: UK
Length: 3⅕in (9cm)
Material: Die-cast metal

Robby the Robot 1956

Based on the character from the film *Forbidden Planet*, Robby has a wind-up motor that allows him to walk as his eyes flash. A typical 1950s robot with his humanoid appearance, Robby was produced by a Japanese company, Ko-Yoshiya.

Specifications
Country: Japan
Height: 8¾in (22.5cm)
Material: Tin plate

Transformer robot 1980s

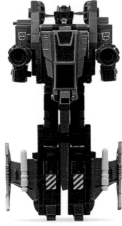

These multijointed armored warriors by Hasbro transform from robots into destructive vehicles. This Turbomaster, with its seven missiles, reflects the growing popularity of aggressive, sci-fi-based toys.

Specifications
Country: US
Height: 7in (18cm)
Material: Plastic

Playmobil 1 2 3 1990s

Playmobil 1 2 3 provides a wide variety of brightly colored, safety-conscious toys for infants, which feature figures and animals in various settings. More challenging versions are designed for older children.

Specifications
Country: Germany
Height: Not applicable
Material: Plastic

Lego 1958

Developed since the 1930s and born in 1958 in the form we recognize today, the Lego block was designed by Ole and Godtfred Kirk Christiansen. Increasingly specialized pieces have made construction possibilities endless.

Specifications
Country: Denmark
Height: Not applicable
Material: Plastic

Scalextric 1950s

Designed by Fred Francis, the first Scalextric cars were wind-up. Later, electric motors and handheld controls allowed the cars to be raced at furious speeds. This track was produced in 1968 by Tri-ang.

Specifications
Country: UK
Length of car: 4¾in (12cm)
Material: Plastic

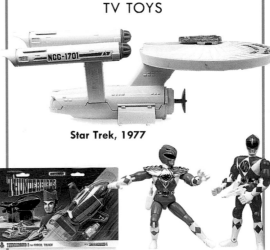

TV TOYS

Star Trek, 1977

Thunderbirds, 1992   **Power Rangers, 1994**

First introduced to enhance the profits of a popular television series, toys based on well-known characters have become an inevitable part of television merchandising. In 1992, the relaunch of 1960s Thunderbirds toys caused so much interest from thirtysomethings that the range sold out by Christmas Eve.

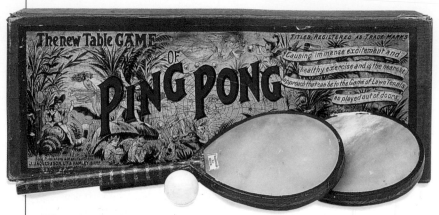

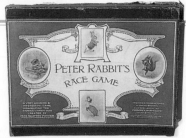

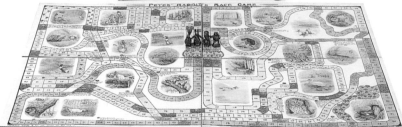

Ping Pong 1900–10

This game was launched in 1905 by Jacques and Hamley Bros., the name derived from the sound of the bat hitting the ball. The bats are beautifully crafted using two sheets of vellum, with the long handles shaped more like lawn tennis rackets than the abbreviated modern table tennis bats we now use. The illustrated box promises "immense excitement and healthy exercise."

Specifications
Country: UK
Length of bat head: 19in (48cm)
Materials: Net, vellum, and wood

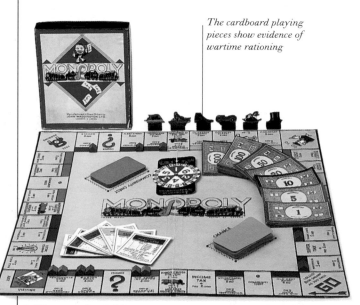

The cardboard playing pieces show evidence of wartime rationing

Peter Rabbit's Race Game 1910

An early example of merchandising a popular children's character, this game is based on Beatrix Potter's well-loved animal creations. Produced by F. Warne and Co., the board is printed with exquisite illustrations.

Specifications
Country: UK
Length of board: 29in (74cm)
Materials: Cardboard and metal

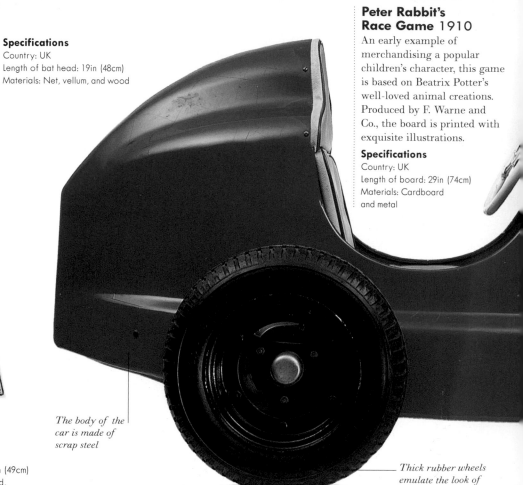

Monopoly 1934

Invented by Charles B. Darrow, Monopoly was based on the street names in Atlantic City. It was so successful that versions set in other cities were quickly introduced, and it is now the world's best-selling copyrighted board game. This British example dates from the 1940s.

Specifications
Country: US
Length of board: 19in (49cm)
Materials: Cardboard, metal, and plastic

The body of the car is made of scrap steel

Thick rubber wheels emulate the look of real racing car tires

GAMES & OUTDOOR TOYS

THERE IS OFTEN LITTLE to distinguish between adults' and children's games. Board games in particular have long been established as favorites with all age groups; most recently, Trivial Pursuit was designed to test and expand knowledge in an enjoyable format. Other games have been conceived with the purpose of promoting physical exercise and good sportsmanship, the most notable being

Ping Pong, now a recognized competitive sport. Perhaps the most significant change in toy design, and the cause of the greatest upheaval in children's play, has been the arrival of computer games. First seen in the 1970s and now showcases for highly complex computer graphics, these stimulate sharp hand-eye coordination, but have been criticized for encouraging a sedentary lifestyle.

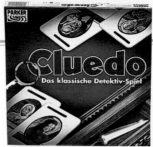

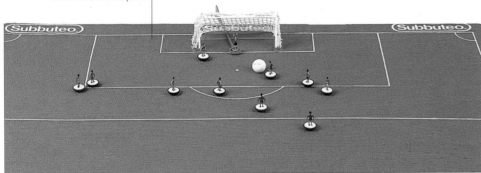

Modern versions of Subbuteo are issued with marked-out pitch

The rooms of the house are laid out around the board

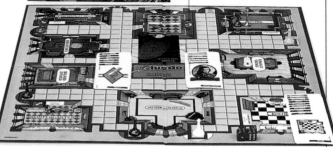

Subbuteo 1947

Invented by Peter Adolph, the first game of table soccer was introduced in Britain in 1947 during severe postwar rationing, and included a piece of chalk and instructions to mark out a pitch on an old blanket. Cardboard players were available in 24 team colors, allowing every child to own his favorite team. Since then, millions of fans have formed special leagues, and even organized a Subbuteo World Cup. This British example by Waddingtons dates from 1995.

Specifications
Country: UK
Width of pitch: 25in (64cm)
Materials: Fabric, plastic, and net

Clue 1949

Devised by Anthony Pratt and designed by his wife in 1944, Clue was launched in 1949. The design of this world-famous game differs from country to country; this 1993 German edition, for example, carries the name Cluedo, as does the British version.

Specifications
Country: UK
Length of board: 19¼in (49cm)
Materials: Metal, cardboard, and plastic

Pathfinder pedal car 1949

Austin produced this child's racing car at its Welsh factory, which was a nonprofit outlet set up to employ ex-miners. Constructed using scrap steel, the car is propelled by the use of pedals. Although they are expensive playthings, toy vehicles have remained popular in many shapes and forms.

Specifications
Country: UK
Length: 63in (160cm)
Materials: Steel and rubber

Space Hopper 1950

The much-loved Space Hopper was introduced at a time when space exploration was becoming a realistic possibility, and science fiction movies were drawing large audiences. The cylindrical ears act as handles for the child, who sits astride the inflated body and bounces.

Specifications
Country: France
Height: Variable
Material: Rubber

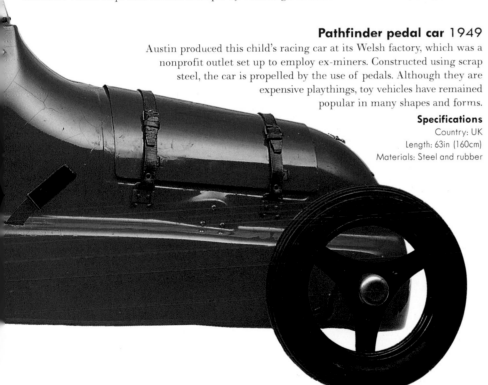

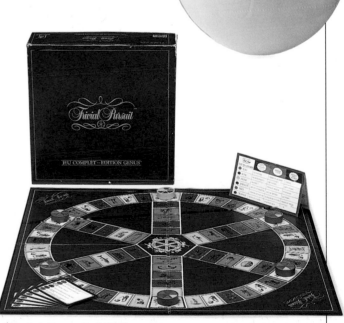

COMPUTER GAMES

By the 1980s, great advances in computer technology meant that game programs could be played on handheld computers, such as Nintendo's GameBoy. The Sony Playstation was formulated in the 1990s, and is operated through a television screen.

Nintendo GameBoy

Sony Playstation

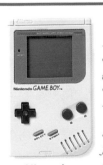

Trivial Pursuit 1982

Conceived in 1982 and designed by Canadian Michael Wurstlin, Trivial Pursuit is played worldwide. Each player answers six categories of trivia questions, filling a circular playing piece with a colored plastic segment at each success. This circular design is echoed on the board.

Specifications
Country: Canada
Length of board: 20in (51cm)
Materials: Plastic and cardboard

DOLLS

UNTIL THE 20TH CENTURY, dolls were typically modeled on adults, often with elaborate wigs, glass eyes, and eyelashes made from human hair. "Baby" dolls were simply smaller versions, and even after the turn of the century very few dolls were made to resemble real babies — the best known being the Kewpie doll. It was in the 1930s that doll design really took off, with more and more models being mass-produced. Baby dolls were fashioned to look increasingly realistic, and to sound and even function like real babies; by the 1960s, dolls could cry and wet their diapers. Adult dolls did not fall out of favor. Barbie and G.I. Joe, first popular in the 1960s, have since been redesigned to appeal to new generations of children.

Tyrolean dolls
early 1950s

Designed by Käthe Kruse, this pair of dolls was manufactured by the famous German Rheinische Gummi- und Celluloid-Fabrik and both bear the trademark turtle label. The factory also made celluloid heads for export to the UK and US, which would be used on composition or stuffed bodies. Celluloid was inexpensive, easy to use, and lightweight. Its drawbacks were its flammability, its crushability, and its tendency to fade in light.

Specifications
Country: Germany
Material: Celluloid

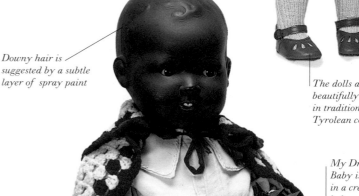

Lead weights in the eyelids allow the doll to "sleep"

Downy hair is suggested by a subtle layer of spray paint

The dolls are beautifully dressed in traditional Tyrolean costume

The Kewpie trademark is printed on a prominent paper label

My Dream Baby is dressed in a cream silk baby robe

Schilling doll c.1900

Relatively large at 23½in (60cm), Stephan Schilling's adult doll is dressed as an English nanny. Parts of the body are made from composition (pulped wood or a paper-based mixture), with upper arms, legs, and mid-torso made from cloth stuffed with straw to allow greater movement. More expensive dolls of the time had a softer stuffing, such as animal hair.

Specifications
Country: Germany
Materials: Composition with straw-stuffed fabric

Kewpie c.1913

Designed by Joseph Kallus and manufactured in the US by George Borgfeldt, this small doll was based on the illustrations of Rose O'Neill featured in the *Ladies Home Journal*. The body and head were cast from liquid clay in a single piece, with arms added afterward. This is a rudimentary design, with definition of the simple form achieved by the painted finish.

Specifications
Country: US
Material: Bisque

My Dream Baby mid-1920s

Manufactured in bisque and composition, Armand Marseille's design is clearly intended to look like a real baby, with chubby legs and a button nose. The arms and legs are moved by means of elasticized string joints, and the large head is painted to give the impression of soft baby hair. Because the facial features were hand-painted, each doll was a unique item.

Specifications
Country: Germany
Materials: Bisque head with composition body and limbs

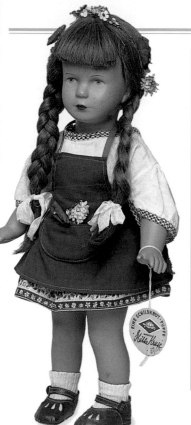

THE CHANGING STYLE OF BARBIE

Probably the most famous of all dolls, Barbie started life in the 1950s as Lilli, named after a risqué German newspaper cartoon character. She first appeared as Barbie in 1959. US manufacturer Mattel's designers have been kept busy ever since, as Barbie has metamorphosed through fashion changes of the past 40 years. While the early Barbies were highly coiffed, heavily made-up ladies, the modern doll is a younger, wholesome all-American girl, with open face, wide eyes, and smiling lips. Eleven inches (30cm) tall and made from molded plastic, with nylon hair rooted into the head, Barbie has hard bent arms and rigid legs. However, flexibility is offered in the jointed hips and swivel waist. Barbie's passion for clothes has ensured a stunning variety of outfits and accessories to fill her pink Barbie closet, each reflecting her ever-changing lifestyle.

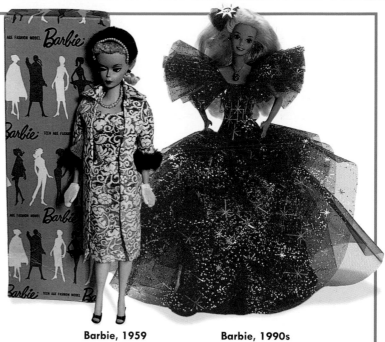

Barbie, 1959   **Barbie, 1990s**

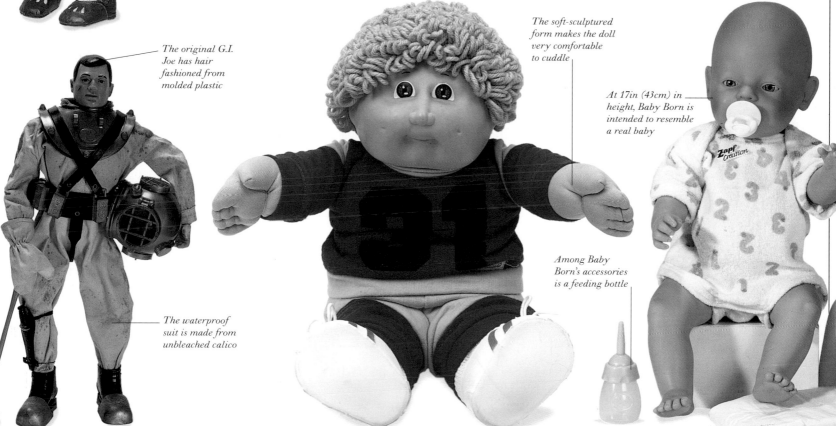

The original G.I. Joe has hair fashioned from molded plastic

The soft-sculptured form makes the doll very comfortable to cuddle

At 17in (43cm) in height, Baby Born is intended to resemble a real baby

The waterproof suit is made from unbleached calico

Among Baby Born's accessories is a feeding bottle

G.I. Joe 1964

First produced in 1964 in response to the realization that boys also enjoy playing with dolls, G.I. Joe – or Action Man, as it was known in the UK – was multijointed to allow him to be positioned in all manner of soldiering positions. The doll was later restyled as a "global adventurer," and was most recently updated and relaunched by Hasbro in 1993.

Specifications
Country: US
Material: Plastic

Cabbage Patch Kids 1983

Between 1983, when they first caught the public imagination, and 1996, when Mattel updated and relaunched them for a new generation, more than 77 million Cabbage Patch Kids were "adopted" by children across the world. Created by Xavier Roberts of the Original Appalachian Artworks, Inc., in Cleveland, Georgia, each soft bodied doll has individual physical details that make it unique.

Specifications
Country: US
Materials: Vinyl and polyester

Baby Born 1989

Designed by Victor M. Pracas and manufactured by Zapf, Baby Born has proved to be one of the most successful dolls of the 1990s, with over three million sold before 1996. Its lifelike appeal rests in the multitude of "bodily functions," which include eating, crying, and soiling its diaper. Joints at the hips, shoulders, and neck allow realistic flexibilty and movement.

Specifications
Country: Germany
Material: Plastic

AROUND THE
HOUSE

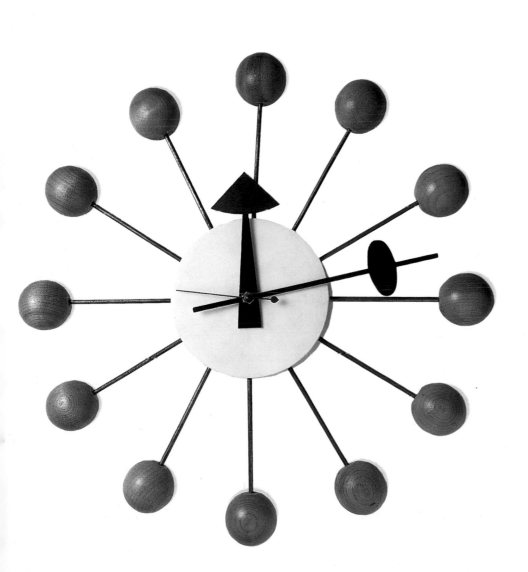

WALLPAPER

SINCE WORLD WAR II, wallpaper producers have been under commercial pressure from the paint industry, which has offered consumers a wide and inexpensive selection of colors in a variety of finishes. In response, new types of wallpapers have been developed, including self-adhesive paper and, in the 1950s, vinyl paper. To breathe more life into the craft of wallpaper design, manufacturers have frequently commissioned highly respected artists to create compositions for them: these include exuberant floral patterning, science-inspired imagery, and abstract designs.

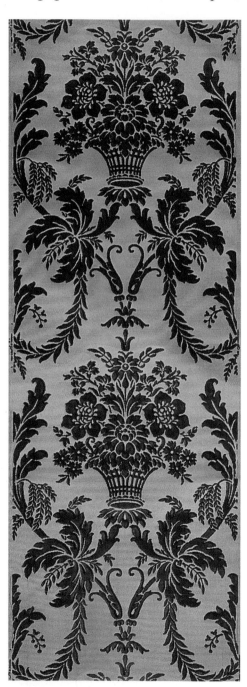

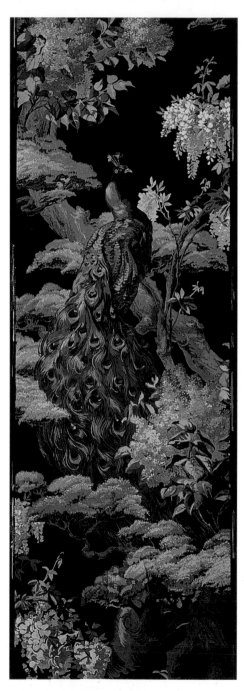

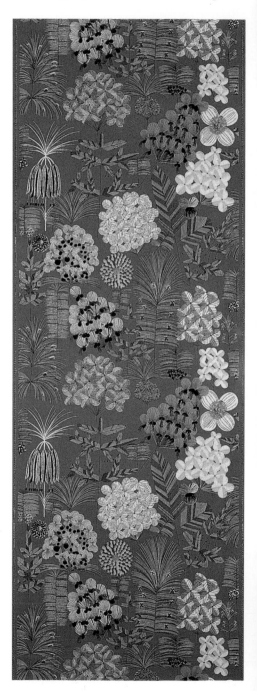

**Block-printed
and flocked wallpaper** c.1900
Flock wallpaper, with its richly textured finish and appearance of velvet, has been produced since the 17th century. In this example from Zuber et Cie, the designer has used a symmetrical floral pattern of red flock over a gold ground.

The Cedar Tree c.1910
This flamboyant design is the work of Louis Stahl for British manufacturers Sanderson & Sons. The rich colors, fine detail, and solid black ground make a striking combination. This paper, hand-printed from carved woodblocks, was still in production in 1957.

Blossom Garden c.1930
Particularly admired for her textile and ceramic designs, Felice Rix was a member of the Wiener Werkstätte and studied under Josef Hoffmann. Her Blossom Garden wallpaper design features a fine pattern of grasses and flowers, machine-printed on an beige ground.

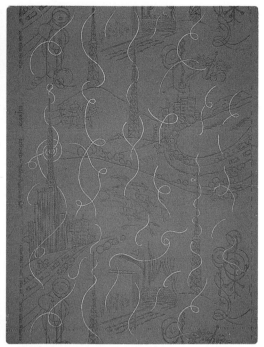

Television 1951
By the 1950s, television ownership was rapidly growing, with over 19 million sets bought in the US by 1952. This screen-printed wallpaper from 1951 represents an enthusiastic response to new advances in the media. The designer, Mildred Coughlin McNutt, has created an image evocative of the many faces of television – sport, theater, music, and urban life.

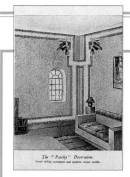

WALLPAPER BORDERS
This illustration from a 1930s wallpaper catalog demonstrates the great revival in borders, either block-printed or sprayed, during the 1920s and '30s. Art Deco lent itself particularly well to this form of decoration. First popular in the final decades of the 19th century, borders retained their place on walls well into the 20th century, and they continue to be used today.

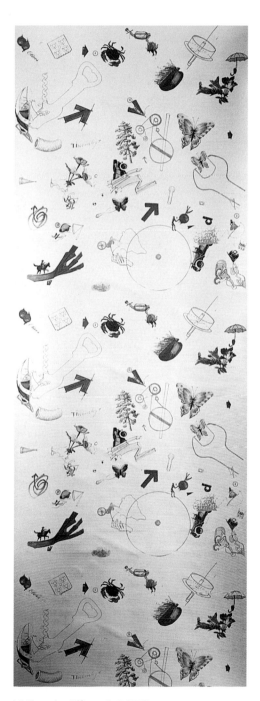

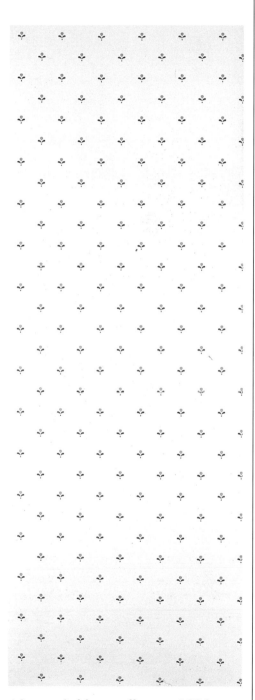

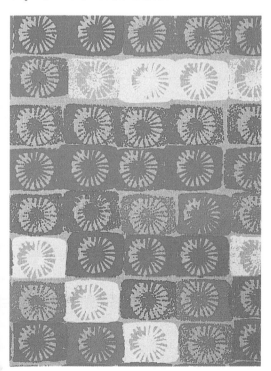

Kyoto Petals 1960
This design by Raymond Loewy was one of several in the Sanderson's Centenary Collection. Composed of an abstract pattern of softly colored rectangles and circles, it was produced in five different colorways. Gio Ponti was also among those to contribute to the collection.

Vive la Liberté 1972
Swiss artist Jean Tinguely's wallpaper composition for the German company Marburger shows freedom from typical imagery by using an unexpected sampling of objects found in modern life. These have been overlaid onto a metallic surface.

Laura Ashley wallpaper 1980
This restrained pattern for the Laura Ashley company consists of a small floral motif printed in blue on a crisp white background. The company was founded by Laura Ashley in the 1950s and has developed a range of products that evoke English country life.

TEXTILES

THERE HAS BEEN A PARTICULARLY STRONG LINK throughout the 20th century between craft and design in the development of textiles. Often the designers themselves are trained weavers or printers, and they bring this hands-on experience to the design process. At the weaving workshops of the Bauhaus, for instance, there was a firm belief in craft-based design being used to support industrial weaving. Painters have also asserted a powerful influence on fabric design. Raoul Dufy has made a direct contribution; the impact of Paul Klee, who taught at the Bauhaus from 1920 to 1931, is evident in the work of Gunta Stölzl, herself an experienced hand-weaver; and the work of Paris-based Ruth Reeves was influenced by her contact with the Cubists. Modern textile designers, such as Susan Collier and Sarah Campbell, have continued the link with the world of fine art by adopting a distinctly painterly approach in their pattern-making.

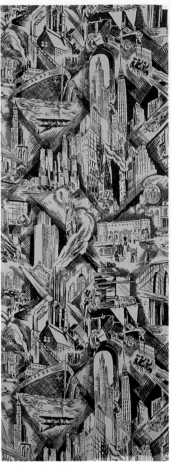

Manhattan 1930
Between 1922 and 1928, Ruth Reeves studied in Paris under the artist Fernand Léger (1881–1955), and became familiar with Cubist painting. This influence was later brought to fruition in her textile designs. The cotton print Manhattan was designed for the New York decorating company W. & J. Sloane. It depicts a lively view of the city, with skyscrapers, boats, airplanes, and factories.

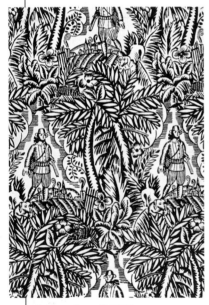

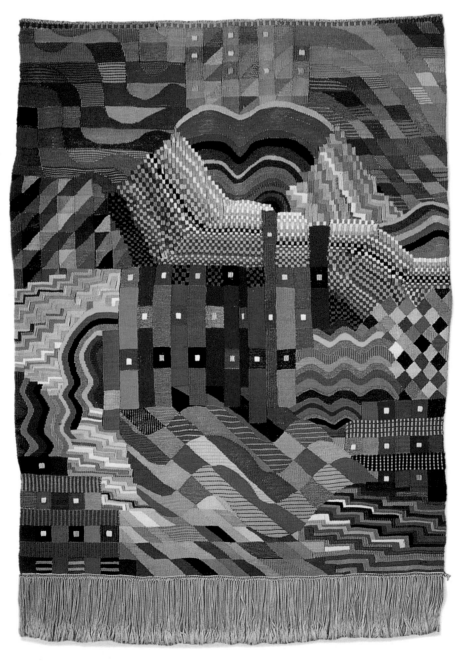

Hunting 1920
Raoul Dufy is best known for his paintings, but he was also an influential textile designer. After studying in Paris, he became associated with the couturier Paul Poiret (see p.142), who set him up in a studio. In addition to the fabrics produced for Poiret, Dufy created bold, decorative textiles, including Hunting, for the Lyons silk company Bianchini-Férier.

Wall Hanging 1927–28
In 1927, Gunta Stölzl took charge of the Bauhaus weaving workshop, where she had studied under the Swiss artist and teacher Johannes Itten (1888–1967). His influence is evident in the mixture of textures, shapes, and colors in this piece. Itten encouraged artists to exploit the expressive value of contrasting colors, in this case reds and greens.

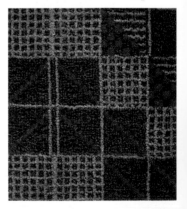

Chevron moquette 1935
Commissioned by Frank Pick, who was responsible for London Transport's corporate identity, this plush fabric was designed by Enid Marx for seating on the trains. Marx produced a number of durable fabrics using tonal variations and abstract patterns of chevrons, stripes, and circles.

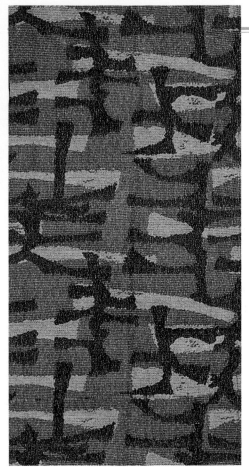

Coral Fotexur c.1960

The work of Tibor Reich epitomizes the design concept of the 1950s and '60s. His richly textured and colored fabrics include designs for Concorde and Lotus cars. The innovative Fotexur system comprised designs, in large repeating patterns, based on Reich's photographs of natural objects.

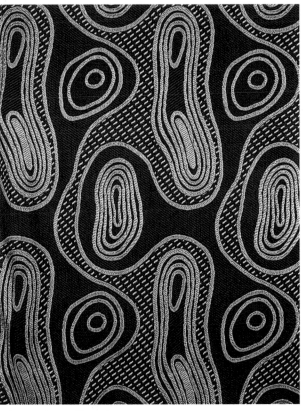

Surrey textile 1951

In 1949, the Council of Industrial Design initiated a program of pattern-making based on images drawn from the structure of crystals, in preparation for the 1951 Festival of Britain. The program, known as the Festival Pattern Group, reflected a growing interest in science. Marianne Straub's Surrey textile, produced by Warner & Sons, is typical of the work produced.

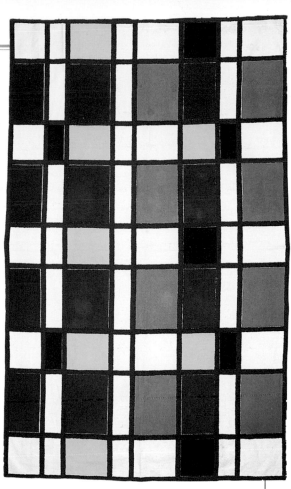

Swedish textile c.1960

Astrid Sampe was head of the Textile Design Studio at Nordiska Kompaniet, Stockholm, from 1937 to 1971. This severely geometric design is typical of Sampe's later work. She described this fabric, with its simple grid colored with blocks of red, yellow, and orange, as "Mondrianist" in style (see p.33).

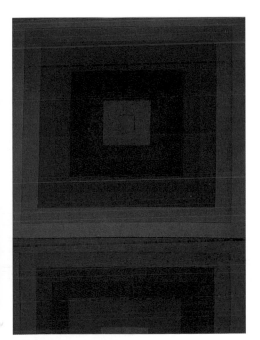

Spectrum 1969

The prolific Danish designer Verner Panton created this textile for the Swiss firm Mira-X. Its strictly geometric layout is in keeping with the abstract OP ART movement of the 1960s, which was concerned with optical illusions, often in the semblance of movement.

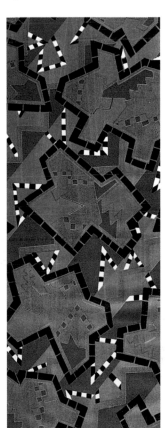

Gabon 1982

French designer Nathalie du Pasquier has designed a large number of fabrics for Memphis, the influential Italian design group. This example uses a series of irregular shapes to make up a complex, colorful pattern. Pasquier's eclectic work draws on influences as diverse as non-Western culture and comic book illustrations.

Côte d'Azure 1983

British designers Susan Collier and Sarah Campbell created Côte d'Azure for their Six Views Collection, which received the Duke of Edinburgh's Design Award. Their work is typified by its painterly quality and use of bright colors. Designing dress and upholstery fabrics for Yves Saint Laurent (see p.144) and Terence Conran has contributed to their international reputation.

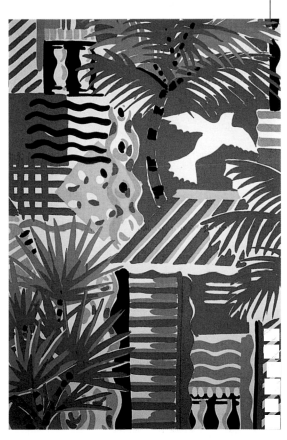

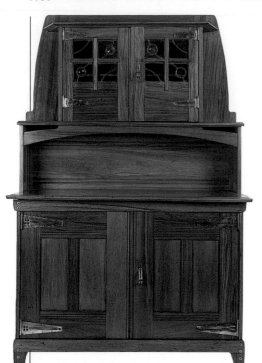

STORAGE

PROVIDING SPACE and protecting items in storage are the key priorities for designers of sideboards, shelving units, and armoires. However, many of these functional pieces have become objects of desire in their own right. Changes in design ethos can be traced through the century, from Gustave Serrurier-Bovy's wooden cabinet, which communicates the craftsmanship of Art Nouveau, through the tongue-in-cheek exercises of Memphis, to Jane Atfield's Made of Waste shelving, which expresses the environmental concerns of the 1990s.

Fruitwood dining cupboard c.1900–10

A classic example of Art Nouveau designer Serrurier-Bovy's work, this cupboard stores its contents behind geometrically styled wooden doors with brass hardware.

Specifications
Country: Belgium
Materials: Fruitwood and brass
Dimensions: h 80in (203cm), w 52¼in (133cm)

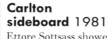

Edelstahl container 1927

Designed by Marcel Breuer in 1927, simplicity is the essence of these "precious steel" drawers. With the ideals of the Bauhaus behind its design, it achieves a compatibility between art and mass production.

Specifications
Country: Germany
Material: Steel
Dimensions: h 39½in (100cm), w 11¾in (30cm)

Carlton sideboard 1981

Ettore Sottsass showed his "programmatic" shelving unit-cum-room divider in the first exhibition by Memphis in Milan in 1981. The show created a stir, and this piece has come to be regarded as an icon of postmodernist design. The substantially sized unit is covered with brightly colored plastic laminate.

Specifications
Country: Italy
Material: Plastic laminate
Dimensions: w 74¾in (190cm), h 77¼in (196cm)

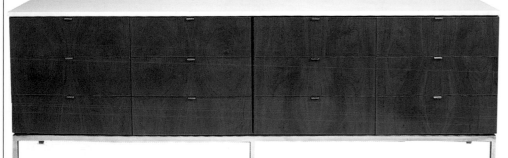

Twelve-drawer sideboard 1950s

This sideboard is an example of American designer Florence Knoll's work from her most influential period, after World War II. Utilizing new techniques and structures, pieces of furniture such as this classically austere twelve-drawer sideboard were widely imitated. It was manufactured by Knoll Associates, a design group founded by Florence and husband Hans in 1946.

Specifications
Country: US
Materials: Steel, wood, and marble
Dimensions: h 24½in (62cm) w 75in (190cm)

Settimanale 1985

This steel cabinet is the work of Matteo Thun, a founding member of Memphis. Its industrial appearance is typical of "micro architecture," a style characterized by its references to architectural concepts. The diamond-shaped holes are punched out in a geometric pattern.

Specifications
Country: Italy
Material: Pressed steel
Dimensions: h 63in (160cm)
w 24½in (62cm)

The angles of the supporting structures create storage spaces of varying volume

The colors of the shelving are determined by the selection of waste bottles used

Made of Waste shelving 1994

British designer Jane Atfield set up the Made of Waste partnership in 1992. She uses recycled plastic bottles to produce furniture in a wild mixture of colors.

Specifications
Country: UK
Material: Plastic
Dimensions: h 72½in (184cm)
w 16½in (42cm)

MOBILE INFINITO

Studio Alchimia was founded in Milan in 1976 by Alessandro Mendini and Ettore Sottsass, among others. This armoire is part of a major project known as Mobile Infinito, in which over 30 artists collaborated in the creation of individual pieces of furniture. Mendini's wardrobe has feet designed by Denis Santachiara (b. 1950), handles by Ugo la Pietra (b. 1938), and flags by Kazuko Sato. The decoration, which can be placed anywhere on the magnetic body, was designed by several artists, including Sandro Chia and Francesco Clemente.

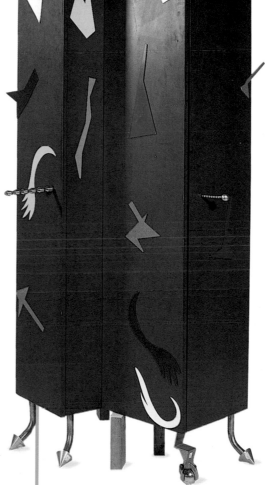

Mobile Infinito armoire, 1980s

PROGRESSIVE STYLE

The Czech designer Borek Sipek created this unique "armoire" for Vitra. A playful combination of colors and materials, it is capped with halogen lighting. Sipek has said of design: "Tradition is the law of progressiveness; progressive design does not destroy that which was, but rather places it in another dimension."

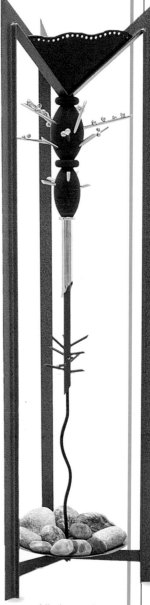

Vitra armoire, 1989–91

Skeleton c.1900

The hugely successful Skeleton model was first produced in the late 19th century by L.M. Ericsson. This elegant telephone was often finished in high-quality black lacquer and decorated with gold decals. The ingenious design utilizes the four curved legs to form the magnets of the generator. The working parts are exposed, as are the bells.

Specifications
Country: Sweden
Material: Brass/
aluminum

TELEPHONES

THE TELEPHONE, INVENTED by Alexander Graham Bell in 1876, is now a common feature in households around the world. Early models were often designed to be wall-mounted, and tended to be cumbersome and delicate. The candlestick was the first successful compact desk telephone, but it was not until the Ericofon of the 1940s that all the components were unified in a single-element instrument. Since then, the use of plastics has given us cheap, lightweight telephones — including the pocket-sized cordless models of the 1990s — in a range of vivid colors.

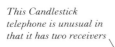

This Candlestick telephone is unusual in that it has two receivers

Candlestick c.1910

The familiar, classic shape of the Candlestick telephone derives from the practical necessity of keeping the transmitter upright. However, the apparent simplicity of the design is misleading, for the telephone requires a separate bellset — containing induction coil, capacitor, and ringer — in order to operate.

Specifications
Country: US
Material: Enameled brass

Second receiver

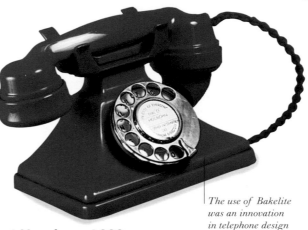

Neophone 1929

Siemens's Neophone, originally made of black Bakelite, was the first completely molded plastic telephone ever produced. Until its introduction, it was still common for telephones to be made from wood or metal.

The use of Bakelite was an innovation in telephone design

Specifications
Country: UK
Materials: Bakelite

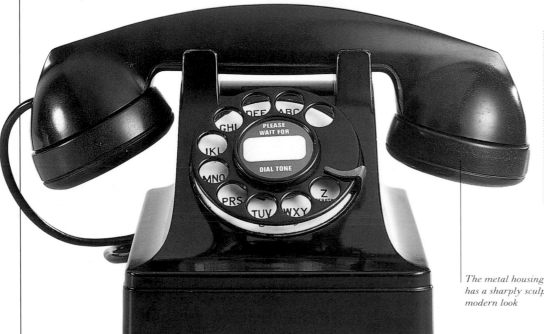

Desk telephone 1937

Inspired by the modern plastic telephone designed by painter Jean Heiberg in 1930, Henry Dreyfuss created this self-contained metal model for American Telephone and Telegraph. It was later produced in Bakelite or similar plastic.

Specifications
Country: US
Materials: Die-cast metal

PLEASE WAIT FOR
DIAL TONE

The metal housing has a sharply sculpted, modern look

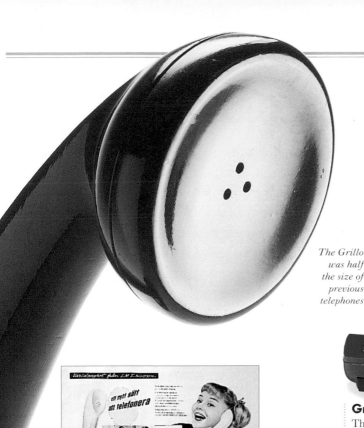

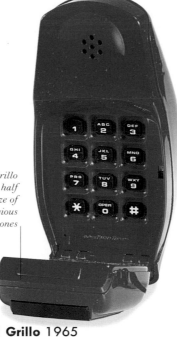

The Grillo was half the size of previous telephones

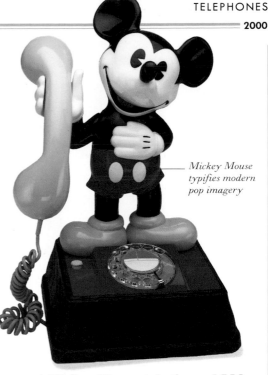

Mickey Mouse typifies modern pop imagery

Single-element telephone 1950s

The first single-element (one-piece) telephone was the Ericofon, designed by Ralf Lysell and Hugo Blomberg in the 1940s. The design of this single element model combines sensuality of form with the function of technology: the earpiece and transmitter are contained in a unified plastic body, and the dial is on the base.

Specifications
Country: Sweden
Materials: Plastic, rubber, and nylon

The dial and circuitry are at the bottom of the phone

Grillo 1965

The stylish, modern-looking Grillo telephone was designed by Richard Sapper and Marco Zanuso in the 1960s; this model dates from the 1980s. It is made from brightly colored plastic, with either push-button keys or a traditional dial. The mouthpiece and main body are hinged so that the unit can be folded away when not in use.

Specifications
Country: Italy
Material: Plastic

Mickey Mouse telephone 1980

The 1970s and '80s witnessed a departure from the restrictive conventions of the past, and a variety of inexpensive plastic telephones were produced. This Mickey Mouse telephone, by the British company Plessey, is lighthearted and fun, and as an item of modern technology, it functions perfectly well.

Specifications
Country: UK
Material: Plastic housing

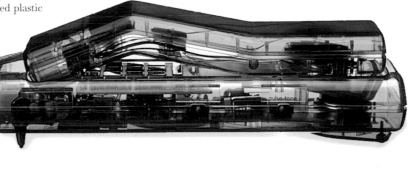

Swatch Twinphone 1994

Although the shape of this model is simple, decoration is provided by the internal wiring and electronics, which are clearly visible through the translucent green plastic.

Specifications
Country: Switzerland
Materials: Plastic

VIDEOPHONE TECHNOLOGY

The 1980s and '90s saw the adoption of more technological advances in the production of telephones, first with cordless models, and then with videophones. Color video pictures are transmitted with sound, enabling callers to see each other during conversations. Although early users experienced a delay of up to half a second between the reception of video and voice signals, newer models make the two simultaneous when used on on a high-speed digital network. Standard calls can also be made to telephones without the video facility.

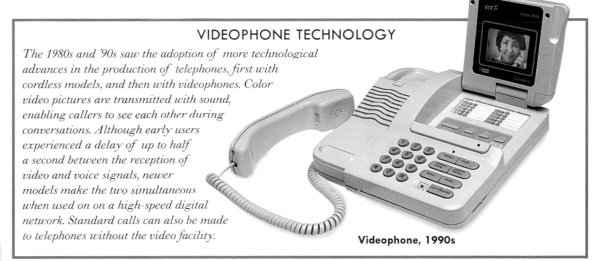

Videophone, 1990s

CLOCKS

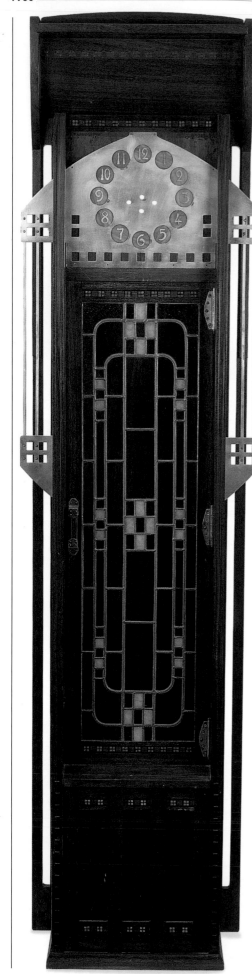

Grandfather clock 1900

Serrurier-Bovy was one of Belgium's leading Art Nouveau designers. Inspired in youth by William Morris, in later years his work showed a German influence. Key hallmarks evident in this partially restored piece include architectural form, geometric decoration, and subtle use of brass fittings.

Specifications
Country: Belgium
Height: 91¾in (233cm)

ALTHOUGH A FORM of electric clock had been invented by 1900, the majority of clocks were mechanical, generally encased in wood or metal. Electric models of increased accuracy became popular in the 1920s, but it was not until 1928, with the design of the first quartz clock, that near-total accuracy was possible – the maximum error being one second every ten years. Smaller movements, together with the development of plastic housings, have since given designers greater freedom for innovation.

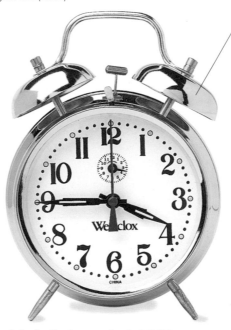

The two earlike bells are linked by a slim, curved handle

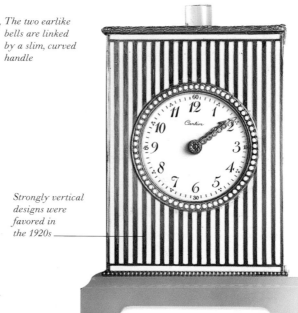

Strongly vertical designs were favored in the 1920s

Double bell alarm clock 1920s

This modern version of the traditional double bell alarm clock, with earlike bells, luminous hands, and slender legs, has a common type of mechanism. It offers the user the option of waking up to a single ring or a repeat ring every few seconds. Many models have an extra seconds dial.

Specifications
Country: US
Height: 6in (15cm)

Cartier clock c.1920

French jewelers Cartier also produced a vast array of clocks. One of the most famous is the Art Deco mantel clock, renowned for its invisible movement. This tiny, exquisite clock is decorated with stripes of gold and white enamel, and has diamond-studded hands.

Specifications
Country: France
Height: 3¼in (8.5cm)

Zephyr c.1930

Kem Weber was a proponent of the streamline aesthetic, which characterized much American design during the 1930s. He has applied that principle in the design of this elegant digital clock for Lawson Time Inc. Zephyr is both the Greek god of the west wind and the name of the streamlined trains that appeared in 1934.

Specifications
Country: US
Length: 8in (20.6cm)

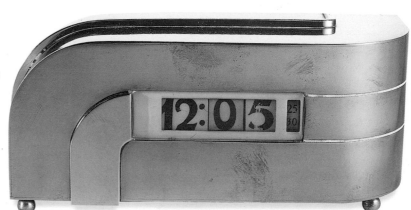

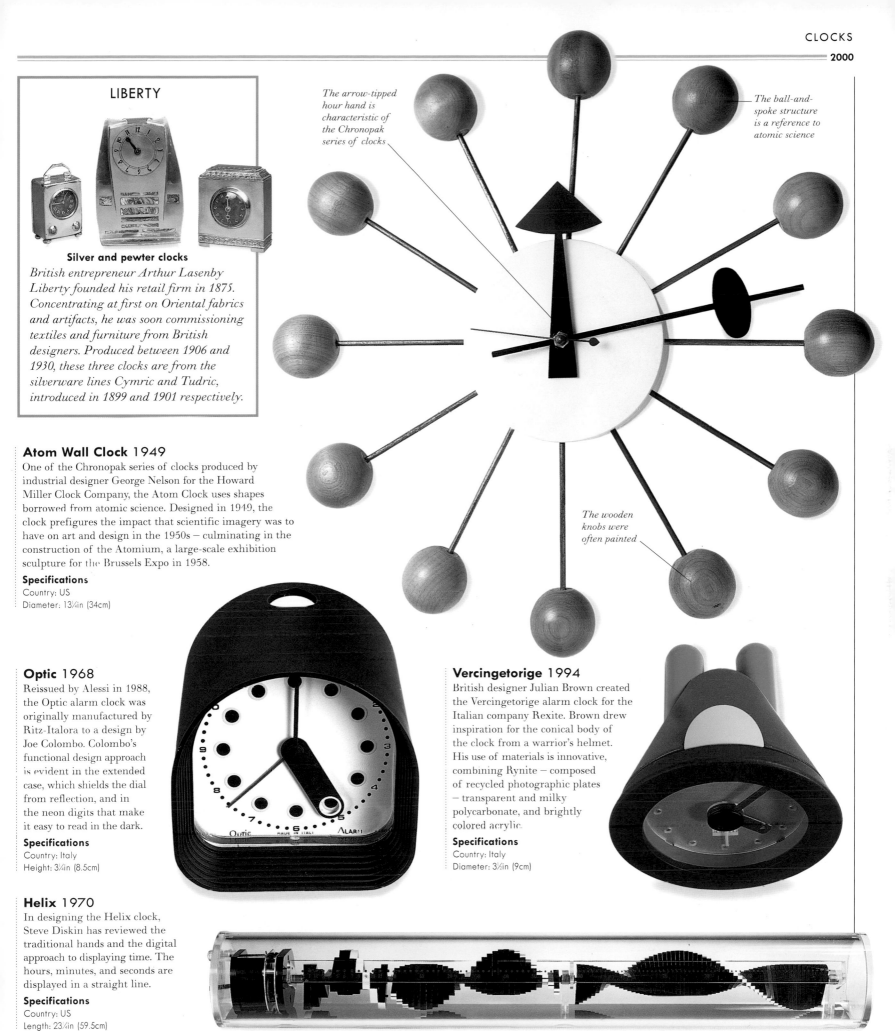

LIBERTY

Silver and pewter clocks

British entrepreneur Arthur Lasenby Liberty founded his retail firm in 1875. Concentrating at first on Oriental fabrics and artifacts, he was soon commissioning textiles and furniture from British designers. Produced between 1906 and 1930, these three clocks are from the silverware lines Cymric and Tudric, introduced in 1899 and 1901 respectively.

The arrow-tipped hour hand is characteristic of the Chronopak series of clocks

The ball-and-spoke structure is a reference to atomic science

The wooden knobs were often painted

Atom Wall Clock 1949

One of the Chronopak series of clocks produced by industrial designer George Nelson for the Howard Miller Clock Company, the Atom Clock uses shapes borrowed from atomic science. Designed in 1949, the clock prefigures the impact that scientific imagery was to have on art and design in the 1950s – culminating in the construction of the Atomium, a large-scale exhibition sculpture for the Brussels Expo in 1958.

Specifications
Country: US
Diameter: 13¼in (34cm)

Optic 1968

Reissued by Alessi in 1988, the Optic alarm clock was originally manufactured by Ritz-Italora to a design by Joe Colombo. Colombo's functional design approach is evident in the extended case, which shields the dial from reflection, and in the neon digits that make it easy to read in the dark.

Specifications
Country: Italy
Height: 3¼in (8.5cm)

Vercingetorige 1994

British designer Julian Brown created the Vercingetorige alarm clock for the Italian company Rexite. Brown drew inspiration for the conical body of the clock from a warrior's helmet. His use of materials is innovative, combining Rynite – composed of recycled photographic plates – transparent and milky polycarbonate, and brightly colored acrylic.

Specifications
Country: Italy
Diameter: 3½in (9cm)

Helix 1970

In designing the Helix clock, Steve Diskin has reviewed the traditional hands and the digital approach to displaying time. The hours, minutes, and seconds are displayed in a straight line.

Specifications
Country: US
Length: 23¼in (59.5cm)

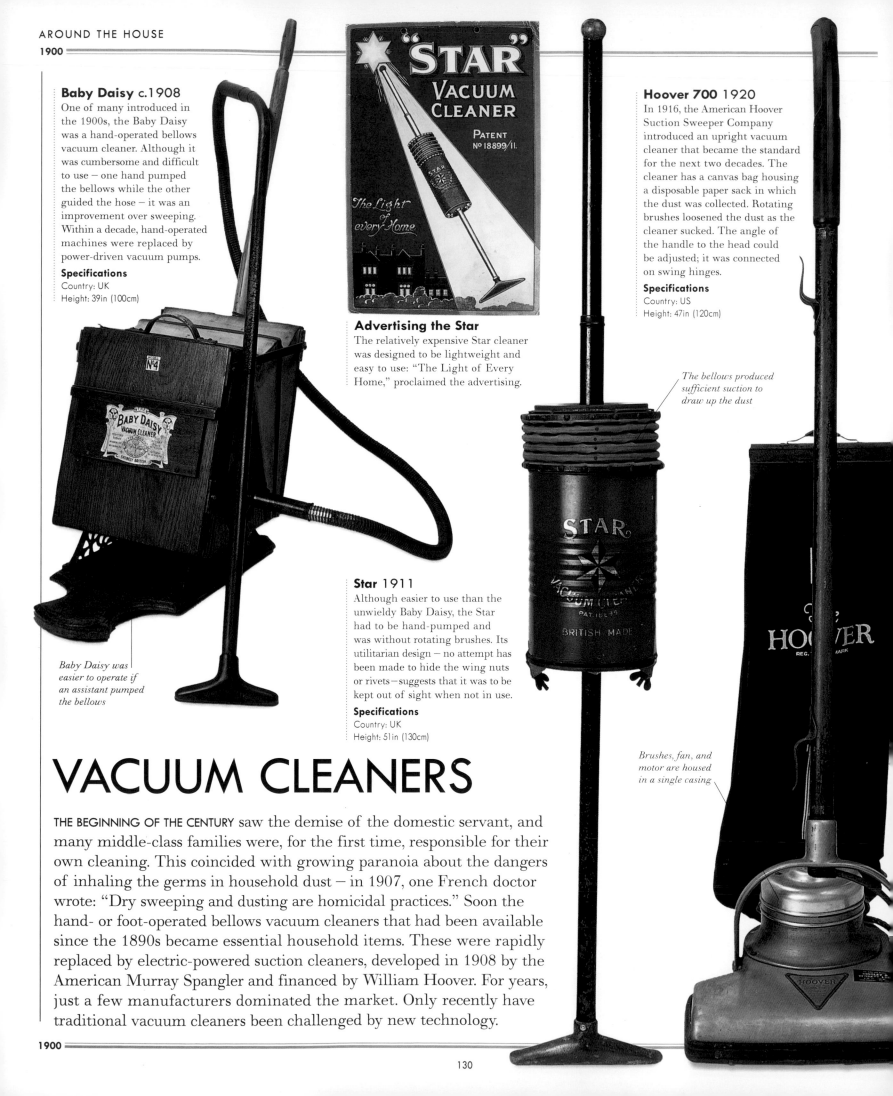

Baby Daisy c.1908

One of many introduced in the 1900s, the Baby Daisy was a hand-operated bellows vacuum cleaner. Although it was cumbersome and difficult to use – one hand pumped the bellows while the other guided the hose – it was an improvement over sweeping. Within a decade, hand-operated machines were replaced by power-driven vacuum pumps.

Specifications
Country: UK
Height: 39in (100cm)

Baby Daisy was easier to operate if an assistant pumped the bellows

Advertising the Star

The relatively expensive Star cleaner was designed to be lightweight and easy to use: "The Light of Every Home," proclaimed the advertising.

Star 1911

Although easier to use than the unwieldy Baby Daisy, the Star had to be hand-pumped and was without rotating brushes. Its utilitarian design – no attempt has been made to hide the wing nuts or rivets – suggests that it was to be kept out of sight when not in use.

Specifications
Country: UK
Height: 51in (130cm)

Hoover 700 1920

In 1916, the American Hoover Suction Sweeper Company introduced an upright vacuum cleaner that became the standard for the next two decades. The cleaner has a canvas bag housing a disposable paper sack in which the dust was collected. Rotating brushes loosened the dust as the cleaner sucked. The angle of the handle to the head could be adjusted; it was connected on swing hinges.

Specifications
Country: US
Height: 47in (120cm)

The bellows produced sufficient suction to draw up the dust

Brushes, fan, and motor are housed in a single casing

VACUUM CLEANERS

THE BEGINNING OF THE CENTURY saw the demise of the domestic servant, and many middle-class families were, for the first time, responsible for their own cleaning. This coincided with growing paranoia about the dangers of inhaling the germs in household dust – in 1907, one French doctor wrote: "Dry sweeping and dusting are homicidal practices." Soon the hand- or foot-operated bellows vacuum cleaners that had been available since the 1890s became essential household items. These were rapidly replaced by electric-powered suction cleaners, developed in 1908 by the American Murray Spangler and financed by William Hoover. For years, just a few manufacturers dominated the market. Only recently have traditional vacuum cleaners been challenged by new technology.

Dyson Dual Cyclone 1986

Not since the introduction of the original Hoover has there been so revolutionary a development in upright cleaner design as the Cyclone. The dust bag has been eliminated; instead, dirt is collected, using G-force technology, in the cylindrical body. Dyson claims 100 percent suction, even when the cleaner is almost full, because centrifugal spin keeps the airstream clear.

Specifications
Country: UK
Height: 42in (107cm)

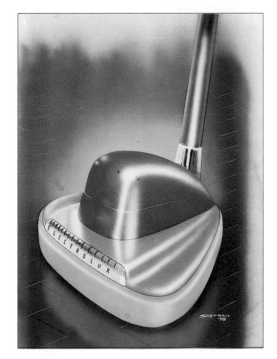

Vacuum cleaner 1948

This illustration shows a futuristic vacuum cleaner design from 1948 as envisaged by Sixten Sason. He produced a whole series of designs for Electrolux, all of them in the newly popular streamlined style championed by Raymond Loewy in the US.

HANDHELD CLEANERS

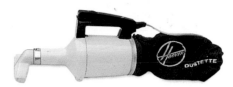

Hoover Dustette

The Hoover Dustette is one of many handheld cleaners designed specifically to dispose of crumbs or pet hairs. Light, portable, and cordless, these appliances are far more convenient than full-size vacuum cleaners for small-scale, precise work. Handheld vacuum cleaners first gained popularity in the 1960s and '70s as a convenient way to clean car interiors. Many could be powered by the car's battery via the cigarette lighter socket.

Electrolux 1920

Despite the prevalance of the upright vacuum cleaner, the cylinder type continues to challenge it in popularity. Manufactured by Electrolux, the original revolutionary design of 1915 had a horizontal cylinder with cleaning brushes attached to a flexible hose. This enabled the user to clean curtains, upholstery, and fabrics at any height.

Specifications
Country: Sweden
Height: Not known

The yellow and gray casing recalls 1950s space-age designs

The cleaner could be carried with a strap or wheeled on castors

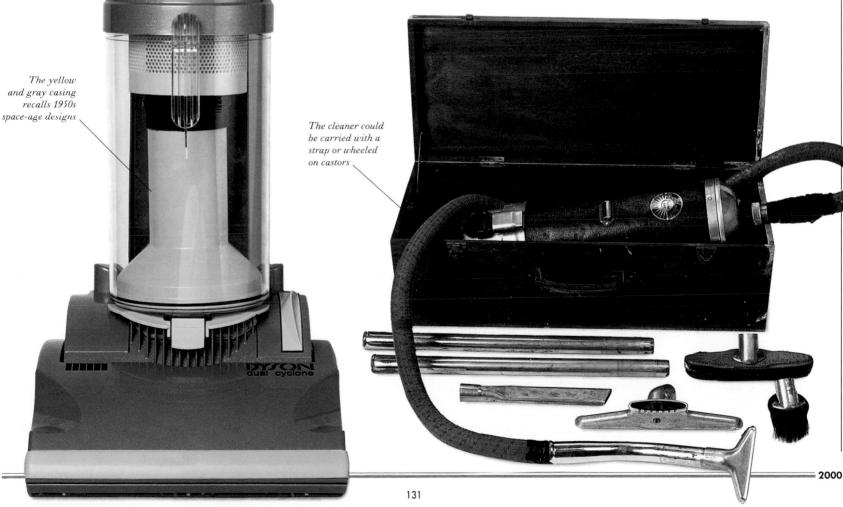

CLOTHING & ACCESSORIES

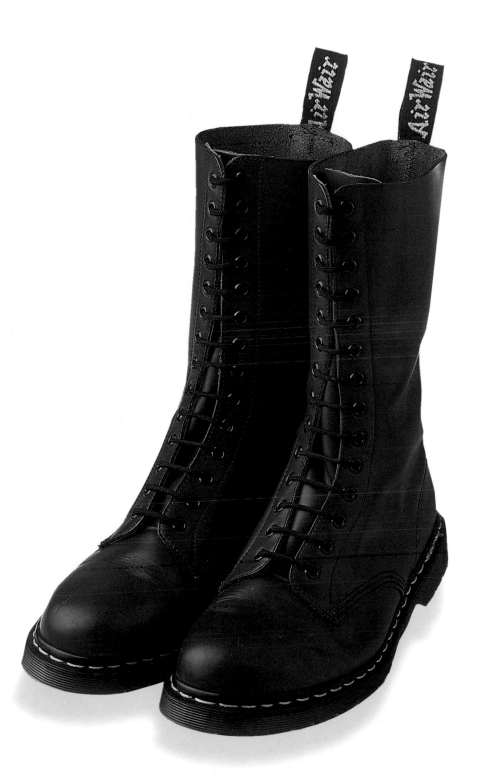

Childrenswear

Women's daywear

Men's daywear

Haute couture

Shoes

Hats

Watches

Fountain pens

Makeup

Jewelry

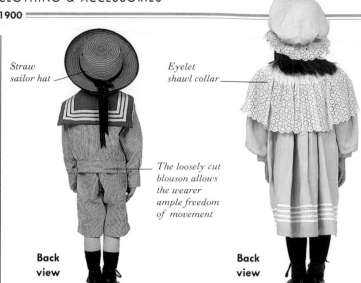

Straw sailor hat

Eyelet shawl collar

The loosely cut blouson allows the wearer ample freedom of movement

Back view

Back view

CHILDRENSWEAR

ALTHOUGH THE CLOTHING REFORMS of the late 19th century prompted a relaxation in public attitudes toward children's dress, it was World War I that witnessed the first significant upheavals. Children were taken out of their heavy, formal outfits — invariably scaled-down versions of their parents' — and dressed in lighter, plainer, less restrictive garments. When, in the 1950s, an array of new man-made fibers, easy-care fabrics, and simpler fasteners emerged, the industry was galvanized anew. The revolution was finally complete with the advent of mass production, when traditional hand-tailored clothes were universally replaced by ready-to-wear outfits.

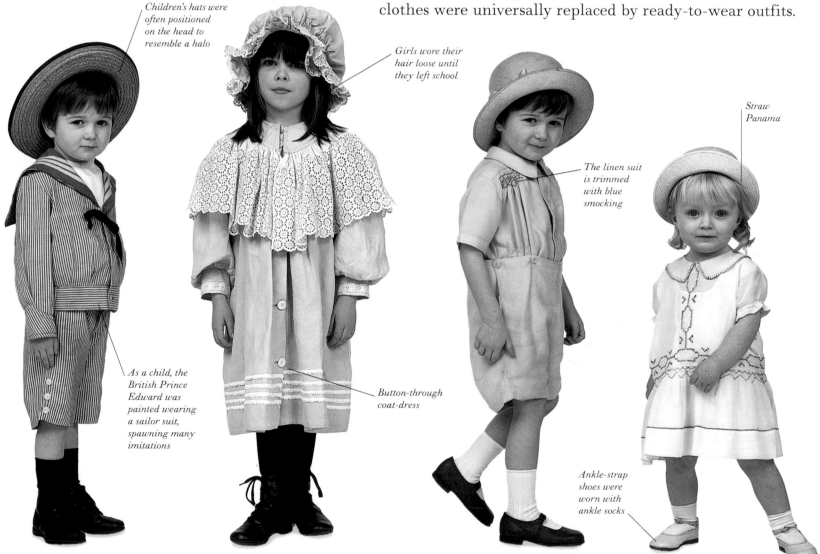

Children's hats were often positioned on the head to resemble a halo

Girls wore their hair loose until they left school

Straw Panama

The linen suit is trimmed with blue smocking

As a child, the British Prince Edward was painted wearing a sailor suit, spawning many imitations

Button-through coat-dress

Ankle-strap shoes were worn with ankle socks

Boys' and girls' daywear c.1900

Although children's sailor suits had been available for decades, they came into their own at the turn of the century, when changes in education meant that clothing had to be suitable for the recently introduced gymnastics and outdoor games that formed part of the revised school curriculum. Looser clothing for girls, like this linen coat-dress, began to gain popularity. Even so, it was still customary to wear heavy, lace-up boots and black cashmere stockings.

Boys' and girls' daywear 1920s

It was after World War I that children's clothes changed most dramatically and universally. This transformation echoed the radical changes taking place in adult fashion. Lighter, less elaborate garments, including soft collars, jerseys, and socks instead of stockings, were adopted, in contrast to the formal styles of the first decades of the century. Girls wore simple dresses with dropped waists and boys wore updated versions of the skeleton suit — brief shorts buttoned onto a shirt top.

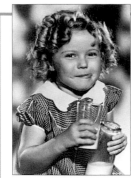

CHILD STAR

In the 1930s, movies played a major role in influencing fashion. Nobody had more impact on children's clothes than Shirley Temple. After her debut at the age of three, she was for a decade one of the biggest stars in the US. She acted in films such as Dimples *and* Curly Top, *and the dresses she wore – with puffed sleeves and Peter Pan collars – became very popular.*

Shirley Temple

Outdoor clothing 1930s

Matching coat and leggings outfits were popular outdoor wear for young children throughout the 1930s and '40s. They were immensely practical because the leggings were loose enough for dresses to be tucked into them, and they could be zipped or buttoned tightly over the shoes for extra warmth.

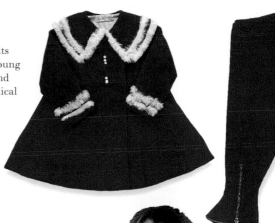

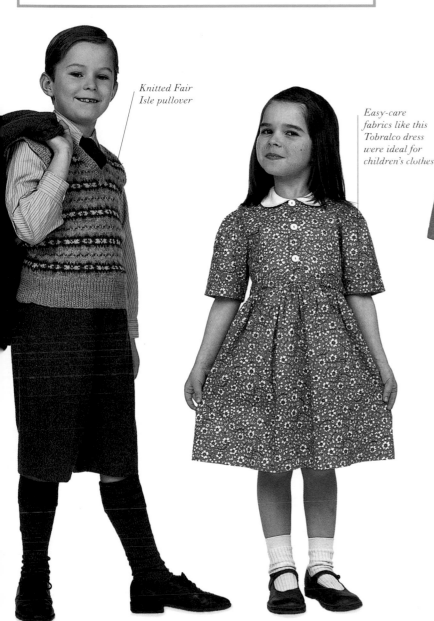

Knitted Fair Isle pullover

Easy-care fabrics like this Tobralco dress were ideal for children's clothes

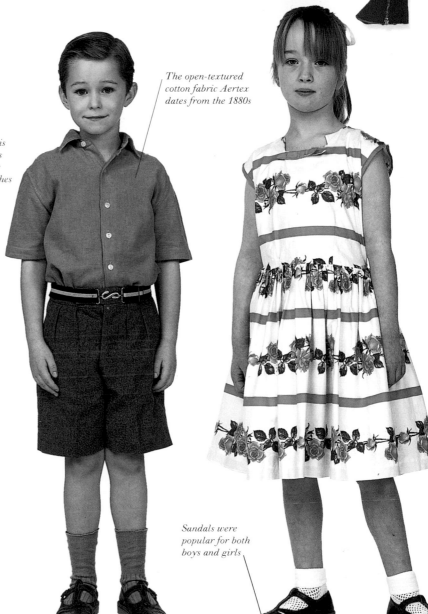

The open-textured cotton fabric Aertex dates from the 1880s

Sandals were popular for both boys and girls

Boys' and girls' daywear 1940s

With the outbreak of World War II children's clothing took on a more practical aspect. Clothes were designed to be comfortable and hard-wearing. Outfits like this double-breasted suit, worn with a knitted sweater, were common. American styles including snowsuits, knickers, and checked shirts — began to filter into Europe with the parcels of clothes sent from the US to aid war-stricken countries. These styles flourished in Europe in the postwar years.

Boys' and girls' daywear 1950s

The postwar baby boom emphasized the potential market for children's clothing. Being economically dependent on their parents, very young children were still influenced by adult styles, but subtle changes did occur, and slowly their dress began to follow teenage rather than adult fashions. Teenagers were an important market force in the 1950s. They used their newfound income to show off their independence, purchasing the clothes, records, and accessories associated with the new pop culture.

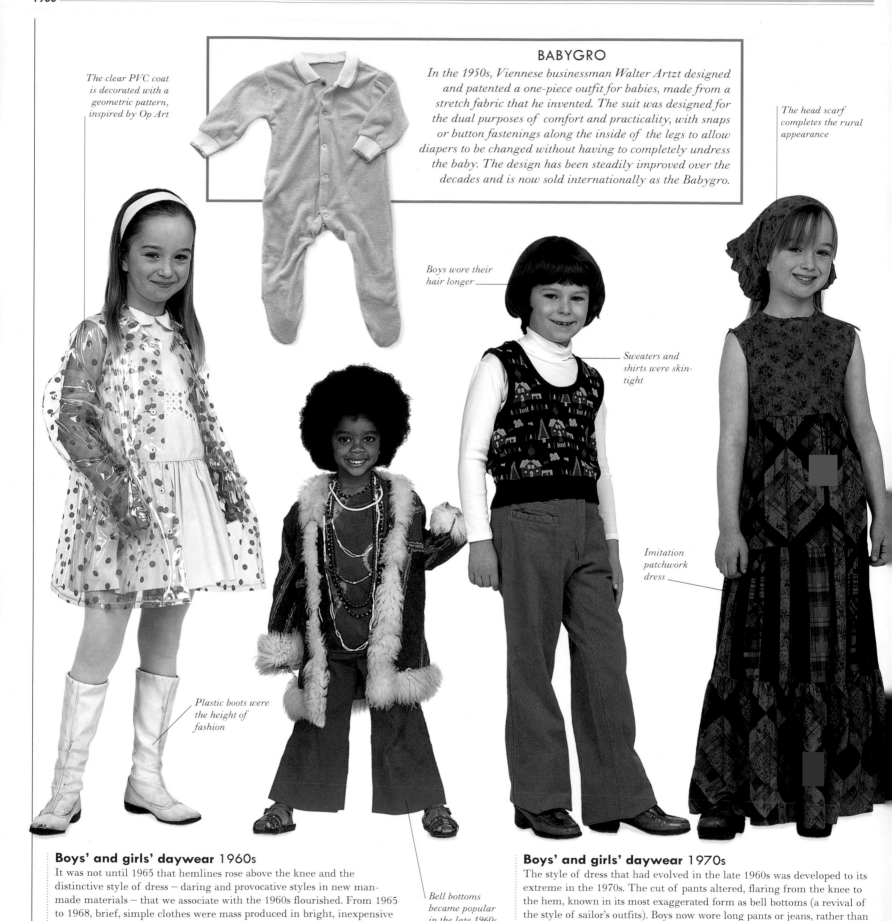

The clear PVC coat is decorated with a geometric pattern, inspired by Op Art

BABYGRO

In the 1950s, Viennese businessman Walter Artzt designed and patented a one-piece outfit for babies, made from a stretch fabric that he invented. The suit was designed for the dual purposes of comfort and practicality, with snaps or button fastenings along the inside of the legs to allow diapers to be changed without having to completely undress the baby. The design has been steadily improved over the decades and is now sold internationally as the Babygro.

The head scarf completes the rural appearance

Boys wore their hair longer

Sweaters and shirts were skintight

Imitation patchwork dress

Plastic boots were the height of fashion

Boys' and girls' daywear 1960s

It was not until 1965 that hemlines rose above the knee and the distinctive style of dress — daring and provocative styles in new man-made materials — that we associate with the 1960s flourished. From 1965 to 1968, brief, simple clothes were mass produced in bright, inexpensive styles, which were ideally suited to the children's market. In the late 1960s, the hippie movement emerged. Developing the experimental nature of the decade, hippies encouraged the adoption of ethnic clothing, long robes in natural materials, exotic beads, and long hair.

Bell bottoms became popular in the late 1960s

Boys' and girls' daywear 1970s

The style of dress that had evolved in the late 1960s was developed to its extreme in the 1970s. The cut of pants altered, flaring from the knee to the hem, known in its most exaggerated form as bell bottoms (a revival of the style of sailor's outfits). Boys now wore long pants or jeans, rather than shorts, from an early age. There was a revival of interest in crafts, such as patchwork, which led to the production of patchwork-printed textiles. Following adult fashions, girls' skirts became longer, and were often worn with frilly blouses inspired by historical or ethnic costume.

LADYBIRD

The history of the Pasold family and its transformation from domestic weavers in the remote village of Fleissen, Bohemia, to mass producers of children's clothing and brand leaders spans 300 years. Two important landmarks in this history were the acquisition of its British plant in 1932, when the company began to shift in production from ladies' to children's garments; and the purchase of the Ladybird trademark in 1938. Today, Ladybird clothes are sold throughout the world — its name is used everywhere except in the US and Spain, but the "bug" motif is universal and instantly recognizable.

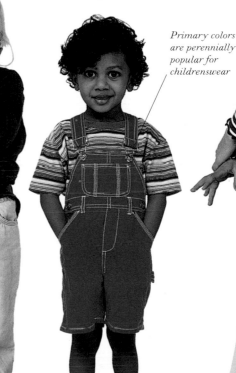

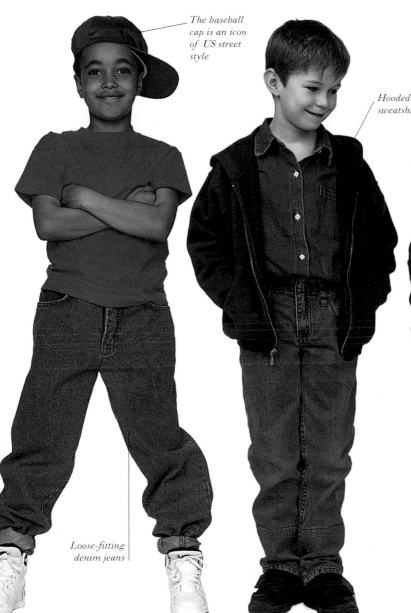

The baseball cap is an icon of US street style

Hooded sweatshirt

Primary colors are perennially popular for childrenswear

Loose-fitting denim jeans

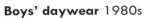

Boys' daywear 1980s

The influence of television and video on childrenswear intensified throughout the 1980s. One effect of this was the spread of American styles to Europe, baseball caps and sneakers became enormously popular. Denim jeans, standard casual wear for the young since the 1960s, returned to a straight-leg style.

Quick-release Velcro fastenings are ideal for children's shoes

Boys' and girls' daywear 1990s

There is no one style that definitively characterizes the 1990s. The number of manufacturers designing especially for children has multiplied and the number of looks available is vast. Many styles or materials have endured or been rediscovered with periodic 1950s, '60s, and even '70s revivals. One children's fashion item that has made a dramatic impact is the athletic shoe, which has become a billion-dollar industry as companies such as Nike and Adidas (see pp.162–63) vie to persuade the young that its product is the coolest.

The sturdy, practical shoe design is enlivened by the decorative trim

WOMEN'S DAYWEAR

THE CHANGING VALUES AND ATTITUDES of the century are clearly reflected in the way women dress: the role of women, the permissive society, and the growth of the youth market have all had an impact. In daywear, restrictive full-length dresses, with a multitude of petticoats, have been replaced by clothing better suited to the lifestyles of modern women. New looks are created through a combination of aesthetic judgment, new materials, and the challenging of past conventions.

NYLON

First produced by the Du Pont laboratories in 1938, nylon was named after the cities where it was hoped it would sell, New York and London. This fine, strong, elastic, synthetic fiber was an ideal substitute for rayon or silk. Research was led by Wallace H. Carothers; after his death the patent was awarded to Du Pont.

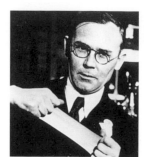

Carothers testing nylon

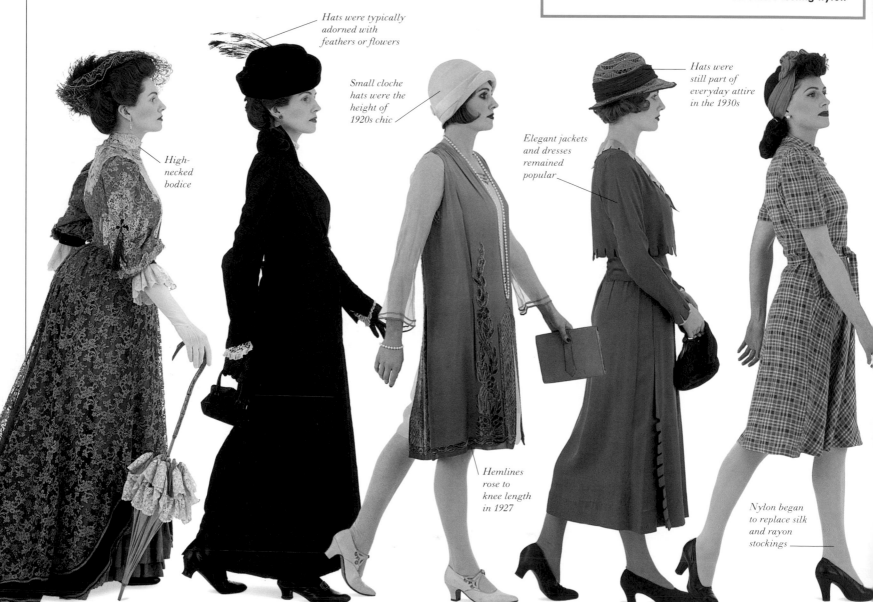

Hats were typically adorned with feathers or flowers

Small cloche hats were the height of 1920s chic

Hats were still part of everyday attire in the 1930s

High-necked bodice

Elegant jackets and dresses remained popular

Hemlines rose to knee length in 1927

Nylon began to replace silk and rayon stockings

Daywear c.1900
Although less restrictive than the multilayered late 19th-century style, women's dress at the turn of the century was still uncomfortable. The "S"-shaped silhouette was molded by a corset, pushing the bust forward and the hips back.

Daywear 1910s
In 1914, Mary Phelps Jacobs designed the brassière – two handkerchiefs with ribbon straps, intended to flatten the bust. World War I brought more women into the workplace, increasing the demand for less restrictive clothing.

Daywear 1920s
In the decade of the tubular silhouette, dresses were shorter, light, and elegant, in silk or crêpe-de-chine, often revealing the arms and back. Beige stockings were worn to suggest bare legs, and rayon provided an affordable alternative to silk.

Daywear 1930s
The Depression influenced fashion in the 1930s. Women's clothes became more sober and the hemline dropped once again. The overall silhouette was more curvaceous. Elegant suits in soft fabrics were popular, often worn with fox fur.

Daywear 1940s
Cloth became scarce during World War II and clothes were plainer and used less fabric than previously. In the UK, clothes were rationed. Nylons were introduced in America in 1940, but were very difficult to obtain in Europe.

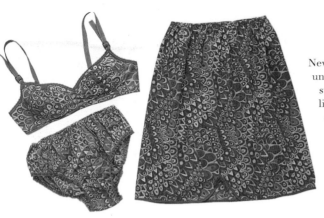

Underwear

New, easy-to-care-for underwear perfectly suited the carefree lifestyles of women during the 1960s. Matching sets of nylon bra, briefs, and half-slips appeared in bold, bright prints.

UNISEX CLOTHING

Although practical, masculine styles had previously been seen in women's sports and casual clothing, it was not until the 1960s and '70s that the gender conventions of traditional dress codes were truly challenged, and unisex clothing gained popularity. Women wore men's pants, often with suspenders, vests, and dinner jackets in the "Annie Hall" look of the '70s. Meanwhile, men took to colorful, floral patterns and flamboyant styling.

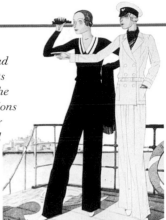

Fashion plate, 1930s

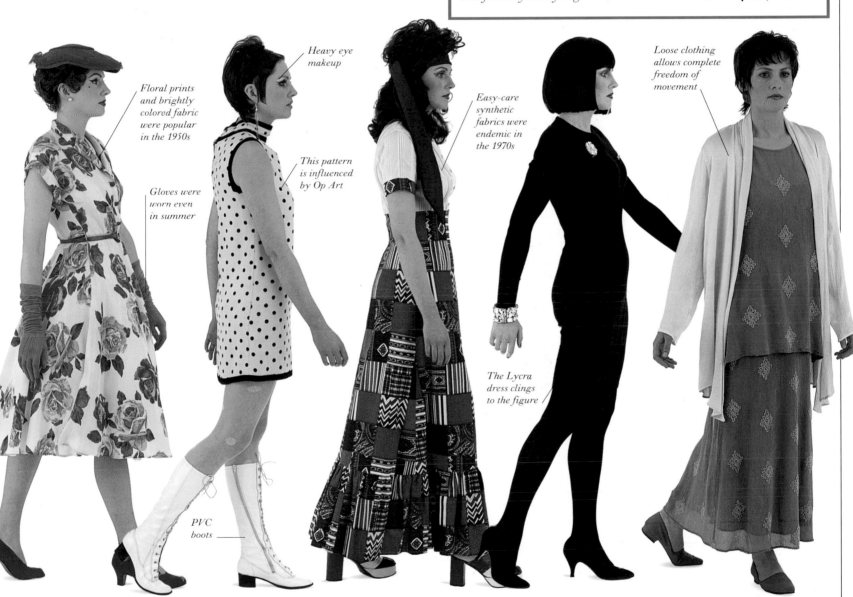

Floral prints and brightly colored fabric were popular in the 1950s

Gloves were worn even in summer

Heavy eye makeup

This pattern is influenced by Op Art

PVC boots

Easy-care synthetic fabrics were endemic in the 1970s

Loose clothing allows complete freedom of movement

The Lycra dress clings to the figure

Daywear 1950s
Christian Dior's "New Look" (see p.142), introduced in 1947, had a huge impact on everyday fashion. The tight-fitting bodice, narrow waist, and full skirt gave a curving silhouette. The brassière was padded and wired to enhance the bust.

Daywear 1960s
Although the decade witnessed a multitude of styles, the 1960s will be forever associated with the miniskirt. It was no longer possible to wear stockings and garter belts, so designers experimented with colored and patterned pantyhose.

Daywear 1970s
In the 1970s, fashion designers drew inspiration from a variety of sources: feminism, the hippie movement, and civil rights. Continuing trends set in the 1960s, easy-care synthetic fibers and psychedelic and patchwork patterns were popular.

Daywear 1980s
Clothes in the 1980s were a mix of glamour, body consciousness, and the casual, multilayered look. Lycra, invented in 1958 in the US and previously used only for underwear, gave rise to the body-hugging designs that went with the 1980s fitness craze.

Daywear 1990s
Unlike previous decades, the 1990s are not epitomized by any single "look"; individualism is the key. There has been a shift in emphasis away from the high achievement that influenced the look of the 1980s and toward a more casual, comfortable style.

MEN'S DAYWEAR

COMPARED TO THE RADICAL changes in women's dress during the 20th century, menswear has appeared more constant in character. The lounge suit, worn at the turn of the century, has undergone changes in material and cut, but remains similar in form to its modern derivative. However, the fashionable male silhouette, like its female counterpart, has been molded to suit changing social values and advances in technology. Heavy Edwardian suits and starched collars have given way to separates in lightweight and synthetic fabrics; waistcoats and hats, once essential components of daywear, are now optional extras. The biggest change in men's dress occurred in the 1960s, when young men adopted colorful, casual clothes that challenged strict gender definitions.

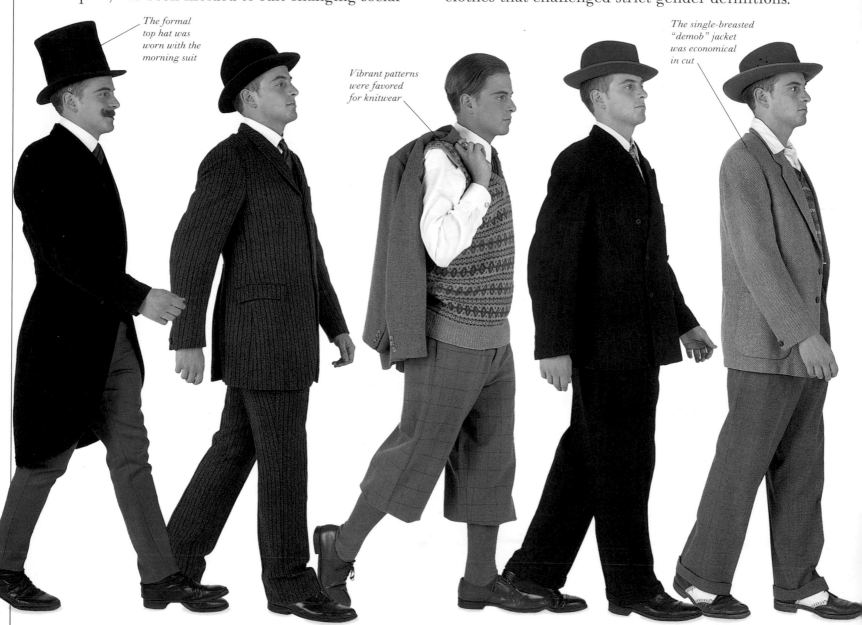

The formal top hat was worn with the morning suit

Vibrant patterns were favored for knitwear

The single-breasted "demob" jacket was economical in cut

Daywear c.1900
Men's dress did not change instantly with the new century. In the first decade the emphasis was on formality; a frock coat or morning suit was correct daywear, worn with a starched shirt collar that averaged 4in (10cm) high.

Daywear 1910s
By 1910, the three-piece lounge suit (waistcoat, pants, and jacket), intended as casual dress, was popular daywear for city dwellers. The jacket had small lapels and buttoned high on the chest. It was worn with narrow pants and a bowler hat.

Daywear 1920s
Equally acceptable on the golf course or as informal daywear, plus-fours became extremely popular in the 1920s. The wide pants, deriving their name from the fact that they fall 4in (10cm) below the knee, were usually made from tweed.

Daywear 1930s
The ideal male silhouette in the 1930s had broad shoulders and narrow hips. These features were accentuated in the cut of the double-breasted suit, which had padded shoulders and wide lapels. Pant legs were cut wide with turn-ups at the hem.

Daywear 1940s
It is difficult to identify any definitive style during the postwar period because the lack of raw materials and, in some countries, rationing meant that many clothes were recycled, a concept unheard of before the war.

THE T-SHIRT

In 1942, the US Navy introduced a knitted cotton undershirt with short sleeves and a round collar. It was known as the T-Type because it formed a "T" shape when laid flat. Initially worn by soldiers and marines, it was later popularized by James Dean, who wore one in Rebel Without a Cause, 1955.

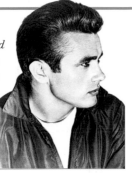

James Dean, 1955

POP CULTURE INFLUENCE

Owing to the immense popularity that followed their first hit records in the early 1960s, the Beatles had an enormous impact on menswear. The collarless jacket shown here, designed by Pierre Cardin (see p.144), was particularly associated with the group. As Beatlemania swept across the world, fans began to mimic the group's style. Although it seems unremarkable now, the "mop-top" haircut, with its thick bangs, was considered shocking at the time.

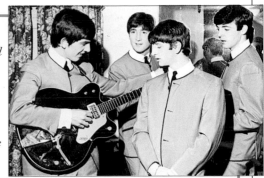

The Beatles, early 1960s

Hats were no longer essential for daywear

The collar on this Armani oufit is inspired by Chinese costume

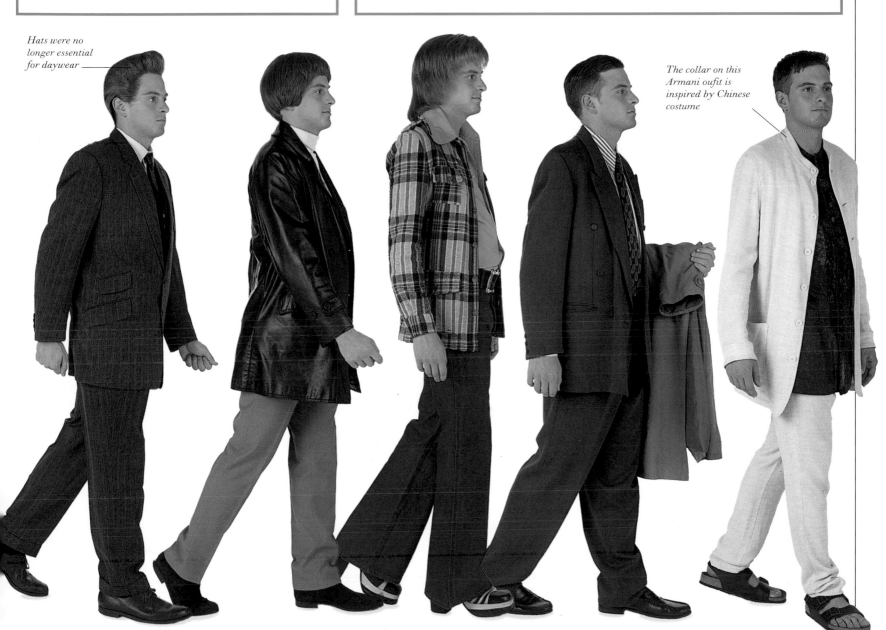

Daywear 1950s
The 1950s saw a steady paring down of the male silhouette. A narrower cut was adopted for suits, with slimmer pants and a long, single-breasted jacket. Known as the drape suit, it was worn in an extreme form by the Teddy boys in Britain.

Daywear 1960s
The male wardrobe underwent a radical transformation in the 1960s. Cheap, colorful clothes were produced for young men and sold in the new boutiques. "Swinging" London, particularly Carnaby Street, was the center of an emerging pop culture.

Daywear 1970s
The traditional suit was, by the early 1970s, an occasional item of dress for most men. In men's fashion, the decade was typified by casualwear and separates. Hip-hugger jeans were popular, cut tight over the hips and thighs and flaring from the knee.

Daywear 1980s
Menswear took a new direction in the 1980s as an increasing number of "boutique" stores began to specialize in clothing for men. The economic boom led to the creation of a new "Wall Street" type with a distinctly corporate look.

Daywear 1990s
The mood has swung again in the 1990s, with a rejection of the professional look that characterized the 1980s. Soft, natural fabrics, such as linen and silk, are favored. Shirts are often worn untucked in a loose, layered style.

HAUTE COUTURE

FRENCH FOR "HIGH SEWING," *haute couture* was originally clothing for the upper classes — high prices prohibiting all but the wealthy from enjoying its luxury. The growth of ready-to-wear clothing since the 1950s has led to a democratization of fashion: couturiers' designs are revealed on the catwalk and then toned down and produced less expensively for the mass market. Although involved in the more lucrative markets of perfume and makeup, the most successful couturiers still produce "one-of-a-kinds."

Dior 1947
The "New Look," presented in Paris in 1947, was Christian Dior's first collection, and it brought him instant fame. After the austere styles of the war years, this elegant, feminine look was a hit with women hungry for something new and glamorous. A narrow waist, tight bodice, and padded hips were features of the New Look.

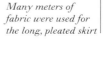

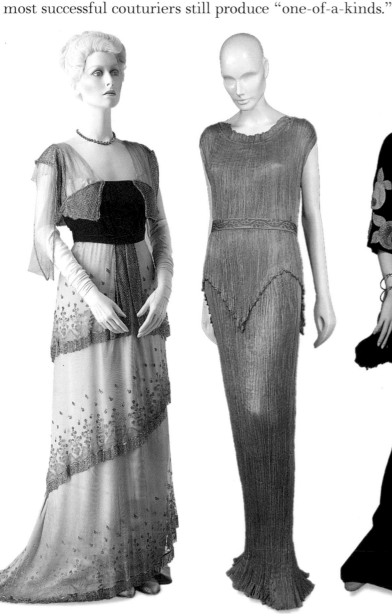

Tiny, nipped-in waist shaped by the "waspie" corset

Many meters of fabric were used for the long, pleated skirt

The high heels and full skirt emphasize the slenderness of lower leg and ankle

Worth 1910–11
Created by the house of Worth for its 1910–11 collection, this velvet and silk evening gown reflects changing fashion trends. The high waistline and narrow skirt represent a move away from the tightly corseted S-bend silhouette of the previous decade.

Fortuny 1912
Mariano Fortuny y Madrazo was an inventor, as well as an artist and couturier. The fine pleats of this silk evening gown were created by his own patented process. This dress shows the influence of classical Greece, and its timeless design would not look out of place today.

Poiret 1912
Paul Poiret is credited with freeing women from the constraints of the corset. This outfit demonstrates several of his signature features — the kimono-style tunic with wired hem, the raised waistline, the turban, the fur trim, and the richly colored and embroidered silks.

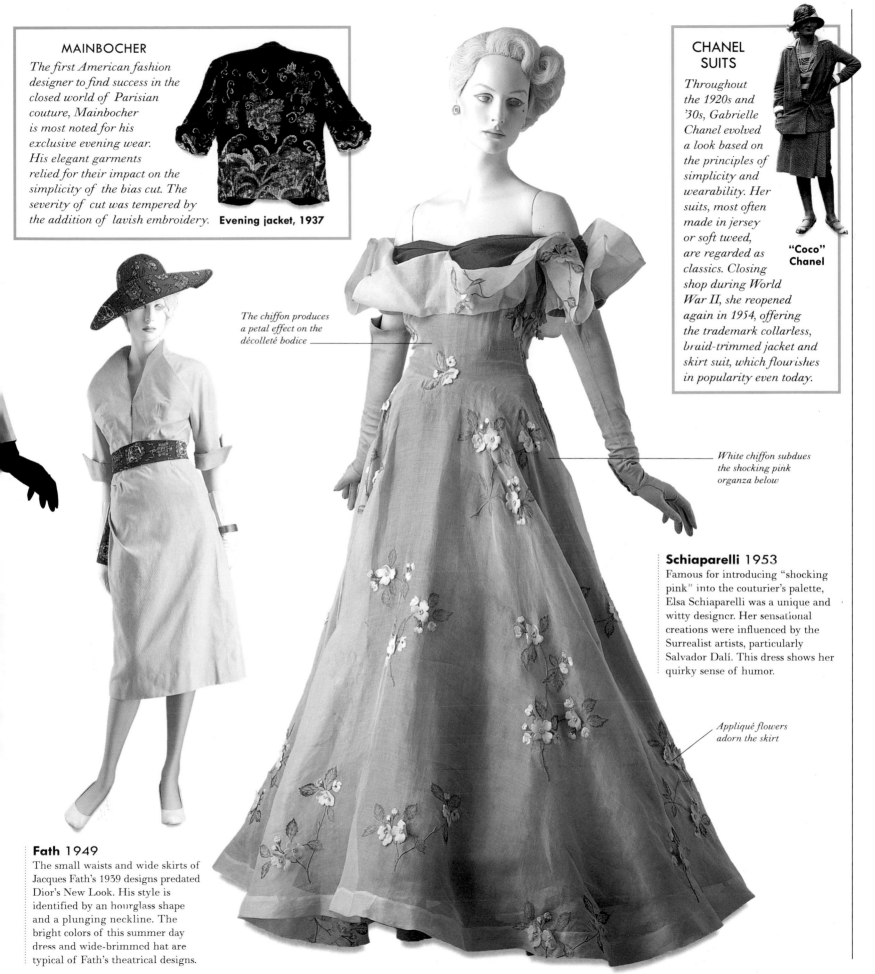

MAINBOCHER

The first American fashion designer to find success in the closed world of Parisian couture, Mainbocher is most noted for his exclusive evening wear. His elegant garments relied for their impact on the simplicity of the bias cut. The severity of cut was tempered by the addition of lavish embroidery.

Evening jacket, 1937

CHANEL SUITS

Throughout the 1920s and '30s, Gabrielle Chanel evolved a look based on the principles of simplicity and wearability. Her suits, most often made in jersey or soft tweed, are regarded as classics. Closing shop during World War II, she reopened again in 1954, offering the trademark collarless, braid-trimmed jacket and skirt suit, which flourishes in popularity even today.

"Coco" Chanel

The chiffon produces a petal effect on the décolleté bodice

White chiffon subdues the shocking pink organza below

Schiaparelli 1953

Famous for introducing "shocking pink" into the couturier's palette, Elsa Schiaparelli was a unique and witty designer. Her sensational creations were influenced by the Surrealist artists, particularly Salvador Dalí. This dress shows her quirky sense of humor.

Appliqué flowers adorn the skirt

Fath 1949

The small waists and wide skirts of Jacques Fath's 1939 designs predated Dior's New Look. His style is identified by an hourglass shape and a plunging neckline. The bright colors of this summer day dress and wide-brimmed hat are typical of Fath's theatrical designs.

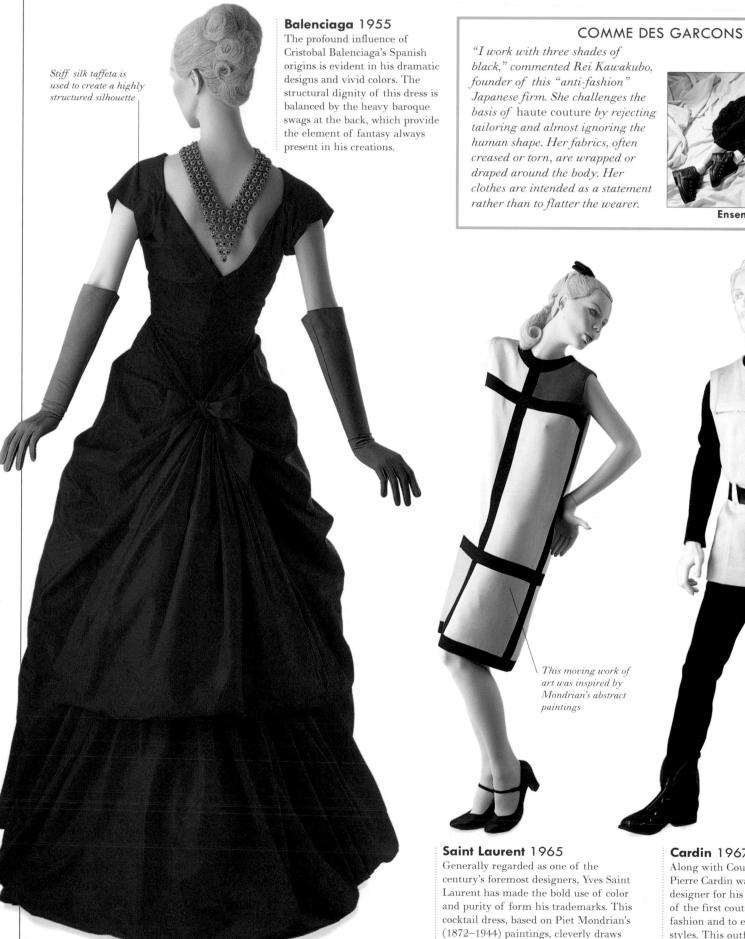

Stiff silk taffeta is used to create a highly structured silhouette

Balenciaga 1955

The profound influence of Cristobal Balenciaga's Spanish origins is evident in his dramatic designs and vivid colors. The structural dignity of this dress is balanced by the heavy baroque swags at the back, which provide the element of fantasy always present in his creations.

COMME DES GARCONS

"I work with three shades of black," commented Rei Kawakubo, founder of this *"anti-fashion"* Japanese firm. She challenges the basis of haute couture *by rejecting tailoring and almost ignoring the human shape. Her fabrics, often creased or torn, are wrapped or draped around the body. Her clothes are intended as a statement rather than to flatter the wearer.*

Ensemble, 1982

This moving work of art was inspired by Mondrian's abstract paintings

Saint Laurent 1965

Generally regarded as one of the century's foremost designers, Yves Saint Laurent has made the bold use of color and purity of form his trademarks. This cocktail dress, based on Piet Mondrian's (1872–1944) paintings, cleverly draws together art and fashion.

Cardin 1967

Along with Courrèges, the avant-garde Pierre Cardin was labeled a "Space Age" designer for his 1964 show. He was one of the first couturiers to consider men's fashion and to experiment with unisex styles. This outfit uses zippers as a design feature, repeated on the boots.

Westwood 1981

Consistently outrageous but nevertheless influential, Vivienne Westwood has always looked to the street for inspiration. Her subversive designs – including ripped T-shirts, necklines cut under the arm, and dangerously tall shoes – do not attempt to approach the traditional concepts of comfort and fit. The Pirate collection of 1981 brought her recognition on the international fashion circuit. This extravagant, multilayered look, dubbed "New Romantic" in the UK, was a maturation of the creative spirit of Punk.

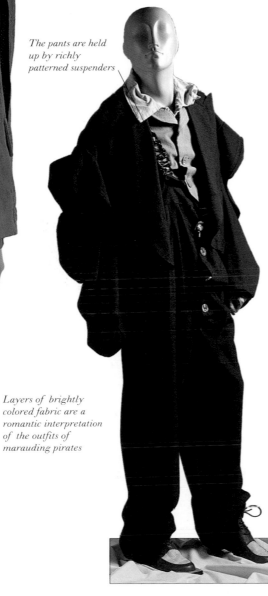

The pants are held up by richly patterned suspenders

Layers of brightly colored fabric are a romantic interpretation of the outfits of marauding pirates

Galliano 1985

John Galliano achieved instant fame with his graduation collection in 1984. Like Westwood, he takes ideas from diverse sources and reworks them in new and unusual ways. His avant-garde designs are often difficult to understand – with complex fastenings and multiple layers – but his brilliance of cut has won him a lasting reputation.

JAPANESE DESIGNS

Ever since the kimono inspired designers such as Poiret at the turn of the century, Japan has played a significant role in Western fashion design. The new generation of Japanese designers is undoubtedly the most important influence on haute couture in recent decades. Designers like Issey Miyake are often concerned with concealing, wrapping up, and disguising body shape rather than enhancing it. Garments are designed to show off the beauty of the fabrics, concentrating on texture rather than form. Japanese design has given us greater flexibility in clothing, allowing a freedom of movement often lacking in Western designs.

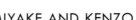

Kenzo ensemble

Miyake ensemble

MIYAKE AND KENZO

Although he received his grounding in the Parisian couture tradition, the success of Hiroshima-born Issey Miyake has been in combining traditional Japanese and African costume to create a loosely wrapped "anti-status" look. He cites the 1968 student revolution in Paris as a formative influence, the event urging him to abandon the restraints of established Parisian couture culture and create less restrictive ensembles for active, modern women. Miyake's compatriot and contemporary, the Kyoto-born Kenzo Takada, has also created an ethnic look, which concentrates on the flow and drape of the fabric. However, he is most famous for revitalizing knitwear design.

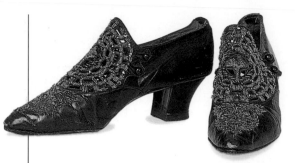

Bead shoes c.1900

These ornate shoes from early in the century combine a high upper with the slightly waisted heel of a court shoe. The pattern cut into the leather is enhanced by an intricate arrangement of tiny steel beads.

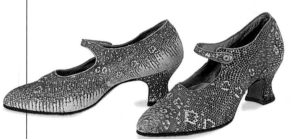

T-strap shoes 1920s

These elegant high-heeled shoes are made from embroidered purple fabric. The ankle-strap shoe is the definitive women's style of the 1920s, the T-strap shown here being a variant of the style below.

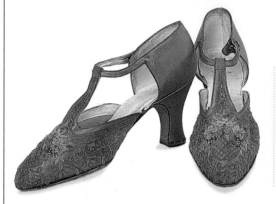

Skin shoes 1920s

Reptile skin has been exceptionally popular in women's shoe design for much of the century. Recently, synthetic copies have developed in response to concerns for wildlife.

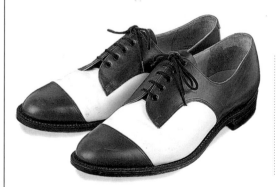

Spectator shoes 1920s

The two-tone spectator, or correspondent, shoe boomed in popularity during the Jazz era. Primarily a fashion for men, these black or brown and white shoes enjoyed a revival in the 1940s.

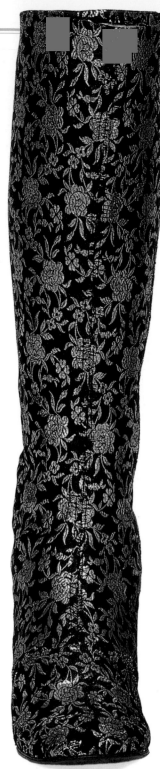
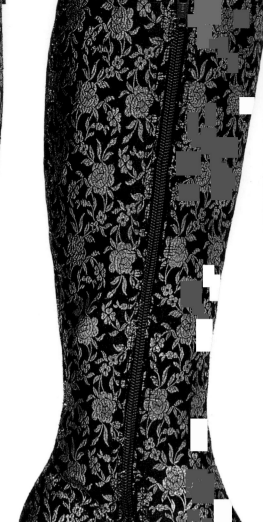

Knee boots 1960s

Although boots were originally made to protect the ankles and calves, by the 1960s they had become more of a fashion statement. Produced in leather or synthetic material, they varied in length from ankle to thigh.

SHOES

REFLECTING AND COMPLEMENTING new styles of clothing, shoe design has always been an important branch of the fashion industry. Italian designer Salvatore Ferragamo was one of the first to put new synthetic materials to use, combining cork platform soles with plastic uppers in the 1930s. Another notable Italian innovation, the stiletto, appeared in the 1950s, and has played a controversial role in women's fashion ever since. Elsewhere in footwear, the distinction between men's and women's styles has lessened noticeably toward the end of the century.

SALVATORE FERRAGAMO

The work of the greatest Italian shoe designer of the century, this "invisible shoe" with nylon toe straps was launched in 1947. It followed the legendary cork wedge heel, patented in 1936 and imitated worldwide. The full Ferragamo collection is celebrated in a museum in Florence.

Invisible shoe, 1947

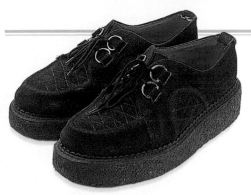

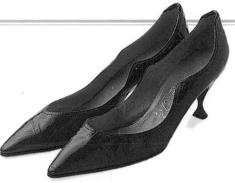

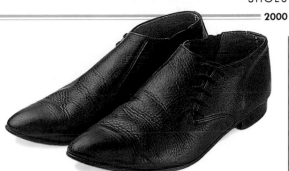

Crepe sole shoe 1950s
Emerging with the cult of the teenager, crepe soles became popular in the 1950s. These shoes were colloquially known as "brothel creepers," because of their thick, rubbery soles and soft suede uppers.

The stiletto 1950s
Since it was introduced in Italy in 1953, the stiletto has varied significantly in shape. Although originally two inches thick and gently tapered, the heel has changed over time to become increasingly tall and pointed.

Winklepickers 1960s
Introduced in the late 1950s, the winklepickers' extreme pointed toes show design influences from as long ago as the 14th century. The name refers to the sharp pin used to pick winkles out of their shells.

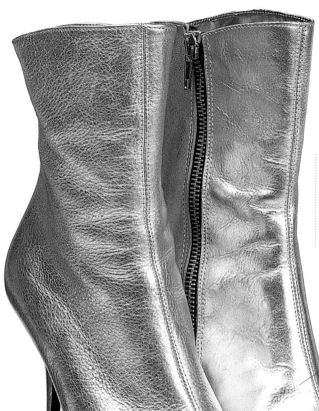

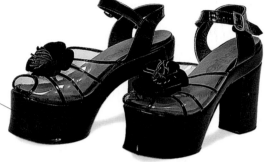

Chunky platform soles have become icons of 1970s street style

Silver boots 1990s
These calf-length silver boots have a central seam running to a pointed toe. The inside zipper is a practical fastening that creates a slimline silhouette, emphasized by the stiletto heels.

Silver has risen in popularity as a color for 1990s fashions

Ladies' platform shoes 1970s
The celebrated platform soles of the 1970s are a radical version of the 1940s wedge. Revived as a fashionable, slightly offbeat shoe, they were made from an affordable combination of leather and plastic.

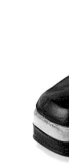

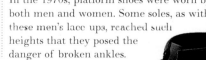

Men's platform shoes 1970
In the 1970s, platform shoes were worn by both men and women. Some soles, as with these men's lace ups, reached such heights that they posed the danger of broken ankles.

RED OR DEAD

Red or Dead was founded in 1982 by Wayne and Gerardine Hemingway. It began as a market stall in London, growing into a chain of international shops. The label's innovative fashions often demonstrate a futuristic, space-age influence.

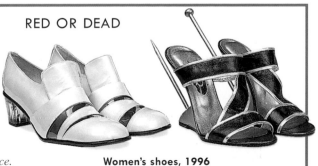
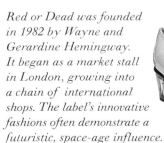

Women's shoes, 1996

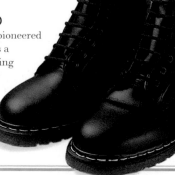

Dr. Martens 1960–90
Dr. Maertens and Dr. Funck pioneered air-cushioned soles in 1945, as a comfortable solution to shodding Maertens's injured foot. They were an instant success. The 1960s "1460" shown here was the first Dr. Martens boot, and has remained a favorite.

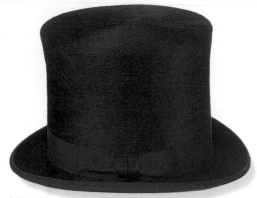

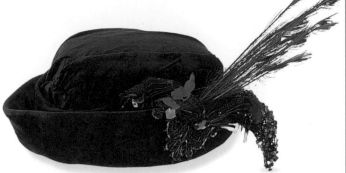

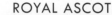

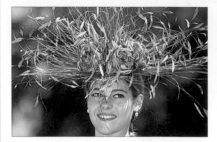

ROYAL ASCOT

Ascot headwear, 1990s

The annual Royal Ascot in Berkshire, England, is a showground for milliners to display their skill and ingenuity. Wildly eccentric creations, which appear to take little account of the wearer's comfort, are paraded for press and public.

Top hat 1900s

Introduced in the early years of the 19th century, top hats have varied greatly in height; there has even been the collapsible black silk version designed to fit under one's seat at the opera. Although this cumbersome formal headgear continued to be widely worn until World War I, it had aready passed its heyday by the turn of the century.

Velvet hat 1910

This black velvet hat, decorated with feathers and appliqued flowers, is discreet and practical compared to some of the richly ornamented, wide-brimmed hats of the period. It was rare at this time to find a formal ladies' hat without embellishment – ribbons, bows, plumes, flowers, and fruit were all used. Gloves and parasol would complete the look.

Bowler hats were designed in sober colors, such as dark brown and gray

The plainness of the style is counterbalanced by the frivolity of the decoration

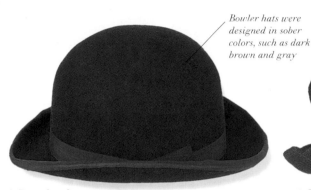

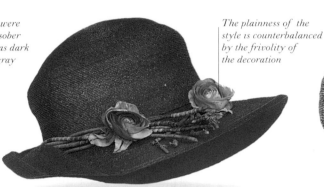

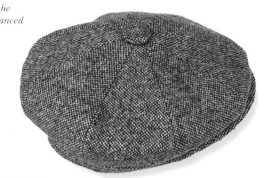

Bowler hat 1910

Originally worn as protective headgear, this hard felt hat with a rounded crown and narrow curved brim was designed by London hatter John Bowler in the 1850s. In the US and Canada, it became known as the derby, after Lord Derby. It gradually replaced the top hat and was still worn by some businessmen until the 1960s.

Straw hat 1918

This simple straw hat, with its elegant silhouette, is a typical example of the gradual transition in style from the wide brims and excessively elaborate trimmings of hats in the early 1900s to the close-fitting helmet-shaped cloche hats of the 1920s. It is made of glossy red straw, with the hatband eschewed in favor of a decorative ring of pale pink roses.

Cloth cap 1920

Over the years, the cloth cap has been produced in countless variations, including the Sherlock Holmes deerstalker look and the pioneering motorist style. The brimless peaked cap shown here would have originally been worn by workmen, but enjoyed a revival in the 1960s, when it was designed in a range of brightly colored PVC and leather.

The 1920s cloche hat is characterized by its deep, rounded crown

The flat top of the straw boater is echoed in the uncurled stiff brim

Traditional baseball cap styles have eyelets for ventilation

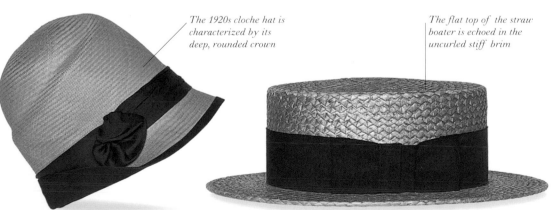

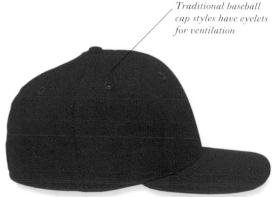

Cloche hat 1920s

This snug-fitting ladies' hat was designed to be pulled low over the forehead and neck. Narrow-brimmed, or even brimless, its shape resembles a bell (*cloche* is the French word for bell), which particularly suited the bobbed hairstyles and short permanent waves that were *de rigueur* from 1915 to the mid-1930s. Both cloche and hairstyle were updated in the 1960s and early '70s, led by Mary Quant and Biba.

Straw boater 1920s

The wide-brimmed, flat-crowned straw boater, complete with broad hatband, was originally worn by men for leisure activities such as boating and seaside excursions. Invariably, it would top a casual summer outfit of flannel trousers and striped blazer. The traditional masculine style has long since been adopted by women to accessorize casual summer fashions.

Baseball cap 1920s

With its close-fitting crown and deep peak, the baseball cap is instantly identifiable as one of the century's most enduring headwear styles. Caps with stiffened visors first appeared for sports in the late 19th century, popularized and renamed in the US through baseball. Today, the cap is produced in an array of colors and logo-intensive designs, often featuring mesh panels for ventilation.

HATS

THIS CENTURY HAS SEEN SWEEPING CHANGES in both hat styles and in the regularity with which they have been worn. While, at the turn of the century, no self-respecting adult would have ventured outdoors without the appropriate headgear, today formal hats are far less frequently seen. Worn by the majority only at social events, they remain otherwise the domain of the fashion individualist. Nevertheless, all the classics of the century – the men's top hat and bowler and the ladies' cloche and pillbox among them – have been revived and reinterpreted by modern milliners. As far as more casual street style is concerned, the common hat of choice is the baseball cap.

PRINCESS DIANA

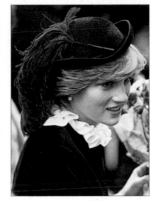

John Boyd hat, 1981

The Princess of Wales's style has always been closely scrutinized by the world's media. This John Boyd bowler-inspired hat, complete with oversized feather, was highly influential, spawning countless copies. The hat was designed to suit the hairstyle of the wearer, the brim seeming to flow with the line of Diana's sweeping fringe.

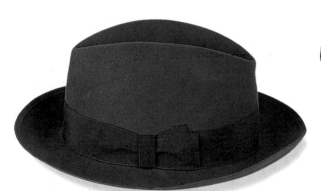

Homburg 1940s
In its smartest form, the ubiquitous men's soft felt hat was known as a homburg, after the German town where it was first made and worn. It has a narrow, curved brim, high, creased crown, dark band, and braid trim around the brim. Its popularity was largely thanks to the Prince of Wales (later Edward VII), who introduced the homburg to Britain and beyond.

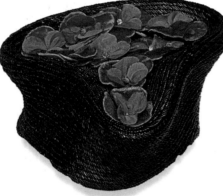

Black straw hat 1940s
The 1940s saw a move to higher crowns and the emergence of the chic pillbox shape (later to be epitomized by Halston's creation for Jackie Kennedy). Although far less flamboyant than earlier styles, this hat has an unusual curved shape and would have been worn tilted to the front of the head to display the decoration of pressed flowers.

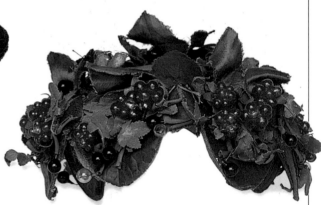

Berry hat 1950s
This delightful summer piece could be described as all trimming and no hat. It is little more than a skullcap strewn with silk leaves and glass beads for berries. Purely decorative, it would have served no purpose as a shield from sun, wind, or rain. Instead, from an era of unfussy headgear in practical fabrics, it represents a welcome exercise in frivolity.

The synthetic furlike fabric is designed to mimic the skin of a leopard

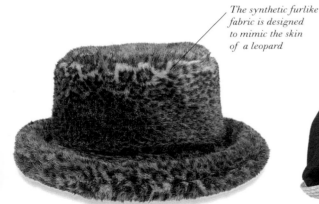

Fake fur hat 1990
While formal millinery plays only a limited role in modern dress, more casual hat styles continue to be worn for warmth and protection. In keeping with the 1990s concerns for animal rights, this hat is made from fake fur. The silk-lined crown is spacious and deep, with the thick brim designed to be pulled down low over the forehead and ears to keep the wearer warm in cold weather.

The simple 1920s cloche shape has been updated to include a jaunty upturn of the brim

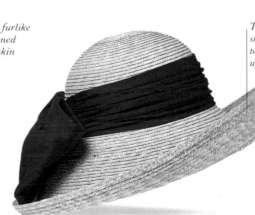

Belgravia hat c.1989
This natural straw and silk hat is made by the British milliner Pamela Bromley. Its streamlined shape echoes the cloche hat of the 1920s, with braids of straw stitched together to create a deep, flared helmet. The colorful ruche is of raw, woven Indian silk. Designed to be worn at outdoor summer social events, the Belgravia is also available in other fabrics and colors.

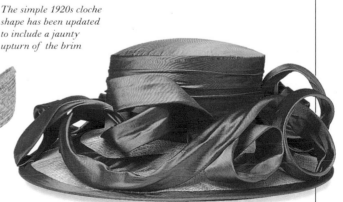

Leonora hat 1995
Also the work of Pamela Bromley, the basic structure of this fanciful creation has been crafted of a woven material made from coconut fiber. The shocking pink and orange decoration is in shot spun silk, the exuberant loops around the brim stiffened with wire. Intended for appearances at weddings or Ascot, the Leonora harks back to the glamorous wide-brimmed concoctions of the early 1900s.

WATCHES

THE FIRST WRISTWATCHES were manufactured in the 1890s and closely resembled the traditional pocket watch. The idea of strapping a watch to the wrist did not meet with instant success; it was considered effeminate for a man to wear a wristwatch. Only when World War I officers found them more efficient than fumbling in their pockets, was this image dispelled. In the 1960s, electronic advances resulted in the digital watch, with its clear display and accurate timekeeping.

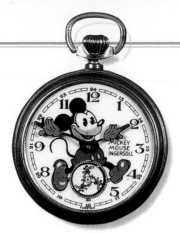

Mickey watch 1930s
This children's Mickey Mouse pocket watch is an early example of a novelty watch. Later, Swatch took the idea of decorated faces to extremes with their adult designs.

Specifications
Country: US
Material: Stainless steel

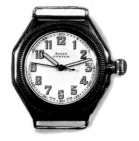

Women's Oyster 1930
Pioneered by Rolex in 1926, the Oyster was the first waterproof watch to be produced. Its case was carved from a solid piece of gold.

Specifications
Country: Switzerland
Material: Gold

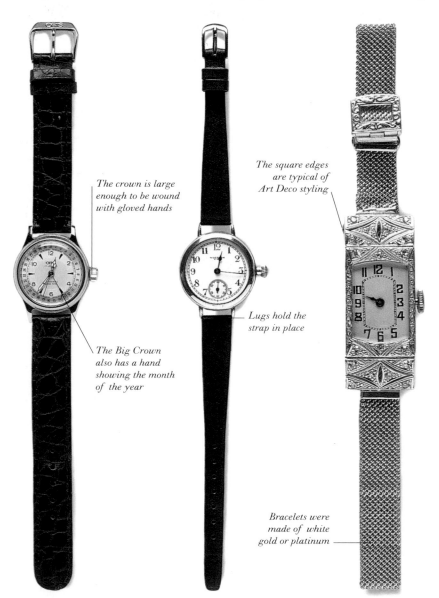

The crown is large enough to be wound with gloved hands

The Big Crown also has a hand showing the month of the year

The square edges are typical of Art Deco styling

Lugs hold the strap in place

Bracelets were made of white gold or platinum

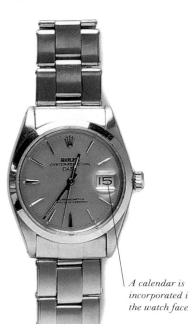

A calendar is incorporated into the watch face

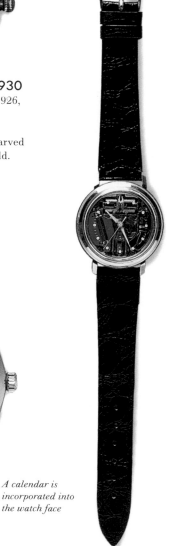

Oris Big Crown 1920s
Named for its oversized winder, the Big Crown was designed to allow early aviators to wind it without removing their gloves. It is still produced today.

Specifications
Country: Switzerland
Materials: Stainless steel and leather

Waltham 1920s
The bulbous case design of this early lady's wristwatch is little removed from the pocket watch. The miniaturization of movements for small women's watches added to their price.

Specifications
Country: US
Materials: White gold and leather

Cocktail watch 1930s
Ornate cocktail watches were prestigious accessories for evening wear during the 1930s. This Art Deco example houses a Swiss movement in a diamond-encrusted case.

Specifications
Country: Switzerland
Materials: Platinum and diamonds

Oyster Perpetual 1965
A twin-lock system seals the winding crown of the Rolex Oyster against water and dust. The Perpetual model winds automatically, powered by the movement of the wrist.

Specifications
Country: Switzerland
Material: Stainless steel

Bulova Accutron 1960s
Engineered by Max Hetzel, the Accutron Spaceview was the first electronic watch. Its time base is controlled by a tuning fork, which was the precursor of the quartz watch.

Specifications
Country: Switzerland
Materials: Stainless steel and leather

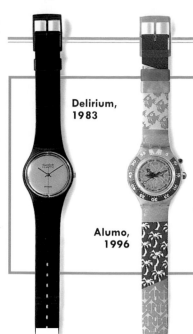

Delirium, 1983

Alumo, 1996

SWATCH

Developed by Ernst Thonke, Jacques Müller, and Elmer Mock in 1983, the Swatch was the first integrated watch; that is, the action was not a separate component from the case. The introductory Swatch model, marketed in 1972, was the Delirium, a modest example compared to the 1990s Alumo, with its brightly patterned strap and face. Swatch has frequently employed artists to create exclusive watches, such as photographer Annie Leibovitz (who made a contribution to mark the 1996 Atlanta Olympic Games) and Vivienne Westwood (see p.145).

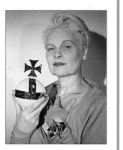

Vivienne Westwood

DIVER'S WATCHES

Omega Seamaster, 1995

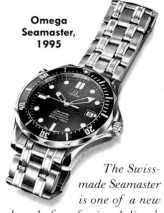

The Swiss-made Seamaster is one of a new breed of professional diver's watches, and was the chosen timepiece of James Bond in the 1995 film Goldeneye. The self-winding chronometer utilizes the movement of the wearer's wrist, making it unnecessary to wind manually. This stainless-steel watch is waterproof to a depth of 1,000ft (300m).

The shimmering bracelet strap is substantially wider than the watch face

The watch is set on an expandable bracelet

The digital face includes alarm, calendar, and stopwatch

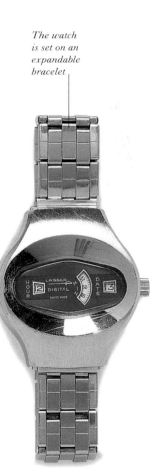

At just ½in (1.2cm) wide, the watch face is a discreet element of the design

This ring turns to indicate the depths reached by divers

Speedmaster 1969
Devised by Claude Baillodin, this Omega watch is the only one to have been worn on the Moon. Tested by NASA, it can withstand temperatures up to 199°F (93°C).

Specifications
Country: Switzerland
Material: Stainless steel

Lasser digital 1970s
Forerunner to the electronic digital, this mechanical version was more common for some time. Its space-age references epitomize the 1970s vogue for futuristic styling.

Specifications
Country: Switzerland
Material: Stainless steel

Gold watch 1970s
From the most affordable to the most exclusive examples, women's watches in the 1970s commonly resembled jewelry. This wide bracelet and small face are typical.

Specifications
Country: Not known
Material: Gold

Casio digital 1990s
The combination of quartz powering and liquid crystal display faces revolutionized digital-watch manufacturing. Low production costs mean they can be sold inexpensively.

Specifications
Country: Japan
Material: Stainless steel

Seiko Kinetic 1990s
An improvement of the Automatic Generating System, introduced in 1988, the Kinetic is one of the most reliable self-winding watches. The need for batteries is eliminated.

Specifications
Country: Japan
Materials: Stainless steel and gold

FOUNTAIN PENS

THROUGHOUT THE 19TH CENTURY, designers experimented with ways to improve dip pens, until then the standard writing instruments. By 1900, the main principles for a successful fountain pen had been established: a reservoir for ink; a filling system; and a method of supplying ink to the nib. Finding the most successful combination has provided a constant challenge, with three American companies – Parker, Waterman, and Sheaffer – dominating the market.

The design of the fountain pen has not relied solely on the demands of engineering, for aesthetics have also played an important role. The look of a pen, its size, weight, color, and the materials used in its construction all contribute to its success. Despite the ascendency of the cartridge pen and ballpoint pen, the nostalgic tastes of the late 20th century ensure the continued desirability of the fountain pen both as collectible item and functional tool.

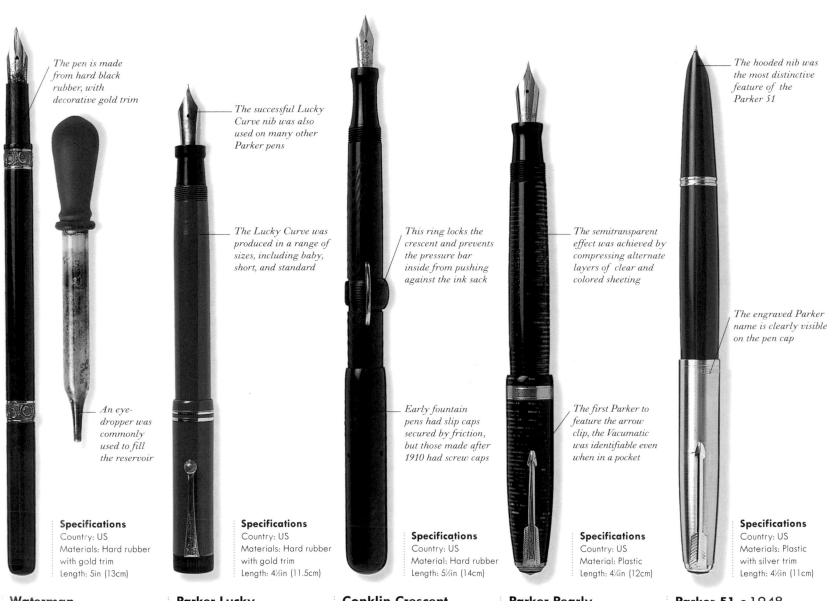

The pen is made from hard black rubber, with decorative gold trim

The successful Lucky Curve nib was also used on many other Parker pens

The hooded nib was the most distinctive feature of the Parker 51

The Lucky Curve was produced in a range of sizes, including baby, short, and standard

This ring locks the crescent and prevents the pressure bar inside from pushing against the ink sack

The semitransparent effect was achieved by compressing alternate layers of clear and colored sheeting

The engraved Parker name is clearly visible on the pen cap

An eye-dropper was commonly used to fill the reservoir

Early fountain pens had slip caps secured by friction, but those made after 1910 had screw caps

The first Parker to feature the arrow clip, the Vacumatic was identifiable even when in a pocket

Specifications
Country: US
Materials: Hard rubber with gold trim
Length: 5in (13cm)

Specifications
Country: US
Materials: Hard rubber with gold trim
Length: 4½in (11.5cm)

Specifications
Country: US
Material: Hard rubber
Length: 5½in (14cm)

Specifications
Country: US
Material: Plastic
Length: 4¾in (12cm)

Specifications
Country: US
Materials: Plastic with silver trim
Length: 4½in (11cm)

Waterman Eyedropper c.1903
Fountain pen pioneer Lewis E. Waterman began his successful company by patenting an improved feed design involving fine grooves under the nib. This was incorporated in this early Eyedropper pen.

Parker Lucky Curve c.1916–23
To prevent fountain pens from blobbing ink onto the paper if left lying horizontally for some time, Parker developed a feed that channeled the ink back into the reservoir. This was used for pens such as the Lucky Curve.

Conklin Crescent filler c.1923
Conklin's crescent filler system, patented in 1901, was copied by all the major pen manufacturers in the world. Air is expelled when the crescent is pressed, and ink drawn into the sack when it is released.

Parker Pearly Vacumatic c.1935
As famous for its handsome appearance as its technological innovation, Parker's Vacumatic design introduced a rubber diaphragm to replace the traditional sack, as well as new mechanisms to draw up the ink.

Parker 51 c.1948
Marking the 51st anniversary of the company's founding, the Parker 51 inspired a fashion for slim, elegant pens with hooded nibs. None reached the commercial success of this original, which was in production in the 1960s.

SNORKEL FILLING SYSTEM

One of a succession of filling systems developed this century, Sheaffer's snorkel method uses a thin tube, which emerges from the underside of the hooded nib when the user turns the knob at the end of the barrel. The tube is then dipped into the ink and, by extending and contracting the plunger, ink is drawn into the rubber sack. The nib remains dry throughout the process.

**Sheaffer
Snorkel pen**

PARKER PEN COMPANY

Born in the US in 1863, George S. Parker worked as a schoolteacher, selling fountain pens to his students to supplement his income. As the school pen repairman, he mastered the inner workings of the pens and decided to put his knowledge to commercial use. His first major success arrived in 1892, when he designed the Lucky Curve pen. Subsequent coups included the mass-produced Vacumatics. As the century draws to a close, there is a growing nostalgia for old-fashioned writing tools, and pre-1920s Parkers are among the most valuable of collectible fountain pens.

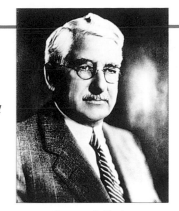

George S. Parker

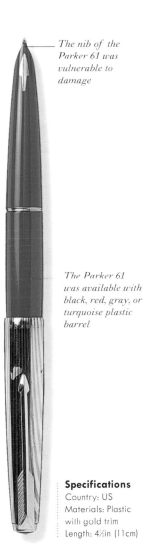

The pen can be filled without the need to submerge the nib in the ink

The Pen for Men was designed with a wide, supposedly masculine-shaped barrel

Specifications
Country: US
Materials: Plastic
Length: 4¼in (11cm)

Sheaffer Pen for Men 1960

Walter A. Sheaffer's 1907 lever filler – widely used for the next 40 years – established him as a leading figure in pen design. The Pen for Men uses the Snorkel system (see above), introduced in the 1940s.

The nib of the Parker 61 was vulnerable to damage

The Parker 61 was available with black, red, gray, or turquoise plastic barrel

Specifications
Country: US
Materials: Plastic with gold trim
Length: 4¼in (11cm)

Parker 61 1956

Although similar in appearance to the Parker 51, the 61 model incorporates an unusual filling system using a new ink called Super Quink. The ink cell, not the nib, is immersed in ink, which is drawn into the cell by capillary attraction.

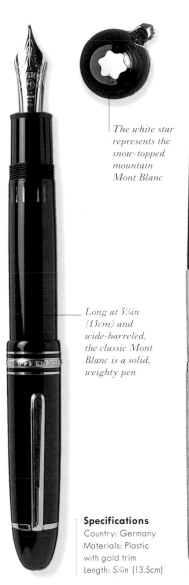

The white star represents the snow-topped mountain Mont Blanc

Long at 5¼in (13cm) and wide-barreled, the classic Mont Blanc is a solid, weighty pen

Specifications
Country: Germany
Materials: Plastic with gold trim
Length: 5¼in (13.5cm)

Montblanc 149 Masterpiece c.1970

The Masterpiece pen dates from 1924, with this 149 model introduced in the 1970s. The figure 4,810, engraved on the nib, refers to the mountain's height and symbolizes the company's high standards of craftsmanship.

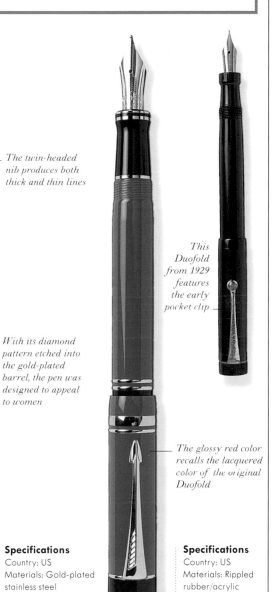

The twin-headed nib produces both thick and thin lines

With its diamond pattern etched into the gold-plated barrel, the pen was designed to appeal to women

Specifications
Country: US
Materials: Gold-plated stainless steel
Length: 4¼in (11cm)

Parker 180 c.1980

This pen is called the 180 because, by turning it by 180 degrees, the user can achieve a fine line with one side of the nib, and a thicker one with the other. The pen originally had a 14k gold nib and often a lacquer-coated barrel with gold trim.

This Duofold from 1929 features the early pocket clip

The glossy red color recalls the lacquered color of the original Duofold

Specifications
Country: US
Materials: Rippled rubber/acrylic
Length: 5½in (14cm)

Parker Duofold 1929; 1994

In keeping with 1990s tastes for retrospective styling, Parker has relaunched its 1920s Duofold. The original could be converted from pocket pen to desk pen by replacing the blind end cap with an extension to the barrel.

MAKEUP

"AT TIMES THE URGE to improve one's appearance, even if only temporary, becomes too strong to resist" said *Vogue*. Through the ages, both men and women have searched for ways to enhance their appearance. The first decade of the 20th century, when the use of cosmetics became widely accepted, is regarded as the heyday of the beauty parlor. The cosmetics industry became even more democratic after World War I, as women's looks attained a classless appearance. Before long, new looks were created as women studiously copied the hair and makeup styles of glamorous movie stars. The 1950s heralded a new era for the cosmetics industry, which turned its attention to a younger clientele, seducing them with novel packaging and seasonal lines.

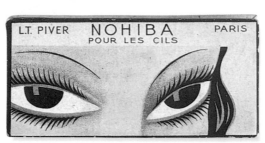

Eye makeup c.1930
The dramatic eye makeup used by actresses and movie stars had a profound influence on every-day makeup in the early part of this century. Diaghilev's Ballets Russes, which arrived in Paris in 1909, had a lasting effect on cosmetics. The dancers' exotic eye makeup created a vogue for colored and gilded eyeshadows, and heavy use of mascara.

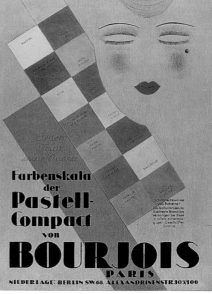

Pastel compact by Bourjois 1928
A growing demand for novelty in cosmetics encouraged manufacturers to introduce new beauty products to the market. Bourjois offered compacts with complementary rouges and lip colors. Vivid lip dyes, applied with a brush, increased in popularity after World War I.

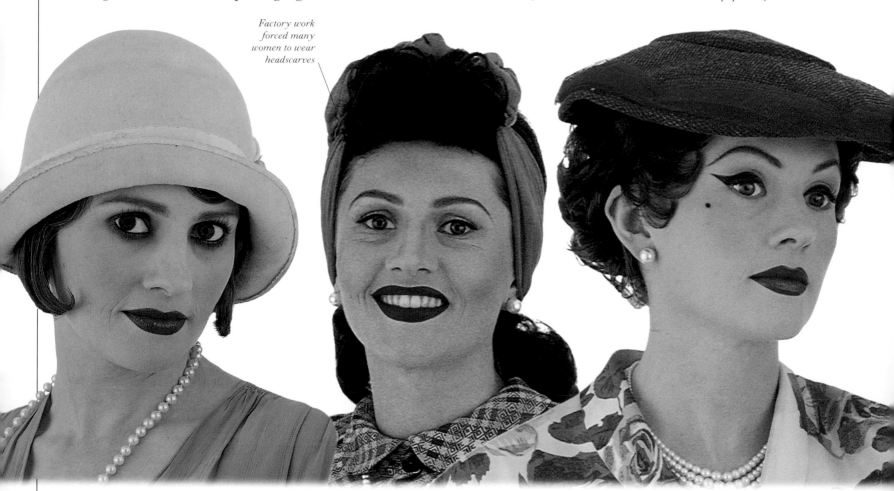

Factory work forced many women to wear headscarves

The Jazz Age 1920s
Lipstick made its debut in the 1920s. The lips were painted to resemble a cupid's bow, in vivid shades designed to shock. The look to aim for was radically cropped, smooth, bobbed hair; kohl around the eyes; severely plucked and penciled eyebrows; and a white complexion. Beauty marks were also penciled in.

Wartime cosmetics 1940s
During World War II, makeup was in short supply, for the petroleum and alcohol used in its manufacture were required for war purposes. Cosmetics were good for feminine morale, and many women improvised with homemade substitutes. Deep red lipstick, available on the black market, was worn with matching nail polish.

Hollywood glamour 1950s
There was a return to a more feminine look after World War II. The eyes were emphasized by shorter hairstyles and by the exaggerated use of black eyeliner on the upper lids. Liquid eyeliner, which was applied with a brush, replaced the pencil, and a variety of new products aimed at a younger market was launched.

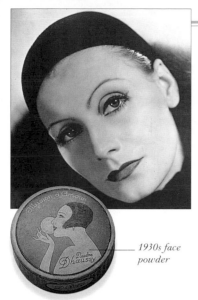

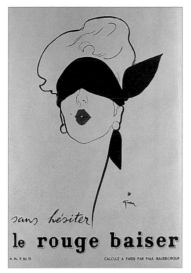

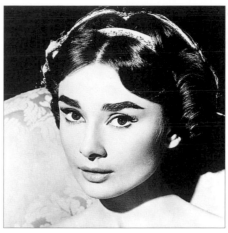

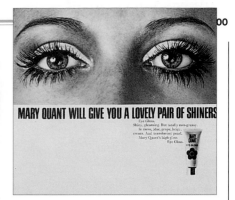

1930s face powder

Greta Garbo 1930s

The sophisticated look of movie star Greta Garbo was widely emulated by women in the 1930s. Garbo wore very pale face powder with no rouge, and accentuated her eyebrows and eyelids with pencil, rather than using tinted eyeshadow.

Red Lips 1949

This provocative poster, by René Gruau, reads "the red kiss." Color is confined to the lips; the contrast with the monochrome illustration makes a stunning impact.

Audrey Hepburn 1956

The gamine charm of Audrey Hepburn captured the imagination of movie audiences worldwide when she made her film debut in 1953. Her short hairstyle accentuated her fine features and her large, dark eyes, which were painted with black eyeliner. She wore pale lipstick, presaging the fashion of the 1960s, and her eyebrows were left unplucked.

Mary Quant 1970

To complement her fashion collection, in 1966 Mary Quant launched a line of cosmetics. The products were strikingly packaged in black and silver, with the famous daisy logo. The lipsticks shown here date from the 1990s, indicating the enduring popularity of Quant's products.

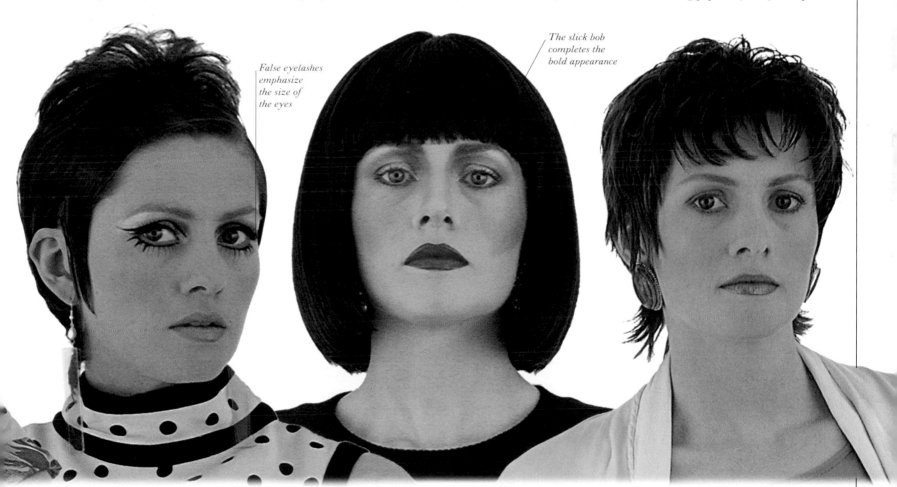

False eyelashes emphasize the size of the eyes

The slick bob completes the bold appearance

The cult of youth 1960s

During the 1960s, cosmetics manufacturers increasingly concentrated on the teenage consumer. Inspired by the Continental look, girls used pale pink or white lipstick and heavy eye makeup. Cosmetics that were quick and easy to use, such as powder compacts and mascara in tube rather than block form, were favored.

Career woman 1980s

A new type of urban professional emerged during the economic boom of the 1980s. This was reflected in cosmetic fashion by a more assertive look, with bold definition of facial features. Manufacturers stressed the longevity of their cosmetics to appeal to women too busy to reapply makeup throughout the day.

The natural look 1990s

Subtlety is the key to applying makeup in the 1990s. Artful application of cosmetics may give the impression of not actually wearing makeup at all. The names of cosmetics hint at the clinically tested ingredients and indicate a move away from the glamour of the early 20th century toward a purer aesthetic.

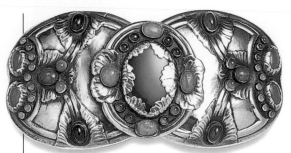

Buckle 1904

The Danish silversmith Georg Jensen was well known for the quality of his craftsmanship, and his impeccable standards are evident in this fine buckle. It is centered on a large piece of agate, which is surrounded by smaller, symmetrically positioned amber and peridot stones.

Specifications
Country: Denmark
Materials: Silver, green agate, amber, and peridot

Used in jewelry since the late 1700s, marcasite became fashionable again in the 1920s as a cheap substitute for diamonds

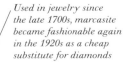

Bakelite was favored in the production of cheap souvenirs

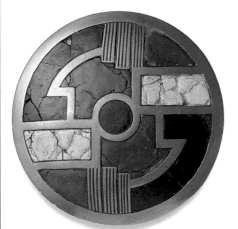

Art Deco brooch c.1925

This enameled piece demonstrates a key hallmark of Art Deco jewelry: geometric combinations of circular and angular blocks of solid color. The influences of Cubism and Fauvism are evident in the bold use of color and geometry.

Art Deco necklace c.1930

The success of this stunning Art Deco necklace lies in the subtle color combination of dulled silver and pale blue moonstones. Marcasite and semiprecious stones are used to create an inexpensive piece that would have been highly popular in the 1930s.

Specifications
Country: Germany
Materials: Silver, moonstones, and marcasite

Bakelite necklace 1936

Lightweight, mass-produced jewelry flourished in the 1930s and designers began to exploit the decorative qualities of Bakelite. The subject matter for such costume jewelry was often inspired by topical events. This necklace was made to commemorate the coronation of King George VI of England.

Specifications
Country: UK
Materials: Bakelite and metal

Specifications
Country: The Netherlands
Materials: Brass and enamel

JEWELRY

JEWELRY CAN BE DIVIDED into three basic groups: classic pieces in high-value metals or stones; paste and metal imitations, orginally produced for security reasons and later known as costume jewelry; and Art Jewelry, a category in which innovation takes precedence over value. The first two are as popular today as they have ever been, with designers using their skills to create subtly modern variations on classic themes. As attitudes toward women's fashions have relaxed, so limitations on jewelry design have been discarded, to the point where a necklace of beaten nails may be as celebrated as a string of pearls.

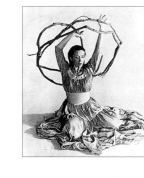

Martha Graham in a production of *Salem Shore*

Dancer brooch 1947

Ed Wiener modeled this brooch on a photograph of Martha Graham taken in 1941. She was a pillar of the modern dance movement and viewed dance as an organic structure – a philosophy reflected in Wiener's design. A biomorphic shape cut from sheet silver defines the body, dress, and right arm; one wire suggests the dancer's head and left arm, and another the skirt frill.

Specifications
Country: US
Material: Silver

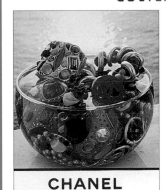

COSTUME JEWELRY

Coco Chanel is largely responsible for the development of costume jewelry as an art form in its own right, rather than as mere imitation. She scoffed at those who desired gems merely for monetary value, and designed "blatantly fake" jewelry of her own. In the 1920s and '30s, the outrageous and witty "jewels" designed and sported by Chanel and fellow couturier Elsa Schiaparelli helped popularize costume jewelry and pave the way for future designers.

CHANEL

26 OLD BOND STREET · LONDON W1 · · 26 SLOANE STREET · LONDON SW1

Advertisement, 1990s

The silver is molded to follow the natural contour of the neck

Silver and quartz neckring 1959

Designed by Vivianna Torun Bülow-Hübe in 1959 and made in 1967, this neckring typifies the simplicity of the Scandinavian approach to jewelry design. Its attraction lies in its unfussiness: an undecorated silver band supports a large quartz droplet.

Specifications
Country: Denmark
Materials: Silver and quartz

LOVE ring c.1966

The Pop artist Robert Indiana's ring is about as close as you can get to summing up the 1960s "Love and Peace" movement in one artifact. Indiana's LOVE motif, first shown in his one-man exhibition in 1962, was also used in a best-selling poster, and has appeared on 400 million US postage stamps.

Specifications
Country: US
Material: Gilded metal

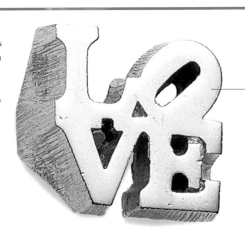

The "O" is positioned quirkily awry

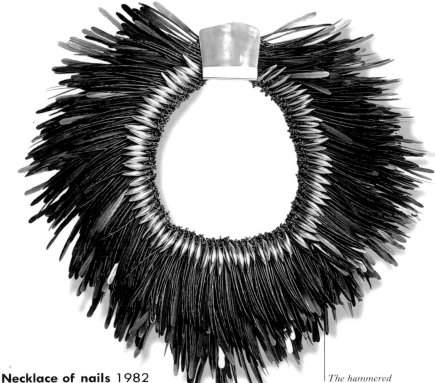

Necklace of nails 1982

At first glance, this extraordinary necklace by Oslo-born Tone Vigeland seems to be made of feathers; it is actually made of hammered steel nails. The nails have been used in such a way that their simplicity is retained while completely disguising their form.

The hammered nails resemble feathers

Specifications
Country: Norway
Materials: Steel, silver, gold, and mother of pearl

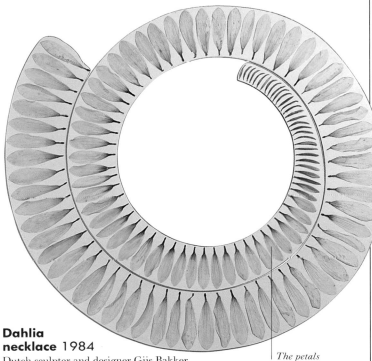

Dahlia necklace 1984

Dutch sculptor and designer Gijs Bakker describes his experimental jewelry as "wearable art." In this piece he has preserved dahlia petals in a flat ring of laminated plastic. His use of ephemeral materials represents a new approach to jewelry design — exploiting nature's intrinsic aesthetic qualities.

The petals diminish in size as they spiral inward

Specifications
Country: The Netherlands
Materials: Plastic and flower petals

LEISURE

Swimwear

Sports equipment

Cameras

Guitars

Jukeboxes

SWIMWEAR

EARLY BATHING COSTUMES were very modest garments, with women's ensembles not dissimilar to regular daywear. However, the adoption of elasticized and synthetic fabrics led to a succession of modifications, and swimsuits became progressively less restrictive – and more revealing. For men, the original one-piece suit was soon abbreviated to shorts. For women, the key innovation was the two-piece suit, launched in the 1940s as a result of US fabric rationing and christened the bikini.

FABRICS

Early in the century, impractical fabrics, such as serge, worsted, and flannel, were still used for bathing costumes. This loose-fitting cotton suit, for example, would have become heavy and uncomfortable when wet. Progress arrived in the form of a light, knitted jersey, which was superseded, in turn, by a new generation of elasticized and synthetic fabrics.

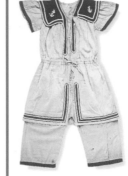

Bathing suit, 1902

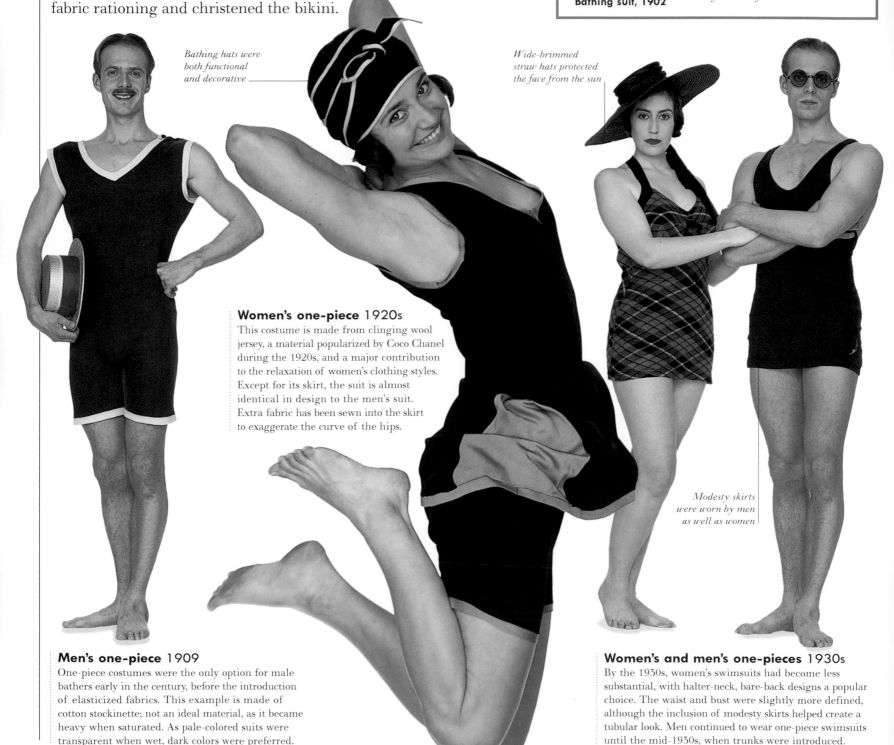

Bathing hats were both functional and decorative

Wide-brimmed straw hats protected the face from the sun

Women's one-piece 1920s
This costume is made from clinging wool jersey, a material popularized by Coco Chanel during the 1920s, and a major contribution to the relaxation of women's clothing styles. Except for its skirt, the suit is almost identical in design to the men's suit. Extra fabric has been sewn into the skirt to exaggerate the curve of the hips.

Modesty skirts were worn by men as well as women

Men's one-piece 1909
One-piece costumes were the only option for male bathers early in the century, before the introduction of elasticized fabrics. This example is made of cotton stockinette; not an ideal material, as it became heavy when saturated. As pale-colored suits were transparent when wet, dark colors were preferred.

Women's and men's one-pieces 1930s
By the 1930s, women's swimsuits had become less substantial, with halter-neck, bare-back designs a popular choice. The waist and bust were slightly more defined, although the inclusion of modesty skirts helped create a tubular look. Men continued to wear one-piece swimsuits until the mid-1930s, when trunks were introduced.

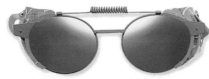

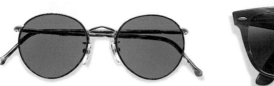

Oakley Jackets

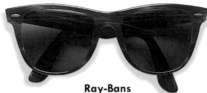

Swatch Snowbuck

Giorgio Armani

Ray-Bans

SUNGLASSES

Although they appeared as early as 1885, sunglasses were widely worn for the first time in the 1930s. Popularized by movie and music stars, their status as fashion accessories has become as great a consideration as the degree of protection they offer from the sun. The 1950s, in particular, witnessed an explosion in the number of frame designs available. The frames shown here are from the 1990s, a health-conscious decade that has seen the refinement of lens quality, with improved filters for ultraviolet light. With eyewear now a highly lucrative area of the fashion industry, many of the world's top designers, including Armani, Valentino, and Gaultier, have ascribed their name to sunglasses.

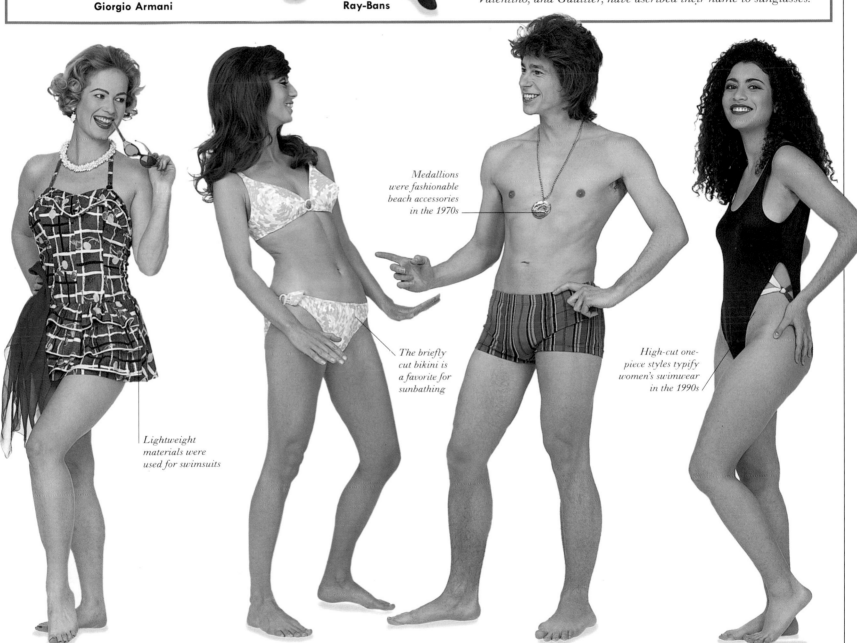

Medallions were fashionable beach accessories in the 1970s

The briefly cut bikini is a favorite for sunbathing

High-cut one-piece styles typify women's swimwear in the 1990s

Lightweight materials were used for swimsuits

Women's one-piece 1950s
With its boned bodice, this suit enhances the wearer's silhouette, emphasizing the bust and reducing the waist. A departure from the tubular style, the influence of Dior's New Look is unmistakable (see p.142).

Bikini 1960s
Pioneered by French couturiers Jacques Heim and Louis Reard in 1946, the bikini was named after Bikini Atoll, where the United States conducted atomic tests. The bikini reached its peak in popularity in the 1960s.

Trunks 1970s
Introduced in the 1930s, swimming trunks allowed men to swim with a bare torso. By the 1970s, tight-fitting, square-legged trunks such as these showcased new, brightly colored, drip-dry synthetic fabrics.

Women's one-piece 1990s
Lycra has made a valuable contribution to the revival of the one-piece swimsuit in the 1990s. Closely sculpted to the shape of the body, modern swimsuits are able to retain their shape perfectly even when wet.

SPORTS EQUIPMENT

THE MAJORITY OF THE SPORTS that we enjoy today have existed for centuries. "Real" tennis and soccer date from the Middle Ages, and American football was first played in the 19th century. The chief contribution to sports in the 20th century has been professionalism, which has brought with it a demand for lighter, stronger, and more flexible sports equipment. Today's professional athletes are now afforded greater precision, control, and protection from injury than ever before, with the combination of sophisticated materials and advanced engineering resulting in masterpieces of sports technology.

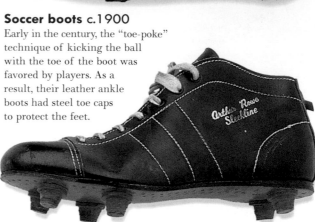

Soccer boots c.1900
Early in the century, the "toe-poke" technique of kicking the ball with the toe of the boot was favored by players. As a result, their leather ankle boots had steel toe caps to protect the feet.

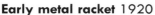

Fishtail tennis racket c.1900
In the early years of the century, with lawn tennis established as a popular sport, tennis racket frames less resembled the loosely strung, pear-shaped Real Tennis racket and now had a symmetrical head. To improve the grip, handles were grooved. Fishtail ends such as this were highly fashionable.

The broad wooden frame is heavy by modern standards

Soccer boots 1950
By the 1950s, soccer boots were lighter, at 1lb (500g) each, and more streamlined in style, with decorative stitching on the leather uppers. Shin pads were now worn inside rather than outside the socks.

Early metal racket 1920
Although most racket frames were made from a solid piece of ash, experiments began in the 1920s with aluminum racket heads that were strung with piano wire. This long-handled grip is made of bare wood, but others at this time were bound in leather to improve the grip.

Wool-covered tennis balls wore out quickly on the piano-wire strings

Soccer boots 1970
These vivid blue and yellow boots, designed by Adidas for the 1970 World Cup in Mexico, are streamlined, supple, and light. They were the first soccer boots with injected nylon soles, and feature removable screw-in studs.

Classic wooden racket 1950
By the 1950s, the wooden racket had reached a design peak, remaining largely unchanged for the next 20 years. The lightweight frame had reinforced shoulders and was laminated in various woods for extra durabilty. It was not until the 1970s that wood was seriously challenged by metal.

TRACK SHOES

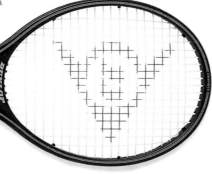

Athletes running in the ancient Greek games 4,000 years ago would have raced barefoot. Today, sprinters practically do run barefoot, so light, supple, and sculpted are modern track shoes, with their optimum cushioning and spiked soles for maximum grip. The Adidas shoe shown here, produced by the giant German sports manufacturer in 1949, was used to make the design application for the three-stripe trim, now instantly associated with the company's footwear and clothing.

Adidas track shoe, 1949

Graphite racket 1980
The lightweight metal rackets widely favored by professionals in the 1970s were soon rendered extinct by molded frames made from a combination of materials that included carbon graphite and fiberglass.

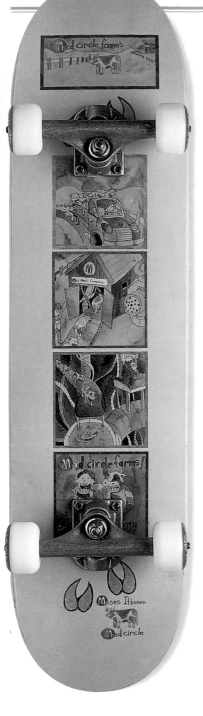

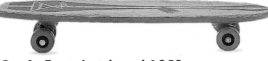

Goofy Foot skateboard 1950

Although skateboarding became hugely popular in the 1970s, the activity was invented in California in the 1950s as a kind of "street surfing." Then, it was a much gentler pastime, with clay-wheeled, flat wooden boards, like this one by Nash Manufacturing Inc., ridden much like scooters.

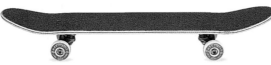

Mad Circle skateboard 1995

Modern skateboards curve upward at either end and feature coarse plastic grips on the upper surface to aid the spectacular leaps and stunts performed by many devotees. Made from Canadian maple, with polyurethane wheels, this Mad Circle board is painted on the underside with a colorful cartoon strip.

FOOTBALL

Helmet

Shoulder pads

The enormous amount of protective padding worn head to toe by football players is essential for this most physical of sports. In 1905, before the introduction of stringent clothing rules, 18 college players died from injuries due to inadequate protection. Those early boiled-leather helmets have now been replaced by helmets of the toughest plastic, with built-in shock absorbers.

The skate has a foam-padded inner boot with anatomical insoles

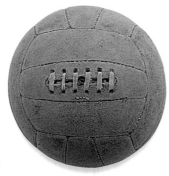

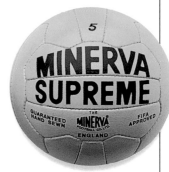

Soccer ball 1930s

Early leather balls were heavier and less waterproof than their modern counterparts. Simple stitching techniques meant that the final seam had to be laced up.

Soccer ball 1990

Stiff, strong, and durable, modern soccer balls are made from 18 panels of waterproof leather. The average weight is 14–16oz (400–450g).

State-of-the-art buckle closure systems replace traditional lacing

Rollerblades 1996

Those who have trundled leisurely around the park on heavy, leather-strapped metal roller skates would barely relate the high-tech modern in-line skates to those traditional "quads." In-line skates, like these by the US manufacturer Rollerblade, are closer in design to ice skates than roller skates. Rollerblades have excellent ankle support, shock-absorbing heel brakes, and "micro-closure" straps to ensure a snug fit. The outer boot and frame are molded from high-quality, lightweight polyurethane.

CAMERAS

THE EASTMAN KODAK box camera of 1888, with its preloaded roll film and widely advertised developing and printing service, opened up photography to the amateur. "You press the button, we do the rest," stated the advertisement. Various designs for small hand cameras existed from the early days of photography, but the Leica, introduced by Leitz optical works in Germany in 1924, had an enormous and lasting impact on camera design and 35mm photographic technique. The 35mm single lens reflex (SLR) camera was developed throughout the 1940s and '50s, attaining true popularity with the Nikon F in 1959. Modern cameras have integral light meters, auto focus, and use highly sensitive film – making the Kodak adage seem truer than ever.

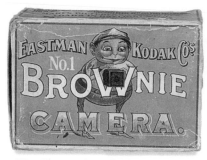
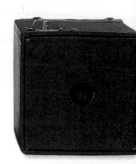

The Brownie 1900

In an attempt to sell more film, Eastman Kodak commissioned Frank Brownell to design a truly low-cost camera. The result was the hugely successful Brownie, a box camera made from the cheapest materials – cardboard and wood.

Specifications
Country: US
Width: 3¼in (8.5cm)

No. 2 Beau Brownie 1930

In 1926, Walter Dorwin Teague set up an industrial design consultancy. For Eastman Kodak, his first major client, he redesigned the Brownie, transforming it from a simple box into a sophisticated camera. He restyled the camera exterior with themes associated with Art Deco.

Specifications
Country: US
Width: 4¼in (10.5cm)

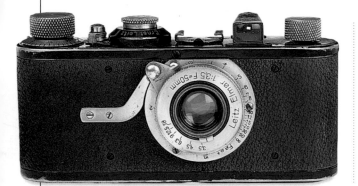

Leica 1A 1929

The Leica, designed by Oskar Barnack in 1913, was the first commercially successful 35mm camera. The Leica 1A, based on the earlier model, was put into production in the mid-1920s. The camera format has become the industry standard.

Specifications
Country: Germany
Width: 5¼in (13.4cm)

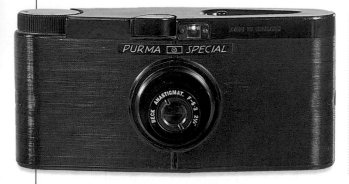

Purma Special 1937

Designed by Raymond Loewy and produced by R.F. Hunter Ltd., the Purma Special was made from black Bakelite and had a unique plastic lens. This cost less than the usual glass lens, so the camera could be retailed at a lower price.

Specifications
Country: UK
Width: 6in (15cm)

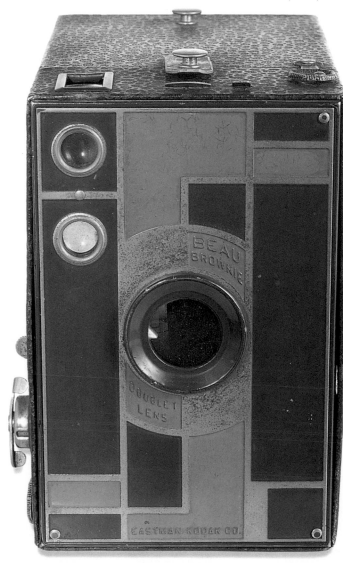

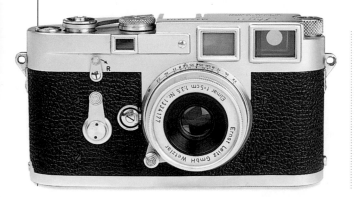

Leica M3 1954

First of a new generation of range finder cameras, the Leica M3 had a bayonet lens mount to facilitate faster lens changes. Although production of this model ceased in 1966, a phenomenal 250,000 cameras had been made since 1954.

Specifications
Country: Germany
Width: 5½in (14cm)

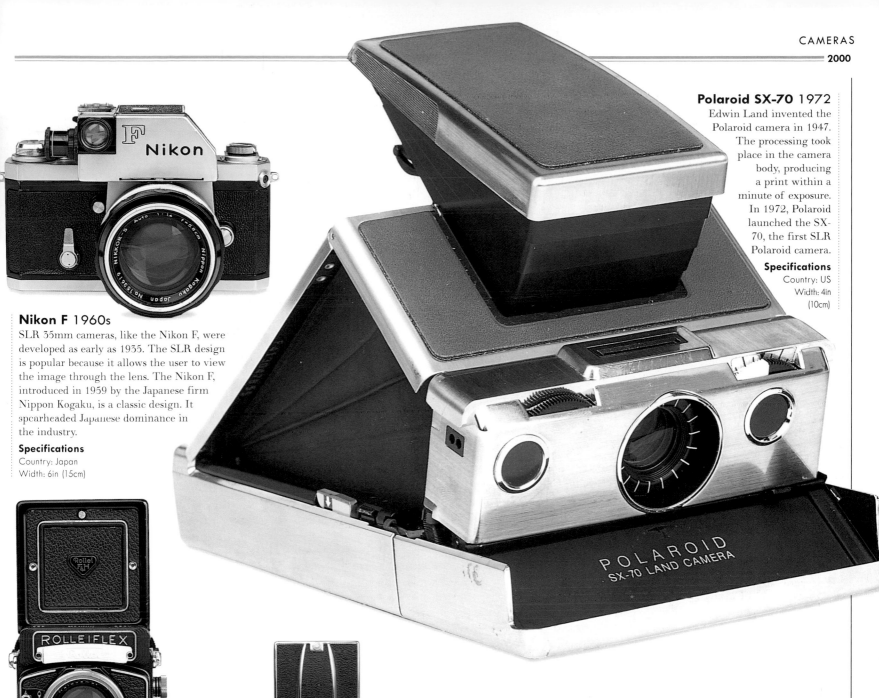

Nikon F 1960s

SLR 35mm cameras, like the Nikon F, were developed as early as 1935. The SLR design is popular because it allows the user to view the image through the lens. The Nikon F, introduced in 1959 by the Japanese firm Nippon Kogaku, is a classic design. It spearheaded Japanese dominance in the industry.

Specifications
Country: Japan
Width: 6in (15cm)

Polaroid SX-70 1972

Edwin Land invented the Polaroid camera in 1947. The processing took place in the camera body, producing a print within a minute of exposure. In 1972, Polaroid launched the SX-70, the first SLR Polaroid camera.

Specifications
Country: US
Width: 4in (10cm)

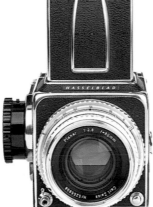

Rolleiflex 2.8F 1965

The twin-lens Rolleiflex is a bulky camera, with a mirror housing and viewing panel mounted above a roll-film box camera. It was favored by professionals because it could take medium-format film, which facilitates high-quality results.

Specifications
Country: Germany
Width: 4⅝in (11.5cm)

Hasselblad 500 1972

This roll-film SLR camera was produced by a firm set up by Victor Hasselblad in 1941 to make aerial cameras. Based on an earlier model designed by Sixten Sason, it is a celebrated professional camera.

Specifications
Country: Sweden
Width: 4⅛in (10.5cm)

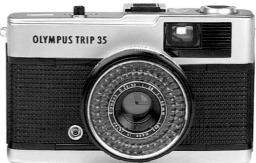

Olympus Trip 35 1968

Grandfather of the compact instamatic, the Olympus Trip 35 is a small, user-friendly camera. It was the first notable departure from the bulky forms of earlier 35mm SLR cameras

Specifications
Country: Japan
Width: 4¾in (11.8cm)

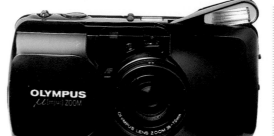

Olympus μ[mju:] Zoom 1993

Designed to slip into a jacket pocket, the stylish μ[mju:] has won many awards. When the sliding lens is closed, the camera is fully protected by its ultra-compact body.

Specifications
Country: Japan
Width: 4¾in (12cm)

GUITARS

ALTHOUGH THE CLASSIC ACOUSTIC VERSION is still widely strummed, it is the electric guitar that has stolen the limelight in this century, determining the evolution of the instrument's shape and sound. Introduced in the 1930s, the first electric guitars merely electrically amplified the acoustic guitar sound, but by the 1940s, solid-bodied guitars with a bright new sound were being designed. In 1950, the pioneering Leo Fender released the first mass-produced solid-body – the Broadcaster – then followed up its success with the legendary Stratocaster. Today, guitars are produced in innovative shapes and constructed of new materials, though rarely do these improve the sound.

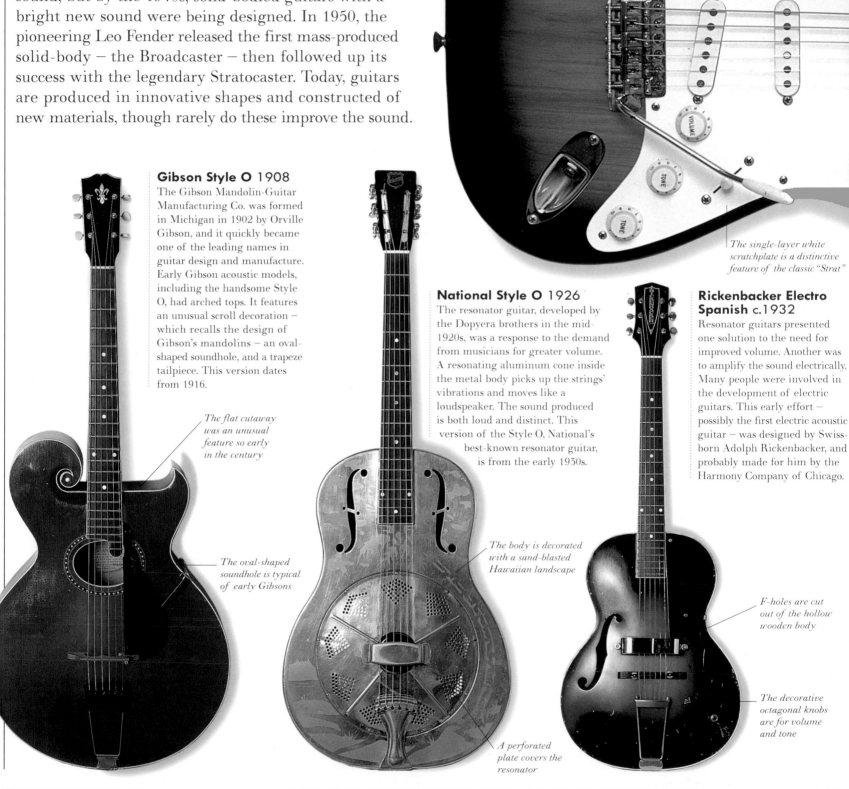

The single-layer white scratchplate is a distinctive feature of the classic "Strat"

Gibson Style O 1908

The Gibson Mandolin-Guitar Manufacturing Co. was formed in Michigan in 1902 by Orville Gibson, and it quickly became one of the leading names in guitar design and manufacture. Early Gibson acoustic models, including the handsome Style O, had arched tops. It features an unusual scroll decoration – which recalls the design of Gibson's mandolins – an oval-shaped soundhole, and a trapeze tailpiece. This version dates from 1916.

The flat cutaway was an unusual feature so early in the century

The oval-shaped soundhole is typical of early Gibsons

National Style O 1926

The resonator guitar, developed by the Dopyera brothers in the mid-1920s, was a response to the demand from musicians for greater volume. A resonating aluminum cone inside the metal body picks up the strings' vibrations and moves like a loudspeaker. The sound produced is both loud and distinct. This version of the Style O, National's best-known resonator guitar, is from the early 1930s.

The body is decorated with a sand-blasted Hawaiian landscape

A perforated plate covers the resonator

Rickenbacker Electro Spanish c.1932

Resonator guitars presented one solution to the need for improved volume. Another was to amplify the sound electrically. Many people were involved in the development of electric guitars. This early effort – possibly the first electric acoustic guitar – was designed by Swiss-born Adolph Rickenbacker, and probably made for him by the Harmony Company of Chicago.

F-holes are cut out of the hollow wooden body

The decorative octagonal knobs are for volume and tone

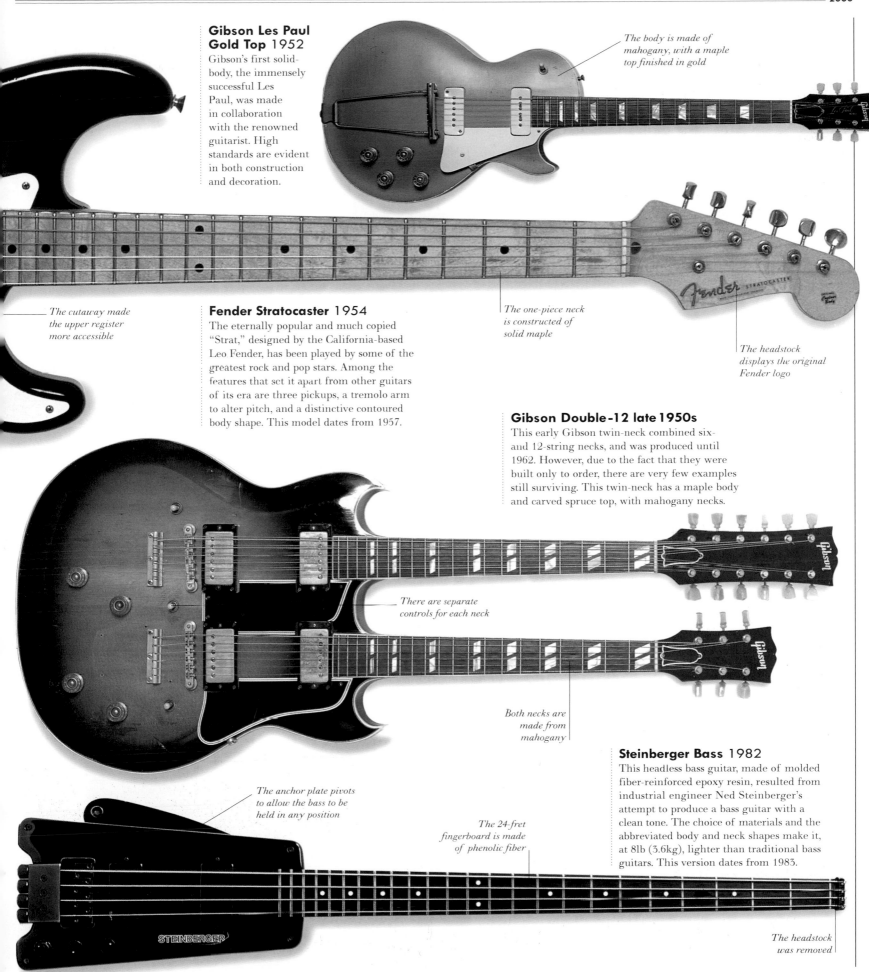

Gibson Les Paul Gold Top 1952

Gibson's first solid-body, the immensely successful Les Paul, was made in collaboration with the renowned guitarist. High standards are evident in both construction and decoration.

The body is made of mahogany, with a maple top finished in gold

The cutaway made the upper register more accessible

Fender Stratocaster 1954

The eternally popular and much copied "Strat," designed by the California-based Leo Fender, has been played by some of the greatest rock and pop stars. Among the features that set it apart from other guitars of its era are three pickups, a tremolo arm to alter pitch, and a distinctive contoured body shape. This model dates from 1957.

The one-piece neck is constructed of solid maple

The headstock displays the original Fender logo

Gibson Double-12 late 1950s

This early Gibson twin-neck combined six- and 12-string necks, and was produced until 1962. However, due to the fact that they were built only to order, there are very few examples still surviving. This twin-neck has a maple body and carved spruce top, with mahogany necks.

There are separate controls for each neck

Both necks are made from mahogany

Steinberger Bass 1982

This headless bass guitar, made of molded fiber-reinforced epoxy resin, resulted from industrial engineer Ned Steinberger's attempt to produce a bass guitar with a clean tone. The choice of materials and the abbreviated body and neck shapes make it, at 8lb (3.6kg), lighter than traditional bass guitars. This version dates from 1983.

The anchor plate pivots to allow the bass to be held in any position

The 24-fret fingerboard is made of phenolic fiber

The headstock was removed

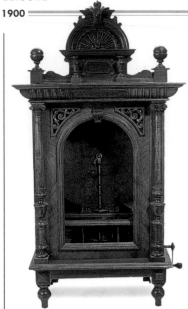

JUKEBOXES

COIN-IN-THE-SLOT MUSIC MACHINES were already well established by the time the Golden Age of the jukebox dawned in the 1940s. While designers of this era, such as Paul Fuller, are particularly revered, design aficionados are beginning to pay closer attention to the two decades that followed. The machines of the rock 'n' roll era scream teenage rebellion with their blatant use of flashy automobile looks. The bold, bright colors of these classics are probably the first thing to cross most people's minds on hearing the word "jukebox."

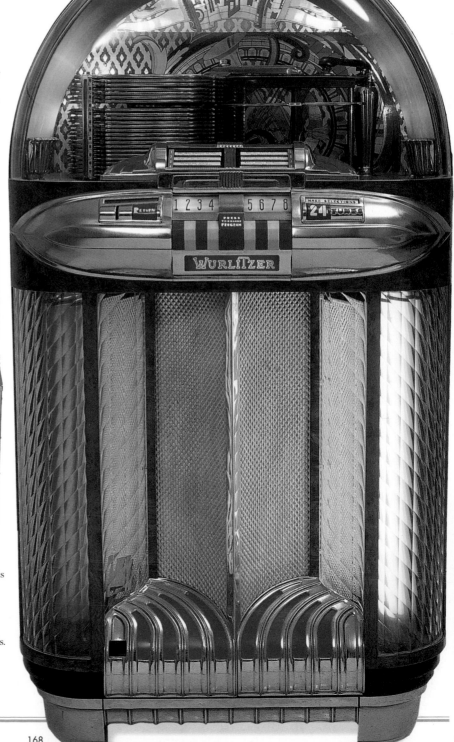

Polyphon c.1900

This wooden, turn-of-the-century coin-in-the-slot machine does not play records – they did not exist – but plays large metal disks with "pins" on. The pins pluck the tuned teeth of a comblike metal plate, as in a music box. This machine must be fully wound before it will play.

Specifications
Country: Germany
Height: 51in (130cm)
Number of selections: 1

Wurlitzer 1100 1948

Paul Fuller is generally considered to be the genius of jukebox design, and the incredible Wurlitzer 1100 was his last jukebox model. It plays from a selection of 78rpm records – seven-inch 45s were still two years away – although the revolving selection display shows only eight at any one time.

Specifications
Country: US
Height: 57in (145cm)
Number of selections: 24

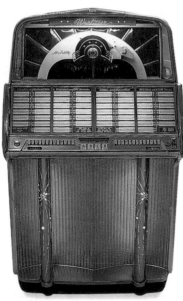

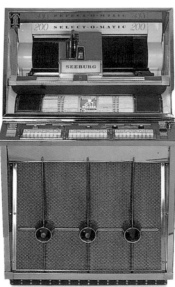

Wurlitzer 1800 1955

At first glance, the design of this jukebox may seem rather muted. However, the colors, the lights, and the generous use of chrome combine to make this machine aesthetically pleasing. In addition, the user has a far greater choice of music than before.

Specifications
Country: US
Height: 53in (135cm)
Number of selections: 104

Seeburg KD200 1957

One quirk of Seeburg jukeboxes is that they play records vertically; this requires only one motor instead of three. The distinctive fins on the front are based on the tail fins and lights of 1950s American cars. The KD200 plays seven-inch vinyl records.

Specifications
Country: US
Height: 58in (147cm)
Number of selections: 200

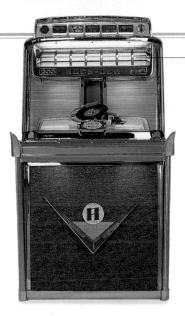

Revolving-drum selection display

AMi Continental 2 1961

This 200 selection stereo machine by AMi (Automatic Musical Instruments) is of particular interest because of its domed glass top. AMi was one of only two jukebox manufacturers ever to do this – the other was UK-based Chantal – because it was very expensive to produce. The design also makes extensive use of the word "stereo." Sharp-eyed viewers of the 1990 Patrick Swayze movie *Ghost* may recognize this machine.

Specifications
Country: US
Height: 64in (162cm)
Number of selections: 200

This stereo machine's curved display represents its "all-around" sound

Rock-Ola Tempo 1475 1959

Many jukeboxes of this era were based on the back ends of US cars, and the very rare Rock-Ola Tempo is no exception. Tailfins make another appearance, though far more subtly than in the case of the Seeburg KD200, and the V-shaped logo on the front of the machine is similar to many automobile logos. Note the revolving-drum selection display at the top of the machine.

Specifications
Country: US
Height: 59in (150cm)
Number of selections: 200

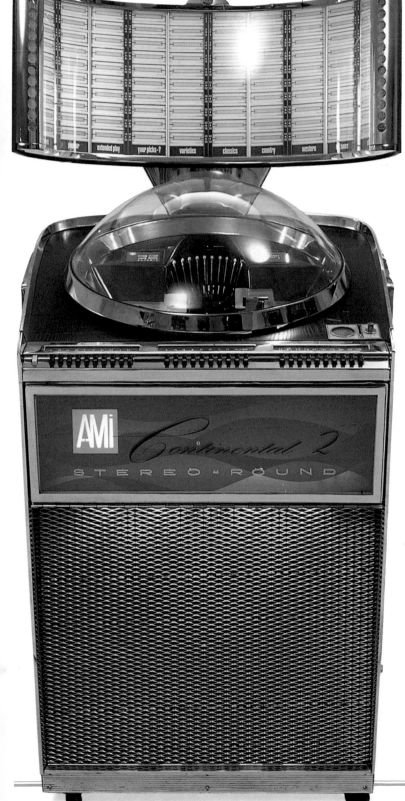

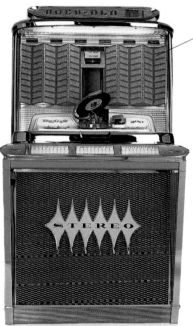

All 200 possible selections are visible at the same time

Rock-Ola Regis 1495 1961

Stereo jukeboxes first appeared in 1959, and one of the most instantly striking design features about the Rock-Ola Regis is the bold emblazoning of the word "stereo" across its front, ensuring that everyone will be well aware of this fact. Another point of interest is the use of pastels in its pink-and-blue color scheme.

Specifications
Country: US
Height: 59in (150cm)
Number of selections: 200

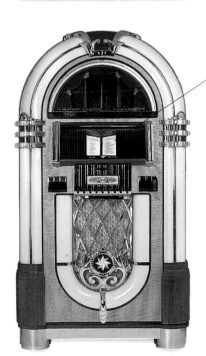

Just one-fiftieth of this jukebox's contents can be viewed at a time

NSM Nostalgia Gold 1995

This machine's design is based on Paul Fuller's 1946 Wurlitzer 1015, the most popular jukebox ever: during 1946 and 1947 Wurlitzer built 56,000 of them. The original would have held twelve 78rpm records, but this replica can accommodate up to 100 compact discs. It would actually be possible to listen to this jukebox for more than five days and nights without hearing the same track twice.

Specifications
Country: Germany
Height: 61in (155cm)
Number of selections: Up to 2,500 (approx.)

TRANSPORTATION

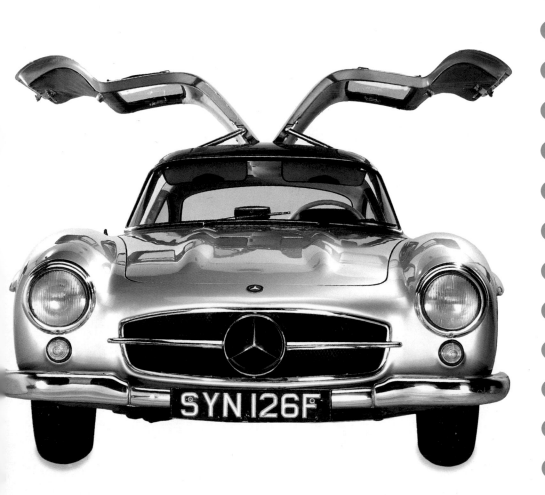

BICYCLES

SINCE THE APPEARANCE of the first "safety" bicycles in the 1870s, a remarkable—and enormously popular—form of transportation has emerged. The modern machine is not only lightweight, strong, and fast, but also easy to ride, comfortable, and safe. Various models have been designed to meet specific market demands: for instance, in the 1900s, versions without high crossbars were introduced to suit women riders, and increasingly aerodynamic models have been developed for the highly competitive sport of bicycle racing. At the end of the century, lighter, more durable materials, such as titanium and carbon fiber, are frequently favored over traditional materials like steel.

Ladies' Humber 1905

By the time the Ladies' Humber was introduced, the key features of the modern bicycle were well established. Instead of the diamond-shaped frame of men's bicycles, the ladies' had an open frame. This catered to the long dresses worn at the time, as illustrated in this poster.

Specifications
Country: UK
Wheel diameter: 28in (71cm)
Material: High-tensile steel

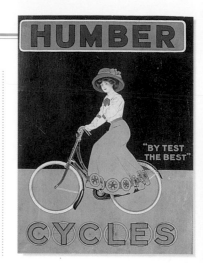

Windcheetah Monocoque c.1986

The essence of this racing bike's prodigious speed is in its streamlined monocoque frame. A single-fork front wheel blade, together with the small front wheel and gull-wing handlebars, make it unusually aerodynamic. The single-body frame meant that the Windcheetah was originally disqualified from official races by the sport's governing body, a ban that was enforced for five years. Built by Mike Burrows, the bike is constructed of carbon fiber, a material as stiff as steel.

Specifications
Country: UK
Front wheel diameter: 24in (61cm)
Material: Carbon fiber

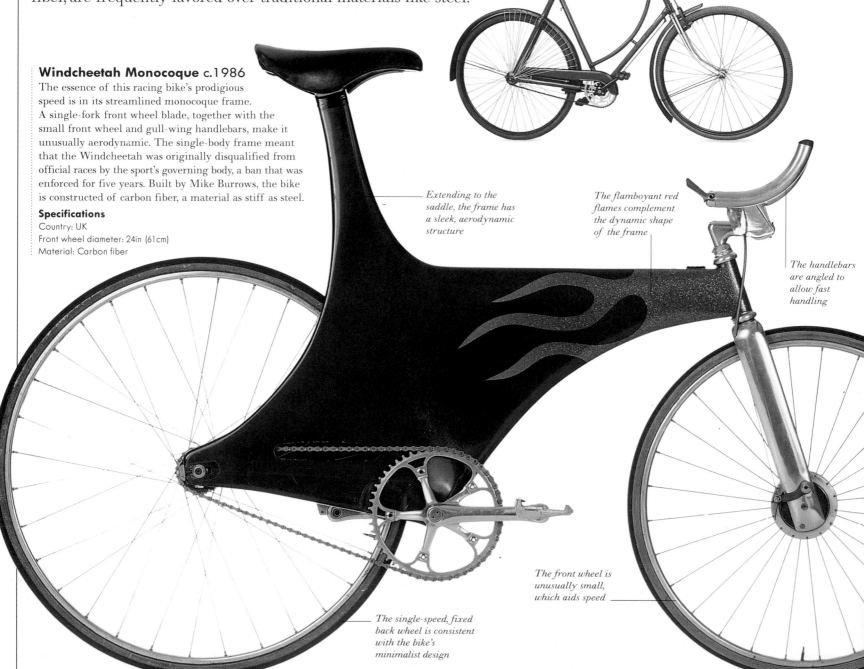

Extending to the saddle, the frame has a sleek, aerodynamic structure

The flamboyant red flames complement the dynamic shape of the frame

The handlebars are angled to allow fast handling

The front wheel is unusually small, which aids speed

The single-speed, fixed back wheel is consistent with the bike's minimalist design

The saddle can be raised above the height of the handlebars

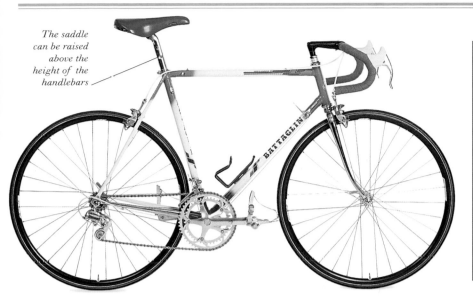

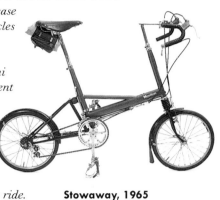

COLLAPSIBLE BICYCLES

For their portability and ease of storage, foldaway bicycles are often favored. Alex Moulton, who worked on the suspension of the Mini in the 1950s (see p.185), went on to design this compact collapsible bicycle. The innovative rubber suspension on both front and back wheels made the bike easy to handle and comfortable to ride.

Stowaway, 1965

Battaglin 1980s

The development of racing bikes, such as this Italian model by Battaglin, saw the introduction of drop handlebars, which reduced body-created wind resistance. The "aero-tuck" body position was further exaggerated by the high placement of the saddle, which is favored by racers.

Specifications
Country: Italy
Wheel diameter: Not known
Material: High-tensile steel

At 2½in (6.3cm) wide, these tires provide good grip even in difficult conditions

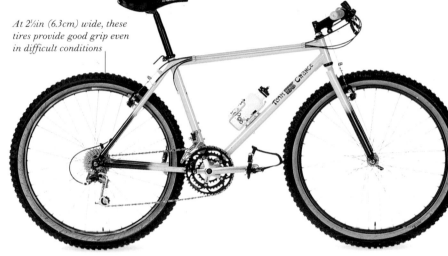

An aluminum frame forms the structure of this bike

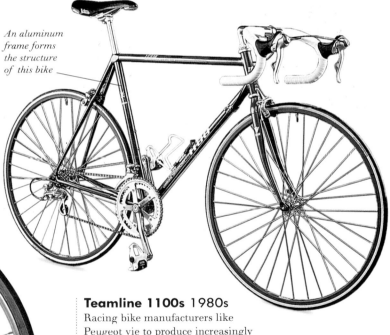

Fat Chance "Yo Eddy" off-road racer 1989

Developed in California by Charlie Kelly and Gary Fisher during the 1970s, mountain bikes have opened up a new experience for cyclists. This model has been refined from the early prototypes, which weighed less than 26lb (12kg).

Specifications
Country: US
Wheel diameter: 26in (66cm)
Material: High-tensile steel

Teamline 1100s 1980s

Racing bike manufacturers like Peugeot vie to produce increasingly lightweight bicycle frames. In the 1970s, versatile, lightweight alloy steels were developed, followed by aluminum tubing in the 1980s.

Specifications
Country: France
Wheel diameter: 26in (66cm)
Material: Carbon fiber

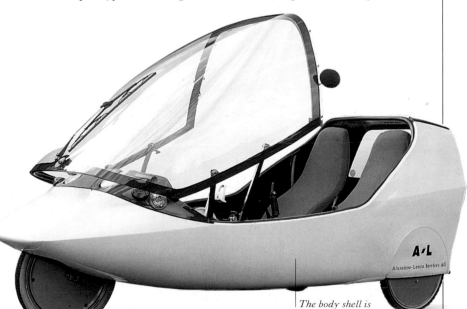

Sociable Tandem 1992

This motor-assisted, three-wheeled recumbent bicycle can accommodate two riders. Using pedals alone, it can reach up to 19mph (30km/h), but with assistance from the electric motor, it can travel over twice as fast.

Specifications
Country: Switzerland
Front wheel diameter: 20in (51cm)
Materials: Fiberglass and aluminum

The body shell is made of fiberglass

SCOOTERS

YOUNG ITALIANS DODGING TRAFFIC through the backstreets of Rome, 1960s "Mods" driving in gangs to British coastal resorts: scooters are synonymous with European street style and youth culture. The machines traditionally favored by both groups are the Italian classics Vespa and Lambretta. These elegant, streamlined machines are notable for their rounded body panels, as opposed to the largely angular bodywork of non-European scooters such as those built by the American company Cushman. Scooters have been popular since the 1920s, when they were little different from the children's toy version. Since then, there have been a bewildering array of these cheap, lightweight, easy-to-ride motorcycles, the two common factors being the small wheels and step-through frame.

Lambretta LD150 1957

Lambretta was the main challenger to Vespa in the 1950s and '60s, and the Lambretta LD150 sold in enormous quantities. It had easily removable engine and gearbox covers, two separate seats, and carried a spare wheel. Like the Vespa, it was rounded in styling, compared with its angular American cousins. The first Lambrettas were built in 1947, and production ended in Italy in the 1970s.

Specifications
Country: Italy
Top speed: 50mph (80.5km/h)

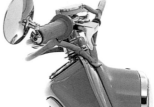

The leg shields were first offered as an option, but became standard

The pressed-steel body panels were mounted on a tubular-spine frame

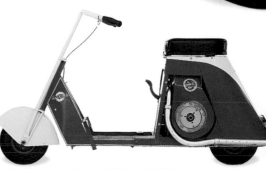

Autoped 1915

Built in the US from 1915 to 1921, the Autoped's key assets were its size and portability. Starkly utilitarian, it was designed to be ridden standing up, with a pressed-steel footplate. The long column for the handlebars can be folded down flat for storage.

Specifications
Country: US
Top speed: 20mph (32km/h) (estimated)

ABC Skootamota 1919

Much in demand after World War I, the British-designed ABC Skootamota had one great advantage over the Autoped: a seat. Designed by Granville Bradshaw, the machine featured the step-through frame that has defined the look of the scooter ever since.

Specifications
Country: UK
Top speed: 25mph (40km/h)

Cushman Auto-Glide 1937

Cushman produced a remarkable range of outlandish scooters in the middle decades of the century. The angular Auto-Glide is the epitome of simplicity in vehicle design: it has neither suspension nor gearbox, and the engine is a simple industrial power unit.

Specifications
Country: US
Top speed: 30mph (48km/h) (estimated)

SCOOTERS AND STREET STYLE

Although originally popularized as a cheap and convenient form of transportation in the postwar era, by the 1960s the scooter had been adopted by young people as a fashion accessory. Members of the British Mod cult rode en masse on customized Vespas or Lambrettas to coastal resorts, where they invariably clashed with rival Rocker gangs.

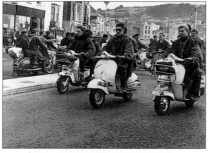

Mods in Hastings, England

Vespa Grand Sport 160 1963

The Vespa (Italian for "wasp" and so named for its buzzing exhaust note) is the most famous of all scooters. It was designed in 1946 by Corradino d'Ascanio, whose previous involvement in aircraft design is clearly evident. It has a waisted rear and a rounded pressed-steel monocoque chassis. One of the most attractive scooters built was the Vespa Grand Sport (GS) 160 Mark 1, considered by many aficionados to be the best Vespa ever designed.

Specifications
Country: Italy
Top speed: 62mph (100km/h)

The rider-friendly build of the GS included a leather dual seat designed for maximum comfort

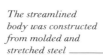

The GS featured a distinctive waisted rear

The streamlined body was constructed from molded and stretched steel

Cushman 32 Auto-Glide 1945

This 32 model first appeared in 1945. Unlike its predecessor, it had lights, "Floating Drive" suspension, and an automatic clutch and transmission system. Designed for convenience, it had a large storage compartment behind the seat for baggage.

Specifications
Country: US
Top speed: Not known

Indian Papoose 1948

The famous American motorbike manufacturer Indian gave its name to a small British scooter originally designed as a folding bike for paratroopers in World War II. The Papoose included a retracting saddle column, which allowed the handlebars to be folded down flat.

Specifications
Country: US
Top speed: 35mph (56km/h) (estimated)

Simplex Scooter 1958

Although it never challenged market leader Cushman, Simplex took advantage of the 1950s scooter boom by introducing this version of its Servi-Cycle. The characteristic clean, straight lines of the American scooter are typified by the simple, tubular steel frame.

Specifications
Country: US
Top speed: 45mph (72km/h)

MOTORCYCLES

THE FIRST MOTORCYCLES were introduced toward the end of the 19th century. With chassis based on the newly developed safety bicycles (see pp.172–73), they lacked power, were difficult to ride, and had inadequate lights and brakes. It was not until the Werner brothers produced their motorcycle of 1901, with its advanced braking system and electronic ignition, that practical motorcycling became possible. Thirty-five years later, Harley-Davidson produced the 61E, a motorcycle that demonstrates just how rapidly technology, performance, and style have evolved. Throughout the century, there have been a remarkable array of weird and wonderful designs. Designers continue to exploit the latest materials and technology to enhance performance and provide a safe ride.

The radical styling is typified by the rounded oil tank wrapped around the battery

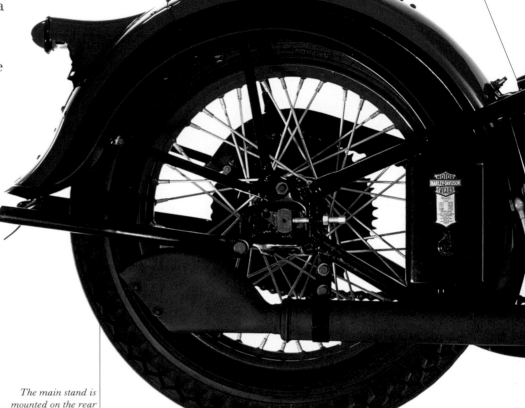

A MOTORCYCLE FOR THREE

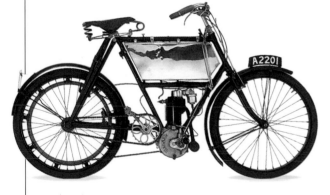

Böhmerland, 1925

The red-and-yellow color scheme and enormously long wheelbase combine to make the Czechoslovakian Böhmerland one of the most bizarre motorcycles ever built. It was created by Albin Liebisch in 1925 (this model is from 1927), and remained in production until 1939, the design changing little over the years.

The main stand is mounted on the rear of the frame

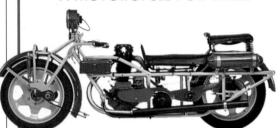

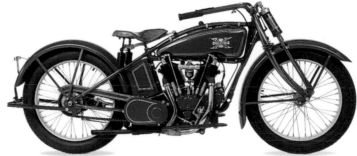

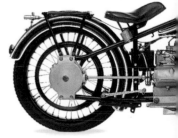

Werner 1901

In 1897, the French brothers Werner made the first motorbike to be sold in significant numbers. The 1901 Werner was one of the first bikes to move from a "bicycle-plus-engine" design to a more integrated look – in some ways, the first "real" motorcycle.

Specifications
Country: France
Top speed: 20mph (32km/h)
Weight: Not known

Excelsior 20R 1912

Until it collapsed in 1931, Excelsior was one of the big three American manufacturers, with Harley-Davidson and Indian. The first bike to break the 100mph (161km/h) barrier, the 20R had a 1,000cc engine. It featured the long, upright handlebars that were prevalent in the US until the 1920s.

Specifications
Country: US
Top speed: 100mph (161km/h)
Weight: 500lb (227kg)

BMW R32 1923

Created by aircraft designer Max Friz, the first BMW was an astonishing leap forward in motorbike design: its 500cc engine was fitted into the frame so that the cylinders were cooled by the air.

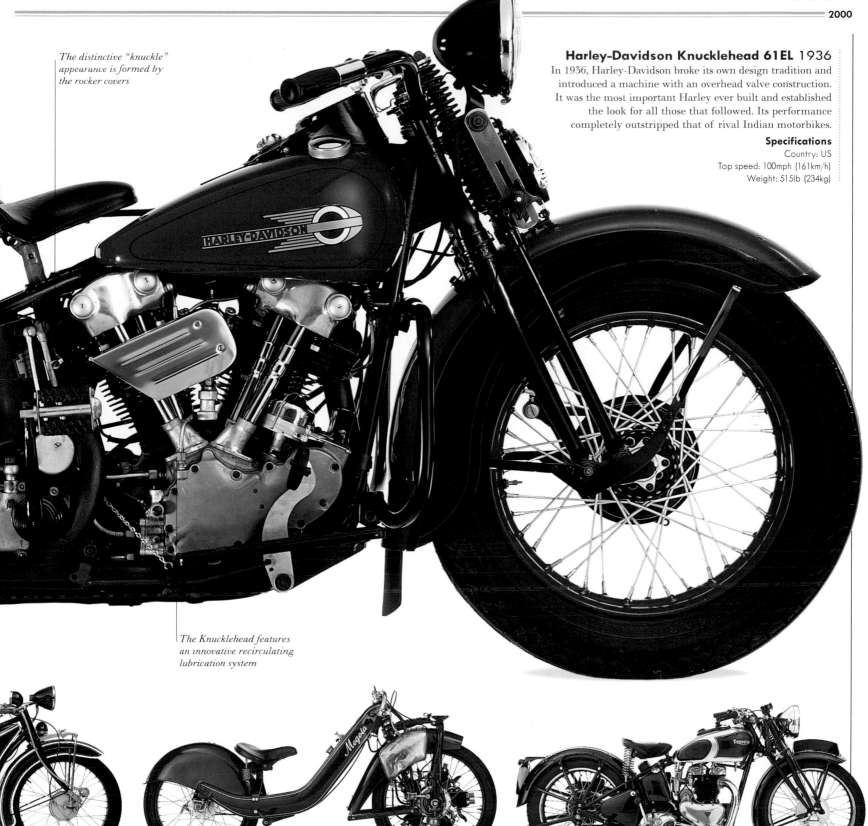

The distinctive "knuckle" appearance is formed by the rocker covers

Harley-Davidson Knucklehead 61EL 1936

In 1936, Harley-Davidson broke its own design tradition and introduced a machine with an overhead valve construction. It was the most important Harley ever built and established the look for all those that followed. Its performance completely outstripped that of rival Indian motorbikes.

Specifications
Country: US
Top speed: 100mph (161km/h)
Weight: 515lb (234kg)

The Knucklehead features an innovative recirculating lubrication system

Megola Racing Model 1923

The Megola rivals the Böhmerland as one of the most unconventional motorbike designs ever. Designer Fritz Cockerell's five-cylinder side-valve radial engine was mounted within the front wheel; as the wheel turned forward once, the engine turned six times in the opposite direction.

Specifications
Country: Germany
Top speed: 53mph (85km/h)
Weight: 269lb (122kg)

Specifications
Country: Germany
Top speed: Not known
Weight: Not known

Triumph Speed Twin 1939

Designed by Edward Turner with speed in mind, the Speed Twin's lines are elegant from any angle. The model formed the basis of Triumph's big bike line for the next 40 years. Turner was also responsible for adapting Triumphs for the American market in the 1950s.

Specifications
Country: UK
Top speed: 93mph (150km/h)
Weight: 378lb (171kg)

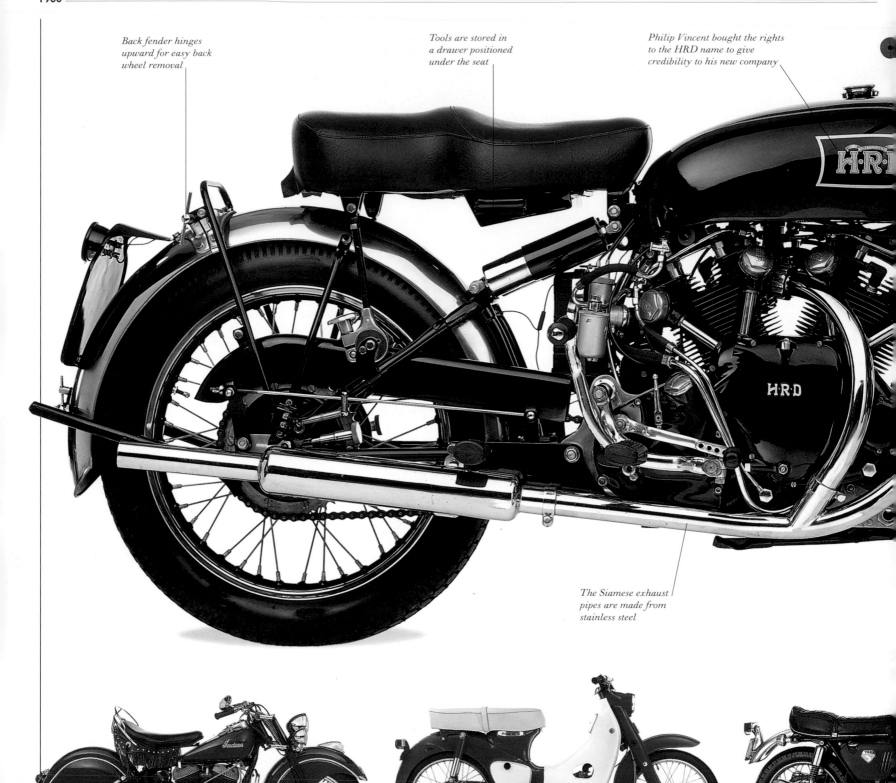

Back fender hinges upward for easy back wheel removal

Tools are stored in a drawer positioned under the seat

Philip Vincent bought the rights to the HRD name to give credibility to his new company

The Siamese exhaust pipes are made from stainless steel

Indian Chief 1947

Built for comfort not speed, the Chiefs were stylish machines that reached their peak with this 1947 design. Valanced fenders and elegant girder forks combined with the sprung leather saddle and chrome-plated details to give an air of streamlined luxury.

Specifications
Country: US
Top speed: 85mph (137km/h)
Weight: 550lb (249kg)

Honda 50 Super Cub 1958

Originally designed as a basic, cheap form of transportation, the ubiquitous Cub is the most successful bike ever made, with sales in excess of 21 million. It was among the first machines to make extensive use of plastic, in the form of the front fender, the side panels, and the leg shields.

Specifications
Country: Japan
Top speed: 43mph (70km/h)
Weight: 143lb (65kg)

Honda CB750 1969

The CB750 launched the era of the Superbike, combining disc brake, five-speed gearbox, electric starter, four-cylinder engine, and 124mph (200km/h) performance all in one powerful machine.

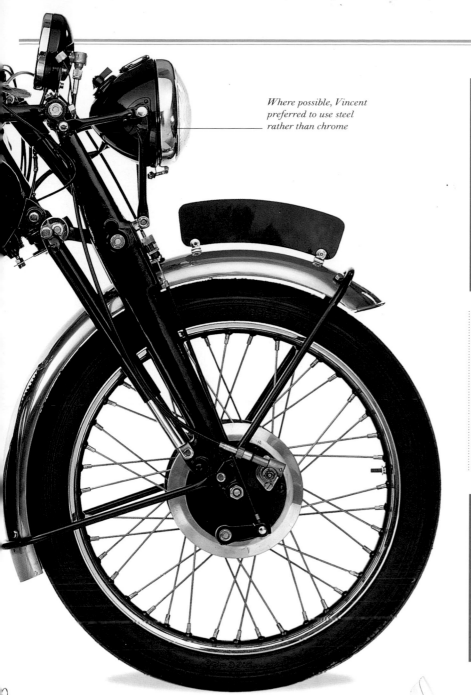

Where possible, Vincent preferred to use steel rather than chrome

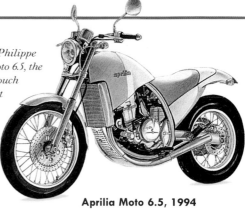

STARCK STYLE

When Aprilia invited Philippe Starck to design the Moto 6.5, the designer's distinctive touch was not compromised at all. His style is evident in both the overall form of the bike and in the details, such as the graphics and paint job. The top speed is 100mph (161km/h).

Aprilia Moto 6.5, 1994

Vincent Black Shadow Series C 1949

In 1949, when the first Vincent C-series Black Shadow was introduced, it was the fastest and the classiest bike in the world. The black bodywork continued in the baked-on black 998cc engine, and the fenders were made in stainless steel, with stainless steel and chrome engine details and exhaust pipes. The Shadow had an oversized speedometer, emphasizing its impressive top speed of 125mph (201km/h).

Specifications
Country: UK
Top speed: 125mph (201km/h)
Weight: 458lb (208kg)

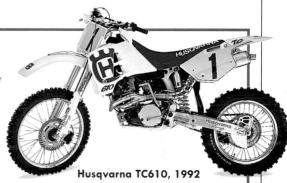

MOTOCROSS

Light, strong bikes with good suspension are required for the grueling sport of motocross, which began as "scrambling" in 1920s Britain. The knobby tires increase grip in muddy conditions.

Husqvarna TC610, 1992

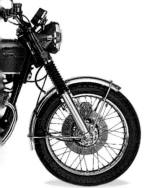

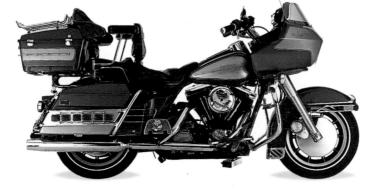

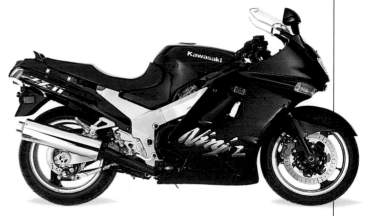

Harley-Davidson Evolution FLTC Tour Glide Classic 1989

In direct competition with Honda's massive Goldwing, the Tour Glide rejected the retro styling of previous Glides. Comfort was the main design objective, with footboards for the rider and armrests and backrests for the passenger.

Kawasaki ZZ-R1100 1990

Everything about the ZZ-R is big, from its top speed of 175mph (282km/h) to its enormous twin front brake discs. Aerodynamic styling (the tank is sculpted to fit the rider's legs snugly) and superb power delivery made the ZZ-R the fastest bike of its day. This model is from 1994.

Specifications
Country: Japan
Top speed: 124mph (200km/h)
Weight: 485lb (220kg)

Specifications
Country: US
Top speed: 110mph (177km/h) (estimated)
Weight: 732lb (332kg)

Specifications
Country: Japan
Top speed: 175mph (282km/h)
Weight: 513lb (233kg)

CARS

FEW THINGS MAP the development of design in this century better than the car. In 1900, cars were just beginning to shed their "horseless carriage" look, yet, by 1915, all of the basic design features of the modern car were already in place. All that remained was for cars to get bigger, smaller, safer, more beautiful, more bizarre, and, of course, faster. At the end of the century, there are nearly one billion cars on the road, including some lovingly restored early models. The history of car design encompasses a vast array of cars: sports cars such as Jaguar's E-type (see p.186); family cars, like Renault's Espace (see p.189); city cars, such as the Fiat 500 (see p.184); outlandish cars such as the 1959 Cadillac Eldorado (see pp.184–85); and supercars like the Lamborghini Miura (see p.186).

1920s RACING MACHINE

Widely regarded as one of the most beautiful motoring creations of the century, this superb racing car by Ettore Bugatti (1882–1947) tapers elegantly at both front and back, the widest point being the two-seat cockpit. Distinctive features include the criss-crossed piano wire cast that braces the car's body and the alloy wheels with integral brake drums. The car has a powerful eight-cylinder engine, which, combined with the four-speed gearbox, took the car up to speeds of 120mph (193km/h).

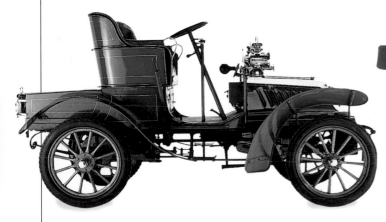

Bugatti Type 35, 1924

Rolls Royce 40/50 1907

In 1907, when Rolls Royce launched the 40/50, or "Silver Ghost" as it became known, it described the model as "the best car in the world." Emphasis was placed on mechanical precision and craftsmanship rather than innovation. The winged figurehead, known as the "spirit of ecstasy," was designed by Charles Sykes and first graced the top of a Rolls-Royce radiator in 1911.

Specifications
Country: UK
Top speed: 55mph (88km/h)

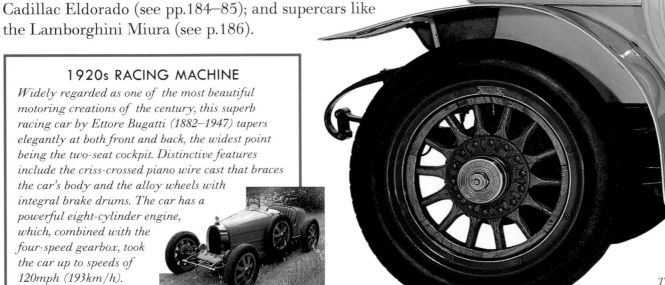

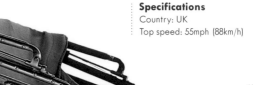

The Ghost has a low-slung "slipper" body

De Dion-Bouton Model Q 1903

The key to the Model Q's success was its powerful 846cc gas engine. De Dion's revolutionary engine design was used in over 100 makes of car from 1898 to 1908, and helped launch companies such as Renault.

Specifications
Country: France
Top speed: Not known

Model T Ford 1908

This was the first car to be mass-produced, with over 15 million made. The car's minimalist design, the use of standardized parts, and new production techniques kept costs down. By the 1920s, every second car on the world's roads was a Model T Ford.

Specifications
Country: US
Top speed: 42mph (68km/h)

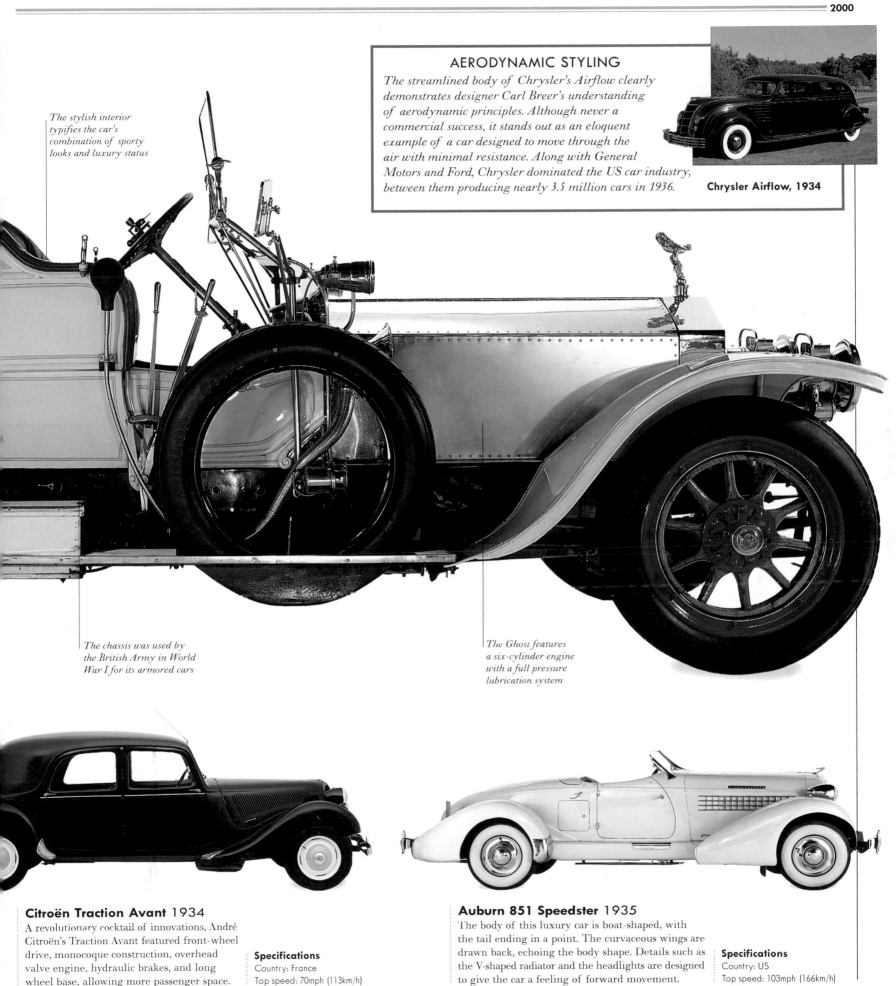

AERODYNAMIC STYLING

The streamlined body of Chrysler's Airflow clearly demonstrates designer Carl Breer's understanding of aerodynamic principles. Although never a commercial success, it stands out as an eloquent example of a car designed to move through the air with minimal resistance. Along with General Motors and Ford, Chrysler dominated the US car industry, between them producing nearly 3.5 million cars in 1936.

Chrysler Airflow, 1934

The stylish interior typifies the car's combination of sporty looks and luxury status

The chassis was used by the British Army in World War I for its armored cars

The Ghost features a six-cylinder engine with a full pressure lubrication system

Citroën Traction Avant 1934

A revolutionary cocktail of innovations, André Citroën's Traction Avant featured front-wheel drive, monocoque construction, overhead valve engine, hydraulic brakes, and long wheel base, allowing more passenger space.

Specifications
Country: France
Top speed: 70mph (113km/h)

Auburn 851 Speedster 1935

The body of this luxury car is boat-shaped, with the tail ending in a point. The curvaceous wings are drawn back, echoing the body shape. Details such as the V-shaped radiator and the headlights are designed to give the car a feeling of forward movement.

Specifications
Country: US
Top speed: 103mph (166km/h)

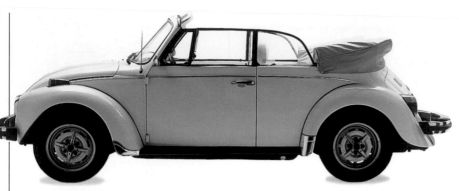

Volkswagen Beetle 1939

In 1973, the Beetle became the best-selling car ever produced. The work of Ferdinand Porsche, it originated in Germany and attracted the attention of Adolf Hitler, who gave the project his personal support. Since the Beetle went into full production in 1945, there have been more than 78,000 design modifications – all of them minor. The Karmann Cabriolet, shown here, is one of the most sought-after models.

Specifications
Country: Germany
Top speed: 82mph (132km/h)

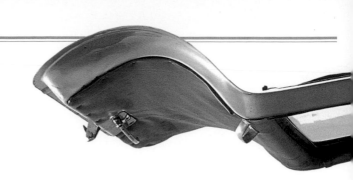

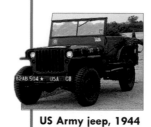

THE JEEP

When it entered production in 1941, the legendary Jeep was made in the US by both Willy's and Ford. Described as "a divine instrument of military locomotion," it was the US Army's "General

US Army jeep, 1944

Purpose" vehicle ("GP" soon became shortened to "Jeep"). Although it was designed for battlefield reconnaissance duties, it soon became clear that the Jeep had more uses. It was light enough to be carried in a glider and tough enough to be dropped by parachute.

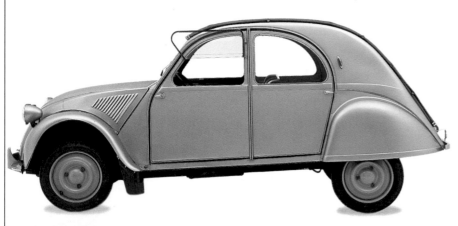

Citroën 2CV 1948

Flaminio Bertone is responsible for the appearance of some of Citroën's most successful cars: the Traction Avant (see p.181), the DS (see p.185), and the 2CV or *Deux Chevaux* ("Two Horses"). Built in part as a response to the Volkswagen Beetle, the 2CV uses a simple construction and simple manufacturing techniques to fulfill a practical need – a cheap and reliable means of transporting people and goods.

Specifications
Country: France
Top speed: 115mph (185km/h)

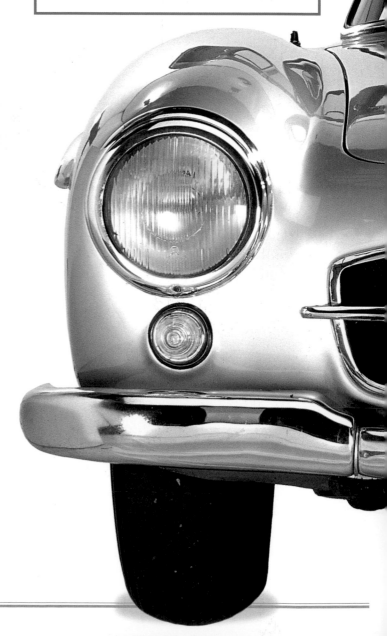

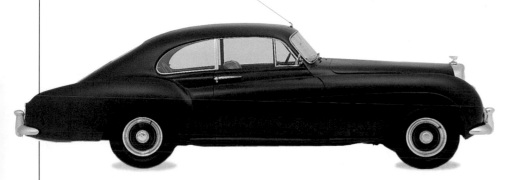

Bentley R-type Continental 1952

Launched in 1952, Bentley's R-type Continental was the fastest production car in the world. Only 208 were made – possibly because it was so expensive – but it was worth every penny to the many who revered it as the greatest car of all time. Described as "a modern magic carpet," the wind-tunnel-inspired lightweight aluminum housing enabled the car to reach 60mph (97km/h) in 14 seconds.

Specifications
Country: UK
Top speed: 115mph (185km/h)

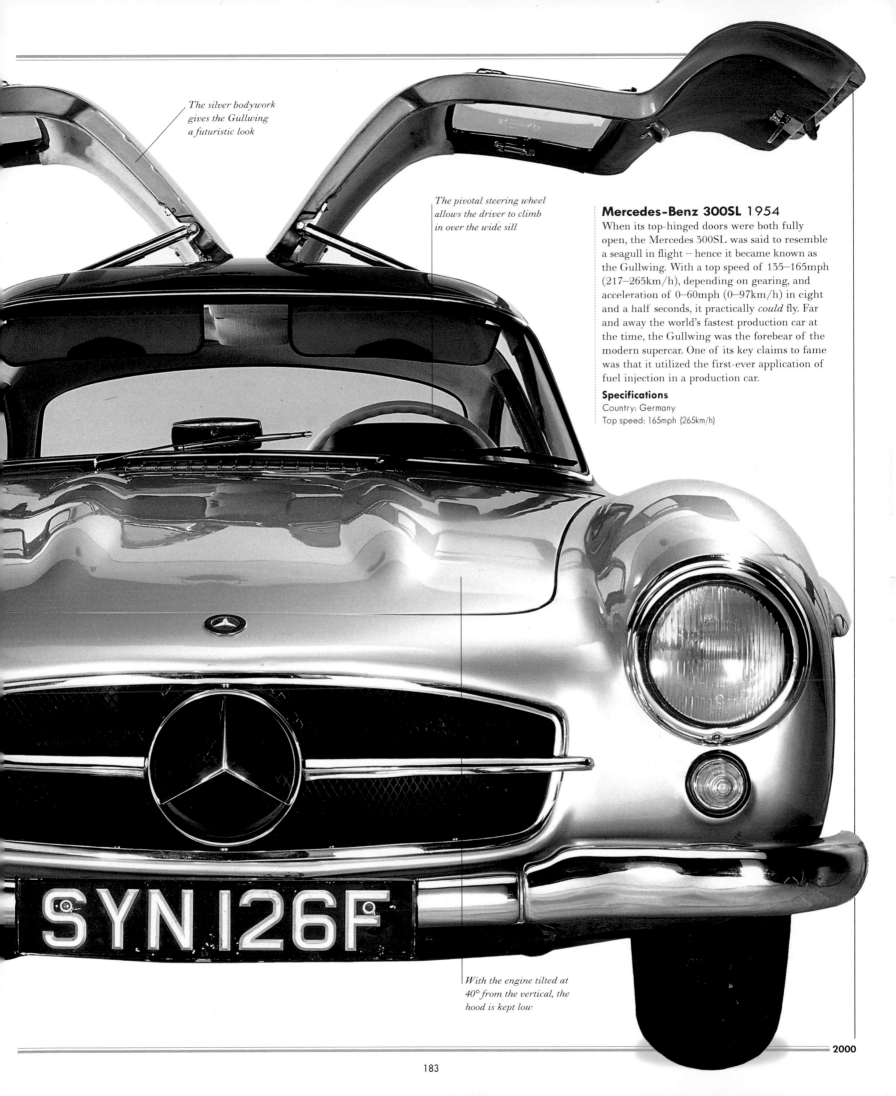

The silver bodywork gives the Gullwing a futuristic look

The pivotal steering wheel allows the driver to climb in over the wide sill

Mercedes-Benz 300SL 1954

When its top-hinged doors were both fully open, the Mercedes 300SL was said to resemble a seagull in flight – hence it became known as the Gullwing. With a top speed of 135–165mph (217–265km/h), depending on gearing, and acceleration of 0–60mph (0–97km/h) in eight and a half seconds, it practically _could_ fly. Far and away the world's fastest production car at the time, the Gullwing was the forebear of the modern supercar. One of its key claims to fame was that it utilized the first-ever application of fuel injection in a production car.

Specifications
Country: Germany
Top speed: 165mph (265km/h)

With the engine tilted at 40° from the vertical, the hood is kept low

Cadillac Eldorado Convertible 1959

Nothing sums up the optimism of the 1950s better than the 1959 Cadillac convertible. The most flamboyant and extravagant of mass-produced cars, this beautiful, brash machine was the creation of automobile stylist Harley Earl. He was influenced by Clarence Johnson, the designer of the Lockheed P38 airplane, which was certainly a source of inspiration. Earl used clay to model the shape of his cars, giving him the freedom to experiment with form. The outcome was a series of cars that owe as much to science fiction and a fascination with space flight as they do to empirical research.

Specifications
Country: US
Top speed: 112mph (180km/h)

The tail fins rise over a yard (1 meter) above the ground

Double headlights are a typical design feature of 1960s American cars

At 20ft (6.1m) in length and two tons (2032.1kg) in weight, the Cadillac was unchallenged in size and power

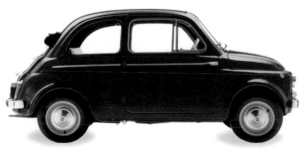

Fiat 500 1957

You could practically fit the Fiat 500 into the trunk of the Cadillac, so opposite are the two cars in philosophy. This charming car's gently rounded body is molded into shape by the one-piece construction. It appeared two years before the British Mini and was 3¼in (8cm) shorter. The Fiat 500, along with the Vespa scooter (see p.175), has come to symbolize Italy's postwar *ricostruzione*.

Specifications
Country: Italy
Top speed: 59mph (95km/h)

Buick Roadmaster 1957

The massive Buick Roadmaster was all about power. At 18ft (5.5m) long and 6ft (1.8m) wide, it needed its V8 engine to propel its mighty bulk to 60mph (96km/h) from standing in just 10.5 seconds. The giant chrome bumpers were just one statement of the car's might. In the 1950s, aircraft design was a major influence on car design, evident here in the wraparound windshield and the tail fins.

Specifications
Country: US
Top speed: 112mph (180km/h)

Morris Mini Minor 1959

Alec Issigonis's legendary Mini Minor is a fine example of the economic use of space. As this advertisement demonstrates, the tiny trunk fits behind the rear passenger seat.

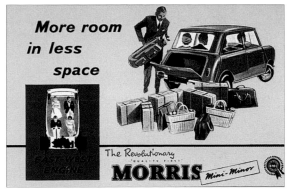

More room in less space

The Revolutionary
MORRIS *Mini-Minor*

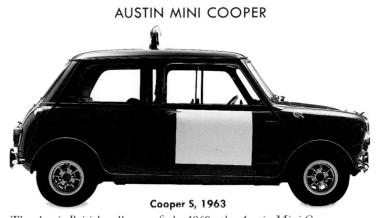

AUSTIN MINI COOPER

Cooper S, 1963

The classic British rally car of the 1960s, the Austin Mini Cooper was a high-performance version of Alec Issigonis's 1959 Morris Mini Minor. These box-shaped vehicles set the standard for small cars and, along with the miniskirt (see p. 139), became British icons of modernity in the 1960s. The rubber suspension was designed by Alex Moulton, who went on to create an innovative collapsible bicycle (see p. 173).

The steel-framed wraparound windshield recalls the styling of a fighter jet

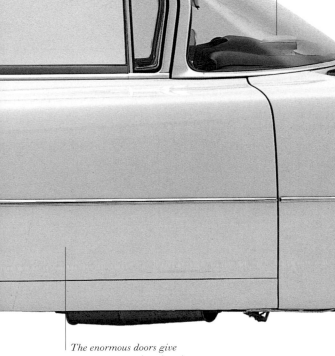

The enormous doors give access to a capacious interior that easily seats six

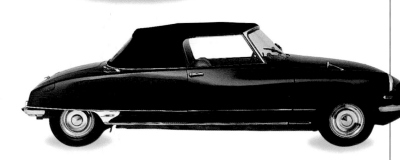

Chevrolet Impala 1960

In 1959, Bill Mitchell succeeded Harley Earl as director of styling at General Motors, but Earl's obsession with all things space-age clearly rubbed off on his protégé: there was even an insignia of a speeding rocket on the rear door of his Chevrolet Impala. Everything about the Impala expresses speed: for example, the antenna appears to bend in the wind even when the car is stationary.

Specifications
Country: US
Top speed: 112mph (180km/h)

Citroën DS 1960

Nicknamed "the Shark," the technically and stylistically daring Citroën DS was an immediate success on its launch in 1960: 80,000 were sold in the first week. The impressive aerodynamic body shape, the wide area of glass, the spacious interior, and the space-age instrument panel all set this car apart from all others.

Specifications
Country: France
Top speed: 116mph (187km/h)

THE LEGEND OF LAMBORGHINI

When tractor magnate Ferrucio Lamborghini had problems with his Ferrari, he went straight to the top with his complaints. Enzo Ferrari refused him an audience, and Lamborghini vowed to build a better car carrying his own name – and so the Lamborghini legend was born. The Miura was capable of 175mph (282km/h), a top speed that was matched by its racy looks – all futuristic, low lines and swooping curves. When it was launched at the 1966 Geneva Motor show, it caused the motoring sensation of the decade.

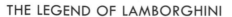

Lamborghini Miura, 1966

The steeply raked windshield typifies the 911's aerodynamic styling

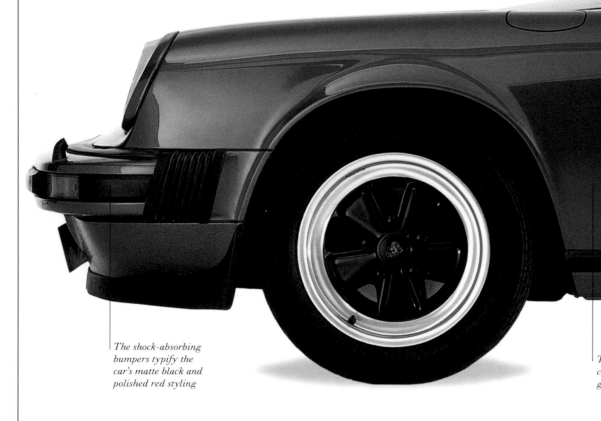

The shock-absorbing bumpers typify the car's matte black and polished red styling

The bodywork is constructed of thin-gauge steel panels

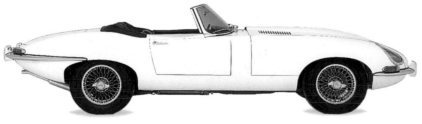

E-Type Jaguar 1961

At its launch in 1961, the E-type caused a sensation. This beautiful sports car's looks, with its distinctive elongated hood, were only part of the attraction, for it was capable of 150mph (241km/h) and was half the price of its main competitors. Designer Malcolm Sayer claimed that the E-type was the first car to be "mathematically" designed.

Specifications
Country: UK
Top speed: 150mph (241km/h)

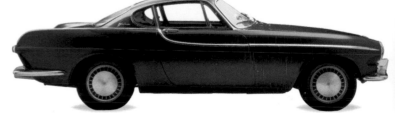

Volvo P1800 1961

From a manufacturer renowned for safe, reliable cars, the stunningly styled PS1800 seems like one of a kind. But closer inspection reveals a car as robust as any other Volvo, mechanically based on the Amazon Saloon and therefore not especially fast. It will always be known as the car driven by Roger Moore in the TV series *The Saint*.

Specifications
Country: Sweden
Top speed: 105mph (169km/h)

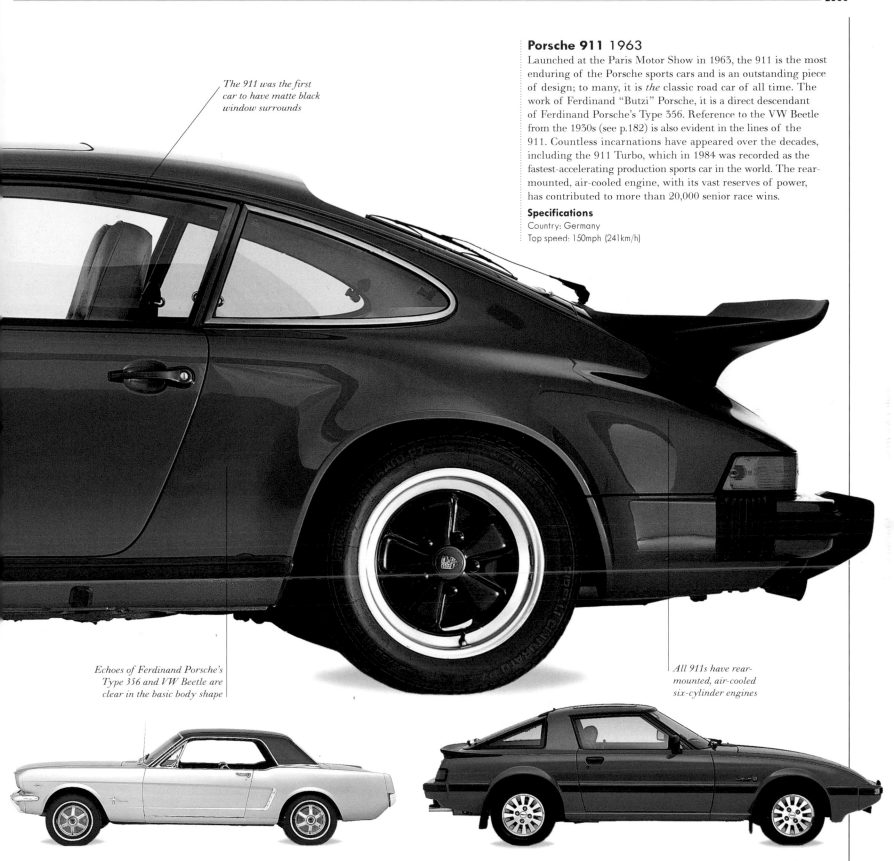

The 911 was the first car to have matte black window surrounds

Porsche 911 1963

Launched at the Paris Motor Show in 1963, the 911 is the most enduring of the Porsche sports cars and is an outstanding piece of design; to many, it is *the* classic road car of all time. The work of Ferdinand "Butzi" Porsche, it is a direct descendant of Ferdinand Porsche's Type 356. Reference to the VW Beetle from the 1930s (see p.182) is also evident in the lines of the 911. Countless incarnations have appeared over the decades, including the 911 Turbo, which in 1984 was recorded as the fastest-accelerating production sports car in the world. The rear-mounted, air-cooled engine, with its vast reserves of power, has contributed to more than 20,000 senior race wins.

Specifications
Country: Germany
Top speed: 150mph (241km/h)

Echoes of Ferdinand Porsche's Type 356 and VW Beetle are clear in the basic body shape

All 911s have rear-mounted, air-cooled six-cylinder engines

Ford Mustang 1964

To most Europeans, the Ford Mustang is a big American car. In fact, when the Mustang was introduced, it was a mold-breaking "compact," conceived as a sports car for the masses. After the excesses of the 1950s, its low-key styling was something of a relief. However, a vast range of options was offered, and, in 1965, the average buyer spent $1,000 on options, almost half the car's price.

Specifications
Country: US
Top speed: 117mph (188km/h)

Mazda RX7 1978

Almost half a million RX7s were sold in seven years of production – 75% of those were sold in the US – making it the most successful rotary-engined car of all time. Pop-up headlights added glamor and reduced wind resistance. Indeed, the car was styled to slice through the air. The car's shape was so well conceived that in seven years only minor changes were made to its design.

Specifications
Country: Japan
Top speed: 125mph (201km/h)

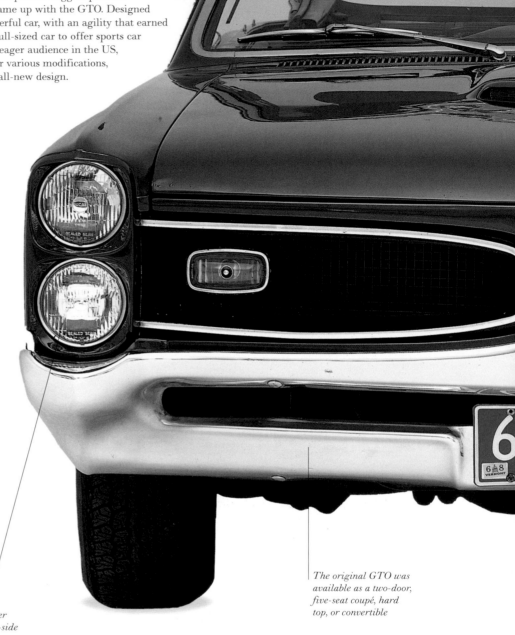

Pontiac GTO 1964

Taking a step back in time toward the big American cars of the 1950s, the innovative division of General Motors put the biggest possible engine into a medium-sized body and came up with the GTO. Designed by John DeLorean (1925–), it was a powerful car, with an agility that earned it the nickname "The Goat." The first full-sized car to offer sports car performance and handling, it found an eager audience in the US, particularly among younger drivers. After various modifications, the car was relaunched in 1970 with an all-new design.

Specifications
Country: US
Top speed: 135mph (217km/h)

A GLIMPSE OF THE FUTURE

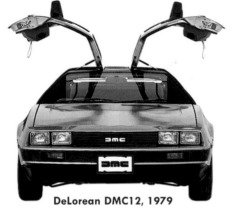

DeLorean DMC12, 1979

Despite £65 million of British government backing and a starring role in the movie Back to the Future, *the DeLorean DMC12 was a spectacular failure. With its stainless steel body and gull-wing doors, the Giorgio Giugiaro design was intended to be a glimpse of the future. In reality, it was dated before it even reached production.*

The vertical twin headlights on this 1966 model were later repositioned side-by-side

The original GTO was available as a two-door, five-seat coupé, hard top, or convertible

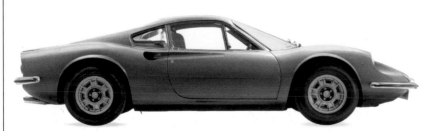

Ferrari Dino 246GT 1969

The beautiful, sweeping lines of the Ferrari Dino are unmistakable: it is the archetypal Italian sports car. Almost invariably red in color (this metallic brown model was rare), it was aimed at the Porsche 911 market and made an immediate impact. The Dino was named after Enzo Ferrari's son, Alfredino, who died at 24 of kidney disease.

Specifications
Country: Italy
Top speed: 148mph (238km/h)

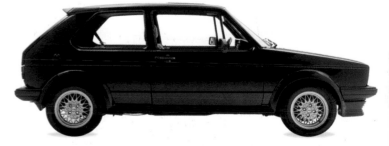

Volkswagen Golf GTi 1976

The car that launched a thousand imitations, the Golf was single-handedly responsible for the craze for hatchbacks that swept the world in the 1970s and '80s. It boasts an appealing combination of good performance and handling, practical design, and immense reliability: the engine was capable of 150,000 miles (241,400km).

Specifications
Country: Germany
Top speed: 111mph (179km/h)

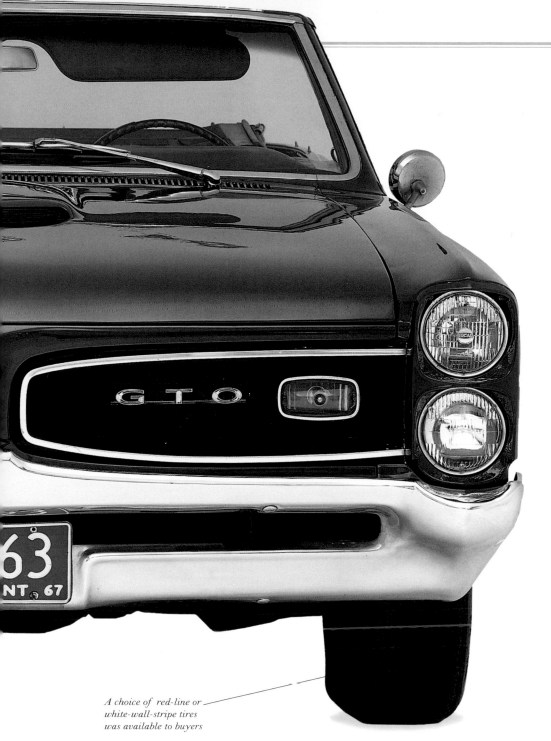

A choice of red-line or
white-wall-stripe tires
was available to buyers

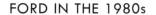

FORD IN THE 1980s

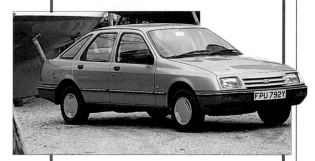

Ford Sierra, 1982

The Ford Cortina, launched in the 1960s, was extremely successful in Europe, thanks to its blend of American styling with the smaller scale and high efficiency expected by its target market. However, by the 1980s, drivers had more exacting demands, particularly in regard to safety and economy. Ford's solution was the Sierra, a collaboration, led by Uwe Bahnsen, between the company's design studios in Cologne, Germany, and Essex, England. The car was launched in 1982, spearheading new, higher standards for "popular price" car production. Its aerodynamic appearance and highly sophisticated engineering placed it indisputably at the cutting edge of technological development. It was also impressively fast: the top-of-the-line Cosworth, which appeared in 1986, was capable of reaching speeds around the 150mph (242km/h) mark.

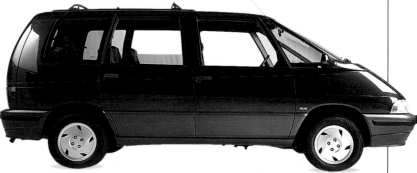

Audi Quattro Sport 1983

The first four-wheel drive road car with impressive all-around performance, Audi's most expensive car, the Quattro Sport, can travel fast in mixed conditions. In looks, it is boxy, with an unremarkable interior. However, the excellent handling and safety-conscious design ensure that it appeals to a wide range of users, from families to long-distance drivers.

Specifications
Country: Germany
Top speed: 155mph (250km/h)

Renault Espace 1984

When it first appeared, the Renault Espace sparked a brand-new philosophy in car design. Its so-called "one-box" construction offers maximum interior versatility, with space for seating and storage utilized according to the number of travelers and the type of trip. It is possible, for instance, to swivel seats or convert seating into a table top.

Specifications
Country: France
Top speed: 118mph (190km/h)

THE OFFICE

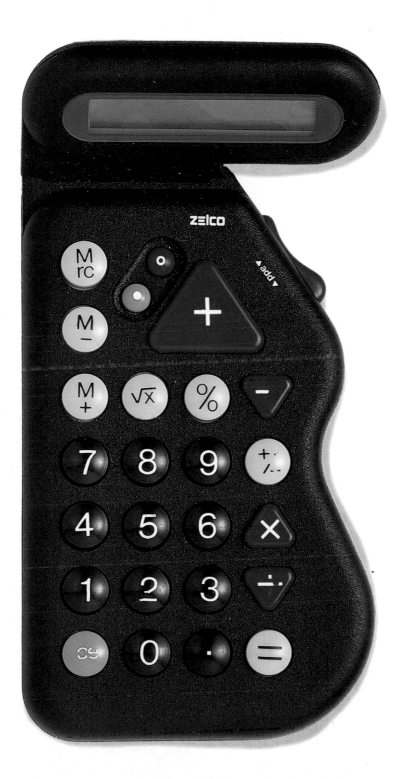

DESKS & CHAIRS

AT THE BEGINNING OF THE CENTURY, desks and chairs were considerable pieces of furniture: they were made of wood, made by hand, and made to last. However, the development of new materials and the introduction of computers made them prime targets for innovation. The traditional solid desk, with its high back and numerous drawers, has gradually been transformed into a simple work surface. Chairs, the items of office furniture most vital to workers' comfort and efficiency, now include unexpectedly comfortable high-tech structures and ergonomic masterpieces. An office planner's choice of both desk and chair is fundamental to the establishment of the company's image, and is often an indication within the office of company hierarchy.

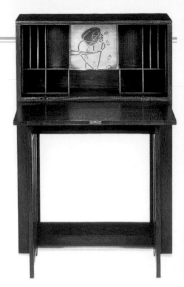

Mahogany bureau 1920s
This solid mahogany bureau by Charles Rennie Mackintosh is one of the designer's numerous furniture designs for the study. The formality of the elongated lines is enlivened by a decorative panel.
Specifications
Country: UK
Material: Mahogany

Synthesis 45 office chair 1972
Ettore Sottsass's chunky secretary chair for Olivetti shows a marked Pop Art influence. Its back and supports are made of bright plastic, and even the spring cover has been styled with great exaggeration.
Specifications
Country: Italy
Materials: Lacquered cast aluminum, plastic, and fabric upholstery

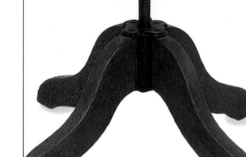

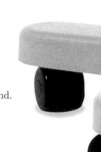

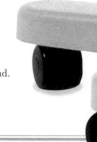

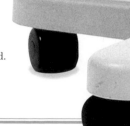

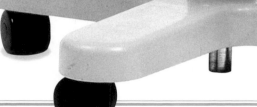

Swivel chair 1930s
This carved and bentwood swivel chair is an attractive combination of sturdiness and elegance, with its solid oak base and slender turned spindles. Originally developed to suit the movements of the user, the chair's height is adjustable. The leather seat covers a web of criss-crossed canvas that provides surprising comfort.
Specifications
Country: UK
Materials: Oak and leather upholstery

Folding chair 1958
This slim-legged, collapsible chair was designed in 1958 by Osvaldo Borsani for his company, Tecno, founded in 1954 with his twin brother Fulgenzio. Leaders in 1950s furniture technology, Tecno designers placed technical research as the top priority, with styling a close second.
Specifications
Country: Italy
Material: Wood

Partners' desk 1930

Made of sycamore, in the style of André Goult, this Art Deco desk was designed with two low, round-backed armchairs so that two "partners" could work opposite each other.

Specifications
Country: France
Materials: Sycamore, goatskin, gilt bronze, and glass

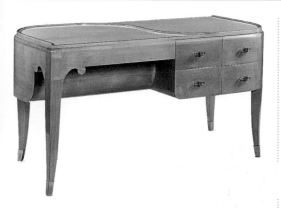

Rosewood desk 1950

The work of Danish designer Nanna Ditzel, this is a classically elegant rosewood desk. The simple design features four identical drawers along the full length of the work surface.

Specifications
Country: Denmark
Material: Rosewood

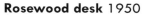

Nomos desk 1987

Norman Foster's line of "Nomos" furniture was designed for Tecno. This glass-topped steel desk has a strikingly high-tech appearance.

Specifications
Country: Italy
Materials: Chromium-plated steel and glass

Pippa folding desk and chair 1985

Rena Dumas and Peter Coles, designers of the impeccably finished Pippa furniture collection for Hermès, claimed that the complexity of the designs demanded "perfect materials."

Specifications
Country: France
Materials: Pearwood, leather, and brass

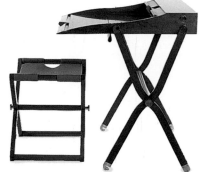

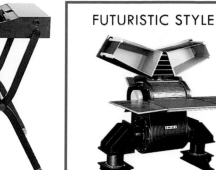

FUTURISTIC STYLE

Robot desk, 1989
Designed by Fred Baier in 1989, it is clear how the Roll-Top Drop Leaf Transformer Robot desk earned its name. The birch plywood and steel desk is fully adjustable to suit most office needs.

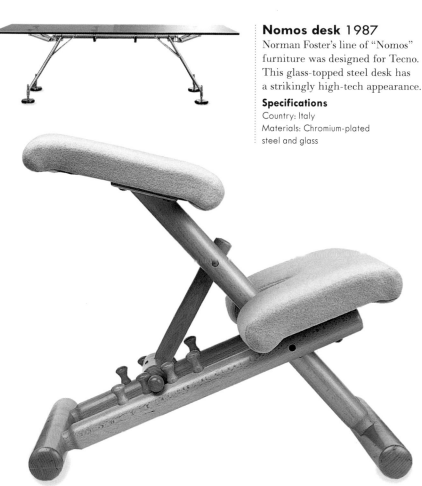

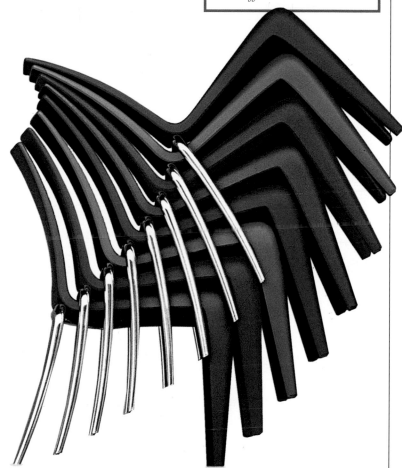

Balans chair 1990s

A product of the Norwegian firm Stokke, the Balans chair represents a complete rethinking of the structure of the office chair. The goal was to reduce the stress on the sitter's spine caused by working all day at a desk. This was achieved by redistributing the upper body weight: the typist perches on the sloping seat, with his or her knees bearing much of the weight as they rest on a cushioned "knee seat."

Specifications
Country: Norway
Materials: Pine and fabric upholstery

Louis 20 chair 1995

The back, seat, and front legs of Philippe Starck's Louis 20 chair are made from a single piece of molded plastic, with the rear legs formed by a bridge of tubular aluminum. These are screwed rather than glued to the body for ease of separating and recycling the different pieces. The chair is available with or without armrests, also constructed of tubular aluminum, and can easily be stacked high.

Specifications
Country: France
Materials: Polypropylene and aluminum

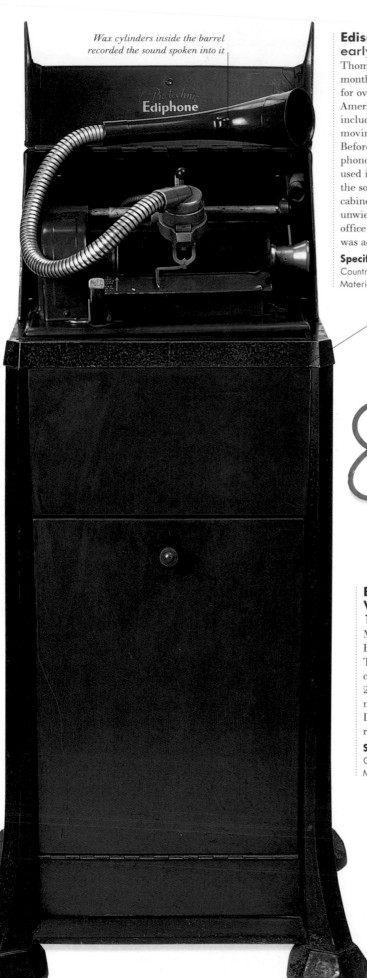

Wax cylinders inside the barrel recorded the sound spoken into it

The cabinet doors have the smooth finish of a piece of furniture

Edison Protechnic Ediphone
early 20th century

Thomas Alva Edison, with only three months of formal education, was responsible for over 1,200 patents and was one of America's greatest inventors. His inventions included the light bulb, the origins of moving pictures, and the phonograph. Before Edison saw the potential of the phonograph for home entertainment, it was used in business to record dictation, with the sound recorded in a wax cylinder. The cabinets of this large early machine were unwieldy, but were one of the few aspects of office furniture design where consideration was actually given to aesthetics.

Specifications
Country: UK
Material: Metal

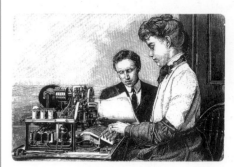

OFFICE LIFE 1903

Early stenographer

Although dictaphones increased efficiency, they tended to depersonalize the office environment. Before their widespread adoption, documents would be dictated to a stenographer — one of the few interpersonal elements of office life.

Edison
Voicewriter
1953

Manufactured by the Ediphone Division of Thomas A. Edison Inc., this compact magnetic tape recorder was produced 22 years after Edison's death, but his influential name appears four times on the machine. Designed by Carl Otto, the Voicewriter was revolutionary for its portability.

Specifications
Country: US
Material: Metal

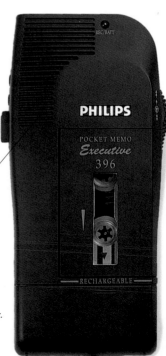

The Pocket Memo is just 5½in (14cm) in length

Pocket Memo 1993

The development of cassette tapes, and now microcassettes, has meant that dictaphones have become smaller and more sleekly styled over the years. The diminutive Pocket Memo Executive 396 dictaphone, manufactured by Philips Dictation Systems, was designed by Austrian Konrad Ellermeier.

Specifications
Country: Austria
Material: Plastic

OFFICE EQUIPMENT

BEFORE WORLD WAR II, the office was a distinctly impersonal place, with the stark, industrial appearance of a factory environment. Office equipment was purely functional; machines such as typewriters and photocopiers had their inner workings exposed (see pp.198–199; 202–203), and the use of dictation machines, commonplace by the 1930s, depersonalized office life further. Decades passed before any link was acknowledged between productivity and environment. It was only as recently as the 1950s that designers began to place the aesthetics of office equipment on a par with technical performance.

The fabric blades exemplify the safety-conscious design of the fan

The bars of the guard resemble ribbons fluttering in a breeze

AEG fan 1911
Peter Behrens was as concerned as any designer of his time with the function of the machinery he designed, but his refined sensibilities meant that his designs stole a march on those of his rivals. This pioneering electric desk fan for AEG is a fine example of Behrens tailoring the design of the item to emphasize its function.

Specifications
Country: Germany
Materials: Cast iron and brass

Bandolero desk fan 1930s
The streamlined Bakelite Bandolero fan was produced by Diehl, the electrical division of Singer, for the Sears catalog. The design dispenses with metal blades, using in their place safer cross-hatched fabric blades, which were replaceable. This removed the need for a protective cage and contributed to the fan's stylish, modern image. The fabric blades were later replaced with rubber versions.

Specifications
Country: US
Material: Bakelite and fabric

PORTABLE STORAGE

The Boby cart was designed by Joe Colombo for the Italian company Kartell in 1970, and is now produced by Bieffeplast. Made of ABS plastic, its ingenious structure is an example of how 1960s and '70s designers mastered the storage potential of plastics. The cart has swing-out drawers and a number of storage compartments. One of its main advantages is that it is so light it can be moved around an office on its large casters.

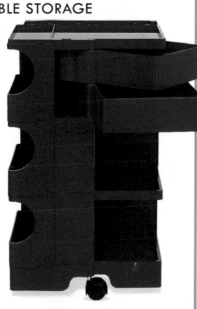

Boby cart, 1970

DESK ACCESSORIES

MOST OFFICE DESKS are littered with items that are, in their way, classics of design. The humble paper clip, invented in 1899 by Norwegian Johann Vaaler, has hardly changed, and the pencil sharpener, developed in Germany in 1908 by the TPX Bias company, remains an essential office item. The Rolodex, which first appeared in 1950, has survived the age of electronically stored information as a simple and efficient means of storing addresses. Even the disposable ballpoint pen has a history.

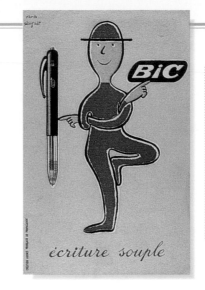

Blotting paper c.1955
In the 1950s, collecting printed blotting paper was popular in many European countries and in the US. The widespread introduction of the Bic ballpoint pen killed off the fad in the 1960s. This advertisement was designed by French illustrator Savignac.

Specifications
Country: France
Material: Paper

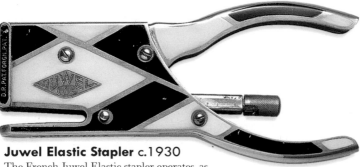

Juwel Elastic Stapler c.1930
The French Juwel Elastic stapler operates, as its name suggests, by means of an elastic band rather than the spring used in modern staplers. The beautiful Deco-inspired geometric enameling in black and white ensures that the Juwel lives up to its name.

Specifications
Country: France
Materials: Metal and enamel

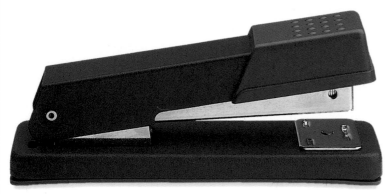

Stapler 1960s
The design of the stapler has changed very little throughout the century. When staplers first appeared, patented by C.H. Gould in 1896, they were used to fasten together the soles and uppers of shoes. The first paper staplers appeared in the late 1890s.

Specifications
Country: UK
Materials: Metal and plastic

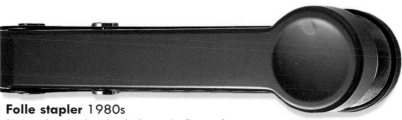

Folle stapler 1980s
Resigned to the fact that little can be done to improve the stapler's function, designers toy with its looks. This round-headed model is available in a range of bright colors. It was designed by Henning Andreasen for Folle APS of Denmark.

Specifications
Country: Denmark
Material: Steel

Index cards are divided alphabetically and rotated to view

Rolodex 1952
Arnold Neudstadter's 1952 design of the Rolodex card file was so successful that the company claimed that "there's a Rolodex file on almost every desk in America." The Rolodex is deceptively simple; made of heavy steel, it rotates "Tuff Fiber" index cards and will stop in any position, thanks to an ingenious ball-bearing clutch mechanism known as the Rolomatic.

Specifications
Country: US
Materials: Metal, plastic, and paper

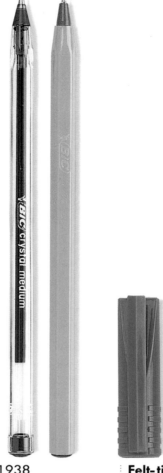

Perpetual calendar 1967

Enzo Mari designed his stylish calendar for Danese in 1967. The innovative design uses PVC cards in three lengths indicating the day, date, and month. The cards were printed in English, Italian, German, and French.

Specifications
Country: Italy
Materials: ABS plastic and PVC

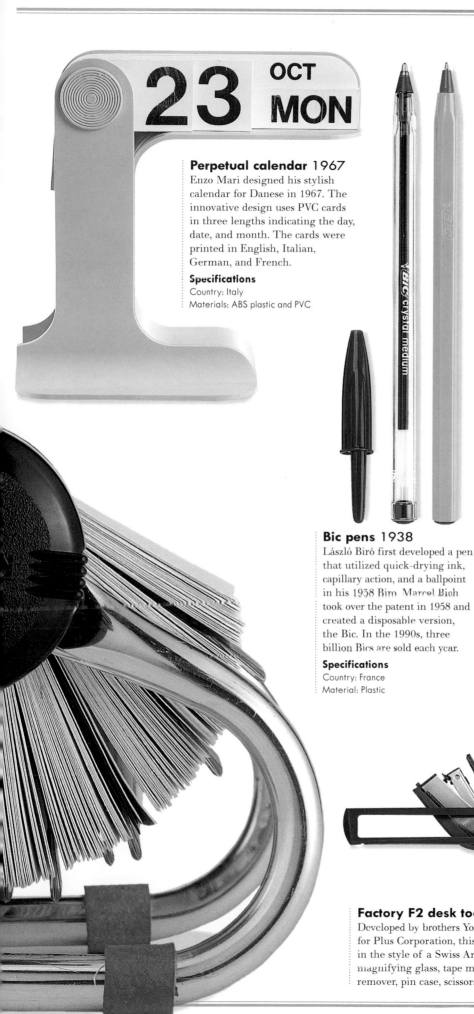

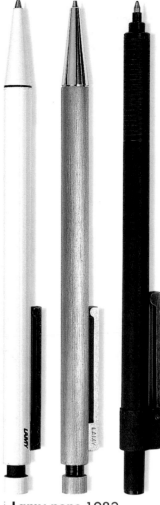

Bic pens 1938

László Biró first developed a pen that utilized quick-drying ink, capillary action, and a ballpoint in his 1938 Biro. Marcel Bich took over the patent in 1958 and created a disposable version, the Bic. In the 1990s, three billion Bics are sold each year.

Specifications
Country: France
Material: Plastic

Felt-tip pens 1963

One of the few advances on the ballpoint, the first fiber-tipped pens, developed in Japan in 1963 by Pentel, used a bamboo inner barrel. This was superseded by a fiber tube that fed ink to the nib by capillary action. This system is still used.

Specifications
Country: Japan
Material: Plastic

Lamy pens 1982

Walter Fabian's pen designs for the German company Lamy were an enormous success, elevating them to classic status immediately. The pens were popular for their styling rather than for any new technical advances.

Specifications
Country: Germany
Material: Plastic

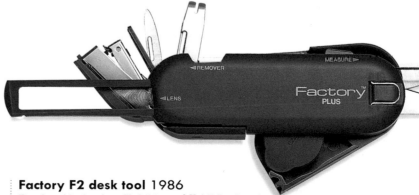

Factory F2 desk tool 1986

Developed by brothers Yoshihisa and Kohji Imaizumi for Plus Corporation, this compact desk accessory is in the style of a Swiss Army knife. It has a stapler, magnifying glass, tape measure, hole punch, staple remover, pin case, scissors, and tape dispenser.

Specifications
Country: Japan
Materials: Plastic and metal

TYPEWRITERS

THE FIRST TYPEWRITERS, made in 1873, had a QWERTY layout, from the word spelled by the first six letters of the top row of keys. This system is based on the positioning of the most-often-used keys is still used today. Early typewriters had an industrial appearance unsuitable for the home market. By the 1930s, portables had been introduced and electric machines were developed. By 1961, when IBM launched the "Selectric", electric models had largely replaced manuals. The advent of personal computers in the 1990s delivered the final death blow to the traditional typewriter.

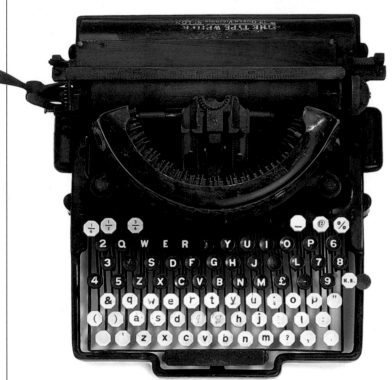

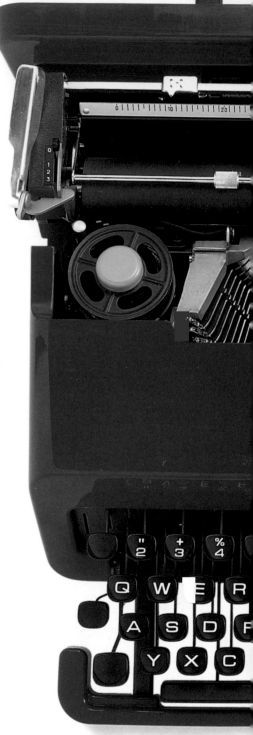

Royal Bar-Lock c.1910

This typewriter has a double keyboard. Without a shift key, which had been developed by Remington in 1878, it was necessary to have two keyboards, one for the upper case and one for the lower. The position of the typebars would have made it very difficult for the typist to see what was being printed. The open body gives the typewriter an industrial look, which would not have appealed to the domestic market.

Specifications
Country: US
Width: 15¾in (40cm)

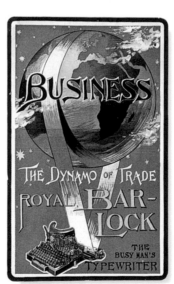

Avertisement for the
Royal Bar-Lock

Multiplex 1919

Hammond produced many innovative typewriters. The Multiplex had a system of interchangeable type shuttles that carried different fonts. The typewriter bears the legend "For All Nations and Tongues," which implies that the various fonts might be used for foreign languages. Most shuttles carried the fonts in three rows, but for specialized shuttles that had four, a second shift key was required.

Specifications
Country: US
Dimensions: h 23in (58.4cm), w 41in (104.4cm)

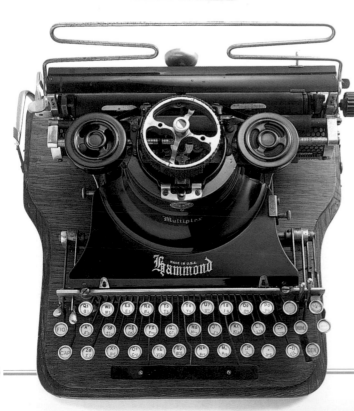

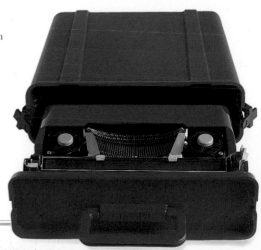

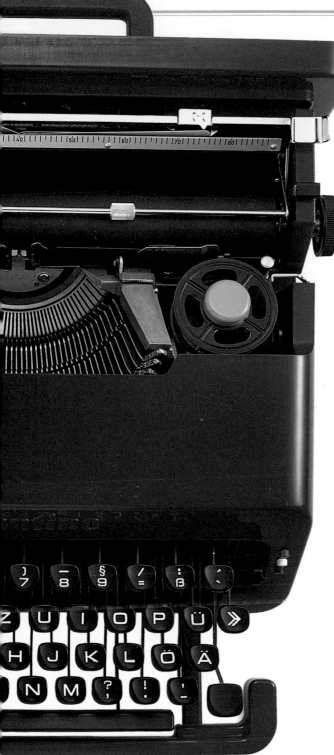

THE SELECTRIC

Eliot Noyes designed the innovative Selectric or "Golfball" typewriter for IBM in 1961. It was a revolutionary design because the typebars were replaced by a small spherical typing head shaped like a ball. This head carried the usual 88 characters, but it moved while the carriage remained stationary. Heads were interchangeable, allowing for a greater selection of typefaces. The Selectric was part of Noyes's corporate identity program for IBM, and its style owes a great deal to Marcello Nizzoli, who was so instrumental in reshaping Olivetti's post-1945 product line.

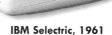

IBM Selectric, 1961

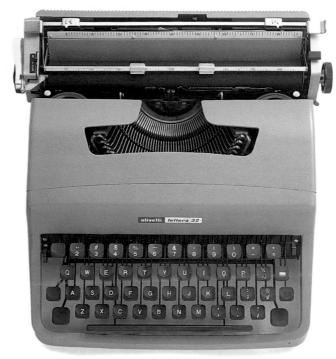

Lettera 32 c.1960
Marcello Nizzoli was Olivetti's first and most influential product designer. In the 1940s and '50s, he created office appliances, including adding machines (see p.207) and typewriters, that have achieved classic status. The Lettera 32 is based on his portable typewriter of 1950, the Lettera 22. The hallmark of Nizzoli's designs was his attention to form and applied graphics.

Specifications
Country: Italy
Dimensions: h 3in (8cm), w 12in (31cm)

Valentine 1969
The Valentine is the ultimate portable typewriter, composed of two simple elements. The machine and handle form one element, and the matching carrying case the other. It was designed for Olivetti by Ettore Sottsass and Perry A. King, who wanted to create a typewriter that would be light enough to carry anywhere and that would not be associated with the work environment. It is made from bright orange-red molded plastic, with yellow caps on the ribbon spools "like the two eyes of a robot," as Sottsass himself described them. It represents a radical departure from traditional office equipment.

Specifications
Country: Italy
Dimensions: h 4in (10.3cm), w 13in (33cm)

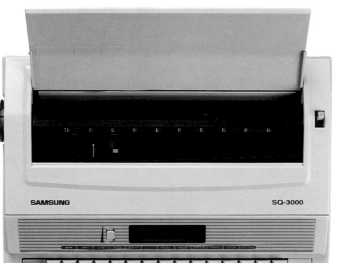

SSQ-3000 1990s
This Samsung is an example of a crossbreed of typewriter that combined a compact electronic machine with a memory facility. The small screen allowed the user to view a line of text before it was printed. Such models were popular from the mid 1980's, until the development of the personal computer rendered their features obsolete

Specifications
Country: South Korea
Dimensions: h 4⅖in (11.3cm), w 15⅜in (39cm)

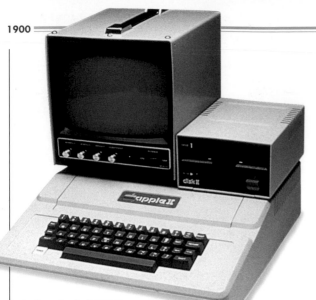

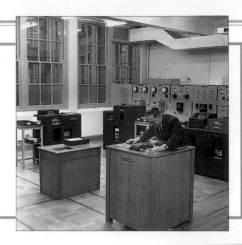

EARLY COMPUTERS

The first electronic computer contained 19,000 electronic tubes, which enabled it to compute 5,000 additions per second, and about 300 multiplications. At the time this must have seemed very quick, but it was child's play compared to the capabilities of modern computers such as the Cray Y-MP (1988), which can achieve more than two billion computations per second.

Apple II 1977

The success of the Apple II, shown here with the Disk II disk drive introduced in 1978, lay in its user-friendliness. Developed by Steve Jobs and Steve Wozniak, it was the first commercial personal computer.

Specifications
Country: US
Dimensions: Not known

The styling of the first personal computers was functional rather than aesthetic

IBM PC XT 1981

The most popular and influential personal computer ever produced, the IBM PC sold over 800,000 units within two years of its launch in August 1981. It was designed by a young team of computer scientists headed by Philip Estridge. Despite its meager specifications, it spawned a whole new industry, setting higher standards in personal computing.

Specifications
Country: US
Dimensions: h 17in (43cm),
w 20in (51cm)

Clean, pale colors, such as beige, have long been favored by the designers and users of computers

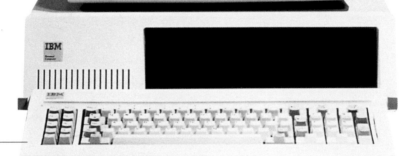

THE APPLE MAC

The Macintosh, designed by frogdesign for Apple Computer and unveiled in 1984, was by far the most original personal computer of its day. With its high-definition screen, graphic icons, and mouse pointing device, it proved exceptionally user-friendly. The disk drive and monitor were built into a single unit, giving the Apple Mac a more streamlined, compact look than its rivals. It was also reasonably priced, which made it as affordable to students as to businesspeople.

**Apple
Macintosh, 1984**

COMPUTERS

THE BOOK THAT YOU ARE READING was written on a computer small enough to fit in a briefcase, and designed and edited on versatile desktop computers. Yet the first electronic computer, the ENIAC (Electronic Numerical Integrator And Calculator), developed as recently as 1946, weighed 30 tons and occupied a surface area of 1,722 sq ft (160 sq m). The invention of the transistor in 1947, and its successor, the integrated circuit in 1959, facilitated the reduced size and greater power that characterize computers today. As more schoolchildren are taught to use computers, the machines are becoming as commonplace in the home as televisions, and, with the advent of CD-ROMs, just as entertaining.

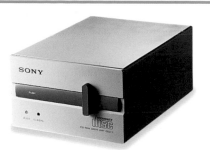

CD-ROM

Invented by Philips, and promoted internationally in collaboration with Sony, the CD-ROM is a laser-read disc that can be used to produce images on a computer screen. It can hold a large amount of information, which is displayed either in the form of text and images, or as narrated animated sequences. Until the 1990s the main market for CD-ROMs was professional, but they are now increasingly available to the home audience.

Sony CD-ROM player, 1985

Amstrad PC1512 1986

The British company Amstrad, established by entrepreneur Alan Sugar, launched the hugely successful PC1512 in 1986. Compatible with IBM's PC, it was, however, easier to use, twice as fast, and substantially lower in price. It made IBM-standard computing, previously restricted to the US market, accessible to the European home user for the first time.

Specifications
Country: UK
Dimensions: Not known

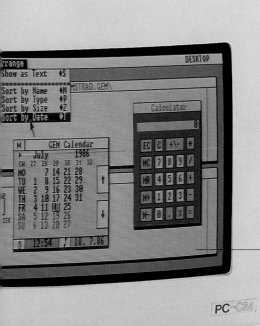

The monitor has an 80-column display and a palette of 16 colors

Psion Series 3 1992

The miniaturization made possible by the microchip is epitomized in this palm-top computer, which incorporates a personal organizer and word processor. It has more power than the computers aboard any Apollo spacecraft.

Specifications
Country: UK
Dimensions: h 2in open (5cm), w 6½in (16.5cm)

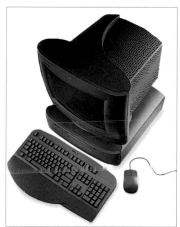

Overhead view of the Acer

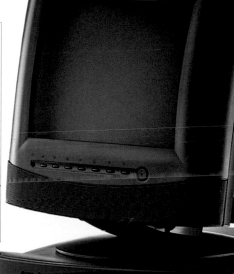

Acer Aspire 1996

In the marketing of computers the emphasis has generally been on function rather than form. Previously, computer use was largely restricted to offices, but the 1990s have seen the emergence of the home office. Companies like Acer have recognized this change in the market, and are offering something more attractive than the ubiquitous beige box. With its decorative surface, sculpted shape, and ultra-modern appearance, the Aspire is an attractive item of home furniture, as well as a powerful computer.

Specifications
Country: Taiwan
Dimensions: h 19¼in (49cm), w 15½in (39.5cm)

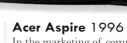

PHOTOCOPIERS & FAX MACHINES

THE PRINCIPLES FOR duplicating and transmitting documents have existed since the beginning of the century. However, it is only with the development of an integrated telephone system and advances in electronics that photocopiers and facsimile machines have come to play such crucial roles in the office. Originally forbidding-looking, the first copiers were transformed as early as the 1930s, thanks to Raymond Loewy's "face-lift" of a Gestetner duplicating machine. Fax machines were developed much later, emerging in Japan and the US simultaneously in 1968, when it took six minutes to transmit a single-page document. Today, communication by fax is an instantaneous and indispensable process.

Gestetner duplicating machine 1920s

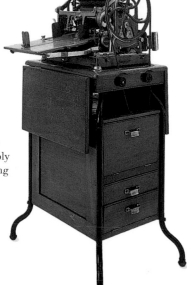

There is no applied ornamentation on this early duplicator by the British manufacturer Gestetner. Instead, the mechanism has been left exposed, giving the machine an unmistakably industrial and uninviting appearance.

Specifications
Country: UK
Materials: Wood and metal
Dimensions: Not known

Specifications
Country: UK
Materials: Wood and metal
Dimensions: Not known

Gestetner duplicating machine 1929

Gestetner commissioned Raymond Loewy to restyle the exterior of its duplicating machine in the late 1920s. In contrast to the overtly utilitarian appearance of the original machine (see above left), Loewy's simplified version is sleek and refined, with the mechanism concealed in a casing. He used a full-scale clay model to achieve the desired sculptural qualities – a working method subsequently adopted by designers in the car industry.

THE FIRST COMMERCIAL COPIER

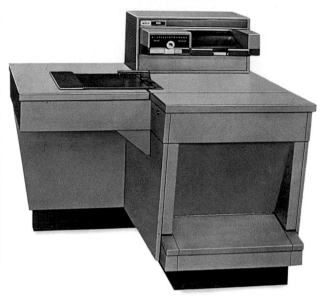

Xerox 914, 1959

The word Xerography was coined by American Chester Carlson in 1937 to describe his invented method for reproducing images. It is derived from the Greek xeros, *meaning dry, and* graphein, *meaning to write. The process, which is still used in modern photocopiers, involves the use of a powerful lamp, dry powder (toner), static electricity, and heat. After years of struggle, Carlson teamed up with Haloid, which later became Rank Xerox, and the Xerox 914 automatic copier was introduced in 1959. It was the first commercially available photocopier, capable of making seven copies per minute. Today, led by the Japanese, manufacturers produce machines that make as many as 100 copies per minute.*

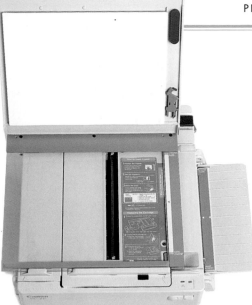

Canon PC-3 portable copier 1993

This personal desktop portable copier by Canon was designed to meet the growing need for a photocopier suitable for infrequent use. It works in the same way as a conventional office photocopier, but is restricted to the most basic operations. It cannot enlarge or reduce documents, and is without a paper stack.

Specifications
Country: Japan
Material: Plastic housing
Dimensions: h 5¾in (14.6cm),
w 15in (38.4cm)

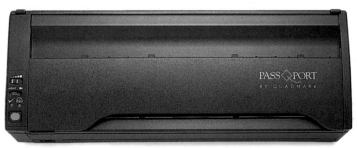

QuadMark Passport portable copier 1993

When Xerox company QuadMark introduced this portable copier in 1993, it was the world's smallest plain paper copier. Battery-operated and cordless, it weighs just 4lb (1.8kg) and is diminutive enough to be stored in a briefcase or desk drawer. Despite its modest size, the reproduction quality is high, with copies printed at 400 dots per inch resolution

Specifications
Country: US
Material: Plastic housing
Dimensions: h 2¾in (7cm),
w 11¾in (30cm)

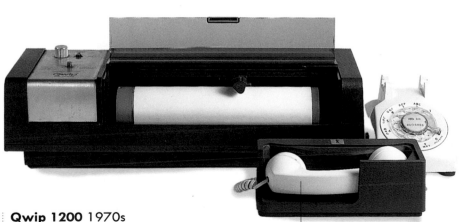

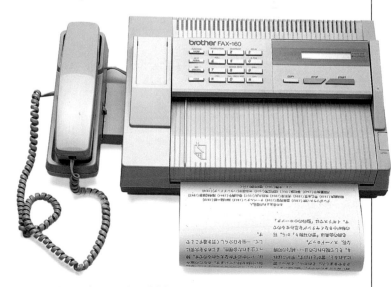

Qwip 1200 1970s

By the 1970s, fax machines were starting to become a familiar feature in modern office environments. By offering companies the very latest technology in a new, compact form, the Qwip 1200 series revolutionized the market. The machine was designed in two sections: the main sender/receiver and the acoustic housing for the telephone headset. It required special paper to receive documents, but otherwise it was simple to use, taking about four minutes to transmit or receive a document.

The headset of a standard telephone is housed in this acoustic shell

Specifications
Country: US
Material: Plastic housing
Dimensions: h 6¼in (16cm),
w 22in (56cm)

Canon Faxphone 8 1988

Compact and unobtrusive, this integrated telephone/fax machine could serve either in the office or the home. The light gray plastic housing conceals all the working apparatus. It has push-button keys and a memory facility. Its great advantage is that it can print onto ordinary paper and can transmit and receive documents in a matter of seconds.

Specifications
Country: Japan
Material: Plastic housing
Dimensions: h 5in (12.5cm),
w 12¼in (31cm)

ADDING MACHINES

WE NOW TAKE FOR GRANTED the use of sophisticated, inexpensive electronic calculators. However, early calculating machines were heavy, slow, and had no stored memory. Computers with this capacity became available for commercial use in the 1950s; they could be programmed to solve complex problems, but their size made them impractical for home use. It was the introduction of the microchip in the 1970s that facilitated massive reductions in the size, weight, and cost of calculators, while transforming their power beyond compare. Today, designers' increased sensitivity to the needs of the operator is reflected in the form of the machine, its graphics, and the grouping of keys.

Victor adding machine c.1935

This mechanical calculator has a two-tone, typewriter-style keyboard, which allows the fast and efficient entry of numbers. Designed by W.A. Knapp for the Victor Adding Machine Co. of Chicago, it is housed in a lightweight Bakelite case. Relatively inexpensive and easy to mold into modern shapes, Bakelite was made popular in the 1930s by the likes of Raymond Loewy, Wells Coates, and Jean Heiberg.

Specifications
Country: US
Materials: Bakelite and metal
Dimensions: h 7in (18cm), w 7¼in (18.5cm), d 12¼in (31cm)

Schubert c.1950

Cumbersome and complicated to operate, the Schubert was one of the last dinosaurs of the adding machine world, doomed to extinction by the advent of the silicon chip.

Specifications
Country: Germany
Materials: Metal and plastic
Dimensions: h 5¼in (13.2cm), w 11¼in (28.5cm), d 5½in (13.8cm)

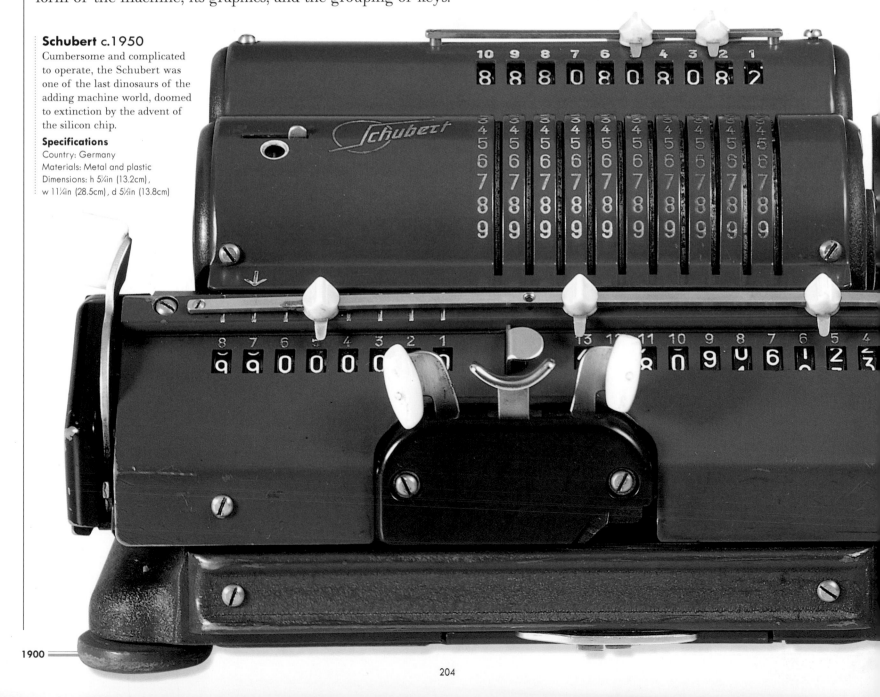

Olivetti Divisumma 24 1956

This calculator is the work of one of Olivetti's most celebrated designers, Marcello Nizzoli. Always mindful of those who will use and maintain his products, Nizzoli has considered the positioning of the keys, the coloring, and the graphics layout to make the machine easier to use. To ease servicing, the two-part plastic casing is removable, allowing maximum access to the mechanism.

Specifications
Country: Italy
Materials: Plastic and metal
Dimensions: h 9½in (24cm),
w 9½in (24.4cm), d 17in (43cm)

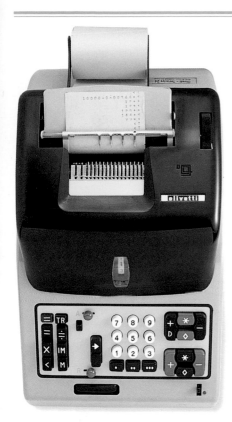

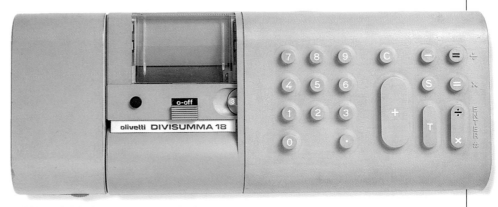

Olivetti Divisumma 18 1973

Like Marcello Nizzoli, Olivetti designer Mario Bellini responds to human requirements in his designs. Although he studies ergonomics, he stresses that they can be merely a starting point, as a person is much more complex than a set of measurements. Divisumma 18 will be remembered as much for its feel as its appearance. Manufactured in brightly colored plastic and covered with a thin sheath of rubber, its soft, tactile keys and the rounded forms made it a pleasure to handle.

Specifications
Country: Italy
Materials: Plastic and rubber
Dimensions: h 1¾in (4.6cm),
w 12¼in (30.9cm), d 4¾in (12cm)

The calculating process relied on mechanical operation

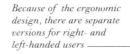

Because of the ergonomic design, there are separate versions for right- and left-handed users

Zelco "Double Plus" calculator 1986

Designed by Donald Booty Jr. for Zelco Industries, this calculator is shaped to be gripped. The name Double Plus derives from the unusual feature of having two plus keys, which allows for a brisker addition function than usual. These, and the other keys, are positioned, shaped, and colored to maximize efficiency.

Specifications
Country: US
Materials: Plastic and acrylic
Dimensions: h 5½in (14.4cm),
w 3in (6.6cm), d ½in (1.3cm)

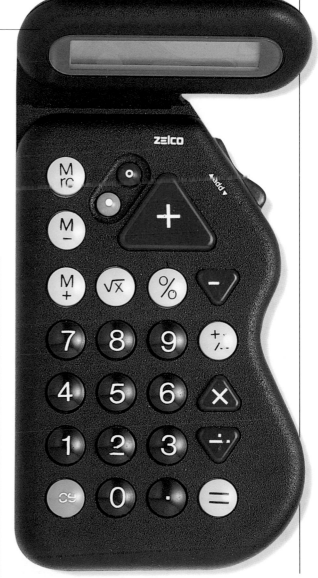

POCKET CALCULATORS

This pocket calculator by Casio is typical of the millions now inexpensively available to all, and in constant use in homes, offices, and schools across the world. It demonstrates the possibilities afforded by modern technology: in addition to its memory storage facility and multitude of mathematical functions, it is powered by a solar cell, and so requires no batteries. The first pocket calculator was introduced in 1972 by Clive Sinclair.

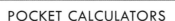

Casio pocket calculator, 1990s

The adding machine sits on soft plastic feet

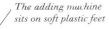

GRAPHICS, ADVERTISING, & PACKAGING

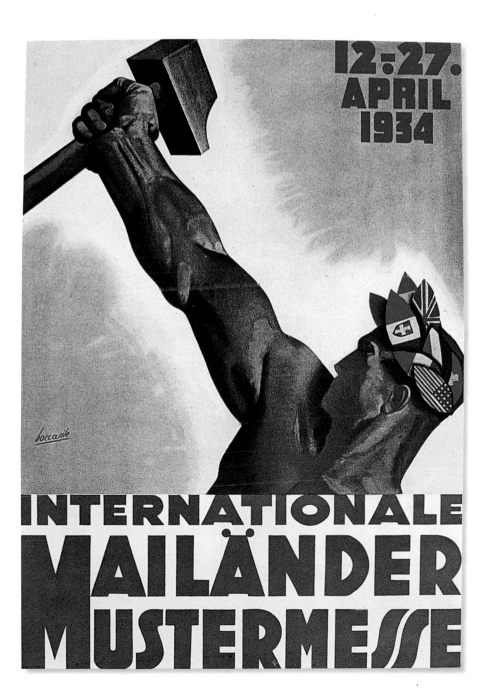

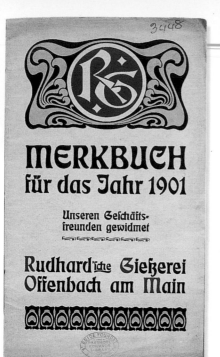

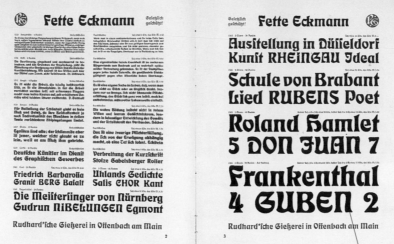

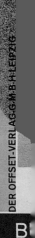

The launch pack for Futura shows a decorative variation of the basic typeface

Even the verticals of Eckmann Schmuck curve organically

TYPEFACES

COUNTLESS PRODUCTS from the 20th century are instantly associated with a particular style of lettering, whether that product is a cereal box, a newspaper, or a subway map. In fact, so powerful is the impact of many typefaces that words are often given expression even before the literal meaning becomes apparent. There are two basic divisions of typefaces: serif faces (those with terminal strokes) and sans serifs (those without terminal strokes), and a multitude of variations exist. Functional and geometric, sans serif letterforms were pioneered by Bauhaus designers in the 1930s and labeled "new typography."

Eckmann Schmuck 1900
Organic and calligraphic influences are clearly evident in this Jugendstil typeface, designed by German typographer Otto Eckmann. The curvilinear strokes of each letter taper and swell, as if with the movement of an italic pen nib. Devised for the Rudhard Foundry, it was also adopted by Klingpor, with which it is most commonly associated.

Underground 1915
In 1915, Edward Johnston was commissioned by London Underground to design a display typeface. He produced a sans serif alphabet that is simple to read and easy to recognize, and it is still used by London Underground today. The typeface is deployed to great effect on the roundel, which appears throughout the system to indicate each station name.

The roundel originally had a solid red disk with a blue bar

Each stroke is of an identical thickness

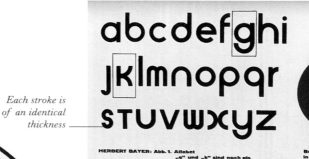

HERBERT BAYER: Abb. 1. Alfabet
„g" und „k" sind noch als unfertig zu betrachten

Beispiel eines Zeichens in größerem Maßstab
Präzise optische Wirkung

Abb. 2. Anwendung

Universal 1925
During his time as head of the print department at the Bauhaus, Austrian Herbert Bayer produced this alphabet. An advocate of modernism, Bayer defended the sans serif typeface as an expression of its time. He denounced serifs as a hangover from handwriting, incompatible with modern typography and printing. His simple, geometric Universal alphabet also suspended the use of capital letters. It was employed in the Bauhaus publication *Offset*, but never released as a typeface.

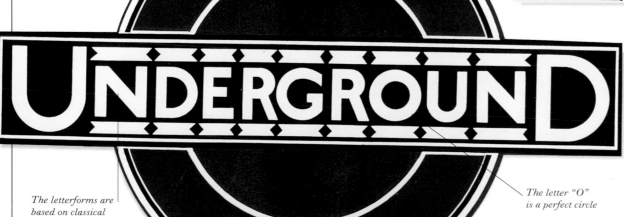

The letterforms are based on classical Roman proportions

The letter "O" is a perfect circle

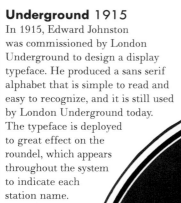

FUTURA fett

FUTURA fett

DIE HEUTIGE ZEIT HAT EIN NEUES FORMGEFÜHL! DAS IST EINE TATSACHE UND MEHR
als das: es ist eine schöpferische Kraft, die in der Kunst wie in den Bezirken des Lebens
wirkt. Der Materialismus versucht die Leistungen, in denen wir diese neue Gesinnung
spüren, zu erklären, als Produkt der Maschine, als Anpassung an die neuen Werkstoffe.

DANN BLIEBE NEBEN DEM TECHNISCHEN STIL JA NOCH PLATZ FÜR
einen reichen handwerklichen! Man hat das wiederholt behauptet,
aber ist es wirklich so? Könnte die Maschine nicht ebensogut auch
reiche, komplizierte Formen massenweise herstellen wie einfache?

DIE MASCHINE HAT DAS DOCH SCHON OFT BEWIESEN.
Aber der Stilwille unserer Zeit will es anders; er ist ein-
heitlich und wurzelt tiefer. Nun erst war die Zeit reif,
auch die Maschine zu verstehen und sie zu bemeistern.

DIE DRUCKTYPE IST DER MASCHINELLE ABDRUCK
maschinell hergestellter Metall-Letter, die mehr
Lesezeichen sind als Schrift. Die Druckschrift ist
keine Ausdrucksbewegung wie die Handschrift.

DIE GROTESKSCHRIFTEN SIND DIE NATUR,

BAUERSCHE GIESSEREI

FUTURA

FRANKFURT AM MAIN

MEISTERKURSUS
Handwerkskunst
MANUSKRIPT
Schriftproben
INDUSTRIE
Neuheiten
BARMEN
Reklame
SCHULE
Malerei

The form of the lowercase "i" is reduced to a dotted bar

Futura 1927–30

The design of the Futura typeface owes more to precision engineering than to the calligrapher's pen. Taking inspiration from Bayer's Universal face, German typographer Paul Renner was one of the first to utilize the revolutionary approach of a completely even stroke throughout the alphabet. Futura is notably more rigid in its geometry than its corresponding British typeface, Gill Sans. As with Universal, the letterforms are based on squares and circles, but, interestingly, the crossbars of the "E" and the "F" are positioned above center. The typeface is still used today in a number of variations.

Gill Sans type is used in this page from the typographic journal The Fleuron

MAY 31
COLLECT FOR
THE FEAST OF S. ANGELA MERICI

DEUS, QUI NOVUM PER BEATAM
ANGELAM SACRARUM VIRGINUM
COLLEGIUM IN ECCLESIA TUA FLOR-
ESCERE VOLUISTI: DA NOBIS, EIUS
INTERCESSIONE ANGELICIS MORI-
BUS VIVERE; UT, TERRENIS OMNIBUS
ABDICATIS, GAUDIIS PERFRUI MERE-
AMUR AETERNIS · PER DOMINUM NOSTRUM
IESUM CHRISTUM FILIUM TUUM QUI TECUM
VIVIT ET REGNAT IN UNITATE SPIRITUS SANCTI
DEUS PER OMNIA SAECULA SAECULORUM

ABCDEFGHIJJKLMN
OPQQRRSTUV
WXYZ
1.2,3:4;5-6!7?8§9*¶()[ ]
40

¶ANNUAL MEETING

FEDERATION

OF

MASTER

PRINTERS

THE LANSTON MONOTYPE CORPORATION LIMITED, LONDON
PRESENT
AN INTERIM PROOF OF THEIR
SANS-SERIF TITLING
DESIGNED BY ERIC GILL

CONGRESS

SELLING

AND

PUBLICITY

BLACKPOOL

Gill Sans 1928

British designer Eric Gill was a highly respected type designer, sculptor, and letter cutter, whose Gill Sans typeface is firmly identified with Modernism. Gill studied under Edward Johnston, whose guidance can be detected in the forms of this sans serif alphabet. The application of subtle stroke variation gives the face greater fluidity, making it easy to read as continuous text. Gill Sans was created for the Monotype Company (renamed the Monotype Corporation in 1931), whose adviser for typographer, Stanley Morison, had earlier supported Gill in the development of his typeface Perpetua. Gill Sans was adopted by London and North Eastern Railways in 1929, and has remained prevalent in the printing of forms.

OFFSET
UND WERBEKUNST

ENTWURF: JOOST SCHMIDT·BAUHAUS IN DESSAU
BAUHAUS-HEFT

A B C D E F G H I J K

Times New Roman 1931

In addition to advising Monotype (see p.209), Stanley Morison was typographic consultant to *The Times* of London for three decades, and he created this typeface for the newspaper. It was used exclusively for one year, replacing a Gothic type that had been favored for more than 120 years. Simplifications in the formation of each letter meant that text could be condensed and remain legible, at the same time saving space.

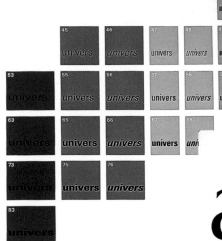

Univers 65

DANS LA PREMIÈRE SÉRIE
Les efforts que l'homme fait pour mieux connaître et pour mieux comprendre rendent

POUR SERVIR D'INTRODUCTION
Les efforts que l'homme fait pour mieux comprendre et pour mieux connaître assouplissent son esprit et le rendent plus apte aux progrès du

UNE IMPRESSION RÉCONFORTANTE SE DÉGAGE
Les efforts que l'homme fait pour mieux connaître et pour mieux comprendre assouplissent son esprit et le rendent plus apte aux progrès du lendemain. C'est un

LE MERVEILLEUX ESSOR DE LA PHYSIQUE
Les efforts que l'homme pour mieux connaître et pour mieux comprendre assouplissent son esprit et le rendent plus apte aux progrès du

UN SUJET ASSEZ DIFFICILE A TRAITER
Les efforts que l'homme fait pour mieux connaître et pour mieux comprendre assouplissent son esprit et le rendent plus

LES DISCIPLINES DE LA SCIENCE
Les efforts que l'homme fait pour mieux comprendre et pour mieux

UN MOUVEMENT RAPIDE
la réflexion de la lumière sur les miroirs et la propagation

RÉSUMONS UN PEU
maintenant que nous devons cesser pour un

BANQUEROUTE
une reproduction authentique de la

PERSUASION
le mouvement qui était prévu

FRANCHE
instruction

21 variations sur un thèr

THE TIMES NEW ROMAN

It may be claimed that *The Times*, with its new titling, its new device, and its new text types, possesses, from the headline on the front page to the tail imprint on the back, a visual unity. But this is no more than the beginning of typographical wisdom, for visual harmony, whatever its

It may be claimed that *The Times*, with its new titling, its new device, and its new text types, possesses, from the front page to the tail imprint on the back, a visual unity. But this is no more than the beginning of typographical wisdom, for visual harmony, whatever its significance for the artist, has little value for the general reader unless and until it accompanies the

It may be claimed that *The Times*, with its new titling, its new device, and its new text types, possesses, from the headline on the front page to the tail imprint on the back, a visual unity. But this is no more than the beginning of typographical wisdom, for visual harmony, whatever its significance for the artist, has little value for the general reader unless and until it accompanies the basic factors of textual legibility. The reader needs a definite

It may be claimed that *The Times*, with its new titling, its new device, and its new text types, possesses, from the headline on the front page to the tail imprint on the back, a visual unity. But this is no more than the beginning of typographical wisdom, for visual harmony, whatever its significance for the artist, has little value for the general reader unless and until it accompanies the basic factors of textual legibility. The reader needs a definite plainness and familiarity of type design;

It may be claimed that *The Times*, with its new titling, its new device, and its new text types, possesses, from the headline on the front page to the tail imprint on the back, a visual unity. But this is no more than the beginning of typographical wisdom, for visual harmony, whatever its significance for the artist, has little value for the general reader unless and until it accompanies the basic factors of textual legibility. The reader needs a definite plainness and familiarity of type design; the greatest possible size and clearness of impression; and that adjustment of the spacing, first, to the single letters, next to their combination in words, lines, paragraphs, columns, and pages which makes the whole "look right" to him. From this point of

It may be claimed that *The Times*, with its new titling, its new device, and its new text types, possesses, from the headline on the front page to the tail imprint on the back, a visual unity. But this is no more than the beginning of typographical wisdom, for visual harmony, whatever its significance for the artist, has little value for the general reader unless and until it accompanies the basic factors of textual legibility. The reader needs a definite plainness and familiarity of type design; the greatest possible size and clearness of impression; and that adjustment of the spacing, first, to the single letters, next to their combination in words, lines, paragraphs, columns, and pages which makes the whole "look right" to him. If anything, was wrong with the founts which served until yesterday? Were the types wrongly designed, or were they wrongly used?

All the current newspaper types—the so-called "moderns"—are designed upon a century-old model; the former type of *The Times* was no exception to this rule, although it was much the best of its kind. But English craftsmen have come to lead the world in all that belongs to the design and printing of books, by studying the art of

MOVABLE TYPE

Printing with metal type has its origins in the invention of movable type by the 15th-century German goldsmith Johannes Gutenberg. Each block has a single letter that can be set, inked, and the relief surface then impressed onto paper. The method was an improvement on woodblock printing, not least because one mistake no longer meant the replacement of an entire printing block. Here, a "forme" is made up of the inked type, wedges, and iron frame, or "chase."

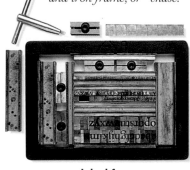

Inked forme

Univers 1957

Swiss designer Adrian Frutiger earned his considerable reputation through the creation of this versatile typeface. Univers 65, shown here, is just one of 21 variations contributing to this universal lettering system, which permits a multitude of combinations and effects. Designed for the purpose of filmsetting, Univers is particularly compatible with printing in condensed spaces, and has frequently been the preferred choice for timetables. In expanded, bolder format, it has been used for large-scale public signage systems. The typestyle is sans serif, with the weight stress balanced on both vertical and diagonal strokes. Univers was taken up by the Monotype Corporation soon after it was launched.

Optima 1958

German type designer Hermann Zapf created this sans serif typeface, the Roman proportions of which have a handwritten quality. Elegant, flowing, and easy to read when reduced in size, the letters end in shallow cups. Initially, Optima was poorly received by critics and designers, but it soon became a highly popular choice for page text. Zapf is internationally recognized for his considerable contribution to the printmaking industry. His celebrated designs include Palatino, in 1949; Melior, in 1952; Zapf Book, in 1976; and Zapf International, in 1979. More recently, he has been involved in the developmental design of digital type.

FIGURENVERZEICHNIS DER OPTIMA

a

ABCDEFGHIJK
LMNOPQRSTUVW
XYZ ÄÖÜ MN
Sonderfiguren
abcdefghijklmnopq
rstuvwxyz äöü

TECHNISCHE ANGABEN

Die Optima ist lieferbar in den Graden: 6, 8, 9, 9/10, 10, 12, 14, 16, 20, 24, 28, 36 und 48 p. Die Schrift ist progetest und ein gesetzlich geschütztes Original-Erzeugnis der D. Stempel AG, Signatur: Hauptsignatur; 6-12 p in allen Garnituren Sondersignatur 3; 6-12 p Halbfette Optima Sondersignatur 3.5. Gleich Hermann Zapfs Melior haben die Brotschriftgrade in drei Garnituren im Handsatz und auf der Linotype-Setzmaschine die gleiche Breite.

AUSZEICHNUNGSMÖGLICHKEITEN

Neben der stehenden Optima laufen die Kursiv und die Halbfette her. Die Grade der Kursiv und der Halbfetten befinden sich in Vorbereitung. Kontraste der Werk- und Akzidenzschriften der Optima mit individuellen Werbeschriften sind sehr wirkungsvoll.

STILGESCHICHTLICHES

Die Optima von Hermann Zapf erschien nach jahrelangen Vorarbeiten zur Drupa 1958. Sie gehört zur Nachfolge der klassizistischen Schriften in ihrer serifenlosen Abart.

Z

ÆŒÇ ÉÊÈË ÅØ åø
æœç chckfffififlftijß
£ 1234567890 $
.,-:;!?'()„" »« &—[]§†*
áâà éêèë íîìï óôò úûù

L M N O P Q R

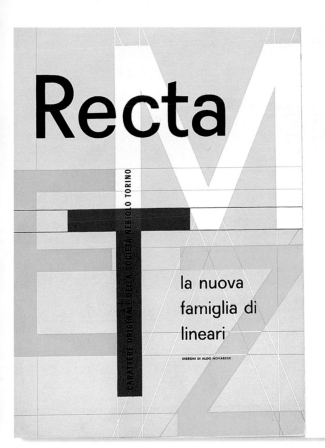

Recta

la nuova famiglia di lineari

CARATTERE ORIGINALE DELLA SOCIETÀ NEBIOLO TORINO

DISEGNI DI ALDO NOVARESE

Una nuova famiglia di stile lineare che sarà pienamente rispondente, nella sua futura gamma di oltre 20 gradazioni diverse, a tutte le esigenze tipografiche moderne

Recta

Serie corsiva nera stretta in corso di lavorazione

Provatevi a respirare artificialmente e a fare pensatamente qualcuno di quei moltissimi atti che si fanno per natura: non potrete, se non a grande stento e men bene. La troppa arte nuoce a noi, e in quello che

L'AVARO PROVA INSIEME TUTTE LE PREOCCUPAZIONI DEL RICCO E TUTTI I TORMENTI DEL POVERO

Alessandro Manzoni nelle Odi

Concorso grafico DIPLOMATICO

Inciso nei corpi
6, 8, 10, 12, 14, 16, 20,
24, 28, 36,
48, 48/60, 60/72

SOCIETÀ NEBIOLO ⬦ TORINO

Recta 1958

This typeface was designed by Italian graphic artist Aldo Novarese, director of its production type foundry, the Società Nebiolo, in Turin. Linear and sans serif in design, the alphabet comprises a series of 21 variations, designed to be compatible with the technical requirements of modern printing. This presentation document has been created to accentuate the geometric propensity of Novarese's typeface.

Sabon 1964–66

Jan Tshichold began his career as a Modernist, advocating simplicity and symmetrical composition. His first book, *Die Neue Typographie*, published in 1928, had a significant impact on members of the Bauhaus. In the 1930s, Tshichold returned to a more traditional style of typography. His Sabon face (see mauve alphabet below) was the first typeface to be designed for linotype, monotype, and hand composition. It is a modernized version of the well-established Garamond.

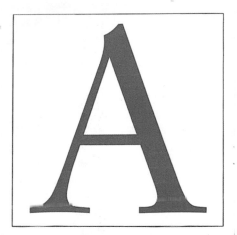

Sabon Antiqua

ABCDEFGHIJKLMNOPQ
RSTUVWXYZÄÖÜ
abcdefghijklmnopqrstuvwxyz
ßchckfffiflft&äöü
1234567890 1234567890
.,;:-!?.'()[]*†×»«„"/£$

—

Sabon Kursiv

Bell Centennial 1978

Devised by British designer Matthew Carter, this typeface was commissioned for use in US telephone directories and was launched during Bell Directories' centennial year. Its key advantage is that it can stand up to compression; unlike Bell Gothic or Helvetica, Bell Centennial can be reduced without blotting or anamorphic distortion.

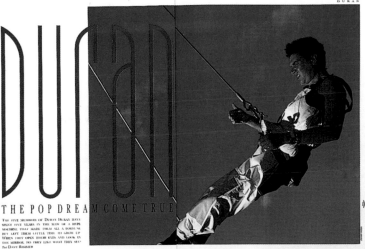

too much too young

DURAN
THE POP DREAM COME TRUE

THE FIVE MEMBERS OF DURAN DURAN HAVE SPENT FIVE YEARS IN THE MAN OF A HYPE MACHINE. THAT MADE THEM ALL A FORTUNE BUT LEFT THEM LITTLE TIME TO GROW UP. WHEN THEY OPEN THEIR EYES AND LOOK IN THE MIRROR, DO THEY LIKE WHAT THEY SEE?

Typeface Six 1986

Postmodernist designer Neville Brody made his name while art editor of the British music and style magazine *The Face* (see p.219). He is one of a number of designers who have taken advantage of technological developments in printing to produce typefaces and layouts that break the rules of traditional printsetting. Frequently aided by computer-generated manipulations, Brody uses letterforms as graphic devices, designing unconventional alphabets that make a dramatic impact. Words, such as "Duran" shown here, take on an expressive quality of their own. His work extends to books, advertisements, and record covers.

STUVWXYZ

CORPORATE IDENTITY

PETER BEHRENS was the original "corporate designer," the first to consider the complete look of a company and the image that it projects to the public. Since his revolutionary work at AEG, most major corporations have paid vast sums to designers to create for them a memorable visual identity. Ironically, one of the world's most successful works of corporate identity, the Coca-Cola script, was designed by the company's bookkeeper.

THE SHELL PECTEN AND LOGOTYPE			
1900	1904	1909	1930
1948	1955	1961	Shell 1971 / Shell 1995

Shell 1900–71

Although primarily a petroleum company, Shell has many other commercial interests, and more than 90 percent of its businesses around the world use the time-honored logo. The picture of the shell has been altered several times over the years, but has been modified very little since 1971, when the name was repositioned below the stylized image.

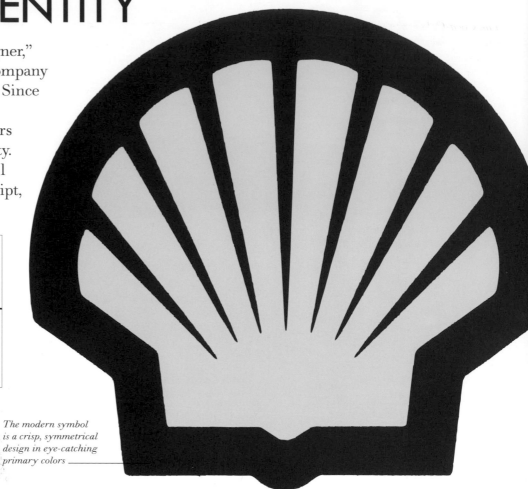

The modern symbol is a crisp, symmetrical design in eye-catching primary colors

MICHELIN MAN

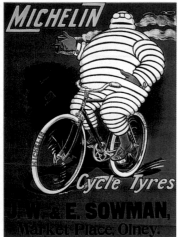

Early 20th-century advertisement

Monsieur Bibendum, the Michelin Man, has been the chief symbol of the French tire company since he was created in 1898. Legend has it that the designer, Mr. O'Galop, was inspired by the sight of a pile of rubber tires. In his earliest incarnations, Monsieur Bibendum had many more thinner rolls, as Michelin made bicycle tires at the beginning of the century; but as the company moved into the production of car tires, his shape changed accordingly. Always depicted as an active, friendly figure, Monsieur Bibendum has achieved lasting success, being both highly memorable and evocative of the product he represents.

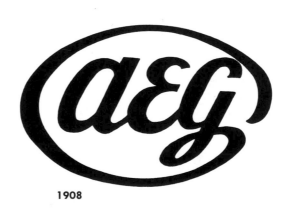

1908

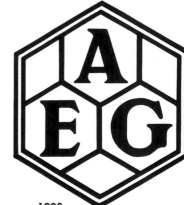

1908

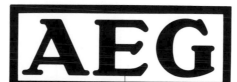

1914

The bold, authoritative style of lettering evokes the might of the company

1960

AEG 1908–60

When, in 1907, Peter Behrens was appointed artistic director of the giant German industrial combine AEG (Allgemeine Elektricitäts-Gesellschaft), one of his first challenges was to redesign the company logo. This he did by dramatically simplifying it to just three letters in a rectangle. The strong, unfussy lettering remains the basis of the logo used today.

COCA-COLA

The Coca-Cola script was designed by an amateur, Frank Robinson, the fledgling company's bookkeeper. He devised both the Spencerian script and the brilliantly concise words beneath: "Delicious and Refreshing." The bottle is among the most recognizable icons in the world, a design that has come to symbolize the youthful exuberance of America. Countless variations have been released over the decades, but the enduring classic is the curved vessel designed by the Root Glass Company of Terre Haute, Indiana, and introduced in 1915. A Coca-Cola dispenser was later designed by Raymond Loewy.

Early poster

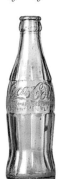 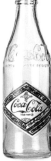 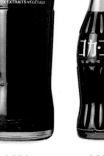 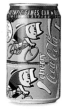 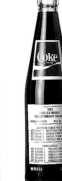

| 1950 | 1980 | 1983 | 1980s | 1980s | 1992 |

Selection of Coca-Cola bottles and can

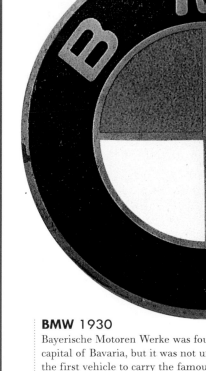

BMW 1930

Bayerische Motoren Werke was founded in 1916 in Munich, the capital of Bavaria, but it was not until 1929 that the Dixi became the first vehicle to carry the famous BMW logo. The symbol is remarkably simple: silver lettering on a circular black band that encases four segments of solid blue and white – the colors of Bavaria. The image has its origins in World War I, when the Bavarian *Luftwaffe* flew planes painted in Bayern blue and white, affording the pilot a view through his propeller of blue and white segments. This inspired the stylized design we now recognize on vehicle logos, such as the one pictured here, and on other BMW products. It has been updated to project an identity that is smart, clean-cut, sporty – and image-conscious.

The shield symbolizes integrity and quality

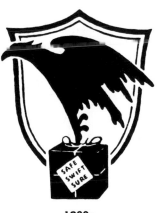

1920s

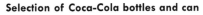

1937

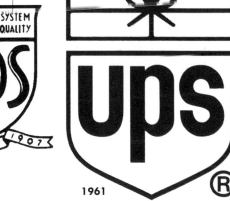

1961

UPS 1920s–61

United Parcel Service developed its first shield logo in the 1920s, using the bold image of an eagle carrying a package labeled "Safe, Swift, Sure." This was simplified in 1937 to a shield outline containing the company initials, with a new message to appeal to the retail trade. In 1961, the current logo was born, the work of Paul Rand. He abbreviated the shield, added a rectangular package, and clarified the lettering. The key to good design, he explained, was "taking the essence of something that is already there and enhancing its meaning by putting it into a form everyone can identify with."

CND 1958

When Gerald Holtom designed what has become the symbol for the British Campaign for Nuclear Disarmament, he was told that it would never catch on. It has since been adopted as the universal image of peace. Designed originally for the Direct Action Committee Against Nuclear War, it works on two levels: it is semaphore for "N" and "D," and it is a self portrait. Holtom explained, "I drew myself, the representative of an individual in despair, with hands . . . outstretched outward and downward in the manner of Goya's peasant before the firing squad."

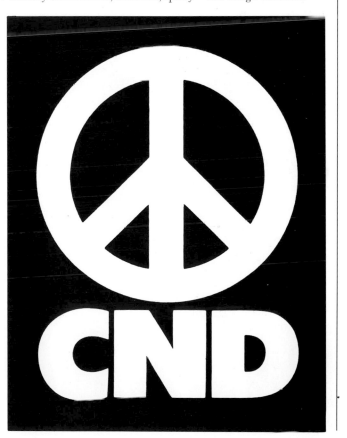

SONY

Sony 1973

The visual simplicity of the Sony logo is pivotal to its design. Easy to understand and pronounce, the name is readable in any language and immediately recognizable. The name derives from the Latin *sonus*, meaning "sound." The design of the logo has been modified only minimally since 1957, when the strokes of the letters were lighter and the word itself more expanded. The version shown here is from 1973; it has remained the same since then.

The thick letters of the Sony logotype always appear in a single color

McDONALD'S

The McDonald's Golden Arches logo was introduced in 1962. It was created by Jim Schindler to resemble new arch-shaped signs on the sides of the restaurants. He merged the two golden arches together to form the famous "M" now recognized throughout the world. Schindler's work was a development of the stylized "v" logo sketched by Fred Turner, which was conceived as a more stylish corporate symbol than the Speedee chef character that had previously been used. The McDonald's name was added to the logo in 1968.

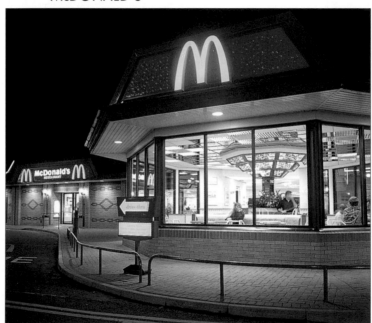

McDonald's restaurant

SNCF 1970

Since it was established in 1938, the French railway SNCF (Société Nationale des Chemins de Fer) has made two significant redesigns of its corporate image. The example shown here dates from 1970, before which the interwoven letters "SNF" were framed by the "C." Updated by Roger Tallon in 1985, a lighter, more fluid-looking logo emerged, based on the italicized outline of its letters.

There is no accompanying image or framing line with the simply composed lowercase letters

olivetti

Olivetti 1970

Like Sony, Olivetti eschews a corporate symbol, instead using the letters of its name to suggest a product of quality and style. Devised by Walter Ballmer, this latest logo, with its rounded, lowercase letters, has evolved from three earlier designs, dating back to a 1934 version by X. Schawinsky.

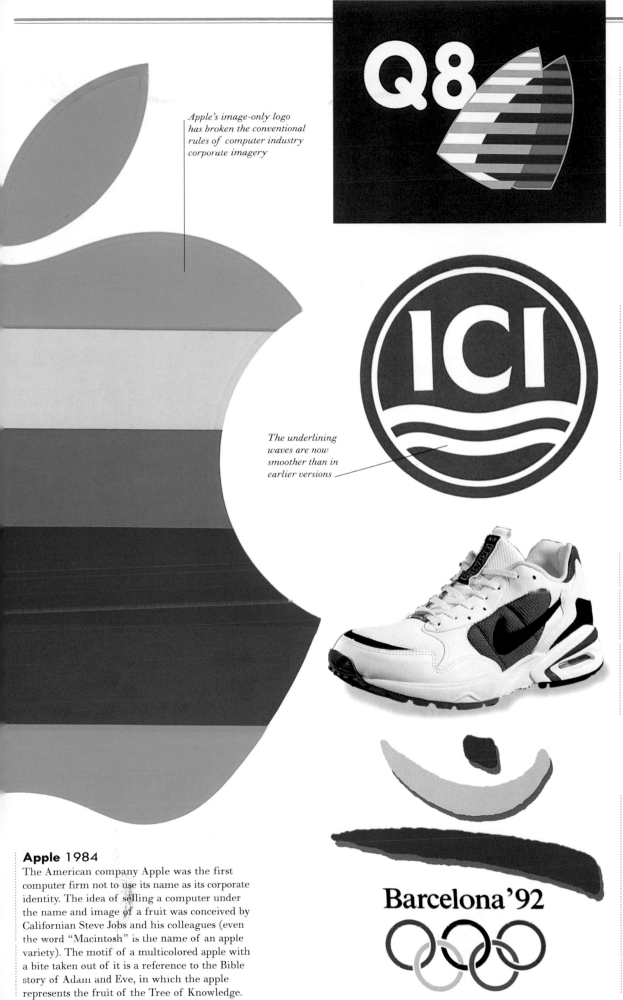

Apple's image-only logo has broken the conventional rules of computer industry corporate imagery

The underlining waves are now smoother than in earlier versions

Q8 1986

In a bid to expand its retail petroleum business into the international market, Kuwait Petroleum took the radical step of completely changing the name of its subsidiary company, Gulf Oil. Gulf became Q8 in Europe in 1986, based on the English pronunciation of Kuwait. Its symbol of twin sails refers to traditional Kuwaiti trading ships, and the bright color combination is intended to improve the visibility of the gas stations in the dark. The new identity was created by Wolff Olins.

ICI 1987

When, in 1926, Nobel and three other large British chemical companies merged to form Imperial Chemical Industries, the existing black and orange Nobel roundel was adopted by the new company. It has been updated several times since, most notably in 1987, when the corporate identity design group Wolff Olins introduced the clean, modern combination of white letters against a blue background. The full name is now used only occasionally; instead, the company is universally identifiable by its initials.

Nike 1989

The Nike logo is a classic case of a company gradually simplifying its corporate identity as its fame increases. The company's first logo appeared in 1971, when the word "Nike," the Greek goddess of victory, was printed in orange over the outline of a checkmark, the sign of positivity. Used as a motif on sports shoes since the 1970s, this checkmark is now so recognizable that the company name itself has became superfluous. The solid, orange check was registered as a trademark in 1995.

Apple 1984

The American company Apple was the first computer firm not to use its name as its corporate identity. The idea of selling a computer under the name and image of a fruit was conceived by Californian Steve Jobs and his colleagues (even the word "Macintosh" is the name of an apple variety). The motif of a multicolored apple with a bite taken out of it is a reference to the Bible story of Adam and Eve, in which the apple represents the fruit of the Tree of Knowledge.

Barcelona Olympic Games 1992

In 1988, José M. Trías, a professor of design and director of Quod Design Company, won a competition that was launched to select the symbol and logotype for the 1992 Olympic Games in Barcelona. The apparently abstract image above the words "Barcelona '92" is based on the stylized form of a leaping human figure. It faces to the right, following the flow of the text, and expresses dynamism, victory, and joy. A shadow has been included to give a sense of height. The five interlocking Olympic rings were designed in 1913 by Pierre de Coubertin; each ring represents one of the five competing continents.

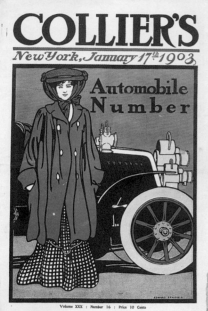

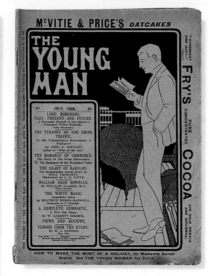

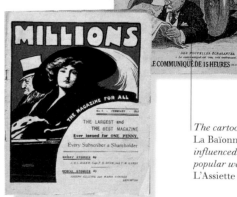

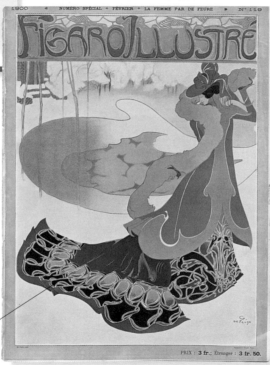

Magazines 1900–10

Figaro Illustré is a fine example of Art Nouveau design. It features the abstract floral motifs and organic forms typical of the French style. Elements of this style were adopted by Edward Penfield, who illustrated this edition of *Colliers*. Penfield was an influential figure in the evolution of the American art poster – a new genre of advertising that was typified by bold, flat colors and unfussy design. *The Young Man*, counterpart to the popular Victorian publication *The Young Woman*, shows elements of the Arts and Crafts style, the predecessor to European Art Nouveau.

Abstract floral patterns were popular in French Art Nouveau graphics

The classic Roman alphabet contrasts with the florid Art Nouveau typefaces

The cartoon style of La Baïonnette was influenced by the popular weekly L'Assiette au Beurre

MAGAZINE COVERS

BEFORE THE 1930s, THE MAJORITY of magazines featured art illustrations rather than photographs on their covers, but, during World War II, designers began to realize the power of the photographic image fully. Often used for political manipulation, pictures such as those showcased by the photojournalism magazine *Picture Post* had enormous impact. After the war, there was a boom in the market for women's journals; this was largely fashion-led and started a trend, which continues today, for glossy, color cover shots of glamorous models. The advent of desktop publishing in the 1980s has enabled designers to create pages on screen and to experiment with unusual typefaces. In some cases, the creative presentation of type and the frank content of the text make the cover lines as eye-catching as the image itself.

Magazines 1910s

There are several subjects that, when featured on the cover of a magazine, are guaranteed to attract a readership. Among these are political satire and lifestyles of the fashionable. The French publication *La Baïonnette* is a prime example of the first, while *Millions* and *Every Week*, with their cover images of chic women, demonstrate the second. In early magazines, it was the illustration rather than the words that conveyed the title's content. It was not really until the 1980s that cover lines became equally influential.

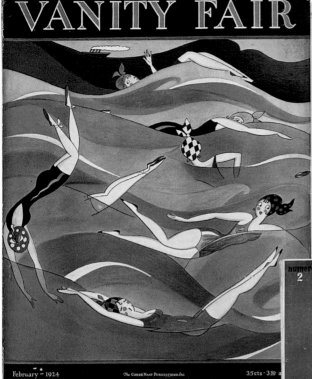

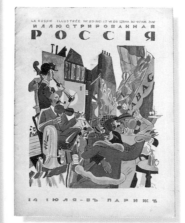

Magazines 1930s

The Spanish Civil War turned Spain into a battleground of rival ideologies. Great political art grew from the conflict, in the form of literature, posters, and magazines. The propagandist cover of *Blanco y Negro* celebrates women's wartime role in industry. Germany continued to be a center for design excellence, exemplified by the assimilation of the Bauhaus school, and by the stream of great designers such as Herbert Bayer (see p.208), who was responsible for this beautiful cover of *die neue linie*.

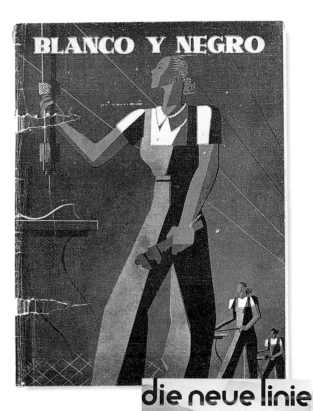

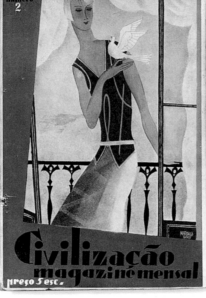

Magazines 1920s

The Art Deco style takes its name from the seminal *Paris Exposition Internationale des Arts Décoratifs et Industriels Modernes*, held in 1925. The style was quickly adopted worldwide, and to such an extent that national origin is often difficult to identify. All of the magazines shown here demonstrate the combination of Cubist and Modernist elements with a bold use of color and stylized forms, which were hallmarks of the Art Deco style in the graphic arts. The images promote the glamorous high living of the 1920s.

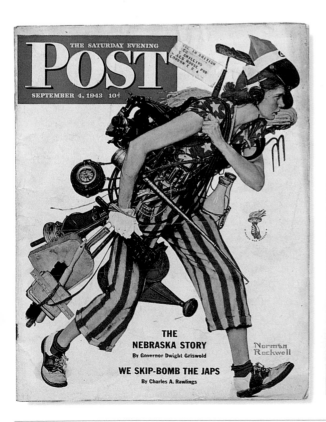

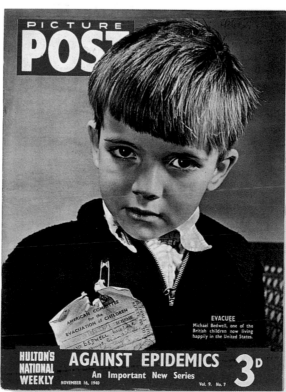

Magazines 1940s

World War II dominated design in the 1940s and is the subject of both the covers shown here. Like *Blanco y Negro*, the witty cover of *Saturday Evening Post*, created by Norman Rockwell, pays tribute to women war workers. Both women hold a monkey wrench; but Rockwell's woman, dressed in the American flag, struggles with the tools of many trades, from milk delivery to nursing. *Picture Post* was one of the first magazines to feature photography inside and out.

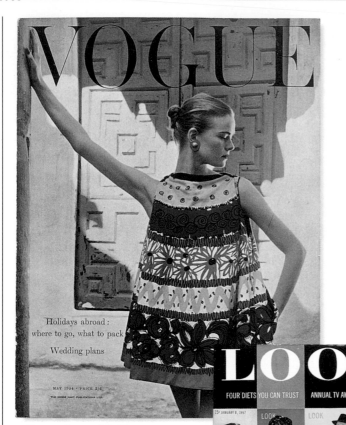

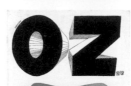

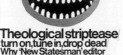

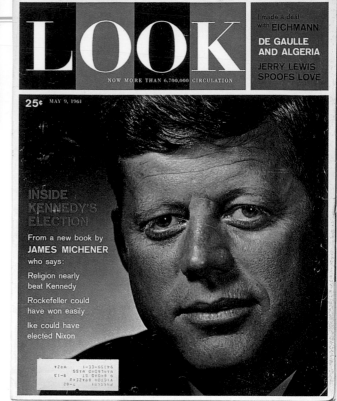

Magazines 1950s

American *Vogue* was established in the early 1890s, followed by the British and French versions in 1916 and 1920, respectively. The early covers showed a commitment to contemporary art movements but, from the 1950s on, color photographs of the latest haute couture fashions were increasingly popular. This copy of the photojournalism title *Look* shows a grid of famous faces that repeats the squares of the masthead.

Magazines 1960s

Among the many underground publications that appeared in the 1960s was *OZ* magazine. Along with contemporaries such as Milton Glaser (see p.22), *OZ*'s designer Martin Sharp was instrumental in setting new standards in graphic design. Their experiments with typography even rubbed off on more conventional women's magazines. While photographs were favored by news magazines like *Look*, *Time*, and *Paris Match*, the satirical journal *Punch* continued to use illustrations.

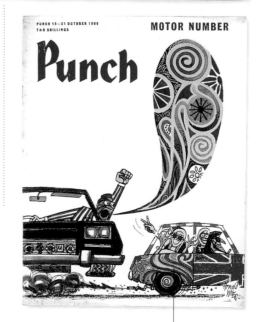

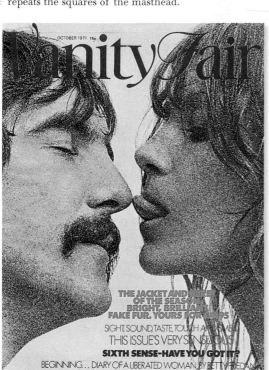

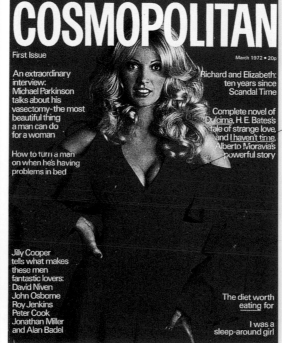

Women's magazine covers typically bear vivid, confident images of femininity

The psychedelic style was a bold adaption of Art Nouveau motifs

Magazines 1970s

By the 1970s, as more magazines appeared on the newsstands, sales became heavily reliant on an arresting cover image. The grainy, tinted photograph used on this issue of *Vanity Fair* demonstrates a technique favored by designers in the 1970s, which was intended to give a sense of realism. The provocative choice of cover image has since come to characterize *Vanity Fair*. *Cosmopolitan*, launched in its present form in the US in 1965, is now an internationally successful title. Shown here, the first British issue prefigures the style of women's magazine covers of the 1980s – strong, vivid, and unmistakably confident.

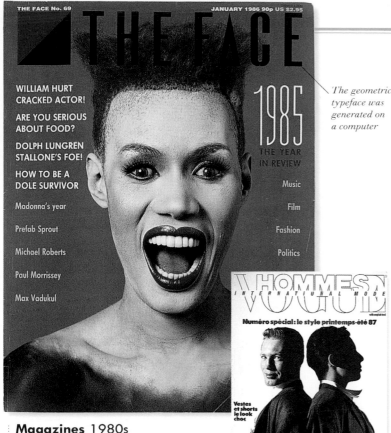

THE FACE No. 69

JANUARY 1986 90p US $2.95

THE FACE

WILLIAM HURT CRACKED ACTOR!

ARE YOU SERIOUS ABOUT FOOD?

DOLPH LUNGREN STALLONE'S FOE!

HOW TO BE A DOLE SURVIVOR

Madonna's year

Prefab Sprout

Michael Roberts

Paul Morrissey

Max Vadukul

1985

THE YEAR IN REVIEW

Music

Film

Fashion

Politics

The geometric typeface was generated on a computer

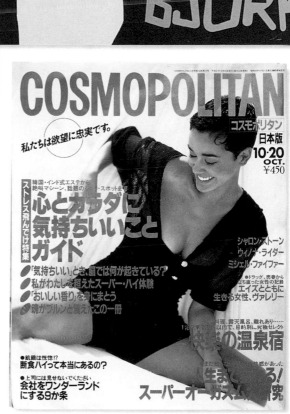

NOUVELLE SÉRIE No 8 - JUILLET-AOÛT-SEPTEMBRE 1995 - 22 FF - 7 FS - 180 FB - 7 SCAN - 600 PTS

vibrations

WORLD JAZZ RAP

vibrations

vibrations

LE MAGAZINE WORLD JAZZ RAP

ISAAC HAYES

KIP HANRAHAN

MENELIK

JAZZMATAZZ II

MO'WAX

JOSHUA REDMAN

DIONNE FARRIS

L'autre BJÖRK

Magazines 1980s

From 1981 to 1986, graphic designer Neville Brody (see p.211) was responsible for the groundbreaking British style and music magazine *The Face*. Like Peter Saville (see p.221), Brody was influenced by the chaotic typography of Punk. He manipulated new and existing typefaces to create a unique visual language that challenged the editorial content of the text. Although *The Face* had a mixed readership, it was aimed more at men than women. *Vogue* took advantage of a gap in the market for a fashion-led men's magazine and launched *Hommes*, presaging the 1990s craze for men's magazines

HOMMES

INTERNATIONAL MODE

VOGUE

with english text

Numéro spécial: le style printemps-été 87

Vestes et shorts le look choc

Supplément
Les collections et leurs coulisses

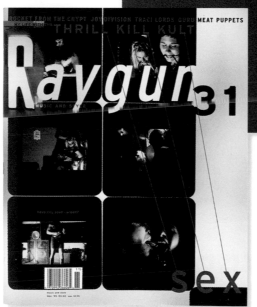

ROCKET FROM THE CRYPT JOY DIVISION TRACI LORDS GURU

THRILL KILL KULT

MEAT PUPPETS

Raygun 31

MUSIC AND STYLE

sex

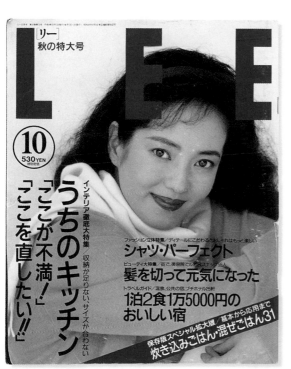

リー
秋の特大号

LEE

10
530 YEN

うちのキッチン
「ここが不満！」
「ここを直したい！！」

ファッション立体特集／ディテールにこだわるときっとそれはもっと楽しい
インテリア徹底大特集 収納が足りない、サイズが合わない

シャツ・パーフェクト

ビューティ大特集／街で美顔器をさがしてみると
髪を切って元気になった

トラベルガイド／温泉、公共の宿、プチホテル65軒
1泊2食1万5000円の
おいしい宿

保存版スペシャル拡大版 基本から応用まで
炊き込みごはん・混ぜごはん31

Magazines 1990s

Over the past decade, Terry Jones's *i-D* magazine and others, such as *Raygun*, have challenged the most basic concepts of magazine design, eschewing the grid (on which designers lay images and text) in favor of a seemingly random, anarchic approach to layout. Desktop publishing has meant that the typesetter's skills have been learned by designers. They now create the pages onscreen and can make immediate changes in typography, rather than sending corrections to the typesetter to be input manually. The ability to manipulate and overlay type directly has resulted in the image almost taking second place to the text in magazines.

COSMOPOLITAN

コスモポリタン

日本版
10·20
OCT.
¥450

私たちは欲望に忠実です。

韓国・インド式エステから絶叫マシーン、話題のスポットまで
ストレス飛んでけ特集

心とカラダに
気持ちいいこと
ガイド

●「気持ちいい」とき、脳では何が起きている？
●私がわたしを超えたスーパー・ハイ体験
●「おいしい香り」を身にまとう
●魂がプルンと震えるこの一冊

シャロン・ストーン
ウィノ・ライダー
ミシェル・ファイファー

●ドラッグ、売春からエイズとともに
生きる女性、ヴァレリー

快感の温泉宿

●肌荒れは性悪！？
断食ハイって本当にあるの？

●上司には見せないでください
会社をワンダーランドにする9か条

生まれ変わる！
スーパーオーガズム研究

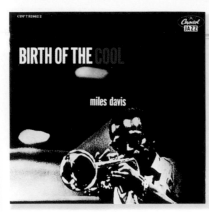

Birth of the Cool 1956
Amran Avakian created the atmospheric image on this record sleeve for *Birth of the Cool* by Miles Davis, released by Capitol Records. The black-and-white photograph is the perfect vehicle for cultivating the ultra-cool persona of this jazz giant.

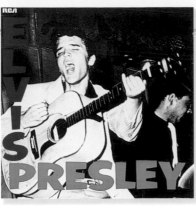

Elvis Presley 1956
The sleeve of Elvis Presley's eponymous first album, produced by RCA, captures the young King of Rock 'n' Roll during a live performance. The red and green lettering that spells out his name was echoed two decades later on *London Calling* by The Clash (see opposite).

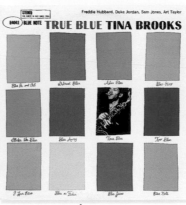

True Blue 1960
Blue Note Records is responsible for some of the greatest album cover concepts ever devised. This sleeve for Tina Brooks's album is a witty example by Reid Miles. Each song contains the word "blue" in its title, and each is represented by a rectangle in a different shade of blue.

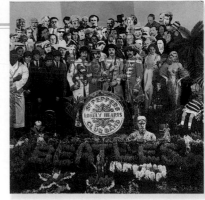

Sgt. Pepper's Lonely Hearts Club Band 1967
Designed by Pop artists Peter Blake and Jann Haworth, this celebrated sleeve for the Beatles' seminal album, released by Parlophone, is probably the most famous ever created. The host of stars includes Marilyn Monroe and W.C. Fields.

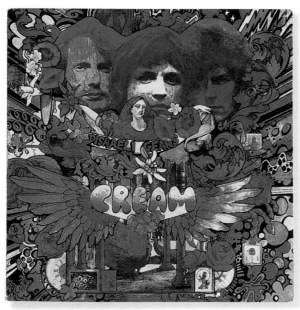

Disraeli Gears 1967
Psychedelic illustration was favored for record sleeves in the 1960s. Martin Sharp's design for Cream's album combines peacocks, flowers, and clocks – all surrealist icons of drug-induced hallucination – in red and acidic yellows. In their midst float the band members' heads, photographed by Bob Whitaker. The album was released by Polydor.

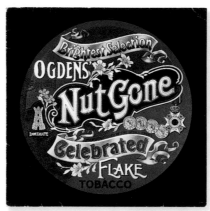

Ogdens' Nut Gone Flake 1968
The British band The Small Faces released this album for the company Immediate Records. Created by P. Brown, the illustration on the sleeve resembles a circular tin of tobacco. Developing this theme, the compact disc version of *Ogdens' Nut Gone Flake* was later released in a tin. This typifies the boom in novelty packaging since the advent of the more manageably sized CD in 1983.

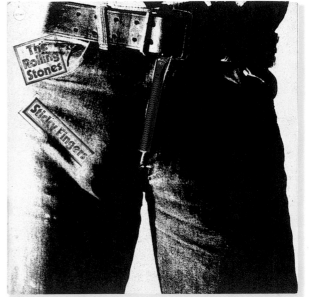

Sticky Fingers 1971
Early editions of this sexually suggestive album cover for the Rolling Stones' *Sticky Fingers* incorporate a real, functioning zipper, while the back of the sleeve shows the rear view of the same denim-clad figure. The concept and photography is by Andy Warhol, whose name appears on the waistband of the briefs on the inner sleeve.

RECORD COVERS

ALTHOUGH POPULAR MUSIC has been available on records since the beginning of the century, only since the 1950s has the design of record sleeves emerged as an art form. The American record company Blue Note was one of the first to develop an apparent design brand, an idea taken to extreme lengths in the 1980s by the British label Factory Records. In the 1990s, the significance of covers to the potential purchaser is recognized by all major record companies, who employ teams of designers to create competitive packaging for releases on vinyl, cassette tape, and compact disc.

Tales from Topographic Oceans 1972
This fantasy landscape for the triple-fold cover of the album by the group Yes is by British artist Roger Dean, a prolific designer of record sleeves and typography during the 1970s. Using illustrations of famous English rocks, including those at both Stonehenge and Land's End, Dean has created a space-age, dreamlike plane with an infinite background. The album was released by Atlantic Records.

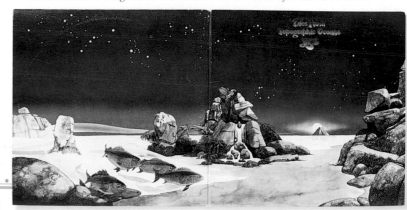

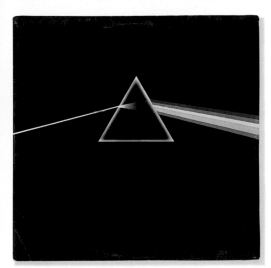

Dark Side of the Moon 1973

Released by EMI Records, this Pink Floyd album was one of the most successful of the 1970s. Its cover is a product of the influential British design group Hipgnosis; George Hardie produced the slick, enigmatic image of a light beam splitting into seven colors as it passes through a prism.

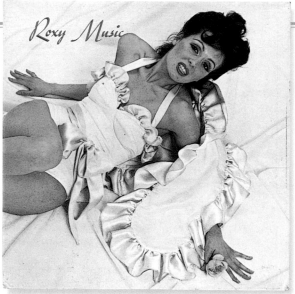

Roxy Music 1972

The term "Art Rock" was coined for Roxy Music, famed for the arty, image-conscious sophistication of their music and personal style. Released by Island Records, this was the first album to contain credits for art (Nicholas de Ville), clothes, makeup, and hair (Anthony Price), as well as photography (Karl Stoecker), and "cover concept" (Bryan Ferry).

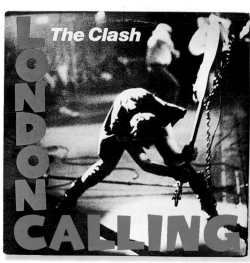

London Calling 1979

Designer Ray Lowry makes overt typographic and photographic references to Elvis Presley's album of 1956 (see opposite) in his sleeve design for the punk rock band The Clash. The powerful photograph by Penny Smith immortalizes vocalist/guitarist Joe Strummer in the act of smashing his guitar.

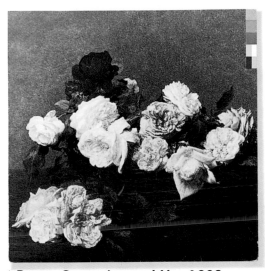

Power Corruption and Lies 1983

Inspired by the painting *Roses* by Henri Fantin-Latour (1836–1904), Peter Saville composed the cover for New Order's album *Power Corruption and Lies* for Manchester's Factory Records. The only alteration to the 19th-century French artist's work is the addition of a color bar in the top right corner. A folded poster is included with the CD version.

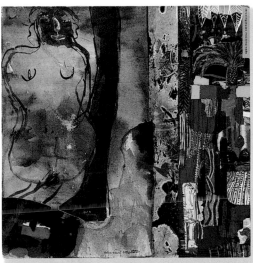

House Tornado 1988

Graphic artist Vaughan Oliver is renowned for his ability to reflect the style of music in the design of its accompanying record sleeve. He established the design studio 23 Envelope, known as v23 after 1988, to create packaging for the British record company 4AD. He designed this album sleeve for the group Throwing Muses, showing painterly influences.

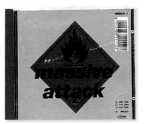

Blue Lines 1991

Designed by Michael Nash Associates, this CD insert features the flame logo that has come to identify Massive Attack albums. The title *Blue Lines* appears in such tiny lettering it looks almost like a copyright mark.

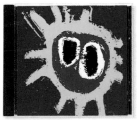

Screamadelica 1991

This CD by Primal Scream was released by Creation Records. The insert design by Paul Connell does not include any text, simply an image typical of the 1990s "rave" scene.

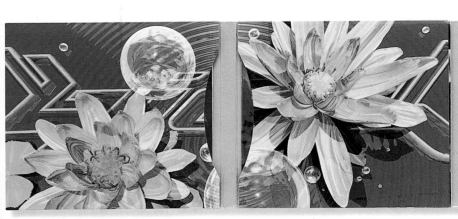

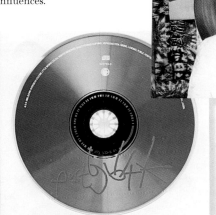

Post 1995

The cover of Björk's album, released on One Little Indian, features the singer against an electronically enhanced background. The pages of the CD insert feature repeated images of a lotus flower.

POSTERS 1900–19

THE DEVELOPMENT OF LITHOGRAPHIC PRINTING in the second half of the 19th century heralded the start of modern poster art. Work by Frenchmen Jules Chéret (1836–1932) and Henri de Toulouse-Lautrec (1864–1901) formed the background to the new art form. By the turn of the century, the most important movement in poster design was Art Nouveau, but William Morris and the Arts and Crafts movement also had a marked impact on the two main centers of design – Glasgow, home to the Glasgow School, and Vienna, birthplace of the Vienna Secession.

Flirt c.1895
The Czech artist Alphonse Mucha is the most famous and flamboyant exponent of the Art Nouveau poster design. His posters featured beautiful women, often with long, flowing hair, framed by floral decoration and organic line. Mucha's break came in Paris in 1894 when he designed a hugely successful life-size poster for Sarah Bernhardt. This example is one of many advertising posters he produced.

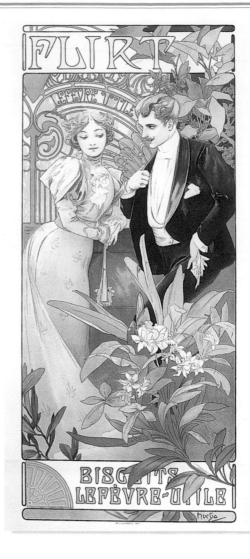

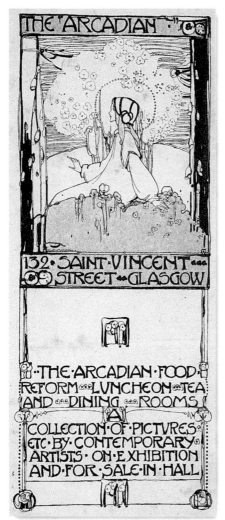

The Arcadian c.1906
During the 1890s and 1900s, the so-called Glasgow School was centered around Charles Rennie Mackintosh, and included Jessie M. King, who designed this poster for the Arcadian Tea Rooms. The Glasgow School took recognizable Art Nouveau elements and added rigid geometry and compositional decoration.

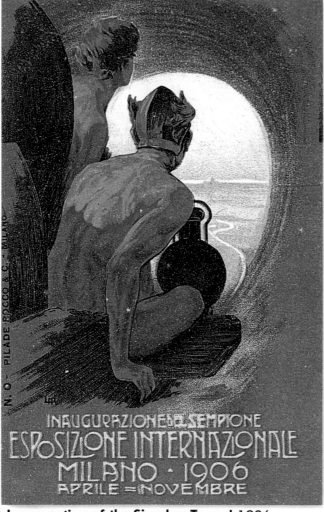

Inauguration of the Simplon Tunnel 1906
Italian designer Leopoldo Metlicovitz created this poster to mark the opening of the Simplon Tunnel at the Milan International Exhibition. The winged-helmeted figure of Mercury, the god of speed, sits at the front of the train as it is about to leave the tunnel. The poster's message is that even Mercury finds it faster to take the train! It typifies Metlicovitz's work, with the painterly figure of a muscular athletic young man, the allegorical subject matter, and subdued brown tones.

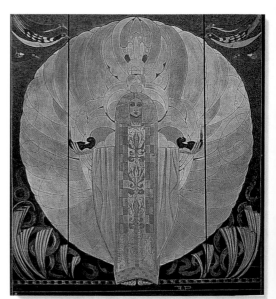

Liberty poster 1907
In Italy, the Art Nouveau movement was known as Stile Liberty (or Stile Floreale), the name making direct reference to the influential store on London's Regent Street. Founded in 1875 by Arthur Lasenby Liberty, the establishment had commercial links with Italy. This leather panel was produced for the Venice International Exhibition in 1907 by Serruccio Pizzanelli.

Vienna Secession poster stamp 1908

The Vienna Secession came into being in 1897 when a number of young artists rebelled over the art establishment's refusal to exhibit foreign work. The Secessionists included Gustav Klimt, Koloman Moser, Josef Hoffman, and J.M. Olbrich. Vienna became the creative design capital of Europe. Berthold Löffler (1874–1960) designed the 1908 Secessionist Exhibition poster. He was also responsible for this poster stamp announcing a procession to mark the Austrian Emperor Francis-Joseph I's 60th Jubilee.

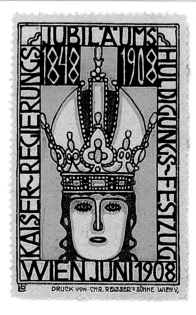

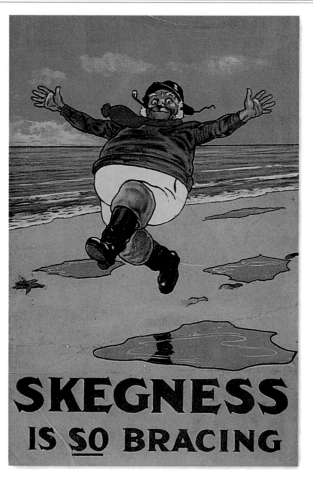

Skegness Is So Bracing 1909

The growth of the British railroads at the start of the century is responsible for some great posters commissioned by London Transport, various rail companies, and tourist resorts served by the railroads. This famous poster by prolific graphic designer John Hassel extols the virtues of the seaside resort of Skegness. Like other seaside destinations, off-season was harder to sell, so Hassel resorts to the invigorating effect of the cold fresh sea air. His comic image is of a portly gentleman skipping along the beach in boots, scarf, and hat. The poster was so successful that Hassel produced different versions of it. It is, in effect, a translation into English design of the French entertainment posters of the 1890s, typified by the work of Toulouse-Lautrec.

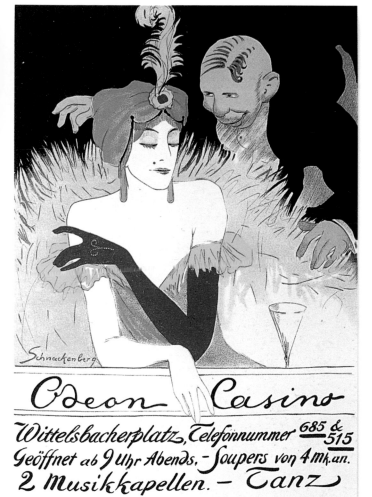

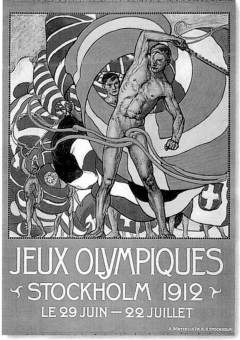

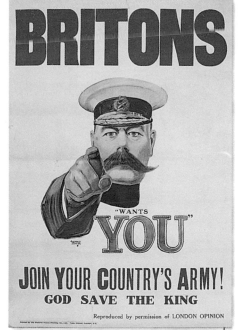

Odeon Casino 1911

The German designer Walter Schnackenberg (1880–1961) produced a series of posters advertising the Odeon Casino. They all featured beautiful, sophisticated women, and most of them also showed handsome men. The bestubbled, ingratiating fellow in this example is presumably a waiter! The poster is striking for its use of bold color. In addition to posters, during his long, successful career Schnackenberg contributed to the German magazines *Jugend* (from which the German form of Art Nouveau, Jugendstil, was named) and *Das Plakat*.

Stockholm Olympic Games 1912

Throughout the century, the Olympic Games has given both athletes and poster designers the opportunity to prove their prowess. In this version, A. Börtzells places center stage a young naked man (his dignity preserved by a well-positioned streamer) swirling the Swedish flag above his head. He is followed by a host of naked men with undulating national flags.

Your Country Needs You 1914

During World War I, many governments made use of posters to aid the war effort. This one, designed by Alfred Leete (1882–1933), gave rise to many imitations, including one by J.M. Flagg for the US Army. Leete's recruitment poster features the inescapable gaze of Lord Kitchener, the secretary of war.

POSTERS 1920–39

THERE ARE AS MANY SCHOOLS and movements in poster design as there are in painting, and from 1920 to 1939 they abounded: Bauhaus, De Stijl, Futurism, Cubism, to name but four. Yet we should be wary of categorizing designers by movement. Certainly, the designer E. McKnight Kauffer, author of *The Art of the Poster*, complained that the public put "Cubist" or "Futurist" tags on anything modern. The majority of the posters produced during these two decades were designed to promote commercial products or cultural events, but propaganda pieces, including the El Lissitsky poster shown here, continued to appear in Russia and elsewhere to support particular causes, such as the Spanish Civil War.

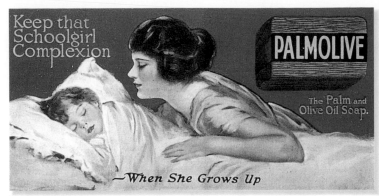

Palmolive early-1920s
This poster exemplifies the technique of selling a product with a slogan. American designer Clarence Underwood (b.1871) was commissioned by J.B. Watson, head of the giant Walter Thompson agency, to produce a series of posters around the same slogan: "Keep That Schoolgirl Complexion." Watson had done extensive research into finding slogans that triggered the "buy impulse."

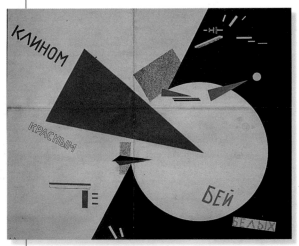

Beat the Whites with the Red Wedge c.1920
El Lissitsky's famous Soviet propaganda poster for the Red Army is an icon of Constructivist design. The poster is typical of Lissitsky's style: simple elements; sharp, dynamic diagonals contrasting with circles; and a bold use of limited color, in this case red, white, and black.

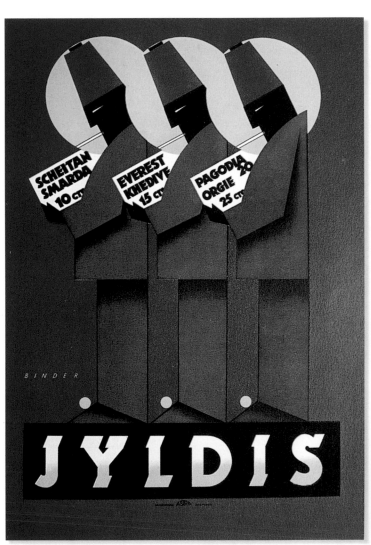

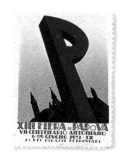

Futurist poster stamp 1931
Through their experiments in typography, the futurists had a direct influence on poster design. Their approach has been called "painterly typography": a visual onomatopoeia, where words look like their meaning. So *Speed* might be in italics, and **Shout** in bold type. Stamp-sized posters, allowing advertising though the mail, were popular in the 1920s.

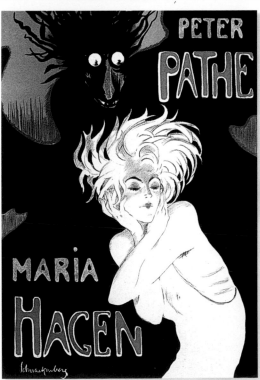

Hagen-Pathé 1920s
German designer, painter, theater set designer, and illustrator Walter Schnackenberg (see p.223) produced a number of high-quality posters, of which this atmospheric theater poster is typical.

Jyldis c.1925
Josef Binder (1898–1972) was an Austrian designer who was described in his day as "the biggest talent and the greatest hope of Austrian graphic arts." His highly individualized, aggressively modern style was hugely successful. He soon turned to theory, though, lecturing regularly in the United States. The basis of his theory was "everything moves faster today; we need the same speed to transmit the message effectively."

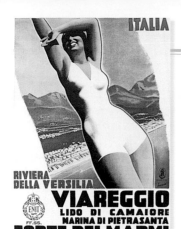

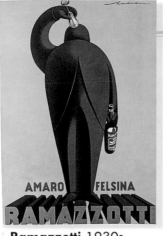

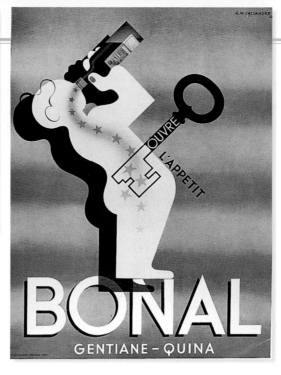

Forte dei Marmi 1930s
One of Italy's lesser-known poster artists, Gino Bocasile designed both the poster featured on p.207 and this beautiful travel one advertising the resort of Viareggio. This is an early example of using sexual imagery to sell.

Ramazzotti 1930s
Federico Seneca (1891–1976), one of the most sought-after poster designers of his day, often featured stylized, Deco-style cartoon characters like this creation. Important clients included Buitoni pasta and Perugina chocolates.

Bonal 1935
A.M. Cassandre believed that the poster was primarily important as the conveyor of the message. Drawing on Cubist and Constructivist ideas, Cassandre's powerful posters dominated French advertising between the world wars. He had particular interest in lettering, believing it to be an integral, but often neglected, part of poster design. Even his hand-drawn letters are indistinguishable from type.

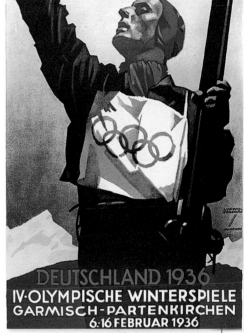

Winter Olympics 1936
Ludwig Hohlwein was the greatest German poster designer of the century, and his work prior to World War I has hardly been equaled. Hohlwein's style remained unchanged – usually one or two figures set against large areas of color, with the lettering confined to a rectangle. Sadly, it is for his last works, celebrating the idealized Aryan race, that he is commonly remembered.

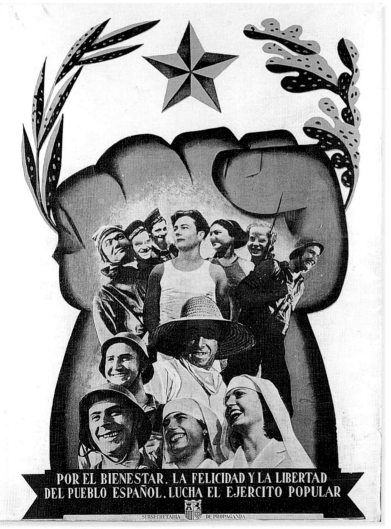

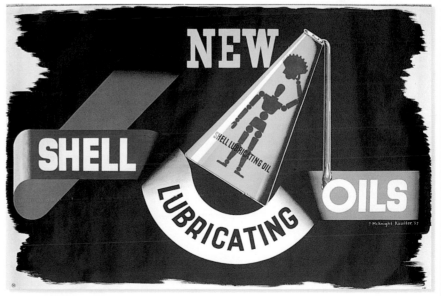

Spanish Civil War 1936–37
The Spanish Civil War attracted the attention of artists and intellectuals the world over, and saw groups of designers collaborating in Madrid and Barcelona on the design of posters in support of the Republican cause. Many of them made use of photography rather than illustrations. This poster shows constructivist influences, with the powerful fist grasping a Laurel wreath and sheltering the people in the foreground.

Shell 1937
E. McKnight Kauffer was one of several designers commissioned to produce posters for Shell Oil in the 1930s. The poster shown is a good example of Kauffer's work, with modernist imagery, bold graphics, stark color contrast, and reductivist typography. The images suggest smooth movement and oil pouring from a can. Kauffer devised the figure that was used throughout the campaign.

POSTERS 1940–59

DURING WORLD WAR II, there was a move away from posters advertising products to those that helped to further the war effort, often by recruiting or giving information. The governments that commissioned these posters urgently wanted direct, effective messages, and so took the risk of employing and giving free reign to young Modernist designers. The results were often controversial, but from this period comes some of the most creative poster designs. The gates were also opened for more inventive commercial advertising after the war was over.

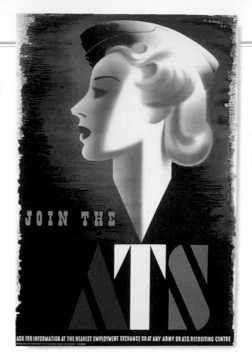

Join the ATS 1941
In his role as Official War Poster Designer for Britain, Abram Games produced nearly 100 posters. This one is a good illustration of his personal maxim, "Maximum meaning, minimum means." It depicts a stylized profile of a glamorous woman soldier, with the simple message plastered across the bottom. The serifs that descend from the crossbar of the white letter "T" form the continuation of the woman's collar, and the post of the "T" suggests a tie.

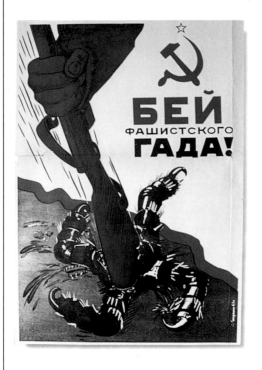

Kill the Fascist Reptile c.1940
Propaganda posters often lacked subtlety. This Soviet example shows the mighty arm of the red soldier smashing the enemy, here depicted as a swastika-shaped reptile. Symbols such as the hammer and sickle make the message easily identifiable.

Budapest Gasworks 1940
This commercial poster makes effective use of color. Its focal point is the flame that forms the engineer's hand and illuminates the lettering above. It was designed by leading Hungarian graphic artist Georg Konecsni (b.1908).

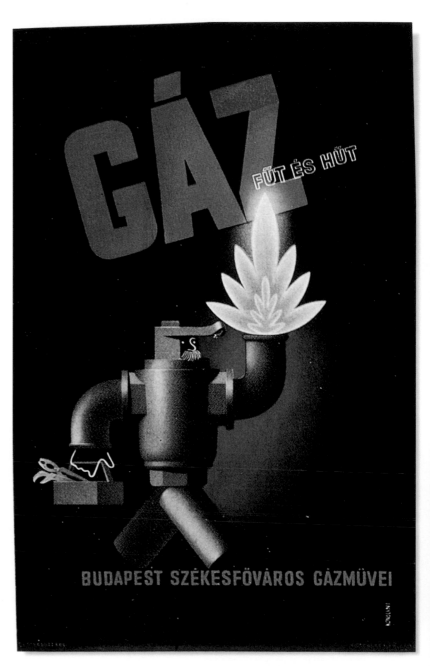

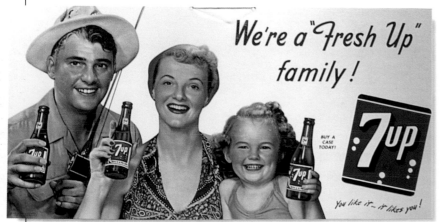

7up family c.1945
This advertising poster portrays an archetypal family enjoying the great outdoors. The fresh-faced beauty, wide smiles, relaxed attitude (the father is holding a fishing rod), and clear imagery present the drink as a healthy, refreshing product.

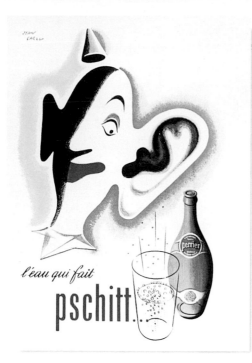

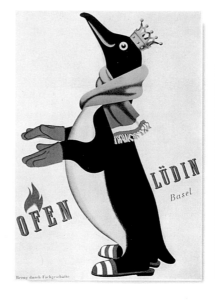

Perrier 1949

The Frenchman Jean Carlu was an important and prolific poster artist. Initially trained as an architect, Carlu turned to graphic design after he lost his right arm in an accident. His early work showed a strong Cubist influence, but, from the mid-1930s, he increasingly championed Surrealist design. Having produced some important political posters during the war, Carlu returned to product advertising for French and American clients. Here, a cartoonlike figure with an oversized ear listens to the fizz emanating from a glass of Perrier mineral water.

Ofen Lüdin 1949

One of Switzerland's most successful poster artists, Herbert Leupin (b.1916) first gained fame for his realistic commercial advertising posters. However, after setting up his own studio in 1939, he developed a distinct style of illustration that earned him commissions from both European and American clients. Many of his posters were humorous, like this penguin warming himself with a Lüdin company heater.

Champagne 1949

During the 1940s, René Gruau's sophisticated women graced numerous French fashion and cosmetic illustrations and advertisements (see p.155). His work often made striking use of a limited number of colors with black and white.

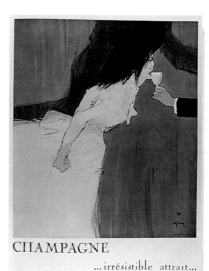

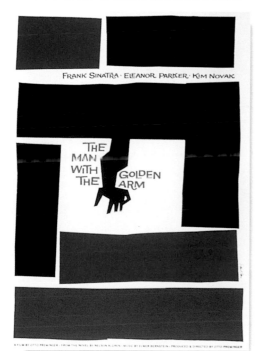

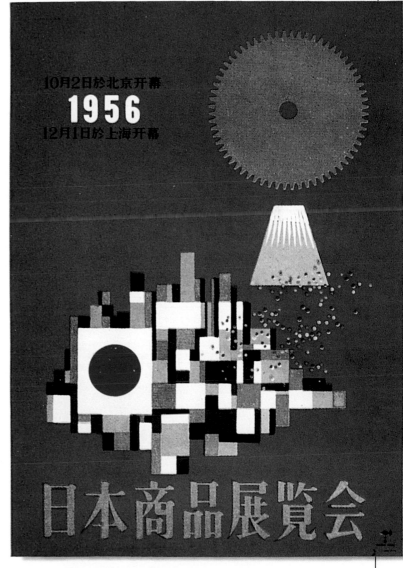

The Man with the Golden Arm 1955

Saul Bass's poster for Otto Preminger's film about a drug addict marked a radical departure in movie advertising. Instead of depicting the storyline, the jagged arm and stark imagery is used to capture the film's essence. Bass also designed the abstract opening credits.

Astral Email 1955

Raymond Savignac was the master of the visual gag. His numerous posters, produced for clients around the world, are all characterized by their direct, simple, witty, and effective designs.

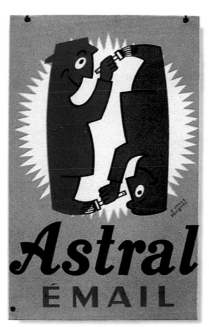

Tokyo International Trade Fair 1956

Takashi Kono (b.1906), who designed this poster, is one of the pioneers of modern Japanese graphic design. The simplified blocks of color incorporating the Japanese flag are reminiscent of 1950s textile design.

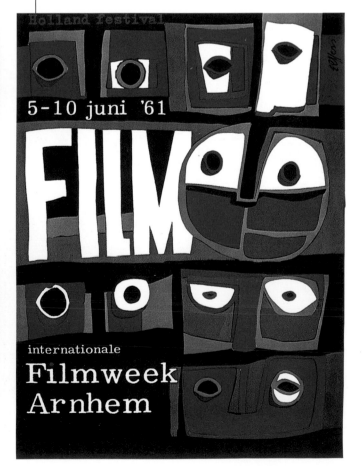

Kobe Workers' Music Council 1961

Tadanori Yokoo was one of the many innovative graphic artists to emerge from studies at the Nippon Design Center, which was founded in 1959. His cultural and commercial posters of the 1960s and '70s drew on both traditional Japanese and Western imagery. Yokoo experimented with different printing techniques, photomontage, and collage.

POSTERS 1960–79

THE PSYCHEDELIC ERA was one of the briefest, but most memorable, movements of this period. Its posters were designed for an exclusive audience with almost illegible lettering carrying the implied message "If you can't read it, it isn't for you." Psychedelia began on the West Coast but spread to Europe with the hippie movement. Elsewhere, Japanese designers were growing in international importance, being more willing than most to embrace new technology. In the 1970s, this gave designers far greater freedom through increased control of typesetting and image reproduction.

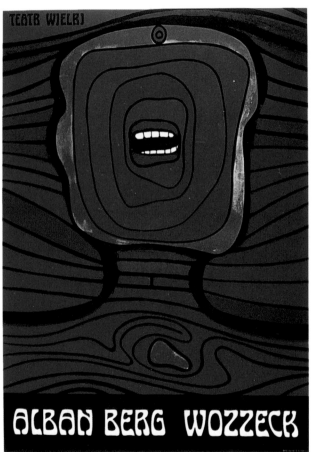

Wozzeck 1964

Jan Lenica's famed poster for the opera *Wozzeck* makes direct reference to the 1893 painting *The Scream* by the Norwegian Expressionist artist Edvard Munch (1863–1944). In both works, the focal point of the image is a screaming mouth, surrounded by resonating lines. Lenica, a prodigiously inventive Polish designer, uses heavy flowing lines that divide the space into solid bands of color: in this instance the whole poster is designed in vibrant shades of red, split by varying thicknesses of black lines.

Paper Dress Show 1967

Designed by Hirokatsu Hijikata, this poster advertises a Japanese fashion show presenting dresses made of paper. It combines a photographic image (the woman's face) with artwork. The design makes striking use of bold graduated colors to evoke the woman's dress and cape.

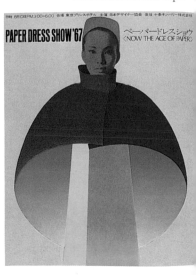

Arnhem International Film Week 1961

This was one of several screenprinted posters created by Dutchman Dick Elffers (b.1910) to promote the Holland Festival of 1961. They featured abstract masked faces rendered with blocks of solid color. This particular example, advertising an Arnhem film festival, displays a mixture of crude typography, including some hand-rendered lettering. In addition to his work as a graphic artist and painter, Elffers taught at the Rotterdam Academy, and he was architect of the interior of the Rijksmuseum in Amsterdam as well as set designer for other cultural projects.

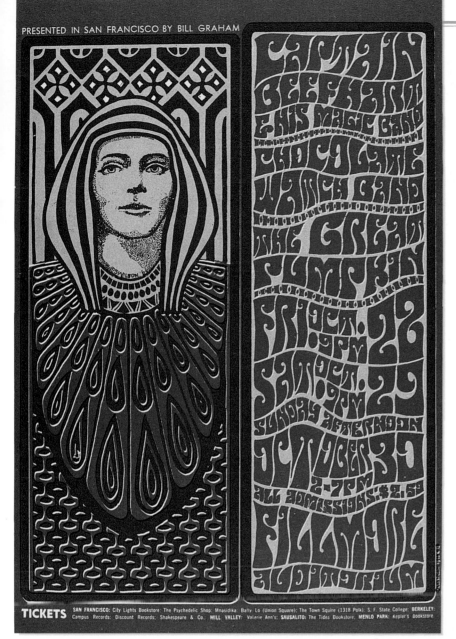

PRESENTED IN SAN FRANCISCO BY BILL GRAHAM

TICKETS SAN FRANCISCO: City Lights Bookstore; The Psychedelic Shop; Mnasidika; Bally Lo (Union Square); The Town Squire (1318 Polk); S. F. State College; BERKELEY: Campus Records; Discount Records; Shakespeare & Co. MILL VALLEY: Valerie Ann's; SAUSALITO: The Tides Bookstore; MENLO PARK: Kepler's Bookstore

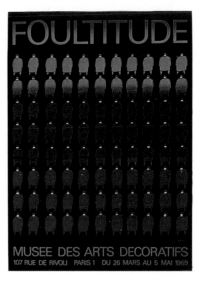

Foultitude 1969

During the 1960s, posters were increasingly viewed and sold as works of art to be framed and hung on the wall. In the US and Europe, museums and art galleries commissioned, published, and marketed posters featuring the work of major artists, including Andy Warhol, Robert Rauschenberg (b.1925), René Magritte (1898-1967), and Roy Lichtenstein (b.1923). The Belgian cartoonist and artist Jean-Michel Folon was commissioned to create a poster to advertise an exhibition at the Musée des Arts Décoratifs in Paris. In it, ranks of anonymous men are differentiated only by bands of color.

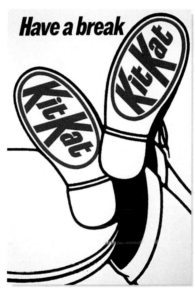

KitKat 1970s

The success of this commercial poster for a well-known chocolate bar relies on the power of the brand name. Many things are suggested but not shown in the design. The slogan "Have a Break, Have a KitKat" is not completed; it is left to the viewer to finish. Likewise, the owner of the feet is not shown; the viewer must imagine him. The product itself does not appear, although the typography and color on the sole of the shoe is the same as the packaging on the bar of chocolate. This kind of suggestive advertising has gained great popularity, particularly with cigarette manufacturers (see p.230).

Captain Beefhart at the Fillmore 1966

The psychedelic artist Wes Wilson borrowed ideas from a variety of sources and fused them together into a style of his own. Using images and lettering from the Vienna Secession (including the flowing hair), Art Nouveau ornamentation, and drug-inspired coloring, he created a language that was aimed an an exclusive "underground" audience. The swirling, multicolored lettering is barely legible.

Chicago 1968

This poster by John Rieben (b.1935) is clearly inflenced by the Swiss magazine *Neue Grafik* (New Graphic Design), which was launched in 1958 by Josef Müller-Brockmann and others. Its designers championed compositions based on grid systems, lowercase sans serif typography, and unornamented images.

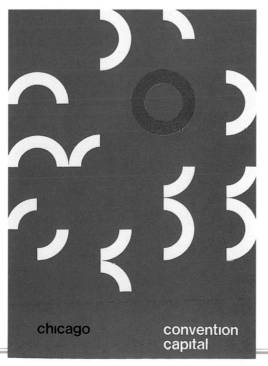

Echos de Grande Bretagne 1970s

Reginald Mount was one of a number of graphic artists who made his name with work commissioned by the British Ministry of Information during World War II. After the war, he produced many commercial and public service posters, including some for the "Keep Britain Tidy" campaign. Humorous, cartoonlike images, sometimes with surrealist elements, are typical of his style. This quirky menu pokes fun at the English etiquette of eating peas with the back of a fork.

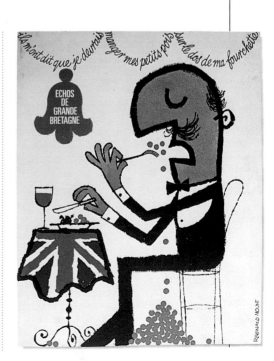

POSTERS 1980–90s

DESPITE THE VAST SUMS OF MONEY that are spent on television advertising campaigns, commercial companies and government agencies have by no means abandoned the poster as a direct and effective means of communication. The computer continues to play an increasingly important role in poster design, and new software allows image manipulation to a degree that was not dreamed of even a decade ago. The resulting work may mix any combination of photography, illustration, and typography.

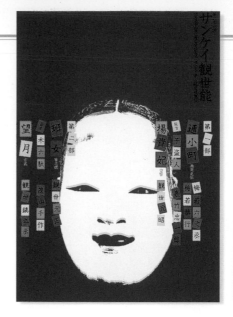

Noh 1981
Ikko Tanaka's posters are renowned for their subtle use of color, and, while they are distinctly Japanese, they do indicate an understanding of modern Western design thought. This performance poster is one of many he produced for the Kanze Noh drama. At either side of the actor's masked head, calligraphic boxes suggest bunched hair.

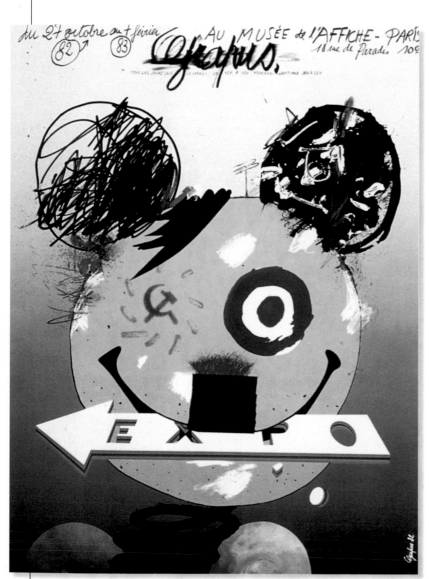

Exhibition poster for Musée de l'Affiche 1981
This striking poster by the French design collective Grapus combines elements of three political philosophies: capitalism – the central image is of Mickey Mouse, and one eye is made up of the US colors; fascism, suggested by the Hitler mustache and flick of hair; and communism, represented by the hammer and sickle forming the left eye. Grapus was founded in 1970 by Pierre Bernard, Gérard-Paris Clavel, and Francois Miehe to produce "social, political, and cultural images." The collage effect, crude drawing, scribbles, and splashes are typical of its acclaimed work.

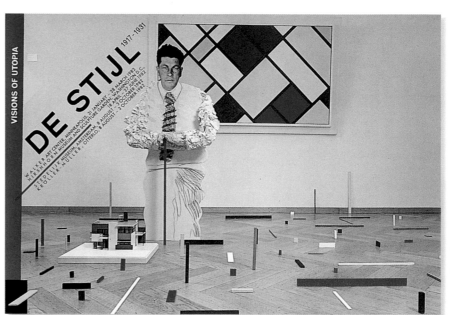

De Stijl exhibition at the Walker Art Center, Minneapolis 1982
By photographing a created "scene," Gert Dumbar broke all the conventions of museum poster design. It advertises an exhibition of the Dutch art movement De Stijl. The movement's originator, Theo van Doesburg, appears, and there are references to De Stijl's ideas, including placing the text at the same angle as the lines in the painting.

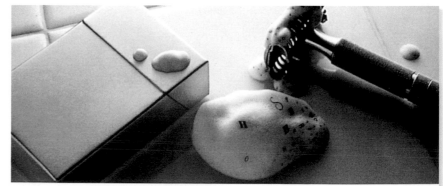

MIDDLE TAR As defined by H.M. Government
DANGER: Government Health WARNING: CIGARETTES CAN SERIOUSLY DAMAGE YOUR HEALTH

Benson and Hedges Shaved Pack 1985
The influential advertising campaign for Benson and Hedges cigarettes has featured a series of increasingly cryptic posters, of which this one, designed by Nigel Rose for the Collett Dickenson Pearce agency, is particularly successful. Although it is impossible to read the product's name (the letters have been shaved off the pack), the gold suggests it.

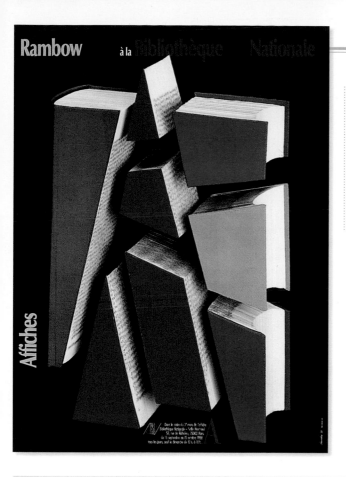

Rambow à la Bibliothèque Nationale

Affiches

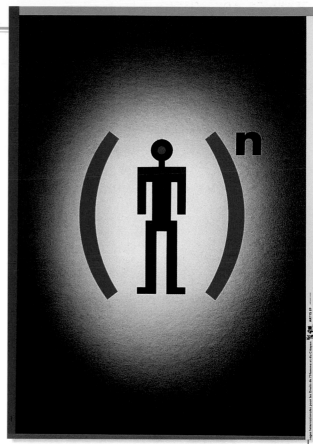

Rambow at the Bibliothèque Nationale 1987

This poster for an exhibition of Gunter Rambow's work was designed by the artist himself, and features a cut-up photograph of a book, rearranged to create a wedge shape that seems to split the book itself in half. Rambow, who typically employs photography and photomontage, is best known for his powerful political and social posters.

Bicentennial Exhibition for "The Human and The Citizens' Rights" 1989

Peret, born Pere Torrent, is a Spanish postmodernist designer. His work often consists of bold, simple graphics in strong colors. He has worked for many humanist organizations, including the Spanish Red Cross and Amnesty International. This simple yet effective poster plays on a mathematical equation, putting a human pictogram in a bracket, multiplied to the power of n, meaning humanity is all-important.

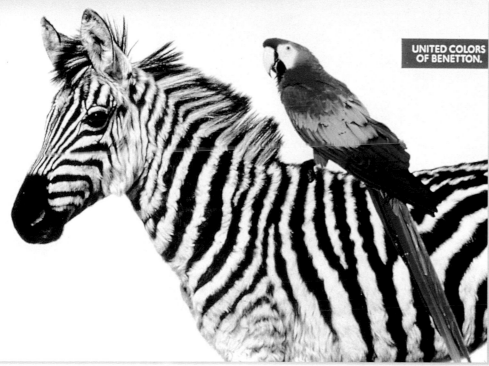

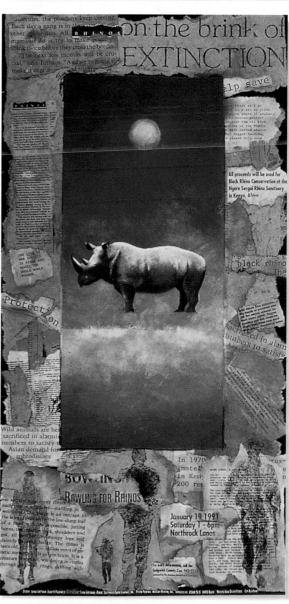

Benetton advertisement 1991–92

Oliviero Toscani has produced some of the most controversial posters of the century for the Italian clothing company Benetton. Under the slogan "The United Colors of Benetton," he has often depicted shocking and disturbing images, including a Christlike man dying of AIDS, a burning car, and a newborn baby. The one thing they all have in common is arresting imagery, and though some have questioned their relevance to the product, they have attracted great attention. This brightly colored example works more obviously with the slogan.

Bowling for Rhinos 1991

The 1980s and '90s have seen the rise of posters supporting a variety of environmental and ecological campaigns. The American graphic designer Sonia Greteman produced this poster for Sedgwick County Zoo to raise funds for black rhinoceros conservation. Its central rhino image is framed by a collage of newspaper clippings about the plight of the species, including one discussing the demand for powdered rhino horn as an aphrodisiac. At the bottom of the poster are the shadowy silhouettes of the hunters who are driving the rhinoceros into extinction.

PACKAGING 1900–09

UNLIKE MOST OTHER AREAS OF DESIGN, packaging can rarely be associated with individual designers. Rather, designs evolve with each new era: by 1900, shopping for groceries was changing from a traditional reliance on a grocer to advise on and wrap items, to allowing the manufacturers' designs to influence choice. Many package designs still reflected late-19th-century tastes, although toiletries and new brands were the exception. Here the flowing, organic style of Art Nouveau was used to attract customers with a "modern" look.

Turnwrights toffees
This tin of English toffees was an attempt to compete with chocolates by presenting them in a gift-style box. Fashionable Art Nouveau graphics decorate the edges.

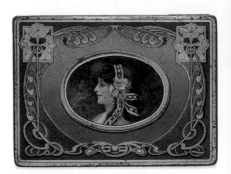

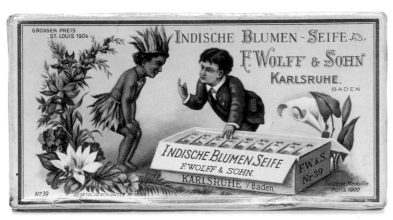

Ivory soap
The name "Ivory" was first used by American manufacturer Procter & Gamble in 1879. For years the traditional appearance of this packaging remained almost unchanged, until a redesign was commissioned in 1940 (see p.241).

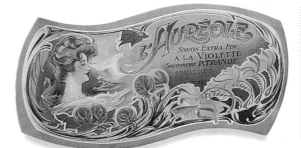

L'Auréole soap
From a box of three individually wrapped French toilet soaps, this label also draws heavily on the Art Nouveau style. The extravagant design was intended to appeal directly to ladies as a luxury product.

Soft pack cigarettes
At about this time, collectible pictorial cards became popular with competing cigarette companies. Besides providing free promotional opportunities, the stiff cards helped protect the cigarettes, as the packs themselves were flimsy.

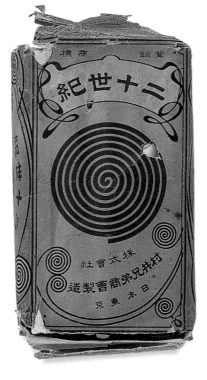

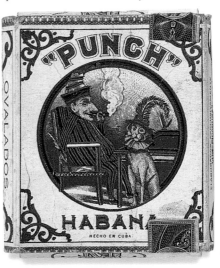

Indische Blumen-Seife
The bright, eye-catching picture on this box of German Indian Flower soap illustrates the product quite literally. The luxuriantly detailed exotic flowers still reflect popular tastes of the late 19th century.

Lübecker marzipan
Somber colors and a picture of an industrial factory lend this box a heavy sense of the past. Two crests appear to give credence to the product.

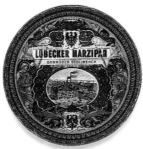

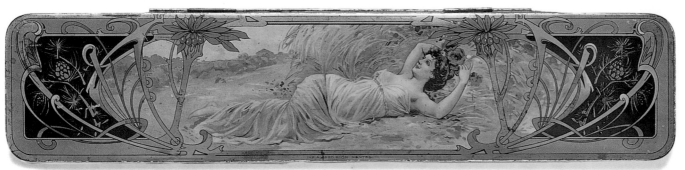

Le Furet corset
The beautiful woman reclining in this idyllic scene is clearly intended to persuade the customer that no other garment could enhance her life so dramatically! The stylish Art Nouveau graphics at each end create a strong sense of refined elegance.

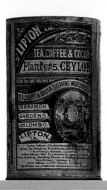

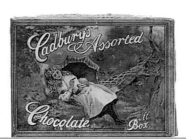

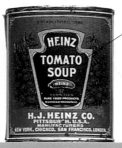

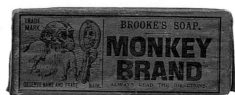

Heinz soup's 19th-century "keystone" logo is still familiar in the 20th century

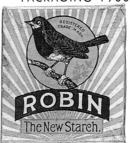

This packaging by a small manufacturer is comparatively crude

The idiosyncratic shape of this Perrier glass bottle, allegedly fashioned after an Indian club, has barely changed through the century (see p.251)

Lefèvre-Utile packages were often stylishly illustrated by famous artists such as the Art Nouveau painter Alphonse Mucha (see p.222)

Quality products

The arrival of individual prewrapped branded goods meant that for the first time the customer had to rely on the look of the manufacturer's packaging to suggest the freshness and quality of a product. Designs that appeared to change little were often meant to give the impression that a product was of consistently good quality.

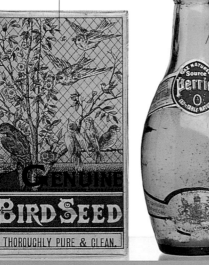

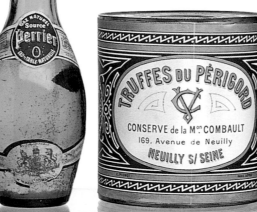

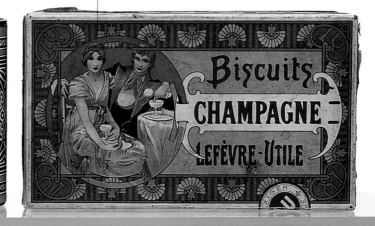

Recurring images

Over the course of the 20th century, certain styles or images have often recurred. Examples include the sunrise motif, such as the Robin starch pack (top right), or intricate graphic patterns as on the Lefèvre-Utile cookies (center right). Women have also become a much stronger selling point, either depicted as strong individuals attractive to men and or as role models for other women.

This American pharmaceutical product is quite traditional, with its information displayed against a white background on the outside of the package

This scene of a woman driving a car reflects the new attraction of automobiles, but it also portrays an independent woman, perhaps to attract more female drinkers

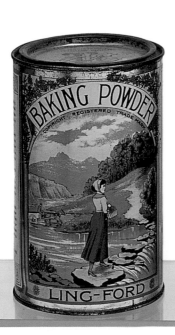

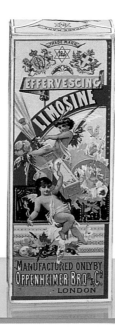

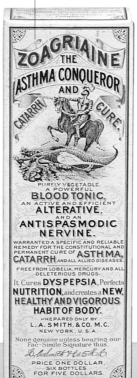

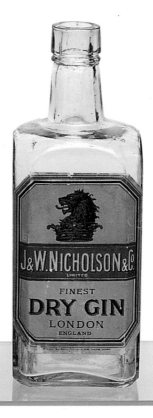

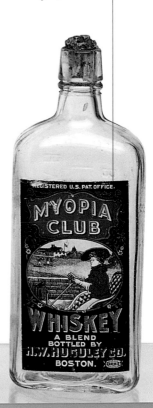

PACKAGING 1910–19

WORLD WAR I ACCELERATED THE TREND toward individual packaging, for it was much easier to distribute and supply rations to the troops in small packages. The world was jolted into a new era by the war and packaging reflected this. Many 19th-century brand labels were updated and more importantly, better packaging techniques improved the possibilities for dispensing or resealing products. Art Nouveau was still popular until about 1915, its characteristic swirls and typography appearing on coffee labels and candy boxes.

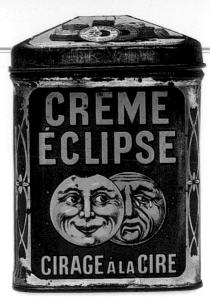

Crème Eclipse
Advertising came into its own as manufacturers jostled for the customer's attention. This tin of string for tying parcels would sit on the shop counter, its sides covered with advertisements, such as the one for shoe polish shown here.

Colgate's ribbon dental cream
This toothpaste package informs the user about the innovative and efficient nature of the product. Previously, tooth powder had been sold in a glazed pot or can; here, a cream is dispensed from a soft metal tube in a flat ribbon, making it more economical and preventing the toothpaste from falling off the brush. Graphic illustrations and simple instructions on the sides of every cardboard package show the user how to fold the tube up as the cream is used and how to squeeze the lower sides of the tube to create a vacuum, drawing back any cream still oozing after use.

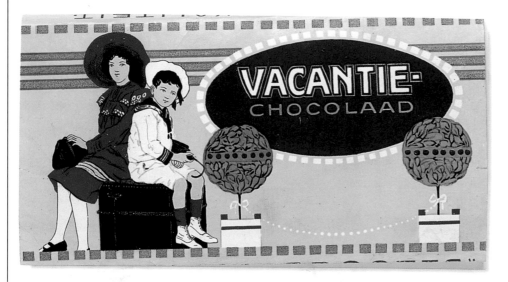

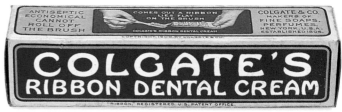

Chocolate wrappers
Commercially sold chocolate bars tasted so similar that the packaging had to attract the eye: the Vacantie wrapper (above), for instance, uses simple colors and looks elegant. By contrast, this German chocolate (right), which was distributed to troops during World War I, shows a patriotic image on a functional wrapper.

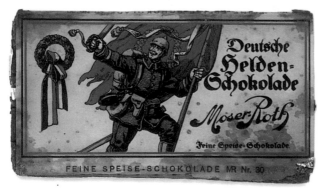

Savon Tatiana
Images from nature were popular with exponents of Art Nouveau, as the snaking golden tendrils and buds on this French soap package reveal. The embossed gold work and rich blue colors make this unusual gift packaging extravagantly beautiful.

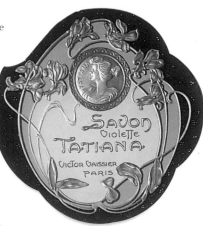

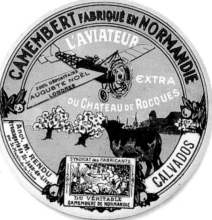

Cherry Kiev drink
This Russian drink label, possibly for schnapps, was manufactured by S. Shagriarskiy in Tbilisi. The simple pattern around the border has a strong Art Nouveau style and shows how much the popular style influenced all types of packaging internationally in this decade.

Camembert cheese
French Camembert cheese box labels traditionally depicted rural scenes or country maids, but instead this label reflects the world's new fascination with machinery and flight. The airplane skimming across this label is an exciting modern contrast to the image of a smiling dairy maid.

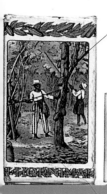

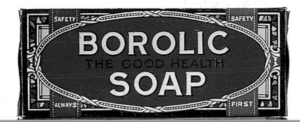

The side of this Horniman's cocoa package illustrates the plantation where the product was grown

Lightweight tins gradually replaced many glazed pot containers and were especially popular for shoe polish

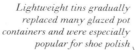
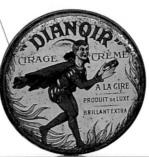
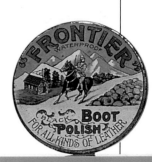

Exotic influences

Some brands, such as the talcum powder (far right), Horniman's cocoa (above left), and dates (below) accentuated the setting of the product's origin or the mystique of the Far East to set the brand apart from others and to sell it.

An elegant Art Nouveau design turns this packet of crystallized chestnuts into a sophisticated gift

Sprinkler tops were one of the new advances made in dispensing products

The flattened oval shape of powder tins appeared after 1909

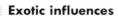
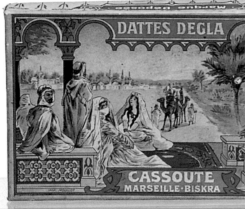
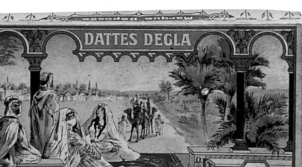
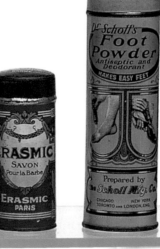
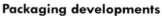
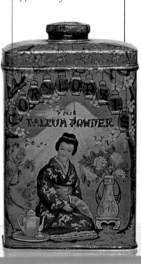

Extraordinary claims

New household products for cleaning and washing made some extraordinary claims on their packaging: for instance, Armour's cleanser (below) "lightens housework," while borolic soap (top) is "the good health soap." The images are also ordered and controlled, with simple, straightforward colors and uncomplicated pictures.

This generic brand is typical of the off-the-shelf design packaging of the period

Packaging developments

By 1910, both the US and UK were producing aluminum foil; in 1908, a Swiss chemist had invented cellophane film. These new materials would revolutionize the way products could be sealed to retain their freshness, but it took time for them to become commonplace. More immediate were the advances made in resealing packages and dispensing the product, such as the sprinkler tops for talcum powder.

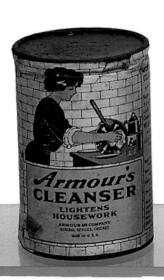
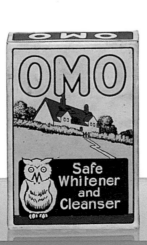
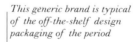
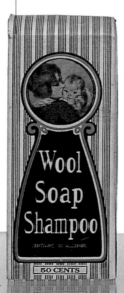
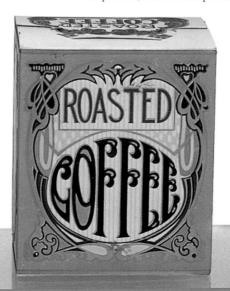
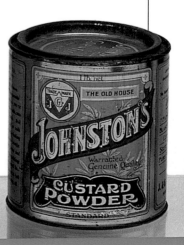

PACKAGING 1920–29

THE YEARS OF CHANGE after World War I continued into the 1920s as the number of servants in the home declined and the family unit reduced, encouraging a trend toward smaller package sizes. Leisure time also increased, and with it came a new breed of snacks and "instant" packaged foods that saved time, such as shelled peas. A different style in packaging gradually emerged through the 1920s, with cleaner, fresher designs influenced by the popular vivid colors and angular lines of the Art Deco movement.

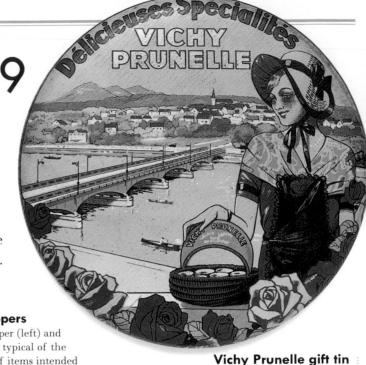

Confectionery wrappers

This 1927 Stolwerck wrapper (left) and Sprengel label (below) are typical of the highly decorative nature of items intended as luxury products. Their extravagant graphics and strong colors contrast distinctively with the American Hershey's bar (below left), its embossed monochrome packaging giving a mass-market appeal.

Vichy Prunelle gift tin

Although not an Art Deco design, this French gift tin has adopted Art Deco colors to give it fresh appeal. This packaging is one version of a traditional design that was gradually adapting to the changing times.

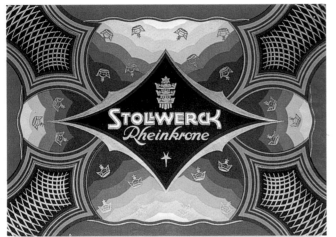

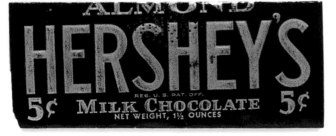

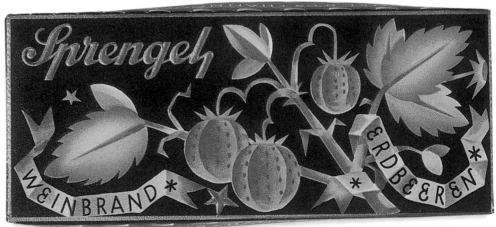

Boyhood fruit crate label

A flourishing fruit trade existed in California by the 1900s, and in order to identify different orchards, pictorial labels were pasted onto each wooden crate of fruit. This label, with its dynamic, stylized image, is quite upbeat, the outsize grapefruit on the cart and the cheerful colors creating a bold, attractive impression.

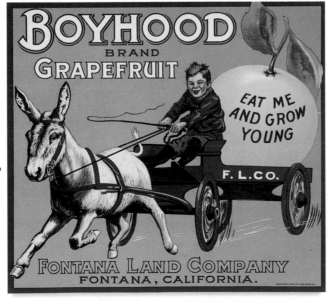

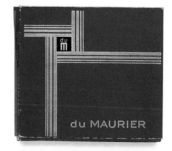

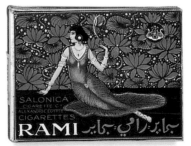

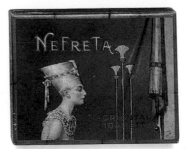

Women's cigarettes

With the increasing emancipation of women in the 1920s came a new breed of products targeted at their leisure time. Aimed at the female smoker, these cigarette packs are stylishly elegant or exotic and use, in the case of the du Maurier pack, an impressive Art Deco design.

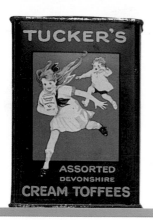

TUCKER'S
ASSORTED
DEVONSHIRE
CREAM TOFFEES

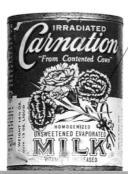

IRRADIATED
Carnation
"From Contented Cows"

HOMOGENIZED
UNSWEETENED EVAPORATED
MILK

The carnation flower on this American evaporated milk can has been used to suggest freshness and sweetness

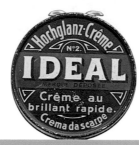

Hochglanz-Crème
N°2
IDEAL
Crème au brillant rapide.
Crema da scarpe.

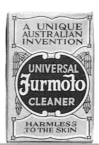

A UNIQUE
AUSTRALIAN
INVENTION
UNIVERSAL
Jurmoto
CLEANER
HARMLESS
TO THE SKIN

Strong, geometric shapes and intense colors defined Art Deco

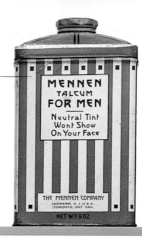

MENNEN
TALCUM
FOR MEN
Neutral Tint
Won't Show
On Your Face

THE MENNEN COMPANY
NET WT. 9 OZ.

Appetizing images

Realistic illustrations printed on the front of packages were becoming commonplace, giving a better impression of what the product actually contained. The sumptuous display of fruit on the Rowntree's pastilles (below) and the juicy peas on the Thorn's package (right) make the brands seem far more enticing.

This American household cleaning product has been continually updated through the century (see p.242)

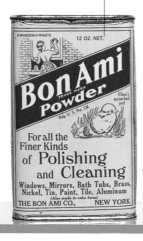

A WINDOW A MINUTE   12 OZ. NET.
Bon Ami
Powder
For all the
Finer Kinds
of Polishing
and Cleaning
Windows, Mirrors, Bath Tubs, Brass, Nickel, Tin, Paint, Tile, Aluminum
THE BON AMI CO.   NEW YORK

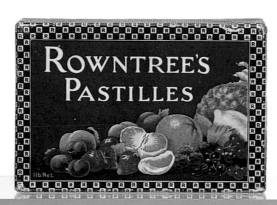

ROWNTREE'S
PASTILLES
1lb Net.

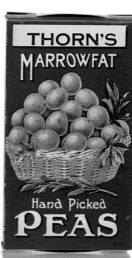

THORN'S
MARROWFAT
Hand Picked
PEAS

This crisp package design, which came out in 1920, lasted until the '50s

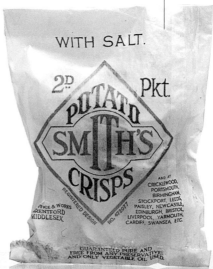

WITH SALT.
2D   Pkt.
SMITH'S
POTATO
CRISPS

Instant snacks

Synonymous with the concept of increased leisure time and convenience food were a new wave of packaged snacks. The popularity of snacks such as potato chips and Pretz Sticks (below) in the US caught on in the 1920s and spread to the UK (see Smith's crisps, above right) and around the world.

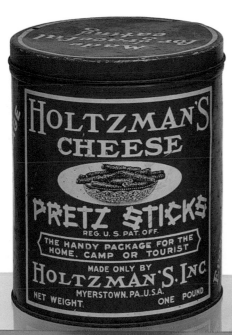

HOLTZMAN'S
CHEESE
PRETZ STICKS
REG. U.S. PAT. OFF.
THE HANDY PACKAGE FOR THE HOME, CAMP OR TOURIST
MADE ONLY BY
HOLTZMAN'S. INC.
MYERSTOWN. PA. U.S.A.
NET WEIGHT   ONE POUND

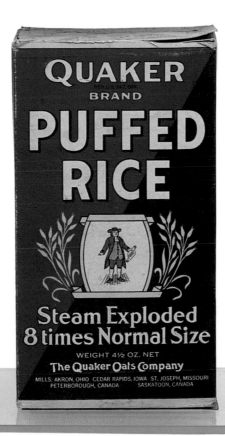

QUAKER
BRAND
PUFFED
RICE
Steam Exploded
8 times Normal Size
WEIGHT 4½ OZ. NET
The Quaker Oats Company
MILLS: AKRON, OHIO CEDAR RAPIDS, IOWA ST. JOSEPH, MISSOURI PETERBOROUGH, CANADA SASKATOON, CANADA

Launched in the US in 1923, this ginger-ale bottle has a clean, fresh appearance

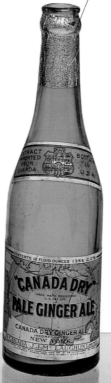

"CANADA DRY"
PALE GINGER ALE
CANADA DRY GINGER ALE
NEW YORK

WORTHINGTON'S
INDIA PALE ALE
BURTON ON TRENT

PACKAGING 1930–39

THE 1930s WAS NOT ONLY A DECADE when Art Deco influenced packaging, but also a time when graphics became noticeably bolder and simpler, catching the eye more immediately; this was a time of rationalization with clear, uncomplicated styles. Packaging technology was also improving: cellophane was a more hygienic overwrap for packed products, keeping them fresher, and plastic and aluminum, although still expensive, were new, lightweight replacements for heavy glass containers.

Gargantua sweet bag

Although a cheap piece of packaging, this waxed paper bag is fun and vital with its simple illustration. Waxy paper cartons were also used for milk, and waxed cardboard cartons for cream, honey, ice cream, and glacé cherries in the 1930s.

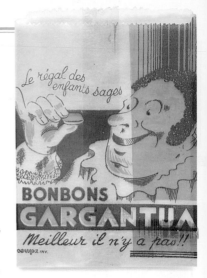

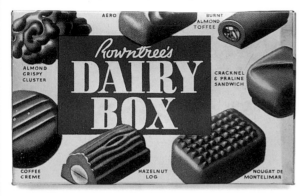

Rowntree's Dairy Box

The chocolates illustrated on this box clearly explain its contents; labels to identify each chocolate are even printed alongside. This realistic format appears to prefigure the photographic packaging of the 1960s and beyond.

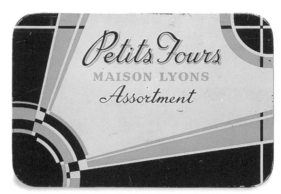

Petits Fours Assortment

A classic example of two popular concepts in packaging at the time, this tin of Petits Fours depicts a sunburst motif in the late Art Deco style using a limited range of striking colors.

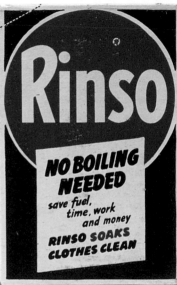

Rinso

A washing powder, Rinso was first launched in 1910 by the American Lever Company to compete directly with Persil (right). This basic design was adapted slightly with each decade (see p.241 and p.243).

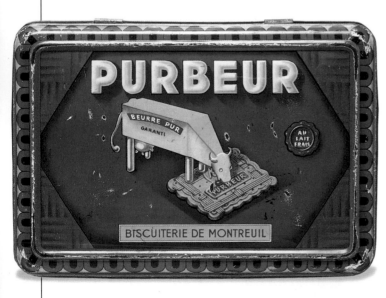

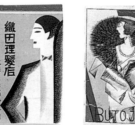

Purbeur butter biscuits

Images of animals were often linked with certain products, such as cows with dairy goods. This stylized illustration makes the cow licking a Purbeur look like a pat of butter.

Japanese matchboxes

The stylish clothes and Art Deco colors on these elegant-looking matchbox covers illustrate the international influence of both Western fashions and Art Deco.

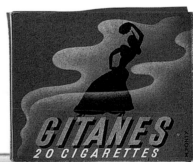

Sacco Bonito Asalmonado

All canned tuna fish tasted much the same, so it was the brand label that had to influence the customer's choice. This label is made more attractive by the realistic illustrations of tuna fish leaping through a stylized sea.

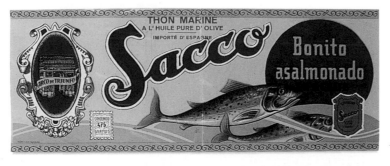

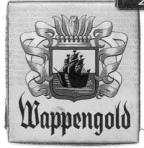

Cigarette packs

By the 1930s, even aluminum containers were used to pack cigarettes and tobacco, as well as round tins and cardboard boxes. Pack designs also changed: this 1930 Gitanes design by Max Ponty has become a classic.

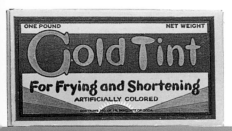

ONE POUND NET WEIGHT

Gold Tint
For Frying and Shortening
ARTIFICIALLY COLORED

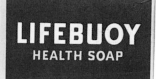

Black Magic's Art Deco chocolate pack remained constant for years

BLACK MAGIC

LIFEBUOY
HEALTH SOAP

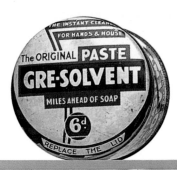

THE INSTANT CLEANER
FOR HANDS & HOUSE
The ORIGINAL **PASTE**
GRE-SOLVENT
MILES AHEAD OF SOAP
6d
REPLACE THE LID

This fun light bulb pack substitutes a light bulb for the body of a butterfly

Sunrise motif
Throughout the history of packaging, the sunrise motif has featured repeatedly as an immediately identifiable symbol. Here it manifests itself in the Gold Tint shortening (above left), Petits Fours (opposite page), and Synergy light bulb pack (left).

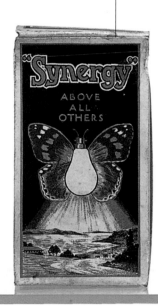

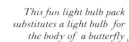

Persil
Wettig gedeponeerd.
VOOR ALLE WAS
Persil
Persil
wast
zonder wrijven
en maakt het linnen
schitterend wit
(Zie gebruiksaanwijzing)
ZONDER CHLOOR

"Synergy"
ABOVE
ALL
OTHERS

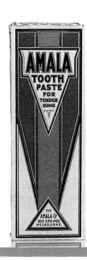

AMALA
TOOTH
PASTE
FOR
TENDER
GUMS
THE
AMALA Cº
BOX GPO 1482
MELBOURNE

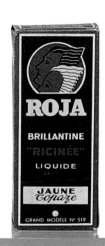

ROJA
BRILLANTINE
"RICINÉE"
LIQUIDE
JAUNE
Copaze
GRAND MODÉLE Nº 519

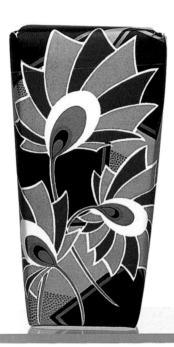

Bold graphics
The influence of late Art Deco can be seen clearly in the 1930s, especially in the way that many packs – Black Magic chocolates (top), Lifebuoy soap (top), and Giant Soap Flakes (right) – use such bold blocks of color, angular lines, and large, clear lettering.

This washing powder pack design, with its bold, unadorned lettering, gives immediate visual impact

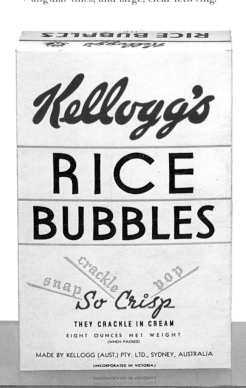

RICE BUBBLES
Kellogg's
RICE
BUBBLES
crackle
snap *pop*
So Crisp
THEY CRACKLE IN CREAM
EIGHT OUNCES NET WEIGHT
(WHEN PACKED)
MADE BY KELLOGG (AUST.) PTY. LTD., SYDNEY, AUSTRALIA
(INCORPORATED IN VICTORIA)

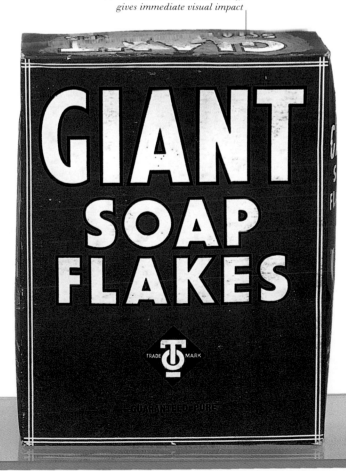

GIANT
SOAP
FLAKES
TRADE MARK

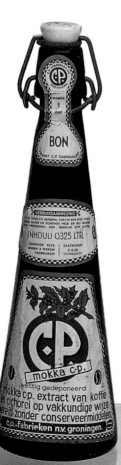

BON
INHOUD 0.325 LTR.
CP
mokka c.p.
wettig gedeponeerd
mokka c.p. extract van koffie
en cichorei op vakkundige wijze
bereid zonder conserveermiddelen
c.p.-fabrieken n.v. groningen.

PACKAGING 1940–49

IN THE 1940s, LIFE WAS DOMINATED, once more, by a world war that affected every aspect of society. Packaging had to adapt in some countries as the availability of printing ink and packing materials was in short supply. Labels became smaller, particularly in the UK, in order to save paper, and the concept of packaging became more of a functional one. Limited natural resources and food shortages persisted in Europe after World War II ended in 1945, so relatively unaffected countries such as the US and Canada continued to export canned or dried produce overseas.

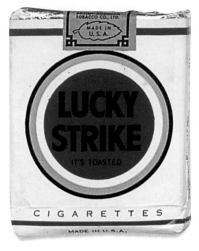

Lucky Strike cigarettes
Lucky Strike cigarettes were introduced to the US in 1917, using the trademark red bull's-eye from the familiar Lucky Strike Tobacco. The pack remained the same until 1942, when Raymond Loewy replaced the green background with a white one. Such minor changes made this a best-selling product: the whiteness of the pack made it look clean, fresh, and stylish.

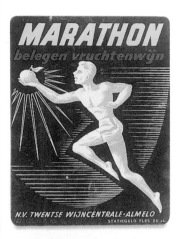

Marathon
The image of this athlete on a Dutch soft-drink label is an epic and heroic one.

Matchbox
Friction matches first became available in 1827, and initially the labels tended to be plain. This Eastern bloc label is just one example of the wide variety of designs that were subsequently produced.

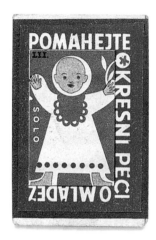

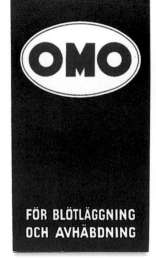

Górnik cigarettes
The stark design on this package has a strong utilitarian feel that is reminiscent of posters of the period.

OMO
FÖR BLÖTLÄGGNING OCH AVHÄBDNING

Omo
The austerity of the 1940s affected even printing ink: the amount of ink used on some labels reduced until only the brand name and instructions were in color (see Rinso, right).

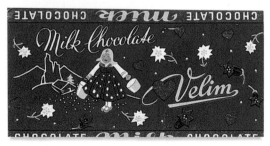

Velim paper wrapper
As a result of paper shortages in the 1940s, some items were sold without any wrappings. Chocolate bars, when they were available, were packaged without silver foil, and for a time even the paper wrappers were replaced by thin transparent ones.

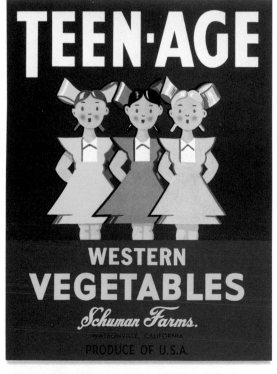

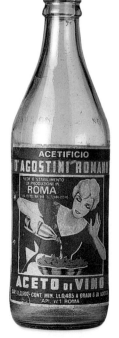

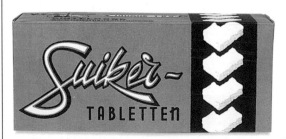

Suiker Tabletten sugar cubes
As the source of raw materials dried up through the decade, the quality of cardboard and paper deteriorated considerably. Simple designs and strong color contrasts were effective substitutes.

Teen-age Western Vegetables label
The airbrush technique and graphics of this label are typically 1940s. As with other American food-crate labels of the period, this is attractive and colorful (see also the Boyhood fruit-crate label, p.236).

Aceto di Vino
The image on this wine vinegar label shows the consumer exactly how to use the product.

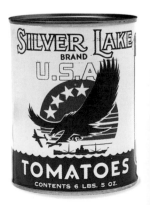

Silver Lake USA tomatoes
Part of the war effort, this can is minimalist in terms of its two-color printing.

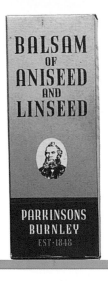

BALSAM OF ANISEED AND LINSEED

PARKINSONS BURNLEY EST·1848

A typically British utilitarian 1940s pack design

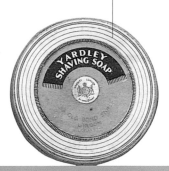

YARDLEY SHAVING SOAP

Utilitarian design

Economic restrictions and limited natural resources in Europe encouraged packaging design in the 1940s to become utilitarian; the products shown here clearly reflect the war years.

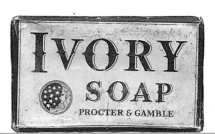

IVORY SOAP
PROCTER & GAMBLE

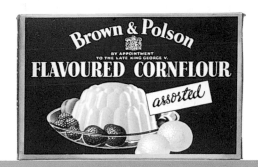

Brown & Polson
BY APPOINTMENT TO THE LATE KING GEORGE V.
FLAVOURED CORNFLOUR
assorted

Special wartime instructions for using Rinso are printed on the back of this package

Heinz's shrunken keystone label (see p.233) is still recognizable without any color

This dried product states clearly that it is wrapped in a "temporary pack"

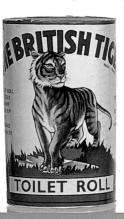

THE BRITISH TIGER
TOILET ROLL

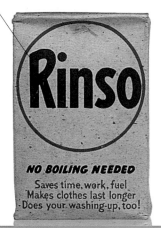

Rinso
NO BOILING NEEDED
Saves time, work, fuel
Makes clothes last longer
· Does your washing-up, too!

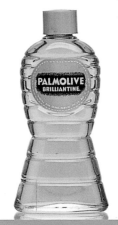

PALMOLIVE BRILLIANTINE

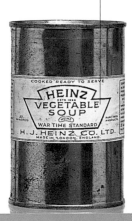

HEINZ VEGETABLE SOUP
COOKED READY TO SERVE
WAR TIME STANDARD
H. J. HEINZ CO. LTD.
MADE IN LONDON, ENGLAND.

GREEN'S SPONGE MIXTURE
SWEETENED
TEMPORARY PACK 6ᴰ NET WEIGHT
BRIGHTON
H.J. GREEN & Cº LTD
ENGLAND

Wartime label reductions

Rationing in Europe extended to paper for a time. This led to the introduction of smaller labels on products, which were packed in poor-quality cardboard packages.

This pack of cleaning powder illustrates well the measures of wartime paper rationing

This Australian wheat flakes package has the feel of the wartime effort

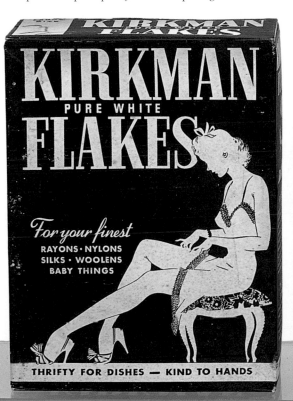

KIRKMAN PURE WHITE FLAKES
For your finest
RAYONS · NYLONS
SILKS · WOOLENS
BABY THINGS
THRIFTY FOR DISHES — KIND TO HANDS

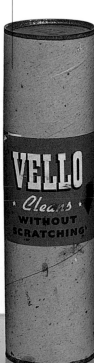

VELLO
Cleans
WITHOUT SCRATCHING

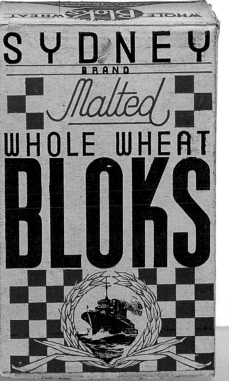

SYDNEY BRAND
Malted
WHOLE WHEAT
BLOKS

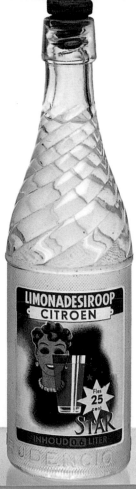

LIMONADESIROOP CITROEN
STAR
25
INHOUD 0.6 LITER

PACKAGING 1950–59

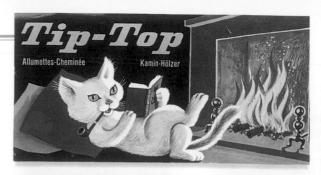

BIGGER, BOLDER, BRIGHTER — by the end of the 1950s, packaging could not have looked more different from that of the '40s. This new incentive for packaging to be more competitive was the rise of the supermarket: by 1950, the vast majority of goods sold were prepacked, and as self-service stores gradually overwhelmed small grocers, the need to create instantly recognizable products that would sell themselves off a supermarket shelf became imperative. Packaging was becoming a true marketing tool, evoking a set of values in the consumer's mind through the images.

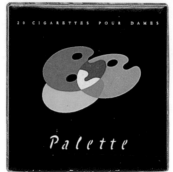 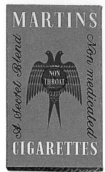

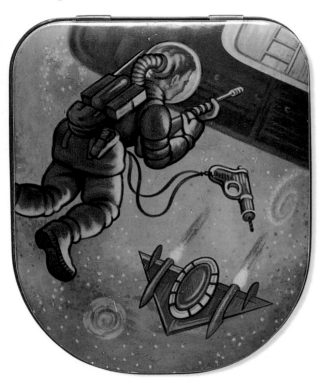

Sharpe's toffee tin
This bright, space-age gift tin lid is redolent of the 1950s fascination with science fiction and popular children's comics. Interestingly, gift tins rarely had the manufacturer's name printed on their lids.

Cigarette packs and Tip-Top matchbox
The manufacturers of products such as these capitalized on the 1950s trend in graphics toward simpler, bolder images or cartoon characters to identify them. The painting palettes and bird are literal visual references to the products' brand names.

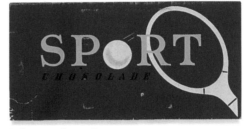 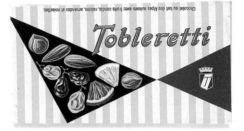

Sport chocolate
This clever Danish design relies on a visual association with the brand name to make a memorable image in the consumer's mind.

Tobleretti chocolate
Visually arresting, this wrapper has an "active" feel, relying on a combination of geometric shapes and detailed illustrations.

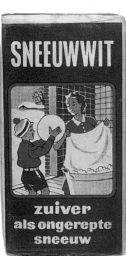 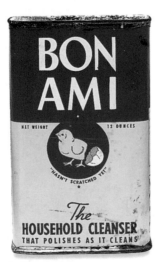 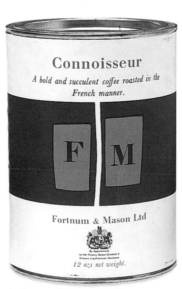 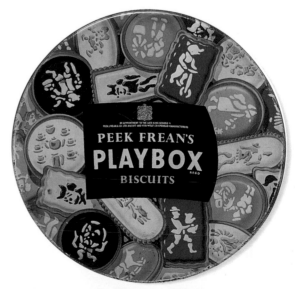

Sneeuwwit
Some well-known household products still had traditional packaging compared to the new wave of soaps and detergents emerging (see Tide, far right).

Bon Ami
The chick motif of the Bon Ami household cleanser, designed in 1901 by Louis H. Soule, was updated in the 1950s (compare with p.237).

Connoisseur coffee
There is little to visually identify what this product is, but the simple, bold graphics make a strong impact. Designed by Ruth Gill, it was retained for many years.

Peek Freans Playbox biscuits
The photorealism of this illustration, displaying the contents of a cookie tin, was typical of the early 1950s. By the end of the decade, photographs were replacing drawn images (see Bird's Eye peas, top right), as they were a cheaper means of producing an image.

This American soap package has a strong, bold design

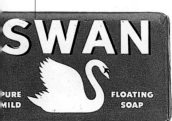

SWAN
PURE MILD · FLOATING SOAP

As with cartoon or comic characters, sales pitches using popular personalities proved successful

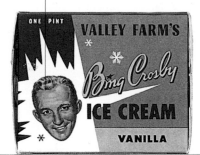

ONE PINT
VALLEY FARM'S
Bing Crosby
ICE CREAM
VANILLA

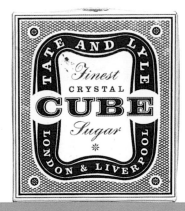

TATE AND LYLE
Finest
CRYSTAL
CUBE
Sugar
LONDON & LIVERPOOL

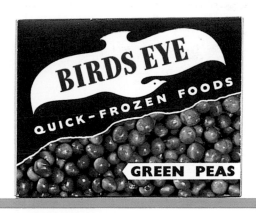

BIRDS EYE
QUICK-FROZEN FOODS
GREEN PEAS

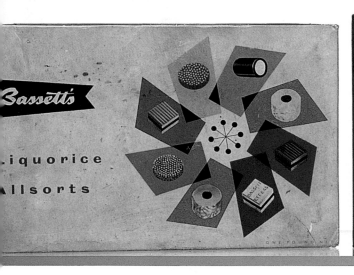

Bassett's
Liquorice Allsorts

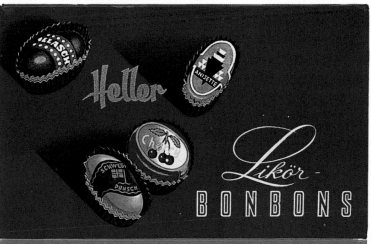

Heller
Likör-
BONBONS

This design attempts a modern feel with its photo-type illustration and gingham tablecloth

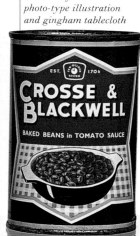

CROSSE & BLACKWELL
BAKED BEANS in TOMATO SAUCE

This Australian pack of Rinso makes good use of simple silhouetted figures for a contemporary feel

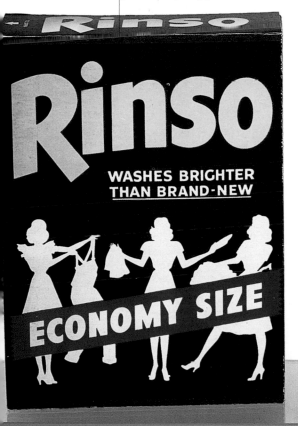

Rinso
WASHES BRIGHTER THAN BRAND-NEW
ECONOMY SIZE

Tide and Surf (Suno) were part of a new type of soapless detergent, that was packaged in active, or busy, bright designs

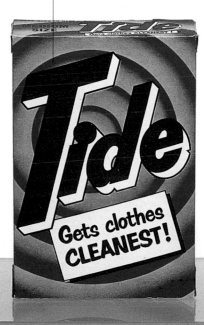

Tide
Gets clothes CLEANEST!

Consumerism in the 1950s

The advertising commercials that first appeared on television in the 1950s were part of a new phase of consumerism. The range of frozen foods available expanded, as did the selection of products on the shelves. As there became more choice, so there was more competition, and products had to compete for the impulse buy. Graphics freshened up, becoming simpler and more recognizable with an emphatic logo or motif.

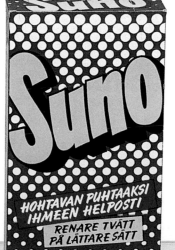

Suno
HOHTAVAN PUHTAAKSI IHMEEN HELPOSTI
RENARE TVÄTT PÅ LÄTTARE SÄTT

This French hot chocolate pack uses "modern" colors to liven up a traditional image

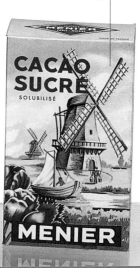

CACAO SUCRE
SOLUBILISÉ
MENIER

PACKAGING 1960–69

THE 1960s WERE TRULY AN AGE of modernity. Fast food, refrigerators, freezers, convenience food, diet products – all these were becoming commonplace, influencing the eating habits and lifestyles of consumers throughout the world. Soft drinks were sold in "throwaway cans" with ring pulls, a dramatic departure from the traditional glass bottle and cork stopper. Cellophane, aluminum, and plastic now sealed up the freshness of a whole variety of products. Packaging designers were preoccupied with conveying a message to buy, while photography and promotional incentives proliferated.

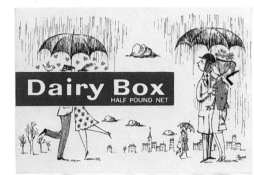

Dairy Box chocolates
The simple, rounded characters on the label of this box are modern and eye-catching. Designed by the artist Raymond Peynet (b.1908), the quirky picture would have been used only briefly as this box was aimed at the gift market.

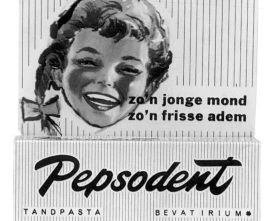

Pepsodent tandpasta
This toothpaste product competes for more shelf space, and therefore more customer awareness, by adding a tall cardboard back to the box. The typography has been updated and the fresh-faced child added to give the product a sense of vitality.

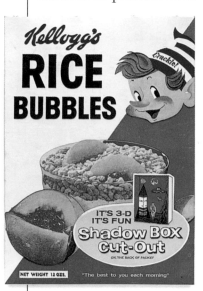

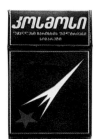

Cigarette pack
The design on this pack of cigarettes is full of dramatic visual impact. A stylized image of a spacecraft, this design was influenced by the contemporary space race between the Soviet Union and the US.

Kellogg's Rice Bubbles
An updated Australian pack (see p.239), this is a modern yet familiar version of Kellogg's designs. The healthy photographic image aims to convince the parent of its nutritious value, while the fun cartoon character and free promotion appeal directly to the child.

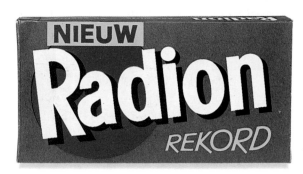

Radion washing powder
In order to stand out from other products on the supermarket shelf, this pack has strong complementary colors and bold, raised letters that appear to jump out from the two-dimensional design.

Siks diet cookies
New fashions in clothes meant that women were more conscious of their figures. Diet-food packages used fashionable images of women and up-to-date designs to attract the consumer.

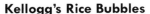
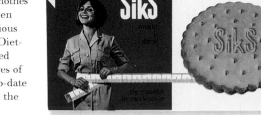

Liga rusks
Household packages increasingly used vibrant designs and active images to capture the attention of customers. This pack was designed to appeal to women who wanted their children to look as healthy as this one.

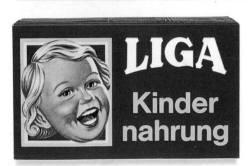

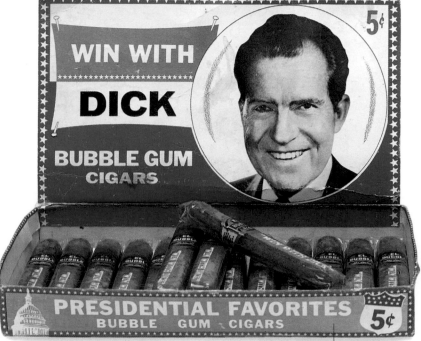

Presidential Favorites bubble gum cigars
Individually packed in cellophane, these bubble gum cigars were sold through another personality sales pitch, promoting Richard Nixon as a candidate for the American presidential elections in 1968. Presumably they were aimed at politically aware adults buying treats for their children.

This cardboard counter box is a traditional selling technique

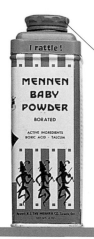

This tin of talcum powder has a free rattle included in the lid

I rattle!

MENNEN BABY POWDER
BORATED
ACTIVE INGREDIENTS
BORIC ACID · TALCUM

ROBINSON'S
orange, egg & honey cereal
INSTANT FOOD FOR BABY

This pack of supermarket store-brand peas is stylistically typical of the 1960s

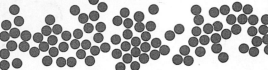

Sainsbury's sweet young
Garden Peas quick dried 1/-

exquis neige
FRAISE
chambourcy
FROMAGE FRAIS A LA CONFITURE

This fun packaging represents a bird's head and beak with its cap and direction pointer

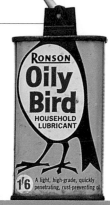

RONSON
Oily Bird
HOUSEHOLD LUBRICANT
1/6 A light, high-grade, quickly penetrating, rust-preventing oil

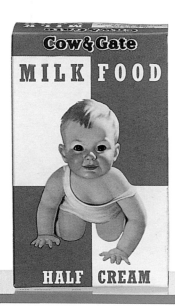

Cow & Gate
MILK FOOD
HALF CREAM

Typography now had little to do with the past unless it was part of an established logo

Although displayed on a tin can, this design depicts a bottle cap from previous packaging

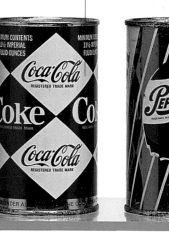

MINIMUM CONTENTS 11½ IMPERIAL FLUID OUNCES
Coca-Cola REGISTERED TRADE MARK
Coke   Co
Coca-Cola REGISTERED TRADE MARK

Pepsi-Cola

Stylish alternatives

Interestingly, some of the more successful designs of the decade were supermarket store-brand packages, such as Sainsbury's Garden Peas (above), which were more experimental, despite being sold as low-price alternatives.

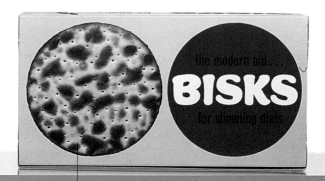

the modern aid...
BISKS
for slimming diets

Soft-drink cans

The 1960s was very much the era of the throwaway soda can. Coca-Cola (above, left) was the first drink to be canned in 1960 and, after the ring-pull opener was developed in the US in 1967, the canned-drink market burgeoned.

Graphically simple yet strong, this design combines a realistic photograph with the claim that a Bisk biscuit is a "modern aid for slimming diets"

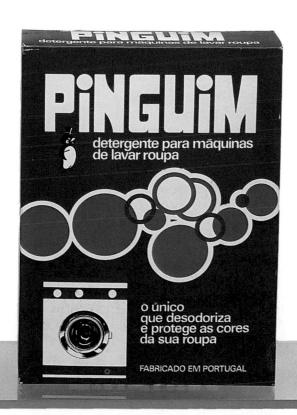

The Purest Made

NICHOLSON
Finest London Dry
GIN
Bottled by the Distillers
J. & W. NICHOLSON & CO. LTD.
CLERKENWELL, LONDON
PRODUCED IN GREAT BRITAIN

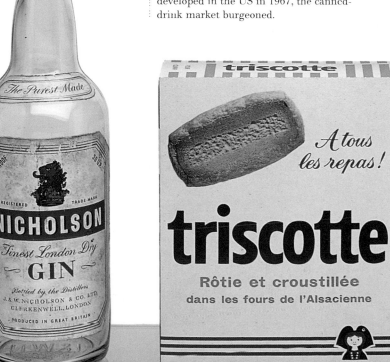

triscotte
A tous les repas!
triscotte
Rôtie et croustillée
dans les fours de l'Alsacienne

PINGUIM
detergente para máquinas de lavar roupa
PINGUIM
detergente para máquinas de lavar roupa
o único que desodoriza e protege as cores da sua roupa
FABRICADO EM PORTUGAL

PACKAGING 1970–79

PACKAGING DESIGN REACHED A CROSSROADS in the 1970s, with a tremendous variety of different styles; the stark new style of some products and supermarket "store brands" provided yet another alternative. Packing technology continued to improve, however, with the arrival of the "Tetrapak" to hold milk, soft drinks, and juices, and molded plastic containers that were all lighter and cheaper to transport than heavy, breakable glass bottles. Consumer tastes were changing as people took more vacations abroad and tasted foreign food, while instant "TV dinners" proved popular alternatives to family meals around the table.

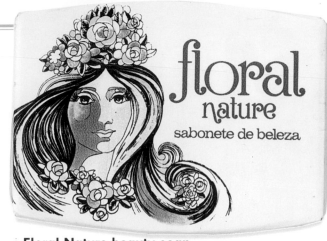

Floral Nature beauty soap
Toiletries continued to represent the latest fashions and popular styles on their packaging, as this line illustration on a pack of beauty soap shows. The white background is used to imply that this is a pure, natural product.

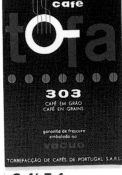

Café Tofa
The modern typography of this stylish Portuguese coffee package has a clever motif of a full coffee cup, seen from above, incorporated into it.

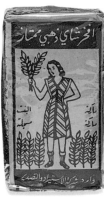

Brooke Bond Girl Brand Ceylon tea
This simply illustrated pack of Syrian tea uses a traditional image to create a sense of symbolism and enduring permanence.

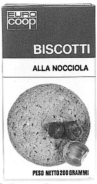

Euro Coop hazelnut cookies
Packaging was generally becoming lightweight, while retaining a pack's freshness. Cookies were often now only packed in tins as gifts.

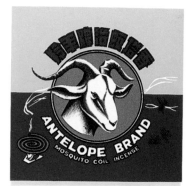

Antelope Brand mosquito coil incense
This conspicuous Indonesian design encapsulates the modern approach to selling a product: using bold graphics and colors to catch the eye.

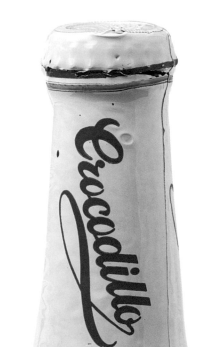
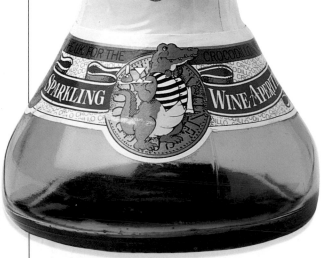

Crocodillo sparkling wine
Developed in 1979, this strangely shaped bottle prefigures some of the gimmicky containers that have appeared in the 1980s and '90s. Shaped like the top part of a glass bottle, it looks as though the rest of the body is missing.

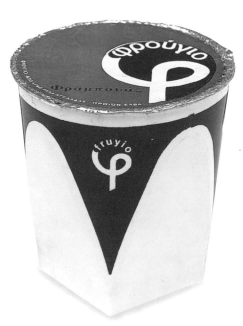

Fruyio yogurt
Yogurt was first packaged in plastic containers in about 1970. Molded plastic containers could literally be produced in any size or shape, as this square-bottomed, round-topped example shows.

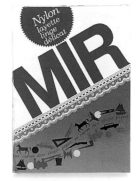

Mir detergent
The colored silhouettes on this pack of French detergent are displayed as examples of the free gifts available in every box.

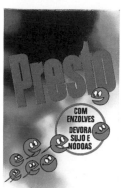

Presto detergent
The age of computer technology took off in the 1970s. These animated enzymes devouring dirt are similar to a popular computer game concept.

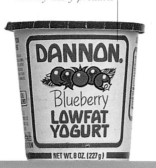

Fruit yogurts were part of a flourishing range of healthy dairy products

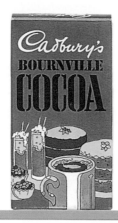

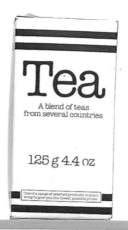

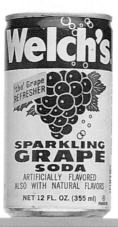

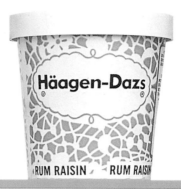

This ethnic TV dinner box is an extreme example of photographic packaging

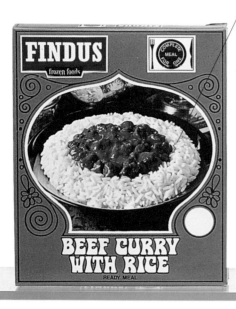

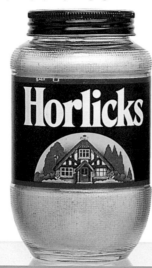

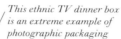

Minimalist design

The bewildering array of styles that appeared in the 1970s was capped by the store-brand packages in supermarkets. This tea package (above) takes the theme of a single color on a white ground to an extreme compared with the Welch's and Dannon brands.

This box of chocolate liqueurs uses retro-styled artwork more synonymous with the 1950s

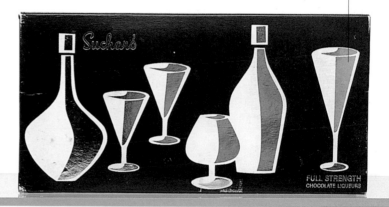

Psychedelic colors

Many of the packages on these pages make use of orange and brown, both strong fashion shades at the time. The garish plastic Aqua Manda container (below) is dyed orange to accentuate the orange-scented talcum powder inside. It is wrapped in a yellow cardboard box purely to create a greater sense of value.

This design by Dick Bruna was intended to appeal to both the mothers buying the product and the children eating it

This British cereal pack – with sunrise motif and earthy colors – captures the essence of California in the 1970s

Another example of personality sales, this orange drink is promoted by comic-book hero Superman

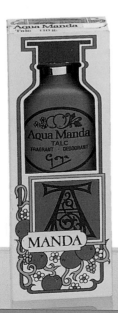

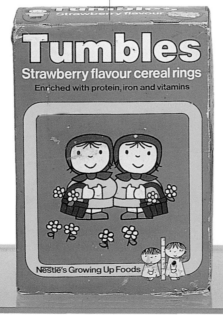

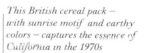

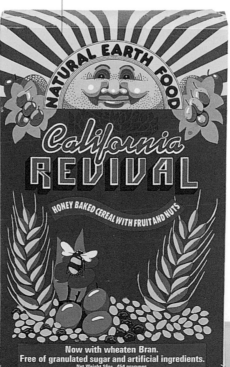

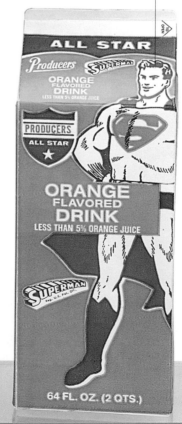

PACKAGING 1980–89

IN THE 1980s, PACKAGING became a stronger selling vehicle for products. Designers realized that packaging could be integrated as part of a brand concept, conveying a total message to the consumer. The technology for cutting and folding materials and molding plastics became less expensive, leading to more innovative packaging ideas. While upbeat, contemporary graphics targeted a younger generation, nostalgia also came back into fashion to stress the wholesomeness and consistent quality of some products.

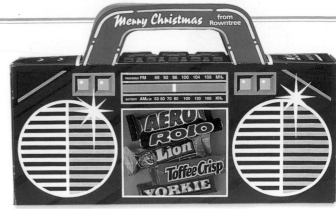

Rowntree Christmas selection pack
A piece of novelty packaging aimed at the youth market, the dynamic graphics and vibrant colors make this molded-plastic chocolate gift box an unusual and exciting one.

Le Sueur canned peas
This functional yet stylish American design is one way of incorporating the packaging material as part of a product. The reflective silver label – imitating a can – stands out on the supermarket shelves, which is surely the purpose of good packaging.

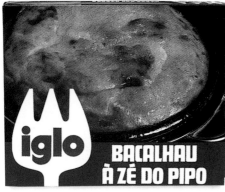

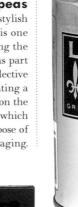

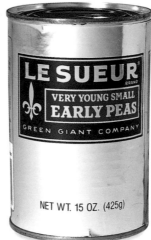

Convenience food
Prepacked ready-made meals such as these reflect a growing trend in the 1980s and '90s: consumers find less time to shop for and cook basic ingredients. The growing popularity of microwaves has meant that these packs really can provide instant cooked food.

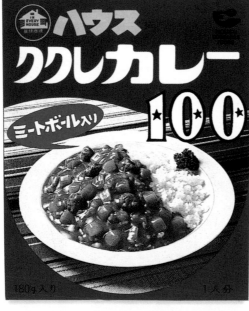

Terry's Le Box
One of the more complicated packaging devices of the 1980s, this origami-inspired box for chocolates looked impressive as a concept on the drawing board but proved too impractical and expensive in reality.

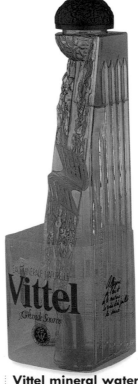

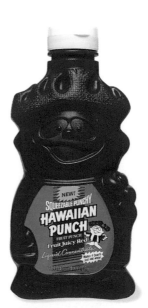

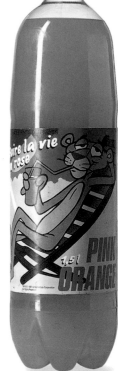

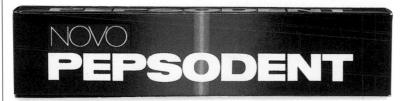

Pepsodent toothpaste
Gone are the pink candy stripes of previous decades (see p.244); this "new" Portuguese version of the American product has a different, very clinical and precise graphic design, with strong, clean white typography.

Vittel mineral water
Created by radical furniture designer Gaetano Pesce, this prototype bottle is shaped like a waterfall.

Hawaiian punch
This startling container is shaped as a character, so creating a product identity through its very form.

Pink orangeade
This small cartoon-character label allows the bright contents to show through.

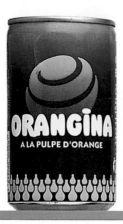
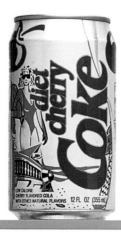
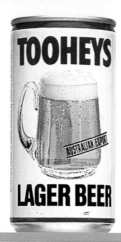
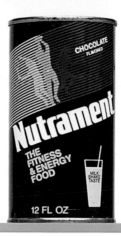
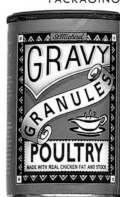

Re-creating identities

Manufacturers have used different strategies to re-create fresh identities for their products. The Coca-Cola can (above) has a 1980s fashion-led design that, although collectible, was intended to have a short shelf life. The traditional look of the gravy granules (top right) gives a nostalgic feel, harking back to a previous era, but it also helps the product stand out on a supermarket shelf. The classic Black Magic chocolates (below) have been updated using a deep red rose (compare with p.239).

Developed in 1988, the bold, stylized image and bright colors help give this hair bleach a summery look

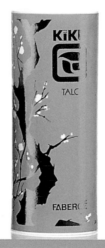
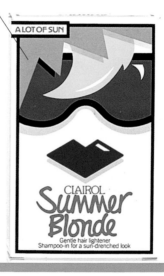
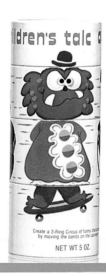

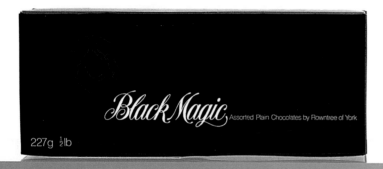

Announcement flashes of the latest changes and improvements, as well as special offers and competitions, have begun to cover much packaging

A bold version of the sunburst motif reappears on a tetrapak carton of milk

Glass bottles

Ironically, after disposable aluminum cans had almost universally dominated the soft-drink market for years, glass bottles (below) began to make a comeback with certain soft drinks. The hope is that the product will be imbued with a greater sense of quality and value.

An embossed basket on the innovative new label makes this modern-looking liqueur bottle a sophisticated one

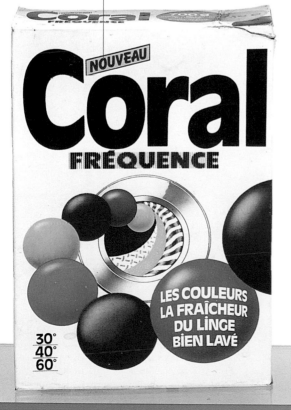
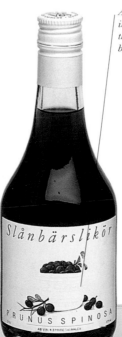
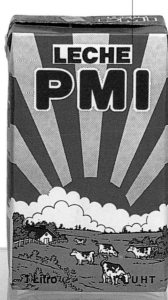
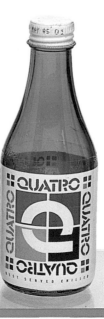

PACKAGING 1990s

CONSUMERISM IN THE 1990s has created a curious juxtaposition. On the one hand, excessive choice has meant that product designs are taken to extremes to attract attention, creating a whole series of novel or gimmicky images. On the other hand, increasing worldwide concern about environmental and ecological issues has put pressure on manufacturers to supply their products in recyclable, biodegradable packaging. There is more variety, with more flavors, bigger sizes, and an "international consumerism" that rejects any regional product varieties – and yet, at the same time, there is a trend toward minimalist packaging with cleaner, purer products that stress a particularly independent and authentic identity.

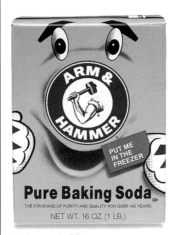

Arm & Hammer baking soda
The nature of the contents seems completely irrelevant to this American packaging design, which has an engaging character to encourage sales.

Body Shop toiletries
The identity and beliefs of this health and beauty company are embodied in its minimalist packaging. This is unusual in the cosmetics world, which is known as primarily a packaging industry. Most Body Shop packaging is also recyclable, enabling customers to return with empty bottles for refills.

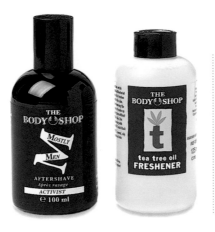

Frufoo Choko-UFOs
Having none of the sophisticated style of adult gift boxes, this pack of German children's chocolates uses every incentive to buy, including a free toy. As with many products on these pages, children are specifically targeted.

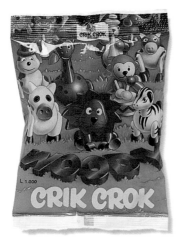

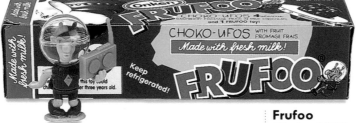

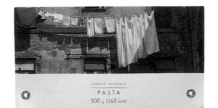

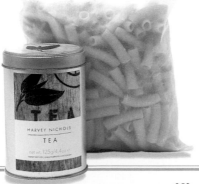

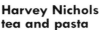

Crik Crok Woody chips
Printing methods are now so advanced that bright, fluorescent colors can be printed most effectively on packing materials. This Italian chip package, with its fun colors and cartoon characters, also contains a novelty toy inside to boost sales.

Harvey Nichols tea and pasta
Although these black and white photographs appear to have little relevance to the produce inside, they do give the utilitarian packaging a sophisticated, alternative image.

Robocop bubble bath
This is an ultimate example of the state-of-the-art plastics technology used in the packaging industry. Aimed entirely at children, the container is molded in the shape of a popular film character, and it can also be used as a toy once it is empty.

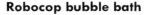

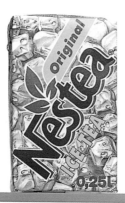

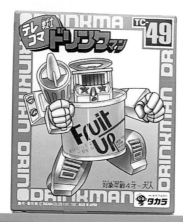

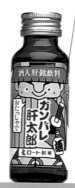

This Japanese energy drink has a quirky, stylized image of a samurai warrior on the label

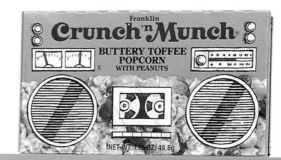

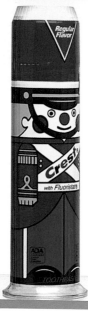

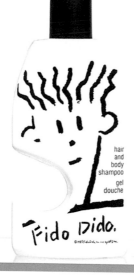

This disk top plastic dispenser allows the product to be opened and resealed easily with just one finger

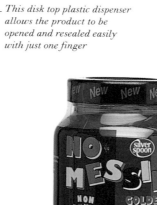

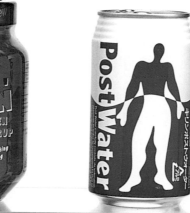

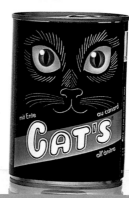

User-friendly

Even mundane household items now have complete packaging concepts. The friendly eyes on this cat food can (below), for instance, are meant to draw the customer's attention to it.

International consumerism

As a packaging material, plastic has been instrumental in transforming our society: plastic packaging, with its robust, durable nature and excellent barrier qualities that prevent contamination, has made it possible to preserve, pack, and transport products from across the world for consumption or use elsewhere, so inviting an international consumerism into our lives.

A transparent plastic bottle helps convince consumers that the water inside is clean and pure

The Perrier bottle is now so familiar that it can be instantly recognized underneath this printed image

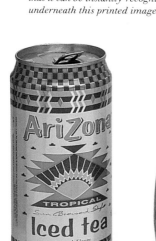

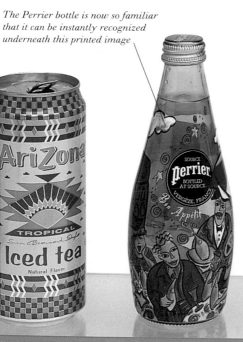

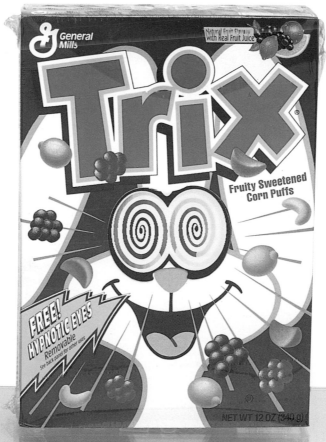

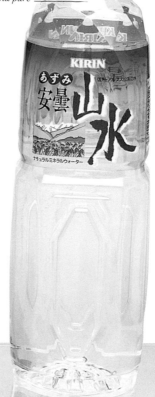

A–Z OF DESIGNERS

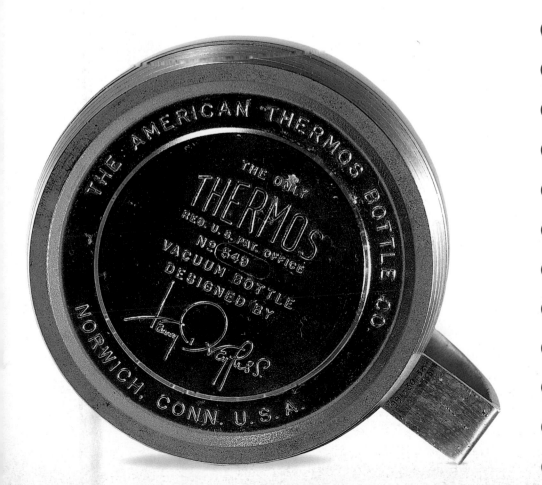

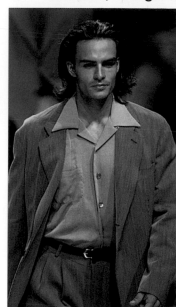

A

AALTO, Aino
1894–1949 Finnish
p.48
Aino Marsio was an architect and designer best known for her glassware and interior designs. She was the wife of Alvar Aalto (see below), with whom she often collaborated.

AALTO, Alvar
1898–1976 Finnish
p.34, 48
One of Finland's most important designers, Aalto designed avant-garde buildings that reflected the close relationship of architecture with nature. During the 1920s, he experimented with wood, especially plywood, and in 1935 founded Artek to produce his furniture and lighting. The company still produces many of his original designs. His work includes the Paimio Tuberculosis Sanatorium, Finland (1929–32), the Viipuri Library (1927–35), the Paimio chair (1930), and the Savoy vase (1936).

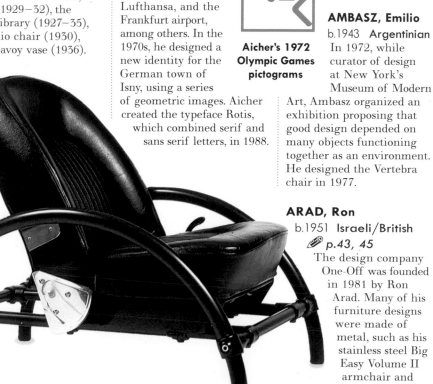

The Rover chair, designed by Ron Arad, 1985

AARNIO, Eero
b.1932 Finnish
p.37
Aarnio studied industrial design before opening his own design studio. He is well-known for his chair design and use of synthetic materials. His early and late works make use of traditional materials, although during the 1980s he used computer-aided design and manufacturing. His pieces include the Ball, or Globe, fiberglass chair with built-in speakers or telephone (Asko, 1963), the Gyro fiberglass chair (Asko, 1968), and the Viking dining table and chairs (Polardesign, 1983).

AICHER, Otl
1922–91 German
A corporate identity specialist, Aicher studied sculpture before establishing a graphics studio. He was the consulting designer for the corporate identity of the 1972 Munich Olympic Games (see right), and produced many corporate identity and visual information systems, working for Braun, Lufthansa, and the Frankfurt airport, among others. In the 1970s, he designed a new identity for the German town of Isny, using a series of geometric images. Aicher created the typeface Rotis, which combined serif and sans serif letters, in 1988.

Aicher's 1972 Olympic Games pictograms

ALBERS, Anni
1899–1981 German
Textile and industrial designer Albers (née Fleischmann) studied at the Bauhaus under Gunta Stölzl (see p.273). In 1933, she emigrated to the US with her husband, Josef Albers (see below). There she taught, experimented with weaving, and designed textiles for industry.

ALBERS, Josef
1888–1976 German
Albers was a painter, designer, and color theorist who taught at the Bauhaus from 1923. After its closure in 1933, he lectured at several universities in the US. A series of abstract paintings entitled *Homage to the Square* epitomize his color theories.

ALISON, Filippo
b.1930 Italian
p.73
Alison is an architect with a special interest in interior design. Among his industrial designs is the Filumena 2 coffeepot (Sabattini, 1984).

AMBASZ, Emilio
b.1943 Argentinian
In 1972, while curator of design at New York's Museum of Modern Art, Ambasz organized an exhibition proposing that good design depended on many objects functioning together as an environment. He designed the Vertebra chair in 1977.

ARAD, Ron
b.1951 Israeli/British
p.43, 45
The design company One-Off was founded in 1981 by Ron Arad. Many of his furniture designs were made of metal, such as his stainless steel Big Easy Volume II armchair and sofa. Possibly his most famous design is the Rover chair (1985; see left), consisting of a salvaged seat from a Rover car fitted into a tubular-steel frame. His later work includes hi-fi systems made of concrete (1985) and the interior design of the Tel Aviv Opera House (1990).

ARAI, Junichi
b.1932 Japanese
A textile designer and manufacturer, Arai gained fame for his experiments with unusual combinations of materials, including celluloid and metallic fibers. His highly complex patterns for weaving using computer punch cards have influenced other textile designers. He now works for his Tokyo-based retail company, Nuno.

ARMANI, Giorgio
See box above
p.141

d'ASCANIO, Corradino
1891–1981 Italian
p.175
In the 1920s, d'Ascanio worked at an airplane factory as technical director. He soon started his own firm and designed a successful helicopter. In 1934, he began working for the engineering company Piaggio, designing aircraft components and helicopters. But it is a 1946 design for which he is best-known – the eternally popular Vespa scooter (see right).

ARMANI, Giorgio b.1935 Italian

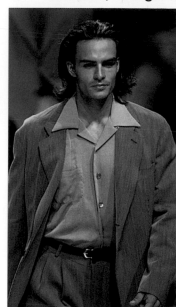

One of the most highly acclaimed fashion designers to emerge from Milan, Armani pioneered a loosely tailored look of casual elegance in the 1980s. After working as a window dresser, he began designing for menswear company Nino Cerruti in 1961. Armani founded his own clothing firm in 1974. Besides his exclusive mens- and womenswear lines, he also mass produces clothing for Emporio Armani stores.

An Emporio Armani design, 1996

ASHBEE, Charles Robert
1863–1942 British
Ashbee was one of the leading figures in the English Arts and Crafts movement. He set up the Guild and School of Handicraft in 1888 and designed many pieces of jewelry, silverware, and furniture for it. His style was linked to Art Nouveau.

ASHLEY, Laura
See box right
p.121

ASPLUND, Gunnar
1885–1940 Swedish
Although usually remembered for his contribution to Scandinavian Modernist architecture and for his interior designs, Asplund also designed furniture. Reproductions of some pieces, such as his Senna chair (1925), are currently manufactured by Cassina.

B

BAHNSEN, Uwe
b.1930 German
p.189
Automobile designer Bahnsen has been head of car design at Ford Europe since 1976. He has overseen the design of the Fiesta, Granada, and Escort, but the most radical and admired of his cars is the Ford Sierra, launched in 1982.

BAIER, Fred
b.1935 British
 p.193
The work of furniture designer and maker Baier is complex, often colorful, and always unconventional. For example, his Roll Top Drop Leaf Transforming Robot Desk (1989) owes as much to science-fiction imagery as traditional furniture design.

BAKKER, Gijs
b.1942 Dutch
✐ p.157
Together with his late wife, Emmy van Leersum, Bakker created a new look for contemporary jewelry. In the 1960s, they made aluminum collars and bracelets. Later, they moved into performance and sculpture, using the body as a part of jewelry design. Bakker has also designed items of furniture, including the Strip chair (1974) and the Finger chair (1979).

BALENCIAGA, Cristobal
1895–1972 Spanish
✐ p.144
Balenciaga is thought by many to be the century's greatest couturier. At the age of 18, he opened his own shop in San Sebastián and began work as a couturier under the name Eisa. In the late 1930s, he opened a couture house in Paris and produced his first collection, consisting of full-skirted crinoline dresses. Like much of his later work, the designs were influenced by his Spanish background and featured brocades, ruffles, black lace, and embroidery. His dramatic evening clothes were strongly colored. In 1957, he produced the "sack" dress, a radical departure from Dior's close-fitting "New Look." He retired in 1968.

BALL, Douglas
b.1935 Canadian
Canada's most successful industrial designer, Ball is best known for the Race office system (Sunar Hauserman, 1978). He has also designed wheelchairs.

BALMAIN, Pierre
1914–82 French
Balmain began his fashion career supplying drawings for the couturier Piguet. After a five-year stint for Molyneux, he worked for Lelong alongside Christian Dior (see p.259). Balmain founded his own house in 1945. His designs found favor with rich, older women and many celebrities. The house diversified into ready-to-wear, sportswear, and perfumes, while Balmain himself designed flight attendant uniforms and numerous stage and film costumes.

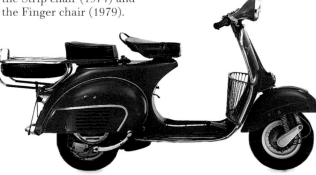

Corradino d'Ascanio's Vespa scooter, 1946

BARNACK, Oskar
1879–1936 German
✐ p.164
Barnack was the inventor of the Leica camera, the first successful 35mm camera.

BASS, Saul
1920–96 American
✐ p.227
Design pioneer Bass established his graphic design company, Saul Bass Associates, in Los Angeles. In movie advertising and credit sequences, he produced groundbreaking work, most notably for Otto Preminger's film *The Man with the Golden Arm* (1955). In addition to his film work, Bass's company has developed many corporate identities including AT&T, Minolta, Quaker Oats, United Airlines, and Warner Communications.

BAYER, Herbert
1900–85 Austrian/American
✐ p.208, 217
The graphic designer most associated with the Bauhaus, Bayer designed and produced all its typography between 1925 and 1928. These lowercase, sans serif typefaces became identified as the Bauhaus graphic style. Bayer left the school in 1928. In the years that followed, he art-directed the German *Vogue*, designed typefaces, and introduced surrealism to the advertising style of the 1930s. In 1938, Bayer emigrated to the US, where he designed graphics and buildings.

BECK, Henry C.
1903–74 British
✐ p.17
In 1931, Beck designed a diagrammatic route map for London Underground. Its geographically distorted and simplified lines were easier to follow than previous maps. Beck developed it until 1959.

BEDINE, Martine
b.1957 French
Bedine moved to Florence, Italy, in 1978. There she worked for the Super-studio group before joining Ettore Sottsass at Alchimia, then Memphis. Her designs include the Super table or floor lamp (1981) and Charlotte sideboard (1987) for Memphis, and luggage for Louis Vuitton. In 1992, she cofounded La Manufacture Familiale to produce mainly wooden furniture.

BEHRENS, Peter
1868–1940 German
✐ p.74, 106, 194, 212
An industrial designer and architect associated with the electrical company AEG, Behrens epitomized the growing relationship between art and industry during the early 20th century. His early paintings and graphic work were influenced by Jugendstil. After joining the Munich Secession, and then the artists' colony in Darmstadt, Behrens worked for AEG between 1903 and 1914. He was responsible for its publicity, packaging, and later

its architecture and general design. His many product designs include kettles and fans. Among his pupils at AEG were Gropius (see p.263), Mies van der Rohe (see p.267), and Le Corbusier (see p.266).

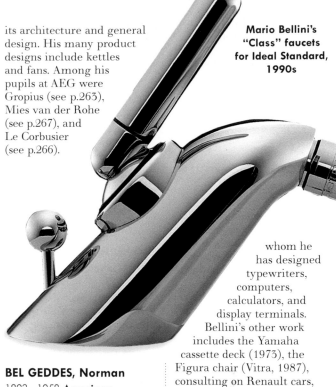

Mario Bellini's "Class" faucets for Ideal Standard, 1990s

BEL GEDDES, Norman
1893–1958 American
✐ p.91
After working as a theater designer and window dresser, Bel Geddes began designing industrial objects in 1927. These included cars, radios, and airplane interiors. Due to the futuristic nature of his designs, few went into production. However, his book *Horizons* helped popularize streamlining and he was the first industrial designer to gain public notice.

BELLINI, Mario
b.1935 Italian
✐ p.62, 87, 99, 205
One of Italy's leading industrial designers, Bellini studied architecture in Milan. Since 1963, he has been consultant to Olivetti, for whom he has designed typewriters, computers, calculators, and display terminals. Bellini's other work includes the Yamaha cassette deck (1973), the Figura chair (Vitra, 1987), consulting on Renault cars, and editing *Domus* magazine.

BENNETT, Ward
b.1917 American
Artist, sculptor, and designer in many other capacities, Ward has also worked as an interior designer. He is now best known for his furniture, textiles, and jewelry.

BERTOIA, Harry
1915–78 Italian/American
✐ p.36
Italian-born Bertoia moved to the US in 1930. After teaching metalwork, he worked with Charles Eames (see p.260) on plywood and wire chairs. In 1950, he set up a studio with help from Knoll International, for which he produced the Diamond chair (1952).

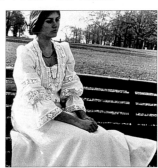

BERTONE, Flaminio
b.1903 Italian
✏ p.181, 182, 185
The man behind the idiosyncratic shape and styling of the Citroën 2CV (1939), Bertone also styled the company's Traction Avant (1934) and DS (1960).

BERTONE, Giuseppe
b.1914 Italian
✏ p.186
"Nuccio" Bertone joined his father's car body shop in 1934 and went on to change it into a successful and influential auto design studio. He was responsible for the design of the Alfa Romeo Giulietta Sprint (1954), Lamborghini Miura (1966), Ferrari Dino 308 (1973), and the Citroën BX (1982), among others.

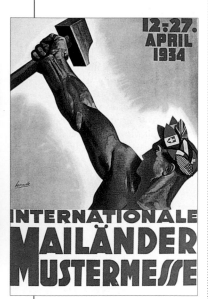
Bocasile's poster for a trade fair in Milan, 1934

BLACK, Misha
1910–77 British
Russian-born Black moved to the UK as a child. During the 1930s, he designed radios and televisions for Ekco, using new plastics. Much of his career was devoted to exhibition design, and he was responsible for part of the Festival of Britain (1951). Between 1959 and 1975, he taught industrial design.

BLAHNIK, Manolo
b.1940 Spanish
Known as the creator of original and extravagant shoes, Blahnik has produced footwear collections for many important fashion houses, including Calvin Klein and Yves Saint Laurent.

BLAKE, Peter
b.1932 British
✏ p.220
Pioneer of the British Pop Art Movement, Blake's most famous design is the LP cover for the Beatles' *Sgt Pepper's Lonely Hearts Club Band* (1967). He is associate artist at the National Gallery, London.

BLOMBERG, Hugo
b.1897 Swedish
✏ p.127
As chief engineer and head of design at the Swedish telecommunications company Ericsson, Blomberg designed the Ericofon one-piece telephone with Ralph Lysell in the 1940s (see p.266).

BOCASILE, Gino
active 1930s Italian
✏ p.225
One of Italy's leading poster designers during the 1930s, Bocasile produced many advertising and tourism posters (see left).

BOERI, Cini
b.1924 Italian
After graduating in architecture, Boeri worked in the studio of Marco Zanuso (see p.275) until 1963, when she became a freelance designer. Although best known for her furniture designs, including the Bobo (1967) and Strips (1972) seating sytems, she has designed showrooms for Knoll International (1976) and a series of prefabricated houses in Japan (1983).

BONETTO, Rodolfo
b.1929 Italian
A furniture and industrial designer, Bonetto first worked in the Pininfarina car design studio. Since setting up his own studio in 1958, he has designed products for Brionvega, Olivetti, Gaggia, Driade, Veglia Borletti, and Fiat. His original use of single-piece plastic molding in the interior of the Fiat 132 Bellini (1980) earned him much acclaim.

BOOTY, Jr. Donald
b.1956 American
✏ p.205
Before founding Booty Design Associates in 1988, Donald Booty, Jr. had studied industrial design in Chicago. The company designs not only for other manufacturers, but also for its own production company, Phorm.

BORSANI, Osvaldo
1911– 85 Italian
✏ p.40
Borsani worked as both an architect and furniture designer. In 1954, with his twin brother Fulgenzio Borsani, he founded the furniture company Tecno. In the early years, Tecno produced Borsani's designs only, but later offered the work of other designers, such as Norman Foster (see p.261). Borsani's most famous pieces are the P40 chaise longue (1954) and D70 reclining sofa (1955).

BOTTA, Mario
b.1943 Swiss
✏ p.92
Botta studied architecture at the University of Venice, and his training included a stint in the Paris studio of Le Corbusier (see p.266). In 1969, Botta returned to Lugano and began work on various public and private buildings that would earn him recognition as an organic, rationalist architect. A recent commision was the San Francisco Museum of Modern Art (1995). Since 1982, Botta has designed a number of pieces of metal furniture for the Italian company Alias. These include the Prima chair (1982), Quarta chair (see right), and Tesi table (1986).

BOUE, Michel
1936–71 French
Automobile designer Boué's career was cut short when he died of cancer at the age of 35. However, he had already produced one major design, the Renault 5 (known in the US as Le Car). The car, which appeared in 1972, was the first of the Superminis, and became the best-selling French car ever.

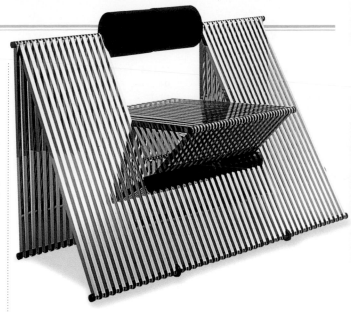
Quarta chair, designed by Mario Botta for Alias, 1984

BOULANGER, Pierre
1886–1950 French
✏ p.181, 182, 185
Boulanger, an engineer, worked for the French tire company Michelin until 1935, when it took over the car manufacturer Citroën. Boulanger became head of the car company and was responsible for the concept of the Traction Avant (1934), 2CV (1939), and DS (1960), all of which were styled by Flaminio Bertone (see left).

BRANDT, Marianne
1893–1983 German
Painter, designer, and metalworker, Brandt studied painting and sculpture in Weimar. She joined the Bauhaus in 1923 and, under the influence of László Moholy-Nagy (see p.267), became one of its best-known metalwork students. She evolved from an Arts and Crafts worker to an industrial designer employing geometric principles. In 1925, she began designing metal lamps at the Bauhaus, and is particularly remembered for the Kandem bedside light (Körting and Matthiesen, 1928.) Between 1928 and 1929, Brandt briefly worked for Walter Gropius's office (see p.263) in Berlin, and after World War II she taught first in Dresden, then in Berlin.

BRANZI, Andrea
b.1938 Italian
An architect and designer, Branzi was an influential member of the Florence-based design group Archizoom (founded in 1966). He moved to Milan in 1979 and worked with Studio Alchimia, then Memphis. His designs for Memphis include the Century couch (1982), Labrador gravy boat (1982), and Magnolia bookcase (1985).
In 1982, Branzi became educational director of the Domus Academy, a postgraduate design school.

BRAUN, Artur
1921–71 German
✏ p.57
Artur Braun took over the Frankfurt-based radio and record-player company, Braun, on the death of his father in 1951, and turned it into the electronics giant it is today. He hired Fritz Eichler (see p.260) as design director. Together they designed the SK 25 radio in 1955 (see below). Eichler employed Otl Aicher (see p.254), Dieter Rams (see p.271), and Hans

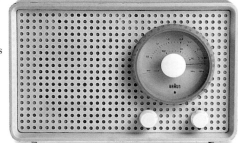
Artur Braun and Fritz Eichler's SK 25 radio, 1955

Gugelot (see p.263), designers with whom he had worked at the Ulm Hochshule für Gestaltung (Ulm College of Design). The Braun products they created displayed a strong company look, epitomized by an unadorned, industrialized style and geometric simplicity.

BREER, Carl
1883–1970 American
p.181
In the 1930s, Breer was chief engineer at the US car manufacturer Chrysler. He was responsible for the unconventional-looking Airflow (1934), which although a commercial failure, was widely commentated on at the time and influenced the design of many other automobiles. Breer retired in 1951.

BREUER, Marcel
1902–81
Hungarian
p.33, 124
After studying at the Bauhaus, Breuer opened an architect's office in Berlin in 1928. His most significant contribution to design this century is his revolutionary tubular-steel furniture (see right). Inspired by the strength and lightness of his bicycle, he first made use of tubular steel for the Wassily chair (1925). The Cantilever chair that followed (1928) was made with an unbroken length of tubing, and became a prototype for countless similar chairs. After a short time working for Isokon in England (for whom he produced a bent plywood chair), Breuer moved to the US, where he built his own house and produced experimental furniture. His major architectural works include the UNESCO headquarters in Paris (1953) and the Whitney Museum of American Art in New York (1966).

BROADHEAD, Caroline
b.1950 British
A prominent figure in European jewelry design, Broadhead first worked with ivory. In 1977, she produced bound-thread necklaces and, in 1978, innovative bracelets.

She was one of the first designers to reject precious materials in favor of everyday materials such as cloth, rubber, and paper. In the 1980s, she created wearable pieces that combined jewelry, clothing, and sculpture.

BRODOVITCH, Alexey
1898–1971 American
Born in Russia, Brodovitch worked in Paris during the 1920s, where he designed books, posters, furnishings, and advertising. He moved to the US in 1930, where he was art director of *Harper's Bazaar* for 25 years.

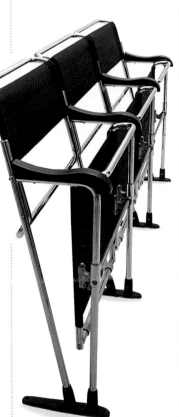

Bauhaus tubular-steel cinema chairs, designed by Marcel Breuer, 1929

Brodovitch revolutionized American magazine design by introducing cropped photographs, spare layouts with ample white space, and illusory effects.

BRODY, Neville
b.1957 British
p.211, 219
A graphic designer who rose to fame in the 1980s, Brody studied fine art and graphic design at the London College

of Printing. He began his career by designing record covers. In 1981, he was appointed art director of the magazine *The Face*, and experimented with unconventional typefaces, logos, and symbols. He continues to run his own design studio in London.

BÜLOW-HÜBE, Vivianna Torun
b.1927 Swedish
p.157
From 1951 to 1956, Bülow-Hübe worked in her own studio, concentrating on wooden and silver jewelry. From 1967 on, she produced various jewelry and watch prototypes for Georg Jensen Sølvsmedie. She later turned her hand to glassware, porcelain, and ceramics, and went on to design kitchen utensils, lamps, baskets, and office equipment.

BURYLIN, Sergei Petrovich
See box right

C

CAMPBELL, Sarah
b.1946 British
p.123, 258
Textile designer Campbell works with her sister, Susan Collier (see p.258); the two founded Collier Campbell.

CAPUCCI, Roberto
b.1929 Italian
Capucci studied at the Accademia delle Belle Arti in Rome, and in 1950 opened a fashion house there. In 1962, he went to Paris, returning to Rome after seven years. He produced many experimental and daring fashion items, using bright colors and sculptural forms, including plastic garments filled with colored water. Capucci was renowned for the skillful cut of his garments.

CARDER, Frederick
1863–1963 British
In 1903, Carder moved to the US, where he cofounded the Steuben Glassworks in New York. Starting out by making iridescent glass, Aurene, in an

Art Nouveau style, Steuben soon became a major player in the glass world. In 1918, the company was taken over by the Corning Glass Works. During the 30 years that Carder was art director there, he designed many of the most successful pieces himself.

CARDIN, Pierre
b.1922 French
p.144
Born in Italy to French parents, Cardin studied architecture in Paris after World War II, and then trained at the fashion houses of Paquin, Schiaparelli, and Dior. In 1950, he opened his own house, showing his first collection in 1953. During the 1960s, he moved into menswear, and came to be considered one of France's most adventurous couturiers. His unconventional designs used bright and patterned materials, some influenced by the space age, and had exaggerated features. Many of his designs were suitable for men or women, and he is said to have invented unisex clothing. Cardin's name is now also associated with cars, furniture, luggage, and wigs.

CARLU, Jean
b.1900 French
p.227
One of France's leading poster designers of the 1920s and '30s, Carlu was clearly influenced by Cubism. Between 1940 and 1953, he lived in the US, and there produced the first US defense poster in 1941.

CARTER, Matthew
b.1937 British
p.211
Today considered to be a master of typography and its technology, Carter designed the Bell Centennial type for the US AT&T telephone directories in 1978. In 1981, he co-founded Bitstream Inc. to produce fonts for computers.

CARTIER, Louis
1875–1942 French
p.128
Grandson of the founder of the jewelers Cartier, Louis Cartier became its most important and innovative designer, improving the types of materials used in jewelry design. From around 1900, he utilized platinum, a suitably flexible metal for his lacelike diamond-set jewelry.

BURYLIN, Sergei Petrovich 1876–1942 Russian

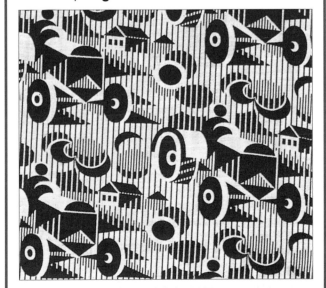

Tractor fabric, 1930

A textile designer, Burylin was active at various textile mills in Ivanovo-Vosnesensk. His most widely known fabric, the Tractor cotton print, is typical of his strong, semi-abstract, Constructivist style.

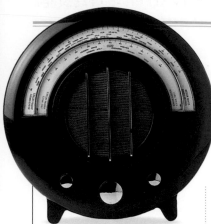

Wells Coates's AD 65 radio, 1932–34

CARWARDINE, George
1887–1948 British
✏ *p.54*

As an automobile engineer, Carwardine was a suspension system specialist; as a lighting designer, he is famous for his 1934 Anglepoise lamp. The springs and hinges of the lamp were designed to replicate the muscles and movement of a human arm. Over 60 years later, the design is still in production and remains virtually unchanged.

CASSANDRE, A.M.
1901–68 French
✏ *p.225*

A.M. Cassandre was the pseudonym of graphic artist Adolphe Jean-Marie Mouron. Between 1923 and 1936, he designed a series of highly successful and influential advertising posters using his idiosyncratic style of bold, geometric abstraction and broad planes of restricted color to integrate images and words. He also created three new typefaces: Bifur (1929), Acier Noir (1930), and Peignot (1936). His Dubonnet poster (1934) and Etoile du Nord poster (1927) have become classics.

CASTIGLIONI, Achille
b.1918 Italian
✏ *p.37*

Innovative industrial designer Castiglioni joined the studio of brothers Livio (1911–79) and Pier Giacomo (1913–68) in 1944, after graduating in architecture from Milan Polytechnic. His work includes lighting, but he is best known for his exploratory furniture design: the 1957 tractor-seat stool Mezzadro and the 1970 kneeling stool Primate.

CHANEL, Gabrielle (Coco)
1883–1971 French
✏ *p.104, 143, 157*

Chanel had no formal fashion training, yet she has proven one of the most enduring fashion success stories. In 1914, she opened her first dress shop; during the 1920s, she responded to women's work and leisure fashion needs with practical but stylish wool jersey and corduroy clothing in neutral shades or red. Hers was a relaxed, unfussy style. Her eveningwear was luxurious, with beading, embroidery, and fur. The look for which she is best known is the jersey or soft tweed collarless suit, with braid trim and many pearls or gold chains. After her death, the House of Chanel remained open and was taken over by Karl Lagerfeld in 1983 (see p.266).

CHASHNIK, Ilia Grigorevich
1902–1929 Russian
✏ *p.15, 83*

Chashnik collaborated with fellow Suprematist painter Kazimir Malevich while working at the Lomonosov State Porcelain Factory design studios between 1922 and 1924. Chashnik designed the enameled decoration for Malevich's witty 1923 porcelain Half Cup.

CHERMAYEFF, IVAN
1932–1996 American

A designer, illustrator, and painter, Chermayeff's major work was in partnership with Thomas Geismar (see p.262). The design group Chermayeff and Geismar Inc. became known for its bold, graphic work in corporate identity. He won many awards, both jointly and individually.

CLIFF, Clarice
1899–1972 British
✏ *p.83*

Cliff is one of the foremost British ceramic designers of this century. She began as a lithographer in 1916 at A.J. Wilkinson Ltd., the Royal Staffordshire pottery works with which she was associated for the rest of her working life. Her best-known design was the Bizarre line, produced from 1927, which was typified by brightly colored, stylized designs against a creamy background, giving a strong Art Deco feel. Despite their unconventional look, Cliff's designs were sold in stores such as Harrods. Her work is enjoying renewed popularity.

COATES, Nigel
b.1949 British

An architect and furniture designer, Coates has achieved notoriety for his extravagant

---

COLLIER, Susan b.1942 British

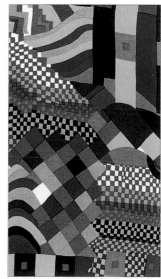

Bauhaus upholstery fabric, 1972

Collier worked as a design consultant for London's Liberty store, before founding her own textile company in 1979 with her sister, Sarah Campbell. Collier Campbell's philosophy was to grow away from the formal, organized graphic designs of the 1950s and produce painterly fabrics with blocks of strong color and abstract patterns. Its concept of "design for now" is still apparent in its fashion, bedding, and furniture fabrics.

---

and unconventional designs for a series of Japanese bar and club interiors. He has also designed fashion shops in London for Jasper Conran and Katherine Hamnett (see p.263). He launched his Metropole and Jazz furniture collections in 1987 and his Noah collection in 1988.

COATES, Wells
1895–1958 Canadian
✏ *p.56*

Born in Tokyo and educated in Canada, Coates settled in the UK in 1929. He is most commonly associated with the Modern Movement in England during the 1930s. His interest in new technologies and materials led him to form the Isokon company with Jack Pritchard in 1931 to design and build modern housing and furnishings. Most of Coates's industrial design work in the 1930s was for Ekco, and he is particularly remembered for his series of Bakelite radios, including AD 65 (see left).

COLANI, Luigi
b.1928 German
✏ *p.85*

Colani's designs are largely influenced by aerodynamic styling, ranging in subject matter from transportation to fashion accessories. Most of his transportation designs have never progressed beyond prototypes, although they have inspired other designers. Among his best-known designs are his 1970 Drop porcelain service for Rosenthal and his cameras for Canon.

COLLIER, Susan
See box, left
✏ *p.123*

COLOMBO, Joe
1930–71 Italian
✏ *p.66, 92, 129*

A painter, sculptor, and designer, Colombo was a leading figure of post-World War II Italian design. He set up his own studio in Milan in 1962, and his works show a

---

concern for the technical problems of design using new materials and techniques. His 1965 Chair 4860, made by Kartell, was one of the first one-piece injection-molded chairs in ABS plastics. His interest in economy and scale led him to design a complete mobile kitchen in 1972. His other clients have included Bernini, Italora, O'Luce, Bieffeplast, and Zanotta.

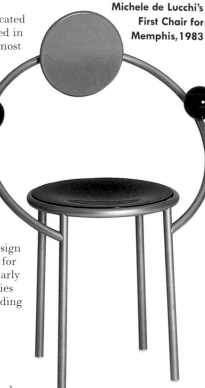

Michele de Lucchi's First Chair for Memphis, 1983

CONRAN, Terence
b.1931 British

Conran has greatly increased Britain's design awareness, bringing "good design" to the masses at affordable prices, largely through the Habitat stores he established in 1964. His early work was inspired by Italian and Scandinavian designs. In 1989, the Conran Foundation funded a Design Museum in London devoted to mass-produced goods.

COOPER, Susie
b.1902 British

An enduring name in British ceramics, Cooper set up her own firm in 1929, producing popular tea and coffee services and decorative items. Her designs feature patterns inspired by nature and strong shapes with clean lines and modern colors.

DEAN, Roger b.1942 British

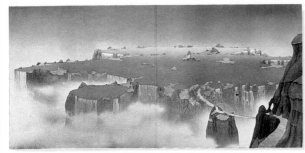

Close to the Edge record sleeve, 1972

Dean has designed stage sets, Teddy Bear Chairs, and seating for a jazz club, as well as illustrating album covers. His work is characterized by fusing natural images with fantastical, unworldly creations. In 1979, he cofounded his own design company, Magnetic Storm, to specialize in product research and development, theatrical construction, architectural design, illustration, and film.

CORDERO, Toni
active 1980s & '90s Italian

✎ *p.109*

Designer of the dramatic Sospir bed, Cordero also built the Alpine Stadium (1985) and the Automobile Museum (1987), both in Turin, Italy. He designs for Artemide, Driade, and Sawaya & Moroni.

COURREGES, André
b.1923 French

Trained by Balenciaga, Courrèges received great acclaim for his futuristic clothes. The 1964 Space Age collection was followed by his 1965 miniskirts and white and pastel pants, which were copied worldwide.

D

DAY, Lucienne
b.1917 British

Day created her famous Calyx fabric design in 1951: its thin black lines, precise graphics, and autumnal colors expressed a new approach to textile design. She has created many elegant screenprinted upholstery fabrics.

DAY, Robin
b.1915 British

Husband of Lucienne (see above), with whom he formed a design studio, Day won a low-cost furniture competition in 1948 at the Museum of Modern Art in New York. He subsequently designed one of the most successful post-World War II chairs for the commercial market, the Polyprop stacking chair (1963).

DEAN, Roger
See box, above

✎ *p.220*

DELAUNAY, Sonia
1885–1979 French

Delaunay's painter husband, Robert, influenced much of Sonia's work: with him she explored dynamism, rhythm, and movement through color.

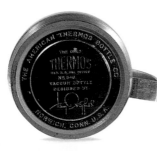

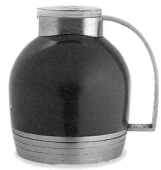

Dreyfuss's Thermos carafe, 1930s

Her work incorporated fabrics, interior design, and theater, designing ballet costumes for Diaghilev's *Aida* and *Cleopatra* productions. By 1925, her bold, decorative clothing designs had become fashionable.

DE BRETTEVILLE, Sheila Levant
b.1940 American

A typographer, graphic designer, and educator, de Bretteville is known for combining social and political attitudes with design. Her early inspiration came from feminist issues, and much of her work promotes women's creative expression.

DE LUCCHI, Michele
b.1952 Italian

✎ *p.24, 25, 43, 45*

De Lucchi was closely linked with the radical international design group Memphis from its initiation in 1981; he worked previously for Studio Alchimia. Like many Memphis designers, de Lucchi used bright, garish colors and asymmetry in his postmodernist work. His best-known piece for Memphis was the 1983 First Chair (see left). He set up his own studio in 1984 and went on to design plastic tableware for Bodum. He has also been a consultant to the office supply manufacturer Olivetti, and designed more than 50 Fiorucci shops.

DE PAS, D'URBINO, LOMAZZI
established 1966 Italian

Originally established as an architectural practice, the firm of Jonathan de Pas (1932–1991), Donato d'Urbino (b.1935), and Paolo Lomazzi (b.1936) turned to furniture design, producing one of the most memorable pieces of Pop-inspired design, the PVC inflatable Blow chair, in 1967.

DEGANELLO, Paolo
b.1940 Italian

After studying architecture, in 1966 Deganello became a cofounder of the radical design group Archizoom in Florence. He has also designed furniture for the Cassina and Driade companies: his 1982 Torso armchair, sofa, and bed for Cassina are particularly important pieces.

DESKEY, Donald
1894–1989 American

✎ *p.44*

An industrial and interior designer, Deskey was a pioneering design consultant and an important exponent of Art Deco in the 1930s. He began in advertising but was later commissioned to design items such as washing machines and printing presses. He was greatly interested in the new materials aluminum, cork, and linoleum. From 1927 to 1931, he worked in partnership with Phillip Vollmer and his work expanded to include interiors, wallpapers, and fabrics. In 1932, he won a competition to design the interior of Radio City Music Hall at Rockefeller Center, New York, which is acknowledged as a piece of classic American Art Deco.

DIOR, Christian
1905–57 French

✎ *p.18, 142*

At his first collection in 1947, Dior launched a totally new look that transformed fashions worldwide. His rise to fame was meteoric: he taught himself to draw, selling his ideas to couturiers and magazines, and then trained formally at the Piguet and LeLong fashion houses. His 1947 New Look captured the postwar mood; his famous A-line collection appeared in 1956. After Dior's death, Yves Saint Laurent (see p.272) became head of design for a brief period.

DORN, Marion Victoria
1899–1964 American

After experimenting with resist-dyed fabrics in the US, Dorn moved to the UK in the early 1920s, making original batiks for interiors. During the 1930s, she became a leading modernist designer, achieving acclaim for her textiles and tufted carpets.

DREYFUSS, Henry
1903–72 American

✎ *p.107, 126*

Industrial designer Dreyfuss's interest in the relationship between man and society led him to incorporate ergonomic features in his work, an approach that influenced later designers. Apprenticed to Norman Bel Geddes (see p.255), he then established his name in the 1930s with the Bell Telephone, designing its classic Bell 300 in 1933. He also designed for companies such as American Airlines, Lockheed, Thermos (see left), and Hoover. His autobiography, *Designing For People*, was published in 1955.

DU PASQUIER, Natalie
b.1957 French

✎ *p.123*

A leading postmodern textile designer, du Pasquier worked first for Rainbow Studio and then Memphis from 1981 to 1988. She is known for her vivid printed patterns. In 1982, she joined the creative staff of Fiorucci. She has also designed furniture, lamps (see below), clocks, and ceramics.

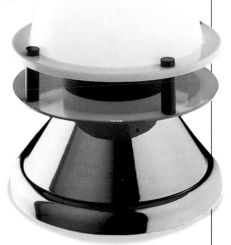

Natalie du Pasquier's Bordeaux Lamp for Memphis, 1986

DUFY, Raoul
1877–1953 French
✎ *p.122*

The early work of painter and decorative designer Dufy was strongly influenced by the bright, strong colors of the Fauves. Later, he designed dress fabrics for couturier Paul Poiret (see p.270) and textiles for the Lyons-based company Bianchini-Férier.

DUMAS, Rena
b.1937 Greek
✎ *p.193*

After completing her studies in Paris, in 1962 Dumas began working as a designer of leather goods for Hermès. She set up her own office in 1971, designing office, home, and store interiors. Working in collaboration with Peter Coles (1954–85), she produced the Pippa collection of folding furniture (Hermès, 1985) and has since created store interiors for Hermès.

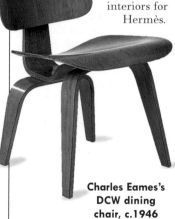

Charles Eames's DCW dining chair, c.1946

DUMBAR, Gert
b.1940 Dutch
✎ *p.230*

A graphic designer and tutor, Dumbar studied painting and graphic arts before joining Tel Design Associates in The Hague in 1967. Tel created the internationally acclaimed corporate identity for the Nederlands Spoorwegan (Dutch Railways). In 1977, Dumbar left the group to set up his own practice. Working in association with Total Design (established 1963), Studio Dumbar produced the corporate identity for PTT, the Dutch Postal, Telegraph, and Telephone authority. Other commissions include the celebrated signage system for the Rijksmuseum and the corporate identities for Westeinde Hospital in The Hague and ANWB (Dutch Automobile Association).

DUNAND, Jean
1877–1942 Swiss

Dunand studied art in Geneva before moving to Paris, where he worked as a sculptor until 1902. He established his own metalwork studio in 1903. Known for his lacquerwork, from 1912 on he studied with the Japanese artist Seizo Sugawara, who also trained Eileen Gray (see p.263). Dunand incorporated lacquering techniques into his metalwork, and later applied them to furniture, screens, and panels. Some of his finest Art Deco creations include the interior of the smoking room of the Ambassade Française at the Paris Expo in 1925, and lacquered panels for the *Normandie* ocean liner (1935).

D'URBINO, Donato
See de Pas, d'Urbino, Lomazzi

E

EAMES, Charles Ormond
1907–78 American
✎ *p.19, 37*

Architect-designer Charles Eames studied architecture at Washington University before setting up in his own practice in St. Louis in 1930. In 1936, he was offered a fellowship at Cranbrook Academy of Art, Michigan, where he met his future wife Ray Kaiser (see right) and Eero Saarinen (see p.271). Saarinen and Eames designed a series of molded plywood seats, which won the 1940 Organic Design in Home Furnishings competition at New York's Museum of Modern Art. In 1941, he and Ray moved to California. The couple were in partnership from 1944 on, creating furniture designs that were mass produced by Herman Miller. They created several notable pieces, including the Lounge chair and ottoman (1956), and later moved into film production, photography, and exhibition design. Their client list included the US government and IBM.

EAMES, Ray
1912–88 American
✎ *p.37*

Ray Eames (née Kaiser) collaborated with her husband Charles Eames (see left) on many of their magazines, exhibition, film, and furniture designs.

EARL, Harley
1893–1969 American
✎ *p.20, 184–85*

Earl was responsible for the styling of General Motors cars from 1927 until his retirement in 1959. His grounding in the glamorous world of Hollywood showed in his flamboyant styling. He was an innovator, introducing yearly model changes and the use of clay models for developing the shape of the bodywork. His most famous model is the Cadillac Eldorado (1959).

EBENDORF, Robert
b. circa 1938 American

Ebendorf is a jeweler whose early work, including coffeepots and umbrella handles, showed both American and Scandinavian influences. In contrast to his early pieces, made from precious and semiprecious materials such as silver, ebony, and moonstone, his jewelry, starting in the 1980s, was produced from a range of nonprecious materials, including paper and wood.

ECKMANN, Otto
1865–1902 German
✎ *p.208*

After starting out as a painter, Eckmann turned his attention to the applied arts, producing illustrations for the magazines *Pan* and *Jugend*. In 1900, he created the Art Nouveau typeface Eckmann Schmuck, one of several designed for the Klingspor foundry, Offenbach. In addition to his work as a graphic artist,

Harley Earl with a futuristic prototype, early 1950s

he also designed textiles, ceramics, and pieces of furniture.

EDISON, Thomas Alva
1847–1931 American
✎ *p.61, 194*

Edison is a key figure in the development of modern technology. Among his many inventions are the phonograph (1878), the incandescent lightbulb (1879), and talking motion pictures (1912).

EICHLER, Fritz
1911–91 German
✎ *p.57, 258*

Eichler began his career in theater set design. In 1954 he was employed by Artur Braun (see p.258) as a program director. Together with the Braun design team, he was responsible for developing the austere functionalist style that has come to be associated with the company.

EISENLOEFFEL, Jan W.
1876–1957 Dutch
✎ *p.82*

After training in Amsterdam in the Hoeker en Zoon silver workshop, Eisenloeffel spent a year learning enameling in Russia. The metalwares and ceramics that he produced for various

Shoe lasts from Ferragamo's studio

Dutch companies, including De Woning and De Distel, all demonstrate his liking for simple, industrial forms that could be mass produced.

ERTE (Romain de Tirtoff)
1892–1990 Russian

Erté took his name from the French pronunciation of his initials, RT. After studying at the Académie Julian, Paris, he was employed as a fashion illustrator by Paul Poiret (see p.270). From 1915, he created drawings for the covers of *Harper's Bazaar* and designed theatrical costumes and sets. Working briefly in Hollywood, he designed sets for Cecil B. de Mille and Louis B. Mayer. Later, he achieved renown when a retrospective of his drawings was shown in New York and London.

ESSLINGER, Hartmut
b.1945 German
✎ *p.200*

Industrial designer Esslinger founded frogdesign, an industrial-design consultancy, in Altensteig in 1969. The firm's first client was Wega Radio, which was later bought out by Sony – establishing a presence for frogdesign in the Japanese market. Esslinger opened an office in California in 1982. His clients include Apple, for which he designed the Apple Macintosh (1984).

F

FARINA, Battista
1893–1966 Italian

Before setting up his own shop in Turin in 1930, automobile designer "Pinin" Farina visited the US to study Ford's production methods. His name is generally associated with the classic Italian makers, such as Alfa-Romeo and Ferrari, but he also designed for mass production. In 1961, the firm was renamed Pininfarina.

FATH, Jacques
1912–54 French
🖋 p.143
Trained at drama school, Fath worked briefly as an actor before establishing a fashion house in 1937. His career as a couturier was interrupted by World War II, but he emerged in peacetime as a successful *haute couture* designer. In 1948, he entered

the American ready-to-wear market, creating biannual collections for Joseph Halpert. Fath was one of the first fashion houses to offer clothes in standardized sizes, which were sold through boutiques. In 1949, Fath received the prestigious Neiman-Marcus Award for his work.

FERRAGAMO, Salvatore
1898–1960 Italian
🖋 p.146
The "shoemaker to the stars," Ferragamo found his vocation early in life, setting up his own workshop in Bonito, Italy, at the age of 14. In 1914, he went to the US, where he opened a shop in Hollywood. He was appalled by the poor

quality of mass-produced shoes and developed his own method of hand production, working directly from the wooden last (see left). In 1927, he returned to Italy, where he continued to produce exciting designs, popularizing the wedge heel in the 1930s. He received the Neiman-Marcus Award in 1947, the year he invented the "invisible shoe."

FERRARI-HARDOY, Jorge
1878–1976 Argentinian
🖋 p.35
Ferrari-Hardoy worked in collaboration with two fellow architects, the Argentian Juan Kurchan (1913–75) and the Spaniard Antonio Bonet

(1913–89), to produce the Hardoy chair, also referred to as the Butterfly chair, in 1938. Its low manufacturing costs made it a popular choice for reproduction by many manufacturers, including Knoll and Artek-Pascoe.

FERRIERI, Anna Castelli
see box above

FOLON, Jean-Michel
b.1934 Belgian
🖋 p.229
Illustrator and graphic artist Folon has produced drawings for various magazines, including *Time*, *Fortune*, and *The New Yorker*. His work,

which highlights human alienation in a technological environment, has also been used extensively in posters and advertisements.

FORD, Henry
1863–1947 American
🖋 p.180
Apprenticed to a machinist in Detroit in 1878, Ford had produced a gas-powered car by 1893. In 1903, he founded the Ford Motor Company. The hugely successful Model T (see right) was the first car to be mass produced on the assembly line. The emphasis shifted from function to styling with the introduction of the streamlined V8 in 1932. Ford was eventually succeeded by his son and grandson.

FORNASETTI, Piero
1913–88 Italian
Fornasetti is recognized for his individualistic decoration. He collaborated on a number of projects with Gio Ponti (see p.270) after Ponti saw his work exhibited at the Milan Triennale in 1940. Famous for his *trompe-l'oeil* designs, his most celebrated commission is the Casino, San Remo (1950).

FORTUNY Y MADRAZO, Mariano
1871–1949 Spanish
🖋 p.142
Working with hand-dyed silks and velvets, artist and dress-maker Fortuny made stunning Aesthetic-style dresses, coats, and capes. His most famous garment is the Delphos dress (1909), for which he employed his patented pleating method. The body-sheathing dress maintained its pleats when twisted into a knot for storage.

FOSTER, Norman
b.1935 British
🖋 p.193
Foster is best known as a high-tech architect, reponsible for the Sainsbury Centre for the Visual Arts, University of East Anglia, Norwich (1978), and the

Hongkong and Shanghai Bank, Hong Kong (1979–85). He also designed the Nomos set of office furniture (1983–87) with Tecno (see below).

FRANCK, Kaj
1911–89 Finnish
An important ceramics and glassware designer, Franck worked for both Arabia pottery and Nuutajärvi glassworks (absorbed by Wärtsilä in 1950) between 1945 and the late 1970s. Through his work, such as the Kilta tableware line (1952), he promoted a distinctly utilitarian aesthetic.

FRANK, Josef
1885–1967 Austrian
Austrian-born designer Frank became a lecturer at the Künstgewerbeschule, Vienna, in 1919. Between 1925 and 1934, he ran an interior design company called Haus und Garten. Moving to Sweden in 1934, he joined Svensk Tenn, where he designed furniture, textiles, and wallpaper. He was an early exponent of the Swedish Modern movement.

FRUTIGER, Adrian
b.1928 Swiss
🖋 p.210
Graphic designer Frutiger earned his reputation in 1957, when he launched the Univers typeface. Creator of more than 20 typefaces, he has also worked on signage, including Charles de Gaulle airport, Paris, and as a consultant for IBM, for which he developed typewriter and computer faces.

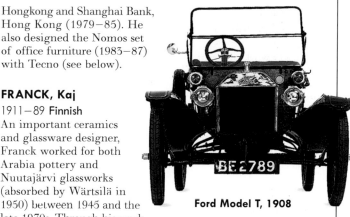

Ford Model T, 1908

FUKUDA, Shigeo
b.1932 Japanese
The witty posters, sculptures, and mosaics of Shigeo Fukuda all demonstrate his playful approach to design. He achieved international acclaim for his posters and signage for the Osaka World Expo in 1970 and since then has exhibited in many group and one-man shows throughout the world.

FULLER, Richard Buckminster
1895–1983 American
Radical architect and inventor Fuller trained in mathematics at Harvard and then at the Naval Academy, Maryland, where he began to develop his humanistic design concepts. His extensive research resulted in the Dymaxion house (1927) and car (1933). His foremost invention was the geodesic dome, which served as a model for future exhibition domes.

Work station by Norman Foster and Tecno, 1983

FERRIERI, Anna Castelli b.1920 Italian

Plastic stacking armchairs for Kartell, 1986

Anna Ferrieri graduated in architecture from Politecnico di Milano in 1943. She married Giulio Castelli the same year and entered into the family business, Kartell, for which she produced plastic furniture, tablewares, and modular storage systems. She set up her own architecture office in 1946, and from 1959 to 1973 worked with architect-designer Ignazio Gardella (b.1905) on furniture and public housing. She has received numerous awards.

G

GALLIANO, John
b.1961 British
✐ p.145

Gibraltan-born fashion designer Galliano graduated from London's St. Martin's School of Art in 1983. In his early collections, ethnic influence blended with his technique of spiral tailoring. When Hubert de Givenchy retired from his Paris couture house in 1995, Galliano became the first British fashion designer to head a French couture house.

GAMES, Abram
See box below
✐ p.38, 72

GAMES, Abram b.1914 British

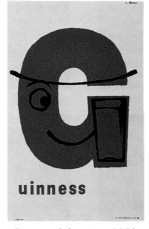

A leading modernist graphic designer, Abram Games is remembered for the posters he produced for the British War Office during World War II. His ideal of "maximum meaning, minimum means" is expressed in the cohesion of stylized images and type. His more commercial designs include symbols for the 1951 Festival of Britain (designed in 1948) and BBC television (1952).

Commercial poster, 1958

GATTI, PAOLINI, TEODORO
established 1965 Italian
✐ p.38

This design association was founded by the Italian trio Piero Gatti (b.1940), Cesare Paolini (b.1937), and Franco Teodoro (b.1939). They acquired early recognition with their Sacco beanbag seating (1968–69).

GAULTIER, Jean Paul
b.1952 French
✐ p.105

After early contact with fashion designer Pierre Cardin (see p.257), Gaultier established himself as a freelance designer in 1976, creating ready-to-wear ranges as well as his own exclusive label. His work, which often utilizes unusual materials, reveals the influence of London street style, particularly Punk. Gaultier has produced glamorous, nonconformist wear for men.

GEHRY, Frank O.
b.1929 Canadian
✐ p.74

An internationally active architect and designer, Gehry has been prolific since the late 1970s. He studied architecture at the University of California and Harvard Graduate School of Design, setting up on his own in 1962. Characterized by irregular, layered shapes and volumes, his buildings have been termed deconstructivist. The fish is a recurrent theme, used in 1983 for his fish light and in his Fish Dance restaurant in Kobe Japan, 1987. The Vitra Design Museum in Germany (1989) and the Pito kettle (1988, see right) are among his works.

GEISMAR, Thomas
b.1931 American

Geismar is most commonly associated with New York graphic design consultancy Charmayeff & Geismar Inc., which he cofounded in 1960. Best known for corporate identity and exhibition design, the Mobil Oil logo (1964) and Xerox logo (1965) are among his works, as well as a number of exhibition advertisements. He received a Presidential Design Award in 1985 for his standardized transportation related symbols.

GIACOSA, Dante
b.1905 Italian
✐ p.184

One of Italy's greatest car designers, Giacosa joined Fiat in 1930. His Fiat 500A, launched in 1936, was the basis for several variations of this small car. He also created the Fiat 124, 128, and 130.

GILL, Eric
1882–1940 British
✐ p.209

Letter-cutter, illustrator, typeface designer, and writer, Gill studied at Chichester School of Art, and later under Edward Johnston (see p.264). After becoming involved with the Roman Catholic Church in 1913, he produced many religious illustrations. During the 1920s, Gill was commissioned by the Monotype Corporation, for whom he produced the typefaces Perpetua (1925–30) and Gill Sans (1928–30).

GIUGIARO, Giorgetto
b.1938 Italian

A prolific contributor to international car design, Giugiaro has produced over 100 designs for several major manufacturers. In 1968, he set up ItalDesign. One of the cars the company worked on was the Volkswagen Golf (1974). Giugiaro's consumer products include appliances for Sony, cameras for Nikon, and lighting for Luci.

GIVENCHY, Hubert Taffin de
b.1927 French

One of the most highly respected fashion designers to emerge from Paris, Givenchy studied at the Ecole des Beaux-Arts and went on to work for the couture houses of Fath, Lelong, Piguet, and Schiaparelli. In 1952, he established his own house, designing traditional, elegant garments. He created Audrey Hepburn's wardrobes for the movies *Funny Face* (1956) and *Breakfast at Tiffany's* (1961), and later expanded into the ready-to-wear clothing market.

GLASER, Milton
b.1929 American
✐ p.22

Illustrator and graphic designer Glaser cofounded Push Pin Studio, New York, in 1954 with Seymour Chwast and Edward Sorel. Although he is often associated with 1960s' psychedelic graphic design, he also created the Twergi line of kitchenware for the Italian design group Alessi and, in 1987, an international AIDS symbol for the World Health Organization.

GOLDMAN, Jonathan
b.1959 American
✐ p.54

Founder of the design consultancy GoldmanArts in 1986, Goldman has been described as an environmental sculptor. His novelty items include an inflatable Sawtooth lamp (1980s) and a 300ft (91m) ribbon for the opening of the Trump Taj Mahal Casino, Atlantic City, in 1990.

Frank Gehry's Pito kettle for Alessi, 1988

GRANGE, Kenneth
b.1929 British
✐ p.78, 79

A London-based industrial designer, Grange advocates that the design of a product should be intrinsic to its manufacturing. His early creations include household appliances for Kenwood and the 1959 Brownie 44A for Kodak. He cofounded the design consultancy Pentagram in 1972. In the 1980s, he was influential in Japan, designing bathroom fittings for Inax and sewing machines for Maruzen. One of his most recent innovative products is his Silk Effects razor for women, developed for Wilkinson Sword and launched by Schick in 1994.

GRAVES, Michael
b.1934 American
✐ p.44

A key protagonist of postmodernism, Graves has been active as an architect and industrial designer. He graduated in architecture from Harvard University in 1959. From the late 1960s until 1977, he was a member of the group of architects

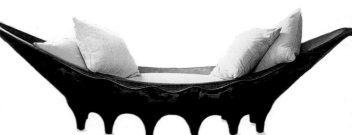

Eileen Gray's chaise longue for a private apartment, 1920s

known as the "New York Five." His many buildings include the Public Services Building in Portland, Oregon (1982), and the Disney World Dolphin Hotel (1989). Among his most celebrated pieces are the Plaza dressing table for Memphis (1981) and the Kettle with a Bird Whistle for Alessi (1983).

GRAY, Eileen
1878–1976 British
p.44
This Irish-born architect and designer studied at the Slade School of Art in London from

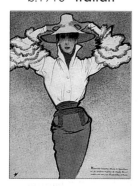

GRUAU, René
b.1910 Italian

Fashion illustration, 1952

After an international education, Gruau settled in Paris after World War II. He contributed frequent illustrations to Vogue magazine, but turned to poster and publicity design as fashion magazines began to make increasing use of photography.

1898 to 1902, then moved to Paris. There she developed skills in Japanese lacquerwork, a technique used to decorate her 1920s Art Deco-styled chaise longue (see left). Gray's production of geometric furniture in aluminum and glass, such as her 1927 table, earned her much respect for her contribution to the Modern movement. Between 1926 and 1929, she designed a house in France for the architect Jean Badovici (1893–1956).

GROPIUS, Walter
1883–1969 German
p.13, 84
A leading figure in modern design, Gropius established the Bauhaus, the most influential design school this century. He assisted Peter Behrens (see p.255) from 1908 to 1910, became a member of the Deutsche Werkbund in 1910, and in 1911, was one of the first to adopt the International Style with his Fagus factory in Germany. Director of the Weimar schools of fine and applied arts, he combined them in 1919 to form the Bauhaus, an exponent of unified arts. When it relocated in 1925, Gropius designed the new building. Nazi criticism forced him to England in 1934, where he designed furniture for Isokon. In 1937, he emigrated to the US. He taught at Harvard and, in 1945, founded The Architects' Collaborative (TAC) in Cambridge, Massachusetts.

GRUAU, René
See box, left
p.155, 227

GUGELOT, Hans
1920–65 Dutch
p.61
An industrial designer and architect, Gugelot was a key figure in reviving the functionalist ideology of the Bauhaus after World War II. Educated in Switzerland, he moved to Germany in 1954, where he became a designer for Braun. Among his major works is Braun's Phonosuper record player (1956). From 1955 to 1965, he was head of product design at the Hochschule für Gestaltung in Ulm.

GUILD, Lurelle Van Arsdale
1898–c.1986 American
p.72
Although he began his career in theatrical design, Guild is best-remembered for his industrial products. Among the most important is the Electrolux vacuum cleaner (1937). He produced several products for the Chase Brass and Copper Co. (see above).

GUIMARD, Hector
1867–1942 French
p.11, 33
A key proponent of Art Nouveau, Guimard studied at the Ecole des Beaux-Arts in Paris. Inspired by the style of the Belgian Victor Horta (1861–1947), he produced architecture, interior designs, and furniture. Many of the buildings featured cast iron florid, curvilinear forms, found in his entrances for the Paris Métro system (1900), typify the style that is simply known as "Guimard."

H

HAFNER, Dorothy
b.1952 American
Primarily a ceramist, Hafner's work is characterized by a lively, graphic style and vibrant colors. These are shown in her Roundabout punch bowl and ladle (1986, see right). A number of her pieces have been produced by Rosenthal Studio Line.

HALD, Edvard
1883–1980 Swedish
p.50
Hald's association with the famous Swedish glassworks Orrefors began in 1917, and continued for the rest of his life, including time spent as its managing director. At the 1925 Paris Expo, Hald won a grand prize for his work. Embracing the features of Swedish Modern design, his engraved wares, some of it colored, reveal a controlled, traditional influence. He also worked as a designer for the porcelain factories Rörstrand (1917–24) and Karlskrona (1917–33).

HAMNETT, Katharine
b.1948 British
A fashion designer whose collections take inspiration from utilitarian workwear, Hamnett founded

her own company in 1979 after freelancing for various foreign firms. She is renowned for bringing political and ecological issues to the forefront of fashion.

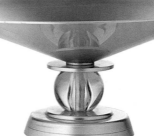
Lurelle Guild's bowl, 1934

HANDLER, Laura
b.1947 American
p.53
Active as an industrial designer in Italy, as well as her native America, Handler produced designs for Sottsass Associati and other Milan-based manufacturers. She designed an award-winning Cat's eye candleholder (1991).

HAUSTEIN, Paul
1880–1944 German
p.52
Active predominantly as an enamaler, Haustein also worked as a ceramist, metalworker, graphic, and furniture designer. He was a cofounder of the Darmstadt artists' colony in Germany in 1903. From 1905 until his death, he taught metalwork at the School of Applied Art in Stuttgart as well as producing silver- and metalware for various manufacturers.

HEIBERG, Jean
1884–1976 Norwegian
p.126
Heiberg's training was as a painter, first in Munich, and then under Matisse, whose influence is clearly visible in his paintings. He was commissioned by the Swedish company L.M. Ericsson to produce a telephone design. It was produced in 1931 and remained internationally the most common design until the 1950s.

HENNINGSEN, Poul
1895–1967 Danish
p.54
Henningsen's PH ceiling and table lamp line, designed for Louis Poulsen in 1924, is his most celebrated work, although he had won many prizes for earlier lighting designs. He initially studied to be an architect, and later supported modernism while employed as editor of the magazine *Kritisk Revy* (1926–28). His architectural works include houses, restaurants, and theaters.

HILTON, Matthew
b.1957 British
p.53
Best-known for his 1987 Antelope and Flipper side tables with animal legs, Hilton also designed high-tech products for the London design group CAPA. He established his own studio in 1984.

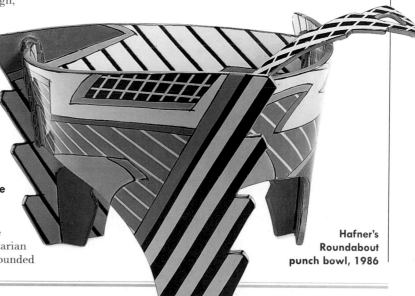
Hafner's Roundabout punch bowl, 1986

HOFFMANN, Josef Franz Maria
1870–1956 Czech/Austrian
✎ p.13, 32, 50, 92

Trained as an architect, Josef Hoffmann worked with Otto Wagner (1841–1918) between 1896 and 1899. He helped found the Vienna Secession in 1897. Inspired by the work of Charles Rennie Mackintosh (see p.266) and C.R. Ashbee (see p.254), Hoffmann, Koloman Moser (see p.268), and Fritz Wärndorfer set up the Wiener Werkstätte in 1903 (see p.12). His architectural achievements include the Purkersdorf Sanatorium (1904) and the Palais Stoclet in Brussels (1905–11), on which he collaborated with Gustav Klimt (see p.265).

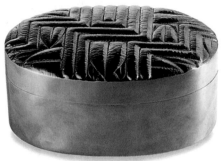

Brass box by Josef Hoffmann, 1915

HÖGLUND, Erik
b.1932 Swedish
✎ p.53, 88

Glassware designer Höglund was employed at Boda from 1953 to 1973. His designs include anthropomorphic candleholders and vases, bowls engraved with primitive figurative drawings, and hand-blown vessels with irregular bubbles (see right). Höglund's approach is unique in that it has challenged the fashion for more formal glassware.

HOHLWEIN, Ludwig
1874–1949 German
✎ p.225

Hohlwein studied architecture in Munich before abandoning this discipline to become a poster artist. In his early work, including a series of posters for the sports tailor Hermann Scherrer, he established a characteristic style that varied little over the next 40 years. Hohlwein created more than 3,000 posters during a career that spanned two world wars.

HULANICKI, Barbara
b.1936 Polish/British

Of Polish descent, Hulanicki moved to Britain in the 1940s. After studying at Brighton Art College, she worked briefly as a fashion illustrator. In 1963, she started a mail order fashion business aimed at teenagers. Encouraged by the response to these designs, she opened a boutique called Biba, which marketed a look that typified the 1960s. In 1969, Biba took over an Art Deco building on Kensington High Street, London. It is for this chic store, with its all-black interior, that Hulanicki is best remembered.

I

IE, Kho Liang
1927–75 Dutch
✎ p.109

Architect and designer Kho Liang Ie trained at the Rietveld Academy of Arts, the Netherlands. Later, he produced furniture designs for the Dutch company Artifort. His commissions have included the interior of the Schipol Airport, Amsterdam, and two rooms for the London home of Sir Robert and Lady Sainsbury.

INDIANA, Robert
b.1927 American
✎ p.25, 157

Artist and designer Robert Clarke renamed himself after his home state. His most famous work, shown in his first one-man show in New York (1962), is based on the word LOVE. The words HUG, ERR, and EAT have also inspired works.

IOSA GHINI, Massimo
b.1959 Italian

A designer of graphics and objects, Iosa Ghini has produced furniture designs for companies such as Moroso (see right) and Memphis. Since 1985, he has acted as a consultant to RAI, the Italian broadcasting service, and in 1988, he designed the Bolidio discotheque in New York.

ISSIGONIS, Alec
1906–88 British
✎ p.185

Born in Turkey, Issigonis emigrated to Britain in 1922. After studying engineering in London, he worked as a draftsman at Rootes Motors in Coventry. In 1936, he joined Morris Motors, Oxford, for which he designed the Morris Minor (1948) and the celebrated Morris Mini (1959). The Mini, with its tiny wheels, transversely placed engine, and front-wheel drive, was a radical departure from conventional car design.

J

JACKSON, Dakota
b.1949 American
✎ p.39

In the early 1970s, Jackson was commissioned by Yoko Ono to design some furniture for John Lennon. Since then, he has manufactured his own furniture, including the 'vik-ter range (1991).

JACOBSEN, Arne
1902–71 Danish
✎ p.21, 36, 91

Born in Copenhagen, Jacobsen trained as an architect before opening his own practice in 1930. Influenced by the work of Gunnar Asplund (see p.254), Le Corbusier (see p.266), and Mies van der Rohe (see p.267), he was an early exponent of the modern style in Denmark. He worked as an architect and product designer, creating furniture for Fritz Hansen and tableware for Stelton (see right), among others. He earned wide acclaim for the SAS Hotel, Copenhagen (1956–60).

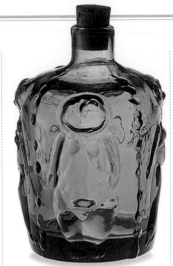

Decanter by Erik Höglund, 1950s

JEANNERET, Pierre
1896–1967 Swiss
✎ p.34, 40

Pierre Jeanneret, cousin of Le Corbusier (see p.266), moved to Paris in 1920. Together they designed various villas in the Parisian suburbs before teaming up with Charlotte Perriand (see p.269) to create the company's iconic tubular-steel-framed furniture. Jeanneret produced some designs independently, such as the Scissor Chair (c.1947) for Knoll. After World War II, he collaborated on projects with Jean Prouvé (see p.270), as well as continuing his association with Le Corbusier.

JENSEN, Arthur Georg
1866–1935 Danish
✎ p.74, 156

Early in the century, Georg Jensen established the famous silver company that bears his name. Together with Johan Rohde (1856–1935), he designed a large proportion of the company's output, including jewelry, candlesticks, tea and coffee sets, cutlery, and other luxury items. By 1924, Jensen had stores in Berlin, Paris, London, and New York. When he retired in 1926, his family took over the firm.

JENSEN, Jakob
b.1926 Danish
✎ p.61

Jensen graduated from and went on to become chief designer for the Copenhagen School of Arts, Crafts, and Design, working under Sigvard Bernadotte from 1952 to 1959. In 1961, he set up a design consultancy; by the late 1960s, his clients included Bang & Olufsen, for which he designed the sleek Beogram 4000 (1972).

JOHNSTON, Edward
1872–1944 British
✎ p.208

A calligrapher and professor, Johnston is best known for his typeface design for London Underground (1915). The sans serif alphabet served as a model for Gill Sans, the face created by his former pupil Eric Gill in 1928 (see p.262). Johnston also published classic calligraphy books, including *Writing & Illuminating & Lettering* (1906).

JONES, Terry
b.1945 British

Jones worked on *Good Housekeeping* magazine before becoming art director of the British *Vogue*. His *Not Another Punk Book*, produced in 1977, represented a turning point in his career. In this title, he first employed instant design, using collage, photocopied distortions, and typewriter print to convey a sense of energy. In 1980, he launched *i-D* magazine, where he developed this approach. He has also worked in video production and as a consultant to Fiorucci.

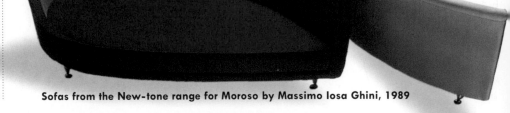

Sofas from the New-tone range for Moroso by Massimo Iosa Ghini, 1989

K

KÅGE, Algot Wilhelm
1889–1960 Swedish
Trained as a painter, Kåge joined the Swedish Ceramic Company in Gustavsberg in 1917. There, he introduced a range of heat-resistant and stackable dinner sets, such as Pyro and Praktika (1930s); as well as more elegant and decorative pieces in the 1940s.

KAMALI, Norma
b.1945 American
Inspired by London designers like Barbara Hulanicki (see p.264), Kamali opened a shop selling imported European fashions in 1967, quickly introducing her own line. In 1978, she established OMO (On My Own), the showcase for her innovative garments.

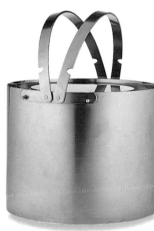

Arne Jacobsen's Cylinder line ice bucket for Stelton, 1967

She popularized the use of sweatshirting and Lycra for everyday wear.

KAN, Shui-Kay
b.1949 British
Born in Hong Kong, Shui-Kay Kan studied and still works in Britain. In the mid-1970s, he established SKK Lighting. He is interested in new lighting techniques and has produced low-voltage and motorized systems. His 1988 Motorized Robotic Light was installed in the London Design Museum.

KAUFFER, Edward McKnight
see box, right
🖋 p.225

KAWAKUBO, Rei
b.1942 Japanese
🖋 p.144
Having studied literature at Keio University, Tokyo, Rei Kawakubo joined the textile company Asahi Kasei. She founded Comme des Garçons in 1969. Her unconventional clothing, including wrapped loosely structured garments, is based on Japanese workwear and ceremonial dress.

KENZO (Kenzo Takada)
b.1939 Japanese
🖋 p.145
Kenzo was one of the first male students to be admitted to the leading Tokyo fashion school, where he was awarded a prestigious prize in 1960. In 1965, he moved to Paris, designing for various fashion houses before establishing his own shop, Jungle Jap, in 1970. Kenzo draws inspiration from Japanese and ethnic costume, adapting the bright colors and dramatic shapes to suit Western tastes. By 1985, his international reputation was well established, with shops in London, New York, and Milan.

KIESLER, Frederick
c.1890–1965 Austrian
An architect, sculptor, and designer of furniture, stage sets, and interiors, Kiesler is best known for his biomorphic designs, including Two-Part Nesting Tables (1935–38). In 1923, he joined the De Stijl group and, in the same year, developed the blueprints for his influential Endless House, which was never built. Kiesler moved to the US in 1926, where he continued to work on a variety of projects.

KING, Jessie Marion
1875–1949 Scottish
🖋 p.222
King is known primarily for her book illustrations. Her name, together with that of Mackintosh (see p.266), is linked with the Glasgow School. From 1905 on, she designed silverware for Liberty, and fabrics and wallpaper for other clients. Inspired by Léon Bakst's drawings for the Ballets Russes, she integrated bright hues into her pastel palette.

KAUFFER, Edward McKnight 1890–1954
American/British

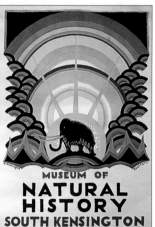

Edward Kauffer adopted the name McKnight in honor of the professor who sponsored his visit to Paris in 1913. In 1914, he moved to the UK, gaining his first commission as a poster designer from London Underground in 1915. His prolific output for clients including Shell and London Transport was greatly influenced by major artistic movements, such as Cubism, Art Deco, Vorticism, and Surrealism.

Museum poster, 1922

KING, Perry A.
b.1938 British
🖋 p.199
An industrial designer, King undertook various projects for Olivetti and Praxis in Milan before teaming up with Ettore Sottsass (see p.273) in 1965. He worked with Sottsass on the design of the Valentine portable typewriter (1969). In collaboration with Spaniard Santiago Miranda (b.1947), he designed typefaces for Olivetti. In 1975, King-Miranda became a formal partnership, concentrating on furniture, lighting, and graphic design.

KJAERHOLM, Poul
1929–80 Danish
Although he is known for his designs for mass-produced furniture, Kjaerholm trained in the traditional craft of cabinet-making. A proponent of the late International Style, he employed chromium and tubular steel in his furniture designs, which were made by Ejvind Kold Christensen and Hellerup, among others.

KLEIN, Calvin
b.1942 American
Inspired by Yves Saint Laurent (see p.272), Klein set up in business in 1968, specializing in classic designs in natural fabrics. His name is associated with jeans, which throughout the 1970s were sought after by the label-conscious. Klein is also known for his perfume, furs, shoes, and underwear.

KLIMT, Gustav
1862–1918 Austrian
🖋 p.13
Painter and designer Klimt studied at the Vienna School of Arts and Crafts, and was one of the founders of the Vienna Secession. He combined the stylized shapes of Symbolism with rich, decorative backdrops inspired by Art Nouveau.

KNOLL, Florence Schust
b.1917 American
🖋 p.124
A furniture designer, Knoll was greatly influenced by the Saarinens (see p.271). In 1943, she joined Hans Knoll (1914–55) in his furniture business, where she headed an interior design service for Knoll customers. With her financial backing, they formed Knoll Associates (now Knoll International) in 1946. The firm manufactured many furniture classics, including designs by Bertoia (see p.255), Saarinen, as well as Florence Knoll.

KOMENDA, Erwin
1904–66 German
🖋 p.182, 187
An automobile engineer, Komenda was a designer for Daimler-Benz before joining Ferdinand Porsche's Stuttgart office (see p.270) in the 1930s. He was responsible for the styling of the original Volkswagen Beetle (1939) and the series of Porsche cars that commenced with the Type 356 (1949) and ended with the Type 911 (1963).

KOPPEL, Henning
1918–81 Danish
Koppel trained as a sculptor in Denmark before World War I, but during the Occupation he worked in Stockholm for the Orrefors glassworks. On his return to Denmark in 1945, he began his long association with Georg Jensen (see p.264). For Jensen he produced some of his finest designs – elegant, sculptural jewelry, flatware, and hollowware. He produced ceramics for Bing Grøndahl from 1961 and glassware for Orrefors from 1971 on.

KURAMATA, Shiro
1934–91 Japanese
🖋 p.24, 39
Kuramata worked for the Teikokukizai furniture factory and the interior design departments of several major Tokyo stores before starting his own business in 1965. His unconventional approach to furniture design won him acclaim in the 1970s. His minimalist designs, executed in industrial materials, such as

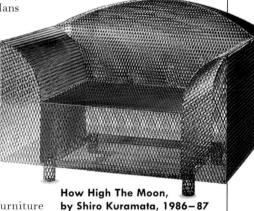

How High The Moon, by Shiro Kuramata, 1986–87

metalmesh (see above), steel cables, and plexiglass, combine Japanese severity with the softer elements of Western design. Important works in the field of interior design include a series of boutiques for fashion designer Issey Miyake (see p.267) and the Seibu store in Tokyo (1987).

L

LAGERFELD, Karl
b.1938 German

A fashion designer best known for his flamboyant evening-wear and fur coats, Lagerfeld has been predominantly active in Paris. At the age of 14, he began working for the couturier Balmain, and later for Patou. In 1983, he became head of Chanel's ready-to-wear, and since 1984 has also worked under his own name.

LALIQUE, René
1860–1945 French
✎ p.11, 104

Lalique is known for his figurative jewelry, in unusual blends of base metals, stones, and enamel, and later, for his glassware. He established Cristal Lalique in 1909, where he produced vases (see below), bowls, perfume bottles, lighting, and other decorative glassware designs produced by molding methods. He was particularly prolific in producing glass, often for architecture, between the wars.

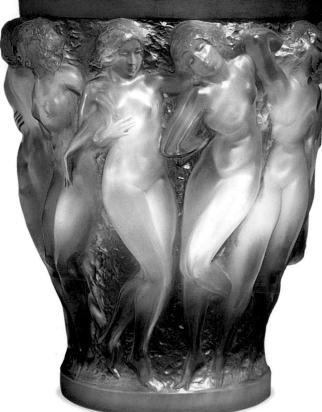

Lalique's Bacchantes Vase, c.1932

LAND, Edwin
b.1909 American
✎ p.165

Physicist and businessman Edwin Land was educated at Harvard University. He is credited with the invention of the Polaroid-Land instant print-processing camera in 1947, and the Polaroid-Land SX70 in 1972, an instant color-processing camera.

LAUREN, Ralph
b.1939 American
✎ p.105

Born Ralph Lipschitz, Lauren had no formal training, but has become one of the most successful fashion designers in the US. Combining American prairie style with traditional English tailoring, he creates a relaxed but elegant finish. His first menswear was for his company Polo in 1968. It has expanded into womenswear.

LE CORBUSIER
1887–1965 Swiss
✎ p.34, 40

An instrumental figure in 20th-century architecture and design, Charles-Edouard Jeanneret-Gris adopted the pseudonym Le Corbusier in the 1920s. His first major piece was the Schwob house in Switzerland (1916). It indicated the purist, austere direction of modernism, setting the style for his future works. In 1922, he set up an architectural office with his cousin Pierre Jeanneret (see p.264). His book, *Vers Une Architecture* (1925), provided some of the fundamental theories of modernism, which were embodied in his Villa Savoye (1929–31) in France. Mainly concerned with urban design, he also produced furniture, and is particularly known for his range of Confort armchairs and sofas during the late 1920s.

LENICA, Jan
b.1928 Polish
✎ p.228

A graphic designer, Lenica studied architecture in Warsaw. In the 1950s and '60s, he designed posters and experimented with film animation. While his earlier works are in keeping with the Polish school of design, his later works, such as the film *Adam 2* (1969), reveal a psychedelic influence.

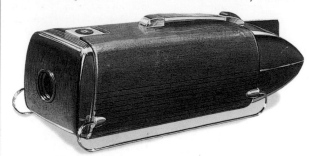

LOEWY, Raymond   1893–1986 French/American

Electrolux cylinder vacuum cleaner, 1939

Loewy is often heralded as the originator of the industrial design profession in the US. He studied engineering in Paris, then emigrated to New York, where he flourished as a designer. His redesign of the 1929 Duplicator 66 for Gestetner, establishment of Raymond Loewy Associates in the same year, and design of the 1934 Coldspot Super Six refrigerator for Sears, Roebuck earned him early respect. His streamlined 1937 S1 locomotive for the Pennsylvania Railroad Company and the Greyhound bus transformed the image of American transportation. In the 1960s, he designed for NASA.

LISSITZKY, Lazar Markovich
1890–1941 Russian
✎ p.224

An innovative typographer, architect, and designer, El Lissitzky followed Constructivist ideology. He was a key figure in adapting these theories to graphic design and internationalizing them through his teaching and traveling. He taught at VHkUTEMAS (see p.15). In 1925, he produced *The Isms of Art 1914–24*, in collaboration with German artist Hans Arp (1887–1966).

LLOYD, Marshall B.
1858–1927 American
✎ p.34

Lloyd patented a twisted paper fiber strengthened with wire that imitated the appearance of wicker. Put into production by the furniture company Lloyd Loom, this method of creating inexpensive furniture became extremely popular during the 1920s and '30s.

LOEWY, Raymond
See box, above
✎ p.68, 81, 121, 131, 164, 202

LOMAZZI
See de Pas, d'Urbino, Lomazzi

LYSELL, Ralf
b.1907 Swedish
✎ p.127

Lysell was the industrial designer who worked with Hugo Blomberg (see p.256) on the development of the Ericofon telephone (1940s).

M

MACKINTOSH, Charles Rennie
1868–1928 Scottish
✎ p.32, 80, 93, 108, 192

Mackintosh was a leading protagonist of Art Nouveau architecture in Britain. His work is unique in its combination of geometric Celtic design and Japanese decoration. Born and educated in Glasgow, it was there that he executed one of his most definitive works, the Glasgow School of Art (1898–1909). In his early years he often worked with his wife Margaret Macdonald (1865–1933), Frances Macdonald (1874–1921), and Herbert MacNair (1868–1953) as members of the Glasgow Four. In 1900, Mackintosh exhibited at the eighth Secession exhibition in Vienna. His architectural works were all in Britain.

MAGISTRETTI, Vico
b.1920 Italian
✎ p.55

An architect and designer, Magistretti benefited from Italy's postwar reconstruction,

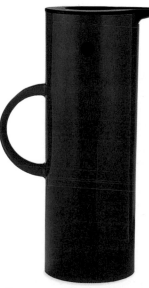

Magnussen's Thermos, 1977

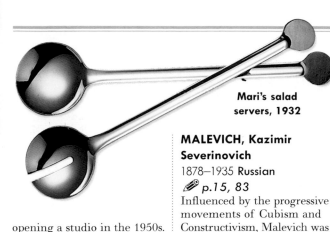

Mari's salad servers, 1932

opening a studio in the 1950s. He developed the Selene chair for Artemide in the 1960s from ABS plastic, providing a new look for Italian plastic goods. His line of Sinbad chairs and sofas for Cassina (1981) emphasizes the importance of structure.

MAGNUSSEN, Erik
b.1940 Danish
Magnussen studied ceramics before establishing his own workshop producing lighting, kitchenwares, and furniture. His range of containers for Stelton (1977, see left) were designed to be entirely functional. From 1978 on, he was employed at the Georg Jensen Sølvsmedie.

MAINBOCHER
1891–1976 American
✎ p.143
Born Main Rousseau Bocher, Mainbocher embarked on his career as a fashion designer in Paris, illustrating for *Harper's Bazaar* (1922). He founded his own couture house in 1930, designing classic, understated clothing, and was the first to create boned, strapless evening dresses, in 1934. He retained his exclusive image by refusing to allow his designs to be mass produced.

MAJORELLE, Louis
1859–1926 French
✎ p.108
A leading exponent of Art Nouveau, Majorelle has become synonomous with the School of Nancy. He inherited his father's furniture business in 1879, updating the traditional styling of its products, and finishing them with naturalistic marqueteries. Mass produced at low cost, these designs were affordable to many. After his factory was destroyed by fire in 1916, Majorelle's success dwindled.

MALEVICH, Kazimir Severinovich
1878–1935 Russian
✎ p.15, 83
Influenced by the progressive movements of Cubism and Constructivism, Malevich was primarily an abstract artist. His work is characterized by strong colors against a white background, a style he described as Suprematism. In 1920, he founded the Unovis group, of which El Lissitzky (see p.266) was also a member. Later, he diverted to product design, as well as architecture.

MARI, Enzo
b.1932 Italy
✎ p.197
Mari promoted the importance of communication through design. A lifelong interest in children's games began with a wooden puzzle he created for Danese in 1957. He continued to work with Danese, experimenting with ABS plastics and producing kitchen products (see above). He also created the 1972 Sof Sof chair.

MARX, Enid
1902–93 British
✎ p.122
Inspired by the patterns of wood engravings, Marx became a prolific fabric and wallpapers designer. She is best-remembered for her upholstery design for London Underground seating (1930s), and was awarded Royal Designer for Industry in 1944. She also created wartime Utility furniture (1944–47) and book jackets for the British publisher Penguin (1950s).

MELLOR, David
b.1930 British
✎ p.80
A leading British kitchenware designer, Mellor studied in Sheffield, where he founded a workshop in 1954. He is widely respected for his

modestly simple but elegant designs for everyday use. He won an award in 1957 from the Design Council for his celebrated Pride cutlery.

MENDINI, Alessandro
b.1931 Italian
✎ p.38, 42, 125
After studying architecture in Milan, Mendini worked for Marcello Nizzoli (see p.268). He expounded radical design as editor of *Casabella*, an Italian magazine (1970–76). He has produced furniture for the design group Alchimia, shown at the Milan Furniture Fair (1981), and silverware for Alessi.

MIES VAN DER ROHE, Ludwig
1886–1969 German
✎ p.34
Mies van der Rohe was trained by his father as a stonemason, and from 1908 to 1911 he was apprenticed to Peter Behrens (see p.255). Many of his early architectural concepts featured steel and glass, but were only realized in the form of the International Style after he moved to the US in 1938. In the 1930s, his tubular steel

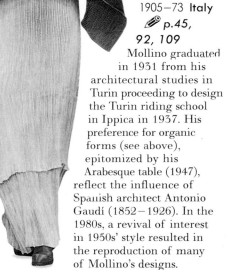

Issey Miyake ensemble, 1994–95

furniture was sold internationally through the German maker Thonet-Mundus. His Barcelona chair (1929) is one of his best-known works.

MIRANDA, Santiago
See Perry King

MIYAKE, Issey
b.1935 Japanese
✎ p.145
Educated in graphic design in Tokyo and fashion in Paris, Miyake founded couture house Issey Miyake International Inc. in 1971. He was among the first to exploit Eastern costume in the West, uniting natural fibers with traditional Japanese lines. He disregarded transient fashions in favor of durable designs (see below).

MOHOLY-NAGY, László
1895–1946 Hungarian
Forced to abandon his law studies by World War I, Moholy-Nagy began painting after recovering from a war injury. He moved to Berlin in 1920, pursuing an interest in photography and the effects of light. After Walter Gropius (see p.263) saw his work exhibited, he invited him to teach at the Bauhaus. Active as a stage and exhibition designer from 1928 to 1933, he created the sets for the Kroll Opera in Berlin. He emigrated to the US in 1937, setting up a school in Chicago based on Bauhaus ideologies.

MOLLINO, Carlo
1905–73 Italy
✎ p.45, 92, 109
Mollino graduated in 1931 from his architectural studies in Turin proceeding to design the Turin riding school in Ippica in 1937. His preference for organic forms (see above), epitomized by his Arabesque table (1947), reflect the influence of Spanish architect Antonio Gaudí (1852–1926). In the 1980s, a revival of interest in 1950s' style resulted in the reproduction of many of Mollino's designs.

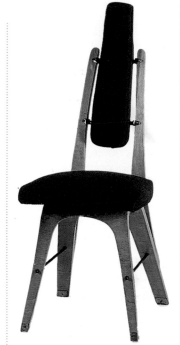

Mollino's Varesio chair, c.1945

MORISON, Stanley
1889–1967 British
✎ p.210
The typographer and type historian Stanley Morison did not have any formal training in design. He acted as typographical adviser to the British Monotype Corporation from 1922 to 1967, during which time he directed the design of types Baskerville (1923), Gill Sans (1928), and Walbaum (1933), later using some of these more radical designs while working for the publisher Victor Gollancz as a book jacket designer. In 1922, he set up the typographic magazine *The Fleuron*, and from 1929 to 1959, acted as typographic advisor to *The Times* newspaper, creating its new face, Times New Roman in 1931–32.

MORRISON, Jasper
b.1959 British
✎ p.39
Educated at the Royal College of Art from 1982 to 1985, Morrison is a London-based designer of unique, offbeat items of furniture and accessories. He cofounded NATO (Narrative Architecture Today), creating designs for Vitra and Aram Designs, among others. His works have appeared internationally in exhibitions, including the 1987 exhibition in Tokyo.

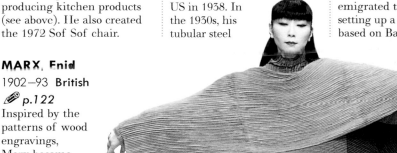

MOSER, Koloman
1868–1918 Austrian

Along with Gustav Klimt (see p.265), Josef Hoffmann (see p.264), Josef Maria Olbrich (see p.269), and others, Moser founded the Vienna Secession in 1897. Trained as a graphic artist and painter, he was involved in the launch of the group's journal *Ver Sacrum* in 1898. In the same year, he designed the stained glass and interior decoration for the Secession gallery, where the members' work was exhibited several times a year. Moser executed furniture, ceramic, silver, and graphic designs for the Secession, as well as pieces for the Wiener Werkstätte, a commercial venture that he set up with Hoffmann in 1903.

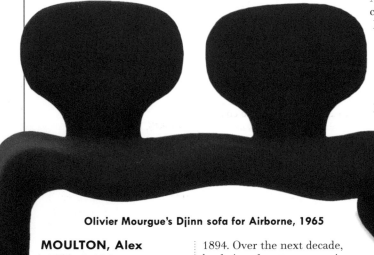

Olivier Mourgue's Djinn sofa for Airborne, 1965

MOULTON, Alex
b.1920 British
✎ p.173, 185

An engineering graduate, during World War II Moulton worked as a researcher at the Bristol Aeroplane Company. Later, he joined his family's rubber-manufacturing firm, developing rubber suspension for cars. In collaboration with Alec Issigonis (see p.264), he designed the suspension for the Mini (1959). In the 1960s, Moulton developed an innovative line of bicycles.

MOURGUE, Olivier
b.1939 French

Mourgue's colorful, gently curvaceous, biomorphic forms epitomize the design aesthetic of the 1960s. Trained in interior architecture and the decorative arts in Paris, he designed his first prototype chair for Airborne while still

a student. The Djinn line (see below), which he created for Airborne in 1965, was used by Stanley Kubrick in the film *2001: A Space Odyssey*. Mourgue has also worked on various domestic projects, including a mobile studio (1970), as well as acting as a consultant to Renault and Air France.

MUCHA, Alphonse
1860–1939 Czech
✎ p.222

Mucha began as a stage set designer in Vienna, moving to Munich in 1885 and Paris in 1887. Settling in Paris, he designed stamps and posters throughout the early 1890s, winning acclaim for a life-size poster of Sarah Bernhardt in 1894. Over the next decade, he designed posters, magazine covers, packaging, textiles, and jewelry – all in a richly decorated Art Nouveau style. Returning to his homeland in 1922, he produced a series of 20 murals, *Slav Epic*, which depicted the history of Czechoslovakia.

MUIR, Jean
1933–1995 British

Distinguished fashion designer Jean Muir served her apprenticeship at Liberty in London before joining Jaeger in 1956. In 1962, she began to design under the Jane & Jane label, opening her own house in 1966. She is known for her classical, elegant, and comfortable womenswear, made up in soft, flowing materials, such as silk jersey, crepe, and suede. In 1983, she was awarded a CBE.

MÜLLER, Gerd Alfred
b.1932 German

Industrial designer Müller is best known for the kitchen appliances (see right) and electric shavers that he created for Braun between 1955 and 1960. In 1960, he set up a design studio in Eschborn, Germany, specializing in appliances and graphics.

MÜLLER-BROCKMANN, Josef
b.1914 Swiss

After studying in Zurich, Müller-Brockmann established his own studio in 1936, concentrating on exhibition design, posters, and corporate graphics. A key figure in the promotion of Swiss International Style, he was a cofounder of the journal *Neue Grafik* (1958), which championed this approach. During the 1950s, he received international recognition for a series of concert posters for the Zurich Tonhalle, and also created powerful public health and safety posters using photomontage. After 1966, he worked with Paul Rand (see p.271) as a consultant for IBM.

MUNARI, Bruno
b.1907 Italian

The early work of artist and designer Munari, from the 1920s and '30s, showed a strong Futurist influence. After World War II, he began designing products and toys. In 1957, he designed the Cube ashtray, the first of many products for Danese. He is a prolific writer, and has taught at both Harvard University and Milan Polytechnic.

N

NELSON, George
1907–86 American
✎ p.41, 129

Architecture graduate Nelson won the Prix de Rome, which funded his visit to Europe in 1931. On his return to the US in 1933, he became an editor on *Architectural Forum*, where

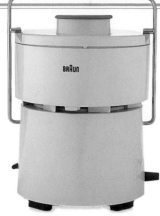

Müller's Multipress MP50 juicer for Braun, 1957

he was able to promote the modernist architecture and design that he had witnessed in Europe. His Storagewall of 1945, shown in *Life* magazine, led to a long association with Herman Miller, for which he executed many furniture designs, including the 1961 Action Office. Though a productive designer, Nelson was perhaps most influential in his writing and teaching.

NIELSEN, Harald
1892–1977 Danish
✎ p.88

Nielsen joined Georg Jensen's Sølvsmedie as an apprentice in 1909, producing the Pyramid flatware service, one of the company's bestselling designs. When Georg Jensen died in 1935, Nielsen became artistic director, a position that he retained for almost 30 years. His jewelry and tableware designs are characterized by smooth, unadorned forms inspired by the Bauhaus.

NIZZOLI, Marcello
1887–1969 Italian
✎ p.199, 205

Nizzoli began as a painter, later turning to poster, exhibition, and textile design. During the 1920s and '30s, he collaborated with architects Giuseppe Terragni (1904–43) and Edoardo Persico (1900–36) on various exhibition and interior projects. In 1938, he was hired as a consultant by Olivetti, where he became the company's most influential product designer. His best-known works include the

Lettera 22 portable typewriter (1950) and the Divisumma 24 adding machine (1956), both for Olivetti.

NOGUCHI, Isamu
1904–88 American
✎ p.17, 45

Born in Los Angeles, Noguchi trained as a cabinet maker in Japan, returning to the US in 1918. During the 1920s and '30s, he worked as a sculptor, visiting Paris in 1927, where he studied under Constantine Brancusi (1876–1957). His first major product was the Radio Nurse of 1937 (see below), commissioned by Zenith. Throughout the 1940s and '50s, he developed a distinctive sculptural style, producing furniture designs for Herman Miller and Knoll, and lighting for Akari. His celebrated paper and bamboo lighting designs have been widely copied.

NOYES, Eliot Fette
see box, right
✎ p.199

NURMESNIEMI, Antti
b.1927 Finnish
✎ p.72

After studying interior design in Helsinki, Nurmesniemi worked for architect Viljo Revell, designing the interiors of banks, restaurants, and hotels. On his return to Finland in 1956, he set up his own office. He has produced popular designs for furniture, household objects – including the Finel coffeepot (1957) – and transportation. A prestigious list of clients includes Artek and Cassina.

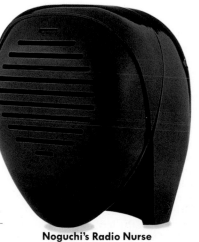

Noguchi's Radio Nurse

NOYES, Eliot Fette 1910–77 American

After studying architecture at Harvard, Noyes joined the Cambridge office of Walter Gropius (see p.262) and Marcel Breuer (see p.257). In 1940, he became a curator at the Museum of Modern Art, New York. After the war, he joined the design consultancy of Norman Bel Geddes (see p.255), starting his long association with IBM. In 1947, he set up on his own, retaining IBM as a client, and created the Model A typewriter, the first in a line of IBM products that established the company's corporate image. Another major client was Mobil, for which he designed the round gas pump in 1964.

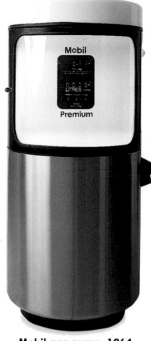

Mobil gas pump, 1964

O

OLBRICH, Josef Maria
1867–1908 Austrian
✎ p.52
Having trained in architecture, Olbrich worked briefly for the Viennese architect Otto Wagner (1841–1918). He was a founding member of the Vienna Secession and, along with Gustav Klimt (see p.265), designed the Secession gallery. In 1899, he was invited by the Grand Duke of Hesse to join an artists' colony in Darmstadt, where he designed numerous exhibition halls and houses, as well as furniture, textiles, metal-, and glassware.

OLINS, Wally
b.1930 British
✎ p.215
Olins teamed up with graphic designer Michael Wolff (b.1933) to form the London-based consultancy Wolff Olins in 1965. The company has created innovative corporate identity programs that have radically transformed major companies. Important clients include ICI, Q8, P&O, and British Telecom. When Wolff left the company in 1983, Olins became chairman.

OLIVER, Vaughan
b.1957 British
✎ p.221
A typographer and graphic designer, Oliver is a prominent figure in record-sleeve art. In 1981, along with photographer Nigel Grierson (b.1959), he formed a design studio called 23 Envelope, which was renamed v23 in 1988 when Oliver went freelance. He is best known for his album sleeves for independent record label 4AD.

P

PANTON, Verner
b.1926 Danish
✎ p.22, 37, 123
After studying in Copenhagen, Panton worked briefly with Arne Jacobsen (see p.264) before establishing a studio in Switzerland in 1955. His work covers the design spectrum, including architecture, textiles, furniture, lighting (see right), and exhibitions. His most famous design, a cantilevered, plastic chair, produced by Herman Miller from 1967, was the first of its kind.

PAOLINI, Cesare
see Gatti, Paolini, Teodoro

PAPANEK, Victor
b.1925 Austrian/American
Born in Vienna, Papanek emigrated to the US in 1939, where he studied architecture under Frank Lloyd Wright (see p.274). From 1964, he ran his own consultancy and lectured widely. Through his teaching and writing, most strongly in his book *Design for the Real World* (1971), he criticized design's slavery to commercialism and the futile waste of resources, winning favor with the emerging ecological movement.

PATOU, Jean
1880–1936 French
After a false start caused by the outbreak of World War I, Patou opened his fashion house to immediate acclaim in 1919. Like his rival, Chanel, Patou realized the marketing potential of simple clothing for the increasingly active woman. Among Patou's clientele were actress Mary Pickford and French tennis star Suzanne Lenglen.

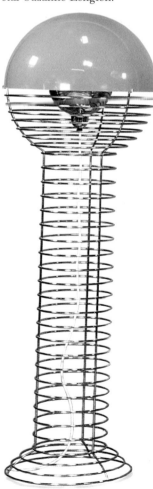

Panton's Wire Lamp, 1969

PECHE, Dagobert
1887–1923 Austrian
✎ p.47
After studying architecture in Vienna, Pêche established himself as a freelance designer, creating wallpaper, textiles, and ceramics. In 1915, he joined the Wiener Werkstätte, developing an ornamental style quite distinct from the geometry of work by Hoffmann (see p.264) and Moser (see p.268). His designs for the Werkstätte included silver, textiles, furniture, ceramics, and glassware.

PERET, (Pere Torrent)
b.1945 Spanish
✎ p.231
Peret began as an illustrator and graphic designer in Barcelona, moving to Paris in 1970, where he worked in a freelance capacity for Citroën and Air France, among others. Returning to Barcelona in 1978, he created cultural posters for the city council and the regional government of Catalonia.

PERRIAND, Charlotte
b.1903 French
✎ p.34, 40
A graduate in decorative arts, Perriand exhibited her metal furniture at the 1927 Salon d'Automne, where it attracted the attention of Le Corbusier (see p.266). It marked the beginning of their productive collaboration, together with Pierre Jeanneret (see p.264), which lasted ten years. Acting as an industrial design advisor in Japan (1940–42), she mounted two exhibitions on French design. On her return to France, she continued her association with Jeanneret, as well as independent work.

PESCE, Gaetano
b.1939 Italian
✎ p.38, 42, 248
Architect, designer, and artist Pesce is known for his radical approach to design. In the early 1960s, he worked on various experimental projects involving programmed and kinetic art. In 1968, he began to explore furniture design,

producing the Up series of chairs, manufactured by B&B Italia in 1969. He is known for his multidisciplinary approach – his Tramonto a New York, a sofa he designed for Italian furniture company Cassina, (1980) is a good example of this. Pesce has worked on projects in Brazil, Japan, Europe, and the US, and teaches extensively.

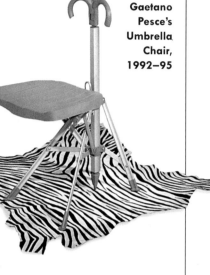

Gaetano Pesce's Umbrella Chair, 1992–95

PETERS, Michael
b.1941 British
Design entrepreneur Peters combines quality design with business acumen. He established Michael Peters & Partners in 1970, handling packaging designs for clients such as Winsor & Newton Inks and Seagram. He is now chairman of a new company called Michael Peters Ltd.

PETERSEN, Arne
b.1922 Danish
✎ p.91
After serving as an apprentice in the gold and silver workshops of C.C. Herman, Copenhagen, Petersen joined Georg Jensen Sølvsmedie in 1948. From 1976, he worked in the hollowware department.

PEZETTA, Roberto
b.1946 Italian
✎ p.69
Pezetta worked for Zoppas and Nordica before joining the domestic appliance company Zanussi in the mid-1970s. In 1984, he was made head of the industrial design section. His best-known design is the Wizard refrigerator (1987).

POIRET, Paul
1879–1944 French

✎ *p.142*

Influential fashion designer Poiret pioneered the use of the brassière. In returning to the loose fit of the Empire-line, he freed women from the discomfort of the corset. After training at the houses of Doucet and Worth, he opened his own salon in 1904, designing lines that clearly show the influence of oriental costume. In 1911, he was the first couturier to launch his own perfume and expand into other areas. He greatly encouraged creativity and spontaneity in students, and in 1911 founded the Ecole Martine decorative arts school.

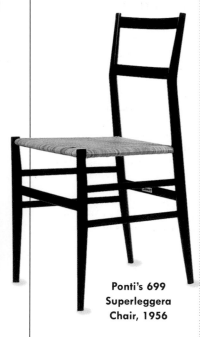

Ponti's 699 Superleggera Chair, 1956

POLI, Flavio
b.1900 Italian

✎ *p.50*

An award-winning glassware designer, Poli joined the glass manufacturer Seguso Vetri d'Arte in the 1930s, becoming its director in 1963. The thick materials and vibrant colors that characterize his work are evident in his bowls and vases (1960s), made by Danese.

PONTI, Giovanni
1891–1979 Italian

✎ *p.98*

Since the 1920s, Gio Ponti has contributed to the icons of Italian design. He studied architecture at Milan Polytechnic, and founded the

magazine *Domus* in 1928, through which he promoted modernism. He cofounded a studio in 1927, seeking to achieve compatibility between tradition and industrial production. The Pirelli Tower in Milan (1956) is considered to be his finest architectural work, while the Superleggera chair for Cassina (see left) has become ubiquitous seating for Italian cafés, compromising between convention and innovation.

PORSCHE, Ferdinand "Butzi"
b.1935 German

✎ *p.55, 187*

One of three designers in the Porsche family, the grandson of car designer Ferdinand Ferry Porsche (1875–1951), who founded Porsche in 1911, was nicknamed "Butzi." The 1963 Porsche 911 is his key car design. He established his own studio in 1972, and in the 1980s, created furniture and lighting, including a range in 1985 for the company Luci.

PRICE, Anthony
b.1945 British

✎ *p.221*

Educated in fashion at the Royal College of Art, London, Price was a prolific designer of 1970s fashions. He is often associated with Bryan Ferry and the Rolling Stones, for whom he designed costumes, sets, and record covers. Since 1979, he has worked under his own name, continuing contact with media and rock stars.

PROUVE, Jean
1901–1984 French

Metalwork designer Prouvé was the son of Victor Prouvé (1858–1943), a key figure of the Nancy School. He opened a workshop in 1923, designing furniture made of bent sheet steel, suitable for industrial production. He created metal furnishings for Le Corbusier's buildings (see p.266) in 1925, and in 1937, codesigned the Roland Garros flying club, acclaimed as the first truly industrialized building. In the 1950s, Prouvé explored the possibilities for mass-produced, prefabricated housing, schools, and offices.

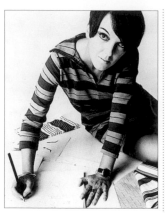

Mary Quant

PUCCI, Emilio
b.1914 Italian

A fashion designer who has concentrated on sportswear, Pucci opened Emilio, his own house, in 1950. He created boldly patterned, brightly colored silk jersey dresses as casualwear for women. His international status earned him the Neiman-Marcus Award in 1954.

PUIFORCAT, Jean
1897–1945 French

✎ *p.82*

Puiforcat apprenticed to his father as a silversmith and studied at the Central School of Arts and Crafts in London. He founded a workshop in 1921, producing clean-lined, unadorned silverware with contrasting materials, such as semiprecious stones and rare wood. The forms of his later works are based on careful mathematical calculations.

Q

QUANT, Mary
b.1934 British

✎ *p.155*

The name Mary Quant (see above) has become synonymous with London in the 1950s and '60s. She opened the boutique *Bazaar* in 1955, responding to the youthful optimism of the time with ready-to-wear fashions for teenagers. Quant helped popularize the miniskirt in the 1960s, also introducing brightly colored tights. Identified by her daisy motif, Quant's range has since expanded to include makeup and accessories.

QUISTGAARD, Jens
b.1919 Danish

✎ *p.91*

Educated as a silversmith in an apprenticeship to Georg Jensen (see p.264), Quistgaard cofounded Dansk International Designs with Ted Nierenberg in 1954. That year, he was awarded the Lunning Prize for his enameled cast-iron cooking pots, designed for the Danish manufacturer De Forenede Jerstøberier.

R

RABANNE, Paco
b.1934 Spanish
See box, below

RACE, Ernest
1913–64 British

✎ *p.36*

An architect and designer of international reputation, Race took his inspiration from 18th-century craftsmanship. He founded

Race Furniture in 1946, setting a precedent for the linear look created with steel rods. This is apparent in his 1951 Antelope and Gazelle chairs, displayed at the 1951 Festival of Britain. In the 1950s and '60s, he received various awards, including Royal Designer for Industry in England 1953, and several at the Milan Triennales.

RAMBOW, Gunter
b.1938 German

✎ *p.231*

Rambow cofounded a graphic design group with Gerhard Lienemeyer (b.1938) in 1960. This was renamed Rambow/Lienemeyer/van de Sand, when Michael van de Sand (b.1945) became a partner. The surreal effects of photomontage are evident in their award-winning 1978 theater poster for a production of *Othello*. The design group also created a corporate identity program for the German publisher S. Fischer Verlag (1976–83).

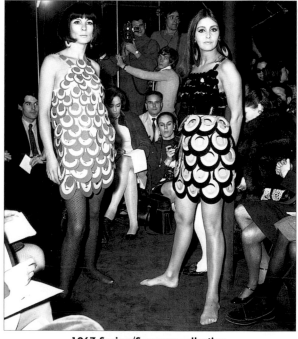

RABANNE, Paco b.1934 Spanish

1967 Spring/Summer collection

This Spanish-born designer of avant-garde fashions was active in France. From 1960 to 1964, he designed fashion accessories for Balenciaga (see p.255), Givenchy (see p.262), and Dior (see p.259). In 1966, he launched a renowned range of body jewelry. The dresses shown above consist of plastic disks linked with metal chains.

RAMS, Dieter
b.1932 German
✎ p.57, 61

An industrial designer and architect, Rams played a pivotal role as a designer for Braun, the German maker of durables. He joined in 1955, and by 1988 was the company's director. Together, Rams and Hans Gugelot (see p.263) developed a functionalist style (see right) that set a criterion for other producers. Among his most celebrated works are his SK4 Record Player (1956) and his KM 321 Kitchen Machine (1957). During the 1950s, he contributed to new forms of lighting, which instigated a change in interior design.

RAMSHAW, Wendy
b.1939 British

Following a training in illustration and fabric design, Ramshaw established herself as a jeweler. She gained recognition in the 1970s with her works in precious metals, and has since experimented with alternative materials, including paper and plastics.

RAND, Paul
b.1914 American
✎ p.213

Influential graphic designer Paul Rand is acclaimed for his adaptation of modernist design philosophies to suit graphic design. His corporate identity program for IBM (1956) set a style for future trademarks, and his influence has also been marked in advertising and editorial design; from 1935 to 1941, he directed the magazines *Apparel Arts* and *Esquire*. His texts *Thoughts on Design* (1947) and *Paul Rand: A Designer's Art* (1985) are well respected among graphic designers.

REEVES, Ruth
1892–1966 American
✎ p.122

A painter and textile designer, Reeves studied under the artist Fernand Léger (1881–1955) in Paris. She is known for her printed fabrics and rugs, which show similarities to her Cubist paintings. From 1931, she worked as a consultant for W. and J. Sloane's furniture store

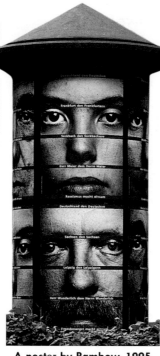

A poster by Rambow, 1995

in New York, which printed her famed Manhattan wallpaper (1931). Reeves was inspired by her extensive travels, including visits to Guatemala in 1934 and India in the 1950s.

REICH, Tibor
1916–1996 Hungarian
✎ p.123

This textile designer united his native background with his formal education to achieve a unique style. His woven fabrics are inspired by the colored ribbons of peasant costume, while showing elements of modernism. In the 1930s, he settled in England, producing woven materials in Stratford, and from the 1950s, also printed fabrics. His theory that "nature designs best" is visible in his 1957 Fotexur range of fabrics, rugs, and ceramics. In 1966, Reich created the upholstery for the Concorde, the first supersonic plane.

RHODES, Zandra
b.1942 British

Rhodes graduated in textiles from the Royal College of Art, London, in the 1960s. Active as a fashion designer, her work reveals the influence of Pop Art. Combining her own textiles and fashions, she creates individual, romantic clothing influenced by her travels, featuring shells, feathers, and zebra-motifs.

RIE, Lucie
b.1902 Austrian

The ceramist Lucie Rie was born Lucie Marie Gomperz. Rich in ornamentation, her works embody the antithesis of modernism. She emigrated to London in 1938, where she established a pottery and button-making workshop. Her ceramics are recognizable by their cross-hatched sgraffito decoration and subtly colored glazes or textured white-tin surfaces. Rie has won various awards and shown her works at several exhibitions.

RIEMERSCHMID, Richard
1868–1957 German

Progressive designer and architect Riemerschmid was one of the first designers to adjust his works to industrial production. In 1887, he cofounded Munich's Verninigte Werkstätten für Kunst im Handwerk, producing simple metal-works. He designed a variety of goods entirely suitable for machine manufacture, including his Maschinenmöbel (1905). Among his architectural work is Germany's first garden city at Hellerau (1907–13). From 1912 to 1924, he directed the Munich Kunstgewerbeschule.

RIETVELD, Gerrit
1888–1964 Dutch
✎ p.33

Architect and designer Gerrit Rietveld is best known for his association with the De Stijl movement. The linear aesthetic with which his work is synonomous is expressed in his Red-and-blue chair (1917–18), the Schröder house in Holland (1924), and his low-cost Zig-Zag chair for Metz & Company department store (1934, see right). Although he favored wood as a material, Rietveld also created some experimental tubular-steel furniture during the 1920s. In the 1950s and '60s, he was predominantly active as an architect and lecturer.

RODCHENKO, Aleksandr
1891–1956 Russian

A leading Constructivist who was active as a painter and designer, Rodchenko brought the aesthetics of the machine age to these fields. He collaborated with fellow Constructivists Kasimir Malevich (see p.267) and Vladimir Tatlin (1885–1953) from 1915 and, in 1921, cofounded the First Working Group of Constructivists. In the 1920s, he designed posters for the government, cinema, and journals *LEF* and *Novyi LEF*.

ROSSI, Aldo
b.1931 Italian
✎ p.73, 87

A postmodernist architect and designer, Rossi graduated from Milan Polytechnic in 1959. Formal and unornamented, his school library at Fagnano Olona in

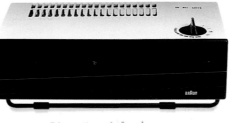

Dieter Rams's fan heater for Braun, 1969

Italy (1972–76) typically draws inspiration from 18th-century neo-classicism. Rossi's product designs for Alessi are commonly based on architecture, such as his 1979 tea and coffee service, which is a scaled-down version of his floating Teatro del Mondo in Venice (1979).

RUHLMANN, Jacques-Emile
1869–1933 French
✎ p.44, 82

Ruhlmann is known for his luxury Art Deco furniture and use of exotic materials. He first exhibited in 1913 at the Paris Salon d'Automne, and later played a significant role in the 1925 Paris Expo, designing the Hotel du Collectionneur, which has been hailed as a high-point in Art Deco design. His furniture for the Maharajah of Indore in the

1920s and '30s, and his 1930 Soleil bed of rosewood veneer, are typical of his furniture.

RUSSELL, Gordon
1892–1980 British

A proponent of the craft ethic, Russell began his education by repairing antique furniture for his father's business. In 1929, he established Gordon Russell Ltd., working on designs of mass-produced radio cabinets for Murphy Ltd. (1930s), and later a line of Utility furniture. In 1949, he became the director of the Council of Industrial Design.

S

SAARINEN, Eero
1910–61 Finnish/American
✎ p.35, 93

Saarinen's designs embrace a diverse selection of styles, from the organic to the strictly geometric. Educated in Paris and New York, he was active mainly in the US. In the early 1960s, he designed Dulles Airport, Washington, and the TWA terminal at Kennedy Airport, New York. He is also renowned for his use of bent plywood and molded plastics, the latter used for his Tulip chairs of 1956.

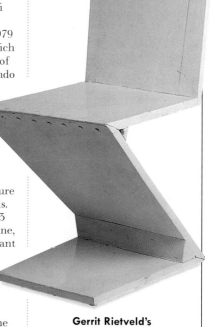

Gerrit Rietveld's Zig-Zag Chair, 1934

SABATTINI, Lino
b.1925 Italian

One of Italy's most inventive silversmiths, Sabattini is known for his fluid silverware, but he has also produced glass and ceramics. From 1956 to 1963, he was design director of the French company Christofle, for which he produced the Como tea service (1960). In 1964, he set up his own silver company in Italy.

SAINT LAURENT, Yves
b.1936 French

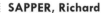 *p.144*

Algerian-born Saint Laurent won the International Wool Secretariat design contest in 1954 with a cocktail dress. The following year, he began work for Christian Dior (see p.259), and in 1957 he took over the great couture house on Dior's death. After fighting in the Algerian war, Saint Laurent opened his own

Sabattini's Estro silver sauceboat, 1976

house in 1962. His early collections were influenced by the Left Bank and the art world, most notably by the work of Piet Mondrian (evidenced in the 1965 collection) and Pop Art (1966). In 1966, he opened the Rive Gauche boutiques for ready-to-wear designs. Saint Laurent has designed film and theater costumes as well as menswear, perfumes, and household goods.

SAMPE, Astrid
b.1909 Swedish

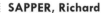 *p.123*

As head of the textile design studio at the Swedish fabric company Nordiska from 1937 to 1971, Sampe designed and commissioned many printed and woven textiles. She favored an abstract geometric style. In 1972, she set up her own studio specializing in fabrics and interiors.

SAPPER, Richard
b.1932 German

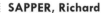 *p.55, 57, 127*

After working in Germany as a designer for Mercedes-Benz, Sapper moved to Milan in 1957. There, he worked first for Gio Ponti (see p.270), and then the department store La Rinascente. Many of Sapper's most interesting designs have been created with Marco Zanuso (see p.275), with whom he began collaborating in 1960. Their work includes televisions and radios for Brionvega, and the Grillo telephone (1965). Among Sapper's other works are the Tizio lamp for Artemide (1972), kettles for Alessi, and car designs for Fiat. Since 1980, he has been a design consultant to IBM.

SARPANEVA, Timo
b.1926 Finnish

A leading figure in modern Scandinavian design, Sarpaneva has produced textiles, graphics, ceramics, and metalware. However, he is best-known for his glass designs, particularly those for the Iittala factory.

SASON, Sixten
1912–69 Swedish

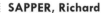 *p.131*

An industrial designer, Sason designed several cars for the Swedish company Saab (see above), including the Saab 92, 96, and 99. He also acted as consultant designer for Hasselblad and Electrolux.

SAVIGNAC, Raymond
b.1907 French

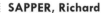 *p.196, 227*

A former assistant to the great French poster designer A.M. Cassandre (see p. 258), Savignac produced theatrical set designs and costumes, as well as posters. He was adept at choosing a single, often humorous, image to convey the message of his posters.

SCHIAPARELLI, Elsa
1890–1973 Italian

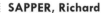 *p.105, 143*

Fashion designer Schiaparelli enjoyed phenomenal success in Paris during the 1930s.

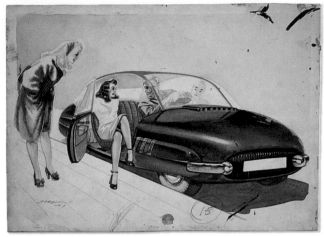

A Sixten Sason car design for Saab, 1947

She started out by selling sweaters knitted by Armenian women. Later, she created interesting fabrics and garments, many decorated with Surrealist-inspired features. Schiaparelli's most famous innovation was "shocking pink," a far more vibrant color than those used by other couturiers. In 1940, she moved to the US, and although she reopened in Paris in 1945, she did not recapture her former glory.

SCHRECKENGOST, Viktor
b.1906 American

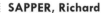 *p.17, 50*

Schreckengost's ceramics were heavily influenced by Viennese pottery. In 1930, while working at the Cowan Pottery Studio, he created a set of punch bowls for Eleanor Roosevelt. The bright blue bowls, which combined words and contemporary images, were later produced commercially. After Cowan closed in 1931, Schreckengost worked for a variety of other ceramic and industrial companies.

SERRURIER-BOVY, Gustave
1858–1910 Belgian

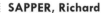 *p.124, 128*

After initially working as an architect, Serrurier-Bovy began making furniture influenced by the Arts and Crafts movement. His Silex range of inexpensive self-assembly furniture was introduced in 1902. It featured wooden bedroom furniture, tables, and chairs, along with metalwork vases and lights.

SHIRE, Peter
b.1947 American

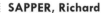 *p.27*

One of the many designers who produced pieces for the Italian Memphis group, Shire contributed brightly colored lamps, tables, a teapot, the Bel Air armchair (1982), and the Big Sur couch (1986). He has also designed silverware and glassware for other Italian companies.

SINCLAIR, Clive
b.1940 British

Sinclair worked as a technical journalist before setting up Sinclair Radionics in 1962. He developed miniaturized electronic goods, including the first pocket calculator (1972) and a miniature television (1977). In 1980, he launched the ZX80, the first of a series of home computers. His C5 electric car (1985) failed to sell.

ŠÍPEK, Bořek
b.1949 Czech

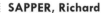 *p.49, 81, 125*

Originally from Prague, Šípek studied architecture in Hamburg, taught in Hanover and Essen, and now works in Amsterdam. The design of his Bambi chair (1983) is typical of his individual poetic approach to functional items. For Vitra, he created the Ota Otanek chair (1988), Wardrobe (1989–91), and a metal waste paper basket (1989). Other works include tableware, glassware, and accessories.

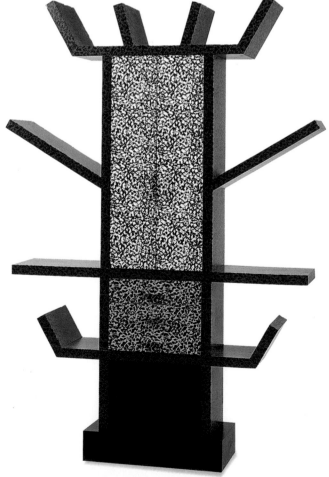

Ettore Sottsass's Casablanca sideboard for Memphis, 1981

SOGNOT, Louis
1892–1970 French
p.108
An architect and furniture designer, Sognot often worked with Charlotte Alix (b.1897) designing interiors and metal and glass furniture.

SOTTSASS, Ettore
b.1917 Austrian/Italian
p.124, 192, 199
One of the best-known names in modern design, Sottsass began work as an architect, opening a design studio in Milan in 1947. In 1957, he became consultant designer to Olivetti, for which he produced various pieces of office equipment and furniture. He exhibited work with Studio Alchimia in 1979, then set up Sottsass Associati in 1980. The following year, he founded

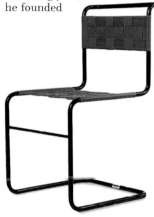

Mart Stam's chair, 1926

the Memphis group, which became a leader of the post-modernist movement. His own designs for Memphis include sideboards (see left), seating, tables, and plates. He continues to design consumer products and exhibitions.

STAM, Mart
1899–1986 Dutch
After studying drawing, Stam worked in architectural practices in the Netherlands, Germany, and Switzerland, and as a town planner in the Soviet Union. He is usually remembered as the designer of the first tubular-steel cantilevered chair (see above).

STARCK, Philippe
See box, above
p.26, 99, 101, 179, 193

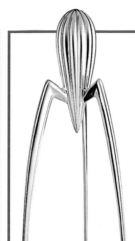

Juicy Salif, c.1990

STARCK, Philippe b.1949 French

Celebrated as one of the most exciting designers of the late 20th century, Starck shot to fame when he refurbished President Mitterrand's private rooms in the Elysée Palace (1982). Other interior designs include the Café Costes in Paris and the Royalton Hotel in New York (both 1984). Starck's architectural projects range from the Nani Nani office building in Tokyo (1990) and the Angle in Antwerp (1991) to La Rue Starck in Paris. He has designed many pieces of furniture, much of it made from pressed metal, as well as products as diverse as motorcycles, lighting, clocks, lemon squeezers, and toothbrushes.

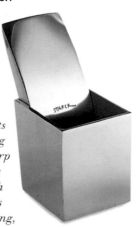

Ashtray, 1988

STICKLEY, Gustav
1857–1942 American
p.10
Stickley was the best-known American exponent of the Arts and Crafts movement. In 1901, he launched *The Craftsman* magazine to popularize the furniture made in his workshops using traditional construction methods. Stickley's company went bankrupt in 1915.

STÖLZL, Gunta
1897–1983 German
p.122
Prominent German textile designer Stölzl directed the weaving workshop at the Bauhaus, Dessau, from 1927 to 1931. In 1931, she set up a textile studio in Zurich with two ex-colleagues from the Bauhaus.

STRAUB, Marianne
b.1909 Swiss/British
p.123
Straub played a leading role in revitalizing the Welsh textile industry in the 1930s. Then, while working for British firms Helios and Warner & Sons, she developed hand-woven fabrics for mass production. Her famous Surrey textile was created for the 1951 Festival of Britain.

SUMMERS, Gerald
1899–1967 British
p.35
In 1929, Summers set up a company called Makers of Simple Furniture, for which

he designed molded plywood furniture similar to that of Alvar Aalto (see p.254). He is best known for the lounge chair he created from one piece of plywood (1933–34).

T

TALLON, Roger
b.1929 French
p.214
Industrial designer Tallon was one of France's first independent designers. His work includes furniture, lighting, and watches. SNCF, General Motors, Daum, Lipp, and Erco have been among his prestigious clients.

TANAKA, Ikko
b.1930 Japanese
p.230
One of the foremost Japanese graphic and exhibition designers, Tanaka has produced some outstanding advertising, cultural, and environmental posters.

TEAGUE, Walter Dorwin
1883–1960 American
p.89, 164
Along with Raymond Loewy (see p.266) and Norman Bel Geddes (see p.255), Teague was a pioneer professional industrial designer, and was one of the first to adopt streamlined styling. His many clients included Eastman Kodak, Corning Glass Works, Ford, Texaco, and Boeing. He designed pavilions for the 1939 New York World's Fair.

TEODORO, Franco
See Gatti, Paolini, Teodoro

THONET, Michael
1796–1871 Austrian
p.32, 92
Thonet's influence extended long after his death through the designs of the furniture company he founded in 1853. Its bentwood chairs have become classics of 20th-century design. In the 1920s, the company began producing tubular-steel furniture.

THUN, Matteo
b.1952 Austrian/Italian
p.81, 125
A partner in Sottsass Associati from 1980 to 1984, Thun was also a cofounder of Memphis. Although he has designed furniture, he is known for his ceramics and computer-aided manufacturing.

TIFFANY, Louis Comfort
1848–1933 American
p.46
A well-known decorative artist of the early 20th century, Tiffany set up an interior decorating firm in 1879, the Tiffany Glass Company in 1885, and Tiffany Studios in 1890. He designed pottery, jewelry, metalwork, furniture, lamps, and windows. His Favrile glass (see below) was hugely successful worldwide.

TSHICHOLD, Jan
1902–74 German
p.211
Typographer Tshichold was the principle champion of the New Typography movement during the 1920s and '30s. He later adopted a more classical style. He also designed books.

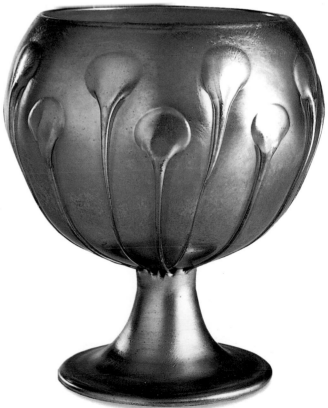

A Favrile glass goblet by Louis Comfort Tiffany, c.1900

TUSQUETS BLANCA, Oscar

b.1941 Spanish

p.85

Tusquets trained as a painter, architect, and designer in Barcelona. In 1965, along with fellow students Lluís Clotet (b.1941), Pep Bonet (b.1941), and Christian Cirici (b.1941), he formed the radical design and architecture group, Studio PER. In 1972, in collaboration with Lluís Clotet, he produced the controversial Belvedere de Regàs, which is generally regarded as one of the first postmodernist buildings. In 1973, Studio PER and other design offices formed B.d. Ediciones de Diseño to produce avant-garde designs. Tusquets created a tea and coffee set for Alessi in 1983.

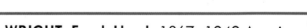

Dinner service by Vignelli Associates, 1986

U

UMEDA, Masanori

b.1941 Japanese

Umeda studied design in Tokyo. He worked at Studio Castiglioni, Milan, until 1969, joining Olivetti as a design consultant in 1970. His best-known piece is the Tawaraya boxing-ring bed, produced for Memphis in 1981. Returning to Tokyo in 1986, he founded U-Meta Design, specializing in abstract furniture, crockery, and interior designs.

V

VALENTINO, (Valentino Garavani)

b.1932 Italian

Valentino studied fashion in Milan and Paris, returning to Rome in 1959, where he set up his own fashion house. His designs were in such demand that in 1969, he opened a boutique for ready-to-wear women's clothing. This was

followed in 1972 by a range of menswear. In the 1970s, he expanded his range to include accessories and perfume.

VENINI, Paolo

1895–1959 Italian

p.48

Venetian law graduate Venini became a partner, together with Giacomo Cappellin (1887–1968), in a Murano glassmaking business in 1921. Initially concentrating on ornamental glass, they began to show more modern pieces at the Monza Biennale in 1923 and later at the Milan Triennale. Venini assumed sole ownership in 1925. He worked with designers such as Gio Ponti (see p.256) and Massimo Vignelli (see right).

VENTURI, Robert

b.1925 American

p.85

In his 1966 book *Complexity and Contradiction in Modern Architecture*, Venturi laid down the basic tenets of postmodernism. Although best known for his architectural achievements, including the Sainsbury Wing extension for the National Gallery, London (1988), he has also designed a tea and coffee set for Alessi (1983) and furniture for Knoll (1984).

VERSACE, Gianni

b.1946 Italian

Versace learned his tailoring skills from his mother, who was a dressmaker. From 1972, he worked as a freelancer, producing a collection of women's ready-to-wear clothes under his own name in 1978. A menswear range followed in 1979. Versace is known for his original use of materials, particularly a soft, metal fabric that he created for his 1983 collection.

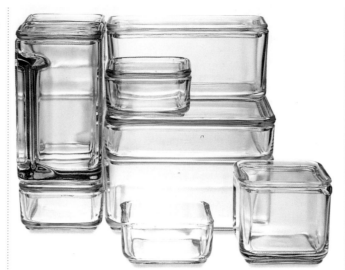

Wagenfeld's Kubus modular storage set, 1938

VIGELAND, Tone

b.1938 Norwegian

p.157

One of Norway's foremost jewelry designers, Vigeland set up her own studio in 1961. Her striking designs evoke her Scandinavian heritage.

VIGNELLI, Lella

b.1934 Italian

p.51

Husband and wife Massimo (b.1931) and Lella Vignelli have introduced a European sophistication into American design through the graphics and products that they have produced since settling in the US in 1965. Working initially for Unimark International, in 1971 they founded Vignelli Associates. Massimo has been largely responsible for the graphic output, including Bloomingdale's corporate image and signage for the Washington subway system; while Lella has headed the furniture and product design branch (see left).

VIGNELLI, Massimo

see Vignelli, Lella

VITRAC, Jean-Pierre

b.1944 French

p.81

Vitrac set up in business in 1974, with offices in Milan, New York, and Tokyo. The company gained a reputation for exploring innovative design concepts, producing furniture, tableware, lighting, and sports equipment.

W

WAGENFELD, Wilhelm

1900–90 German

Entering the Weimar Bauhaus in 1923, Wagenfeld studied under László Moholy-Nagy (see p.267). He remained there, teaching in the metal workshop, until 1927, when he went freelance. Concerned with function, economy, and purity, Wagenfeld designed utilitarian ceramics, metal-, and glassware (see above) for companies such as Rosenthal and the Jenaer Glassworks.

WARHOL, Andy

1928–87 American

p.220

Although famed for his role in Pop Art, Warhol also created advertisements for *Vogue* and *Harpers Bazaar* and record sleeves for Columbia Records. He was awarded the Annual Art Director's Club Medal in 1956 and '57 for his I. Miller shoe and hat advertisement. His paintings and films drew on themes from the commercial world.

WEBER, Kem

1889–1963 German

p.128

In 1914, Karl Emanuel Martin (KEM) Weber went to assist on Germany's exhibit in the Panama-Pacific International Exposition in San Francisco. Trapped by the outbreak of war, he settled in the US. In 1927, he established himself as an industrial designer in Hollywood. Weber developed a distinctive style, openly embracing modernism.

WEGNER, Hans

b.1914 Danish

p.93

Trained first as a cabinet-maker and later as a furniture designer, Wegner worked in the office of Arne Jacobsen

WRIGHT, Frank Lloyd 1867–1949 American

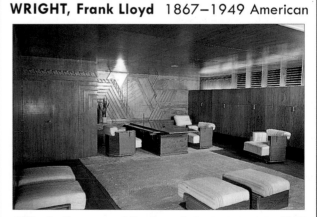

Office for the owner of Kaufmann's department store, 1937

Primarily remembered as America's most creative architect, Wright was also an important design theorist. Working at the architectural office of Louis Sullivan (1856–1924), he was first exposed to the concept of functionalism. His interest in Japanese architecture led to the development of his own style of work, which he called "organic architecture." This was characteristically low and simple and made use of natural materials. He designed 800 buildings, 380 of which were realized.

(see p.264) from 1940 to 1943, when he established his own studio. In 1940, he began his long and illustrious association with furniture maker Johannes Hansen, which produced his famous piece, The Chair, in 1949. Wegner's designs, mostly executed in natural materials, are characterized by their elegance and visual simplicity.

WEIL, Daniel
b.1953 Argentinian
p.57
Born and trained as an architect in Buenos Aires, innovative industrial designer Weil went to London in 1978. He received recognition for a series of clocks, radios, and lights that he designed in 1981 as part of his degree show for the Royal College of Art, London. Together with Gerard Taylor, he has worked on various interior and product designs for Sottsass Associati, Knoll, and Alessi.

WEINGART, Wolfgang
b.1941 German
As a typography teacher at the Basle School of Arts and Crafts since 1968, Weingart has been instrumental in overturning the conventional Swiss graphics approach. He rejected strict adherence to the grid and introduced wide type spacing, step rules, and mixing of type weights. He is credited with bringing New Wave graphics to the US via his extensive teaching.

WEISS, Rheinhold
b.1934 German
p.107
Weiss remained at the Hochschule für Gestaltung, Ulm, as associate director of the product design section, after studying there. The products that he created for Braun in the 1960s reflect both his training at Ulm and Braun's functionalist aesthetic. In 1967, he moved to Chicago, setting up a studio in 1970.

WESTWOOD, Vivienne
b.1941 British
p.145
Generally recognized as the most influential and original British fashion designer of

the 1970s and '80s, Westwood has played an important role in reasserting London on the international fashion stage. Inspired by the street style of rebellious urban youth and historical and ethnic costume, she has created a series of outrageous collections.

WEWERKA, Stefan
b.1928 German
p.67
Artist, architect, film-maker, and designer Wewerka worked initially as an architect and sculptor. He made his debut as a furniture designer in 1974, when he was commissioned by Tecta to design a classroom chair for its trade fair stand. Since then, he has produced a number of asymmetrical furniture designs for Tecta and, from 1981, irregularly shaped clothing, which he constructs on the body.

WIENER, Edward (Ed)
b.1918 American
p.156
Wiener began working as a jeweler in 1946, establishing himself in New York in 1947. Spirals, figures, and fish are familiar motifs in his work.

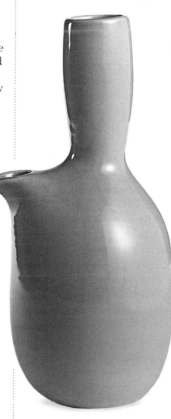

Iroquois carafe by Russel Wright, 1950

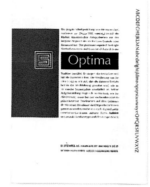

ZAPF, Hermann b.1918 German
An outstanding typeface designer, Zapf's work spans five decades. Self-taught from the writings of Rudolf Koch (1876–1934) and Edward Johnston (see p.264), he began his career at Paul Koch's foundry in Frankfurt. It was for the Stempel foundry, where he worked from about 1940, that he created his finest typefaces, such as Palatino (1949) and Optima (1958).

Optima typeface, 1958

WILSON, Wes
b.1937 American
p.229
Underground cartoonist Wes Wilson was a chief exponent of Psychedelia. Drawing on Secessionist lettering, Art Nouveau patterning, and East Indian motifs, he produced numerous posters for West Coast rock concerts, principally at the Fillmore and Avalon venues in San Francisco.

WIRKKALA, Tapio
1915–85 Finnish
p.89
One of the finest postwar Scandinavian designers, Wirkkala won international acclaim for his entries for the 1951 Milan Triennale. His glassware, produced by Iittala from 1946 to 1985, reflected his grounding in sculpture and his interest in organic forms. His famous Kantarelli vases, created in 1946, typify this approach. He also worked on a freelance basis, creating glassware for Venini, ceramics for Rosenthal, and lighting for Airam.

WORTH, Jean Philippe
1853–1924 French
p.104
When his father, Englishman Charles Frederick Worth, died in 1895, Jean Philippe assumed responsibility for the house of Worth. Jean Philippe handled the creative output, while his brother Gaston (1856–1926) provided the business acumen, hiring designers such as Paul Poiret (see p.270). Retiring in 1910, Jean Philippe was

succeeded by his nephew, who kept the name of Worth in the forefront of fashion during the 1920s. The house of Worth finally closed in 1954.

WRIGHT, Frank Lloyd
See box, left
p.86

WRIGHT, Russel
1904–76 American
p.80, 86, 89
Wright was born and raised as a Quaker in Lebanon, Ohio. His functional designs reflect his puritanical outlook. He began in theater design, but by 1930, he had established a studio in New York, producing metalware. He introduced his hugely successful Modern Living furniture line, which was mass produced by Conant-Ball and sold through Macy's store, in 1935. Wright is best known for his ceramics (see left), particularly the American Modern dinnerware manufactured by Steubenville Pottery from 1939 on.

Y

YAMAMOTO, Yohji
b.1943 Japanese
Yamamoto studied at Keio University and later at the prestigious Bunka College of Fashion in Tokyo. He founded his own company in 1972, showing his first collection in 1976. Like many Japanese fashion designers, Yamamoto concentrates on daywear. His garments are typified by loose, asymmetrical forms.

YOKOO, Tadanori
b.1936 Japanese
p.228
Working as a freelance graphic designer, Yokoo's striking posters from the 1960s and '70s earned him international recognition. Mixing Western images with Eastern graphics, he explored the impact of pop culture on Japanese society.

Z

ZANUSO, Marco
b.1916 Italian
p.127
Zanuso studied architecture at Milan Polytechnic, where he later taught. He established his own design office in 1945. He is known for employing innovative materials, such as foam rubber and sheet metal,

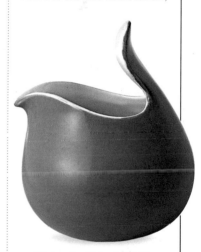

Pitcher by Zeisel, 1946

in his furniture designs for Arlex, among others. From 1958, he collaborated with Richard Sapper (see p.272) on various projects for Brionvega and Siemens.

ZAPF, Hermann
See box, above
p.210

ZEISEL, Eva
b.1906 Hungarian
p.86
A Hungarian-born ceramist, Zeisel worked extensively in Europe before settling in the US in 1938. Her early work reflects the prevailing trend for geometric patterns, but she adopted the emerging style of organic modernism (see above) with her move to the US.

GLOSSARY

ABS plastic
An acrylonitrile-butadiene-styrene thermoplastic with superior ductility, high-impact strength, good colorability, and a high gloss, making it suitable for molded and decorative objects. It is most commonly used in electrical goods, telephone handsets, and furniture.

Aesthetic movement
An artistic movement that evolved in the 1880s and was devoted to "art for art's sake." Leading to the Arts and Crafts movement, it adopted an extravagant ideal of beauty and led to freer expression in art and design.

Anti-design
A movement that emerged in the late 1960s rejecting established design theory and reacting to the rise of consumerism in the 1950s and '60s. It was thought to promote "good design" to enhance sales. Anti-design sought to redefine design through its garish colors and unconventional shapes and proportions.

Art Deco
A decorative style, its name originated from the 1925 Paris *Exposition Internationale des Arts Décoratifs et Industriels Modernes*. Its influences were diverse, from Cubism to Egyptian art to an appreciation of modern machinery. Characterized by simple geometric patterns, sharp edges, and bright colors, the style was applied to a wide range of disciplines.

Art Nouveau
An international decorative style that began in Europe in the 1880s and reached the height of its popularity by 1900. Based on forms of plant-life, the style created a new unity across the visual arts. It is characterized by the whiplash curve, suggestive of organic fluidity.

Arts and Crafts movement
An English and American movement, first established in England in 1882 and named after the Arts and Crafts Exhibition Society. In its prime, between 1888 and 1910, it sought to revive the ideal of the hand-crafted object in an industrial age, a notion that had both social and aesthetic implications. Characterized by medieval and Gothic references, its products were often robust and simply constructed.

Austerity
A period during World War II when governments in Europe, Japan, and the US limited the use of strategic materials and instead commissioned a range of consumer products using basic or new materials.

Avant-garde
Meaning "the vanguard," a group of innovators. In art and design, it refers to developments in the use of materials and styles.

Bakelite
The trade name for a thermosetting plastic, Phenol-Formaldehyde, invented and patented by Leo Baekeland in 1907. An early, brittle plastic, its streamlining qualities, cheapness, and similarity to wood made it ideal for consumer products such as radios and televisions.

Bauhaus
An influential art school, founded in 1919 by Walter Gropius, which ran until 1933 when it was closed by the Nazis. One of its aims was to forge links between art and industry. In the 1920s, the Bauhaus became the leading intellectual and creative center of design, playing a key role in the development of modernism.

biomorphic design
A style of design in which an object is styled to imitate the appearance of a living organism.

Brussels Expo, 1958
A world's fair that was dominated by the Atomium, a huge structure built specifically for the exhibition, which accurately represented an atomic molecular structure.

cantilever
An engineering term to describe a projecting bracket that supports a load. The concept of a cantilever has been applied by innovative 20th-century designers to furniture, producing some highly original, modern chairs.

Classicism
A design style based on abstract principles of organization and order found in Greek and Roman antiquity. The style is simple, harmonious, and well-proportioned.

Compasso d'Oro
Established in 1954, this design award for excellence is presented every year by the Italian chain store *La Rinascente* to Italian designers for outstanding, often domestic, products.

Constructivism
A movement that emerged in Russia after the 1917 Russian Revolution. Partly influenced by Cubism and Futurism, it ignored fine art in favor of applied art: design for mass production was an important ideal. Its largely abstract, "sculptural" works were assembled rather than painted or carved, influencing design in the West.

Cubism
Developed in France in 1907 by Pablo Picasso and Georges Braque, Cubism was a reaction against the optical realism of Impressionism. Images were depicted in geometrical form from multiple viewpoints but displayed on one plane on the canvas. Though short-lived, the movement had a major influence on 20th-century art and design.

De Stijl
A multidiscipline Dutch modernist movement founded in 1917 by Theo van Doesburg. Its name derives from the *De Stijl* journal, meaning "the style." It used abstract geometric forms, with neutral and primary colors in place of natural form, in the search for a visual language to express the new machine aesthetic.

Deconstructivism
A term that emerged in the 1980s to describe visually complex forms with geometrically arranged areas of vibrant colors. Most designs never progressed beyond the stage of plans or models.

determinism
A philosophical theory that humans do not act out of free will, but are directed by external forces.

eclecticism
The term for borrowing from, often combining, a variety of historical sources. This practice was prevalent between 1900 and the 1950, and later re-emerged in postmodernism.

ergonomic design
A scientific approach to the relationship between humans and their environment. Products are designed to suit the human form.

Favrile glass
The trade name registered in 1894 for a high-quality glass produced by Louis Comfort Tiffany.

Festival of Britain, 1951
This festival reflected a new, postwar British approach to architecture and industrial design characterized by light metal structures and modern materials.

Functionalism
Louis Sullivan coined the phrase "form follows function" in 1896. The term embodied the belief that an object's function is of primary importance in determining its appearance.

Futurism
An Italian movement launched in 1909 by Filippo Tommaso Marinetti. It extolled the virtues of modernity, demanding the inclusion of new technology and dynamism in art.

Glasgow School
A group led by the innovative Scottish architect and designer Charles Rennie Mackintosh. His interpretation of Art Nouveau in the 1890s and 1900s resulted in a linear, less ornamental style.

graphic design
A generic term for photography, drawing, typography, and printing.

high-tech
An architectural and design style that rejects decorative elements in favor of industrial equipment.

International Style

An architectural style adopted worldwide that epitomized the simple, functional approach of modernism. Leading exponents were Walter Gropius, Mies van der Rohe, and Le Corbusier. It was characterized by new materials, such as steel, reinforced concrete, and plate-glass windows.

Jugendstil

Meaning "young style," a term used in Germany, Austria and Scandinavian countries for a style closely related to Art Nouveau.

kinetic art

A form of art that depends on movement for its effect.

kitsch

A critical term used to describe pretentious, cheap, ugly, or sentimental work. The style has flourished since the rejection of modernism by some designers in the 1960s. Gillo Dirfles's 1969 *Kitsch: An Anthology of Bad Taste* is the definitive book on the subject.

machine aesthetic

A term describing the appearance of an object that has been determined by its manufacturing process.

Milan Triennale

An art exhibition held every three years in Milan, it is a showcase for modern designs, generally Italian.

modernism

Not representative of one group, but a general reaction in art, design, technology, and society in the 20th century against traditional styles that emphasized the simple, functional aspect of forms without decoration. Its aim was to produce high-quality designs for a mass population.

motif

A distinctive feature or dominant idea. Also an ornament identifying a maker or model.

Nancy School

The school of craftsmen set up in Nancy, France, by Art Nouveau exponent Emile Gallé in 1890 to promote naturalism in design.

New York World's Fair, 1939

The theme of this exhibition was "Building the World of Tomorrow." It was dominated by the American concept of streamlining, revealed in the cars, model buildings, and futuristic products on show. For the first time, the decorative arts were overshadowed by industrial designs strongly influenced by modernism.

Op Art

An abstract movement that developed in the 1960s and exploited various optical effects. Illusions of movement were produced by graphic processes or by overlapping patterns.

organic design

A style of design that echoes the curvilinearity of natural forms. In recent years, it has been aided by the improvements in plastics and computer technology in production.

pâte-de-verre

A glass making technique that involves grinding down glass and reforming it in a mold.

Paris Expo, 1925

This exhibition, also known as *Exposition Internationale des Arts Décoratifs et Industriels Modernes*, focused on the decorative arts and first introduced the Art Deco style.

Pop Art

An abbreviation of Popular Art. The movement grew in the 1950s and '60s drawing its inspiration from aspects of commercial culture such as packaging, advertising, and comics. Its irreverent images were based on consumerism, and its exponents, such as Andy Warhol, were opposed to contemporary aesthetic standards.

postmodernism

In rejecting modernism, with its innovations that alienated the masses, the postmodernists relied on historical references. The movement became increasingly influential through the late 1960s, and can be characterized by a rejection of the logic and simplicity of the modernists. Instead, designers used an eclectic range of references, styles, and eras.

Psychedelia

An influential 1960s style that sought inspiration from mind-expanding hallucinogenic drugs for its bright, bold, often abstract designs.

Punk

A British street culture movement that developed in the 1970s.

Rationalism

An Italian movement rejecting Futurism that made efficient use of resources, space, and visual impact.

Romanticism

Containing the distinctive qualities or spirit of the Romantic movement. Considered a state of mind rather than a style, it encompassed diverse artists, whose use of grandeur and the picturesque aimed to invoke a powerful emotional response.

sgraffito

A ceramic decorative technique in which a different, underlying color is revealed by scratching through the surface of a material.

signage

The arrangement or design of graphic images, often involving text, in a sign that is intended to convey information to the public.

Social Realism

Expressing social or political tendencies as part of a practical approach in art and design.

Stile Liberty (or Stile Floreale)

Term used in Italy for Art Nouveau, deriving its name from the British decorative arts retailer Liberty & Co., which sold the designs of its progressive craftsmen in Italy. The style was revived in design as Neo-Liberty in the 1960s.

Streamlining

Aerodynamic experiments to reduce wind resistance on aircraft in America were subsequently applied to cars and other design work in the 1930s and '40s, giving objects gentle curves free of projections. Equated with functional excellence, the style was also used for purely visual effects, and by the 1950s often appeared in a highly exaggerated form.

Suprematism

Developed by Kazimir Malevich in Russia, this concept was concerned with the reduction of forms to a simple geometric arrangement in pure colors to represent the "supremacy of pure emotion."

Surrealism

Surrealists sought to go beyond the accepted conventions of reality and explore the subconscious mind. Representations were presented as depictions of a dreamworld, and objects were deliberately constructed in strange conjunctions. The play on the meanings of objects was picked up by the Anti-design movement.

Utility

Furniture and textiles produced in Britain between 1941 and 1951 in response to the economies of war.

Vienna Secession

Considered the Austrian version of Art Nouveau, the movement was founded in 1897 when a group of artists and designers seceded from the Vienna Academy. It utilized natural images and curving forms, but its designs were more geometric than those of French and Belgian Art Nouveau.

vitreous china

A type of china so fine, hard, and transparent it is almost glasslike.

Vorticism

An aggressive movement between 1912 and 1915 that attacked sentimentality in favor of violence, energy, and machinery. Bold and abstract, it drew from Cubism and Futurism, often creating angular, machinelike objects.

Wiener Werkstätte

A cooperative group of workshops that grew out of the Vienna Secession in 1903. Incorporating artists, designers, and craftsmen, it flourished as a center of progressive design until 1932. Although initially rectilinear, it later developed a more curvilinear, eclectic style.

zoomorphism

A style of designing objects that imitate or represent animal forms.

INDEX

ACKNOWLEDGMENTS

Picture Credits

Abbreviations: a=above b=below
c=center l=left r=right t=top

Alvar Aalto Foundation: **p34bl**, **p48b**
Acer UK Ltd.: **p28tr**, **p201br**
©ADAGP, Paris, and DACS, London, 1996: **p11tr**, **p104c**, **p225tc**, **p227tl**, **p266l**
Adidas Archive: **p162crb**, **br**
Advertising Archives: **p155tr**, **p157tr**
AEG: **p106cl**, **p212br**
Aga-Rayburn: **p66r**
AKG London: **p13tr**, **p155tcr**
ALIAS: **pp92–93b**, **p256t**
Alessi spa Italy: **p85c**; Design by Philippe Starck, 1991: **p273tl**; Design by Michael Graves, 1984: **pp74–75c**
Alternative Plans: **p66t**
Amstrad/Michael Joyce Consultants: **p201l**
Apple Macintosh/Bite Communications Ltd.: **p200tl**, **bl**
Aqualisa Products Ltd.: **p98tr**
Arcaid: Richard Bryant: **p10t**, **p24t**; Dennis Gilbert: **p29cl**; Peter Mauss/Esto: **p14br**
Giorgio Armani/Mana GA Press Office: **p254tr**
©ARS, NY and DACS, London 1996: **p274b**
Laura Ashley: **p255br**
Atelier de Création Graphique Pierre Bernard: **p230l**
Atrium Ltd.: **p43b**, **p264br**
Bang & Olufsen: **p61bc**
The Bathroom Works: **p255tr**
Bass Yager Associates: **p227cl**
Bauhaus Archive: **p122c**
BayGen Power (Europe) Ltd.: **p28cl**
Benetton/Modus Publicity: **p231bl**
Dieffeplast: **p123tc**
Courtesy of Bonhams Fine Arts Auctioneers, London: **p67c**, **p93t**, **p109tr**, **p109c**, **p125cr**, **p269b**
RGA Bott Ltd.: **p69br**
Andrea Branzi: **p41b**
Bridgeman Art Library: Bonhams, London: **p150t**, **cra**, **p268l**; Fine Art Society: **p192t**; JCK Archive: **p121 bl**; Musée d'Orsay, Paris: **p108t**; Neue Galerie, Linz: **p13t**; Private Collection/Clarice Cliff ® and Bizarre™ are trademarks of Josiah Wedgwood & Sons Limited/All rights reserved: **p83tr**; Private Collection: **p139tr**, **p262l**; By courtesy of the Board of Trustees of the V&A, London: **274b**
Courtesy of Torsten Bröhan, Düsseldorf: **p80l**
Neill Bruce/Peter Roberts Collection: **p260t**
BT Archives: **p126t**, **cl**
BT Museum: **p126c**, **p127tr**
BT Pictures: **p127br**
Camera Press: **p149tr**
Chanel: **back jacket** tr; **p104t**
Jean-Loup Charmet: **p214clb**
Christies Images: **p11tr**, **p14l**, **p44cl**, **p45br**, **p92c**, **p124tl**, **p128l**, **p129tl**, **p193tr**, **p192bl**, **p224cl**, **p266l**, **p267u**, **p272b**
CND: **p213br**
The design of the Contour bottle is reproduced by kind permission of The Coca-Cola Company. "Coca-Cola," Coke and the design of the contour bottle are registered trademarks of the Coca-Cola

Company: **front jacket flap, spine**, **p12l**, **p213t**, **p245cl**, **p249tcl**
Collection of the New-York Historical Society: **p9bl**
Collier Campbell: **p123br**, **p258b**
Colorsport: **p215b**
Corbis-Bettmann/UPI: **p270br**
© DACS, 1996: **back jacket** c; **p14l**, **p33t**, **p34tl**, **p40t**, **p74tl**, **p105tl**, **p122l**, c, **p157br**, **p195cl**, **p196tr**, **p208br**, **p223bl**, **p224cl**, **p225cr**, **p227cb**, **p228c**, **p229tr**, **p271b**
© Design Council: **p69cr**
Dupont Information Service: **p138t**
Ergonomi: **p27l**
M. Espues y Peret Asociados SCP, Barcelona: **p231tr**
E.T. Archive: **p18tr**
Mary Evans Picture Library: **p12b**, **p194tr**
EWA: **p22tr**
Museo Salvatore Ferragamo/Aurelia Public Relations: **p146br**, **p260b**
Fiell International Ltd.: **p19l**
Gallaher Ltd.: **p230br**
Frank O. Gehry & Associates Inc: **pp38–39c**
Giraudon: **p52tr**
Milton Glaser Inc.: **p22bl**
The Ronald Grant Archive: **front jacket** cl; **p58cl**
Greteman Group: **p231br**
Manufactured since 1955 by Fritz Hansen A/S. Allerødvej 8, DK-3450, Allerød, Denmark; tel: +45 48172300, fax: +45 48171948: **p36br**
C.P. Hart Group/Halston PR Ltd: **p96tc**, **p99cr**
Hasbro: **p117bl**
⌘ Approved and Licensed by Josef Hoffmann Stiftung-Vaduz: **p13br**, **p32t**, **p50cl**, **p92l**, **p264l**
Angelo Hornak Library: **p14tr**
Hulton Getty: **p20bl**, **pp22–23b**, **p109tl**, **p135tl**, **p143tr**, **p155tl**, **p156br**, **p175tl**, **p200tr**
© Hunterian Art Gallery, University of Glasgow: **p108br**, Mackintosh Collection: **p32l**
Courtesy of International Business Machines Corporation: **p200c**
ICI Corporate Slidebank: **p215ca**
Ideal Standard Ltd: **p98tc**
Ikko Tanaka Design Studio: **p230t**
Inskip/Pepsi-Cola International: **p28b**
Kartell, Milan: **p261l**
Katz: **p141tl**
Kenzo: **p145tr**
Eero Saarinen Womb Chair, Courtesy of Knoll: **p35br**
J.F. Hardoy Chair, Courtesy of Knoll Archives: **p35cr**
Käthe Kruse: **pp116–117t**
Kuramata Design Office: **p24l**, **p39tr**, **p265br**
Kuwait Petroleum (GB) Limited: **p214tr**
Ladybird/Coats Viyella: **p137t**
London Transport Museum: **p17tl**, **p126br**, **p208bl**
Michele de Lucchi: **p24cr**, **p25tr**, **p43t**
Mark Hall Cycle Museum: **p172cr**
Barbie ® photography reproduced with kind permission of Mattel Toys: **p117tr**
McDonald's Restaurants Ltd.: **p214c**
Memphis, Milan: **pp44–45c** photo: Studio Aldo Ballo, **p123cb** photo: Studio Azzurro, **p259br** photo: Robert Gennari
Alessandro Mendini: **p38bl**, **p42c**
Miele/Elizabeth Hindmarch PR: **p71br**

Issey Miyake: **p145br**, **p267b**
Alex Moulton Bicycles: **p173tr**
National Library of Scotland/Reproduced by permission of Stewartry District Council and the E.A. Hornel Trust: **p222l**
National Motor Museum, Beaulieu: **p180cl**, **p181tr**, **p182tr**, **p189tr**
Neff UK/ RSCG Conran Design: **p67r**
George Nelson Associates: **p41t**
Peter Newark's American Pictures: **p16l**
Nike UK Ltd.: **p215cb**
Olivetti UK Limited: **p214bl**
Omega: **p151r**
The Robert Opie Collection: **p15tl**, **p16ct**, **p18cr**, **p34tr**, **p60bl**, **p60br**, **p66b**, **p70cr**, **p87tr**, **p105tr**, **p110c**, **p121tc**, **p130ct**, **p131tr**, **p154ct**, **p172tr**, **p185tl**, **p198c**, **p207**, **p212bl**, **p222tr**, **p223bl**, **br**, **tr**, **p224bl**, **br**, **tr**, **p225tl**, **c**, **br**, **p226bl**, **cl**, **t**, **p229cr**, **br**, **p256cl**, **p265t**
Panasonic: **p59crb**
Verner Panton: **p22tl**; **p36c**, **p269b**
Parker Pen Company: **p153tr**
Pepsi-Cola International: **p245c**
Gaetano Pesce: **p38tr**, **p42bl**, **p269cr**; **p248bc**
Philips: **p59tr**, **p61br**, **p62tl**, **p63tr**
Popperfoto/Stuart Forster: **p148tr**
Mary Quant, Europe: **p270t**
Gunter Rambow Graphik Design: **p231tl**, **p271t**
Retrograph Archive Ltd: **p154tr**, **p155ctl**, **p196tr**, **p213ct**, **p217tr**, **p217br**, **p222c**, **br**, **p223tl**, **p224c**, **p225tc**, **cr**, **bl**, **p226br**, **p227tl**, **p227tr**, **c**, **br**, **cb**, **p228**, **p229tl**, **tr**, **bl**, **p262l**, **p263l**
Rex: **p141tr**
Rowenta: **p75br**
Sawaya & Moroni, Milan: **p109b**
Scala/Museo Statale Russo, Leningrad: **p257r**
Science & Society Picture Library: **p71l**, **cr**, **p199tr**
Sears, Roebuck & Co.: **p68tl**, **p70b**
Seiko: **p151br**
Shell UK Limited: **p212t**
SMEG/Phyllis Oberman Consultants: **pp68–69c**
© Smithsonian Institution: **p67t**
Sony: **back jacket** tl, **p59tl**, **bl**, **p63bl**, **p201tl**, **p214t**
Sony Computer Entertainment, Europe: **p115bc**
Sotheby's, London: **p108bl**
Ettore Sottsass: **p128r**, **p192br**
Studio Dumbar/photo: Lex van Pieterson: **p230br**
Design Studio 65 (1970) Designers: F. Audrito, A. Garizio, G. Paci, A. Pozzo, A. Sampaniotou, M. Schiappa, F. Tartaglia: **p42tl**
Superstock: **p69tr**
Swatch/Marianne Egli Communications: **p127c**, **p151tl**, **ctl**, **ctr**, **p161ct**, **p223cb**
Swid Powell: **p85c**
Tecno: **p40b**, **p193cl**, **p261br**
Tecta: **p67c**, **p124cl**
Gebrüder Thonet GmbH: **p32l**
Topham Picture Source: **p18l**
UPS: **213bl**
By courtesy of the Board of Trustees of the Victoria and Albert Museum, London: **p24l**, **p45cr**, **p122l**, **p122tr**, **p123ct**, **p142**, **p143tl**, **l**, **c**, **p144**, **p145l**, **c**
Courtesy of Virgin Records: **p220cr**, **p221ccr**
Vitra Ltd.: **back jacket flap**; **p125r**, **p193br**, **p265r**
Collection Vitra Design Museum, Weil am Rhein, Germany: **p10l**, **p21tr**, **p32r**, **p32t**, **p33t**, **p34tl**, **bl**, **c**, **p35tr**, **cr**, **br**, **p36tl**, **br**, **c**, **pp36–37c**, **p37br**, **p38tr**, **bl**, **pp38–39**, **p39tl**, **tr**, **p40b**, **p41t**, **b**, **p42tl**, **bl**,

pp42–43c, **p43tr**, **p192br**, **p254bl**; **p259cr**; **p273cl**; **p270l**
Volkswagen: **front jacket flap**
W.M.C.N.A.: **p179tr**
Peter Williams: **pp126–127c**, **p131tr**, **p202r**, **p257l**, **p266t**, **p269tl**, **p272t**
Xerox: **p203tl**
Zapf Creations: **p117br**.

The following were photographed at Cooper-Hewitt, National Design Museum, Smithsonian Institution:
p1r: Gift of Georg Jensen, Sølvsmedie A/S **p2cl**: Museum Purchase through the Decorative Arts Association Acquisition Fund **p2–3c**: Gift of Rodman A. Herren **p3cl**: Gift of Mel Byars **p4r**: Gift of Julia Haiblen **p5l**: Gift of Carlo Moretti **p8c**: Gift of Mel Byars **p13br**: Ely Jacques Kahn **p15c**: The Henry and Ludmilla Shapiro Collection, Partial Gift of Purchase through the Decorative Arts Association Acquisition Fund and Smithsonian Collections Acquisition Program **p16cr**: Museum Purchase through the Decorative Arts Association Acquisition Fund **p17tr**: Gift of Mrs. Homer D. Kripke; **bl**: Gift of Mel Byars **p19br**: Gift of Christian Rohlfing **p23br**: Gift of Deane Granoff **p25tl**: Gift of Barry Friedman and Patricia Pastor **p26br**: Gift of Clotilde Bacri **p27tr**: Gift of Denis Gallion and Daniel Morris **p30l**: Gift of Garry Laredo **p33bl**: Gift of Mme Hector Guimard; **br**: Gift of Gary Laredo **p36cl**: Gift of Knoll International **p37tl**: Gift of Robert Blaich; **tr**: Gift of International Contract Furnishings, Inc. **p38tl**: Gift of ICF, Inc. New York **p39br**: Gift from the Collection of Zoe and Pierce Jackson **p44c**: Museum Purchase through the Decorative Arts Association Acquisition Fund **p46l**: Gift of Mme. Hector Guimard; **r**: Gift of Stanley Siegel **p47bl**: Gift of Ely Jacques Kahn; **tl**: Gift of Marcia and William Goodman; **ct**: Gift of Danese Milano **cr**: Purchased in memory of Georgiana L. McClellan; **r**: Museum Purchase through the James Ford Fund; **p48bl**: Gift of Harmon Goldstone; **tr**: Gift of Mrs. Jefferson Patterson **pp48–49c**: Gift of Christian Rohlfing **p49ct**: Gift of Danese Milano; **r**: Museum Purchase through the James Ford Fund; **b**: Gift of Gallery 91 **p50bl**: Museum Purchase; **cl**: Gift of Ely Jacques Kahn; **tl**: Gift of Denis Gallion and Daniel Morris; **pp50–51cb**: Gift of Mrs. Homer D. Kripke; **ct**: Gift of the Italian Government **p51tl**: Gift of Robert and Frances Diebboll; **tr**: Gift of Lella and Massimo Vignelli; **cr**: Gift of Robert Kent; **br**: Gift of Mel Byars **p52bl**: Gift of Vivianno Torun Bülow-Hübe and Royal Copenhagen; **cl**: Gift of Denis Gallion and Daniel Morris; **br**: Gift of Julia and Fred Haiblen **p53cl**: Gift of Design Ideas; **tl**: Gift of Harry Dennis, Jr.; **c**: Gift of Mel Byars **p54bl**: Museum Purchase through the Eleanor G. Hewitt Fund; **tl**: Gift of Margaret Carnegie Miller **pp 54–55c**: Museum Purchase **p55c**: Gift of Anglepoise, Ltd.; **tr**: Gift of Mel Byars; **br**: Gift of Coch & Lowy **p56bl**: Gift of Barry Friedman and Patricia Pastor **p57cbl**, **ctl**: Gift of Barry Friedman and Patricia Pastor; **cr**: Gift of Max and Barbara Pine **p61bl**: Gift of Barry Friedman and Patricia Pastor **p62cl**: Gift

of John W. Fell **p64**l: Gift of Württembergische Metallwarenfabrik AG **p72**bl: Gift of Antti Nurmesniemi; cl: Gift of Mel Byars **pp72–73**c: Gift of Maura Santoro **p74**bl: Anonymous Gift; tl: Museum Purchase through the Decorative Arts Association Acquisition Fund made possible by a gift from Theodore Dell **p76**tl: Museum Purchase through the Decorative Arts Association Acquisition Fund **pp77–77**c: Museum Purchase through the Decorative Arts Association Acquisition Fund **pp78–79**c: Museum Purchase through the Decorative Arts Association Acquisition Fund **p80**cl: Gift of Russel Wright; r: Gift of Mel Byars **p81**cb: Gift of Württembergische Metallwarenfabrik AG; l: Gift of Stephen and Dorothy Globus; t: Gift of J. P. Vitrac Design; r: Museum Purchase through the Decorative Arts Association Acquisition Fund **p82**tr: Museum Purchase **pp82–83**c: Museum Purchase through the Decorative Arts Association Acquisiton Fund **p83**cl, tl: The Henry and Ludmilla Shapiro Collection, Partial Gift and Purchase through the Decorative Arts Association Acquisition Fund and Smithsonian Collections Acquisition Program; br: Museum Purchase through the Decorative Arts Association Acquisition Fund **back jacket** cr, **pp84–85**c: Gift of Rosenthal Glas and Porzellan AG **p85**tr: Gift of Rosenthal Glas and Porzellan AG **p86**bl: Gift of Russel Wright; cl: Gift of Roger Kennedy; br: Gift of Paul F. Walter **p87**bl: Anonymous Gift **p88**bl: Gift of Carlo Moretti; tl: Gift of Justin G. Schiller; tcl: Gift of Mrs. Jefferson Patterson; ctr: Gift of Harry Dennis, Jr.; r, c: Gift of Mr. and Mrs. Burton Tremaine and Mrs. John McGrew **p89**tl: Gift of Iittala Glassworks tr: Museum Purchase through the Sir Arthur Bryan Fund; b: Gift of Paul F. Walter **p90**bl: Anonymous Gift; tl: The Henry and Ludmilla Shapiro Collection, Partial Gift and Purchase through the Decorative Arts Association Acquisition Fund and Smithsonian Collections Acquisition Program; c: Gift of Rodman A. Herren **pp90–91**c: Gift of Paul F. Walter **p91**tl: Gift of Mel Byars; ctl: Gift of Peter Condu; ct: Gift of Mel Byars; c: Gift of Gallery 91; br: Gift of Dansk Designs, Ltd.; tr: Gift of Paul F. Walter **p92**l: Purchased with Combined Funds and Crane and Co. **p100**r: Anonymous Gift **p101**c: Gift of Julia Haiblen **p102**bc: Gift of Barry Friedman & Patricia Pastor **p103**bc: Gift of Diane and Mauro Genneretti, Italianissimo, Inc.; **p104**bl: Anonymous Gift **p105**tl: Gift of Monique Fink in memory of Peter Fink; ct: Gift of Primary Design Galleries **p107**: tl: Anonymous Gift; tr: Gift of Henry Dreyfuss **p118**l: Gift of Mel Byars **p120**l: Gift of Mr. Henry Spencer **p121**c: Museum purchase **p126**bl: Museum Purchase through the Decorative Arts Association Acquisition Fund **p127**ct: Gift of Becker, Incorporated **p128**cr: Gift of Mr. and Mrs. Arthur Wiesenberger; br: Museum Purchase through the Decorative Arts Association Acquisition Fund **p129**cl: Gift of Barry Friedman and Patricia Pastor; tr: Gift of Mel Byars, cr: Gift of REXITE. b: Gift of Ivy Ross and Robert Ebendorf in memory of Herbert Ross **p156**cl, tl: Museum Purchase through the Decorative Arts Association Acquisition Fund; tc: Gift of Sally Israel in Memory of Fredericka Steinbach; cb: Gift of Michele Wiener **pp156–157**c: Gift of Deane Granoff **p157**bl: Museum Purchase made possible in part by the Decorative Arts Association Acquisition Fund; tl: Gift of Vivianna Torun Bülow-Hübe and Royal Copenhagen; br: Museum Purchase through the Decorative Arts Assocation Acquisition Fund; cr: Gift of Deane Granoff **p164**cl: Gift of Barry Friedman and Patricia Pastor; br: Gift of Mr. and Mrs. Maurice Zubatkin **front jacket** cr, **p191**l: Gift of the Arango Design Foundation **p193**ct: Gift of Hermes, SA **p194**cr: Anonymous Gift; br: Gift of Philips Dictation System USA **p196**bl: Gift of Arango Design Foundation and Steelcase Design Partnership; tl Gift of Rodman A. Herren **pp196–197**c: Gift of Rolodex Corporation **p197**tl: Gift of Max and Barbara Pine; tr (three pens): Gift of Arango Design Foundation and Steelcase Design Partnership br: Courtesy of Plus Corporation of America **p198**bl: Museum Purchase through the Decorative Arts Association Acquisition Fund; br: Gift of Barry Friedman and Patricia Pastor **back jacket** br, **pp198–199**c: Gift of Barry Friedman and Patricia Pastor **p199**c: Gift of Mel Byars **p203**bl: Gift of Olentangy Associates; cr: Gift of QuadMark **p204**t: Gift of Max & Barbara Pine **pp204–205**c: Gift of Barry Friedman and Patricia Pastor **p205**tl, tr: Gift of Barry Friedman and Patricia Pastor; br: Gift of the Arango Design Foundation **p252**l: Gift of Paul F. Walter **p256**br: Gift of Barry Friedman and Patricia Pastor **p259**bl: Gift of Paul F. Walter **p260**cl: Anonymous Gift **p263**tr: Gift of Mel Byars, br: Gift of Dorothy Hafner **p264**cl: Gift of Mr. Phelps Warren; tr: Gift of Harry Dennis, Jr. **p265**cl: Gift of A/S Stelton **p266**br: Gift of A/S Stelton **p267**tl: Gift of Smart Design, Inc. **p268**tr: Gift of Barry Friedman and Patricia Pastor; br: Gift of Mel Byars **p271**br: Museum Purchase through the Decorative Arts Association Acquisition Fund **p272**l: Gift of Lino Sabattini **p273**tl: Gift of Joseph L. Morris; tr: Gift of Clotilde Bacri; br: Gift of Joseph L. Morris **p274**t: Museum Purchase; cl: Gift of Lella and Massimo Vignelli **p275**bl: Gift of Dalmar Tifft; cr: Gift of Paul F. Walter.

Every effort has been made to trace the copyright holders. Dorling Kindersley apologizes for any unintentional omissions, and would be pleased, if any such case should arise, to add an appropriate acknowledgment in future editions.

Dorling Kindersley would like to thank the following for the kind loan of props for photography:
ABC Business Machines: **p199**br; Simon Alderson, Twentieth Century Design: **p22**tl, **p23**tr, **p45**tr, **p57**br, **p59**c, **p123**bl, tr, **p124**bl, **p193**tcl; Algerian Coffee Stores: **p72**tl, r, **p73**tr, br, **pp74–75**c, **p262**tr; Angels and Bermans: **p139**cl, c, **p140**l, cl, c, cr, **p148**cl, **p149** cl; Laura Ashley: **p121**r; Jane Atfield, Made of Waste: **p29**r, **p125**bc; The Back Shop: **p193**bl; BBC Costume Store: **p136**l (boots and coat), cr, c; Andrea Black, Artistic License: **p140–43** (makeup); Pamela Bromley: **p149**cb, br; The Business, 0181-963 0668: **front jacket** br, **p5**r, **p139**cr; Butler & Wilson: **p5**r (jewelry), **p139**cr; Joe Carroll, Rare Camera Company: **front jacket flap** ctl, **p15**b, **p163**tl, bl, **p164**bl, tl, cb, br, tr, cr; The Contemporary Wardrobe: **front jacket** tl, **back jacket** cbl, **p147**tl, ct, tr, **p148**ct; Cos Prop: **back jacket** cbl, **p138**l, cl, c, cr, r; **p139**l, **p148**ct; Classic Restorations: **pp181–82**c; Roy E. Craig: **p188**br; Garry Derby, American '50s Car Hire: **pp184–85**c; The Duffer of St. George: **p163**ct; D.H. Evans: **p61**br, **p77**cbr, br, **pp102–03**c, **p107**c, **p271**c; Max & Beverly Floyd: **p187**bl; Freuds: **p4**l, **p93**r; Ghost: **p139**r; Jack Hampshire Baby Carriage Collection: **p110**bl, cl, tl, **pp110–11**c; c/o Hendon Way Motors: **pp186–87**c; Phil Hester: **p186**bl; D Howarth: **back jacket** cb, **p188**cl; Nick Hughes & Tim Smith: **p182**tl; Ideal Standard: **p98**l, **pp98–99**c, **p99**br, tr; Jenny Jordan: **pp138–139**, **pp154–155** (makeup); The Juke Box Showroom, RS Leisure, 0181-451 6124/5: **p168**c, **p169**tr, cr, br; Austin Kaye & Co. Ltd: **p150**cl, c, cr, r, **p151**l, c, cr; Lawleys Ltd.: **p84**t; The London Toy and Model Museum, Paddington, London: **p112**tl, ctl, cbl, bl, br, **pp112–13**c, **p113**l, ct, tr, c, cr, br, **p114**bl, tl, tr, **pp114–15**c, **p115**tl, br; Anna Lubbock: **pp134–37** (makeup); Graham Mancha, Design for Modern Living: **p34**cl, **p40**t, **p44**bl, **p92**r, **p93**cl, **p195**bl; Carlo Manzi Rentals: **p2**, **p140**b, r, **p146**bl, **p148**tl; Dr. Martens: **p133**l, **p147**br; The Robert Opie Collection, The Museum of Advertising & Packaging, Gloucester, England: **front jacket** cl, **back jacket** bl, cc, **p4**cl, **p8**r, **p17**br, **p19**tr, **p20**tr, **p21**l, cr, **p56**tl, **p57**bl, tl, tr, **p58**cl, **pp58–59**c, **pp60–61**c, **pp62–63**c, **p66**cl, **pp66–67**c, **p68**bl, cl, **p70**tl, tr, **p71**tr, **p75**tr, **p77**tr, **p78**bl, **p91**cbr, **p100**l (six toothbrushes), **p101**tl, **p102**l, tc, **p104**cb, br, **p106**t, c, bl, **p119**c, **p130**l, c, r, **p131**br, **p159**, **p164**tr, **p168**tl, bl, r, **p169**l, **p194**l, **p195**cl, **p198**cl, **pp232–51**; Dennie Pasion: **pp138–139**, **pp158–159** (hair styling); Penfriend: **front jacket** ctl, **p1**cl, **pp152–53** (all pens); Pentagram Design Limited, London: **front jacket** cb, **p6**, **p103**br; A J Pozner (Hendon Way Motors): **p189**bl; Kevin Price, Volvo Enthusiasts' Club: **p186**br; Reckless Records: **p220**cl; Red or Dead: **p147**bl, cb; Tibor Reich Collection, Stratford-upon-Avon: **p123**tl; Road Runner: **p163**b; Rosenthal: **pp86–87**c, **p87**cr, br; Courtesy of Peter Rutt: **pp188–89**c; Gad Sassower, Decodence, 13 The Mall, 359 Upper Street, Islington, London N1 0PD: **p1**r, **p56**r, **p76**bl, **p195**r; Slam City Skates: **p163**l, c; St. Bride Printing Library: **p208**t, **pp208–09**ct, cb; **p209**cb, br, **p210**l, b, c, t, br, **p211**tl, cr, cl; Sunglass Hut: **p161**tl, cl; Le Tout Petit Musée/Nick Thompson, director Sussex 2CV Ltd: **p182**cl; Tom Turkington (Hendon Way Motors): **p185**tr; Irene Turner: **p187**br; The Water Monopoly, 16/18 Lonsdale Rd, London NW6: **p11**br, **p95**l, c, r, **p96**l, **p97**bl, cl, tl, ct, r; "57th Heaven" Steve West's 1957 Buick Roadmaster; Janet & Roger Westcott: **p184**bl; Wig Specialities: **p138**l, cl, c, cr, r, **p139**c, cr, **p154**l, c, **p155**c; Margaret Wicks: **p134**tl, tr, bl, bcl, bcr, br, **p135**l, cl, cr, r; Courtesy of Mr. Willem van Aalst: **p182**bl; Lawrence Zeegen: **p1**l, **p12**l, **p213**cr.

Cooper-Hewitt, National Design Museum, Smithsonian Institute is grateful to the following staff for their generous support on this project:
Linda Dunne, Assistant Director for Administration; Brad Nugent, Head of Photo Services; Greg Heringshaw, Technician, Wallcoverings Department; Cynthia Trope, Technician, Department of Applied Arts and Industrial Design; Todd A. Olson, Assistant, Department of Applied Arts and Industrial Design; Cordelia Rose, Registrar; Steven Langehough, Associate Registrar; Larry Silver, art handler; Honor Mosher, art handler.

Thanks are also due to:
Hugo Wilson, Laurent Marceau, The British Dental Association, and VolksWorld Magazine for their help and advice; Helen Castle, Adrian Craddock, DNH Camcorder Repairers, Victoria Elvines, Gloria & John Jacobson, Nicky Munro, and Andrew Pucher for the loan of props; models Sarah Foster, David Gillingwater, Emily Gorton, Thomas Green, Hayley Miles, Susannah Marriott, Jacqueline Phillips, David Terrey, Ryan Thomas, and Patricia Wright; and Susannah Steel, particularly for her help with the packaging section. Additional thanks to Kirstie Hills, Caroline Hunt, Claire Legemah, Neil Lockley, Heather McCarry, Claire Naylor, Julie Oughton, Claire Pegrum, Nicola Powling, Catherine Shearman, Nichola Thomasson, Tracy Timson, and Joanna Warwick.

Additional photography
Lynton Gardiner; Clive Streeter; Gary Ombler; Sarah Ashun; Dean Belcher; Terence Sarluis; and Jonathan Keenan.

Author's acknowledgments
I particularly thank the staff at Dorling Kindersley, who have shown dedication, and have encouraged and guided me with enthusiasm. I am especially grateful to Janice Lacock, who has managed the project with skill and commitment. I thank Carla De Abreu, Louise Candlish, Stephen Croucher, Jo Evans, Tracy Hambleton-Miles, Claire Pegrum, Jane Sarluis, Susannah Steel, Dawn Terrey, and David T. Walton for their remarkable efforts. Finally at DK, a special thanks to Sean Moore for his support and advice. My thanks also to Deborah Sampson Shinn at Cooper-Hewitt Museum, New York; Mike Ashworth and David Ellis at the London Transport Museum; Peter Barnet; The Victoria and Albert Museum, London; Hamish MacGillivray at the London Toy and Model Museum; Robert Opie; the Vitra Musuem; Julia Tambini; Patricia Wright; Sandra Millichip; Hal Haines; Shirley Finch; and Stephen Le Flohic.